COLLOQUIUM OF THE SEVEN ABOUT SECRETS OF THE SUBLIME

Credit: H. Roger Viollet, Paris

Colloquium
of the Seven about Secrets of the Sublime

Colloquium Heptaplomeres de Rerum Sublimium Arcanis Abditis

BY JEAN BODIN

TRANSLATION
WITH INTRODUCTION, ANNOTATIONS,
AND CRITICAL READINGS, BY

Marion Leathers Daniels Kuntz

PRINCETON UNIVERSITY PRESS

Published by Princeton University Press
Princeton and London

Library of Congress Cataloging in Publication Data
will be found on the last printed page of this book

Printed in the United States of America by
Princeton University Press
Princeton, New Jersey

For

CHARLES and ALAN DANIELS,

my beloved sons,

and for

PAUL OSKAR KRISTELLER,

incomparable scholar
and friend,

and

Paul, Gregor, Richard,
and the memory of Otto Asa.

Contents

Preface

SEVEN years ago the *Colloquium heptaplomeres* was brought to my attention for the first time. Since that time it has seldom been out of my consciousness. When the *Colloquium* was suggested to me by Professor J. Russell Major as a work appropriate to my interest, I readily accepted the challenge because at the time I was unaware of the intellectual and physical demands of this book. However, after the *Colloquium heptaplomeres* and I had been constant companions for six months, it captured me completely. My work on the *Colloquium* has been long, difficult, often lonely, as well as inspiring, exciting, and rewarding. Indeed it has been a labor of love.

The *Colloquium* has led me to exciting cities—Venice, Rome, Paris—to search out its secrets. It has led me to new friends who share mutual interests. It even led to me a man who wanted to know about harmony in the *Colloquium heptaplomeres* and who soon thereafter became my husband, Paul Grimley Kuntz. Therefore, in spite of the long years of labor I owe much to the *Colloquium*.

I am indebted not only to the *Colloquium*, however, but also to many friends and colleagues who by their advice, encouragement, and effort have helped me bring this work to completion. I am grateful to Professor J. Russell Major and Professor Francis Manley for suggesting this work to me and for their advice and reading of the manuscript in an early version; to Professor Joseph Conant for his careful reading and corrections on the first four books of translation; to Professor Gregor Sebba who encouraged me to complete the work and rendered excellent criticism of the introduction.

I am also indebted to Professor Donald Kelley for his helpful criticism on specific points in the introduction and his interest and enthusiasm about the book; to Professor Brian Armstrong for his sustained interest and criticism; to Professor Richard Popkin for his indispensable criticism and his illumination on a host of vital questions including Jewish mysticism, Cabala, and skepticism; and to Professor Morton Smith for his help in transliterating and interpreting the Hebrew in Bodin's book. Dr. Frederick Prussner has also been very helpful to me in questions concerning Hebrew.

I am indeed grateful to the libraries in this country and abroad for the use of materials. In particular I want to thank Miss Ruth Walling, acting director, and Miss Joyce Werner, formerly of the staff, of Emory University Library, and also Miss Frances Muse, Reference Librarian, of Georgia State University; Dr. O. B. Hardison, Dr. Richard Schoeck, and Miss Dorothy Mason of the Folger Renaissance Library; to the libraries of Columbia University, Yale University, and Princeton University for use of materials. I am especially indebted to the Very Reverend Monsignor José Ruysschaert, Vice-Prefect of the Biblioteca Vaticana, for his help in locating rare materials and for the use of these; and to Dr. Giorgio Ferrari, Director of the Biblioteca Marciana, whose courtesies are too numerous to mention; also to the Directors of the Bibliothèque Nationale and the Bibliothèque Mazarine.

To my colleagues and administrators at Georgia State University whose interest has supported me, I am grateful. Thanks go to the typists, Mrs. Frances Stewart and Mrs. Joe Tignor. Thanks also to my sons and their wives, especially Sarah Schroth Daniels for proofreading. For typing the index special thanks are due to Gerard Elfstrom and my secretaries at Georgia State University.

I am especially indebted to the careful editing of Mr. Sanford Thatcher and the staff of Princeton University Press.

I am also very grateful to the American Council of Learned Societies for a grant-in-aid which fostered the final research on the book.

I have delayed my thanks until last to the two men without whom this work would never have been. No words can express what I owe to Professor Paul Oskar Kristeller for his diligent attention to every detail of the manuscript, for the laborious task of checking every word of my translation against the Latin text and making corrections, for his constant advice and encouragement, and for the inspiration of his scholarship and his *aretē*. Indeed no part of this work is without his influence, and I hope it is worthy of his interest and efforts.

And to my husband, Professor Paul G. Kuntz, who has for the three years of our marriage offered daily encouragement and an attentive ear to my discussions of the *Colloquium*, I am forever thankful; for his advice on philosophical questions, for the laborious task of proofreading the annotations, for his many trips to the typist and the library in my behalf, and most of all for his faith in me and the *Colloquium heptaplomeres.*

MARION LEATHERS DANIELS KUNTZ

Atlanta, Georgia
1974

INTRODUCTION

CHAPTER I

Religion in the Life of Jean Bodin

AMONG the many paradoxes of the Renaissance one of the most striking was Jean Bodin. Truly a man of the Renaissance, he harked back to the ancients of Greece and Rome for much of his inspiration and style, yet he pointed the way to the modern age with his definition of sovereignty, his quantity theory of money, his liberal approach to religion, and his emphasis on toleration.

Bodin's influence[1] was secured by his most famous works, *Methodus ad facilem historiarum cognitionem* (1566), *Response aux paradoxes de M. de Malestroit* (1566), and *Les six livres de la république* (1576). Concerning his influence, Kenneth McRae says: "His concept of sovereignty, his theory of climate, and his advocacy of religious toleration have today become commonplace in practically all the histories of political thought."[2]

The three works of Bodin's life which reveal most vividly the enigmatic nature of the man and his stimulating religious views are the *Universae naturae theatrum* (1596), *De la démonomanie des sorciers* (1580), and the *Colloquium heptaplomeres*. But all of his writings in some measure reveal his concern with the religious basis of human existence.[3] "He thought of the natural order as contained

[1] *Les six livres de la république* were published in 1576, and their success was so great that even women were eager to read them, according to the article on Bodin in *Dictionnaire de biographie française* (Paris, 1954).

[2] Jean Bodin, *The Six Bookes of a Commonweale*, translated by Richard Knolles, edited by Kenneth D. McRae (Cambridge, Mass., 1962), A, vii.

[3] John William Allen, *History of Political Thought in the Sixteenth Century* (New York, 1928), p. 400.

within an eternal order comprehending the universe and all particulars within it, in a single system of relationships. . . . The proper motion of the heavenly bodies can be determined by observation because in them there is no imperfection. But when one comes to consider men, the divine and natural intention has been disturbed by the Fall. The proper order of human society cannot therefore be determined by observation simply, because men are imperfect. To know that order we must consult natural reason and with even more certainty, the law of God revealed in the scriptures. . . . In fact Bodin's political thought was rooted in a body of dogma, the law of God."[4]

Though the facts of Bodin's life are incompletely known, religion seems to be a key for understanding the man and his works; from the beginning of his life to the end the aura of religion surrounded him. He was born in June 1529 or 1530, perhaps at Angers, although the place of his birth is not absolutely certain. If Angers was not his birthplace, at least in his later life he thought of it as such because he refers to himself as an Angevin. His father was Guillaume Bodin, a master tailor of Angers, who, though not of the nobility, was secure enough financially to provide comfortable dowries for his four daughters and an inheritance for his three sons.

Contemporaries often said that Bodin's mother was a Jewess whose ancestors had fled from Spain during the persecutions of 1492 and had come to France, where they preserved their customs and religion in secret.[5] Perhaps the legends about his mother spring from the important role Bodin gave to Salomon in the *Colloquium*, his numerous citations in this work from the Old Testament, and the conclusion of the *Colloquium*, where he shows obvious sympathy

[4] Jean Bodin, *Six Books of the Commonwealth*, translated by M. J. Tooley (Oxford, 1955), pp. XIX–XX.

[5] Henri Baudrillart, *Bodin et son temps* (Paris, 1853), p. 112. See also, Jacques Levron, *Jean Bodin et sa famille* (Angers, 1950); Roger Chauviré, *Jean Bodin, auteur de la république* (Paris, 1914), pp. 1–22; Aldo Garosci, *Jean Bodin* (Milan, 1934). Cf. also N. Planchenault, "Études sur Jean Bodin," *Mémoires de la société académique de Maine et Loire*, I (Angers, 1857), 11–105. This article is interesting and eloquent, though filled with non sequiturs; e.g., "A Jewish mother of Bodin! One has forgotten the traditional hatred, I should have said providential, of the two races, Jew and Gentile!" (18); also p. 22, "Bodin dedicated his book to Gabriel Bouvery, Bishop of Angers; this would not have been if Bodin had been a Jew." All translations are my own.

for the Jews who were persecuted in Spain. The mysterious aura of a Jewish mother has been diminished by new evidence, however.[6] His mother was Catherine Dutertre, and one of her brothers was prior of the Carmelite monastery in Angers.

Records reveal that Bodin entered the Carmelite house at Angers at an early age and later was sent to Paris to study at the Carmelite house.[7] Gabriel Bouvery, a great patron of letters and Bishop of Angers, to whom Bodin dedicated his translation of Oppian, *De venatione*, in 1555, was influential in Bodin's profession as a Carmelite.[8]

While in Paris he came in contact with the old and new learning and the intellectual controversies that were raging in the capital. Bodin displayed an affinity during this period with an exponent of the new learning, Peter Ramus. Though forbidden by royal edict in 1543 to lecture in logic or philosophy, Ramus obtained a repeal of the ban in 1547 because of the patronage of the Cardinal of Lorraine. Bodin probably listened to Ramus' lectures while in the order at Paris, and afterward when Ramus took over the administration of the Collège de Presle in 1545. The Ramist method divided the subject of logic into two sharply distinct compartments. The first part, known

[6] See Kenneth D. McRae's unpublished dissertation, "The Political Thought of Jean Bodin" (Harvard, 1953), for the most complete and up-to-date account of Bodin's life. Also cf. Pierre Mesnard, *Oeuvres philosophiques de Jean Bodin*, I (Paris, 1951), pp. VII–XXI.

[7] Jacques-Auguste de Thou, *Historiarum sui temporis* (n.p., 1620), V, liber CXVII, 701. McRae, "Political Thought," p. 9, has proof of Bodin's Carmelite relationship from the discovery at Ham, in the Somme département, of a volume of sixteenth- and seventeenth-century documents; among these is the sworn statement, made by four priests of the Carmelites at Paris, that they had known Jean Bodin, who attended lectures in philosophy and left the order after two or three years. Professor Richard H. Popkin, however, is not convinced that the evidence about his mother or anything else really settles the question of his Judaism. He says the fact that Bodin and his uncle belonged to the Carmelite monastery makes him more suspicious than otherwise, since, in Spain, at that time the only religious orders that accepted members of Jewish ancestry were the Carmelites and the Jesuits. The Carmelites in Spain were heavily Jewish, and the same may have been true in France.

[8] Garosci, *Jean Bodin*, p. 15, makes an interesting comment about the Carmelites: "It is interesting to note that the protector of the Carmelites is the holy prophet Elias, which name Bodin gave to the first of his sons." The name Elias may have even greater significance than Garosci suggests, but this will be discussed later in the introduction.

as invention, was intended to lay bare the irreducible components which go to make up any discourse; the second part, the disposition, concerned the proper use of these basic arguments. The technique to be used in invention was a skillful division of the topic by successive stages, and regardless of the nature of the subject, Ramus insisted on reasoning deductively from general principles to the particular.[9] Bodin's interest in philosophy and logic continued throughout his life, and his Ramist background suggests an explanation for his criticism of Aristotle, his diatribes against the grammarians' devotion to "words" rather than "things," and his insistence that knowledge is for use.[10] The *Universae naturae theatrum* perhaps shows the Ramist method most clearly. But in the *Colloquium heptaplomeres*, too, one speaker presents the general topic, and then the other interlocutors probe the details.

The reasons for Bodin's departure from Paris and the Carmelite order after three or four years are uncertain. He may have been released because he had professed at an early age, or his lack of orthodoxy may have become apparent. In 1548 the prior of the Carmelites of Tours, René Garnier, and two religious brothers of Paris, one of whom was named Jean Bodin, were summoned as heretics before the Parlement of Paris.[11] Venot, one of the brothers, suffered martyrdom along with Leonard Gallimard, a Protestant who arranged the escape of other Protestants to Geneva. It is uncertain whether our Jean Bodin was the brother summoned with Venot, and if so, what were the reasons for his escape.[12] Bodin's late

[9] See Kenneth D. McRae, "Ramist Tendencies in the Thought of J. Bodin," *Journal of the History of Ideas* 16 (1955), 306–23. For Ramist influence on another great religious thinker, John Wesley, see W. J. Ong, "Peter Ramus and the Naming of Methodism," *Journal of the History of Ideas* 14 (1953), 235–48. I am indebted to Professor Donald R. Kelley of the University of Rochester for his suggestion that Ramus' "influence" on Bodin has been overdone.

[10] McRae, "Political Thought," p. 320 says that Bodin mentions Ramus in a short tract, known only in the Latin translation of the French by the German Johann Bornitius, *Consilia Johannis Bodini Galli, & Fausti Longiani Itali, de principe recte instituendo* (Erfurt, 1603), fol. B-2–B2v, on the education of a prince in which he declares the superiority of the Ramist logic above all other disciplines as a general training for the youthful mind.

[11] Mesnard, *Oeuvres philosophiques*, p. XIII.

[12] See McRae, "Political Thought," pp. 18–25, for a complete discussion of the heresy trial of 1548.

works, however, make it clear that he might easily have gotten into difficulty in his youth because of his religious views, because control of men's consciences was always repugnant to him. Gabriel Bouvery may have intervened on his behalf, if the Jean Bodin cited before the Parlement was indeed his protégé. However, it seems unlikely that Bouvery would support a heretic, at least one who acknowledged the fact. Bodin, at any rate, maintained the bishop's good will, because in 1555 Bodin dedicated a book to him and was effusive in his praise of the bishop.[13]

Bodin may have left the Carmelites because he was in sympathy with the spirit of religious reform. This sympathy and interest may have inspired Bodin to pay a visit to Geneva in 1552 to observe Calvinism at first hand. *La France Protestante* cites one Jehan Bodin of S. Amand as a resident of Geneva in that year.[14] The archives of Geneva reveal a marriage contract on August 25, 1552, between Jean Bodin of Saint-Amand and Typhaine Reynaude, resident of Geneva and widow of Leonard Gallimard, mentioned above as the Protestant who was put to death along with Venot, companion of Jean Bodin. If the Jean Bodin who was in Geneva in 1552 was our Bodin, the marriage of Bodin to Gallimard's widow sheds remarkable light on Bodin's sojourn in Paris in 1548 and supports the theory that he was one of the brothers cited for heresy in 1548.[15] Bodin's name is inscribed in the registry of residents of Geneva on November 22, 1552, and there are a few other references to Jean Bodin and his wife, but none later than 1553. McRae suggests an interesting hypothesis for the entry in the register of "Jean Bodin of Saint-Amand,"[16] and Saint-Amand was always linked with our author's name after 1576.[17]

With the facts as they now stand, it seems likely that the Jean Bodin of Saint-Amand, a resident of Geneva in 1552, was indeed

[13] See Mesnard, *Oeuvres philosophiques.* Also Planchenault, "Études sur Jean Bodin," p. 22. Gabriel Bouvery was the nephew of Guillaume Poyet (1473–1548), an Angevin, who became chancellor of France in 1538.

[14] *La France Protestante* 2 (Paris, 1879), 671.

[15] Mesnard, *Oeuvres philosophiques*, p. XI. Cf. also McRae, "Political Thought," pp. 18–26.

[16] McRae, "Political Thought," pp. 28–31.

[17] Mesnard, *Oeuvres philosophiques*, p. XI.

our Jean Bodin, for the general tenor of Bodin's inquisitive mind might well have led him to pay a visit to Geneva and observe Calvinism at first hand.[18] Although Bodin was often accused in his later life of being a Calvinist, his *Colloquium heptaplomeres* gives no indication that he favored Calvinism as a religion.[19] However, he did share intellectual interests with many of the Protestant group, and he had a detailed knowledge of Genevan history.[20]

The burning of Michel Servetus on October 27, 1553, surely must have caused a crisis in Bodin's intellectual attachment to Protestantism. If Bodin had expected Geneva to provide a refuge for his increasingly liberal religious views, which reach their climax in the completely tolerationist attitude espoused in the *Colloquium heptaplomeres*, the case of Servetus certainly brought the intolerance of Geneva into sharp focus. This intolerance and the tragedy of Servetus were perhaps instrumental in Bodin's decision to leave Geneva.[21] It is worth noting that the brilliant and free-thinking countryman of Bodin, Guillaume Postel, who was hospitably received by the Swiss in Basel in 1553 after he had been forbidden to teach in Paris,[22]

[18] See the introduction to McRae, ed., *Six Bookes*, p. A4. Also Tooley's introduction to Bodin, *Six Books*, edited by Tooley, p. VIII.

[19] Pierre Mesnard held the opinion that Bodin's interest in Calvinism was intellectual rather than a matter of deep commitment. See Pierre Mesnard, "La Pensée religieuse de Bodin," *Revue du seizième siècle* 16 (1929), 77–121. Note especially page 86: "Let us then summarize the theology of Bodin at the stage which concerns us: antipapalism, professed sympathy with the Protestants with whom he had associated, a grand conception of salvation open to all, Christians or pagans on equal footing. The historic Christ conceived as the final term of an abundant series of prophets; moreover, the Judaeo-Christian tradition, pagan terminology and symbolism, thought strongly permeated with Paduan Platonism. I doubt for my part that such a doctrine was agreeable to the ears of Calvin and that if Protestantism it is in the letter to Bautru des Matras, the latter must have had something in common with the religious spirit which, after having inspired the martyrs of Paris, was soon to kindle the pyres of Geneva."

[20] Beatrice Reynolds, *Proponents of Limited Monarchy in Sixteenth Century France: Francis Hotman and Jean Bodin* (New York, 1931), p. 107.

[21] All the Swiss cantons voted for Servetus's death; Castellio was the only Protestant who refused to support the burning. See Jaques George de Chaufepié, *The Life of Servetus, Being an Article of his Historical Dictionary*, IV, translated by James Yair (London, 1771), p. 119.

[22] William J. Bouwsma, *Concordia Mundi: The Career and Thought of Guillaume Postel (1510–1581)* (Cambridge, Mass., 1957), pp. 19 ff.

left in the fall of the same year and shortly thereafter composed an *Apologia pro Serveto.*[23]

Ten years after the supposed date of Bodin's departure from Geneva, he was practicing law in Paris, and at that time all the members of the Parlement of Paris were required to take oaths of loyalty to the Catholic faith. On June 10, 1562, Bodin's name, along with three hundred and sixty-seven others, appeared on the list of those faithful to the church. It is impossible to say if this was a sincere profession of religious conviction or a necessary gesture of conformity for a struggling young advocate. By 1562 Bodin's religious views reflected Protestant positions, if the letter to Jan Bautru des Matras be genuine, though Bodin tells his friend that differences of religion are of no account among friends.[24]

As the Wars of Religion increased in vehemence, a royal edict was passed in 1568 which decreed severe punishment for those of the reformed faith, dismissed all Protestants from offices of the Crown, and renewed the oath of catholicity upon the parlements and the universities. Bodin's religious views made him suspect. On March 5, 1569, his career as deputy for the *procureur-général* at Poitiers was interrupted by his arrest and imprisonment for a year and a half as an adherent of the new religion. He was released as a result of the Edict of Pacification of August 11, 1570. This episode is important because it witnesses to his continuing lack of religious orthodoxy during middle life and offers strong support to later testimony which might otherwise have been considered biased. From Blois, where the

[23] *Ibid.*, p. 23. This work was circulated in manuscript and was first printed in 1748 from a manuscript in Basel.

[24] Mesnard, *Oeuvres philosophiques*, p. XVI, says: "The repression of heresy, of which the Parlement de Paris remained the active center, gathered to its bosom more and more numerous sympathies. The great majority of lawyers did not object to taking the oath of Catholicity which was demanded of all officers of justice and royal functionaries. The historians of Jean Bodin have not up to now drawn attention to this important fact: he had signed the formula of June 1562, though the two Bautru des Matras, the Parisian lawyer and his father the Angevin judge, refused, as also du Moulin and de la Noue. There is no more common attitude between the two correspondents: the letter to Bautru des Matras could not therefore have been earlier than 1562." Also cf. Allen, *History of Political Thought*, pp. 400–401.

Estates General were in session, William Wade wrote home to Lord Burghley in February 1577: "I have good and famylyar acquaintance with Bodinus, his profession is the Cyvill law though he is constrayned to retire him selfe from the practice for his safety being of the Religion [Protestant] and therefore his estate is poore."[25]

In 1571 he was appointed *maitre des requêtes et conseiller* for Francis, duke of Alençon. The duke was the official leader of the *Politiques*, who maintained, in an age of rising fanaticism, that the state's primary concern was the maintenance of order, not the establishment of true religion. The *Politiques* also espoused religious toleration rather than religious conflict. This party and the Huguenots often shared common political theories. Yet the *Politiques* did not believe that religious differences gave men the right to resist the monarchy. In 1574 Alençon used the aid of the Protestants in furthering his plans to succeed Charles IX as king of France instead of his brother, the king of Poland. Although the plan was abortive, it is important to us because Bodin's name was mentioned during the trial of two of the conspirators who implicated him in the plot.[26]

In spite of Bodin's service to Alençon he found favor with the new king, Henry III, who perhaps enjoyed his erudition among the sophisticates of his court. Bodin attempted to explain to the king the ideals of the *Politiques* and the basis for a solution to the religious and political crisis.

In 1576 Bodin served as representative of the third estate for Vermandois at the Estates General. At a meeting of representatives of the Île-de-France Bodin was successful in blocking the extremist course of the Paris representative concerning the articles of religion. In the end, however, the *Politiques* lost the vote of the entire third estate, and the king was requested to unite his subjects in the Catholic faith.[27] Although the *Politique* viewpoint in regard to religion was defeated, they were more successful in the question of financing the reunion which could be brought about only by war. Bodin opposed

[25] McRae, ed., *Six Books*, introduction, pp. A7–8.
[26] McRae, "Political Thought," pp. 60–67.
[27] *Ibid.*, pp. 72–74.

the king's proposal to alienate the lands from the domain of the Crown and successfully blocked the king's efforts to raise money by constitutional methods.[28] Bodin was now the leading spokesman at the Estates of Blois for the moderate party.

Since Alençon had been unsuccessful in his bid for the French throne, as an alternative he aspired to a marriage with Queen Elizabeth. On his second visit to England in 1581 Jean Bodin accompanied him. Bodin had made clear in the *République* (1576) his admiration for English institutions, and he was on intimate terms with Mr. Secretary Walsingham and the queen herself.[29] When Bodin arrived in England, the Spanish ambassador Bernardino de Mendoza referred to him in a letter to Philip II as a "great heretic, as is proved by the books he has written."[30]

Though called a heretic by Mendoza, Bodin obviously did not approve of the Protestant government's policy of imprisoning and hanging Catholics. He makes this clear in a letter addressed to the queen, the *optimates*, and *senatores* of England on the occasion of the hanging of the Blessed Edmund Campion in 1581:

> I will not here, in so great variety of people so much differing among themselves in religion take upon me to determine which of them is the best (howbeit that there can be but one such, one truth, and one divine law, by the mouth of God published) but if the prince well assured of the truth of his religion would draw his subjects thereunto, divided into sects and factions, he must not, therein, use force. For that the minds of men, the more they are

[28] *Ibid.*, pp. 75 ff.

[29] Bodin's *République* was well known in England before his arrival and had won for its author widespread admiration. Bodin sought out the nobles and ministers at the court and soon impressed them with his scholarship and wit. The queen herself was charmed with Bodin's erudition, and she often enjoyed his conversation concerning forms of government and his theory of climate. This warm relationship was short-lived, however; a crisis developed between Bodin and the queen when it became apparent the queen had no intentions of marrying Alençon. For additional information on Bodin's relationship to Walsingham and the queen before 1581, see McRae, "Political Thought," pp. 62–65.

[30] Summerfield Baldwin, "Jean Bodin and the League," *Catholic Historical Review* 23 (1937–38), 165.

> forced, the more forward and stubborn they are, and the greater punishment that shall be inflicted upon them the less good is to be done, the nature of man being commonly such as may of it selfe bee led to like of anything, but never enforced so to do.[31]

A disillusioned Bodin left England a year later and arrived in Antwerp, where Alençon had preceded him. The intolerant attitude of the Protestant government there disturbed him. Before citizens could go to Mass, they were forced to take an oath renouncing the Catholic king, Philip II, and his party. The Calvinists by this oath hoped to trap the Catholics whom they believed would refuse to sign. Jean Bodin advised the duke to urge everyone to sign the oath, and he also tried to impress upon Alençon the need to maintain freedom of religion.[32] In addition, Bodin disapproved of the duke's use of force to establish his position as prince of the Netherlands. Bodin's visits to England and the Netherlands seemed to crystallize his thoughts regarding toleration and freedom of conscience.

Alençon's death in 1584 left Bodin again without employment, and he settled at Laon, retiring permanently from national politics. In 1576 he had married the widow of a Laon official and succeeded to her brother's office of *procureur du roi* upon that official's death in 1587.

Bodin's views, however, were far too controversial to leave him in obscurity for long. The English authorities sought his arrest because he had predicted in his correspondence in 1585 that Elizabeth would be overthrown. He expressed sympathy for Mary Queen of Scots and was aware of the Babington plot against the queen's life. He dated letters to friends in England on August 28, 1587, referring to the date as the last day of the queen of England. It is significant that Bodin knew of the plot and did not reveal it until the appointed day.

Bodin's catholicity was not accepted by some princes of the Catholic League, for they complained to Catherine de' Medici that certain men of the new faith had been appointed to public office, and they mentioned Jean Bodin's name.[33] As a result of this complaint, Bodin

[31] *Ibid.*, p. 166.

[32] *Ibid.*, p. 167.

[33] The following poem, which I believe is heretofore unpublished, is written by a sixteenth-century hand. Of particular interest is the last line, which seems to refer

was questioned by the lieutenant-general of Laon in June 1587, but was cleared by the testimony of several witnesses, including two priests.

Bodin's life was saved a year later in Paris by a Catholic friend, the advocate Dauger, on the famous day of Barricades, May 12, 1588, when rioters for the League captured Bodin. Dauger, recognized as a good leaguer, presumably testified that Bodin was a good Catholic.[34]

The operations of the Catholic League became more pronounced

---

to Bodin's trouble with Catherine de'Medici. Biblioteca Vaticana *Urbinates Latini* 1619, fol. 88.

De Johanne Bodino

Magnus es historia, Bodine, magnus Latinis
Juribus, et magnus Graiugenum Sophia.
Plurima civili promis ratione, docesque
Queis urbes possint ipsaque regna regi.

Daemonas exagitas, exosus verba Magorum
In campos nebulas disjicis aerios.

Si quis ad annales curam protendat avitos
Per salebras tutus te duce signat iter
Salve magne parens, salve notissime Mundo,
Si te doctiloquum non regia ulla silet.

About John Bodin

You are great in history, Bodin, great in
Latin laws and great in the wisdom
of the Greeks.
You relate the most in statesmanship,
and you teach
how cities and kingdoms can be ruled.

You stir up demons, hating the words
of the magicians.
You scatter darkness into airy fields.
If anyone should direct his attention to
ancestral records,
he safely designates the route through the
rough places with you as his guide.

Hail, great parent, hail, most famous one
in the world,
If no palace silences your learned tongue.

[34] Baldwin, "Jean Bodin," pp. 171–72. Also see J. Moreau-Reibel, "Bodin et la ligue d'après des lettres inédites," *Humanisme et renaissance* 1–3 (1934–35), 422–40.

after the death of Alençon, for the leaguers feared the ascent to the throne of Henry of Navarre. Henry III was so fearful of the League's power that he ordered the assassination of its leaders, Henry, duke of Guise, and Louis, cardinal of Lorraine, in December 1588. This act erupted into increased violence, and orders were sent by the Parlement of Paris to the officials in the provinces to rebel against the king. Bodin, as a supporter of the monarchy and *procureur du roi* for Laon, found himself in a difficult position. He delayed his decision as long as possible, yet in the end there was only one course of action possible—other than flight—if he remained in Laon; and that was to declare for the League, which he did on March 21, 1589.

Bodin has been accused of hypocrisy by this declaration for the Catholic League. Yet it must be realized that his family and property were at stake, and since he was devoutly religious, he believed that the League, though evil, was an instrument of God for working out His divine purpose for France. Earlier Bodin had stated that Catholicism was the best civil religion for France because it was a better foundation for a just constitution and for good citizenship. Here we see that even Bodin's political judgments were in part religious. His true opinion concerning the League can be found in his private correspondence during these years. He voiced the hope that the king and the League would come to some agreement and not ruin the "flower of the whole world, France." When it became obvious that more bloodshed would follow if the oath was not carried out, Bodin addressed the people and administered the oath. A revealing statement by Bodin in a letter of 1590 indicates his attitude toward the Wars of Religion. "Victory depends on God, who, without doubt, will reveal a turn of His hand, for the sake of Religion, and will punish those who, on either side, are covering their ambitions and their thefts under the veil of Religion."[35]

The tensions of war subjected Bodin to a search of his house in January 1590, and certain of his books were publicly burned. Bau-

[35] Baldwin, "Jean Bodin," p. 181. McRae says in his introduction to Bodin, *Six Books*, pp. A11–12, that Bodin believed that God would intervene directly to destroy the House of Valois and establish a new line of kings; therefore devout men could only wait for the divine plan to be fulfilled.

drillart states that the search and burning were the result of a charge of magic leveled against him as a result of his *Démonomanie.*[36]

During the precarious years following Henry III's assassination (1589–1593) Bodin believed that God desired the duke of Mayenne, not the king of Navarre, to be the king of France. This position seems strange in view of the fact that he had been in the service of Alençon, a *Politique*, and had rendered numerous services to the king and queen of Navarre.[37] One must remember, however, that Bodin desired peace and stability for France above all, and he believed that the Catholic church was the religious organ that could best accomplish this. When the king of Navarre abjured Protestantism on July 23, 1593, Bodin's attitude toward Henry surely shifted, for he had always been in sympathy with the party of moderation, and he slipped away in April 1594 to join Henry and the royalists before they reached Laon.

In spite of the fluctuating position of Bodin's fortunes during the League's supremacy, he continued to write, and the work of his last sixteen years reveals his acutely religious and philosophical nature, which was apparent as early as the publication of the *Methodus* in 1566. *De la démonomanie des sorciers* (1580), though filled with lurid cases of witchcraft, explores the metaphysical realm of spirits and demons as agents of God's divine plan. *Universae naturae theatrum* (1596) presents a dialogue on the wonders of natural science and the universal nature of God's unchanging plan. Perhaps the most revealing and interesting of all his works is the *Colloquium heptaplomeres*, a dialogue among men of seven different faiths. This work is boldly critical of the superficial nature of organized religion and was not published until the nineteenth century, although it was widely circulated in manuscript. The *Methodus*, the *Theatrum*, the *République* were all placed on the Index of prohibited books, and his broad interpretation of religion caused him to be constantly under suspicion. Bodin was always a controversial subject, for as Bayle relates, "those who mount the pulpit here tell

[36] Baudrillart, *Bodin et son temps*, pp. 134–51. Chauviré shares the same view of the episode.

[37] Reynolds, *Proponents of Limited Monarchy*, p. 192.

stories, declaim against Bodin through a whole sermon, and pull him to pieces, without remembering that the villain had been of the League and died a Jew, without speaking of Jesus Christ in his last words, which I have in verse."[38] Perhaps Diecmann's remark is nearer to the truth: "About the religion of the man nothing can be said more certain than that his religion varied with the various years of his life."[39]

Paradoxical to the end, Bodin requested a Catholic burial in the Church of the Franciscans at Laon, and his wish was carried out on June 7, 1596.

[38] Pierre Bayle, *A General Dictionary—Translation of that of the Celebrated Mr. Bayle,* translated by J. B. Bernard, Thomas Birch, John Lockman (London, 1735), p. 439.

[39] Ludovicus J. Diecmann, *De naturalismo* (Leipzig, 1684), p. 3.

CHAPTER II

Religious Views in His Works

The Relationship of the *Colloquium heptaplomeres* to the *Universae naturae theatrum* and *De la démonomanie des sorciers*

WHAT were Bodin's religious views? This difficult question can perhaps be answered more readily from his works than from the facts of his life. During his life he had been accused of being a Jew, a Calvinist, a heretical Catholic, an atheist. Bodin seemed to be none of these, surely not the latter; indeed, it is impossible to read Bodin's works and not to sense the profoundly religious nature of the man. True religion to Bodin was an extremely personal matter practiced in his search for God and the eternal praise of His Majesty. True religion, he felt, requires no church; in fact, the church often impedes true worship. True religion cannot be controlled by the state, for to forbid men the private exercise of their religion is to make them oftentimes atheists. Although Bodin was tolerant of all religions, the one thing he could not abide was atheism. "So the greatest superstition that is, is not by much anything so detestable as Atheisme. And truly they (in mine opinion) offend much, which think that the same punishment is to bee appointed for them that make many gods, and them that would have none at all: or that the infinitie of gods admitted, the almightie and everliving God is thereby taken away. For that superstition how great soever it be, doth yet hold men in feare and awe, both of the laws and of the magistrats, as also in mutuall duties and offices one of them towards another; whereas meere Atheisme doth utterly root of mens' minds all the fear of doing evill."[40]

[40] Bodin, *Six Bookes* p. 539.

A thorough understanding of Bodin's religious thinking can be attained only by a careful analysis of his last three works. In the *Universae naturae theatrum* he gives a detailed account of the universe and God's relation to this theater of nature. In *De la démonomanie des sorciers* he expands his theory of the universe to include the world of spirits, both angelic and demonic. In the *Colloquium heptaplomeres* he incorporates his ideas about the universe and the spirit world, but he expands these concepts into a full view of man in the universe, who is searching for his own personal relationship to the cosmos and a comprehension of true religion.

In the *praefatio* of the *Universae naturae theatrum* Bodin explains why he turns to the theater of universal nature to explore the question of God. Man's laws are often irrational and full of error, but the laws of nature are logical and fixed, for God himself is their author. The contemplation of nature is of prime importance, for it often leads a man to thoughts of God.[41] "And indeed the Theater of Nature is nothing other than the contemplation of those things founded by the immortal God as if a certain tablet were placed under the eyes of every single one so that we may embrace and love the majesty of that very author, his goodness, wisdom, and remarkable care in the greatest matters, in moderate affairs, in matters of the least importance. For as Aristotle writes, the one who doubts whether there is a God or not must be refuted by no weak arguments."[42] Nature not only brings pleasure to the beholder but also such a desire for the Founder that we, though unwilling, are seized, stupefied, and amazed at the love of Him.[43] All the ornaments of the world, the more beautiful manifestations of the angels, and the immortal spirits show the work of the Master Builder.

God is the prime mover of the universe, and creation is so unique to the prime cause that it is communicable to no creature.[44] God is the principle that sets the universe in motion. "The ultimate principle is eternal, and nothing can be previous to it, nothing like it,

[41] In the *Theatrum*, Bodin's views on nature are quite close to the tenets of Stoicism.

[42] Jean Bodin, *Universae naturae theatrum* (Lyon, 1596), pp. 3–4.

[43] *Ibid.*, p. 4.

[44] *Ibid.*, pp. 16–17.

nothing contrary to it, and nothing equal to it."[45] "Principle is singular nor can it be more than one, and it is without beginning; for if anything was before the principle, it can not even deserve to be called the principle, since it owes its origin to another, either from nature or time: but principle ought to be of this sort, according to the teaching of Aristotle himself, so that things arise neither from themselves nor from others, but from the principle."[46] The principle is eternal; if it were not, "it would be necessary that God either have his origin from another, or from himself; it could not be from another, because it would not be a principle; not from himself because nothing can be made from itself . . . therefore it is necessary that principle be eternal."[47]

God, the principle, the prime mover, alone is infinite and eternal. In things eternal there is no first cause, no last. The world has a first cause; consequently it is not eternal. Nothing can be eternal in its own nature whose first cause is voluntary, and since the first cause of the world is voluntary, and its station and conditions depend on the will of another, the world is not eternal.[48]

Cause cannot precede principle; God, the principle, created the universe not from necessity but from free will. Causes proceed from the first cause in a fixed order, as though a golden chain had been let down from heaven, but causes are not unchangeable because God alone is changeless.

It is impossible for the human mind to comprehend the principle because the principle cannot be known by comparison. Although Bodin states that man cannot understand God, he presents three views of the origin of the world. The Chaldaeans and Hebrews say that it was created and came into action from pure privation and that it will return to nothingness. The Academicians, Stoics, Epicureans, ancient Latins, and some Arabs, except Averroës, say that it was not created but came into being from misshapen matter and that it will perish and all things will return to chaos. Aristotle says that it has neither beginning nor end but existed from eternal

45 *Ibid.*, p. 16. 46 *Ibid.*, p. 22. 47 *Ibid.*, p. 58.

48 *Ibid.*, p. 37; cf. also Jean Bodin, *Colloquium heptaplomeres de rerum sublimium arcanis abditis,* edited by Ludovicus Noack (Schwerin, 1857), p. 27.

time and would exist forever. Bodin's own views are similar to the Chaldean-Hebraic interpretation, although he states that matter cannot be corrupted because nothing is corrupted which was not born; so all things in this way will return where first they were begun and will return to their own beginnings.[49] There can be nothing in the middle between being and nonbeing.[50]

The world and all that is in it is corporeal and therefore *divisibile, patibile, ac dissolubile est.*[51] Bodin cites Psalm 101 and Isaiah 65 to substantiate the claim that the Master Builder (*opifex*) has decreed that at some time or other the universe will perish. God alone is incorporeal and the Hebrews call "God, maqom, that is, place, because above the sky his divine majesty and essence embrace the universe. They do not say that God is in the world, but the world is in God, since He is not inclosed in the world nor shut out from the world, although the sky is called the abode of God."[52]

God's relation to the universe and to man is emphasized by the epithets Bodin used to describe Him. God is called *conditor, rex, opifex, architectus, deus optimus maximus, principium*, and *lux sempiterna.* God is without body and indivisible and is able to communicate no part of his essence to another. "For if a creature should have any part of the divine essence he would be God completely because God does not have parts nor is divided into parts."[53] Because man is finite, he can never grasp the infinite mind and goodness of God. Man may question the phenomena of nature and the dire happenings on earth, but he should be ever mindful that God made

[49] Bodin, *Theatrum*, p. 83. Bodin in the same section describes matter as a *meretrix* who puts on and takes off forms.

[50] *Ibid.*, p. 71. On being and nonbeing Bodin says: "Because nothing can be fashioned in the middle between being and nonbeing: For we see the beginning of generation is made in the natural body, with matter and form attendant, as in an end from which, and this generation extends itself into the completed body: indeed the change [*mutatio*] which precedes generation has a foundation residing in its own matter and form; consider the embryo, or blood or seed or roots of plants or buds or the beginnings of fossils or metals, all of which have their own form and matter; wherefore that figment, which Aristotle in his thinking imagined between being and nonbeing [*non-ens*], never existed in nature, moreover cannot even be captured in thinking."

[51] *Ibid.*, p. 41.

[52] *Ibid.*, p. 107.

[53] *Ibid.*, pp. 629–30.

all things good. Evil is nothing else than the privation or the lack of good. As jailers, magistrates, and judges are necessary in states, so in this state of the world "God himself for the generation, care, and safeguarding of things has placed angels in all places, in states, provinces, families, as leaders and moderators, and also he placed avengers in all places who do nothing and punish in no way except ordered by God."[54] Though man may not understand, God is ever planning for his welfare. When God noticed that man was carried by base desires away from the contemplation of intelligible things, He willed for man to be involved in agriculture and the care of animals so that this concern would lessen man's mad desires.[55] Indeed, there is a marvelous power of nature placed in the minds of men which inspires them to piety, justice, and virtue. But how do they follow divine knowledge unless God has given them the breath of life?[56]

God alone is simple and can impart no part of his infinity to any creature. How then can God the Creator, eternal principle, without cause, be known? Bodin's answer is Platonic-Augustinian: there are ideas shared between the Creator and the things created. "God had created every seed of the field before it was in the land, which cannot be interpreted in any other way than as the archetype and eternal example in the mind of the Creator."[57] Other values are not all equally remote from God, for there is a chain of being. Next to God in created nature are two Seraphs which stand by the eternal Creator and have six wings and eyes in all parts of the body.

Although knowledge of created things is known through cause, as the Aristotelians said, God is known in a different way, through his creative influences. "God cannot be known from higher causes or antecedent causes, which are none, but can be known only from the rear, that is, from effects."[58] God used good and bad angels, the stars, and other natural causes to bring about all things, and there is no action, no calamity, which has not come from God.[59] Although

[54] *Ibid.*, p. 632. [55] *Ibid.*, p. 273. [56] *Ibid.*, p. 207.
[57] *Ibid.*, p. 630. [58] *Ibid.*, p. 633.
[59] Jean Bodin, *De magorum daemonomania* (Basel, 1581), pp. 13–15, 36–38, 92–94. The Latin edition, translated by Franciscus Junius, was used for all the citations from this work.

man can never know "who and what God is . . . ,"[60] Bodin constantly emphasizes that nature is the key to understanding God. In the conclusion of the *Universae naturae theatrum* Bodin says that he wrote about nature so that we might grasp even a shadowy recognition of the Creator and "break forth in his praises with so much force that at length we might be carried on high by these steps; which indeed is the highest and final good of man."[61]

God created the universe through the exercise of His free will, and He bestowed free will on man. "But if this world is ruled by the highest fairness, also we must confess that the wicked are punished by right, nor is any necessity for sinning due to the higher causes, but free will is granted to man by which he may be higher not only than the lascivious desires but also than the stars."[62] Man was made a little lower than the angels, and since angels are good and devils bad, man also has a free choice to be good or bad.[63] Citing Deuteronomy 30, Bodin presents God's words:

> I have placed before your eyes good and evil, life and death; choose therefore the good and you will live. . . . After God created man, he gave him free will and said 'If you wish, you will keep my commandments; and they will preserve you; I have given fire and water to you, you can direct your hand to one and to the other; you have good and bad, life and death, and whatever you wish, you will have.'[64]

In 1578 Bodin presided as judge in a case of witchcraft brought against Joanna Harvilleria. Bodin found the woman guilty as charged and condemned her to death. In the *praefatio* of *De la démonomanie* (1580) Bodin explains the charge and the penalty, and with the witchcraft case as a starting point, Bodin unfolds in the rest of the book his concept of the world of spirits. He defines a magician as one who is wise and prudent in the ways of the devil and so perverts the law. The devil has devised superstitions and impieties and has taught these to his slaves, the magicians, for the

[60] Bodin, *Colloquium heptaplomeres*, p. 42.
[61] Bodin, *Theatrum*, p. 633.
[62] *Ibid.*, p. 32. [63] *Ibid.*, pp. 14–15. [64] *Ibid.*, p. 16.

destruction of the human race. Lest anyone be doubtful concerning the spirit world, Bodin cites the philosophers and the sacred writings to prove that spirits do exist. Good spirits are called angels, and evil spirits are known as demons, according to the opinion of the Sorbonne in September 1398. From the beginning of the universe God created angels and that great Satan whom the Scripture calls Behemoth and Leviathan. On the nature of demons Bodin cites ancient authorities who believed demons were of two orders, good and bad, but he follows the opinion of the theologians in believing that all demons are bad.

In discussing the association of spirits with men, Bodin reiterates his view stated in the *Universae naturae theatrum* that the *anima* of men is between demons and angels, placed in the middle as it were, and since men are created a little lower than angels, men have the choice of following angelic or demonic natures. Magicians are filled with evil spirits who deceive in two ways, either openly with expressed pacts with the devil or by idolatry in the guise of religion. Magicians pretend that they can foretell the future, but true divination comes from God who speaks to His prophets in dreams, in visions, or through angels. All other divination is human and diabolic. The hymns of Orpheus call upon the oracles of Pan, which is Satan to the Hebrews. Plutarch calls Pan the great leader, and Caesar and Pompey relied on Pan and soothsayers, but all these are human predictions.

Bodin says that in pursuing legitimate goals men often find no help from nature or human faculty but, instead of turning to God who can help most of all, turn to magicians who invoke the devil. Bodin details the several kinds of diabolic divinators: (1) people who send their children through fire; (2) judges who judge with money and priests who divine with silver; (3) sorcerers who rely on lots and numbers; (4) those who fool the eyes of men; (5) those who beg the oracles of evil spirits or consult the devil hidden in bones of beasts; (6) those who consult the dead. All these divinators are abominations to God.[65] God ordained natural divination from

[65] Martin Luther was also strongly opposed to magicians and astrologers. See Carlo Ginzburg, *Il nicodemismo: simulazione e dissimulazione religiosa nell' Eu-*

the creation of the universe, as the Cabala shows, in secret intelligence of divine miracles and in allegories woven throughout sacred scripture. The sacred writings show that it is not necessary to insist on literal interpretation because God speaks in allegories and parables, and His secrets hang as if from a chain let down from heaven. Since God is the first and eternal cause, all things, all spirits and divinations come from him.

Bodin places astrologers in the same category as magicians, and he says it is wrong to trust in astrologers since God is above all. Astrologers are unworthy to make judgments about spirits, virtues, merits, or punishments, and it is most unworthy for astrologers or anyone, for that matter, to argue about religion. Bodin does not deny that magicians are able to cause storms, sickness, sterility, and to kill men and flocks, but he cites Augustine who says that demons have no power of themselves, but God has given them power for punishing men. He continues by saying that God has thousands of ways for vengeance: first through Himself, then through angels, then through demons, men, and beasts, and finally through nature. God brings about all things by means of angels, demons, stars, and other natural causes. He increases our plenty through good servants and punishes us through evil agents.

Through this often tedious book Bodin constantly emphasizes that magicians are shrewd men who are under Satan's power, yet Satan himself can do nothing except what God wills. With this as his major theme he returns at the end of the book to the case of Joanna

---

ropa del '500 (Turin, 1970), p. 30: "In 1520 Luther had published a comment to the decalogue, including among the violators of the first commandment also magicians, necromancers, and astrologers. Luther's hostility toward astrology was great; moreover, this anti-astrological polemic on a religious basis was widespread enough as was the traditional, contrary attempt to show—if the words of Psalm 18 are recalled, 'The heavens declare the glory of God'—the religious legitimacy of astrology. But, coming from a heretic such as Luther, this new attack on astrology could very easily be turned around. Laurent Fries, a physician and astrologer of Colmar, intervened in defense of the science of the stars with a short work (*Ein kurtze Schirmred der Kunst Astrologie* . . . [A Brief Defense of the Art of Astrology . . .], J. Grüninger, Strasburg, 1520) written in the form of a dialogue between Fries himself and Luther. In this work Fries tried to show that astrology was, from a Christian point of view, perfectly orthodox and not therefore, as Luther had maintained, a pagan science."

Harvilleria. He defends the death penalty for magicians and sorcerers because they have allied themselves on the side of Satan, whose aim is to destroy the works of God.[66]

In the *République* Bodin had said that prevention of crime was a more proper remedy than punishment; however, he theorizes, in keeping with the premises of canon law, that the principal benefit derived from punishing crime is that citizens succeed in appeasing God's wrath, and they gain God's benevolent care for the good of the whole commonwealth. Sorcerers, then, must be punished because their crime is aimed at God's majesty. "As Bodin had stated elsewhere, it is not customary for jurists to make codes of law for the sake of vindicating the theories of philosophers, but rather for the sake of serving those practical ends at which the majority of people wish to arrive. Expediency is thus a matter of principle for our author. Had he not explained this to us, we might have considered that in estimating sorcery as the most heinous of crimes, he was making an undue and hypocritical concession to God."[67]

Although it may seem strange that a man of Bodin's erudition and legal training would believe in witchcraft and magic, he was not unlike many of his age in this belief. The spirit world to which angels and demons belonged was a vital part of Bodin's religious thought; consequently, magicians and sorcerers were part of his world view.[68]

The key to Bodin's religious thought is found in the *Colloquium heptaplomeres*, the intriguing work which Bodin completed in 1588[69]

[66] For Bodin's place in the history of magic, see Lynn Thorndike, *History of Magic and Experimental Science*, VI (New York, 1941), pp. 525–27. Thorndike stated that few people were as credulous regarding the powers of witches as Bodin, yet Bodin distinguished "natural means of knowing secret things" from witchcraft.

[67] H. E. Mantz, "Jean Bodin and the Sorcerers," *The Romanic Review* 15 (1924), 174–75.

[68] Bodin's view was surely not uncommon in the sixteenth century. See Daniel P. Walker, *Spiritual and Demonic Magic from Ficino to Campanella* (London, 1958).

[69] Diecmann and Guhrauer believed that 1593 was the correct date because at the end of Bibliothèque Nationale fonds latin 6564 and other manuscripts the letters H.E.J.B.A.S.A.AE. LXIII seem to indicate that Bodin wrote the *Colloquium* when he was 63 years old, that is, in 1593. See E. Guhrauer's introduction to *Das Heptaplomeres des Jean Bodin, zur Geschichte der Kultur und Literatur im Jahrhundert der Reformation* (Berlin, 1841). However, 1593 is not the correct date

but did not publish. Guhrauer believed that Bodin never intended the book to be published during his lifetime because he knew his age too well. The German scholar stated that the *Colloquium heptaplomeres* should be regarded as Bodin's religious testament for a later age, which he worked out only for his inner satisfaction.[70] Contrary to Guhrauer's statement, I believe that Bodin would have published the *Colloquium heptaplomeres* had he lived longer. In spite of the dangers involved,[71] Bodin must have felt a great need to publish the *Colloquium heptaplomeres* because this work is truly the key to the other two works and, perhaps to all his works.

The *Colloquium heptaplomeres* expresses the basic ideas of the *Universae naturae theatrum* and *De la démonomanie* and then advances a step farther. In the *Colloquium heptaplomeres* Bodin presents the problems of the creation of the universe, which constituted a great portion of the *Theatrum*, and of God's revelation of Himself through the order of nature and through the spirit world, the theme of *De la démonomanie*. Then he advances to the problem of man in the natural world, in the world of spirits, and in his quest for God or, as Bodin poses the problem, his quest for true religion.

The *Colloquium heptaplomeres* is a dialogue between men of seven different faiths or points of view. Coronaeus, at whose home the conversations take place, represents the Catholic viewpoint, Salomon the Jewish, Toralba the philosophic naturalist, Fridericus the Lutheran, Curtius the Calvinist, Senamus the Skeptic, and Octavius the Islamic. In the *Theatrum* Bodin uses a pseudodialogue form, but the dialogue is soon forgotten for the exposition. In the *Colloquium heptaplomeres* the dialogue form is maintained throughout, each man presenting his opinions on the various points under discussion.

In Book II of the *Colloquium heptaplomeres* the men, with Toral-

---

because a manuscript of the *Colloquium* which I discovered in the Bibliothèque Mazarine (Bibliothèque Mazarine fonds latin 3527) carries the date 1588. This evidence opens up many new problems for Bodin scholars. Either Bodin was not born in 1530 (for he could not have been 63 years old in 1588), or A.AE. LXIII (anno aetatis LXIII) does not refer to his chronological age. An article by the author on this manuscript and Bibliothèque Mazarine fonds latin 3529 is now in progress.

[70] Guhrauer, *Das Heptaplomeres*, p. 6.

[71] The *Methodus*, the *République*, and *De la démonomanie* had already been placed on the Index.

ba dominating the conversation, debate the causes of things. Toralba points out that God did not create the universe from necessity, which is one of the central arguments of the *Theatrum*. Toralba says: "Still nothing is more foolish than to say that the first cause is the producer and preserver of all things and to find this same first cause by servile obligation and necessity and yet to assign to oneself free will. . . . That God is immutable is agreed by all natural scientists and theologians. But they think that higher causes are checked by the force and power of lower causes. More credible is the opinion of the poets, who, in their fictions, profess that Jupiter is loosed from the power of lower gods but still is bound by the higher laws of Nemesis. . . . Augustine thinks that fate applies to God alone or to no one."[72] Salomon agrees with Toralba and says that fate is God who receives all things within himself and encompasses all things with free will. Toralba then proffers an opinion which contains much of the thought of the *Theatrum* and *De la démonomanie*: "Natural things do not happen by chance, at random, or in blind sequence but proceed uniformly according to the same laws, so that given the cause the effect follows, unless they are kept from doing so by the divine will in all things or human will in some or by the power of demons in many."[73]

Throughout the *Colloquium heptaplomeres* Bodin emphasizes that demons and angels are emissaries from God to man, and just as in the *Démonomanie*, he cites numerous examples of strange events that happen apart from nature and consequently must be a result of demonic power. He constantly repeats, however, that demons have no power of themselves and can do nothing unless ordered by God.

Bodin reiterates the fact that God alone is eternal, and he departs from Aristotle's teaching that the world is eternal. In the *Universae naturae theatrum* Bodin also states this idea and adds that the world cannot be eternal of its own nature since it depends on the will of another.[74] In contrast man has been granted free will by God. If a

[72] *Colloquium heptaplomeres*, Book II, p. 20.

[73] *Ibid.*, p. 24.

[74] "Nothing can be eternal in its own nature, whose first cause is voluntary: the first cause of the world is voluntary; therefore, the world cannot be eternal in its own nature, since its state and condition depend on the freedom and will of another." *Universae naturae theatrum*, p. 37.

man chooses the good, he will live; if he chooses evil, he will suffer punishment. Man is also free to obtain knowledge of the good. If man chooses to find God, God reveals Himself by a process of emanation rather than by any particle of God being implanted in man, which would be impossible because it would destroy the Unity which alone is eternal.[75] Bodin posits a certain kind of immortality for the soul and envisions a life after death in which the just will be rewarded and the unjust punished. To Bodin, however, punishments are not infinite.[76]

The ideas which are expressed in the first three books of the *Colloquium heptaplomeres* are paralleled by the same ideas in the *Universae naturae theatrum*. The main theme of the *Theatrum* is that God can best be known from the theater of universal nature,[77] and

[75] *Ibid.*, pp. 629–30. Bodin's concept of free will reflects the influence of St. Augustine. Cf. Augustine's *On the Free Choice of the Will*, Book I and Book III, chapters XI–XVIII. The emanation theory which Bodin emphasizes in the *Colloquium heptaplomeres* reflects the influence of the Neoplatonic "stages" and also the emanation theories of the Cabalists. In the *Theatrum* and *De la démonomanie* Neoplatonic influence is more apparent; in the *Colloquium* there is increased attention to Cabala. For a concise statement concerning Neoplatonic and Cabalistic theories of emanation, note Gershom G. Scholem, *Major Trends in Jewish Mysticism* (New York, 1954), pp. 208–209. "According to the Kabbalists, there are ten such fundamental attributes to God which are at the same time ten stages through which the divine life pulsates back and forth. The point to keep in mind is that the Sefiroth are not secondary or intermediary spheres which interpose between God and the universe. The author does not regard them as something comparable to, for example, the 'middle stages' of the Neoplatonists which have their place between the Absolute One and the world of the senses. In the Neoplatonic system, these emanations are 'outside' the One, if it is possible to use that expression. There have been attempts to justify an analogous interpretation of the theology of the Zohar and to treat the Sefiroth as secondary stages or spheres outside of or apart from the divine personality. . . . True the Zohar frequently refers to the Sefiroth as stages, but they are plainly regarded not as the steps of a ladder between God and the world, but as various phases in the manifestation of the Divinity which proceed from and succeed each other."

[76] See *Colloquium heptaplomeres*, pp. 102–103, 342–43, 344–46. Also *Universae naturae theatrum*, pp. 536–41. For a recent treatment of the question of eternal torment in the seventeenth century, see Daniel P. Walker, *The Decline of Hell* (Chicago, 1964).

[77] "In this elegant allegory it is indicated that God cannot be known from higher or antecedent causes, which are none, but only from behind, that is, from effects . . . and He placed man not in a hidden recess but in the middle of the world, so that he might contemplate more easily and better than if he were in the heaven the universe of all things and all His works, and from the wealth of His works man

Toralba, who dominates Books II and III of the *Colloquium heptaplomeres*, constantly expresses this view. In fact, many passages are so similar that only a few words are changed. Bodin was fascinated by certain stories, and he repeated them in both books. He was so impressed with accounts of Egyptian mummies, their powers of stirring up storms, and their powers of healing that he repeated this story in all three of these works.[78]

More important still for an understanding of Bodin's thought is the discussion of harmony with which he begins Book IV and which is also developed in the *Universae naturae theatrum* (pp. 143 ff.). He begins by showing the harmony in numbers, as in geometric progressions, then the harmony in musical systems, then the harmony most perfectly expressed in nature. Harmony in nature includes harmony in religion and toleration, which is central to Bodin's thinking. The harmony of nature is based on multiplicity, which is the aspect of creation in the world. The unity of Divinity is apart, however, from every multiplicity.[79] Bodin calls upon the concept of harmony to show that, as there is need for multiplicity in nature, so also there is need of this multiplicity in religion. When the dialogue ends with the statement that no further discussions will be held on religion, the concept of harmony takes on additional significance. There is no rejection or acceptance of any one religion, but rather a recognition of the divine descent of all religious beliefs

might probingly view the Sun, that is, God Himself." *Universae naturae theatrum*, p. 633. For Toralba's identical view compare his speeches throughout Books II and III.

[78] *Colloquium heptaplomeres*, pp. 66 ff., *Universae naturae theatrum*, pp. 143–44, *De magorum daemonomania*, p. 197.

[79] For an excellent discussion of the *Colloquium heptaplomeres* see Giorgio Radetti "Il problema della religione nel pensiero di Giovanni Bodin," *Giornale critico della filosofia Italiana*, VI, fasc. 4–5 (1938), 277–94. On the question of harmony he says: "As in nature the elements are comparable to voices, to notes which, even though diverse and, in fact, for this very reason, form a harmony ('From whence the sweetest elements, etc.'—cf. *Universae naturae theatrum*, p. 143). So in the human world the state has as its goal the foundation of this harmony among men; the last page of the *Republic* is a complete exaltation of the harmony which regulates and unifies the universe. Cf. *De la rép.*, p. 1060, cf. *Methodus*, p. 294. Moreover, the same doctrine of climates is bound to this doctrine of universal harmony," p. 293.

and a universal brotherhood of men in the worship of divinity and in a moral life and a free conscience for everyone.[80]

Bodin's emphasis upon harmony and toleration, coming as it did in the midst of an age of religious conflicts, makes him an innovator in the religious thinking of the Cinquecento, because the complete tolerationists' view that Bodin was offering was not held by anybody before Uriel da Costa and Spinoza. In contrast to da Costa and Spinoza, who developed a tolerationist attitude because they had given up any historical religion, Bodin remained religious throughout his life.[81]

To summarize, the relationship of the *Colloquium heptaplomeres* to the *Universae naturae theatrum* and *De la démonomanie* is that of a synthesis to its parts: each of the other works contains many of the same ideas as the *Colloquium heptaplomeres*, but the *Colloquium heptaplomeres* contains *all* the ideas inherent in the other two. The first three books of the *Colloquium* reflect the emphasis in the *Theatrum* on the theater of nature as the work of the Master Builder. The laws of nature reflect the wonder of their Creator. The first three books of the *Colloquium* also reflect the spirit world of *De la démonomanie*. Everything which does not happen from God or through the laws of nature must happen because of the action of demons or angels.

The line written at the end of the *Theatrum* gives a clue to another strong relationship between the three works. Bodin says that he wrote the book when all France was burning with civil war. ("*Finis Theatri Naturae, quod Io. Bodinus Gallia tota bella civili flagrante conscripsit.*") The point that Bodin seems to be making is that France is burning because she has not applied the harmonious laws of nature

[80] Radetti, "Il problema della religione," p. 294. Bodin had already stated in the *République* that a man of no religion could not be obedient to the law, yet he stressed in the *Colloquium heptaplomeres* the fact that no one can be forced to believe. His plea for toleration was witnessed as early as 1576 by his conduct in the Estates General of Blois as representative of the third estate. See Joseph Lecler, *Toleration and the Reformation* (New York, 1960), pp. 179–85.

[81] Professor Richard H. Popkin called to my attention the relationship of Bodin, da Costa, and Spinoza in regard to toleration. It might be added that Guillaume Postel (1510–1580) expressed tolerationist views that were very similar to those expressed in the *Colloquium heptaplomeres*.

to the question of religious toleration, and France (and the world) will continue to burn until the harmony of nature becomes a symbol for universal harmony, especially in the area of religion. This is, of course, the theme of the *Colloquium heptaplomeres*. The last three books of the *Colloquium* are concerned with the question of true religion. The harmony of nature and the spirit world which reflects the higher Unity of God serve, then, as a base upon which Bodin builds the main structure of the *Colloquium heptaplomeres*: the nature of true religion, which reveals and accepts the multiplicity of ways to approach God and the multiple revelations of God to man. True religion is tolerant, for it sees the harmonious multiplicity of religions. No religion is true whose point of view is not universal, whose expression is not free, whose center does not reflect the intimate harmony of God and nature. The *Démonomanie* reflects this emphasis on true religion and so is related not only to the first part, but also to the second part of the *Colloquium heptaplomeres*. Bodin says in his book on witchcraft that true religion is the recognition of God, and that God has revealed himself in multiple ways through miraculous allegories which we read in the Cabala.

It is interesting to note also the progression in form of presentation through the three works. In *De la démonomanie* Bodin uses pure exposition. The dialogue appears, to a limited degree, in the *Universae naturae theatrum*. The *Colloquium heptaplomeres* then shows the full development of the dialogue style, while incorporating all his religious and philosophical thought.

When one looks back from the *Colloquium heptaplomeres* to his earlier work, one realizes that the *Politique* of 1576 has become progressively more liberal in his religious views. When Bodin published the *République* in 1576, it was difficult to determine precisely what his religious views were, but he maintained in 1559 in his *Discours au senate et au peuple de Toulouse* that people should be brought up publicly in one religion, as an indispensable element in the cohesiveness of the state; he also avowed that care should be taken to preserve religious unity, and religion should not be cast in doubt by becoming a subject for disputation. Religion, according to Bodin in 1576, provides the unity of the state and underlies the king's power, the execution of the laws and respect for the laws, and obedience of the subjects.[82] Between 1580 and 1596 his liberal views became even more apparent, until they reach a climax in the *Colloquium heptaplomeres*, in which his religious opinions seem to have developed into a kind of theism which leaves each man's religion, provided he has some, to his own personal conscience. In the *Colloquium heptaplomeres* atheism alone is intolerable to Bodin.

Scholars have held diverse opinions concerning which speaker represents Bodin's thinking. Baudrillart, Noack, Guhrauer, and with some limitation, Dilthey think Toralba speaks for Bodin; Huet and Guttmann say Salomon does; Chauviré seems to choose Salomon and Toralba, and Mesnard points to Coronaeus.[83] Nearer to the truth, I believe, is the view that all the speakers represent Bodin's thinking at one time or another. No one represents his thinking exclusively, but Bodin is sympathetic to some views of each as the dialogue develops. The point seems to be, however, that regardless of Bodin's approval or disapproval of the religious views represented in the dialogue, he constantly stresses the need for toleration of all religions.

Coronaeus the Catholic, the gentle peacemaker who does not want to offend anyone, represents authority and tradition. Salomon the Jew, who commands respect by his erudition and his advanced age, displays a vast knowledge of the Cabala and the Old Testament. The other speakers find it very difficult to refute Salomon. Octavius, a convert from Catholicism to Islam, points out that Muslims have ideas common to both the Jewish and Christian religions. He believes that many religions can be received by a state. Octavius also describes exotic places and strange customs in the East, and he has a good knowledge of demons and angels. Curtius, the Calvinist, represents the Reformed religion with its emphasis on inner piety. He holds fast to his belief in the Incarnation, the Virgin birth, and the immortality of the soul, but he is not nearly so dogmatic as the Lutheran Fridericus, a mathematician who displays a wide knowledge of demonology. Fridericus is the least tolerant of the seven.

82 *République*, Book IV.

83 See Radetti, "Il problema della religione," p. 278.

Senamus is the skeptic who questions the beliefs of all but says that all religions are good. He also displays a subtle wit, which may reflect a trait of Bodin, who was said to possess a genial disposition and a lively wit.[84] Toralba believes that true religion consists in the simple adoration of God and following the laws of nature. He thinks rites and ceremonies are unnecessary. Salomon disagrees with him on this point, but both agree that the oldest religion is the best, the religion of the earliest man and the patriarchs, Adam, Enoch, Job, Abraham, Isaac, and Jacob.

Perhaps some additional remarks are in order concerning Coronaeus' role in the dialogue. Although fewer speeches are allotted to Coronaeus than to the other speakers, his position is central for a proper balance among the various opinions. The importance of his role gradually evolves as the dialogue progresses, until Coronaeus becomes the mediator, as it were, between the non-Christians (Salomon, Toralba, Octavius, and Senamus) and the Christians (Curtius, Fridericus, and, of course, himself). He often remarks that he believes in the authority of the church, but his belief does not keep him from an appreciation of the non-Christians nor does he answer the harsh words of Curtius and Fridericus in kind but with love.

The role of Coronaeus is more representative of the *Colloquium* in its entirety than is that of Senamus, who is also tolerant. Senamus approves of all religions and pays homage to all, but his skepticism does not allow a real belief in any. On the other hand, Coronaeus' tolerance leads him to agree even with some points that the non-Christians bring forth, yet he is firm in his Catholic faith. If Bodin himself could not possess the certainty of Coronaeus' faith, he, nevertheless, seemed inspired by his portrayal of a liberal sixteenth-century Catholic, who in several ways resembles the eminent Cardinal Gasparo Contareni.

We may say then, in summary, that the *Colloquium heptaplomeres* is one of the great expressions of religious synthesis. There is an

[84] Senamus cleverly misquotes Horace (*Graecia capta ferum victorem cepit, Epist.* II. I. 156) as an answer to Salomon, who has been pointing out the superiority of the Jewish religion. Senamus says: "Judaea capta ferum victorem cepit." (Captured Judea captured the savage conqueror.) *Colloquium heptaplomeres*, p. 201.

essence shared by all historical faiths but never exhausted by any one. Hence in the great tradition of universalism we find a sixteenth-century voice. It was not left to the later centuries to have this message expressed by Shaftesbury, Locke, Spinoza, Hume, or Lessing. The very age that bred rancor and bloodshed also produced its opposite, harmony and toleration.

CHAPTER III

The *Colloquium heptaplomeres* and the Sixteenth Century

THE relation of the *Colloquium heptaplomeres* to the intellectual currents of the sixteenth century is as involved and complicated as everything else about the work. The colloquy requires opposing participants, and truth is preserved by conflict and resolution of diverse opinions. This dialogue form was a favorite literary type, and there are many Renaissance examples. Perhaps the form was popular during the Renaissance and Reformation period because the dialogue provided a *persona* for the author whose views might not find favor with the authorities; he could always say the speakers in the dialogue said it, not he. Although the *Praise of Folly* is not a dialogue, Erasmus used "Folly" as such a *persona* to criticize the social scene and the church. The *Praise of Folly* is also similar to the *Colloquium heptaplomeres* in that no real conclusion is reached but rather the problem is boldly displayed.

The setting of Bodin's dialogue reflects the ideal societies depicted in Renaissance utopias. The home of Coronaeus is a utopia that provides all the aspects of life dear to the well-versed man of the Renaissance—intelligent conversation, polished manners, wit, good food, music, indeed all the arts. Coronaeus' home recalls Castiglione's *Courtier* and looks forward to Bacon's *New Atlantis.*[85]

[85] The enlightened atmosphere of Coronaeus' home also recalls the well-ordered and tolerant government of the Khazars, whose king in 960 A.D., could boast of a broad-minded and just administration when fanaticism, ignorance, and anarchy reigned in Western Europe. Those who were persecuted because of their religion could find refuge there. The supreme court of justice was composed of seven judges,

In the sense in which "Renaissance," describing an individual man, signifies universal breadth of interest, the *Colloquium heptaplomeres* is truly a Renaissance book. The philosophical orientation of the work is Neoplatonic, especially of the Florentine variety. Bodin is close to Ficino in his admiration for the "divine" Plato, whose *Timaeus* and *Phaedo* he constantly cites. To Bodin, as to Ficino, Plato represents the perfection of an ancient tradition of theology. Bodin, following Numenius, calls Plato the Attic Moses.[86] In the introduction to his translation of the *Corpus hermeticum* Ficino writes:

> Mercurius Trismegistus was the first philosopher to raise himself above physics and mathematics to the contemplation of the divine. . . . Therefore he was considered the original founder of theology. Orpheus followed him and held second place in ancient

two of whom were Jews, two Mohammedans, two Christians, and one pagan. The "Khazari Letters," which detailed the affairs of this tolerant state, were first published in 1577 by Isaac Aqrish into whose hands these documents had fallen while on a journey from Egypt to Constantinople. Cf. also A. Garosci, *Jean Bodin* (Milan, 1934), p. 110, note 4: "This reminds us of the *Book of the Khazars*, where a Rabbi, a Mohammedan, and a Natural Philosopher converse in the presence of a King. But it is not credible that Bodin had directly imitated Jewish sources. Rather, it is evidently the imitations of the anti-Christian discourse of the Rabbi in Celsus, preserved in Origen, *Contra Celsum*." For a thorough and fascinating account of the Khazars see D. M. Dunlop, *The History of the Jewish Khazars* (Princeton, 1954). *The Khazar* was written originally in Arabic in A.D. 1140, by Judah ha-Levi and later translated into Hebrew. Dunlop states, p. 116, that ha-Levi's work is "a defense of Rabbinic Judaism cast in the form of a dialogue which is represented as having taken place in Khazaria 400 years before the author's own time. In this dialogue the interlocutors are the Khazar and others. Ha-Levi is not concerned to enlarge on the setting, his main interest being theological not historical, but he regards the conversion of the king to Judaism at this date as an accepted fact." The Khazari Letters, which were in existence in ha-Levi's time, were supposedly an interchange of letters between Hasday ibn-Shaprut, a well-known Jew in Spain, and Joseph, king of the Khazars. Dunlop points out that the expression "books of the Khazars" is not applicable to the letters and important details given by ha-Levi are not in the letters. Where Isaac Aqrish obtained the text of the Khazari Letters is unknown. As to the authenticity of the letters, Dunlop, p. 130, states: "If anyone thinks that the Khazar correspondence was first composed in 1577 and published in *Qol Mebasser*, the onus of proof is certainly on him. He must show that a number of ancient manuscripts, which appear to contain references to the correspondence, have all been interpolated since the end of the sixteenth century. This will prove a very difficult or rather an impossible task."

[86] *Colloquium heptaplomeres*, p. 187.

> theology. Aglaophemus was initiated into the Orphic mysteries. Aglaophemus' successor in theology was Pythagoras, and his pupil was Philolaus, the master of our divine Plato. So six theologians, in wonderful order, formed a unique and coherent succession in ancient theology, beginning with Mercurius and ending with the divine Plato.[87]

Throughout the *Colloquium heptaplomeres* Bodin shows admiration for this ancient tradition and these ancient theologians.

With Pico, Bodin shares perhaps an even greater affinity. The *Colloquium heptaplomeres* is surely a work in which the right of the individual to intellectual and spiritual freedom is proclaimed. Pico's philosophy is pervaded with emphasis on the right and duty of man to search freely in the intellectual and spiritual world. "Pico rejects any inquisition, in the domain of knowledge as in that of faith. For him there are no heretics of the intellect. The intellect can be moved to accept a determinate proposition only when it produces the conviction of that proposition in itself; and this conviction must be founded on determinate grounds."[88] Bodin also reflects Pico's thinking on the question of original sin and the Fall. Bodin speaks of the golden age of man transmitted through the noble heroes of our ancestors, and he does not look back to Adam but to those after the Fall, namely, Abel, Enoch, Noah, Abraham, Job, Isaac, and Jacob.[89] To Pico also man's sin and consequent Fall do not stand "as an indelible stain upon his nature; for in it he sees nothing but the correlate and counterpart to something other and higher. Man must be capable of sin, that he may become capable of good."[90] Pico defends the teaching of Origen, whom Bodin also cites, that there can be no eternal punishment. "An eternity of punishment would imply a form of finality which according to Pico's basic con-

[87] Quoted by Paul Oskar Kristeller, *The Philosophy of Marsilio Ficino* (Gloucester, Mass., 1964), pp. 25–26.

[88] Ernst Cassirer, "Giovanni Pico della Mirandola," *Journal of the History of Ideas* 3 (1942), 328.

[89] *Colloquium heptaplomeres*, p. 172 and throughout.

[90] Cassirer, "Pico della Mirandola," p. 329.

ception would contradict the real meaning of human existence."[91] Bodin presents the same view, which has been referred to earlier in this introduction.

Bodin's Neoplatonism also has its roots in Plotinus, Augustine, Proclus, and Dionysius the Areopagite. Nor is he completely separated from the medieval theological tradition, for he shows great admiration for St. Thomas, even when he allows one of the speakers to refute him. Bodin shows the same respect for Aristotle and Averroës, whom he often refutes. Pico also displayed profound respect for Averroës, although he disagreed with him.

In addition to the religious views discussed earlier, the *Colloquium heptaplomeres* represents many of the ideas of the Brethren of the Common Life, the Christian humanists, such as Erasmus, who emphasized inner religion and true piety, and the Reformers. Curtius in the *Colloquium heptaplomeres* expresses the Reformed concern with the worship of saints, "idols," and with other "empty rites."

The rising interest in science during the Renaissance appears in the *Colloquium heptaplomeres*. Reference is made to gunpowder, new stars that have appeared, and the scientific investigation of nature. Geography, travel, and the studies of navigation which flourished in Portugal and Spain were of keen interest to the man of the Renaissance as they were to the scholars at Coronaeus' house.

The role of a Renaissance prince as portrayed by Machiavelli also concerns Bodin's scholars, for Octavius says that it is sometimes justifiable for physicians and princes to lie.

Senamus with his constant doubting and questioning reflects the revival of Skepticism in the sixteenth century. Perhaps the most significant influence of Pyrrhonism was on the theological disputes of the period. "This initial version of this style of argumentation was intended to show that as soon as the Reformers had admitted that the church could err, thus denying the traditional rule of faith, they could then be reduced to skeptical despair. If the alternative criterion of true faith is Scripture, then, according to St. Francis de Sales, Cardinal du Perron, Pierre Charron, Bishop Camus and others, no

[91] *Ibid.*, p. 330.

one can tell by Scripture alone what it says or means. All the Reformers have to offer are the dubious opinions of Luther, Calvin, and Zwingli."[92] Montaigne and Charron tried to undermine the reasoning abilities of man and consequently cast doubt upon the reasons of the Protestants for their faith. Although Senamus represents the skeptic point of view, all of Bodin's speakers agree that it is wicked for a person to destroy a man's religious beliefs and have nothing to put in their place.

Bodin favors the "new learning" of the Renaissance, and he has Toralba say that the more he knows, the more he knows that he does not know. Curtius says that this is characteristic of most learned men and that when a man can freely view the lands and heavenly bodies from the top of a mountain, he is struck by his old earth-bound ignorance. He also explains that many have refused to learn because of the power of empty authority.

Closely connected with the "new learning" was the Renaissance idea of wisdom, which the *Colloquium heptaplomeres* develops throughout the work. Though the "new learning" reflected wisdom on one level, to most Renaissance men true wisdom was the "knowledge of divine things," as Ficino said. True wisdom was mysterious and veiled from the eyes of the profane. Pico said that God created from eternity the *prima mens*, wisdom, and from this divine intellect or wisdom come all the ideas or forms by which God created all things. "It is because a knowledge of Ideas is the result of divine illumination that wisdom is said to come from God. Not only do the sacred texts of Jews and Christians say that only God can teach wisdom, and that it can only be got by faith, hope, and charity, but Plato also tells how he daily asked God for wisdom. This is the divine meaning hidden in the Orphic fable of the birth of Minerva from the head of Zeus. Explained by Ficino and his followers, who were themselves following Boccaccio, the myth meant that all wisdom has its origins in God and is mysteriously infused in us by God. . . . At this crucial point Ficino joins Nicholas of Cusa and the

[92] Richard H. Popkin, *The History of Scepticism from Erasmus to Descartes* (Assen, 1960), p. 69.

Christian mystics; wisdom is a gift of the Holy Spirit, a supranatural infusion of divine light."[93]

The *Colloquium heptaplomeres* emphasizes this Renaissance concept of wisdom perhaps more than any other single idea, as the complete title of the work suggests. Salomon is repeatedly asked to explain these secrets of divine things which were hidden from the average man. Salomon professes that he "drinks from the same springs" as everyone else, yet he does unfold some mysteries that he says are locked in the divine words of the Old Testament and the Cabala. By the numerous discussions that the participants in the dialogue have about allegories which the untutored never comprehend, Bodin reveals his interest in Renaissance wisdom. Salomon says that the Old Testament is filled with allegories so that the secrets of God may not grow stale in their commonness. "Therefore we must exercise our mind on rather obscure divine words so that we may not only abstain from faults and embrace true glory but also seek the body's health, the mind's prudence and wisdom, and the closest union with immortal God."[94]

Many Renaissance figures agreed that the Bible held secrets for the wise. Pico said that the Bible had a literal meaning and a secret meaning; the literal meaning can be grasped by the *vulgus*, but the secret meaning needs the expert intellect. Savonarola also believed in the hidden meaning of the Bible. Sebastian Franck called the Bible a book sealed with seven seals. Campanella pointed out the scriptures' ambiguous character.[95] To these men and to Bodin the ambiguous nature of the scriptures was part of their idea of wisdom, but there were other factors which colored their premises. "They were inspired by very diverse motives: Pico della Mirandola by his desire to reconcile pagan philosophy with Christian faith, Savonarola by his efforts aimed at a fundamental reform of the Church, and Cam-

[93] Eugene F. Rice, Jr., *The Renaissance Idea of Wisdom* (Cambridge, Mass., 1958), p. 67.

[94] *Colloquium heptaplomeres*, pp. 74–75; Eng. transl. below, pp. 96–98 f. Bodin begins Book III with the question of the allegory, and he develops thoroughly the idea of wisdom in this book.

[95] See Edward E. Lowinsky, *Secret Chromatic Art in the Netherlands Motet* (New York, 1967), p. 137.

panella by his enthusiasm for the new science. Since they remained in the Roman Catholic camp and had to justify their views, they had to resort to the theory of an esoteric meaning of the Scriptures which would support their beliefs."[96] All these diverse motives seem applicable to Bodin and help explain his emphasis on secret meanings.

Bodin begins Book IV, as he did Book III, in the *Colloquium heptaplomeres* with a discussion that reflects this hidden meaning. The conversation begins with comments on geometrical progressions and then develops into a discussion of musical theories and practices; from music the discussion drifts into the nature of harmonies (nonmusical), and if one looks at the last book of the *Colloquium heptaplomeres*, the hidden meaning of the musical discussion becomes clear. It was appropriate for Bodin to use music as a springboard for broader questions of harmony. The musical world of the latter part of the Cinquecento was very different from the early years of the era, and the revolutions in religion, science, and philosophy may be compared to that in music.[97]

Lowinsky, in his excellent study of Renaissance music,[98] points out that the new chromaticism in the music of the Renaissance met with a hostile attitude from the church. "The defense of the diatonic system of the Ecclesiastical modes against the rising wave of chromaticism presents one of the most fascinating chapters of Renaissance

[96] *Ibid.*, pp. 137–38.

[97] The fifteenth century is called by Donald F. Tovey "the Golden Age" of music. It began with the inherited "modes" and ended with the basis of the modern major and minor scales. Thus the very concept of harmony changed, and what had been rejected, even regarded as illegal and blasphemous, became the very norm. Whereas we think of Palestrina's masses as the most appropriate and fitting music for the Sistine Choir to sing in St. Peter's, the Council of Trent discussed whether to permit polyphony. We may well link Bodin's problem of harmonizing the new religious and philosophic thoughts with Palestrina's problem of how to incorporate the experiments in disharmony. Tovey asks the question if there is anything deeper in the use of A♯ than "a desire for a sensational variety of harmony." The problem was to find limits to the novelty. When the *Colloquium heptaplomeres* was written (1588), the great careers of Orlando de Lasso and Palestrina were almost finished; both died in 1594. Josquin des Prés and Monteverde were flourishing. When Monteverde introduced discords and experimented with new rhythmic principles, his problem was like Bodin's, whether the old styles could establish order in the new materials. Article "Music," *Encycl. Brit.* (11th ed.), XIX, 75–77.

[98] Lowinsky, *Secret Chromatic Art*; see also his article, "Music in Renaissance Culture," *Journal of the History of Ideas* 15 (1942), 509–53.

theory. A study of the material available reveals with the utmost clarity that the Church took a most lively and serious interest in the matter of preserving the old diatonic system of modes."[99]

The question of Renaissance wisdom and secret meanings leads us to the secret meaning in the *Colloquium heptaplomeres*, and for this we must turn our attention to Hermes Trismegistus and the Cabala. As Frances Yates has pointed out,[100] the core of the Renaissance Neoplatonism was Hermetic. The core of the *Colloquium heptaplomeres* is also Hermetic. Bodin's concept of man who can be in tune with God and the cosmos by the demonic agents of God is very similar to the Hermetic concept of man. Yates says: "Contrast this Hermetic Adam with the Mosaic Adam, formed out of the dust of the earth. It is true that God gave him domination over the creatures, but when he sought to know the secrets of the divine power, to eat of the tree of knowledge, this was the sin of disobedience for which he was expelled from the Garden of Eden. The Hermetic man in the 'Pimander' also falls and can also be regenerated. But the regenerated Hermetic man regains the dominion over nature which he had in his divine origin. When he is regenerated, brought back into communion with the rule of 'the all' through magico-religious communion with the cosmos, it is the regeneration of a being who regains this divinity. One might say that the 'Pimander' describes the creation, fall, and redemption not of a man but of a magus. . . ."[101]

This concept of man who is in tune with the mysteries of the universe is a theme that runs throughout the *Colloquium heptaplomeres*, not specifically stated by one of the participants but gathered from

[99] *Ibid.*, p. 111.

[100] Frances E. Yates, "The Hermetic Tradition," in Charles S. Singleton, ed., *Art, Science, and History in the Renaissance* (Baltimore, 1967), p. 255. See also Frances E. Yates, *Giordano Bruno and the Hermetic Tradition* (Chicago, 1964).

[101] Yates, "Hermetic Tradition," p. 257. Jean Thenaud, a sixteenth-century Franciscan, wrote a book about the Cabala (*La saincte et trescrestienne cabale*), in which he condemns as superstitious the use of the Cabala by believers in magic. "He disapproves particularly of the attribution of 'superstitions, curious writings, and vain fictions' not only in philosophy but even in theology, to great men of past ages and of the consideration of Moses as 'prince of magic.' Among the books which he censures are the Hebrew *Raziel* and the works of Hermes Trismegistus." Cited by Joseph Leon Blau, *The Christian Interpretation of the Cabala in the Renaissance* (New York, 1944), p. 95.

the conversations of all, and especially articulated by Salomon and Toralba. The emphasis is on man after the Fall, who by all the magico-religious forces of the cosmos can unfold the secrets of divine things and thereby regain a harmony with the universe and with God.[102] Bodin follows Trismegistus' theory of the emanation of the divine presence into man.[103] There are repeated references to the Cabala and to Hermes, whom the Neoplatonists believed to be an Egyptian priest, perhaps prior to Moses, from whom much of the ancient wisdom flowed to Plato. Salomon gives lengthy explanations about how the Hebrews came in contact with the Cabala, which was an oral tradition for many centuries. Salomon places the Cabala as equal in divine revelation to the Old Testament and other prophetic writings. The references to Hermes and the Cabala in the *Colloquium heptaplomeres* are too numerous to cite. Bodin thus places himself in the midst of one of the most important aspects of Renaissance Neoplatonism, the Hermetic tradition.

102 This concept is very akin to Pico's use of the Cabala as one element in a universal synthetic system of thought. Franciscus Georgius of Venice, a follower of Pico in Cabalistic thought, published *De harmonia mundi totius cantica tria* in 1525 and therein revealed that the harmony of which he spoke was the nature of Pico's synthesis of all philosophies. For an excellent study of the Christian use of the Cabala, see Blau, *The Christian Interpretation of the Cabala.* Other illuminating works on the Cabala and Jewish mysticism are Gershom G. Scholem, *On the Kabbalah and Its Symbolism* (New York, 1965); Gershom G. Scholem, *The Messianic Idea in Judaism* (New York, 1971); Gershom G. Scholem, *Major Trends in Jewish Mysticism* (New York, 1954); Wolfgang S. Seiferth, *Synagogue and Church in the Middle Ages: Two Symbols in Art and Literature* (New York, 1970). Also, Joseph Leon Blau, "Postel and the Significance of Renaissance Cabalism," *Journal of the History of Ideas* 15 (1954), 218–32; François Secret, "Les Jesuites et le Kabbalisme Chrétien à la renaissance," *Bibliothèque d'humanisme et renaissance* 20 (1958), 542–55; P. Zambelli, "Il «De auditu Kabbalistico» e la tradizione lulliana nel Rinascimento," *Atti e mem. dell'Accad. Toscana . . . «La Colombaria»* 30 n.s. 16 (1965), 113–247.

103 Bodin's theory of emanation was also very close to that of the Spanish Cabalists. See Scholem, *The Messianic Idea in Judaism*, p. 44. "To the question of how the world came into being the Spanish Kabbalists had proffered their doctrines of emanations. From the abundance of His being, from the treasure laid up within Himself, God 'emanated' the *sefirot*, those divine luminaries, those modes, and stages through which He manifests Himself externally. His resplendent light emanates from stage to stage, and the light spreads to ever wider spheres and becomes light evermore thickened. Through the descent of the lights from their infinite source all the worlds were emanated and created; our world is but the fast and outward shell of the layers of divine glory."

Bodin's use of the Cabala in the *Colloquium* is analogous to the Cabalistic thinking of his learned and strange countryman, Guillaume Postel (1510–1581). Of all the famous Renaissance Cabalists, Postel was perhaps the only one who had read all the Cabalistic writings in the original tongue. Whereas Pico had relied mainly on a commentary on the *Zohar* for his knowledge, and Reuchlin's sources were chiefly pre-Zoharic, Postel was acquainted with all the major documents of the Cabala. Bouwsma says that "of all the intellectual strains with which Postel was acquainted, this comes closest to a source for him in the most literal sense. No doubt the Cabala reinforced tendencies already present in his mind. But Postel so venerated the authority of Cabalistic writings that they constantly influenced the development of his ideas (after 1545) and the manner of his expression."[104]

There were three elements of Cabalistic thinking that were especially dear to Postel, and they appear throughout his writings.[105] They are the sacredness of the Hebrew language, cosmic sexual dualism, and universal harmony. This is not to say that other Renaissance Cabalists did not also display keen interests in these areas. Postel, however, emphasized these aspects and centered much of his thought around them. This is of particular interest when one observes that these ideas are the major Cabalistic themes expressed by Bodin in the *Colloquium*.[106]

The Hebrew language had special significance for Postel, as indeed did all language which enabled man to communicate with the ultimate source of truth. Postel shared the Cabalistic view of Hebrew as the holy tongue and the original common language for communication between God and man. Hebrew was reverenced, almost

[104] William J. Bouwsma, *Concordia Mundi: The Career and Thought of Guillaume Postel* (Cambridge, Mass., 1957), p. 138. Cf. also Blau, *Christian Interpretation of the Cabala*, pp. 97–98.

[105] For the most complete account of Postel's writings, see François Secret, *Bibliographie des manuscrits de Guillaume Postel* (Geneva, 1970). I have read a number of Postel's major works, and it is indeed striking how often Postel's ideas reappear in Bodin's *Colloquium*, and also to a lesser degree, in the *Theatrum* and the *Démonomanie*.

[106] These themes appear very often in the *Colloquium*.

worshipped, by Postel, as the key to wisdom and sublime things. "It thus represented ultimate human order, and its recovery by Renaissance scholarship therefore signified far more to Postel than an impressive academic feat; it suggested to him the approaching reunion of the human race under God."[107]

Similarly, in the *Colloquium* Bodin's Salomon, perhaps the most important of the seven speakers, and certainly the most learned, constantly reminds his friends that ignorance of the holy tongue has led to many errors in translation and interpretation of scripture and therefore separates man from divine wisdom. In explaining the works by which eternal God is indicated, Salomon says "this secret lies hidden to those unskilled in the holy tongue."[108]

The holy tongue is related to numbers, especially the number four. Salomon in the *Colloquium* shows a marked preference for the number four because the holy, most sacred name of God, which cannot be uttered by man, the sacred tetragrammaton, contains four letters. Bodin's Salomon prefers the number four to the number three, and he reminds his friends that the voice of God repeated the four names of God to Moses.[109] Postel earlier had shown an affinity for the number four. "Four indeed eventually supplanted

[107] Bouwsma, *Concordia Mundi*, p. 105.

[108] *Colloquium heptaplomeres*, p. 184; "quod arcanum latet imperitos linguae sanctae."

[109] *Ibid.*, pp. 282–83. "It would be much more likely to contrive a quaternity from the name tetragrammaton than a trinity, as did Basilides the evangelist, whose opinion the Noetians and Lombard himself, the Master of the Sentences, seem to follow, as Abbot Joachim wrote, because, in addition to three persons, they substituted a fourth which they called *hypokratora.* The Pythagoreans seem to have held this opinion. They had been accustomed to swear to a holy quarternity. Timaeus Locrensis indicated that by means of a tetragonal pyramid this quaternity held many thousands of worlds together. The powerfully sagacious reasoning by the Master of the Sentences concerning the quaternity either established the quaternity or overturned the trinity, because he opposed the two relations of things produced to the two relations of things producing, namely, the thing begetting, the thing begotten, the thing breathing, the thing neither begotten nor begetting nor breathing. The four wheels would be appropriate to this opinion, and also the four animals of divine vision, and that voice of God repeating to Moses the four divine names, namely, the God of your father, the God of Abraham, the God of Isaac, the God of Jacob." Emphasis upon the number four and the sacred tetragrammaton pervade the *Colloquium.*

three in Postel's thought as the number for God Himself, whom Postel analyzed into essence, unity, truth, and goodness, of which the first three find fulfillment in the fourth."[110]

Cosmic sexual dualism was a key to Postel's concept of the universe. The idea of a masculine and feminine principle in the universe is ancient and widespread, and Postel had many sources from which to draw, especially from the Neoplatonists and the Cabala. A sexual dualism is fundamental to the Cabalistic picture of the universe. That basic Cabalistic text, the *Zohar*, is permeated with a concern to establish the masculine and feminine identities of things: rich and poor, right and left, sun and moon, heaven and earth. Ultimately the work conceives of God Himself in terms of a sexual dualism which explains His generative power. "From the Neo-Platonists Postel absorbed suggestions about the order prevailing among the masculine principle, the feminine principle, and God; he conceived of the sexual principles as emanations from God which correspond to the common Neo-Platonic principles of the universal Mind and, following from it, the universal soul."[111] Postel saw these sexual principles working throughout the universe, and this concept of sexual dualism is a dominant force in Postel's thoughts. In *De Etruriae regionis . . . originibus* Postel says that after Noah's arrival in Etruria this dualism was revealed in names attributed to the goddesses.[112] Postel was so absorbed with cosmic dualism that his ideas

[110] Bouwsma, *Concordia Mundi*, p. 107. See Guillaume Postel, *De Etruriae regionis, quae prima in orbe Europaeo habitata est, originibus institutis, religione, et moribus et imprimis* (Florence, 1551), pp. 145–53, 188 ff.; for a lengthy discussion of the primacy of the number four also see Postel [Elias Pandocheus], *De nativatate mediatoris ultima* (s.l., s.d.), pp. 31 ff.

[111] Bouwsma, *Concordia Mundi*, p. 109.

[112] Postel, *De Etruriae regionis . . . originibus*, p. 104. "From Noah . . . the wife of Noah and the mother of the world, preserved from the line of Cain, assumed various names in Italy. She has been called Vesta, Rheack, Maiach, Arezia, from the property of the four elements," pp. 106–107. "The fiery Spirit is the basis of a rational nature and because it has been fastened on matter, it is accustomed to be ascribed to the feminine: . . . For it is altogether necessary that, just as in the whole nature of things we see Form, which is the image of the masculine and is called Mind, and Matter which gives its basis to the feminine and to mothers. . . ." Also note p. 144. "The higher are Idea, Mind, Masculine, Agent Intellect, and Man turned

on this subject even appear in his letters to friends. For a restitution of all things Postel believed there was need for a double spirit. One for the higher part, paternal and mental, was for the restitution of souls (*animorum*). The other for the lower part, maternal and spiritual, was for the restitution of spirits (*animarum*).[113]

In the *Colloquium* Bodin has Salomon explain in a lengthy passage the allegorical meaning of male and female elements. I quote only a brief section: "woman in an allegorical sense everywhere means body. . . . The word man indicates natural form, and woman indicates matter, which also is often called in Proverbs *Meretrix* (harlot), since as a harlot takes pleasure in a number of men, so matter delights in a number of forms."[114]

Universal harmony is the central theme of the *Colloquium heptaplomeres*, and in this concept Bodin's thought reveals great similarity to that of Postel. Postel's belief in the unity of all things led him to stress the similarities of people's beliefs. In *De Orbis Concordia* Postel said that all men were brothers,[115] and he emphasized the fraternity

inward; the lower are Similitude, Spirit, Feminine, Passive Intellect and Man exterior and apparent."

[113] *Alia Postelli Epistola ad D.C.S.*, 1553, bound in Guillaume Postel, *Absconditorum a constitutione mundi clavis, qua mens humana tam in divinis, quam in humanis pertinget ad interiores velaminis aeternae veritates* (Amsterdam, 1646), p. 107. "There is need for a dual Spirit in the restitution, . . . one for the higher part, paternal and mental, in the understanding, for the restitution of [masculine] souls: and this was given to the Apostles. The other, for the lower part, maternal and spiritual (For the mind and spirit are as masculine and feminine) in the heart, for the restitution of [feminine] souls. Let it be and seem to be spiritual which was a living being." This letter was written by Postel on 14 August 1553 while he was staying in the house of the Giunti.

[114] For the complete passage, see Salomon's second speech, *Colloquium heptaplomeres*, p. 73. Also see Salomon's reference to the Greeks who gave their gods male characteristics, and the Latins who gave theirs feminine characteristics, p. 119.

[115] *De orbis terrae concordia* (Basel, 1544), p. 276. "If then we ought to be moved especially by the example of the highest divine will, we who will be sons against brothers . . . in so fierce a soul: in addition, he who hurls back injury in that he condemns in another what he approves in himself." Also note p. 275, "also from the example of the supreme God who is exceedingly kind toward all (even ungrateful and wicked men), He orders and persuades us to honor with kindnesses not only friends, but also enemies and to condone their injuries: He wishes that this be done because of fear of our eternal damnation, or desire of everlasting happiness, or, that which is most excellent, the example of God and the love of virtue: it

among men when he proclaimed that all men believe in God.[116] In the *praefatio* of *De nativitate mediatoris ultima* he said that divine truths have been revealed from many sources such as the Targum, Zohar, Midrash, and Rabboth, and God's providence toward mankind is so great that His truths were made known to all people so that they might know Him.[117] Differences among men are the result of ignorance or difficulty of understanding, but God does not condemn mankind because of ignorance.[118] God is the same God for all men, and all men must be as one. All men who do good are acceptable to God.[119]

The title of Bodin's work, *Colloquium heptaplomeres de rerum sublimium arcanis abditis*,[120] indicates the primacy of harmony in Bodin's thought and also suggests a relation to the theory of universal harmony which was dear to Postel. The Greek word *heptaplous* means "seven times" and the noun, *meros* means "part." Seven speakers say their parts in the freedom of Coronaeus' home, and although the seven often disagree, they respect the others' opinions, and recog-

cannot be allowed that anything greater can be imagined for the preservation of nature."

116 *Panthenōsia* (s.l., s.d.), p. 10. "And so let us rejoice, O sons, brothers, fathers, daughters, sisters, mothers, in this alone, that Turks, Jews, Christians, Heretics, Pagans, and all the nations of the world believe that God is, and all either have or seek Jesus."

117 *De nativitate mediatoris ultima* (s.l., s.d.), p. 9. "They exist in the Targum, Zohar, Midrash, Rabboth, and in many other interpreters. One must not think that the providence of God is so small toward the human race that the people pardoned by the blessing of Ismael are deprived of their truths by which God, the giver of light, forgave them in their darkness."

118 *Ibid.*, pp. 150–51. "All men are harmonious in principles, but they only disagree in manner. Still it is true that all men seek the good in order that not only men but all things created with them, with nature as guide, may accomplish this. . . . Wherefore, whatever difference there is among men, it resides in ignorance alone or in the difficulty of understanding. . . . For what parent would condemn a son because of his true ignorance?"

119 *Ibid.*, pp. 151–52. "But since God and man are one in Christ, it is then necessary that both gentiles and Israelites become one. . . . For he who does good in every nation, this one has been accepted by That One, whether he is excellent or not in the practice of sacred rites."

120 The *Colloquium heptaplomeres* may reveal by its title the influence of two earlier works whose themes are compatible with the ideas of the *Colloquium heptaplomeres*. They are the *Heptaméron* of Margaret of Navarre and the *Heptaplus* of Pico della Mirandola.

nize the right that each man has to state his opinion and live according to his own religious beliefs. These seven "parts" indicate Bodin's insistence upon harmony among all religions. The seven parts may also refer to the seven-branched candelabra of Moses, which Postel used in his book, *Candelabri typici in Mosis tabernaculo . . . interpretatio*, to indicate the universal significance of Israel and France in establishing the kingdom of heaven on earth.[121]

The prophet Elias has a very prominent place in Zoharic writings and in the eschatology of the Cabalists; Elias was assigned the task of bringing world peace and religious harmony to men. Elias is the prophet who, along with Isaiah, is most frequently quoted in the *Colloquium*. Postel identified himself with Elias as the preacher of eternal truth and the one to bring universal harmony. He took the

[121] Antoine Teissier in his additions to the *Histories* of Jacques-Auguste de Thou (1553–1617) suggested a relationship between Bodin and Postel. In *Éloges des hommes savants, tirés de l'histoire de M. de Thou, avec des additions*, edited by Antoine Teissier (Leyden, 1715), pp. 210–11, he made this very important statement concerning the *Colloquium* and its relation to Postel:

> Henri Etienne assures us that he saw Postel at Venice publicly proclaiming that if one wished to have a good religion, it would be necessary to compose a religion from those of the Turks, the Jews, and Christians. Moreover, Mr. Naudé said that at the time when Postel was at Venice there were four men who gathered twice every week to discuss with complete freedom all the religions of the world and that Postel wrote what took place in their discussions. After the death of Postel, these writings fell into the hands of Bodin and became the material for the book entitled, *About the Hidden Secrets of Sublime Things*. . . .

In 1684, Diecmann made a similar statement in *De naturalismo*, p. 3:

> And so it was pleasing to arrange his whole scene with Bodin as chorus-leader so that any religion might be applauded more than the Christian religion, or that religion might be mingled by Samaritan confusion with Jewish and Turkish treachery; that he seems to have wished to unite himself clearly to the intention of his most insane citizen, Guillaume Postel, whom Henricus Stephanus heard saying publicly now and then at Venice that whoever wishes to fashion a form of good religion ought to blend this from those three—the Christian, Jewish, and Turkish religions. I am not at all deceived in this conclusion which I learned not so long ago from a certain French manuscript which mentioned that Guy Patin, physician and royal professor at Paris, had heard from Gabriel Naudé, whom he knew very intimately, that there had been at Venice four men who had met twice a week for the purpose of establishing philosophical discussions about the various religions. Among those were Coronaeus of Rouen and the one whom I mentioned, Guillaume Postel, who acted as a stenographer. His [Postel's] manuscripts, after he had died at Paris in 1584, came into the hands of Bodin and were used to complete this work.

pseudonym Elias Pandocheus and published the *Panthenōsia* under this name. Bodin named his first son Elias, and Bodin also published a book, *Sapientiae moralis epitome quae bonorum gradus ab ultimo ad summum hominis extremumque bonum continua serie deducit* under the name of Elias Bodin. In the *Colloquium heptaplomeres* Bodin makes a striking reference to Elias which may, indeed, refer to Postel. Salomon has been speaking of the prophet Elias and his struggle with the priests of Bahal. Then Bodin has Fridericus say: "I would wish that now a certain Elias would give proof from heaven in view of kings and people to explain what is the best among so many and so great religions."[122]

Although the answer to this question is never formulated in the *Colloquium heptaplomeres*, harmony with its handmaiden, toleration, is from the beginning of the *Colloquium* posited as the real answer to religious questions and indeed all questions concerning the cosmos. The home of Coronaeus and the attitude of the seven men toward each other provide a harmonious setting from the outset. Although all were well trained in the liberal arts, "each seemed to surpass the other in his unique knowledge."[123] However, they lived together with such harmonious understanding that "no one so much resembled himself as all resembled all."[124]

Music as a reflection of the music of the spheres, the divine harmony, is central to Bodin's concept of harmony in the *Colloquium heptaplomeres*. At the close of each day's discussion Coronaeus summoned the boys "who were accustomed to soothe their spirits by sweetly singing divine praises with a harmony of lyres, flutes, and voices."[125] The blending of voices and instruments in praise of God serves to bring the seven speakers back into a harmonious relationship with each other after their divergent opinions have been expressed. The harmony of the seven-stringed lyre reminds the seven of the divine music which is a leitmotif of the *Colloquium*.

Although the new chromaticism in the music of the Renaissance met with a hostile attitude from the church, Coronaeus reflects Bodin's belief that a Catholic should be able to entertain opinions

[122] *Colloquium heptaplomeres*, p. 132.
[123] *Ibid.*, p. 2. [124] *Ibid.* [125] *Ibid.*, p. 19.

which differ from the church's when he finds delight in chromatic systems. No longer does the single mode reign supreme; a contrapuntal scheme with voices pitched against each other entails a harmony to which the "enlightened" (*auribus eruditis*) can truly respond. When there is no harmonious blending of sounds (or opinions), one overpowers the other, and "the dissonance offends the delicate senses of wiser men."[126]

All participants in the discussion agree on a concept of harmony that envisions a unity based on multiplicity (*concordia discors*), and one may safely say that this is the only subject discussed in the *Colloquium heptaplomeres* in which the scholars share a common opinion. From the question of musical harmonies Bodin directs the discussion toward harmony in the natural world. Toralba, the natural philosopher, dominates this conversation and adds a new dimension to the concept of harmony when he states that there is a basic harmony in each harmonious element. Toralba later remarks that things which are contrary to each other in nature herself cannot be mingled by design but only blended or united so that they seem to be one. This statement is revealing for the question, which is posed later in the dialogue, whether it is proper for men to discuss religion, since opinions on this subject show such variance. Yet, as Toralba cogently states, the opposites in nature, when united with certain interventions in their midst, safeguard the remarkable harmony of the universe, which would perish if it were all fire or moisture.[127]

Even in a well-ordered state, Toralba continues, men of justice, integrity, and virtue would not be perceived unless wicked men were mingled with the good, sane with the mad, brave with the cowardly, rich with the poor, low with the noble. Senamus rejoins that a state would be happier if all wicked men were driven out. Curtius counters that "as the variances of individual matters combine for the harmony of one universe, so also do the hostilities of individual citizens foster the harmony of all peoples."[128]

[126] *Ibid.*, p. 112. In addition to Lowinsky's studies on chromaticism already cited, see Kathi Meyer-Baer, *Music of the Spheres and the Dance of Death* (Princeton, 1970).

[127] *Colloquium heptaplomeres*, p. 114.

[128] *Ibid.*, p. 116.

There can be no doubt that Bodin believed that many factions protect the harmony and stability of the state because a state split into two opposing camps would fall prey to civil wars such as France was suffering during Bodin's lifetime. From the consideration of political factions Bodin directs attention to the question of the multiplicity of religious opinions, and the question of religious harmony dominates the last two books of the *Colloquium.*

The reconciliation of all citizens and foreigners in a remarkable harmony, even though they differ among themselves and with the state in matters of religion, is achieved, according to Octavius, when the state admits every kind of religion. Coronaeus prays that there be a harmony of all mortals about divine matters and one religion, provided it is the true religion. Although one may assume that Coronaeus was referring to the Catholic religion, he never makes this plain but only posits the statement, which leads to a lengthy discussion of the true religion. The role of Coronaeus in the *Colloquium heptaplomeres* is important in that he typifies an enlightened Catholic position in the Cinquecento. Of the seven, Coronaeus is the peacemaker, the harmonizer. When the discussions become harsh because of the conflicting opinions of the speakers, Coronaeus speaks conciliatory words which indicate some validity for every contradictory opinion. Although Bodin does not give the shrewdest or the lengthiest speeches to Coronaeus, the importance of his harmonizing role cannot be minimized, for it is at the home of Coronaeus that these discussions with seven different points of view take place.

The statement that Adam had been instructed in the best religion and had worshipped eternal God to the exclusion of all others stands unrefuted. The argument becomes intense, however, when the question of rites is mentioned. The discussants share no harmonious opinion on the true function of a sacred rite. Nor can they agree on the meaning of Jesus as Messiah or the unity in the Trinity. Yet at the end of the *Colloquium* Bodin says that the seven scholarly friends continued to cherish the integrity and piety of life by their common interests and manner of living with a remarkable harmony (*mirabili concordia*). Although they never discussed religion again, each protected his own religion through the greatest holiness of life.

The dialogue ends without rejection or acceptance of any one religion but rather with recognition of the divine descent of all religious beliefs and the universal brotherhood of men in the worship of divinity and in a moral life and free conscience for everyone.[129] As the harmony of nature is based on multiplicity, and the oldest religion is the natural religion of the parents of the human race, so there is need for the harmony of nature, based on multiplicity, to be applied to questions of religion and therefore a tolerance of all religions.[130] Atheism alone is detestable to Bodin.

The harmony which Bodin focuses upon in the *Colloquium heptaplomeres* implies much more than mere toleration. Toleration is an important theme, especially religious, but it is a by-product of harmony. The harmony of nature must be a pattern for world harmony which will permeate the lives of all men. Men who live in harmony, as Bodin conceived it, must of necessity be tolerant of each other.

Until the harmony of nature becomes an exemplar for earthly

[129] Bodin had already stated in the *République* that a man of no religion could not be made to obey the law, yet in the *Colloquium* he stresses the fact that no one can be forced to believe.

[130] For additional sources on the religious questions in the *Colloquium heptaplomeres*, see Friedrich von Bezold, "Jean Bodins Colloquium Heptaplomeres und der Atheismus des 16. Jahrhunderts," *Historische Zeitschrift*, 113 (1914), 3F.17, 260–315; George Holland Sabine, "The Colloquium Heptaplomeres of Jean Bodin," in *Persecution and Liberty. Essays in Honor of G. L. Burr* (New York, 1931), pp. 271–309; Ernst Benz, "Der Toleranz-Gedanke in der Religionswissenschaft (Über den Heptaplomeres des Jean Bodin)," *Deutsche Vierteljahresschrift* 12 (1934), 540–71; Pierre Mesnard, "La pensée religieuse de Bodin," *Revue du seizième siècle* 16 (1929), 77–121; Roger Chauviré, "Grandeur de Bodin," *Revue Historique* 188–89 (1940), 378–97; Lucien Febvre, "L'universalisme de Jean Bodin," *Revue de sythèse*, 7–8 (1934), 165–68; Georg Roellenbleck, *Offenbarung, Natur und Jüdische Überlieferung bei Jean Bodin. Eine Interpretation des Heptaplomeres* (Studien zur Religion, Geschichte und Geisteswissenschaft, 2) (Gütersloh, 1964); Joseph Lecler, *Toleration and the Reformation* (New York, 1960); Don Cameron Allen, *Doubt's Boundless Sea* (Baltimore, 1964), pp. 97–110; Ernst Gustav Vogel, "Zur Geschichte des ungedrückten Werks Colloquium Heptaplomeres," *Serapeum* 1 (1840), 113–16; also the very important article of Giorgio Radetti, "Il problema della religione nel pensiero di Giovanni Bodin." Although the following articles do not deal with the *Colloquium* specifically, they are very useful for an understanding of the religious aura of the *Colloquium*. See Paul Oskar Kristeller, "The Myth of Renaissance Atheism and the French Tradition of Free Thought," *Journal of the History of Philosophy* 6 (1968), 233–43; also Hubert Jedin, "Gasparo Contarini e il contributo veneziano alla riforma cattolica," in *La civiltà veneziana del Rinascimento*, edited by Diego Valeri (Venice, 1958), pp. 103–24.

harmony, a harmony based on multiplicity, the lives of men may necessarily reveal contradictions if the state or society or religion allows no multiplicity (*concordia discors*), no blending of opposites, no dissonant sounds.

Perhaps the poem of Curtius in which he proclaims the contrariety in all things tempered by immortal God reveals most clearly Bodin's concept of harmony in the *Colloquium heptaplomeres*:

> Creator of the world three times greatest of all,
> Three times best parent of the heaven,
> Who tempers the changes of the world,
> Giving proper weight to all things,
> And who measures each thing from His own ladle
> In number, ratio, time,
> Who with eternal chain joins with
> remarkable wisdom two things opposite in every way,
> preparing protection for each,
> Who, moderating melody with different sounds and
> voices yet most satisfying to sensitive
> ears, heals sickness, has mingled cold with heat
> and moisture with dryness,
> The rough with the smooth, sweetness with pain,
> shadows with light, quiet with motion,
> tribulation with prosperity,
> Who directs the fixed courses of the heavenly
> stars from east to west,
> West to east with contrary revolutions,
> Who joins hatred with agreement,
> A friend to hateful enemies.
> This greatest harmony of the universe though discordant
> contains our safety.[131]

131 *Colloquium heptaplomeres*, pp. 114–15.

CHAPTER IV

Manuscripts, Editions, and the Translation

A COMPLETE account of the manuscript tradition of the *Colloquium heptaplomeres* can be found in the introduction to E. Guhrauer, *Das Heptaplomeres des Jean Bodin* (Berlin, 1841) and Roger Chauviré's edition, *Le colloque de Jean Bodin des secrets cachez des choses sublimes* (Paris, 1914). Chauviré lists four sixteenth-century and seven seventeenth-century Latin manuscripts as well as several French manuscripts from the sixteenth and seventeenth centuries. He considers Bibliothèque Nationale fonds latin 6565 (Mazarinaeus, 16th century) an excellent manuscript,[131a] while Guhrauer states that Bibliothèque Nationale fonds latin 6564 (ex Bibliotheca Memmii, 16th century) is the oldest and the best. Chauviré did not investigate the manuscripts which were in the libraries of Germany and elsewhere.

The fate of the autograph is almost impossible to determine. According to one tradition, Bodin's heirs gave the manuscript which was found at his death to the president of the Parlement of Paris, Henri de Mesmes; this report of the manuscript was recorded in a letter written by Gabriel Naudé to his learned friend Guy Patin.[132] Guhrauer, however, did not believe that this manuscript, now in the Bibliothèque Nationale (fonds latin 6564), was the autograph because immediately following the *Colloquium* is a letter of Bodin to his nephew. The *Colloquium* and the letter are written by the same

131a While stating the excellence of BN 6565, Chauviré says that he prefers BN 6564 on superstitious grounds because it belonged to Henri de Mesmes.

132 Diecmann, *De naturalismo*, pp. 12 ff. Also see Guhrauer, ed., *Das Heptaplomeres*, pp. lxii ff. and Roger Chauviré's introduction to Jean Bodin, *Le colloque de Jean Bodin des secrets cachez des choses sublimes* (Paris, 1914), p. 4.

hand, and Guhrauer thought it unlikely that the letter would be attached to the autograph of the *Colloquium*.[133]

According to another tradition, it was not Mesmes who had received the autograph but Johannes Cordesius, canon of Limoges. Claude Sarrau confirmed in a letter to Isaac Vossius that the original manuscript was in the hands of Cordesius.[134] After Cordesius' death his inheritance came into the library of Mazarin.[135]

Guhrauer stated that some believed that the autograph was either the manuscript in the British Museum (Ms. lat. 9002) or in the Biblioteca Vaticana in the Queen Christina collection (Reginensis 1313). As one can gather from the various opinions, the real fate of the autograph is unknown.

Manuscripts of the *Colloquium heptaplomeres* were very rare and

[133] I concur with Guhrauer's opinion not only for this reason, but also because on page 345 of the manuscript, in the marginal notes which appear to be written by the same hand as the text, I discovered that the copyist had written "does that wicked Bodin pay eternal penalty in Hell?" All the words in the marginal note are not legible; however, the words, *sceleratus ille Bodinus*, are certain. The marginal notes seemed to have been written by the author of the manuscript. However, the copyist in recording the marginalia perhaps added a note of his own. It would appear very unlikely that Bodin would call himself *sceleratus*. Consequently, if the handwriting of the marginalia and that of the text are the same, as I believe, then BN fonds latin 6564 could not be the autograph. For the dating, see above, note 69.

[134] Chauviré, ed., *Colloque de Jean Bodin*, p. 4. Also see Bezold, "Jean Bodins Colloquium Heptaplomeres" pp. 281 ff. Bezold says that one can believe with reasonable certainty that Canon Cordesius had Bodin's autograph, but that it disappeared after the canon's death.

[135] In 1634 Canon Cordesius sent the autograph (if indeed it was the autograph) to his friend, Hugo Grotius, and gave him permission to keep it or send it back. Perhaps Grotius returned the manuscript when he visited France in 1635. That Grotius had received the *Colloquium* from Cordesius is confirmed in a letter to Cordesius written on Sept. 19, 1634 [*Epistolae Hugonis Grotii* (Amsterdam, 1687), letter 353, p. 124]. "Reverend Elder, your Cramoisius blessed me with many things at the same time; he brought me long letters from you, and more pleasing than this, the book written by Bodin, most worthy to be read. . . . In that work sent to me I have recognized Bodin of the sort as I have always considered him; a man more devoted to things than words, using Latin which is not completely polished, boyishly unskilled in metrics, not well-versed in Greek, whose knowledge of Hebraic customs and opinions stems not from a deep understanding of that language but from the friendship which he cherished with very learned Hebrews, whose friendship in no small way weakened in that one the full persuasion which is required of Christians. In citing histories and records I see that he often strays from the truth; I prefer to believe from neglect rather than deceit. And yet at times he hardly escapes the suspicion of trickery."

very difficult to obtain in the seventeenth century. Queen Christina of Sweden was eager to secure a copy and commissioned the French scholar Sarrau to buy the manuscript from the library of Mesmes, but he was not successful in his attempt.[136] Nor was it available in the libraries of de Thou, Richelieu, Mazarin, Guy Patin, or the brothers du Puy.[137] Isaac Vossius had by now begun the quest and was advised to search for the manuscript in the library of Cluny, but here he found hostility instead of the manuscript. The queen had to content herself with the first book for a time, but finally, she came into possession of the manuscript. Queen Christina's manuscript may have been a copy or the original manuscript of Canon Cordesius.[138]

Manuscripts of the *Colloquium heptaplomeres* made their way to England and John Milton possessed a copy.[139] Although the *Colloquium* was attacked constantly during the latter part of the seventeenth century, and copies were extremely difficult to obtain, it continued to be reproduced more and more, so that at the beginning of the eighteenth century almost every scholar of importance had his copy.

In addition to the manuscripts listed in Chauviré, Professor Kristeller notes an eighteenth-century manuscript in the Biblioteca Palatina at Parma (Fondo Parmense 1121).[140] Guhrauer stated that there were several eighteenth-century manuscripts of the *Colloquium* in German libraries. The library at Dresden has five copies, Göttingen three, Hanover two, and Zittau one.[141]

[136] Guhrauer, ed., *Das Heptaplomeres*, p. lxxv.

[137] Chauviré, ed., *Colloque de Jean Bodin*, p. 5, note 7, where he says: "One will consequently see that the cabinets of Richelieu, Mazarin, Guy Patin each possessed a *Hept.* and they concealed the fact to the emissaries of the Queen."

[138] See Bezold, "Jean Bodins Colloquium Heptaplomeres," p. 293, n. 2. Bezold is not convinced by Baudrillart's assertion that Queen Christina had Cordesius' manuscript. However, he says that Sarrau had obtained the first book of the *Colloquium* from Canon Cordesius. Also see Chauviré, ed., *Colloque de Jean Bodin*, p. 6.

[139] Guhrauer, ed., *Das Heptaplomeres*, p. lxxvii. Also see Louis I. Bredvold, "Milton and Bodin's Heptaplomeres," *Studies in Philology* 21 (1924), 401.

[140] Paul Oskar Kristeller, *Iter Italicum* II (Leiden, 1963), 40. Professor Kristeller also lists the Reginensis 1313 in the Biblioteca Vaticana. See *Iter Italicum* II, 402 and 597.

[141] Guhrauer, ed., *Das Heptaplomeres*, p. lxxxvii.

In 1719 there was a public announcement that an edition of the *Colloquium* was being prepared by Polycarp Leyser, professor of law at Helmstedt. In 1720 a note appeared in a Leipzig newspaper that the printing had begun; a short time later the printing was forbidden by a decree of the city officials.

The *Colloquium heptaplomeres* fell more and more into oblivion, so that even Lessing ignored it when it would have seemed apropos to mention it. However, at the close of the eighteenth century Heinrich Christian von Senckenberg occupied himself with a critical analysis of the manuscripts. He collated five manuscripts, one of which, an excellent one, had been given to him by Heyne from the Göttingen library, together with conjectures about passages that were difficult to read. Senckenberg stated that he believed he had produced a version which was very close to the autograph and on which a future edition could be based.[142]

In 1841 Guhrauer published an abridged edition of the *Colloquium*. He gave a summary in German of Books I–III; he printed the Latin text of the last part of Book IV and all of Book V. The last book, which is crucial to an understanding of the *Colloquium*, he completely omitted. Guhrauer used Bibliothèque Nationale fonds latin 6564 for his abridged edition.

In 1914 Roger Chauviré published excerpts of the *Colloquium* based on a seventeenth-century French translation in manuscript.[143]

Ludwig Noack published in 1857 the first complete edition of the *Colloquium heptaplomeres* after almost three hundred years of its circulation in manuscript.[144] Noack's edition was based on the Senckenberg codex, collating it with other manuscripts in Giessen, Göttingen, and Altona.

This translation of the *Colloquium heptaplomeres*, which is the first published, complete translation, is based on the 1857 edition

[142] *Ibid.*

[143] See Chauviré, ed., *Colloque de Jean Bodin*, pp. 12, 21.

[144] Jean Bodin, *Colloquium heptaplomeres de rerum sublimium arcanis abditis*, edited by Ludovicus Noack (Schwerin, 1857). In 1966 a facsimile reprint of the Noack 1857 edition was published (Stuttgart, 1966). It is interesting to note that Guhrauer's 1841 edition has also been reprinted in facsimile (Geneva, 1971). The *Colloquium* is finally being rescued from oblivion.

of Noack. As a control on Noack's text I have collated Bibliothèque Nationale fonds latin 6564 and Reginensis 1313, Biblioteca Vaticana. The former is the manuscript which belonged to Henri de Mesmes. It is a beautiful and excellent manuscript, one of the oldest. By using this manuscript as well as the Reginensis it has been possible to correct Noack and render, I believe, a sound text.

Noack's text was based on the Senckenberg codex, and Senckenberg evidently had made use of BN f. lat. 6564, because Noack's apparatus almost always records the readings of this manuscript; he often states "one codex" records this, and the reading will indeed be the reading of the Memmius. (BN f. lat. 6564.) Unfortunately, Noack does not provide a sigla, and his text reveals careless proofreading. However, Noack's readings are occasionally preferable to those of the manuscripts.

The Reginensis and the Memmius are similar, although the Memmius has fewer mistakes. I have examined the Grotius (BN ms. f. lat. 16139) which was copied from the Cordesius, and it appears that the Reginensis was copied from the Cordesius or the Grotius.[145] Even the style of the chapter designations is the same. I have examined all the Latin manuscripts of the *Colloquium* in the Bibliothèque Nationale; the Reginensis, which is in the Vatican Library, is the most beautiful in appearance, although the Memmius is preferred for accuracy and completeness.[146]

It is indeed unfortunate that the Reginensis is incomplete. One cannot be certain that Queen Christina ever had the complete manuscript; however, the sources indicate as much, and I personally believe she did possess the complete manuscript. The queen's great desire to possess it and the Reginensis itself lead me to this conclusion. The Reginensis breaks abruptly in Book V in the middle of

145 See above, notes 134 and 138.

146 Dr. Katharine Davies of Edinburgh, Scotland, has collated Bibliothèque Nationale fonds latin 6566, a sixteenth-century manuscript once belonging to Guy Patin, with Noack's text. She reports in a letter of January 8, 1972, that Noack and BN f. lat. 6566 differ considerably in detail of expression, although most of this does not seriously alter the meaning; she also states that BN f. lat. 6566 could not stand without Noack because of some essential omissions which Noack supplies. I am very grateful to Dr. Davies for the information which she gave me concerning this manuscript. Ssee above, note 69.

a sentence, not at a good stopping place for a copyist. The remaining pages may have been lost while in the queen's possession, later found, then bound in another volume.[147]

The *Colloquium heptaplomeres* presents many problems for the translator in addition to length of the text. The Latin is often difficult. The sentences are very long, and the ideas complex, thereby posing the problem of breaking a sentence without altering the idea. Accuracy throughout has been my chief priority, but it is hoped that accuracy has not impeded a smooth rendering. As a translator, I felt obligated to maintain the formal tone of the colloquy of the seven learned men, because the dialogue never lapses into a familiar conversational style; rather, it always maintains a cultured formality. I have also tried in the translation to reveal the unique personality and attitude of each speaker which is apparent in the Latin text.

Passages from classical authors are located by the system used in Oxford texts, which most editors now follow. Passages from the Bible are located in the Douay version, but where the King James differs, it is cited second in parentheses. I have not used any standard translation of Biblical quotations, but translated directly from Bodin's Latin.

Generally no specific published volume is cited, because the reference can be found in any edition. Only if the edition is obscure or idiosyncratic is it specified. When there is no difference between editions, no specific publication is cited for any author's work.

Collation of the Noack text revealed differences from various manuscripts. Citations which I chose to read from the Memmius are designated by "M" and likewise citations from the Reginensis are noted by "R." A difference of both from the Noack text is indicated by "MR." Page references to the Latin text are in the margins.

[147] I searched recently in the catalogue of the Queen Christina collection at the Biblioteca Vaticana for some indication of the lost pages but to no avail. However, not enough time was available for a thorough reading of all the entries. This I hope to accomplish in the near future, for one of my goals is to locate the missing pages of the Reginensis 1313 which may shed some light on the autograph.

Bibliography

Primary Sources

Agrippa, Henry C. *De incertitudine et vanitate scientiarum et artium atque excellentia verbi dei declamatio* (s.l., 1530).

Bellarminus, Robertus. *Disputationum de controversiis Christianae fidei, adversus huius temporis haereticos*, II (Venice, 1721).

Bodin, Jean. *Colloquium heptaplomeres de rerum sublimium arcanis abditis*, edited by Ludovicus Noack (Schwerin, 1857).

———. *Consilia Johannis Bodini Galli, & Fausti Longiani Itali, de principe recte instituendo*, translated by Johann Bornitius (Erfurt, 1603).

———. *Das Heptaplomeres des Jean Bodin, Zur Geschichte der Kultur und Literatur im Jahrhundert der Reformation*, edited by Dr. E. Guhrauer (Berlin, 1841), abridged edition.

———. *De la démonomanie des sorciers* (Paris, 1580).

———. *De magorum demonomania*, translated by Franciscus Junius (Basel, 1581).

———. *Le colloque de Jean Bodin des secrets cachez des choses sublimes,'* edited by Roger Chauviré (Paris, 1914), abridged edition.

———. *Les six livres de la république* (Paris, 1576).

———. *Method for the Easy Comprehension of History*, translated by Beatrice Reynolds (New York, 1965).

———. *Methodus ad facilem historiarum cognitionem* (Paris, 1566).

———. *Six Books of the Commonwealth*, translated by M. J. Tooley (Oxford, 1955).

———. *The Six Bookes of a Commonweale*, translated by Richard Knolles, edited by Kenneth D. McRae (Cambridge, Mass., 1962).

———. *Universae naturae theatrum* (Lyon, 1596).

Grotius, Hugo. *Epistolae Hugonis Grotii* (Amsterdam, 1687).

Haywood, William. *The Hierarchie of the Blessed Angells* (London, 1635).

Paolini, Fabio. *Hebdomades* (Venice, 1589).

Pico, Giovanni della Mirandola. *On the Dignity of Man; On Being and the One; Heptaplus* (New York, 1965).

Postel, Guillaume. *Absconditorum a constitutione mundi clavis, qua mens humana tam in divinis quam in humanis pertinget ad interiores velaminis aeternae veritatis* (Amsterdam, 1646).

———. *Candelabri typici in Mosis tabernaculo iusso divino expressi brevis ac dilucida interpretatio* (Venice, 1548).

———. *De Etruriae regionis, quae prima in orbe Europaeo habitata est, originibus institutis, religione, et moribus et imprimis* (Florence, 1551).

——— [Elias Pandocheus]. *De nativitate mediatoris ultima, nunc futura et toti orbi terrarum in singulis ratione praeditis manifesta, quae in theosofiae et filosofiae arcanis hactenus fuere* (s.l., s.d.).

———. *De orbis terrae concordia* (Basel, 1544).

———. *De rationibus spiritus sancti* (Paris, 1543).

———. *Descriptio Alcahirae urbis quae Mizir et Mazar dicitur*, edited by Angela Codazzi (Varese, s.d.).

———. *Guillaume Postel (1510–1581) et son interprétation du candélabre de Moyse*, edited by François Secret (Nieuwkoop, 1966).

———. *Panthenōsia* (s.l., s.d.).

Secondary Sources: Books

Albert-Buisson, François. *Michel de l'Hôpital* (Paris, 1950).

Allen, Don Cameron. *Doubt's Boundless Sea; Skepticism and Faith in the Renaissance* (Baltimore, 1964).

———. *The Legend of Noah* (Urbana, 1963).

———. *The Star-Crossed Renaissance* (Durham, 1941).

Allen, John William. *History of Political Thought in the Sixteenth Century* (New York, 1928).

Amphoux, Henri. *Michel de l'Hôpital et la liberté de conscience au* XVI *siècle* (Paris, 1900).

Baron, Salo Wittmayer. *A Social and Religious History of the Jews.* XVIII, *Inquisition, Renaissance, and Reformation*; XIV, *Catholic Restoration and Wars of Religion* (New York, 1969).

Baudrillart, Henri. *Bodin et son temps; tableau des théories politiques et des idées economiques du seizième siècle* (Paris, 1853).

Bayle, Pierre. *A General Dictionary Historical and Critical: A New and Accurate Translation of that of the Celebrated Mr. Bayle*, translated by J. B. Bernard, Thomas Birch, John Lockman (London, 1735).

Blau, Joseph Leon. *The Christian Interpretation of the Cabala in the Renaissance* (New York, 1944).

Boas, George. *The Happy Beast in French Thought of the Seventeenth Century* (Baltimore, 1933).

Bouwsma, William J. *Concordia Mundi: The Career and Thought of Guillaume Postel (1510–1581)* (Cambridge, Mass., 1957).

———. *Venice and the Defense of Republican Liberty. Renaissance Values in the Age of the Counter Reformation* (Berkeley, 1968).

Brush, Craig B. *Montaigne and Bayle* (The Hague, 1966).

Bury, John B. *The Idea of Progress* (London, 1920).
Butler, Sir Geoffrey. *Studies in Statecraft* (Cambridge, 1920).
Cassirer, Ernst. *Descartes, Corneille, Christine de Suède* (Paris, 1942).
———. *Individuo e cosmo nella filosofia del Rinascimento* (Florence, 1935).
Charbonnel, J. Roger. *La Pensée italienne au* XVIe *siècle et le courant libertin* (Paris, 1919).
Chauviré, Roger. *Jean Bodin, auteur de la république* (Paris, 1914).
Church, Frederic C. *The Italian Reformers 1534–1564* (New York, 1932).
Church, William F. *Constitutional Thought in Sixteenth Century France* (Cambridge, Mass., 1941).
De Chaufepié, Jaques George. *The Life of Servetus, Being an Article of his Historical Dictionary*, IV, translated by James Yair (London, 1771).
Diecmann, Ludovicus J. *De naturalismo, cum aliorum, tum maxime Jo. Bodini, ex opere ejus MSC anekdotō, de abditis rerum sublimium arcanis* (Leipzig, 1684).
Dunlop, D. M. *The History of the Jewish Khazars* (Princeton, 1954).
Febvre, Lucien. *Le Problème de l'incroyance au* XVIe *siècle* (Paris, 1942).
Franklin, Julian H. *Jean Bodin and the Rise of Absolutist Theory* (Cambridge, 1973).
———. *Jean Bodin and the Sixteenth-Century Revolution in the Methodology of Law and History* (New York, 1963).
Fulton, John F. *Michael Servetus, Humanist and Martyr* (New York, 1953).
Garin, Eugenio. *Scienza e vita civile nel Rinascimento italiano* (Bari, 1965).
Garosci, Aldo. *Jean Bodin, politica e diritto nel Rinascimento francese* (Milan, 1934).
Gentile, Giovanni. *Studi sul Rinascimento* (Florence, 1936).
Ginzburg, Carlo. *Il nicodemismo: simulazione e dissimulazione religiosa nell' Europa del '500* (Turin, 1970).
Hoefer, Dr., ed. *Nouvelle biographie général* (Paris, 1855).
Hofmann, John J. *Lexicon universale* (Leyden, 1693).
Jones, Percy M. *French Introspectives from Montaigne to André Gide* (Cambridge, 1937).
Jones, Rufus M. *Studies in Mystical Religion* (London, 1919).
Katz, Jacob. *Exclusiveness and Tolerance. Studies in Jewish-Gentile Relations in Medieval and Modern Times* (New York, 1961).
Kelley, Donald R. *Foundations of Modern Historical Scholarship: Language, Law, and History in the French Renaissance* (New York, 1970).
Kristeller, Paul Oskar. *Iter Italicum* I, II (Leiden, 1965, 1967).
———. *The Philosophy of Marsilio Ficino* (Gloucester, Mass., 1964).
———. *Studies in Renaissance Thought and Letters* (Rome, 1956).
Lecler, Joseph. *Toleration and the Reformation* (New York, 1960).
Levron, Jacques. *Jean Bodin et sa famille* (Angers, 1950).
Lowinsky, Edward E. *Secret Chromatic Art in the Netherlands Motet* (New York, 1967).
McRae, Kenneth D. "The Political Thought of Jean Bodin" (Ph.D. dissertation, Harvard, 1953).

Merritt, Arthur Tillman. *Sixteenth-Century Polyphony* (Cambridge, Mass., 1954).
Mesnard, Pierre. *L'Essor de la philosophie politique au* XVIe *siècle* (Paris, 1951).
———. *Oeuvres philosophiques de Jean Bodin*, I (Paris, 1951).
Meyer-Baer, Kathi. *Music of the Spheres and the Dance of Death* (Princeton, 1970).
Mondolfo, Rodolfo. *Figure e idee della filosofia del Rinascimento* (Florence, 1963).
Morhof, Daniel G. *Polyhistor* (Lubeck, 1732).
Olgioti, Francesco. *L'anima dell' umanesimo e del Rinascimento* (Milan, 1924).
Ong, Walter J. *Ramus, Method, and the Decay of Dialogue* (Cambridge, Mass., 1958).
Owens, John. *The Skeptics of the Italian Renaissance* (New York, 1893).
Picot, Émile. *Les Français italianisants au* XVIe *siècle* (Paris, 1906).
Popkin, Richard H. *The History of Scepticism from Erasmus to Descartes* (Assen, 1960).
Possevino, Antonio. *Iudicium de nuae militis Galli scriptis, quae ille discursus politicos et militares inscripsit, de Joannis Bodini methodo historiae: Libris de republica et demonomania* (Roma-Vaticana, 1592).
Prevost, and Roman D'Amat, eds. *Dictionnaire de biographie française* (Paris, 1954).
Puteanis, Petro and Jacobo, eds. *Catalogus bibliothecae Thuanae* (Paris, 1679).
Rekers, B. *Benito Arias Montano (1527–1598)* (London, 1972).
Reynolds, Beatrice. *Proponents of Limited Monarchy in Sixteenth Century France: Francis Hotman and Jean Bodin* (New York, 1931).
Rice, Eugene F., Jr. *The Renaissance Idea of Wisdom* (Cambridge, Mass., 1958).
Robertson, J. M. *A History of Free Thought, Ancient and Modern to the Period of the French Revolution*, I, II (London, 1969).
Roellenbleck, Georg. *Offenbarung, Natur und Jüdische Überlieferung bei Jean Bodin. Eine Interpretation des Heptaplomeres* (Studien zur Religion, Geschichte und Geisteswissenschaft, 2) (Gütersloh, 1964).
Rosenthal, Franz. *Knowledge Triumphant. The Concept of Knowledge in Medieval Islam* (Leiden, 1970).
Scharbau, M. Henrico. *Judaismus Detectus in quo vindicantur et restituuntur, qui vel injuste inter Judaeos relati, vel ex Judaeorum numero immerito exclusi sunt* (Lübeck, 1722).
Scholem, Gershom G. *Major Trends in Jewish Mysticism* (New York, 1954).
———. *The Messianic Idea in Judaism* (New York, 1971).
———. *On the Kabbalah and Its Symbolism* (New York, 1965).
Secret, François. *Bibliographie des manuscrits de Guillaume Postel* (Geneva, 1970).
Seiferth, Wolfgang S. *Synagogue and Church in the Middle Ages: Two Symbols in Art and Literature* (New York, 1970).

Simone, Franco. *The French Renaissance: Medieval Tradition and Italian Influence in Shaping the Renaissance in France*, translated by H. Gaston Hall (London, 1969).

Singleton, Charles S. *Art, Science and History in the Renaissance* (Baltimore, 1967).

Spink, J. S. *French Free-Thought from Gassendi to Voltaire* (New York, 1960).

Taylor, Henry Osborn. *Thought and Expression in the Sixteenth Century*, I, II (New York, 1920).

Tetel, Marcel. *Marguerite de Navarre's "Heptameron": Themes, Language, and Structure* (Durham, N.C., 1973).

Thorndike, Lynn. *Alchemy during the First Half of the Sixteenth Century* (London, 1938).

———. *History of Magic and Experimental Science*, V, VI (New York, 1941).

Thou, Jacques-Auguste de. *Les Éloges des hommes savants, tirés de l'histoire de M. de Thou*, edited by Antoine Tessier (Leyden, 1715).

———. *Historiarum sui temporis* (n.p., 1620), V, liber CXVII, 701.

Von Tieghem, Paul. *La Littérature latine de la renaissance: étude d'histoire littéraire européenne* (Geneva, 1966).

Walker, Daniel P. *The Decline of Hell* (Chicago, 1964).

———. *Spiritual and Demonic Magic from Ficino to Campanella* (London, 1958).

Yates, Frances E. *The French Academies of the 16th Century* (London, 1947).

———. *Giordano Bruno and the Hermetic Tradition* (Chicago, 1964).

Articles

Bainton, Roland H. "Wylliam Postell and the Netherlands," *Nederlandsch Archief voor Kerkgeschiedenis* 24 (1931), 161–72.

Baldwin, Summerfield. "Jean Bodin and the League," *Catholic Historical Review* 23 (1937–38), 160–84.

Baudrillart, Henri. "Jean Bodin et l'heptaplomeres" in his *Publicistes modernes* (Paris, 1862), pp. 229–40.

Bauer, Robert J. "A Phenomenon of Epistemology in the Renaissance," *Journal of the History of Ideas* 31 (1970), 281–88.

Beinart, Haim. "The Records of the Inquisition. A Source of Jewish and Converso History" in *Proceedings of the Israel Academy of Sciences and Humanities* II (Jerusalem, 1968), 211–27.

Belladonna, Rita. "Sperone Speroni and Alessandro Piccolomini on Justification," *Renaissance Quarterly* 25, no. 2 (1972), 161–72.

Benz, Ernst. "Der Toleranz-Gedanke in der Religionswissenschaft. (Über den Heptaplomeres des Jean Bodin)," *Deutsche Vierteljahresschrift* 12 (1934), 540–71.

Bezold, Friedrich von. "Jean Bodins Colloquium Heptaplomeres und der Atheismus des 16. Jahrhunderts," *Historische Zeitschrift* 113 (1914) 3F.17, 260–315.

Blau, Joseph Leon. "Postel and the Significance of Renaissance Cabalism," *Journal of the History of Ideas* 15 (1954), 218–32.

Boas, George. "Recent Books in the History of Philosophy," *Journal of the History of Ideas* 19 (1958), 581–84.

Buonaiuti, Ernesto. "La filosofia religiosa del Rinascimento," *Religio* 15 (1939), 335–55.

Bouwsma, William J. "Postel and the Significance of Renaissance Cabalism," *Journal of the History of Ideas* 15 (1954), 218–32.

Bredvold, Louis Ignatius. "Milton and Bodin's Heptaplomeres," *Studies in Philology* 21 (1924), 399–402.

Cassirer, Ernst. "Giovanni Pico della Mirandola," *Journal of the History of Ideas* 3 (1942), 123–44, 319–46.

———. "On the Originality of the Renaissance," *Journal of the History of Ideas* 4 (1943), 49–56.

Chauviré, Roger. "Grandeur de Bodin," *Revue Historique* 188–89 (1940), 378–97.

Clive, H. P. "The Calvinist Attitude to Music," *Bibliothèque d'humanisme et renaissance* 20 (1958), 79–107.

De Chaufepié, Jaques George. "Guillaume Postel" in his *Nouveau dictionnaire historique et critique* 3 (Amsterdam, 1750), 215–36.

Drake, Stillman. "Renaissance Science and Music," *Journal of the History of Ideas* 31 (1970), 483–500.

Droz, E. "Le Carme Jean Bodin, hérétique," *Bibliothèque d'humanisme et renaissance* 21 (1959), 453–67.

Durand, Dana B. "Tradition and Innovation in 15th Century Italy," *Journal of the History of Ideas* 4 (1943), 1–20.

Febvre, Lucien. "L'universalisme de Jean Bodin," *Revue de synthèse* 54 (1934), 165–68.

Ferguson, Wallace K. "Renaissance Tendencies in the Religious Thought of Erasmus," *Journal of the History of Ideas* 15 (1954), 499–508.

Gianturco, Elio. "Bodin's Conception of the Venetian Constitution and His Critical Rift with Fabio Albergati," *Revue de littérature comparée* 18 (1938), 684–95.

Gray, Hanna H. "Renaissance Humanism," *Journal of the History of Ideas* 24 (1963), 497–514.

Hirsch, Elisabeth F. "Erasmus and Portugal," *Bibliothèque d'humanisme et renaissance* 32 (1970), 540–49.

Hughes, Merritt Y. "Spenser's Acrasia and the Renaissance Circe," *Journal of the History of Ideas* 4 (1943), 381–99.

Jedin, Hubert. "Gasparo Contarini e il contributo veneziano alla riforma cattolica," in *La civiltá veneziana del Rinascimento*, edited by Diego Valeri (Venice, 1958), pp. 103–24.

Keller, Abraham C. "Zilsel, the Artisans, and the Ideas of Progress in the Renaissance," *Journal of the History of Ideas* 11 (1950), 235–40.

Kristeller, Paul Oskar. "The Humanist Bartolomeo Facio and His Unknown Correspondence," in *From the Renaissance to the Counter-Reformation: Essays in Memory of Garrett Mattingly*, edited by C. H. Carter (London, 1966), pp. 56–74.

———. "The Myth of Renaissance Atheism and the French Tradition of Free Thought," *Journal of the History of Philosophy* 6 (1968), 233–43.

———. and Randall, John H., Jr. "Study of Renaissance Philosophies," *Journal of the History of Ideas* 2 (1941), 449–96.

Levron, Jacques. "Jean Bodin, Sieur de Saint-Amand," *Bibliothèque d'humanisme et renaissance* 10 (1948), 69–76.

Linder, Robert D. "Pierre Vinet and the Sixteenth Century French Protestant Revolutionary Tradition," *Journal of Modern History* 38 (1966), 125–37.

Lowinsky, Edward E. "Music in Renaissance Culture," *Journal of the History of Ideas* 15 (1942), 509–53.

Mantz, Harold E. "Jean Bodin and the Sorcerers," *The Romanic Review* 15 (1924), 153–78.

Marongiu, A. "Jean Bodin e la polemica sulle «assemblee di stati»," in *Gouvernés et gouvernants,* 3e partie, I (Brussels, 1966), 49–70.

McRae, Kenneth D. "A Postscript on Bodin's Connections with Ramism," *Journal of the History of Ideas* 24 (1963), 569–71.

———. "Ramist Tendencies in the Thought of J. Bodin," *Journal of the History of Ideas* 16 (1955), 306–23.

Mesnard, Pierre. "La Démonomanie de Jean Bodin," in *L'Opera e il pensiero di G. Pico della Mirandola*, II (Florence, 1965), pp. 333–56.

———. "Jean Bodin à la recherche des secrets de la nature," in *Umanesimo e esoterismo* (1960), 221–34.

———. "Jean Bodin fait de l'histoire comparée la base des sciences humaines," *Organon* 3 (1966), 181–84.

———. "La Pensée réligieuse de Bodin," *Revue du seizième siècle* 16 (1929), 77–121.

Michel, François. "Adrien de Thou et l'heptaméron de Marguerite de Navarre," *Bibliothèque d'humanisme et renaissance* 5 (1938), 16–36.

Monter, E. William. "Inflation and Witchcraft: The Case of Jean Bodin," in *Action and Conviction in Early Modern Europe*, edited by Theodore K. Rabb and Jerrold E. Seigel (Princeton, 1969), pp. 371–89.

Morandi, Carlo. "Botero, Campanella, Scioppio e Bodin," *Nuova Rivista Storica* 13 (1929), 342–50.

Moreau-Reibel, J. "Bodin et la ligue d'après des lettres inédites," *Humanisme et renaissance* 1–3 (1934–35), 422–40.

Ong, Walter J. "Peter Ramus and the Naming of Methodism," *Journal of the History of Ideas* 14 (1953), 235–48.

———. "System, Space, and Intellect in Renaissance Symbolism," *Bibliothèque d'humanisme et renaissance* 18 (1956), 222–39.

Pineas, Rainer. "Polemical *Exemplum* in Sixteenth Century Religious Controversy," *Bibliothèque d'humanisme et renaissance* 28 (1966), 393–96.

Pines, Shlomo. "The Jewish Christians of the Early Centuries of Christianity According to a New Source," in *Proceedings of The Israel Academy of Sciences and Humanities,* II (Jerusalem, 1968), 237–309.

Planchenault, N. "Études sur Jean Bodin," *Mémoires de la société académique de Maine et Loire* I (Angers, 1857), 11–105.

Ponthieux, A. "Quelques documents inédits sur Jean Bodin," *Revue du seizième siècle* 15 (1928), 56–99.

Popkin, Richard H. "Skepticism and the Counter-Reformation in France," *Archiv für Reformationsgeschichte* 51 (1960), 59–87.

Radetti, Giorgio. "Il problema della religione nel pensiero di Giovanni Bodin," *Giornale critico della filosofia Italiana*, VI, fasc. 4–5 (1938), 277–94.

Randall, John H., Jr. "The Development of Scientific Method in the School of Padua," *Journal of the History of Ideas* 1 (1940), 177–206.

Reynolds, Beatrice. "Shifting Currents in Historical Criticism," *Journal of the History of Ideas* 14 (1953), 471–92.

Sabine, George Holland. "The Colloquium Heptaplomeres of Jean Bodin," in *Persecution and Liberty. Essays in Honor of G. L. Burr* (New York, 1931), pp. 271–309.

Screech, M. A. "The Illusion of Postel's Feminism," *Journal of the Warburg and Courtauld Institute* 16 (1953), 162–70.

Secret, François. "Jean Macer, François Xavier et Guillaume Postel, ou un épisode de l'histoire comparée des religions au XVIe siècle," *Revue de l'histoire des religions* 170 (1966), 47–69.

———. "L'Emithologie de Guillaume Postel," *Archivio di Filosofia, Umanesmo e Esoterismo*, nos. 2–3 (1960), 381–437.

———. "Les Jésuites et le kabbalisme chrétien à la renaissance," *Bibliothèque d'humanisme et renaissance* 20 (1958), 542–55.

———. "Notes pour l'histoire des juifs en France," *Revue des études juives* 125, fasc. 1–3 (1966), 233–43.

———. "Notes sur les hébraisants chrétiens," *Revue des études juives* 123, fasc. 1–2 (1964), 141–68.

———. "Notes sur les juifs d'Avignon à la renaissance," *Revue des études juives* 121 (1962), 178–87.

Tindall, William Y. "James Joyce and the Hermetic Tradition," *Journal of the History of Ideas* 15 (1954), 23–39.

Tuve, Rosemond. "Imagery and Logic; Ramus and Metaphysical Poetics," *Journal of the History of Ideas* 3 (1942), 365–400.

Ulph, Owen. "Jean Bodin and the Estates-General of 1576," *Journal of Modern History* 19 (1947), 289–96.

Vogel, Ernst Gustav. "Zur Geschichte des ungedrückten Werks Colloquium Heptaplomeres," *Serapeum* 1 (1840), 113–16.

Wagner, Robert L. "Le vocabulaire magique de Jean Bodin dans la demonomanie des sorciers," *Bibliotheque d'humanisme et renaissance* 10 (1948), 95–123.

Walker, Daniel P. "The Prisca Theologia in France," *Journal of the Warburg and Courtauld Institute* 17, nos. 3–4 (1954), 204–59.

Weisinger, Herbert. "Ideas of History during the Renaissance," *Journal of the History of Ideas* 6 (1945), 415–35.

Wilson, Harold S. "Some Meanings of 'Nature' in Renaissance Literary Theory," *Journal of the History of Ideas* 2 (1941), 430–48.

Zambelli, P. "Il «De auditu Kabbalistico» e la tradizione lulliana nel Rinascimento," *Atti e mem. dell' Accad. Toscana . . . «La Colombaria»* 30 n.s., 16 (1965), 113–247.

Zilsel, Edgar. "The Origins of William Gilbert's Scientific Method," *Journal of the History of Ideas* 2 (1941), 1–32.

COLLOQUIUM
OF THE SEVEN ABOUT SECRETS
OF THE SUBLIME

BOOK I

To N.T.

You ask me in letters to write to you about my foreign travel. Everything would have happened to my liking, if I could have taken delight in your companionship. If I shall ever meet with you again, I shall never allow myself to be separated from you. When we had a difficult time sailing along the coast of the Adriatic sea, we reached Venice, a port common to almost all nations or rather the whole world, not only because the Venetians delight in receiving strangers hospitably, but also because one can live there with the greatest freedom. Whereas other cities and districts are threatened by civil wars or fear of tyrants or harsh exactions of taxes or the most annoying inquiries into one's activities, this seemed to me to be nearly the only city that offers immunity and freedom from all these kinds of servitude. This is the reason why people come here from everywhere, wishing to spend their lives in the greatest freedom and tranquillity of spirit,[1] whether they are interested in commerce or crafts or leisure pursuits as befit free man. P. 1

It was very fortunate that in my quest for educated and excellent men, I met Paulus Coronaeus, who was very eagerly[2] investigating, in every nook and cranny of the city, all the monuments of antiquity and had joined with the most scholarly men in an intimate society, so that his home was considered a shrine of the Muses and virtues. And although he was very slight in stature and too weak to endure stormy seas and distant sojourns, he had an incredible desire to understand the language, inclinations, activities, customs, and virtues of different peoples. At[3] his home he had admitted a gathering of men from abroad—Fridericus Podamicus,

[1] *animi* MR [2] *studiosissime* MR [3] *ad* MR

Hieronymus Senamus, Diegus Toralba, Antonius Curtius, Salomon Barcassius, Octavius Fagnola. Although they were exceptionally well trained in the disciplines of the liberal arts, nevertheless each seemed to surpass the others in his unique knowledge. Moreover, while living together in Coronaeus' house, they had easy access to anything new or worthy of note anywhere in the world by means of letters from friends whom they had made a point of acquiring at Rome, Constantinople, Augsburg, Seville, Antwerp, and Paris.

P. 2 They lived not merely with sophistication of discourse and charming manners, but with such innocence and integrity that no one so much resembled himself as all resembled all. For they were not motivated by wrangling or jealousy but by a desire to learn; consequently they were displaying all their reflections and endeavours in true dignity. Most important, however, was the fact that Coronaeus' home was filled not only with an infinite variety and supply of books and old records, but also instruments either for music or for all sorts of mathematical arts. Still nothing seemed to me more unusual than the pantotheca six feet square. Each foot was divided into six square[4] compartments. The square number 36 multiplied by itself produced 1296 small boxes. Coronaeus had chosen the number six because this one number among the digits[5] was perfect. It appeared most widely in all of nature because most living things terminate in this number. Also in all nature there are only six perfect bodies, only six simple colors, six simple tastes, six harmonious harmonies, only six simple metals, six regions, also six senses including common sense.

Coronaeus had instructed that the pantotheca be built from olive wood, an almost indestructible material, to house the universe, its goods and materials. To begin with he had prepared likenesses of sixty fixed stars, then the replicas of planets, comets and similar phenomena, elements, bodies, stones, metals, fossils, plants, living things of every sort, which he could secure each in its own class. But since the form of all plants and insects could not be contained in the limited pantotheca nor, because of their rarity, acquired, each was marked in its box by a drawing or a description or according to its own classification, as rhinoceros, an Indian goat, and things like these. He had provided that the rest be imported, or he had bought them when they were available.

Moreover, he had complete plants or the roots displayed separately on rather larger charts so that each box contained a particle of plant and

[4] *quadratas* MR

[5] *digitos* MR

animal life and in this arrangement: the last was connected to the first, the middle to the beginning and the end, and all to all in its appropriate class. In fact, between the earth and stones he had placed clay and chalk, between water and diamonds, crystal, between stones and metals, flint and marcasite, between stones and sprigs, coral, between animals and plants those which are called zoophyta, between sea and land animals, amphibians, between water birds and land birds, flying fish, the kite and the cuttle-fish, between the winged and landed wild life, the bat.

Moreover, he had arranged the pantotheca so that the boxes could be easily identified for firmer recollection by six simple colors, and he had positioned them to face the light for easy viewing. He did not place them P. 3
in a perpendicular arrangement lest something spill from the boxes; nor did he place them horizontally, for they would not receive the light. But he placed each species at an angle for easy viewing when the curtain was drawn, so that after lengthy study they could be remembered more easily.

And indeed in this Coronaeus was so proficient that he remembered all the goods in the little cupboards and knew the use not only of those things in the pantotheca, but also of all things which he heard of or read about. To preserve his strength he did not waste his time in writing or reading;[6] rather he had developed the sharpest[7] critical faculty by listening, discussing, and contemplating. At mealtime, he had readers present who would read a little something until he had finished his repast in pleasure and without the harassment of conversation. He did not hold discussions while walking about, in the manner of the Peripatetics, because he thought the motion of the body hindered his judgment and memory; nor did he imitate the Stoics who dispute while standing because he thought that this could not be done for long without fatigue and the danger of a joint disease; nor did he prefer the Academicians' reclining position which encouraged wantonness and sleep. He chose rather a sitting position.

Indeed he had added me to his household as reader, following the custom of the ancient[8] Romans, who even at their banquets used to feed their minds along with their bodies with readings of memorable experiences. Although the Romans were rather negligent in their conclusions, Coronaeus would postpone the question to the following day if any difficulty occurred, so that no one being unprepared would give an opinion which would cause embarrassment later.

I used to take down almost everything in a kind of shorthand as for-

[6] *legendo* MR [7] *acerrimam* MR [8] *veterum* MR

merly stenographers did. Then I transcribed the notes, and since I had done this for some time, I collected many questions about nature, mathematics, the preeminence of laws, the best form of governments; also about medicine and about the reliability of histories.

Still I thought no discussion was richer or worthier in its argument than the one which began with the voyage of Octavius. For when Coronaeus had seated himself for dinner along with those whom I have mentioned I was bidden to continue the reading of Plato's *Phaedo*, which I had begun, when I had reached the passage where Socrates said that the bodies of the Egyptians had been preserved with such skill that they escaped putrefaction for an incredible length of time,[9] Octavius asked Coronaeus to have me reread this passage, and so I did. This section as well as the preceding one described the power of immortal souls, which they had discussed fully on those[10] previous days. Therefore CORONAEUS said: "Don't you think we have talked enough about the immortality of souls?"

P. 4 "More than enough," said SALOMON. "Even if there were no proofs, we have been persuaded for a long time of that immortality and that eternal rewards are fixed for the good and punishments decreed for the wicked."

TORALBA said: Indeed I consider it very useful to seek clear proofs of all things and especially of those which pertain to piety, lest we through lack of preparation are tripped up by the Epicurean mockers[11] of divine matters.

Then SENAMUS spoke: I have known many who scorn the gods, even more who are no different from beasts except in form. Up to now, however, I have found no Epicurean, that is, one who piously worshipped the gods with no hope of reward, who lived most frugally and temperately, who embraced continence, justice, faith, integrity of character, as Epicurus did,[12] but who believed that souls were mortal and that immortal God did not interfere or threaten anyone's affairs. In short, one who would place the highest good and final goal for man not in bodily pleasures, but in the serene peace of a noble soul.

Next TORALBA spoke: Granted that Epicurus excelled in all these virtues. Still what benefit were they to him, when he severed from the root, as if by an ax, the fear and reverence of deity? For when the hope of rewards and the fear of divine punishment are removed, no society of men can endure. Indeed what place can faith and justice hold among

[9] *Phaedo*, 80 d.

[10] *illis* MR

[11] *irrisonibus* MR

[12] See Diogenes Laërtius X. 16 ff.

those who fear nothing except a witness or a judge?[13] Therefore, Epicurus' integrity was false, since he was so unjust toward immortal God that he snatched all justice from Him; that is, the power of rewards and punishments. Indeed he wrote books about religions[14] for no other reason than to escape the punishment of Diagoras[15] and Protagoras.[16]

Then SENAMUS said: What is the reason then that many leave other sects for the Epicureans, but none returns to other sects from the Epicureans?

CORONAEUS said: This is no more strange than the fact that men can become eunuchs, but no eunuch can become a man. The paths from modesty to lewdness are enticing and easy, but all returns to modesty are blocked.

OCTAVIUS spoke next: It is pleasing to remember dangers that are past and to "watch from the shore Neptune raging at a distance"[17] so that we may withdraw as far as possible from the opinion of that most loathsome man, for

> The temple wall with its votive pictures shows that I have hung up my wet clothes for the powerful god of the sea

as the poet writes.[18] The account from Plato's *Phaedo* which the lector just read recalled to me a most hazardous sea voyage which I would gladly describe to you if it were not tiresome. P. 5

CORONAEUS: Who indeed[19] would not be most delighted[20] to hear Octavius?

OCTAVIUS: When I was in Egypt, I explored the city of Cairo,[21] which the inhabitants describe as a "brooding hen" because of its numerous citi-

[13] *judicem* MR

[14] *religionibus* MR. Diogenes Laërtius X. 26 said that he wrote about 300 volumes, although not all were about religion.

[15] Diagoras, a Melian philosopher of the 5th century B.C., denied the direct interference of God with the world and hence was called an atheist. He was condemned to death and fled. His teacher was Democritus.

[16] Protagoras, a Sophist of the 5th century B.C., maintained that everything is motion and that out of motion everything comes into existence. He also believed that we are not able to know whether and how the gods exist. Because of this position, he was said to have been banished (Diogenes Laërtius IX. 52; Cicero, *De nat. deor.* I. 23; Eusebius, *Praep. evang.* XIV. 19).

[17] Horace, *Epist.* I. 11. 10.

[18] Horace, *Carm.* I. 5. 16.

[19] *vero* MR

[20] *libentissime* MR

[21] *Cairam* N *Cahiram* M *Cahriam* R

zens and vast size, and the ancient pyramids near the city. Then a certain Genevan "Empiricist," whom I had taken as a companion persuaded me that we should steal an "Amomia." He used this term to describe Egyptian corpses because from antiquity they had been soaked for a long time in balsam, cardamon, salt, vinegar, honey, myrrh, aloe, nard, wild cinnamon, resin, and other preservative potions. He stated that there was so much healing power in these corpses that they warded off almost all diseases. Although I have doubts about empiricists, I gave in to this one. We went among the pyramids, opening as many tombs as we could, and dragged out a corpse wrapped[22] in a leather covering. Under the leather narrow strips of linen, which were not worn out in any part, were wound around and around each part of the corpse and covered the gilded skin; for as you know, gold is a very enduring preservative not only for corpses, but also for wood, metals and other things. The flesh with its covering seemed gold-colored and tawny because it was soaked in the substance which the ancient Cretans used for sugar. The corpse was very dry inside since the viscera were removed. In place of the heart was a stone image with the name of Isis, once an Egyptian queen, whose tomb is in the city of Nysa in upper Arabia and whose epitaph was carved on a marble column:

> I am Isis, queen of Egypt, trained by Mercury;[23]
> No one will loose my statutes.
> I am the mother of Osiris;
> I am the first inventor of crops;
> I am the mother of king Horus.
> I am the gleaming dog in the skies.
> The city of Bubastis has been founded in my honor.
> Rejoice, rejoice O Egypt, you who have nurtured me.

The sacred rites of Isis were abrogated in the reign of Constantine the Great,[24] if I am not mistaken, so the corpse was buried 1300 years ago or

[22] *obvolutum* MR

[23] Hermes Trismegistus.

[24] It is possible that Bodin was referring to Eusebius' comment that Constantine prohibited "the vile rites of idolatry which were practiced of old in town and country, so that no one should dare to erect images, or to attempt divination and other vanities, or sacrifice at all." (Quoted in A. H. M. Jones, *Constantine and the Conversion of Europe*, New York, 1949, pp. 211–12.) Jones says that Eusebius exaggerates the actions of the emperor and that pagan religions were not really outlawed, although certain rites such as ritual prostitution were banned in particular cases. Constantius in 341 ordered "that superstition and the madness of sacrifices shall

possibly two or three thousand years ago. Moreover, the body was a male body and completely odorless because of its very dry state. For feminine cadavers more easily might have developed stench and decay because their flesh is more plump and moist and because the bodies of young girls and women, who were not yet withered by old age, were not entrusted to the undertakers and embalmers for three days lest they debauch the corpses, as you have read in Herodotus.[25] P. 6

SALOMON: That sort of lust seems incredible to me.

CORONAEUS: Many fabulous things are read in Herodotus which gave Plutarch the occasion to write against him.[26]

FRIDERICUS: Since we shrink from vices of that sort, we consider things incredible which time has proved quite true. And not to go too far away from our own city, Malatesta, a prince of Rimini, within the memory of our grandfathers received with hospitality the noble wife of a certain German count who was en route to Rome on a pilgrimage. But when he failed to seduce her with flattery or force, he cruelly ran[27] a sword through her throat so that he might sate on the mutilated and bloody corpse the lust which he could not when she was alive.

CURTIUS: Crimes of such enormity are not restricted only[28] to Egypt or Italy but have advanced even into Gaul. Indeed I myself saw a surgeon in Toulouse who was said to have satisfied an illicit lust on the body of a woman dead[29] of the plague. Since he was caught "having limbs on limbs" to use the legal word, he was consigned[30] to avenging flames, and the people looked on in horror. This sort of thing seems to confirm completely what Herodotus wrote.

SENAMUS: Since Plutarch wished to safeguard the honor and dignity of his city, he scorned Herodotus who harshly had reviled it. Marcus Tullius, however, called him the "father of history."[31] And although many people did not believe things that Herodotus said, time has proved them to be quite true. For example, the accounts of the lycanthropy of the

---

cease." The rites of Isis had been in trouble before. They were prohibited during Tiberius' reign because of a scandal, but they were restored under Caligula. W. R. Halliday, *The Pagan Background of Early Christianity* (New York, 1970), pp. 276–77.

[25] *Hist.*, II. 89.

[26] *De Herodoti malignitate, Moralia*, XI. 854.

[27] *hausit* MR [28] *tantum* MR [29] *mortua* MR

[30] *deprehensum* MR

[31] Cicero, *Leg.* I. 1. 5; *De orat.* II. 13. 55; cf. Quintilian, X. 1. 73. Also Gellius, *Epist.* V. 12. 3 [ad Lucceium].

Nervii and the eruption of the winds are found to be familiar even in this age. And what he tells of girls ready for marriage, the ugly ones being dowried out of the price of the beautiful, has been carried over into the most powerful and flourishing republic of Siena.

CORONAEUS: Let us listen to Octavius as he continues the story.

OCTAVIUS: I would have brought you this same cadaver which I brought out of those tombs if the Tritonian spirits had allowed. I had made arrangements for its transportation home and had placed it in a box as if it were a purloined Palladium. Pistacus the merchant was waiting with a loaded ship for good winds in the port of Alexandria, where I had gone in order to return to Italy after my long travels. When the wind Vulturnus began to blow, he summoned the deck hands to make ready the sails. I put the chest quickly on board. Since the ship was very large, it held a
P. 7 large crew of sailors and hands. As you know, Alexandria is a very populous city where many foreign merchants gather.

When we set sail, Vulturnus was blowing. The Greeks call this wind Euronotus, unless I am mistaken; the Egyptians call it Syrochus from its origin in Syria, and Horace calls it the "white Notus," and it gave us that calm air which he describes in this verse:

> As the white Notus often scatters
> the clouds from a murky sky[32]

Homer in the same sense calls it "clearing."[33]

CURTIUS: But the same Argestes shakes our region of Provence with such force that it often has hurled down rocks and uprooted forests and homes. The local people still call the wind Albanus, which is the same name our forefathers used, as Pliny says.[34]

OCTAVIUS: We notice that the wind which is rather gentle at first becomes more violent as time passes. Moreover, when we were far out to sea, a storm was stirred up by Circius, the most blustering of all the northwest winds. Homer describes it as "clearing and stormy."[35] Circius blew directly opposite to Vulturnus, and as a result, the angry waves began to shake the ship's sides with such force that we were forced to draw in sail and to toss overboard the heavier cargo. The storm had already buffeted the ship for a day and night. The sailors, hoping for its

[32] *Carm.* I. 7. 16. For the other winds mentioned see L. Apuleius, *Opera Omnia* II (Hildesheim, 1968); *De mundo* XI.

[33] *Iliad* XI. 306; XXI. 334.

[34] *Hist. nat.* II. 119.

[35] *Odys.* V. 295; XII. 289.

cessation, said a tempest of such intensity usually spent itself in that length of time and rarely lasted two days, never more than three. Still because one blast was blowing opposite the other, the waves had swollen with much greater violence than before.

SENAMUS: I had learned from Aristotle that winds never blow at the same time with a contrary blast.[36]

OCTAVIUS: Perhaps Aristotle wrote this in the shade of the Lyceum, not in the school of sailors, who say that the severest storms are stirred up only by the opposing blasts of winds. Hence those words of Maro:[37]

> Together Eurus[38] and Notus and Africus
> clash rapidly with their blasts;

Likewise Horace:[39]

> He did not fear rash Africus fighting
> with Aquilo;

And again Vergil:[40]

> The vying winds and resounding
> tempests.

In the same way Homer[41] represents Africus and Aquilo blowing together:

> As the two winds, Boreas and Zephyr, are
> stirring up the fishy sea.

At first the skipper had urged us to be courageous and hope for better things. When he fully realized the situation, he was terrified, "a sailor conquered by the violent northwest wind," to use the poet's words.[42] Then he made everyone empty the ship which was being filled with the P. 8 unceasing waves. All, however, shirked their jobs because their bodies were wracked with pain from the ship's violent lurching. After he dropped the anchors, he groaned and urged each one to pray to God. Then a certain Florentine began to call upon Catharine of Siena; another the Virgin of Loreto, very well known to this city. Many were praying to Nicolas; others to Clement. Several with mournful wails were singing "Hail, star of the

[36] *Meteorologica* II. 6. 364a, Par. 30.
[37] *Aen.* I. 85.
[38] *Eurusque* MR
[39] *Carm.* I. 3. 13.
[40] *Aen.* I. 53.
[41] *Iliad* IX. 4–5.
[42] Lucan, *Pharsalia* VII. 125.

sea." The Greek merchants in the common speech began to repeat *sōson hēmas, kyrie, eleēson, hēmas, eisakouson despota*, "Save us, O Lord, have mercy on us, hear us, O Master." The Jews were chanting again and again *shema' 'adonai* "Hear, O Lord." The Ismaelites of Alexandria were saying: *Ejuche nahbudu, Alla, Alla, Alla, malah, resulala.* (It is you we worship, Allah, Allah, Allah, Lord of the Prophet of Allah.) A certain Venetian priest, kneeling and taking from his bosom the consecrated host in a round glass container, said:

O saving host who spreads open the doors of heaven.

You know the rest. Then someone from Calabria was crying out with a loud voice: "Against You alone, against You, O God, we have sinned; help comes not from mortals but from the Lord God; have mercy, O God, on us blind mortals." A merchant from Marseilles said:

"The Spirit, if God commands it, blows violently and an
impetuous wave swells over the vast sea;
But if there is need,
God suddenly puts those who cry to Him in lamentation far
from the evils that torment them and makes the stormy wind
abate its fury and calms the sea and the waves."

They said other things, which I do not remember. Since I knew that vows had always been most effectual when dangers approached, I prostrated myself and begged immortal God for forgiveness for my sins. I made a vow that if I should escape from this peril and arrive safely into port, I would observe that day with a yearly feast. But a Spanish soldier, as he was drenched with a huge wave, cursed God abominably with the customary Spanish insults—"in disgust," etc. I shall not say the rest: "malgrado," etc. "pere," etc., "a la virgen sa madre." Finally he added the following: "Your power cannot be compared to the devil." He was thinking of that mad song—"If I cannot move heaven, I shall move hell."[43]

When a certain merchant had heard these abuses, he became very angry and urged the captain to punish the monstrous impiety of the curser by torturing the Spaniard or by throwing him overboard; otherwise they would all perish for the sin of one.

P. 9 SALOMON: If a storm arose and could not be calmed with prayer, men of old used to cast lots and throw overboard the one on whom the lot had fallen. Thus when the prophet Jonah,[44] on whom the lot had fallen, was

[43] *Aen.* VII. 91. 312.

[44] Jonah 1: 15.

thrown overboard, the storm suddenly subsided. I think the same thing would have happened in the case of the Spaniard who was spewing out so many insults against God. Would that custom were again put into practice. The lot used to fall rather often upon a very influential man, though never unless he deserved it.[45] However, because of his powerful bodyguard he was able to elude the sacred lots. Therefore, the lots on ships fell into disuse.

Nevertheless I maintain that no one would die except for his own sin; on the contrary it often happens that one man's integrity may save the rest from imminent dangers, or one alone is snatched from shipwrecks, fire, and epidemics.

Octavius: When it was evident that we had poured out our prayers in vain, a good spirit prompted the captain to order death for anyone who did not throw overboard any Egyptian corpses which happened to be on the ship. I was terrified at this order, and under cover of night's darkness I drew out the cadaver from the box and threw it in the sea, without anyone's knowledge. Suddenly the force of the winds lessened, and favorable winds carried us safely to Crete. At this point a venerable old man with white hair, extending his hands to Heaven and giving thanks to immortal God, forced the others by his example to praise God. Remembering my vow I then wrote this dithyramb:

> Now pour out to God holy songs
>   from sweet tongues,
> You who have been snatched from the
>   waves marvel at the roaring
>   of the harsh sea, as your
>   quick feet toss up sand
>   along the shore.
> Unholy spirits, depart.
> Yield to God, masterful and awesome
>   power of the sea,
> Who strikes the lofty stars with His
>   head,
> Who molds the watery masses in a ball
>   and suspends them in the deep . . .
> From His restraining breast the winds
>   breathe on the terrestrial mass,

[45] *merentem* MR

Corus and Africus and gentle
Vulturnus and Auster pregnant
with rains which with encircling
blast quickly stir up the black
swill from the abyss of the
raging storm.
Then the water resounding with
its mighty groan strikes the
air and flows over the ships
as the sailors tremble.
But if anyone in terror should invoke
You with sacred prayers,
O Father of the Sea, three times great,
Forthwith He puts the sailors safely
P. 10 on shore, recalling the peace of
Halcyon,
And they praise him gloriously in song.

SALOMON: Oh, if only all who have been snatched from dangers would give thanks to immortal God in this way. But the hope of the ungrateful dwindles away as the teacher of wisdom divinely wrote.

OCTAVIUS: I asked that old man who seemed to me exceptionally wise and experienced in nautical matters why the captain had ordered any Egyptian corpses aboard to be cast into the sea. He answered that the transportation of Egyptian corpses always stirred up storms, and he said that the nautical laws of Egyptians scrupulously prohibited this. If anyone acted contrary to the law, he must throw overboard his cargo and pay damages to the merchants. When I learned this, I decided to keep quiet lest someone demand damages from me, although I knew I had erred.

CORONAEUS: Not only is the story of this sea voyage interesting, but it also seems useful because it could supply abundant material for conversation if we had none. In the first place, why should storms arise from Egyptian corpses, when no such thing happens when other bodies are being transported from one place to another? Still I am inclined to think that the same thing would happen to other corpses if the tomb had been violated. Next, are the seas stirred up by the power of demons, or only from exhalations, as the physicists say? Finally, with such a variety of religions represented, whose prayers did God heed in bringing the ship safely into port?

At this[46] point all were silent. Then they looked at Toralba because he was very well versed in physics. But he did not dare say anything in matters so complicated.

But CORONAEUS, breaking the silence said: "It is enough to have proposed the topics which we shall discuss tomorrow, so that we may return better prepared, as we did in the case of other questions." Since the others agreed, he called the boys who were accustomed to soothe everybody's spirits by sweetly singing divine praises with a harmony of lyres, flutes, and voices. After the music was ended, each one received permission to depart and went his way.

[46] *hic* MR

BOOK II

THEY returned on the next day, and after warmly greeting each other and discussing what each had learned in the colloquium, in a happy mood they soon sat down. At this time Coronaeus gave me, in place of the *Phaedo*,
P. 11 letters which he had received from a merchant of Corcyra. These related the news of Constantinople—the circumcision of the first-born son of the Turkish king, the visiting ambassadors, the influx of travelers, the parade of the Circesian games, the banquets, the largess, and the circumstances of each event. Since these spectacles seemed remarkable and even incredible unless performed in a crowded theater and before a crowd as large as ever assembled in that city, Coronaeus urged me to reread the passages which were especially admirable. For example, they related the speed and daring of the rope dancers who would run and leap very gracefully on the ropes which were stretched from the loftiest summits of the pinnacles; and likewise the daring of that rider who would pierce with an arrow the iron shoes of the hind hooves of the horse on which he was riding very swiftly from behind, and also of the rider who stood on the saddles of two swiftly galloping horses. The letter also told how two horsemen, standing on the saddles of two horses, were carrying another man on their shoulders[1] who was standing erect, all the while goading to the swiftest pace with an arrow the horses on which they were standing. Moreover, we read how another broke an iron beam with a violent blow from his bare shins with no blood or bruise; he also broke the iron shoes of the horses with his hands and bit the broken parts with his teeth. Also while he was lying down huge beams were placed on his arms, and men were violently striking an anvil which was placed on his chest; nevertheless he would rise up very easily against all the resistance.

[1] *hominem super humeros in pedes* MR

Many events such as these were described in the letter which had been posted at Corcyra on July 14 and delivered on July 15 to Venice, which is about 250 miles from Corcyra.

FRIDERICUS: Then the ship must have gone ten miles an hour.

CURTIUS: With an east wind blowing this would be possible, provided a sleek ship or a pirate's vessel was spurred on by many sails of the sort that pirates use when they follow merchant ships.

SENAMUS: I am not sufficiently informed how fast each ship can travel. Yet we know from an unknown source that Aemilius Paulus'[2] victory over King Perseus in Macedonia was reported four days later at Rome during the theatrical games. Similarly, a victory of the Romans near the Sagras River[3] was proclaimed in the Peloponnesus on the same day; and still another battle against the Medes near Mycale,[4] a city of upper Asia, was known on the same day in the Greek camp near Platea. Also when Domitian was emperor the story reached Rome that Antonius,[5] who had taken up arms against Domitian, had been conquered in Germany, and this on the very day he had been beaten and killed, even though he had been 2,400 miles away from the city. And at the same moment in which P. 12 the Romans had routed the Tarquins and the Latins in a great battle,[6] this very event was reported at Rome, though on uncertain authority.

FRIDERICUS: These things seemed remarkable to the ancients, though nothing occurred more frequently through the work of magi and demons who display for observation, even in mirrors fused and penetrated with magic arts, all the events in the world. Others have dogs as messengers who report in human speech all the words, deeds, actions, victories, and

[2] Lucius Aemilius Macedonicus defeated Perseus on June 22, 168 B.C. near Pydna.

[3] A river by Bruttium on the east coast of Italy between Caulonia and Locri. It is famous for the great battle fought on its banks in which an army of 130,000 Crotoniats is said to have been defeated by 10,000 Locrians. This was regarded as so incredible that it became a kind of proverb for something incredible but true. The date of the battle is uncertain, but it probably took place between 560 B.C. and 510 B.C. Cf. Cicero, *De nat. deorum* II. 2. 6; III. 5. 11; Pliny, *Hist. nat.* III. 10. 15; Strabo, VI.

[4] The Persians were defeated at Mycale in 479 B.C.

[5] Lucius Antonius Saturninus was governor of Upper Germany in the reign of Domitian. He raised a rebellion against Domitian in A.D. 91 because of personal hatred but was conquered by L. Appius Maximus, the emperor's general. See Dion Cassius, LXVII. 11; Suetonius, *Domitian* VI. 7; Martial, IV. 11; IX. 85; Plutarch, *Aemil. Paul.* XXV.

[6] Rome conquered the Latins at Lake Regillus in 496 B.C. in a battle in which Castor and Pollux were said to have intervened. Cf. Livy, II. 9.

misfortunes that have taken place. His pupil Wierus and Paulus Jovius wrote that Cornelius Agrippa had such a dog, and when its master died, a large crowd of people saw the dog deliberately jump in the Rhone river.

SENAMUS: Franciscus[7] of Siena raised a dog like this. Not too long ago, when Franciscus was burned to death, the Roman people saw this and heard the dog speak.

FRIDERICUS: Many things which are rather customary are considered incredible. Near the distant shores of the North men go with bird-like swiftness into the most distant places. Philostratus[8] wrote about Apollonius of Tyana that he quickly flew from Aethiopia and the sources of the Nile to Rome. Plutarch reports the same about Romulus, Aristaeus of Proconnesus and Cleomedes of Stampalia,[9] and Hugo Floriacensis wrote the same about the Count of Macon. Sprenger, Olaus Magnus and Paulus Grilandus, Sylvester Prierias, Molitor, and Wier are full of similar stories about airy flights, which not only theological decrees[10] but also divine and human laws have confirmed. When Plato in the second book of *Laws*[11] was deciding the punishments for those who used the wicked arts of magic, he wrote that incredible things were done by those. Apuleius, himself charged with that same magic art and on that account condemned publicly, nonetheless confirms these things. "You will not be wise," he says, "if by the most corrupt opinions you think those things are lies which seem new to hear or strange to see or difficult to comprehend. If you consider them more accurately, you will realize that not only are marvels evident to ascertain[12] but also rather easy to do."[13] And in the same vein he says: "Lest you doubt any longer, first I shall swear by the all-seeing God that I am telling things that are true and certain."[14] From this one realizes that things which happen not according to nature or human power are wrought by divine power or the power of demons.

[7] *Franciscus N Francisca* MR

[8] Flavius Philostratus was born about A.D. 170. He studied at Athens and later joined the philosophical group patronized by Septimius Severus and his wife Julia Domna. At the empress' instance he wrote the *Life of Apollonius of Tyana*; Apollonius was a mystic of the first century A.D. On his aerial flights cf. Philostratus, *Apollonius of Tyana* VIII. 10. 12.

[9] Plutarch, *Parallel Lives, Romulus* XXVII, XXVIII; cf. Pausanias, IX. 6.

[10] Augustine, *De civ. Dei*. VIII. 15. 16.

[11] Bodin's citation is incorrect. See *Laws* X. 909b; XI. 933a.

[12] *compertu* MR

[13] Apuleius, I. 3. 4. Also cf. Augustine, *De civ. Dei* XVIII. 18.

[14] Apuleius, *ibid*.

SENAMUS: I often wanted to see those air-borne messengers who could fly in a moment over vast regions without any horses or whips.

CURTIUS: I remember that when Petrus Corsus was seeking auxiliaries from the king of the Turks along with the French legate Vinea, he had a mirror in which he saw his wife at Marseilles making love with adulterers from Constantinople. The adulterous woman also saw her husband P. 13
in the mirror just as though he were present, when he sailed from port and on the day before he was to arrive at Marseilles. But before her husband arrived, her guilty conscience caused her to flee to Antipolis where her husband pursued her and killed her along with her illegitimate children and her maid. This is a recent story, well known to the whole province, which is not unlike an event which took place at about the same time near Aqua Sextia in the same province. When Guarinus, a fiscal counsellor, left his wife to plead for his life in the Senate of Paris, he promised her that he would announce his death to her should he die. On the very day that the hangman broke his neck, his wife showed to many her husband's image lightly marked in the palm of her right hand. Grignanus, prefect of the province, informed Henry II, king of France, of this strange occurrence.

FRIDERICUS: In a similar vein Thomas Aquinas wrote that it is a kind of necromancy if someone exacts a promise from a dying man to report after his death in what condition he will be.

SENAMUS: Indeed it would be desirable that proofs of such things were to be found in "mirror books."

CURTIUS: The account of actions depends upon the senses, the "that it is," but the proof of causes, namely the "why it is," must be sought more deeply from the hidden secrets of philosophy. More remarkable to me than all these things which the letter from Corcyra contains is the story which Suetonius Tranquillus,[15] Pliny, Dio Cassius, and Xiphilinus related about a well-known Roman knight who in the public games with a crowd looking on had run over a rope while sitting on an elephant. Xiphilinus explains "catadromus" as a rope stretched from the highest pinnacles of towers. The Roman people were especially amazed to see an elephant walking on a rope, as Pliny writes. Hence, the ancients had ropewalking elephants, and nothing can be more remarkable than this.

CORONAEUS: The causes of these things are difficult and lie hidden in the mysteries of nature. Only Toralba can unfold them for us.

[15] Suetonius, *Nero.* 11.

TORALBA, whose modesty was mingled with mannerliness, said: Truly I would[16] be foolish to acknowledge these praises which Coronaeus has granted to me wrongly. For if I held the secrets of nature, which Coronaeus admits are hidden, still it is not up to the natural scientist to solve such questions, since he contemplates only those things which are in nature. But the examination of the actions of demons and angels does not seem to me to pertain to natural science, but to those who study meta-
P. 14 physics, since it is evident that they take place by the will and power of demons. However, since Fridericus is an excellent mathematician and has zealously studied the things included in the arts of magic, as you have often heard in his discussions, I think no one is better qualified to explain the causes of these things than he, if he is willing.

FRIDERICUS: I am often rightly irritated with lawyers who have pronounced[17] as legitimate principles of the science[18] which they profess to be of this kind: Error makes the law; it is permitted to deceive each other; it is[19] also law when the judge makes a wrong judgment. I was never more justly angry with those than when they grant the names of mathematician and magi, that is, names of divine wisdom, to the most loathsome and wicked men. For there is a rubric in the *Codex* of Justinian Augustus[20] about magicians and mathematicians, both condemned for the same great wickedness and impiety. Now what can be more unfair than this?

CURTIUS: Fridericus is accustomed to revile this jurisprudence which we profess and cherish. He was trained in the surest proofs of the mathematicians, but whenever he abandons Euclid for Accursius, he thinks he has fallen from the brightest light into the black murk and entangling labyrinth of errors. Toralba also you have often heard scorn this legitimate knowledge; he is so well indoctrinated in the recognition of truth that he can neither say nor hear anything false which happens to those who have cleared away all the cobwebs of their minds by clear reasonings. Just as nurses are wont to talk baby-talk to babies, so it is inevitable that legislators often err along with the people. For since the Chaldeans debased the science of the Magi—that is, the knowledge of divine and sublime matters—into the foulest association with demons, the magicians by a vulgar error were called Chaldeans, "magi" and mathematicians instead of magicians. But let us not delay over the subtlety of words.

[16] *sim* MR [17] *prodidere* MR [18] *scientiae* MR
[19] *est* MR
[20] *Codex iuris civilis* IX. titl. 18.

SENAMUS: I would gladly hear one talking of his science, whether we call him a magus or magician, because no one can understand this skill unless he has had experience with it.

FRIDERICUS: There is a danger, Senamus, that the same thing may happen to you that, according to Sylvester Prierias, happened not long ago to a legate of Pope Clement. He was holding in jail a crowd of fortune tellers who admitted the usual flights through the air or the foulest copulations with demons, dances, feasts or worship of demons, which things physicists and physicians affirmed to be the sport of maniacs. The judge himself with his deputy prosecutor of impiety trials decided to run a risk and promised impunity to one of the fortune tellers if she would lead them to a place designated by the demons. The place where the fortune teller led them was very near the city, and they hid in a spot covered with branches of trees. About midnight, they saw a crowd of people, men P. 15
and women, flying as if they were birds gliding down from the clouds, and they saw things being done which they had reported most truly they did. After the witches had worshipped the demons and in their accustomed manner had taken the poisons for killing animals and plants and nothing else[21] remained except dismissal, as Apuleius says,[22] the leader of that gathering ordered the legate of Pope Clement and his deputy to be summoned because they had not been ashamed to dishonor the holy of holies of the fortune tellers or to view their sacred rites with profane eyes. And so, dragged from their hiding place and reviled with insults, they were so severely beaten and mangled with sticks that they returned home with difficulty and died eight days later.

CORONAEUS: I remember that when news of their unexpected misfortune reached the city, Pope Clement ordered the matter to be published abroad just as it had happened, so that no one afterwards should be so incredulous as to dare to doubt or so wicked as to dare run the risk.

CURTIUS: Indeed, I have been overcome before this with an incredible desire to view with these eyes the flights of witches and the meetings with demons. However, when I had compared all the writings on this subject of the ancients, Greek and Latin, and all the divine and human laws from the most remote antiquity with the accounts of fortune tellers, the charges, confessions and depositions of witnesses to such associations, I decided I must give assent at the least to their existence. I also thought I ought not to set my life in jeopardy as to whether the things which

[21] *nec . . . aliud* MR

[22] *Metamorph.* XI. 17.

were being commonly reported were true or not. Furthermore, I was mindful of Aesop's fox who, when invited by the lion, refused to go to his cave to dine "because footprints that lead all in one direction and none in the other terrify me."[23]

FRIDERICUS: As a monkey clad in purple is still a monkey, so the power of demons is the same everywhere in the world.

OCTAVIUS: Many people wonder at many things in the vast realm of nature, but nothing is more amazing than this, namely, the prevalence of lycanthropy and *onanthrōpia*[23a]. Formerly I had considered ridiculous what was being reported in Cairo—that men were changed into asses and did incredible things in public view. Also I thought fabulous the story about Ammonius who had an ass that was a student of philosophy, as well as the golden ass of Apuleius and Lucian.[24] But when I sailed from the port of Arcione, which is now called Kneza, and was coasting the shores of Arabia, frequently I saw the magic of sorceresses who turned men into asses or wolves and then restored them to human form. There-
P. 16 fore, I considered not only probable but virtually certain and verified the things that Homer wrote about Circe,[25] Herodotus[26] about the Nervii, Varro,[27] Pausanias,[28] Plato[29] and Pomponius Mela[30] about the lycanthropy of Arcadia and Lycaonia.

CORONAEUS: I would have considered them as incredible as you did, and I would not have trusted my eyes or my senses if I had not read in the sacred writings of the transformation of Nebucadnezar[31] from human form into cattle and[32] of branches into serpents. I thought thereafter that there

[23] Horace, *Epist.* I. 1. 74.

[23a] The manuscripts read *onanthrōpia*, although *enanthrōpia* (changing of one's nature), is the proper word.

[24] Loeb Classics Library (hereafter abbreviated LCL), Lucian, VIII. 47, lists *The Ass* as a work of Pseudo-Lucian, stating that the most helpful accounts of the problem of the authorship and its relation to the *Metamorphoses* of Apuleius are found in B. E. Perry, *The Metamorphoses Ascribed to Lucius of Patrae* and in P. Valletti's introduction to the Budé edition of Apuleius' *Metamorphoses.*

[25] *Odys.* X. 226–43.

[26] Herodotus, IV. 17. 105.

[27] The reference should be to Pliny, *Hist. nat.* VIII, Par. 34.

[28] Pausanias, VIII. 2, Par. 1.

[29] *Res pub.* VIII. 16. D.

[30] Pomponius Mela of Tingentera wrote under Gaius (A.D. 37–41) or early in Claudius' reign *De chorographia*, a geographical survey in Latin of the inhabited world. The work gave some details of physical nature, climate, and customs of lands.

[31] Dan. 4:32–33.

[32] *et* M

was no further room for doubt unless one should think Circe and the magi bewitched the eyes.

SALOMON: If it were merely bewitchment and madness induced in people's minds and not a real metamorphosis, the rod of Moses[33] could not have destroyed the rods of the magicians, nor would Nebucadnezar be paying the penalty for his arrogance. We have the testimony of sacred writings[34] that for seven years he was covered by claws and hairy skin and garbed in the appearance of an animal of the herd; maddened, he had gone so far as to feed on hay. For Moses writes that the magicians of the Egyptians had made the same things which he himself had made with divine power—namely, serpents, frogs, blood.[35] But Moses bewitched no one, and therefore neither did they (since he writes that they did the same as he) nor would Daniel, most famous of all prophets, have said that the mind of Nebucadnezar was snatched and restored along with his human form.[36]

CURTIUS: Homer seems to imply a similar thing about Circe's suitors whom she changed into swine; their heads, voices, and hair were like swine, but their minds and bodies remained unchanged.[37] Boëthius renders it thus: "Though voice and body be destroyed, the mind alone steadfastly endures the monsters it produces."[38]

FRIDERICUS: Philo Judaeus[39] says that a witch cannot only change the shape of the body but also can destroy the mind's reasoning power, though the human body remains. I could never have believed this unless I had satisfied myself that a young relative of mine had been spoiled of his mind by the criminal sorcery of a certain magician and lived mindless ever after. Actius Sincerus[40] indicates this in these verses:

> I shall try to destroy that one with magic rites,
> the one who miserably deprived me of my reasoning.

Lucan's[41] verses are similar:

> The bewitched mind perishes, though polluted with
> no poison brew.

[33] Ex. 7:9–12. [34] Dan. 4:32–33. [35] Ex. 7:9–25; 8:1–15.
[36] Dan. 4:34–37. [37] *Odys.* X. 239. [38] *Consol. phil.* IV. 3. 28.
[39] *De specialibus legibus* I. 59, Par. 319–21; III. 18, Par. 100–102.
[40] Actius Sincerus was the pseudonym of Jacobus Sannazarius, Italian poet (1485–1530), who wrote pastorals and whose poem, *De partu virginis*, won for him the title of the "Christian Vergil." See *De scriptis et scriptoribus anonymis atque pseudonymis* (Hamburg, 1674), p. 135.
[41] *Pharsalia* VI. 454.

SENAMUS: What was easier for Circe than to change her suitors (*procos*) into pigs (*porcos*)? For this is done with the change of a single letter.

P. 17 CORONAEUS: The change of suitors into pigs is easier because their manners are more similar than the letters. For I think that those who had given themselves over to gluttony and lust and had succumbed to Circe's enticements had lost their reason and mind and had no likeness to man except in their appearance; Homer,[42] however, wrote that they had lost their human form but had retained a stable and undisturbed mind.

FRIDERICUS: Clever and true. But if we accept this interpretation alone, the other things which are found in divine and human laws will be thrown into doubt. That metamorphosis of men into cattle is described as most true[43] not only by Herodotus,[44] Vergil,[45] Homer,[46] and Plato[47] but also by Moses,[48] Isaiah,[49] and Daniel,[50] the most famous theologians. Even in these same times among those Nervii of Herodotus, whom we call Livonae, every year about the winter solstice a large crowd of soothsayers jumps over the local river and are changed into wolves; then they most cruelly set upon the flocks, men, and cattle, and after the twelfth day they cross over the same river and again receive their human form. For this reason criminal courts are appointed. Those who are changed in this manner are judged to be convicted sorcerers. This happens very often to those who feed on human flesh. Pausanias[51] says that Lycaon, king of Arcadia, poured out human blood as a libation to Jupiter Lycaeus. Marcus Varro[52] and Copas,[53] who wrote the *Olympionica*, tell of Demarchus[54]

42 *Odys.* X. 239.

43 *pro verissima* MR

44 Herodotus, IV. 17. 105.

45 *Ecl.* VIII. 69–70.

46 *Odys.* X. 226–43.

47 *Res pub.* VIII. 16. D.

48 Ex. 7:9–12.

49 Bodin seems to be stretching the point with reference to Isaiah. In Isaiah 65:25 there is a transformation, but it is of animals eating together in an unlikely manner. In the references to Moses and Daniel, there is again no transformation of man into animal as in the pagan references.

50 Dan. 4:32–33.

51 Pausanias, VIII. 2, Par. 1–6.

52 Bodin's reference to Marcus Varro is erroneous. The citation is found in Pliny, *Hist. nat.* VIII. 34, Par. 82. Also Augustine, *De civ. Dei* XVIII. 17.

53 Copas is mentioned in Pliny, *Hist. nat.* VIII. 34, Par. 82, as the author of the *Olympionicon*, and the story which Bodin relates is also detailed by Pliny in the same reference. Variant spellings of the name are given. Bibliotheca Teubneriana, *C. Plinius Secundus*, II, 106, lists Apollas, Agriopas, Copas and Scopas. An *Olympionicon* is attributed to Phlegon of Tralles, a freedman of Hadrian, but the work is lost. See Felix Jacoby, *Die Fragmente der griechischen Historiker* (Leiden, 1926 ff.) IIB. 257a. Also cf. Albin Lesky, *A History of Greek Literature* (New York, 1966), p. 853. Copas and Phlegon may indeed be the same person.

54 Demarchus, the spelling in Noack and the manuscripts MR, appears as De-

of Parrhasis who, after offering human sacrifices to Jupiter, ate the sacrifice and suddenly changed into a wolf; after ten years he recovered his human form and won the prize, so they say, at an Olympic boxing match. After the Arcadians had investigated this matter, by consecrated laws they forbade anyone, under penalty of death, ever to go to the temple of Jupiter Lycaeus.

SENAMUS: It seems reasonable to me that no one could change from man to animal without the man's death. I would think it more logical that fallible human eyes or, as Heraclitus says,[55] false witnesses were deceived by witchcraft.

FRIDERICUS: I do not doubt that magicians work magic, but not all the time nor for everyone. When I went to Thuringia in Lower Germany, there was a certain quack in town who received pay for feeding the inexperienced people on empty wonders. He gulped down a four-horse team loaded with hay—horses and driver—while the crowd watched. Then saying he wished to scale the heavens, he was suddenly raised from the earth. His wife followed, holding onto his feet; then the maid followed her mistress, the servant the maid. When all were suspended in the air, as if needless on a magnet, they remained immovable for a long time, much to the amazement of all.

CURTIUS: I believe the devouring of the steed and driver was the work P. 18
of witchcraft, but I do not doubt that the ascension was accomplished with the help of a demon. For Simon Magus,[56] with Nero[57] and the courtiers watching, ordered that he be cut into pieces, and then limb by limb he was restored to life. After this he was carried into the heavens and obtained divine honors and a statue from Caesar. Indeed what is so difficult, so contrary to the power of nature, but that witch says she can accomplish it:

> At my will rivers to the surprise even of their banks return to their springs. Disturbance I calm, calmness I disturb. Low-lying clouds I scatter or send with a song and to my voice all winds bend. Serpents

---

maenetus in Pliny, *Hist. nat.* VIII. 34, Par. 82. Pausanius, II. 8. 2. also relates the story; however, he remarks that he cannot believe that Damarchus (note spelling) turned into a wolf but only that he won an Olympic victory.

[55] *vel ut Heraclitus* M

[56] Justin Martyr, *Apol.* I, XXVI and LVI.

[57] Irenaeus, *Adv. haeres.* I. 20, says it was reported that Claudius Caesar had erected a statue to Simon.

I tame and forests move. Cause mountains to tremble, lands to moan and Shades to leave tombs. Oh Luna, I also bring you down.[58]

CORONAEUS: Toralba, do you think these things are wrought by nature or with the help of a demon?

TORALBA: I shall frankly reveal what I think, but I beg you, Coronaeus, not to expect answers to these difficult questions beyond my ability.

CORONAEUS: I would be out of my mind if I were to want to know what you do not know.

TORALBA: Although I was not sure I could attain to truth in other arts, I tried to investigate nature itself and its hidden causes, and I had the same experience that voyagers have. For the farther they go from shore, the deeper the waters they find. When they are as far as possible[59] from land, they lose the use of the leads because of the depth of the sea. In like manner, as I study the nature of elements, fossils, metals, plants, animate and celestial bodies, and finally delve more deeply into the remarkable power of angels and demons, reason seems to leave me completely. Also the more I wish to know and the more carefully I direct my attention to minute details, the more I realize I do not know.

CURTIUS: This is characteristic of the most learned men. When I inquire the reason for this, Franciscus Fuxaeus, a noted mathematician who had been summoned by King Charles IX of France and who taught in Paris before many listeners what Archimedes long ago had stated, namely to move a given weight, said that a knowledge of ignorance was the surest beginning for understanding the more perfect sciences and also that none were more unlearned than those who think they know everything. He used as an example those who had always lived in a hovel or the cave of
P. 19 Socrates[60] and whose view of the sky was no wider than three ells. When they get a better vantage point and see the neighboring regions which they have never seen before, they are amazed. When they are lifted to the tops of the mountains they freely view the lands and seas and the heavenly bodies most remote and stand struck with their old ignorance. Also empty authority draws along many whom reason ought to have led. And yet they hurry along like cattle, not where or whither they ought, but wherever others are going.

TORALBA: Granted most live this way. For who would not reply to one seeking the origin of storms or the wind that these things are produced

[58] Ovid, *Metamorph.* VII. 200–207.
[59] *quam longissime* MR
[60] Plato, *Res pub.* VII. 1–3, 514–18B.

by warm dry[61] exhalation. Now if you seek the reason, they will say "Aristotle said so," as the pupils of Pythagoras used to say, he said. Still no one is so foolish to think that warm dry vapors in the coldest winter in the deepest abysses of the ocean opposite each pole have any power, as often as they swell with storms. There are some, however, who are moved by reason alone, not by authority; but they believe that they will furnish the causes of all things, although they cannot even attain to the reasons of less weighty matters—namely, the things which reside in us and happen before our eyes. How much more modestly did Pliny,[62] that wisest, most keen-scented hunter of nature, write when he said we ought in most matters to admire the majesty and divinity of nature rather than to engage in over subtle enquiry. Also Alexander of Aphrodisias,[63] a very astute Peripatetic, did not hesitate to admit that nature had hidden the reason why teeth are sensitive to an iron file.[64] Of all the innumerable errors that our natural scientists can make, there is none more serious than to think that all things which are outside man's power come from the necessary causes of nature[65] or fortune. Those who think this try[66] to snatch away free will from God. They believe that demons and angels have no power unless[67] necessary or that demons do not even exist, but only those things which encounter the brute senses. They think it base to admit that they are ignorant of the causes of the things which fall under the senses. And if they cannot deny it, they consider it better to give an absurd reason than no reason at all. It must be stated and confirmed by principles and careful proofs, unless I am mistaken, against the Peripatetics, so that some conclusion to the proposed questions can be found, that the first cause is bound by no necessity to act, but tempers all things with this freedom so that it can, if it wishes, restrain the attacks of men and beasts, control lifeless natures, keep fires from burning, shake the world at will or raise it up again. On the other hand, the whole assembly of Peripatetics, Epicureans, and Stoics had decided that not only is the first cause moved to action by necessity, but even that God has no power to prevent things that occur by nature.[68]

[61] *sicca* MR
[62] *Hist. nat.* II. 63, Par. 154–59.
[63] Cf. Aristotle, *Problem.* VII. 5. 886b. 12.
[64] *ad ferri limam agitatam* MR
[65] *a naturae causis necessariis* MR
[66] *conantur* MR
[67] *nisi* MR
[68] Toralba's interest in the freedom of God from necessity and God's power to act independently of natural necessity was not only a traditional question, but also one with great contemporary and future interest. The following century was to see the most subtle original philosophies of Spinoza and Leibniz, among many other

P. 20 FRIDERICUS: There is no one of those who has now assumed[69] any opinion of piety who thinks that God is bound by any necessity. However, about these matters the natural scientists reach one conclusion, the theologians another.

SALOMON: What is true must always be one and the same, and the same matter cannot be true to theologians but false to natural scientists, even if the judgments of theologians and scientists about the same matters often are contrary.

CORONAEUS: Proceed then, Toralba, to reveal a clear demonstration of this matter.

TORALBA: Aristotle writes many intolerable things about God as when he calls Him "animal."[70] This was unseemly for not merely a natural scientist but even for a metaphysician—an investigator or observer of divine things—since by this definition he admits that God is corporeal by himself defining "animal" as *corpus animatum*. Still nothing is more foolish than to say that the first cause is the producer and preserver of all things[71] and to bind this same first cause by servile obligation and necessity[72] and yet to assign to oneself free will; for Aristotle maintains that man is free because he is the cause of himself,[73] and no outside power can compel him. What is more arrogant or alien to physical laws? Indeed Plutarch[74] did not have a stronger argument to upset the Stoics' opinion of fate than that they removed God as helmsman of the world by admitting necessity, that is, "If necessity is mingled with action, God does not have power over all, nor does everything live through his reason."

FRIDERICUS: To be sure elementary works have great variety and flux, but the most certain and immutable revolutions of the heavenly bodies, which hasten themselves in mutual encirclings, prove that they depend upon an immutable cause.

---

natural theologies. Although Spinoza tended to deny contingency in God, yet God by his nature is supreme. There can be nothing "beyond God," for this is absurd. It is difficult to assert a greater absurdity "of God, whom we have shown to be the first and only free cause of the essence of all things and their existence." *Ethics.* Leibniz stresses the choice of God (of the best of all possible worlds), yet God's knowledge of things as they will be, is of things as they must be. Even if some are contingent, is this not because they are possible, and can God make the possible impossible? Hence is not God necessitated? See *Discourse on Metaphysics*, etc. A profound source for these and others is Charles Hartshorne, *Philosophers Speak of God* (Chicago, 1953), especially pp. 192–94 and 137–42.

[69] *induerunt* MR [70] *Metaphys.* XII. 7. 9. [71] *Ibid.*, XII, 7, 1–8.

[72] *Phys.* VIII. 1. 8–9; *De generatione et corruptione* II. 9–11.

[73] *Metaphys.* VII. 7. 3; *Eth. eudem.* II. 6. 1–6.

[74] *De defect. orac.* 425F, Par. 29.

TORALBA: That God is immutable is agreed by all natural scientists and theologians. But they think that higher causes are checked by the force and power of lower causes. More credible is the opinion of the poets who, in their fictions, profess that Jupiter is loosed from the power of lower gods but still is bound by the higher laws of Nemesis.[75] Parmenides used to say this Nemesis or fate embraced the world, but Chrysippus said that eternal motion, beautiful and fitly applied, Zeno said that Providence, Augustine that fate applies to God alone or to no one.[76]

SALOMON: A Hebrew interpreter writes similarly that fate, *kodesh*, is that in which the holy of holies is contained, that is, God, receiving all things within himself and encompassing all things with free will.

TORALBA: If it is true, as Aristotle writes, that no one deserves praise or blame for that which he does of necessity,[77] then surely he thinks that eternal God does not deserve praise, or thanks for His benefactions toward us, since He is forced by necessity to do them. It follows then that God P. 21
is freed from administration of all things, since providence is discerned in only two matters: first, that each single thing be; second, that it be good. But necessity excludes both of these because a necessary series of causes effects a stable and unchangeable order of things. So that he who is in a furnace cannot be saved from the burning of the fire, nor can a man's safety be provided for contrary to the power of nature. But if providence is removed (by which all things visible and invisible stand), it is necessary that the whole world be overturned. Rather than admit this, Aristotle usurped a saying of Plato's from the *Phaedo*:[78] namely, it is reasonable that God has care for us.[78a] The same Plato in the *Statesman* calls God the Shepherd of the human race.[79]

SENAMUS: This argument seems probable, though not inevitable, that the world would be destroyed if providence were removed. Because if God provides for the universe, He does it either for Himself or for the world. Now, He does this not for Himself because He can easily do without the world; otherwise He would not be content in Himself, that is *autarkestatos*, which not only Plato and Aristotle[80] call him, but also He calls Himself *Shaddai*, which is the same thing. Indeed, He does not pro-

[75] Aeschylus, *Prometh.* 936.

[76] Parmenides in Hermann Diels, *Die Fragmente der Vorsokratiker*, 6th ed. (Berlin, 1954), I, Par. 8, line 30, p. 23F.

[77] *Eth. eudem.* II. 8. 17–23. *Eth. nicomach.* III. 1. 11–26.

[78] *Phaedo* 62D.

[78a] Mazarine f lat. 3527 *nostri*.

[79] *Polit.* XIV. 271E.

[80] Plato, *Philebus* 67A; Aristotle, *Metaphys.* XII. 9. 1–6. Also cf. Proclus, Prop. 10 and Prop. 40. in E. R. Dodds, *Proclus, The Elements of Theology* (Oxford, 1963), pp. 12 and 42. (Hereafter referred to as Dodds, *Proclus*).

vide for the world on account of the world because the world would be God's end, and He would be gladdened on its account; for the end (i.e., final cause) always surpasses those that are directed to the goal.

Toralba: Indeed, Senamus, Alexander used this argument to defend the judgments of Aristotle. And yet at the same time he departed far from this opinion when he said: "To say that God is unwilling to govern our affairs is alien to the divine majesty; for it is envious and wicked not to want better matters when you can."[81]

Salomon: The argument of Senamus is convincing in part, because it does not suit divine majesty to do anything for anything except for Himself. He said: "I have created all these things for Myself, even the wicked for the day of vengeance."[82] He would not have been better or happier because of the creation or administration of the world because He would have been neither best nor happiest before. Still in this God pleases Himself to make His power manifest to all created beings and intelligences, impelled by no stronger force, no stronger necessity, and finally with no stronger happiness. Nor can one say God is envious,[83] if He does not make things better than is possible. Proclus was not correct in determining the eternity of the world[84] from this, since the nature of finite things is such that no such way can or ought to be made equal to the Creator in the best degree of time or happiness.

Coronaeus: The question does not yet seem settled to me how the first cause is immutable if the series or progression of lower causes is
P. 22 changed. But if the progression of lower causes is immutable, one must admit that this world exists from necessity, and that the things which happen are caused by the immutable force of higher causes and by the power of necessity.

Salomon: Indeed God, giving a witness about Himself, says: "I am the Lord eternal; I am not changed."[85] Likewise, "The heavens will decline and perish, but You are Yourself the same, always like unto Yourself."[86] These words indicate that the divine majesty and nature is always stable and eternal, but still they do not destroy but rather confirm the free will of God.

[81] *Phaedo* 62D.

[82] Prov. 16:4.

[83] Aristotle, *Metaphys.* I. 2. 12.

[84] See Dodds, *Proclus, Of Time and Eternity*, Prop. 55, and commentary on this proposition, p. 301, where Dodds states that in the scheme of Proclus the physical universe is finite except in the sense that finite bodies are potentially divisible *ad infinitum*, p. 229; also see Prop. 198 and commentary.

[85] Isaiah 40:28.

[86] Psalm 101:27–28.

SENAMUS: What does this verse mean then? "The fates rule the world, and all things exist according to a fixed law."[87]

TORALBA: That is correct. Either fate is nothing, or it is God, who has prescribed fixed laws for all natures which He alone can change or upset. The Lawgiver of nature is freed from His own laws, not by the senate or people but by Himself alone. Why is the earth not covered by waters since the earth is heavier? Aristotle says this was done for the protection of living things. It would have been more honest to imitate the tragedians who, when they cannot explain a difficult matter, bring forth a *deus ex machina* (God from a machine). Therefore, from this demonstration we gather that nothing in nature is necessary which could happen otherwise.[88] Algazel, the shrewdest of the Arab philosophers, perceived this learnedly in contradiction to Averroës. For what is more frequent than for winter wheat to spring from rye? Not always but all too often tares come from grain. Or on the contrary a serpent is produced from a man; very often monsters spring up from the race of all living things. We have seen new and unheard of illnesses advance, great floods, unexpected fires, prodigious births, rains of stones, blood, milk, and wheat, and finally awesome portents. Antiquity is full of examples of these things, as are the books and the literature of the Greeks, Hebrews, and Latins, so that it is necessary that they happen not only apart from nature but even in opposition to nature.[89]

OCTAVIUS: Since our Hippocrates had always noticed that the power of epidemic, incredible, and incurable diseases transcended nature, he wrote that they were evoked by a certain divine power.[90] Fernelius, a leading physician, illustrated this principle by the various and amazing actions of demons which were contrary to the usual progressions of natural causes and symptoms.

TORALBA: Although Alexander himself usually defended Aristotle, he departed from the text of his teacher and wrote that nature is often

[87] Marcus Manilius, *Astronomicon* IV. 14. *Iulii Firmicima* (Basel, 1533).

[88] *quod aliter fieri* MR

[89] *Julii Obsequentis prodigiorum liber . . . integritate suae restitutus, P. Vergilii de prodigiis libri III, J. Camerarii de ostentis liber II* (Paris, 1553). Listed in *Br. Mus. Cat.* (1963), CLXXIV, 230.

[90] This statement seems strange in view of the fact that *On the Sacred Disease* abjures any appeal to nonnatural causes. "Men regard [this disease] as divine from ignorance and wonder. . . ." Hippocrates, *Genuine Works*, translated by Francis Adams, II (London, 1849), "On the Sacred Disease," p. 843. "Of the Epidemics" is thoroughly naturalistic.

changed at one time by force, at another time by customs, next by prayers to God.[91] By this he asserts that sickness and evils are mitigated or changed. Indeed, we read that these things happen constantly from the
P. 23 criminal acts of magicians. And also keep in mind the things which Fridericus related and the things our lector read that happened earlier at Constantinople to the amazement of the people. All of these, you realize, happened with all nature opposing. These things do not prove sufficiently, do they, that the power of nature is not necessary and unchangeable? For it cannot be in any way that things are necessary which happen otherwise, as Aristotle himself admits,[92] who, nevertheless, fixing chance and fortune in nature, has removed necessity from nature in conformity with the opinion of the people.[93]

SENAMUS: What then will happen to Plato[94] who, in accordance with the opinion of Homer,[95] represents a golden chain let down by Jupiter from heaven? Must we not grant that the series of natural causes is inviolable and completely unchangeable?

TORALBA: In my opinion Homer explains himself sufficiently when he recognized that those lower gods can be drawn upward by the higher, but the Supreme Deity cannot be drawn down by the lower.

SALOMON: I think the Homeric chain is nothing other than the ladder represented in the nocturnal vision of Jacob the Patriarch; God was at the top of the ladder, and angels descended from the top of heaven to the earth and then ascended again to heaven.[96]

OCTAVIUS: At least Proclus the Academic and Plutarch seem to confirm Salomon's interpretation when they place demons between the nature of men and gods, carrying divine things to men and human things to the gods.[97] But the difference is that he called God by the name of *demon*; they only include evil demons. Even Plato called God the greatest of all demons,[98] but the younger Academics more often than not interpreted demons as mean and evil.

TORALBA: From either interpretation it follows that angels and demons have less power than God but greater power than men; yet this force and power would be equal to the power of God if God were bound by the

[91] This is indeed a contradiction to Aristotle, for in *Magna Moralia* I. 6. 1186a. 5 he states that nothing that is by nature becomes another by training.

[92] *Metaphys.* VI. 2. 6.

[93] *Metaphys.* VI. 2. 6–13; VI. 3. 1–4.

[94] *Theaet.* 153C.

[95] *Iliad* VIII. 19.

[96] Gen. 28:12.

[97] Dodds, *Proclus,* Prop. 128. Plutarch, *De defectu oraculorum* 436F.

[98] *Polit.* 272E; also cf. *Leg.* IV. 713D., *Apol.* 27C.

necessity of action, since every cause produces greater effects the more powerful it is. If, however, the first cause would act from necessity, the power of all consequent causes would be infinite, and the power of a finite thing cannot be infinite.

CORONAEUS: That argument would be most effectual if the antecedent could be arrived at by proof.

TORALBA: Whatever acts naturally acts to the limit of its own power and ability; for example, fire burns to the limit, not with restraint nor within limits but to the extent assigned it by nature. Therefore, if the first cause acts naturally, as Aristotle[99] says, it is necessary for all its own power, which indeed is infinite, to spill over into the second cause, P. 24 and by the same rationale the second cause must grant infinite power to the third and then likewise passing it on to the ensuing causes even down to the last, which is to say, to enrich and increase the things which are finite, changing, and fleeting by a certain infinite power, since all schools of philosophers even to the Epicureans admit that the first cause is of infinite power and goodness. And so in that way the power of all causes would be equalled; likewise, the second cause being united to the finite and bounded heaven, with that infinite power would neither act nor move temporarily. This seemed absurd to Averroës so he, breaking with Aristotle's opinion, separated the first cause, because it was infinite, from the action of heaven and joined the second cause to the first and finite orb, lest finite things unite with infinite, eternal with fleeting, by a necessary series of connection. This necessary connection is all the more absurd because Aristotle[100] wrote that all minds and forms separated from matter once and for all hang from the first cause. Avicenna and Averroës following the Academics repudiated this opinion because they believed that the second cause was derived from the first, the third from the second in a fixed order.

SENAMUS: This proof of Toralba has been presented subtly and cleverly, but from this same explanation the whole science of nature is overturned.

CORONAEUS: How is this?

SENAMUS: It is needful that there be necessary causes for those things of which there is any science, but the explanation of Toralba removed the necessity of causes. Therefore, all the science of nature is bound to be turned upside down, since there can no more be a science of things

[99] *Metaphys.* III. 2. 2; XII. 4; XIII. 10. 5–9.

[100] *Metaphys.* II. 2. 1–10; I. 7. 4; VII. 8. 4 ff.

which happen by chance or which can be done otherwise than there can be a science of finding a buried treasure.

TORALBA: Natural things do not happen by chance, at random, or in blind sequence but proceed uniformly according to the same laws so that given the cause the effect follows, unless they are kept from doing so by the divine will in all things or human will in some or by the power of demons in many. For if you keep a rock from falling down or fire from rising up, the proof is not thereby invalidated—namely, that a stone tends downward because it is heavy, and fire upward because it is light.

OCTAVIUS: From the reasoning of Toralba we gather that the first cause is free, not natural, not violent. For if the first cause were forced, there would be no free will in God, but rather He would be necessarily forced either by a higher cause or by an equal one or by a lower cause. The first cause is not forced by a higher cause because nothing is higher than the highest; not by an equal, because it would not be equal if it could be forced. It can be forced not by itself, much less by a lower or weaker cause, since the supreme cause is rich in so many and so great resources that a higher cause cannot exist.

The nature of God, moreover, would not be very powerful and out-
P. 25 standing if it were subjoined to this necessity or nature by which the sky, seas, lands, and this whole world are ruled and if this power were equipped with greater and better power than God himself.

SALOMON: Impressive as this proof of Toralba's is, more impressive still is that proof which issues from the mouth of omnipotent God himself. "All things," He says, "which I have wished, I have made."[101]

CORONAEUS: This is clear enough but one thing remains, viz., that the younger Peripatetics imbued with a more divine doctrine, lessening the impious conclusions of Aristotle, do not take will away from God but think that in God willing and being are the same thing, so that what He wills is, and what is, that He wills.

TORALBA: Just as the sick have their beds and their positions changed but cannot escape the illness, so also descendants fall into the same difficulties as their predecessors because more severe problems follow from Coronaeus' remarks than from the earlier because the substance of God cannot be changed. But the will of God, if it cannot be changed, is not will and is not free for this or that, but only for this and this alone. For God could have made two or three suns, but He did not will to. Thus God wills many things, but He is one God not many. Therefore, willing

[101] Isaiah 46:11.

and being are not the same in God because He wills that many and varied forms exist but not infinite, eternal, or simple. Whereas He himself is infinite, simple, eternal, not numerous and manifold. It is necessary that God be the same in all forms. But if we say that the world also exists from necessity, as those think, willing and being cannot be the same in God because the necessary existence of the world excludes completely the will of God. For nothing voluntary can happen when violent necessity forces it.

CORONAEUS: Let us grant then that all things exist by the will of God, and willing and being are not considered to be identical in God. What follows from this?

TORALBA: In the first place, the world is preserved by another than itself.

SENAMUS: Aristotle also writes that the world is preserved by the first cause.[102]

TORALBA: Quite so, but he thinks it is preserved of necessity, and for this reason he decided it was eternal. If the world depends on a voluntary cause, as I am sure has been proved, it cannot be eternal of its own nature. Since there are two principles of action, one is brought about by the impulse of nature, the other by no necessity whether for generation or management and protection of the things produced. Therefore, since it has been shown that the productive and preservative cause of the world is free and loosed[103] from the fates and the laws of Nemesis, and that will is not the same as essence, it follows that God can desert what He has made whenever He wishes. Destruction necessarily follows desertion, since nothing can be preserved or come about by itself. Therefore the work which depends on another's judgment and will for its safety is not eternal. Since Avicenna, preeminent for his scholarship, was aware of this, he P.26
said: "The creature is nothing and from nothing, and has its existence in accordance with essence from the first cause. But there can be no first cause if the world is eternal." From this another proof follows, no less productive and useful than the former; however, I do not wish to weary you with a longer discussion.

CORONAEUS: Surely we shall not grow weary of this discussion from which we derive not only the greatest pleasure but also even greater profit.

TORALBA: In eternal objects there is no first, no last cause, as Alexander himself admits.[104] But the world has a first cause, as all the scientists agree;

[102] *De generatione et corruptione* II. 10.
[103] *liberam et solutam* MR
[104] Alexander Aphrodias, *In metaphys.* I. 12.

therefore the world is not eternal. Inasmuch as Aristotle[105] had seen this, he made all causes eternal, especially first causes. Why first causes rather than middle or final, if all are eternal and begin to exist at the self same moment. Or if there is one first cause, how are consequential causes eternal and contemporaneous with the first, when the rationale of prior and posterior has in view not time but rank, as they themselves say. Since these things are foolish, we must admit that the world is not eternal. If it is not eternal, it must have had a beginning and also will have an end. This indeed has been decreed by all divine[106] and natural laws[107] that whatever will have an end had a beginning and what had a beginning of its own origin will perish at some time or other. For if anything[108] can always be, it has an immutable nature: if it has immutable power[109] in its own nature, it will never be able to be changed. If it could never be changed, it could not even have been produced; but if it has been produced, it must also have been changed in order to pass from potentiality to actuality. Therefore if anything is changeable of its own nature, it cannot be eternal. And so when Plato[110] attributed to the world a beginning of existence, he knew it would end; nevertheless he thought that the same would be everlasting by virtue of God's goodness, not by its own nature. All things, then, which had a beginning will perish, unless they are supported by the nod of the builder, by his judgment, will and power. From this one plainly sees that Galen[111] wrote with no reason that the following principle seemed to him not to be necessary: "Everything begotten is transitory."

SALOMON: If a builder said that this building constructed by himself would collapse some day, nothing can stand contrary to his decrees. Now the Eternal Builder decreed that the world would perish at some time. And yet our Hebrew Philo,[112] following the opinion of Plato, thinks that the accidents of the heavens, not the essence, will be changed and that it is very shameful even to conceive the destruction of the world; yet, dear is Plato, dear is Philo, but more dear is the voice of God which allows
P. 27 no one to doubt. The stars and the heavens are very ancient, but, as a garment they will fade and die.

105 *Phys.* VIII. 6; *Metaphys.* VII. 7; XII. 8. 4–5.
106 I Kings (I Sam.) 3:12; also cf. Rev. 8:1.
107 Aristotle, *Metaphys.* V. 17. 2. Plato, *Timaeus* 28C.
108 *quid* M
109 *si vim habet immutabilem* MR
110 *Timaeus* 29D–30C.
111 *De sanitate tuenda* I. 5.
112 *De opificio mundi* II.

CORONAEUS: The Epicureans and Stoics declared the world would be destroyed by fire, as Lucretius[113] the Epicurean says:

> One day will give it to destruction, and the mass and machinery of the world, sustained for many years, will fall.

Those wrote this with no proof. Although this surely has very great weight and influence, not only in refuting the opinions of the Peripatetics which leave no place for divine laws or authority, but also that they, who are aware that they themselves and the whole world depend upon and are preserved by so glorious a source, may be seized with a more ardent desire for God the best and greatest and break into His praises.

CURTIUS: All nature perceives the decline and old age of the world. Writers say with continuous complaints that men cannot be compared with their ancestors in size or strength, as is attested by the remains of their bones and the life of these little men and little lads when compared with the gigantic size of those men who were seven,[114] eight, or nine cubits taller. This fact bears witness to the senility of the world and its future destruction.

TORALBA: The proof of the world's destruction is no less inevitable from its change than from the will of the Creator Himself. Since the heavens are moved, they must be corporeal; moreover, whatever is corporeal is likewise divisible, passive, and dissoluble,[115] as the physicists and theologians agree with one accord. That the heaven is corporeal is seen not only from the fact that it is mobile, but also because, confined by its own boundaries and limits, it encompasses other things in its sphere, having multitudinous divisons, also a finite and commensurable form and quantity. But corporeal quantity contains matter[116] within itself, likewise motion shaping quality, all of which are accidents. But they say that matter exists nowhere without form. Aristotle[117] says: "When I say the heavens, then I mean form; when I say this heaven, I mean this form in this matter." By these words he admits that heaven is formed from matter, form and accidents, as do also his interpreters.

CORONAEUS: Consequently we have the first part of the discussion explained fully and accurately—namely, that the universe and the things which are held in the most ample bosom of the world and are loosed at the will of the eternal artisan and, besides that, so many wonders which

[113] *De rerum natura* V. 96.
[114] *qui tribus desunt in* MR
[115] *ac dissolubile* MR
[116] *materiam* MR
[117] *De caelo* I. 9, Par. 278b.

stupefy men, so many tricks and levitations of magicians, are accomplished not by nature but by the power of angels and demons outside of or contrary to nature.

P. 28 SENAMUS: If demons were corporeal, it would be less confusing.

TORALBA: The question about the nature of immortal souls, that is, about angels and demons, always seemed very difficult and obscure. Although Aristotle almost everywhere calls demons living, still he does not explain whether or not they are bodies because he calls God living[118] as well as demons. "Some one may ask," he says, "why the spirit which wanders in the air is better and more immortal than the spirit which is in living beings."[119] Here he admits that either demons or the minds of men separated from the bodies wander away in the air. Plato,[120] however, acknowledges that a disputation about demons exceeds the capacity of the human mind; still we must give assent to the opinions of our ancestors.

Often, however, there is a discussion in Plato about demons—in the *Symposium,*[121] *Protagoras,*[122] *Critias,*[123] *Politics,*[124] *Epinomis,*[125] *Phaedo,*[126] *Sophist,*[127] and in the *Laws.*[128] In the *Theages*[129] also he openly says that we like sheep always need the wonderful care of divine shepherds, and he thinks it is as foolish to entrust men to the care of men as the care of sheep and goats to sheep and goats. He also praises in the *Cratylus*[130] the opinion of Hesiod who calls demons good and wise men who have died, and in the *Symposium*[131] he placed them midway between gods and men, composed of an airy nature. In the *Phaedo*[132] he openly stated that angels, whom he always calls gods, were our guardians. In the *Sophist*[133] he even writes that a guardian angel, which the younger Academics call "the demon that sits beside," accompanies us wherever we go

[118] On demons as living, see *Metaphys.* XII. 8. 19–20; on God as a living being see *Metaphys.* XII. 8. 9.

[119] *Metaphys.* XII. 10. 12.

[120] *Timaeus* 40E.

[121] *Symp.* 202E.

[122] Demons are not discussed in the *Protagoras.*

[123] Demons are not mentioned in the *Critias.*

[124] *Polit.* 272E, 274B, 271D, 309C.

[125] *Epinomide* MR. *Epin.* 992D.

[126] *Phaedo* 107D, 113D, 108B.

[127] *Soph.* 266B.

[128] *Leg.* 713D, 717B; V. 729E, 738D; VIII. 848D; IX. 877A; X. 906A; XI. 914B.

[129] *Theages* 122C, 128D–131.

[130] *Cratylus* 397E, 398B.

[131] *Symp.* 202E.

[132] *Phaedo* 62D.

[133] *Soph.* I. 1. 216b.

and examines our thoughts. Also in the *Theages*[134] he says: "I have a certain demon by some certain divine allotment who has followed me from boyhood." With his argument as a starting point, all the Academicians began various disputations about the nature of demons, and they agreed on this point—that a demon was granted to each man at birth by a divine gift to be his leader. Menander[135] expresses it thus: "For every man who is born there is a demon who is the guide of life for all." When Socrates was still a little boy his father received the prophecy that he had a leader better than six hundred teachers, as indeed Plutarch[136] says in the book, *About the Demon of Socrates*. Empedocles, who is said to have been carried off alive and breathing by demons on the summit of Mt. Aetna, used P. 29
to say that a good and bad demon was granted to each person.[137]

SALOMON: Rabbi Moses of Egypt, who was instructed not by Empedocles but by his elders, also declares that each person has a good and bad angel.

SENAMUS: If as great a power of demons and angels as you imagined existed, it seems strange to me why the Epicureans removed the substance of demons from nature.

CURTIUS: We ought to remove the Epicureans from the register not only of philosophers but also of human beings, first because they differ very little from the opinions of beasts, next because they rely only on the senses.

CORONAEUS: Since philosophers and theologians, or rather all mortals agree there are demons, as is clear from their manifest actions, let us discuss, if you please, whether demons differ in essence and sensible quality or only in the difference of good and evil, and likewise in what actions and affairs they are involved. When we see and understand this, it will be clear what we ought to think about prodigies, portents, witchcraft, and finally about the amazing actions of magicians and lycanthropy. And since Fridericus seems diligently to have made a thorough study of the nature and power of demons, I do not doubt that he will easily settle all these matters for us.

FRIDERICUS: If so many philosophers of such great learning throughout

[134] *Theages* 122C.

[135] LCL, *Frag.* 549K. 7–8.

[136] *De daemone Socratis* 588C.

[137] Many marvelous happenings were attributed to Empedocles. See Diogenes Laërtius VIII. 67, 69, 70, 71. Also cf. *Porphyrii de philosophia ex oraculis haurienda*, edited by Gustavus Wolff (Hildesheim, 1962) (hereafter referred to as Wolff, *Porphyry*), p. 217. "Demons whom Empedocles granted to each man, are not so much divine-wills as forces of the mind by which each one is led to honor and blame."

the ages could not or did not wish to make statements about the nature of demons, what can you expect from a man who is not a bit of a philosopher? Indeed I have carefully read as many books about witches and fortunetellers as I could get my hands on to understand to some extent the actions of witches. These matters will be boring to describe, since from those same springs from which I have drunk, each one can also drink to the same effect. I would be foolish, indeed, should I wish to affirm anything about the nature, origin, and essence of demons.

Toralba: There are two methods of proof, one from causes, the other from effects. Therefore, if the causes are obscure, one can search these out from the effects, so that if we cannot understand the nature of demons, surely we can know from their actions that they exist.

Fridericus: I do not refuse to tell you the bare factual account in order to humor you, provided you do not require any more of me. Although Apuleius, who was accused of witchcraft and poisoning, confessed that he had experienced *onanthrōpia*[137a] in his own person and could more cleverly explain the essence of demons than the others, I doubt whether he wished to do what he was able to do. At any rate he defined demons thus: "They are animal in kind, rational in nature, passive in soul, aerial in body, eternal in time."[138] I marvel that Augustine[139] followed this description
P. 30 in all passages, especially in this where he writes that their nature is eternal, although Porphyry, Plutarch, and Plotinus say they are mortal[140] and confirm[141] this by the oracle of Apollo, that is, the witness of the greatest demon himself: "Alas, O tripods, weep for me. Apollo is dead, vanished. A heavenly flame exerts violence upon me!" Even Plutarch,[142] following Cicero's opinion[143] in this, writes that oracles have failed because the demons who once reported the oracles have died. But if demons, who are companions and friends to the human race, lie so much about themselves, what can we expect from the more sublime and divine nature of heavenly angels? To be sure, Philo Judaeus[144] describes angels as some

137a See above note 23a.

138 *De deo Socratis* XV; also see Augustine, *De civ. Dei* IX. 8, for the exact quotation.

139 *De civ. Dei* VIII. 14.

140 Cf. Wolff, *Porphyry*, pp. 30, 144–50, 152, 157, 177, 185, 214 ff. For Plutarch, cf. *De defectu oraculorum, de Pythiae oraculis, de Iside et Osiride*. For Plotinus, see Augustine, *De civ. Dei* IX. 10, where he says that the bodies of demons are eternal.

141 *confirmant* MR

142 *De defectu oraculorum* 419B–420, 434C–F.

143 *De divinat.* I. 51. 116.

144 *De opificio mundi* XXVIII. 84.

more divine and separate natures, subject to the power of all-powerful God, whom He uses as lieutenants; still, in the book *De mundo*[145] he writes that angels and demons are the same in essence, although the good differ from the evil in quality.

SENAMUS: I cannot pretend that I would not be delighted to hear when demons were first born, by what nurses they were raised, and how long is the life of each.

FRIDERICUS: Toralba has neatly proved that demons are not eternal, since eternity is suitable to God alone, the Father of all things, but I believe that no one knows how long their life is. Plutarch, Proclus, and Porphyry[146] limit it to a thousand years on the basis of Herodotus'[147] dictum that the nymphs live ten centuries in Phoenicia. Jerome Cardan writes about his own father Facius that he had a demon, as an assistant, for more than thirty years and had learned from him that a demon's life is limited to three hundred or four hundred years at most. This is as if one said that man's life is limited to a hundred years or at most 969 because Methusalah, who is said to have lived longest, did not live longer.

SENAMUS: Apuleius,[148] Porphyry,[149] and Cardan give evidence of a variety of opinions, since one limits the life of demons to three hundred years, another to a thousand, and another thinks they are eternal.

CURTIUS: At least it is clear from Toralba's explanation that they are not immortal. This is confirmed by the statement of Eusebius, bishop of Caesarea, which he lifted from Plutarch[150] into his book, *Praeparatio Evangelica*.[151] In it we read that when a ship put into the Echinades islands during Tiberius' reign, a voice was heard crying: "Thamus! Thamus!"[152] When the shipmaster Thamus answered the voice, the voice was heard again speaking these words: "When you come to the Paludes, announce in a loud voice—Pan[153] is dead!" The sailor, terrified of shipwreck if he did not obey the god's commands, cried out in a loud voice when he had come to the Paludes—"Pan is dead." When he had said this, suddenly the voices of men wailing and sighing were heard—though P. 31
there were no men there.

145 The title of Philo's work is *De opificio mundi*.
146 See Wolff, *Porphyry*, pp. 216–29.
147 Hesiod, *Theog*. 130, attributes unusual longevity to nymphs.
148 Apuleius says demons are eternal in time. *De deo Socratis* XIII. 148.
149 Wolff, *Porphyry*, pp. 216–29.
150 *De defectu oraculorum* 419B–420, 434C–F.
151 *Praep. evang*. V. 3. 182C.
152 *clamantis Thamus! Thamus!* MR
153 *Pana* MR

SALOMON: It is not strange if they said "Pan is dead," because the Scripture attested that Leviathan, the chief demon, would die.[154]

SENAMUS: I had heard before that demons fly over lands and seas and transport even people in an instant as if on the fastest horses. If these things are true, why did the demons of the Echinades islands learn of the death of their leader from men, since *daemones* is derived not *para tou deimainein* (from fear) as Eusebius thinks,[155] but from *daēmenai*,[156] as it were, with the same meaning as the Hebrew *Yidde'onim* (diviners) from the verb *Yada'* meaning to know.

FRIDERICUS: I think demons know the things which they can induce, but it is truer that spheres have been circumscribed for them by immortal God, and they cannot go beyond them. Proof of this is what Caesarius writes: namely, that the daughter of a certain priest of Cologne who was possessed of a demon was carried on her father's order across the Rhine. The demon left her at once, but her father was beaten and struck down by so many fierce blows that he died shortly afterwards. It is clear from this that the power of that demon was bounded by the river. Hermias describes a similar story. When a certain parricide had killed his mother and was being severely tormented by demons, he consulted Apollo, who answered that he should seek another region; and so he crossed over to an island that had emerged in a river, and his torments ceased.

SALOMON: Fridericus' statement seems to be supported at least by what we have read in the Scripture that an angel of God had bound in upper Egypt the demon Asmodeus, who had already killed the seven husbands of Sara. For in this story the highest goodness of God is apparent because He ordered not only serpents and wild beasts to be carried into the desert, but also harmful demons, lest they harm the society of men, nor were they to be loosed except for the most just punishment of the wicked. Moreover, according to divine law on the solemn day of atonement the priest is instructed to choose by lot two goats, one to be sacrificed to eternal God, the other to be given to Azazel[157] which the seventy-two interpreters call the scapegoat. It was the custom to lead the goat to the top of a mountain and hurl it off headlong.[158] It was said that the red thong[159]

[154] Job 40:15–25. Isaiah 27:1.

[155] *Praep. evang.* IV. 5, Par. 142B.

[156] The Greek verb daō, daēmenai means to learn.

[157] *Azazeli* MR

[158] See Justin Martyr, Fr. 11. [J. P. Migne, *Patrologia Graeca* (Paris, 1857), VI. 1596B.]

[159] *corium M lorum* corr. N

with which the goat had been bound became white if God was appeased.[160] A goat's horn relayed the good news with a joyful noise, and the neighboring regions indicated their public joy with a similar noise. Moreover, nowhere in the lands was a goat called Azazel found. They say that this is the reference of the passage in Isaiah: "If your sins have been redder than scarlet, they will become whiter than snow."[161] This is P. 32
indeed in agreement with what Rabbi Moses relates from the ritual accounts of the Chaldaeans and Sabeans; the ancient idolators sought demons in the desert and were accustomed to sacrifice to them by incantations performed over ditches and by the effusion of blood; then they customarily feasted and caroused. This is prohibited by the holiest divine law, and for that reason the blood of sacrifices is ordered to be poured out at the northern part of the altar.[162] I do not mean to say that there are not demons everywhere unremittingly testing all the words, actions, and deeds of all men. But the great majority of them roam around tombs and gibbets, or in caves, on mountains, through forests, or around the shores. The Greeks call them Satyrs, Sylvani, Tritons, Manes, Nymphs, Dryads, Hamadryads and Oreads.

OCTAVIUS: It is not true then, is it, that those sepulchral demons who watch over the corpses of Egyptians are freed from their bonds and transgress their appointed limits, crossing over seas and raising tempests to get the stolen corpses returned to them?

SENAMUS: If it is true that the demon of Cologne, who killed the father after leaving the daughter, could not leap across the Rhine nor swim across this very rapid river, we would have a present remedy against demons which besiege so many women that in one day at Rome we saw more than eighty women who had been very severely tormented, incapable of being freed by any incantations of the exorcists.

FRIDERICUS: The power and nature of demons was never more apparent than in the possessed ones whom the Greeks called possessed and divine and frenzied and ventriloquists and ones who prophesy from the belly and familiar spirits and Eurycles (ventriloquists), and we have read there

[160] Levit. 16:8–26.

[161] Isaiah 1:18.

[162] Cf. Origen, *Contra Celsum* IV. 36 (Migne, *Patrologia Graeca* XI. 1084C). Celsus was censured for calling depraved pagan nations inspired by God and for withholding this epithet from the Jews. Also see Theodoretus Cyrrhensii, *Quaest. in Leviticum* I. 207 and *Commentarius in Isaiah* XIX. 3 [A. Möhle, *Mitteilungen des Septuaginta-Unternehmens* (Berlin, 1932)]. Eurycles (Wolff, *Porphyry*, p. 47), who lived at the time of the Peloponnesian War, was said to have predicted the future with the help of a demon enclosed in his stomach.

were once many of them everywhere. We ourselves saw in the Kentorpian monastery in northern Germany pious virgins who were being tossed up and down by demons and sometimes were carried high off the ground and returned very gently with no feeling of pain; then they cackled with constant laughter, beat each other like bacchants, and defiled the surrounding air with their most loathsome breath. For it is characteristic of demons that they imbue the neighboring areas with the vilest smell, like the odor of sulphur and decayed bodies. On the other hand angels give off an ambrosial odor from their heads. We also discovered that if anyone uttered sacred prayers in the presence of those demoniac vestals or occupied himself with divine praises, the possessed would be wracked with the sharpest pains; whereas if they themselves said the hourly prayers in Latin or paid attention to those telling a story, the possessed would be relieved of their torment. When the magistrates asked who had delivered them to the demons, they accused Elsa Kama, a servant of the convent, a charge she did not blush to confess, and, condemned as a witch, she was burned at the stake.

P. 33 SENAMUS: I remember that a Benedictine exorcist at Rome asked women possessed by demons who they thought had caused their possession, and the demons answered that they had accomplished it with the help of the Jews because the Jews were angry with the women who had turned from Judaism to Christianity.

SALOMON: The fact that they had turned away from the religion of their forefathers to a foreign religion perhaps gave an opportunity for possession to the demons, but no one can believe that this was accomplished with the help of the Jews. The demons rather wanted the Jews to be beset by false accusations and charges. They have always been most hostile to the Jews.

FRIDERICUS: There is a rather famous account of a knight and senator, Antonius Segnetus[163] of Belgium, whose son had a witch as a concubine. When the young man at his father's command had married a noble woman, the witch, wildly jealous like Medea over Jason's marriage to the daughter of Creon, king of Corinth, disturbed her rival so much with the help of a demon that very often she was lifted on high and then, after being tossed hither and thither, thrown down. When the wife was in labor, the witch approached the bed of the woman as she was giving birth and put her in such a sound sleep and stupor that she snatched away the foetus without the mother's knowledge.

[163] *Antonii Segneti* N *Antonii Hugeti* M *Antonii Sugueti* R

SALOMON: What if the father had vowed his son to demons from the womb? For this is the wont of witches, and it is for this reason that divine law condemns with the most severe curses those who dedicated their children to the god Moloch.

FRIDERICUS: No less worthy of record is the fact that in a convent on a mountain of Hesse holy virgins had been so possessed with demons that they were seen to copulate with black dogs and then to be tossed up and down and breathe out the foulest smells.

SALOMON: Perhaps God granted it as a vengeance on the demons that they should copulate with dogs as sometimes happens. For nothing is more detestable than to prostitute a virgin, dedicated to God, to the filthiest beast. And that is why the divine law in the same chapter forbade the price of a dog and the wage of a prostitute to be offered to God; in the following chapter[164] the law demands death for those who copulate with animals.[165]

CURTIUS: That monstrous crime is called by nuns a silent crime, and this is not new if we believe Aelian who says that a Roman citizen charged a dog with being the corrupter of his wife. And in Celtic Aremorica a cow gave birth to a girl, who was cow-like in no way except for one foot, which gave rise to grave controversies.

FRIDERICUS: It is not so strange that a man copulate with an animal as with a demon. But not so long ago in the monastery of Gertrude at Cologne a girl had a demon as a lover, and in her lettercase love-letters between the girl and the demon were found. Soon all the nuns were possessed with demons. P. 34

TORALBA: It is easier to wonder at these stories than to ascertain the reasons for them. For I remember, when I was in Spain, that Magdalena de la Cruz, head of the convent of Cordova, had secured a pardon from Pope Paul III because she had lived more than thirty years with a black demon, Ephialtes; yet she had displayed such integrity in her life and religion that during Mass she was carried on high from the earth, as if by an angel. Porphyry also relates this happened to Jamblichus while celebrating sacrifices.[166] Even the host[167] in its glory, when a side of the altar burst, was seen[168] to fly into the nun's mouth. The fathers and priests used to seek answers[169] from her as if from an oracle. The story is well known every-

[164] *sequenti capite* MR
[165] Deut. 23:18, 27:21; Levit. 18:23, 20:15.
[166] See Wolff, *Porphyry*, p. 208.
[167] *quin etiam hostia* MR
[168] *videbatur* MR
[169] *responsa* MR

where, and similar is what Franciscus Picus writes; namely, that he saw Benedict Berna, a priest, consumed with flames because he had had Hyphialtes as concubine for more than forty years, as she had lived with Ephialtes.

Senamus: Does[170] Italy produce demons of each sex—*incubi* and *succubi*? I fear that these things will seem insane to physicians.

Fridericus: But Fernelius, a very famous physician of Henry II, King[171] of France, writes of a youth of noble birth, who was possessed by a demon and though the boy had never learned his letters, he nevertheless could speak in Greek. Philip Melanchthon says that a certain little woman, when she was tormented by a demon, was accustomed to speak in Greek and had announced a holy war, with which almost all of Germany raged, in this song: "There will be suffering upon the earth and violence in this nation." While physicians and theologians were expressing various opinions about this matter, a certain quack doctor, in order not to seem ignorant, said that a foreign language could be aroused by melancholy, but he was openly mocked with laughter and hissing.

Octavius: That could easily be refuted since ventriloquists with mouth closed or even with tongue stuck out spoke clearly even from the belly.[172]

Coronaeus: But it is strange that those possessed by demons shrink from the sprinkling of holy water, as Cyprian writes and experience proves.[173] But Philip Melanchthon boasted that he had deceived a demon because, when he had sprinkled the demoniac with pure water, he fled this water just the same as the holy water.

Salomon: I think demons despise holy water for two reasons. First, it removes the stains by its purity, whereas demons delight in impurity.
P. 35 It is for this reason that divine law orders[174] frequent washings, which magicians curse. Second, holy water is sprinkled with salt by which all things are preserved from decay, whereas the function of demons is to destroy and corrupt.[175] And so divine law orders salt to be sprinkled on all sacrifices.[176] Since Plato knew the power of salt, he writes that salt is pleasing to the gods.[177]

[170] *etiamne* MR [171] *regis* MR

[172] Wolff, *Porphyry*, p. 47.

[173] Cf. Epiphanius, *Panarion seu adversus LXXX haereses* XXX. 10; XXX. 12; *Constitutiones apostolorum* VIII. 29. 3.

[174] Psalm 25 (26):6; Psalm 50 (51):4; Ezech. 16:9; especially Lev. 18:16.

[175] Cf. *Nomocanon* 127. [176] Levit. 2:13.

[177] *Timaeus* 60E.

CORONAEUS: By discoursing as we have been doing, one perceives what the power and nature of demons are. For Paulus Grilandus, a lawyer and judge of questions of impiety, writes a certain neophyte was carried by his wife with the help of a demon to a banquet of soothsayers near a Beneventan tree, far removed from his home, and when the food for the feast was spread, he constantly asked for salt. Finally something similar to salt was brought, and he said: "Thanks be to God. This salt has finally come!"[178] At these words the whole gathering of demons[179] and witches, along with the illusory food, vanished. After the neophyte was left alone, he returned naked to his home which was fifty miles away.[180]

FRIDERICUS: All farmers are in the habit of putting salt on babies' faces as an amulet against the witchcraft of soothsayers.

OCTAVIUS: Do you suppose it is because the ancients all agree the sea cleanses all impurities? For Hippocrates[181] writes that exorcists in his life-time were accustomed to rid of spells by dipping in the sea all the things from which spells were said to threaten.

CURTIUS: I suspect those exorcists, whom Ulpian calls imposters, are guilty of impiety because they have conversations with demons and abuse sacred rites by mingling the ridiculous with the serious. Very often in their rash wantonness they are seized by demons or cruelly tormented. For example, when those seven exorcists in the Acts were accosting the demon in one possessed with these words—"I adjure you by Jesus, whom Paul proclaims"—the demon answered: "I know Jesus and Paul, but who are you?"[182] And the demon, rushing at them, drove them all mad.

OCTAVIUS: I remember reading in Pope Gregory that a certain priest had been seized by a demon when he had laid a sacred shawl on a possessed girl; also Origen in commenting on Matthew strongly forbids demons in possessed people to be questioned.[183]

TORALBA: Hippocrates was the first to tear to pieces in his writings exorcists as the wickedest men, who formerly were considered very holy

[178] *evenuto* M [179] *daemonum* MR [180] *distabat* MR

[181] Again this statement seems unlike Hippocrates because he says that "the cause is no longer divine, but human. . . . But this disease seems to me to be nowise more divine than others; but it has its nature such as other diseases have, and a cause whence it originates, and its nature and cause are divine only just as much as all others are. . . ." Hippocrates, *Genuine Works*, pp. 845, 847.

[182] Acts 19:13–15.

[183] Celsus defends the invocation of demons, urging that the Christian who enjoys the bounties of nature ought to give thanks to the powers of nature. See Origen, *Contra Celsum*, VII. 62 and VIII.

and divine.[184] When he saw that they used the emptiest formulas for expiations, he said: "God alone is our salvation and freedom." Although he was so great as to have no equal in his time, not yet had any age understood how great is the difference between sacred illness or epilepsy
P. 36 and demonic frenzy. Later physicians took more precise notes on symptoms, many similar, many dissimilar. For example, epileptics foam at the mouth, but demoniacs do not. Demoniacs have loathsome breath, epileptics do not; the demoniacs prophesy by mixing truth with lies; epileptics are silent; demoniacs are seized and freed at the demon's will, but not so epileptics. If any magician whispers these words in a demoniac's ear—"Leave, demon, because the Ephimolei order!" suddenly the demoniacs fall as if in a dead sleep. Then after a short time they rise up and tell all the things which had happened afar as if they had been present. Finally, epileptics never use foreign tongues, as demoniacs do.

FRIDERICUS: One thing that worries physicians is that they cannot heal in any way the sicknesses caused by witchcraft, nor can the magicians heal customary illnesses without harm, as formerly Philo the Hebrew,[185] and in our time, judges of impiety very often understood. Whether the sickness is a result of evil or of natural weakness, soothsayers seek to ascertain by pouring hot lead in a small vessel placed over the patient. Indeed, Galen,[186] in writing of Homeric medication, says that unskilled men are cured of illnesses with the power of words, and the healing is effective in proportion to their faith. For we have seen that magicians cannot heal unless the sick man admits that he has faith that the magician can heal him;[187] and so they first proclaim—"Believe and you will be healed!"

[184] Toralba's statement is in accord with Hippocrates' naturalism. See above, note 181.

[185] See article, "Magic," in James Hastings, *A Dictionary of the Bible* (New York, 1900), III, 206–12.

[186] A profound issue, for which I can find no specific text! Does Galen ever defend a form of mental or faith healing? If so, it is most untypical and even inconsistent with his main argument. For he follows Hippocrates in using the physiological, for example conditions of climate, to explain the mental, that is, temperament. Moreover, he is what we moderns would call a "determinist." See Arthur J. Brock, *Greek Medicine, Being Extracts Illustrative of Medical Writings from Hippocrates to Galen* (London, 1929), pp. 231–44. The same author, in the introduction to Galen's *On the Natural Faculties* (London: LCL, 1916) pp. xxviii–x, attributes to Galen an organic viewpoint compared to Bergson's with the doctrine of "the interdependence of [the organism's] parts." This would of course permit influence of thought upon bodily health.

[187] *quam si aeger fidem habere profiteatur sortilegium curare posse* MR Missing in N

SENAMUS: I fear that we may take the false for true, like those whose eyes were bewitched by that deceiver[188] the man who seemed to have devoured a wagon full of hay along with the horses and driver.

FRIDERICUS: I do not doubt that a spell can be put on the eyes, but the ears cannot be bewitched[189] so that Greek is thought to be Latin. Also it is clear that the storms and winds that were aroused because of the theft of the Egyptian mummies were not feigned, but very real, and the destruction of the men and ships was certain.

CORONAEUS: Although we were to grant that the wagon could not have been devoured, still it is contrary to nature to blind the eyes with witchcraft or to infuse madness into husbands so they are not able to copulate with their wives or beget children.

SENAMUS: I think that all substance is divided into body and spirit and that demons are angels of this kind—minds snatched from bodies. But if this is true, how does it happen that incorporeal demons are able to strike[190] or be struck or to be bound or restrained in definite places and abodes? For nothing except the corporeal can be restrained in a place, and it can suffer only from a body. But if we grant that demons, angels, and minds are corporeal, we must also admit they are passible and dissoluble according to that explanation of Toralba which taught that the world P. 37
would perish for the very reason that it is corporeal.

TORALBA: I am sure that both have been already proved, that nothing can be everlasting which is not eternal, nor can anything be considered eternal except the first cause of all things; wherefore not even angels will be eternal from their own nature but are sustained solely by the goodness of God.

CORONAEUS: Therefore, because learned men have many various opinions, we must consider whether demons are corporeal or incorporeal.[191]

TORALBA: We must foresee, I think, the consequences of each proposition and what is harmonious with each. It is most important to know whether demons are corporeal, as many affirm, but angels incorporeal, as theologians say with one accord, or whether both angels and demons put on and take off a bodily nature according to the circumstances, although they are incorporeal, as Homer, who calls demons "of all kinds," seems to imply.[192] For if we were to grant that they are corporeal, we shall have

[188] *praestigiator* MR

[189] *fascinari nequeunt* MR

[190] *caedere* MR

[191] *an incorporei* MR

[192] See *Eustathii commentarii ad Homeri Iliadem* (Hildesheim, 1960), I–II. 200. 9; 651. 11.

much more to admit that human minds, snatched from these bodies, exist in a corporeal nature. But if we think that angels and all heavenly beings are without body, as does Aristotle,[193] who calls angels separated forms and intelligences, movers of the celestial orbs, this discussion will belong not to natural science but to metaphysics.

CURTIUS: I do not see that Aristotle consistently defines anything about separated minds, but Apuleius, Porphyry, Jamblichus, Psellus, Plotinus, Philoponus, Ammonius, Alexander, and Augustine are in complete agreement about the corporeal nature of demons.[194] Hesiod[195] seems to concur in this verse—"Clothed with air they wander over all the earth." Orpheus, the priest of magicians, makes demons partly celestial, partly terrestrial, partly aerial, partly aqueous, partly subterranean, partly nomadic. From this it follows that minds, both celestial, and elementary, are corporeal, since place can belong only to bodies. Plotinus[196] says a demon qua demon must be with some body. Although Augustine[197] has written that angels are without bodies, very often he affirms they consist of a body. "It is certain," he says, "that every spirit is body and of spiritual matter." Likewise Damascenus[198] says: "All things which have been created, if compared with God, have something crass and material; and God alone is incorporeal and without matter." Basil,[199] who calls angels rational beings, writes that mind is free from place, that is, it is altogether incorporeal; but the other theologians say that not only angels, but also demons and the minds of men are incorporeal.

P. 38 OCTAVIUS: The authority of important men has the greatest influence in making faith more enduring than any opinion. However, as a few adopt this or that opinion because it pleases them to, most people wish to be convinced by necessary proofs to agree, as after a questioning, in

[193] *Metaphys.* XII. 6. 4.

[194] Apuleius does not belong in this group because he said demons have immortality in common with the gods and suffering in common with man. He also says demons are living in kind, rational in mind, passive in soul, airy in body, and eternal in time. See *De deo Socratis* XII.

[195] *Opera et dies,* 121–25.

[196] See *Ennead* III. 3–5.

[197] *De civ. Dei* XIII. 22. Also cf. XIII. 9. 16. 18.

[198] See Books I and II, *The Orthodox Faith.*

[199] *De paradiso* according to the marginal note in M. On the Platonic concept of the soul as immaterial and independent of space, see article, "Soul (Christian), Patristic and Medieval." James Hastings, *Encyclopedia of Religion and Ethics* (Edinburgh, 1909), XI, 735–37.

order that by attaining knowledge they may throw off all opinion. Knowledge and opinion can no more exist at the same time than faith and knowledge.

TORALBA: If it is proved that no essence except God is incorporeal, it will also be clear that the essence of God alone is infinite, which Johannes Scotus[200] said could not be demonstrated. Even this clever theologian admits that he has no proof of the infinite essence of God. Nevertheless, we will accomplish[201] that by this proof of the incorporeal nature of God. In addition to this, the very dangerous opinion of the Thomists and Averroists about one mind for all men, which Albumazar Maurus too zealously clings to, will be completely overthrown. For they have declared that all the minds of the wicked as well as the good come together in one and the same soul, and no statement can be more ridiculous and wicked than this. Finally from this proof, namely, that all substance except God is corporeal, there are evident punishments for the wicked which the Epicureans, however, deny only for the reason that they admit no action upon bodies except by bodies themselves; and they think that incorporeal natures are not capable of suffering from bodies.

CORONAEUS: Well then, Toralba, unless it is too much trouble, please give us this proof which includes so many advantages.

TORALBA: Then let us establish this first, if you please: every substance which is encompassed in the circuit of the greatest orb is finite. Human minds, angels, demons are contained in the heavenly orb; therefore, they are finite because nothing infinite can be enclosed in a finite orb.

CORONAEUS: Indeed that is clear in its own light.

TORALBA: Whatever is finite has boundaries by which it is limited, a place in which it is enclosed, and nothing incorporeal is enclosed by boundaries or is contained in places; therefore angels are not incorporeal since they are limited to their own bodies and boundaries. If they are not incorporeal, it follows that they have a corporeal nature, since all substance is either corporeal or incorporeal; it must be one of the two. Next, all substance, except God, has finite power; all finite power has limited distance;[202] from this it follows that demons, angels, and minds which leave the body at death are enclosed in bounded abodes and do not exist everywhere or in many places at the same moment, as of course is admitted by the very people who think that angels and minds are in-

[200] *Liber sent.* IV. 4. [201] *consequemur* M [202] *distantiam* MR

P. 39 corporeal. For if the same finite substance should exist in two places at the same time, they could also be moved and be at rest at the same time, contrary to the clear proof of the philosophers.[203]

Senamus: Granted these things to be true, still I do not yet see by what boundaries or limits demons are enclosed.

Toralba: The limits or boundaries of a substance cannot be thought of apart from surface. Surface, however, is a property of body alone. Therefore, every finite and bounded substance must be corporeal; otherwise it would be infinite because there is no third possibility. But it is absurd to think that human minds, demons, and angels, who are enclosed in limits and boundaries of the world are infinite; otherwise infinite things would be enclosed by finite.

Senamus: What keeps angels, demons, and human minds from being enclosed in some fixed and definite abode but not bounded by surface?

Toralba: To be sure this is the opinion of those who admit that angels, demons, and separate minds are in place, but still not limitedly, to use their words, but definitively. Since this distinction seems empty to many, they preferred to say neither definitively nor limitedly in place but only effectively. Though this statement has less error than the other, because it does not involve affirming and denying at the same time; still it has the problem of denying that angels and demons are moved in place. With this reasoning the good could not go to heaven nor the wicked to hell, since to be everywhere is fitting only for incorporeal substances.

Senamus: I am afraid that the argument advanced by you is very like this one of Aristotle:[204] "If form is not limited to matter, while outside matter it is infinite." This is no more logical than if one would say: "If body is not limited by body, it is infinite." For by that reasoning the highest sphere which is limited by no body would be infinite.

Toralba: I shall explain this more clearly. Every substance which is enclosed in the bosom of the highest tomb we established as finite, a point we all admit; moreover, there are no boundaries of finite substance except the surface which is characteristic of body alone, which is clear from geometric principles. Likewise all minds have a prescribed and limited place—that is, it is not limited to the greatest nor the smallest place ever, but to a place equal to its own essence. From these statements then it is shown that separated minds and angels are connected by a certain corporeal nature. Therefore if we grant that that body is spiritual, as Paul[205]

[203] Scotus, *Liber sent.* I. 2. quaest. 4. [204] *Metaphys.* VII. 10. 16–XI.
[205] I Corinth. 6:20; 7:34; Eph. 4:4; Rom. 8:11; 12:1; I Corinth. 6:15; 15:40.

and Damascenus say, still it will be body, however tenuous we say it is, and it will no more be able to be with another body of the same nature than the thinnest air will be with aqueous and terrestrial matter.[206] P. 40

SENAMUS: Is it so out of harmony with nature for anything incorporeal to be in a place, when incorporeal points and accidents themselves are enclosed each in its own abode and place?

TORALBA: Senamus, you are thinking of points and accidents which in themselves and without bodies have no substance, which can never exist of themselves nor be in any place nor even be moved except for the movement of bodies. Our discussion, however, is about the substance, that is, about an angel, about a mind that survives the body which they admit is finite; still they say it is incorporeal, something that cannot be conceived by any human ability unless we grant that affirming and denying are true. That substance which they represent as incorporeal, they establish in only one place, and this a definite place, outside of which nothing of itself can be found nor do they mean it to be everywhere but[207] have its own location, or to use their words, its own "whereness." So that if we should ask where an angel is, the reply could be given—in the sky or on the earth, but not in both places, but only there where its action or suffering is, and nowhere else. Nevertheless they deny they are circumscribed by place or change place, when they are hurled down headlong from high to low places or fly back from low to high places. From this evolves the paradox—an angel is in heaven, an angel is not in the heaven—obviously contrary to nature. But what does "to define place" mean except to define limits of place around a body? Now if to be limited by place or to be circumscribed are the same, then to be in place circumscriptively and definitively will also be the same, as Damascenus admits in two places. And so Thomas, rejecting the definitions of his predecessors, wrote that an angel was in place not by action[208] but by inclination; in refutation Scotus concluded that the presence of an angel was necessary before action[209] and indeed commensurately in place. He speaks thus, since an angel is not everywhere, neither in the greatest place nor smallest place ever, but in a place equal to its own substance and cannot occupy a greater or smaller place than this. From this it follows also that descent and ascent must of necessity be attributed to separated minds. But whatever is moved from place into place must be corporeal because it first passes through space less than itself, then through space equal to itself

[206] *materia* MR [207] *sed* MR [208] *actione* MR
[209] *actionem* MR

before it traverses spaces greater than itself. But incorporeal substance cannot pass through space less than itself[210] because nothing incorporeal can be assigned largeness or smallness, and so we must admit that whatever is moved is corporeal. Likewise, all motion takes place in time, and we must assume a lesser time than any other in which the less movable may be moved. Therefore for every movable object something less mobile will be assumed to infinity. From this it follows that nothing incorporeal or indivisible[211] can be moved. Likewise the succession of motion, which is precluded in motion, may be a resistance of the movable to the moving object, or of the interval to the movable object or of the mover to the
P. 41 interval. But there would be no resistance for an angel if it were incorporeal, for it would not resist the interval nor would the interval resist the angel, nor would the angel resist himself as mover. But the human mind does not have the ability to understand how motion takes place between extremes without the transition of the intervening space. Wherefore if place, body, space are divisible, angels, human minds, demons must also be corporeal and divisible, contrary to their opinions and writings.

SENAMUS: Why then are the Peripatetics so scrupulous to divide metaphysics from physics, since they wish the entire subject of physics to be the natural body, but they assign to metaphysics substances free from all concreteness[212] of body, in which statement they say separated minds and intelligences are included.

TORALBA: Those who confuse metaphysics with physics make a serious error, that is, to confuse the natural with the divine, except to the extent that one is better understood from the other. Moreover, no subject is possible for the metaphysician except the first incorporeal cause. For although Aristotle[213] tried to overturn Plato's ideas everywhere because the ideas had no actualization in nature, nevertheless he posited intelligences or separated minds in nature with these words: "Is it pertinent to physics to talk about every soul? Or only about that which is called matter?"[214] This last question seemed so foolish to Alexander of Aphrodisias that he affirmed that there was no substance at all without body. And rightly, if he had excepted the first cause which must be incorporeal because it is infinite.

210 *non potest decurrere spatium se ipsa minus majusve* MR; *lacuna* N

211 *indivisibile* MR

212 *concretione* MR

213 *Metaphys.* I. 9. 9; VII. 11. 6–9; VII. 14; X. 10. 1–5; XIII. 4. 5–18.

214 *Phys.* II. 2. 194b; 1. 10; for a full discussion of the scope of physics, see *Phys.* II. 2, throughout.

OCTAVIUS: Cleverly spoken, Toralba. The thing that bothers me, however, is that, since an angel is a certain particle, a spark as it were, of that divine and eternal mind, how does it happen that a corporeal mind can spring from incorporeal nature?

TORALBA: You are assuming that which is in question, Octavius, namely, whether the human mind is a particle of the divine mind, an opinion,[215] I see, adopted by some who do not hesitate to cite the authority of Plotinus[216] because he said that the mind of man was of the same substance with God Himself. But the human mind is not even like God, much less the same substance as God. False also is that which Arrian[217] writes to Epictetus, whom he represents speaking to a man as follows: "You, a portion of God, have a part of Him in yourself." Trismegistus[218] addresses an opinion different from that to Asclepius. He says: "The mind has not been cut away from the substance of God, but has been unfolded, as the light of the sun." For if an angel or the human mind were plucked from the essence of God, that is, if it were a particle of God, God would be corporeal, which all admit is foolish. Likewise, the entire man would be God; for that must be entire from which no part can be taken. Like- P. 42
wise, the nature of God would be divisible and dissoluble if it had parts; accordingly the Scriptures call the mind of man, not the substance of God, but the breath, that is, *Ruah* (spirit) and an image, not a part of Him, since nothing of the sort can be conceived in the incorporeal divine nature.

SALOMON: Wise indeed are those who have separated body altogether from the nature of God, for this is the principal point of our creed.

SENAMUS: What then does it mean that God is everywhere? For if He is everywhere, He is in place; if in place, He must also be corporeal.

FRIDERICUS: God is everywhere and nowhere.

SENAMUS: Therefore contradictions are at the same time true; if God is here, God is not here.

CURTIUS: Augustine[219] says we believe God is everywhere in presence, in essence, in power, in every place without circumscription, in all time without change.

[215] *id* MR

[216] *Ennead* IV. 4. 28; IV. 7. 10.

[217] *Epicteti dissertationes ab Arriano digestae*, edited by Henry Schenkl (B. G. Teubner, 1965), II. 8. 11.

[218] Apuleius, *Asclepius sive dialogus Hermetis Trimegisti* VII. Also see II–VI. [L. Apuleius, *Opera Omnia*, edited by G. F. Hildebrand (Hildesheim, 1968)], II.

[219] *De civ. Dei* XII. 15–19; *De trinitate* V. 17.

OCTAVIUS: More modest,[220] in my opinion, is Chrysostom[221] who admits he cannot comprehend how God is everywhere.

SALOMON: That one speaks truly, for God, speaking about Himself, says: "I fill heaven and earth!"[222] Also, "Heaven is My abode, but the earth is the footstool of My feet."[223]

SENAMUS: These things seem to pertain to his infinite power, not to His essence, as Elias the Thesbite acknowledges in these words: "God is not in the wind, not in the earthquake, not in the fire."[224] Otherwise there would be one and the same essence for creator and created; if the two were mingled promiscuously, the worship of the creator and the created would also be considered the same. Because of this God is called the Highest, that is, *'Elyon*, because He is in the heavens. By the Hebrew interpreters God is called *maqom*, that is, the place of the blessed, because the world is in God, not God in the world—which is indeed most vast, but in comparison with that infinite essence, a thin little body; not because God is kept from access to the world but that we may know that He is not held by the capacity of innumerable worlds and that His purest and most incomprehensible essence is not mingled with foul, fleeting and perishable things. For the world is everywhere very full of bodies, and nothing is free from matter.[225] But who God is and of what nature God is (although there is no quality in Him) no mortal will know, however long he may live. For God said to Moses, when he asked God to show Himself to him: "No one living will see God,"[226]—that is, know clearly. And that is why He is said to abide in black obscurity and to have established His hiding places in the shadows. In other words the understanding of God seems most obscure and difficult for men grounded in pitch-black darkness, although He, Himself, the Author of light, fills all things with His own brightness. Although it is noble to proclaim
P. 43 all His works, words, deeds, laws in frequent song, still there is no truer or better way to praise Him than by the silence of contemplation. Therefore David[227] wisely observes this when he says: "Silence is Your praise." The common interpretation, "a song, O God in Zion, befits You," does not explain David's words. Rabbi Moses and also the Chaldean para-

[220] *modestius* M

[221] The apocryphal "Letter to Caesarius" contains a passage on the Eucharist which seems to favor the theory of impanation, which has been the occasion of many disputes.

[222] Jer. 23:24.

[223] Isaiah 46:1.

[224] III Kings (I Kings) 19:11.

[225] *materiam* M

[226] Ex. 33:20.

[227] Psalm 44 (45):2.

phrast learnedly interpret the Hebrew words, *Leka dumiyah tehillah* when they say: "In Your presence silence is considered to be praise, because God, who or what He is, cannot be described by any words nor even understood by any reasoning power."

CURTIUS: Pythagoras intimates this in one of his symbols when he urges that God ought to be praised by silence and cherished with the pure love of the mind because speech itself is base and cannot mount to the true praise of God. Porphyry and Jamblichus interpret this silence to mean when the pure mind of man raised up in an ecstasy of divine love, is offered to God.[228] The ancients meant this when they said in their sacrifices, "Be silent!" or as Homer[229] says: "Cut out your tongues," so that by the contemplation of sublime and divine affairs men's hearts may be carried on high above all heavens where the essence of God abides in separation from all thought of the world. This happens most of all when, in an attempt to know God, we contemplate His power, goodness, wisdom, and all His words, deeds, judgments, and actions; we are stunned into silence by the enormous infinity of wonderful and sublime things.

TORALBA: Yet I shall break the silence and sing unceasing praises to immortal God, even in heroic verses:

The great glory of your works captures
    me, all powerful God.
The mob of foreign gods flees and with
    them the picture of false piety.
Angelic choruses, make haste, make haste,
    O poets
As many as adore the sacred name
    in piety
And pour out God's praises from pure
    lips!
But here is where there is the power of words
    and greatest wisdom which orders by
    eternal laws the sea, the lands, the
    orbs of heavens,
All in a moment's time.

CORONAEUS: Therefore we believe God has placed His own abode above the heavens, outside the matter and pollutions of the world, as also the

[228] See Wolff, *Porphyry*, p. 110 n. 15.
[229] *Odys.* III. 332.

vision of Ezechiel[230] and seventy-two prophets whom God inspired with the spirit of Moses plainly declare.

SALOMON: This is indicated even more evidently by the condition of man whom God created in His own image, according to the interpretation of Rabbi Moses who states that just as the intellect (as agent or attained) is outside man and free of man's materiality, so also is God free from the matter and pollution of the world.

P. 44 CORONAEUS: We have Toralba's explanation that not only is the nature of angels and demons corporeal but also that no substance is incorporeal except God; but someone may ask whether the essence of demons and angels is the same as that of human minds.

CURTIUS: Augustine[231] teaches that the essence of angels is purer than that of demons, and their bodies are brighter. The bodies of bad angels have been changed in their fall into a meaner quality of denser air. He also says that the delicate bodies of angels have been changed into meaner and denser bodies for them to be able to suffer from fire.

TORALBA: Porphyry[232] in Homer's cave writes that angels and demons consist of and are clothed with an airy body so that they can suffer from fires, and confirming this Philoponus[233] says: "Otherwise intellectual nature could suffer nothing."

SENAMUS: If there are in air no sense organs, no instruments of sight, touch, taste, and not even any nerves from which we could have sensation, and no brain whence the nerves originate, how[234] could airy minds suffer from fires? Likewise if human minds are composed of an igneous nature, as Vergil[235] says—"Man has fiery vigor and a heavenly origin," fire can suffer nothing from fire. Much less if they are formed of an airy compound. Otherwise all the air, however much there is, would have long since perished, consumed by the flames. But if separated minds are composed of an aqueous nature, they could extinguish the flames rather than feel the force of fire.

OCTAVIUS: The opinion that souls are constituted of a nature of fire is a very old one. Therefore Synesius in a certain letter to the bishop of Cyrene writes that those who had feared death at sea made use of a dry sheath so that they might cast forth the soul and keep it from being sub-

230 Ezech. 1:1; 3:13; 10; 11:1.

231 *De civ. Dei* XI. 22.

232 See Wolff, *Porphyry*, p. 215.

233 *Ibid.*, pp. 108, 177.

234 After *quo nam modo* R has a lacuna of 121 speeches. It commences again with Senamus (*itaque providendum est de maritandis angelorum*), Noack, p. 69.

235 *Aen.* VI. 730.

merged, as Homer[236] indicates, and for this reason Philostratus[237] wrote that before Ajax, the son of Oïleus, who died at sea, it had never been customary to offer sacrifices for men lost at sea. This is the meaning of the utterance of the Sibyl to Palinurus:[238]

> Without burial will you see the Stygian waters and the harsh river of the Eumenides or approach the bank before your time?

Is Philo[239] any nearer to the truth when he calls demons a group of spirits deprived of body? Or why would the Hebrews say the soul, which surviving the body, has flown off widowed if it had been joined with another body after deserting the first body? For the mind could not properly be called widowed if, after leaving the corpse, it united with another body as if in a second marriage.

FRIDERICUS: If Senamus' argument, in which he concludes that souls, demons, angels are without sensations, were inevitable, not even God himself would hear or see. But what is more stupid than for Him, who P. 45
gave the remarkable faculty of sound and sight even to brute animals, to be considered blind and deaf because He does not have eyes, ears, and the other instruments of the senses? I think it is doubtful to no one that[240] the voices of angels and demons are heard by others who have attendant demons, though it is admitted that they lack these senses. Indeed demons' voices seem high and pleasing at one time, at another low and terrible as if they uttered them from the belly. For this reason a bad demon is called by the Hebrews *'ov*, from the belly.[241]

CORONAEUS:[242] I remember Hermolaus Barbarus, a patrician, who was exiled from Venice because on a mission to Rome he had accepted from the pope the rank of cardinal without the senate's approval. Since he did not understand the word for entelechy in the definition of the soul, he decided to ask his attendant demon which he had welcomed as judge in the matter, along with Georgius della Placentinus. The demon answered so obscurely in such a high voice that his meaning could not be understood.

236 Although I cannot ascertain the reference in Homer, I found a reference to a soul deprived of its sheath in Pliny, *Hist. nat.* VII. 52. 174.

237 Philostratus, *The Life of Apollonius of Tyana* IV. 13.

238 Vergil, *Aen.* VI. 374–75.

239 *De somniis* I. 22. 135.

240 *quin* M

241 Cf. Lev. 20:27; see also Wolff, *Porphyry*, p. 47.

242 *Coronaeus* M *Toralba* N

TORALBA: Therefore the lungs, larynx, tongue, palate are not necessary for speech, but we must admit that the power of the senses is of one kind in God, another in heaven, another in angels and demons, another in animals.

OCTAVIUS: If there were no sensation in separated minds, there would be no punishments for the wicked and rewards for the good.

SALOMON: Senamus, I want to know if you have not often seen in dreams, with the mind alone, while your eyes were closed and all the senses numbed, the images of things as if you had your eyes wide open? Now if you admit this, why do you hesitate to admit that the sight of the mind is sharper for seeing than that of the eyes. Marcus Tullius[243] wrote as elegantly as truthfully that minds themselves are most sensitive and active when they have left the bodies.

CORONAEUS: It would be useless to go over again the matters already clearly explained. For from those proofs of Toralba about the corporeal nature of demons and souls, we have plucked this fruit, as well, namely, that the pernicious opinion of the Thomists and Averroists is removed. They said that there is one soul for all, diffused into each individual man, and that separated at death, it enters again into itself. Thus those thirty arguments which the Averroists specify to strengthen this error all fall at one and the same time. But it could not have befallen these [i.e., arguments] so neatly at the hands of those who have taken the position that souls are without body, since incorporeal substances, if any were to exist, might easily be wrenched from their bodies and come together into one, whereas it is entirely impossible for bodies to penetrate one another. Therefore, it remains for us to learn how, from this proof, the essence and infinite power of God are deduced, a proof Toralba promised us earlier, unless I am mistaken.

P. 46 TORALBA: Indeed I said that, as that man in a light matter, but I did not promise. For who would be bold enough to believe that he could promise this to himself or to another? I yield to Coronaeus, however, to whom nothing can be denied, for I prefer to seem foolish rather than disobedient.

Every corporeal substance is finite, whereas incorporeal substance is enclosed by no limits; but substance which is enclosed by no limits is infinite. This corollary is derived from the preceding demonstrations. Now in the opinion of all theologians and philosophers the first cause is in-

[243] *Tusc. disp.* I. 66.

corporeal; therefore the first cause alone is an infinite essence, and if its essence is infinite, its power, goodness, and wisdom are infinite. Because if finite power should coincide with an infinite subject, infinite power could even coincide with a finite subject, and a finite creature would be possessed of infinite power. This consequence is absurd, so also therefore is the antecedent. Therefore nothing finite can be imagined in infinite God. To enlarge on this, God alone is simple, whereas all corporeal things are made up of parts, and God alone is impassible and indissoluble, contrary to what is the case with compound substances, which are composed of those things into which they are dissolved and are dissolved into those things from which they are composed. But, that which is simple cannot be divided into parts of which it has none or dissolved into other elements.

SENAMUS: If God is incorporeal, why is it that He is given ears, eyes, nose, fingers, feet, arms, and face?

SALOMON: Also very often anger and passion; now on this account shall we say that He is angry and passionate? But nurses and parents must stammer with babies and human attributes must be transferred to God, since divine things cannot be translated to men. It is worth noting that the senses of taste and touch are never attributed to God although other senses are, because they always inhere in the body, and the sensibles of touch and taste cannot be perceived without bodies, as other sensibles, so that more and more it appears that God is completely incorporeal. But, if an angel were incorporeal, as Aristotle and many theologians think, its substance would exist in every place and would have an infinite extension and essence; nay, even intelligences and demons would have to be one and the same with God, and also good with evil, eternal with perishable, changing with continual, holiest with foulest. Finally the Creator would be mixed indiscriminately with the created, which is not only absurd but wicked to utter. Also if an angel were eternal, it would now have total duration, which it is going to have, and, to speak more strongly, one formally infinite. Philosophers and theologians agree that being (*esse*) and being able (*posse*) are the same in divine essence; likewise, to have been, and to be about to be are considered one and the same in eternal beings because there is no before or after in God, as Rabbi Moses very accurately writes. Isaiah[244] indicates the same thing when he writes each angelic Seraph had six wings and with two covered its face, with two

[244] Isaiah 6:2.

its feet, and flew with the other two, so that we can know that angels had
P. 47 a beginning and will have an end. To man, however, the beginning and end are unknown, but God alone is without beginning and end and all succession of time. For where there is succession, there is renewal and change, so that an angel is not the same as before because it does not hold what has passed and waits for the future; it is therefore changeable and will have an end. For unless different things were in motion, not even in time could before and after be perceived. Toralba has clearly shown that angels have motion; we are often told by scripture not only that angels have motion but they even mention the speed and agility of the motion, giving four or six wings to angels. This indicates that their nature is changeable and dissoluble.

CORONAEUS: We have then a clear and positive proof about the power and essence of God. He is infinite in all ways, and alone is eternal, but angels, demons, minds are corporeal and finite, changeable and soluble in their own nature. These things seem to pave the way for a discussion of what is said about the actions of demons, elephant rope-dancers, trees and speaking animals, flights of magicians.

SENAMUS: We must be careful, I think, not to take as starting point the very thing which has been placed in question—these miracles which we watch are stirred up by demons. For even if we grant that demons are corporeal, it does not follow that the flights of magicians are true.

TORALBA: That which cannot come about by nature or men must be done by God or by an angel or by demons. But those flights of magicians through the air cannot be accomplished through nature or through action of men; therefore they must be accomplished by God or by angels and demons.

OCTAVIUS: We are taught that after the creation of the world God rested from all action and did nothing except by mediate causes;[245] yet it seemed to me very dangerous to decide anything about matters so difficult and removed from the feeling and understanding of men.

TORALBA: If we admit God is mobile, we must confess He is both passible and mutable. This is absurd; therefore, the other is. But to understand better the actions of angels and demons, we must prove not only that the first cause is immobile, but that it does not ever move, contrary to the opinion of Aristotle[246] who bound God with eternal motion.

CORONAEUS: Come, then Toralba! Explain, as you are doing, these

[245] Gen. 2:2–4.

[246] *Metaphys.* IV. 8. 8; XI. 1. 4; XII. 4. 8; XII. 6; XII. 7; XII. 8. 4.

things which have been for so long involved with the vague errors of petty philosophers.

TORALBA: The old error of Aristotle has deceived many, who, if they would view more closely the order of movable and moving things, would have departed from the opinion they had adopted. For certain things are only moved; for example, matter which suffers all movements, as though it were the dregs, but does not itself move [i.e., other things]. Some things move and are moved, as form and natural bodies; some things move but are not moved, as the prime mover, who indeed moves *primum mobile* but is not moved.[247] Given this order of mobile and moving things it is necessary that something be the final thing which does not move nor is moved. This is the first cause of all mobile and moving things, and it enjoys perpetual quiet. P. 48

OCTAVIUS: This order of mobile and moving things is very pretty, but I do not see that it is necessary.

TORALBA: There are other demonstrations which necessarily prove that the first cause of all things neither is moved nor moves any thing else.

CORONAEUS: Since in a matter of such seriousness we must try everything, therefore please tell us, unless it is tedious, how we can refute the Epicureans with arguments powerful enough to make them agree with us.

TORALBA: It is as foolish for infinite essence to be joined to a finite little body in a finite manner as to assign infinite power to a finite nature, since there is the same discipline for opposites. It is stupid and completely alien to reason to assign infinite power to a finite body; therefore it is also stupid to join the infinite essence of God to a little body, the finite world. That even seemed too incongruous to Averroës and so foreign to nature that he repudiated Aristotle's opinion and granted to the second cause the turning of the *primum mobile*. But forgetful of his own premise, he said that the universe was eternal. With this reckoning he binds the second cause, which he confesses is finite, to eternal, that is, infinite, motion. And he falls into the same error as he charged Aristotle had fallen.

CORONAEUS: Indeed this proof is as powerful for uprooting the opinion of Aristotle and Averroës about the eternal world as that former discussion was about the corporeal nature of demons and angels. To establish God as a restless mover is alien not only to the divine nature but also to Aristotle's writings which are themselves inconsistent. Aristotle[248] says: "We think gods are happy and blessed. But since they are hindered by

[247] See *Metaphys.* XII. 8. 4.
[248] *Eth. nicom.* X. 8. 7. Also cf. *Magna Moralia* I. 3 and 4. 1–6.

no actions, and do not sleep like Endymion, it remains that they enjoy eternal contemplation." If Aristotle thinks that God enjoys contemplation, which is the opposite of motion, or blessed quiet, why does he weary Him with ceaseless motion? For God is said to have rested after the creation
P. 49 of the world. What is more alien to the world than quiet? Since this is true, the consequence is that the heavens are moved through themselves and from form inherent in them or by angels.

Octavius: I see that we have gradually slipped from metaphysics to physics if it has been proven that angels, demons, and human minds flourish in a corporeal connection and that no essence at all except God is incorporeal.

Toralba: The whole argument and subject of metaphysics pertain to incorporeal essence. Because other things, being bodies, are natural, let us say they are appropriate to the natural sciences. But who would say that the actions of angels and demons, which are voluntary, pertain to nature? It is as though[249] one were to think that the free actions of men, having originated from the will, are natural, although man, as far as his body is natural, will be a subject for the natural scientists.

Curtius: Aristotle is ambiguous about the human mind and removed the discussion of this from his *Physics*.[250]

Toralba: There comes to mind the opinion of a certain Helvetian who gave himself the elegant name of Theophrastus Paracelsus.[251] He introduced new dreams by destroying from the roots the teachings of all physicians. After he repudiated the agreement of learned men, he substituted this opinion, that the actions of demons are natural.

Coronaeus: Therefore we must first decide what action deserves to be called natural.

Toralba: Action cannot be natural which happens either from God, with no help from lower causes, or from an angel or a demon or from the judgment of divine will or finally from chance. I call chance the union of many causes with unexpected effects; with these exceptions we shall say the rest are done by nature.

[249] *perinde est enim ac* M

[250] See *Phys.* III. 4. 203a–204a.

[251] Paracelsus (1493–1541) is also known as Theophrastus von Hohenheim and Bombastus von Hohenheim. Because of his opposition to the prevailing Galeno-Arabic system of medicine, he was hated by the authorities and was considered a charlatan. Trained in alchemy as well as surgery, Paracelsus, a phenomenon in the history of medicine, had as his aim the discovery of a specific remedy for every disease. He was one of those satirized by John Donne in his *Conclave of Ignatius* (1610).

Fridericus: No one surely, unless he is mad, thinks the ascent of a man into heaven or the flights of magicians through the air are natural, since nature opposes these actions by the force of gravity, unless some vacuum follows, as when rain water is snatched upward from the lakes. Then heavier objects are borne up and lighter ones down for the safety of the whole world.

Curtius: I think this world ought to be ruled just as a republic after the image of a republic of this world, or rather our state ought to be a pattern of that exemplar and archetype of a mundane state. For whoever has looked deep into the order of the universe will much better regulate the affairs of his state.[252] Furthermore, in a well-ordered state certain laws of *maiestas* and *imperium* are continual, but some are changed during various times and circumstances. Likewise, there are certain customary P. 50
legal magistrates for the administration of justice, for safeguarding the treasury, for repairing the state buildings, for food supply, for the care of public safety. Likewise ministers of the magistrates are sent out in all places to carry out the orders of the leaders and magistrates. Thus it is also appropriate that God, the provident parent of nature, has ordained certain laws to be perpetual and inviolable; for example, the fixed paths and returns of the orbs which have so great stability that they do not wander off their primordial course even for a moment. There is no doubt that He has placed together angels, leaders, as it were, in heaven, and lower ones than these in the elements. Some He directed to look after the sacred rites, who, as if priests, sacrifice purer and holier minds, as if victims, to immortal God and also offer prayers and vows. Some He put in charge of states and empires. The Greeks used to call them guides of the universe;[253] the Latins called them tutelary gods,[254] and they believed states could not be stormed or captured before those protectors and leaders of cities were called away with offerings and entreaties. Hence, this saying: "The gods who have upheld this imperium have departed."

Fridericus: Plato calls the directors of states "messengers and demons, according to their positions under the gods who rule all the things of the world, the parts having been divided."[255]

Salomon: Plato had received that secret as he did all the best things

[252] With Curtius' speech, cf. Philo, *De opificio mundi* XXVII and XXVIII. Also cf. Aristotle, *De mundo,* VI. 400b.

[253] *Kosmagous* M. Cf. Synesius Cyrenensis, *Hymn.* III. 271 (Migne, *Patrologia Graeca* LXV), 1597; and Dasmascius Philosophus, *De principiis* 112.

[254] See Macrobius III. 9.

[255] Plato, *Leges* X. 888D.

from the Hebrews, for we read in the sacred documents that God established limits and boundaries for people according to the number of angels. We must not doubt that some angels are in charge of the heavens, some in charge of the elements, some in charge of man; some are appointed to distribute rewards for the good and punishment for the wicked. This is the reference of the Psalm of David:[256] "The leaders of the peoples have been gathered together with the God of Abraham, since the guardians of the lands have directed their attention toward God." For this is what is meant by *Maginné 'eretz* (the shields of the earth); and these in the same verse he calls leaders of the people, *Nedivé 'ammim*. Although Plato writes that they had been appointed by the gods, still he calls the leader of all these and the ruler of the armies of demons and gods the thrice greatest god, whose chariot the others follow:[257] "The great leader in the heaven, Zeus, has winged chariot, and the army of gods and demons follows him." This has also been expressed by the Psalms of David[258] in this verse: "The chariot of God's rejoicing armies—thousands upon thousands." The Chaldean paraphrast translates it thus: "The chariots of God—twenty thousand of glowing fire—two thousand angels lead them. The divinity of God is above them so that we may know that God, enjoying peaceful quiet, uses the services and obedience of angels and demons."

CURTIUS: We also observe in nature that which we see in a well-ordered state—namely, that laws are sometimes changed and extraordinary officers are appointed, instead of ordinary magistrates, for the safety of the state. P. 51 And so the laws of nature are sustained[259] and certain new marvels, prodigies, plagues, fires, floods are stirred up outside of nature lest any one think that God is bound by the necessity of natural laws, as Toralba cleverly[260] showed. For what would be more foolish than for a king to be loosed from his edicts and laws in his own state so that he could correct and emend the laws, contingent upon circumstances, and yet for God, the ruler and parent of the world, to be bound by his own laws? The things which happen outside the customary order of nature—rivers flowing backward, seas being divided, flames leaping down—ought not to be considered as natural actions of angels and demons, since these would not be done without divine power and approval.

SENAMUS: Nothing seems good to me which happens outside of nature, as Aristotle writes.[261]

[256] Psalm 46 (47):10. [257] *Phaedr.* 246. [258] Psalm 67 (68):18.
[259] *sustineri* M [260] *argute* M
[261] *Phys.* II. 8; *Metaphys.* V. 4; XI. 8. 12.

SALOMON: I think we should forgive Aristotle, who was ignorant of divine matters, even contemptuous of them.

SENAMUS: Then what keeps us from saying that all things which happen from nature are accomplished by demons and angels?

SALOMON: We see many things arise and increase gradually by the power which God imparted in the beginning of the origin of each without any actions from demons or angels. Consider for example plants and living things which produce their own kind by their own power granted by God in the beginning of their kind. Likewise think about rocks, metals, fossils, which the land, cultivated or not, brings forth of its own accord. Moreover, aside from this generating of animals and plants, there is another usual and customary one which recurs yearly, yet outside the laws of nature. From these kinds are propagated from seed, so that all those schools of fish spring up, full grown from the shores yet without seeds or any traces of their parents on the shoals or shores or on the rocks and algae. Those who originate from their parents have their own seeds and increase, and as they gradually grow, so also they gradually fade away. But the others in a moment break forth in a great size; after a little while, unless they are caught, they disappear, as lines of tunny fish, which in a cubic shape swim with so much force and number from Pontus into the Hellespont that they often overturn ships and nets with their great strength. Not only in the Hellespont but also in the waters around Rhodes swordfish of the same great size come forth in such large schools that they can supply food for the Rhodians for a long time. I do not doubt that on other shores also a similar supply of fish is divinely granted to relieve the poverty and need of the inhabitants.

FRIDERICUS: Indeed near Holland I have seen such a large catch of salmon and sturgeon, which they call sheat-fish, that they were sold for a P. 52
large profit in the neighboring regions. Not far from Holland around the Strait of Ixion there are so many thousands of fish in the month of October that a great crowd of fishermen can never pull in all the fish. These fish are shipped through France, both Germanies, and Britain for a handsome profit. But it is strange that, although they come forth full grown in a moment, no seeds, no offspring, nor even any traces of offspring are seen. When I was inquiring about these things from fishermen and merchants, they said that near the Orkney Islands fishermen find a remarkable abundance in their fish traps every year, and on the Celtic shore they catch whales in the month of March, then mackerel in April. Where such a mass of fish came from no one knows.

Curtius: I have very often seen schools of mullet return at the same time every year on the coast of Gallia Narbonensis, and on the shores nearest to Marseilles schools of trout[262] return; likewise on the opposite coasts of Africa there are chub every year. The natives call these fish *jurata*, but we call them shad, and they are rarely seen on other shores.

Coronaeus: Also every year the Cretans have thousands of fish which provide food for the island in marvelous fashion but in such numbers as to seem to have been born from the same womb, in the same hour, in the same moment or to have fallen down from heaven or to have come forth from the inner depths of the land. Likewise a very large supply of murena appears on the Sicilian shore every year.

Toralba: The most generous parent of nature has provided not only for your men but also for ours. Every year the Calaeans around the shores of Portugal catch a kind of herring which they call sardines, and in the Atlantic far from the shores of Europe fishermen are delighted with the great abundance of haddock which appears a little after the summer solstice. But when we say the fishermen were intent on profit and were awed by such bounty so suddenly supplied, we hurled invectives against the greedy fishermen in these iambics:

Greedy fisherman, who crosses the churning straits as you
strive after fishing,
Tell if you can (but who can?)
What is the source of so many fish suddenly appearing
with their gleaming scales?
At birth they are all the same size and equal in
weight.
P. 53 Soon after birth their size increases.
No seed was there nor any traces of seed.
Neither does the worthless algae germinate the snails
from its stock
nor does the vast depths of the sea
nor the rocks with lofty crags
nor the pure shores
nor the sea-foam mother of shining
Aphrodite produce them.

262 The names of the fish are perplexing, and it was necessary to make certain emendations. Since *apica* could not be located, *lapicadus* (a fish that lives in rocky streams, the trout) is suggested. For *trissa* or the variant *frissa* I read *frisgula* (the chavendar or chub).

Who directs that cubic line of fish
and from whence does the shiny alex
    come to the strait of Ixion,
Breaking the nets stretched from the
    struggling ships?
Should I recall others?
There is hardly a shore which from the heavenly largess
    does not abound in fish and birds[263] that[264]
    feed at a distance from the sea-shores
Or in a hoard of crickets.
They fly away sated to their solitary nesting places
    to be just punishments for the wicked
    and for the good just rewards,
O remarkable divine will!
O loftiest summit of the best provider
who nourishes all things with your sway!

OCTAVIUS: I see you have spent more leisure in fishing than in fowling. With my neighbors at Volterra I have often watched with admiration the flight of a flock of pigeons, although no pigeons were to be found on P. 54 the mainland or any sign even of eggs or nests, much less on the nearby islands. Now if anyone thinks he can fly across the Mediterranean sea from Africa with a west wind blowing, he is easily refuted by the great distance of 1,200 miles; yet all the inhabitants agree that [the birds] fly from the seacoast inland.

CURTIUS: When I was in France, a certain clever fowler at night by torch light hunted with no effort many thousand ring doves which had flown from the ocean to the shore of Rouen. When I asked him where so many doves came from, he answered that they only fly there in those years when the beech nuts are plentiful for them to feed upon. Furthermore, huge flocks of those bluish birds which he called *pluviers* [plovers] in his native tongue, of the family of doves, rained down into the fields of Orleans, yet no nests were found and not even any trace of food in their crops or stomachs. Moreover, in the province of Anjou forest geese came down from the sky, and after they fattened themselves on the grass in the pasture, they provided plump provisions for the inhabitants.

SENAMUS: On the Neapolitan shore you could see every year the fishing for quail; when they try to fly across the Mediterranean with the north-

[263] *alite* MR   [264] *qui* MR

west wind, they sink and are tossed dead upon the shore. Also I think that whereas flocks of birds such as cranes, swallows, storks, hawks, geese, wood ducks, and quail fly back and forth crossing rivers, seas, and mountains, they sink, however, weak because of the shortness of their wings and heavy because of fat. Indeed wherever you may search in winter you can still never find swallows.

SALOMON: Senamus tries to direct everything clearly to natural causes. But, in fact, in the beginning God ordered the waters to produce not only sea animals but also flying creatures.[265] And so in Scripture[266] we read that such large numbers of quail were scattered by God's spirit from the shore to the camp of the Israelites that they filled the camp on all sides to a height of two cubits for the space of a day's march. One can know how great the camp was from the fact that 600,000 citizens who bore arms had been registered.[267] The number was three times greater because old men, young boys, women, and foreign slaves had not been counted. And nevertheless it is a fact that the quail satisfied the people's desire for eating meat for a whole month but also made them sick at the thought of meat. Therefore when we read that so many flocks of quail
P. 55 had been wrenched by the spirit of God from the seacoast, it plainly means that their generation [i.e., birth] was out of the order of nature by the agency of angels on the authority of a divine grant and gift. So also are those unexpected hoards of birds and fish provided for man's nourishment by the wondrous concern and goodness of God. In like manner, that manna on which the Israelites fed in the desert for more than forty years was expressly called food of the angels,[268] not because angels eat manna, but because it was furnished daily by the agency of angels and by none of the ordinary causes of nature.

SENAMUS: I do not see why there is need for the care of angels or demons if the things you speak of can happen from God's will alone.

SALOMON: It is one thing to talk about divine will, another thing to talk about divine power. It is written that God rested from all labor after the creation of the world[269] and that in all places angels served God diligently and followed his orders.[270] This is what is meant by the saying that God calls together assemblies of angels, which Rabbi Moses interprets as meaning that he uses the services and functions of angels.

[265] Gen. 1:20.
[266] Num. 11:32; also cf. Ex. 16:13 and Psalm 77 (78):27–29.
[267] Num. 2:32–33.
[268] Psalm 77 (78):23–25; Ex. 16:4–36.
[269] Gen. 2:3.
[270] Psalm 102 (103):20–21.

When He had said that He would kill the first-born of the Egyptians, nevertheless in the same chapter, He said that He would not allow the executioner to go to the homes of His people in that destruction.[271] Likewise He said: "I shall rebuke that evil demon from the north to keep it from destroying the crops."[272]

SENAMUS: Why does He so many times and so often call His people to witness that often plague, hunger and all calamities have been brought upon them by Him?[273]

SALOMON: In order that they not fall into the worship of angels and demons, but believe that all things depend on the hand and power of God alone whose decrees, however, demons execute always at His bidding. As proof let us take the following. When King Ahab had done many wicked things, he at length was persuaded by soothsayers to war against the king of Syria for a third time, but first he decided to consult the prophet Micah. This prophet[274] said: "I saw God sitting on a lofty throne and a whole army of angels standing around; God said to them: 'Who of you will persuade Ahab that he begin the battle and be killed?' " And when they all gave different answers, a certain spirit stepped forth and standing before God said: "I shall persuade him!" Certain theologians say that spirit was Naboth's, whom Queen Jezebel with the king's consent P. 56 had falsely accused and then had cruelly killed by treacherous murder so that the king might enjoy the property which he could not extort by entreaty or money.[275]

CURTIUS: The Academicians and the leader of the Platonists believed that those dead from murder, overcome by the desire for vengeance, demand vengeance in every way.[276]

SALOMON: God could have destroyed King Ahab with a single command, but you see that at the fitting moment for war He summoned a council of angels to be false prophets and bring vengeance finally as administrators of the divine decree.[277] In like manner it is said that a council was convened before the devil obtained any power against Job, and it is said that Satan had been present in the council.[278] By analogy one knows that it is inconsistent with divine majesty to act through itself what it can perform through the action of angels. Harmonious with this is the

271 Ex. 12:23.
272 Mal. 3:11; Joel 2:20.
273 Lev. 26:14–46; Deut. 28:15–69.
274 III Kings (I Kings) 22:14–23.
275 III Kings (I Kings) 21:4–16.
276 Plato, *Locr.* 104E; *Pol.* VIII. 565E; IX. 571D.
277 III Kings (I Kings) 22:14–23.
278 Job 1:6–12; 2:1–6.

statement of Jedacus the Levite in the *Door of Light* that all things are filled with angels and demons from the depths of earth to the vault of heaven. Likewise in another place he writes that the angels breathe from the boundaries and limits of heaven and that good angels attend to good things and bad angels attend to wars, unfruitfulness, common illnesses, and harmful beasts for the punishment of crimes.

FRIDERICUS: Though in nature nothing has been established in vain, if all things were done only by God's command, as in the beginning all things were created by the will of God alone, so many angels and demons would have existed in vain.

TORALBA: Certain living things are generated for a short time and then vanish when their duty has been completed. Indeed, Pliny[279] was wondrously amazed that Syrian birds fly to the Casion mountains during the summer solstice to destroy a multitude of insects so that they may not, living, harm the crops nor, dead, spoil them with their stench. When the birds have eaten the insects, they disappear in such a manner that they are found nowhere. The birds were not accustomed to fly every year but only in those years when the insects were prevalent. Aristotle, along with Pliny, said that hoards of field mice which are not often seen—but still too often according to the farmers—disappear after they have eaten the crops and are never again seen above or below the earth.[280]

SALOMON: We have also a witness to this in Scripture that when God had covered all of Egypt with a swarm of locusts, all flew away at the same time because of the repentance of Pharaoh and the prayers of Moses, and none remained in that vast and widespread region.[281]

SENAMUS: It is not strange if they flew away well fed, since they flew in when they were hungry. But who went down to the caverns of the earth to sacrifice to the corpses of dead mice? Many things are entangled
P. 57 in popular mistakes which we have finally seen explained. Swallows which were born for extermination fly inland with the sea winds blowing but fly back with the southwest wind and hide all winter under rocks along the shores; they are said to have been caught often by fishermen in the Swedish sea, since places along the coasts are always warmer than other places because of the heat which rises from the tossing of the sea and often from the force of storms, just as things boil when fire is placed beneath them. Also some think that swallows penetrate the lowest depths of the sea.

279 *Hist. nat.* X. 39. 280 Cf. *ibid.*, X. 85. 281 Ex. 10:14–20.

Toralba: It is utterly impossible that swallows hide in the lowest depths since animals which have lungs die suddenly if air is removed. For even though dormice sleep all winter sunk in slumber and cannot be aroused by any blows or wounds, they leap out if they are submerged in water.

Curtius: But we nevertheless see nests and eggs so that swallows, cranes, and storks may return, but no eggs of fish, ring doves, or wood swans are ever found. Granted that roots, beetles, locusts, wingless locusts, mice, and frogs owe their beginnings without seed to decayed ground, still it cannot happen that such great schools of fish and swarms of birds have so sudden an increase through nature and through neglect vanish completely.

Toralba: Since it is not possible to persuade Senamus that the origin and destruction of living things happen other than from natural causes, I shall gladly learn in earnest from all those who deal with the natural sciences whence such a multitude of frogs, with the heat and dryness beginning in the summer, in a moment descend in a heavy rainstorm. Indeed they cannot be produced in the upper air from seed or mating of their parents or from the mire of the land or water.

Senamus: I always thought that very warm rains falling on the dusty earth produced the most suitable material for generating tadpoles.

Toralba: But the generation of the most perfect living things cannot happen in a moment through nature. I have often tested this by experiment. I filled a ditch with water in the heat of summer and after a month, in the ditch which was now dry, the beginnings of tadpoles, covered with black follicles and tails, appeared; we saw groups of these swimming in the marshes where there are many frogs. The next month they shed the follicles and four-legged frogs leaped forth. But I do not think it possible by nature that four-legged frogs, complete in every part, are produced in the very short space of one hour and as proof of the fact that it is evident that frogs are suddenly produced high in the air, let it suffice that very often on trees, especially willow trees whose pruned tops are broader, as well as on the ground, fallen tadpoles are found after summer P. 58
rains.

Coronaeus: It seems more likely that the mass of dust and particles is carried with exhalations and moisture into the middle region by the force of the winds whence frogs and stones often are produced and rain down. When in my youth a storm had begun at Crema, rocks mixed with rain fell, and one was of such great weight that it equalled ten pounds; it was a gray color and smelled of sulphur. Moreover, the brief time in which the rains are condensed clearly shows these things (as well as the tadpoles which the magicians in Egypt summoned before the eyes of Pharaoh)[282] are the work of demons.

FRIDERICUS: If God gave to living things the power of propagating their own species and also imparted to the elements the power of producing plants and animals, how much the more did he assign the same power to angels and demons? In fact, this was clear from that procreation of frogs at Pharaoh's court, which Moses affirms was most authentic.[283]

SENAMUS: What keeps one from admitting that storms, thunder, lightning, and winds are stirred up by demons if we grant that these things are wrought by them? But if these things happen without demons because of a secret harmony and will of nature, it is consistent that those other things also depend upon nature.

OCTAVIUS: Previously I had always thought that winds and storms were stirred up by nature herself until I had tossed into the sea at the captain's orders that Egyptian corpse which I had carried on board; for at once the most violent storms subsided. Nor would I think now that it had befallen on account of this if I had not confirmed and ascertained it by the words of all the sailors, by long experience, and by nautical laws and trials themselves.

FRIDERICUS: I remember Heraclitus, Theophrastus, and Plutarch complained that the diffidence and unbelief of men hindered us from pursuing the surest knowledge about the greatest hidden matters.[284] For I think we ought neither to agree too rashly and frivolously nor disagree too persistently.

TORALBA: Although I had been satisfied for a very long time with the teachings of the Peripatetics and thought that one should attribute many things more to authority than to reason, nothing freed me from these misconceptions as much as the movements of the elements and especially the sea. For Aristotle posited a miracle of nature as it were, namely, that the limits of moving and movable things are the same.[285] When this foundation has been shaken, other things also with the slightest pressure threaten ruin and lead us to the point of being constrained to confess the
P. 59 actions of angels and demons and all immortal things are alien to nature.

SENAMUS: That conclusion seems to rest not only on the authority of

282 Ex. 8:3.

283 Ex. 8:1–2, 4–11.

284 Heraclitus 86: "Many things of the gods flee from our knowledge because of disbelief."

285 *Phys.* III. 2. 202a; III. 3. 202a.

Aristotle and almost all philosophers but also upon so many powerful reasons that it is very difficult to overturn. For if it is logical that efficient causes are present to their effect, surely it is necessary for the limits of the moving thing and the movable thing to coincide. If the former is true, then this is true. Whereas all things move spirit; spirit moves muscle; muscles move arms; arms move a sling; a sling moves a rock; a rock moves a beast or something does; still it happens that the limits of movable and moving things coincide.

TORALBA: Granted this is true in these examples, still it is false in a magnet attracting iron, in amber drawing out the dust, in naphtha catching[286] fire from a distance, in the electric-ray fish shocking fishermen, in an enemy arousing pallor or a blush, in the moon moving the ocean though separated by infinite space.

SENAMUS: But who does not see that the power of a magnet or an electric-ray fish or the moon penetrates from one end to the other through the middle. We may take as proof the fact that iron is not moved by a magnet at a greater distance than that to which the power of the stone [i.e., magnet] can reach.

TORALBA: That may be true. Nevertheless this is not the reason that the nets and rods of a fisherman are shocked or the sea moved by the moon, the air by fire, and water by air. In the supreme purity and tranquility of heaven, however, the ocean rolls in and out, to be sure, not the whole ocean but only the parts that are nearer to the shore, as many think the ocean breathes in and out like a living thing; or the parts of the ocean which are not too far from the shore they believe to be as still as a marble slab when the sky is tranquil and serene.

SENAMUS: From the writings of Aristotle we can thus interpret his saying to mean that a part of moving objects is moved, a part is at rest; for example, when one foot moves, the other will be at rest.[287]

TORALBA: This will also be found to be false in the flight of birds, in moving weapons which are moved altogether with no part stable, false in heavenly masses which orbit together with no part at rest, as has been shown in the clear proofs of Eudoxus[288] and is known from experience. We can also remember that when the moon rises above the horizon, the ocean overflows into its customary estuaries in six hours in which time

[286] *corripiente* M

[287] *Phys.* III. 3. 208a.

[288] *Eudoxi* M. Eudoxus of Cnidos (408–355 B.C.) was a brilliant mathematician and astronomer. He attended lectures by Plato, studied astronomy in Egypt, founded a school at Cyzicus. See Aristotle, *Metaphys.* XII. 8. 9.

the moon advances to its meridian. When the moon declines from its meridian, the ocean returns to the shores in the same amount of time. After the moon sinks from the horizon all the way to the nocturnal and meridian, the ocean again flows on those same shores in the same amount of time and then returns onto the strand, with the moon returning to the horizon in the marvelous harmony of each's nature.

P. 60 SENAMUS: That motion does not seem to be constant or uniform since the swell of the ocean is much greater when the sun and moon are in conjunction and opposition.

FRIDERICUS: When I sought the causes of this variation, I noticed that the moon in its conjunction or opposition reaches its apogee of the eccentric, but in its quadratures reaches its hypogee, as if it could draw the ocean's swells along with it the higher it is borne from the lands, since the hypogee of the moon is not farther distant from the ocean than the apogee of the moon is from the hypogee. One knows from this that the moon with a double interval is distant from the lands in the apogee of the eccentric the more it is situated in the apogee of the epicycle. However, in the Mediterranean sea and especially in the narrow straits of the Adriatic almost no fluctuation is perceptible as long as the moon remains in the hypogee of the eccentric, that is, in the orbits of its quadratures with which the moon is the closer to the lands.

SENAMUS: But the nearer a movable object is to the mover, the more actively it is moved. For example, in a magnet we have seen the heavier needles touch the magnet, and the lighter ones follow by contact with the heavier.

FRIDERICUS: Indeed it is logical that the moon, drawn farther away from the lands, draws the ocean along with it, as it were.

TORALBA: Accordingly we see the efficient cause of the ocean's movement is referred to the moon, since the motion of waters as of all heavy matter is directed to the center. For there is another motion of the waters from the agitation of air, and another without any agitation, though less often. Pliny[289] wrote about a certain lake of Italy which swelled with waves not only without any blast of winds, but also under the calmest sky. But now since no inanimate thing is moved by itself, we must admit that this agitation of waters is stirred up by demons, and that is the sense of the following about the remarkable power of witches:[290]

[289] On the marvels that Pliny details concerning springs, rivers, and lakes see *Hist. nat.* II. 56 ff.

[290] Lucan, *Pharsalia* VI. 465–71.

And the heaven thunders with those
 same voices though Jupiter is unaware,
They have shaken the mists and clouds[291]
To pour out water far and wide, their locks[292]
 being loosed; though the
 winds are quiet the sea
 swells; again refusing to acknowledge
 the blasts it becomes quiet
 though the south wind is blowing.

SENAMUS: Granted that these things are true which are unknown to me at least, and possibly not really known by anyone, still they ought not to be drawn out for an example.

CORONAEUS: Lest we cling to minutiae, it must be proven, I think, that the movement of air is caused by the sun or by living things or by demons. There is no fourth.

TORALBA: I declare that just as the ocean is stirred up and moved by the moon, so the air is moved by the sun. And as the ocean's waves are increased or decreased by the violent motion of the air, so the movement of the air that is ordinary and congruent with nature is often disturbed by the extraordinary force and power of demons. P. 61

SENAMUS: If the wind rises from a hot dry vapor which sets in motion successively the vapor nearest to itself in an oblique motion,[293] as Aristotle[294] says, I do not see why we ought to decide that the extraordinary disturbances of air are the work of demons.

OCTAVIUS: The definition of the ancients seemed much truer to me, namely, that the wind is a current of air.[295] Many prefer to read *fluctus* (wave), but the Greek word *reusis tou aeros*[296] (flowing of air) removes the ambiguity with *fluctus* (wave), which is expressed by *kuma* (swell).

TORALBA: Aristotle, dislodging this definition, as all the principles of the natural philosophers, relates it, for no credible reason, to the smoky vapors.[297] Nevertheless, nothing is more imperceptible than these vapors, yet nothing can be more violent than a storm. But that which happens

291 *nimbosque* M

292 *comis* M

293 *motu* M

294 *Meteorologica* II. 4. 359b–360a.

295 Cf. Aristotle, *Meteorologica* I. 13. 349a and note a, where he says that some (Hippocrates and Anaximander) say that the wind is simply a moving current of air. Also see Pliny, *Hist. nat.* II. 44. 114.

296 Aristotle, *Meteorologica* I. 13. 349a and note a.

297 *Ibid.*, II. 4. 359b–360a; I. 4. 341b.

from nature cannot be violent. Indeed we see winds of such force that they uproot forests, hurl down towers, crumble buildings, twist huge trees in whirlwinds, sink ships in whirlpools, although the air does not move in a circular path nor with downward motion by nature.[298]

SENAMUS: You have also seen, I believe, and often read that when a small dust of nitrate and sulphur is ignited, huge towers and walls are destroyed from the foundation.[299]

TORALBA: This happens lest[300] in underground places a penetration of bodies results. However, no penetration can exist in very thin air, and this is the reason why in overturning towers and walls through tunnels one must be especially careful that there be no crack or fissure. Now not only those thin vapors which escape our eyes because of their thinness but also heavier vapors with black mist are carried very rapidly upward and overcome the heavier air. Indeed the wind is borne in a slanting movement or is hurled down from the clouds with the quickest force. Therefore the wind is not from vapor which by its own nature tends upward, whence clouds originate which have increased with the vapor and exhalation in the cold region of the higher air, and by these the forces of the winds are usually calmed, not aroused. Likewise, if the wind were from vapor, since it always rises from the earth, it would be stirred up always from the same region, not from opposite or different regions. Besides, all vapor is warm, but no wind is warm. Therefore no vapor can stir up the wind. Indeed the colder the winds are, the stronger they are; wind, therefore, is not from warm vapor. Likewise if wind were from
P. 62 vapor, it would be felt more strongly when the supply of vapor is greater —that is, in summer, especially at noon, when the earth splits open. But at both those times the winds are quiet; however, in winter and autumn very violent storms arise, for as Pliny[301] noted, it was at those times that the seas were closed to navigation. Likewise the force of the winds is rather often stirred up in the deepest abysses of the ocean where no warm dry vapor is present, but only cold damp vapors. Although Aristotle's opinion is plainly wrested from its position by these arguments, still the

298 Cf. Aristotle, *Problem.* XXVI and *Meteorologica* III. 1. 370b–371b.

299 Roger Bacon's *De mirabili potestate artis et naturae* (1242) is the most important work on the history of gunpowder; however, one should not overlook Albertus Magnus, *De mirabilibus mundi* and Marcus Graecus, *Liber ignium.*

300 *ne in subterraneis locis penetratio corporum sequatur* M. Note a similar passage in *Theatrum*, p. 174: *Nihil mirum debet videri si terra discedit dehiscit: id enim fit, ne corporum penetratio sequatur.*

301 *Hist. nat.* II. 47. 122–29.

opinion common to all the physicists clearly proves that nothing is moved by itself, otherwise actuality and potentiality would be one and the same[302] at the same time. And if air were moved by vapor, it would be moved by itself since vapor is nothing other than warm misty air. Therefore wind is not from vapor.

CURTIUS: This abundance of arguments sufficiently convinces us that the origins of winds are not due to vapors. The most convincing proof is that in the coldest winter when the lands and seas are frozen from cold, the power of the winds is much greater than in the summer when the lands are gaping, and in the midday heat in summer the winds are completely calm, as Aristotle[303] writes and as experience forces us to admit. And for that reason, that shepherd of Theocritus[304] forbids flute-playing at midday because he feared that Pan returning from the hunt, might vent his anger against the flocks and cattle. This is the interpretation that the commentator on Aristophanes gives to *empousa* [hobgoblin][305] and "midday demon,"[306] because when demons are at rest from stirring up the air, then they rage against flocks, crops, and people. For this reason the ancients sacrificed a black animal at midday, according to Festus Pompeius.

SALOMON: Rabbi Salomon Jarchi, the son of Gerson, concerning the passage from Psalms[307] about the evil spirit of midday, interprets *Midderer* as a demon, who kills in the middle of the night but *Miqqeṭṭev* as one who kills at midday.[308] From this arose the custom of appeasing God with prayers at midday and midnight. The Psalm expresses it this way: "I used to rise at midnight to sing praise to Your name."[309] Likewise: "Evening and morning and midday I shall tell Your wonderful works."[310] This too is worthy of notice that the winds in almost all places in sacred Scripture are attributed to God.[311] Nay God is even said to draw the winds from His own storehouse[312] and summon them from the four

302 *et idem* M

303 *Meteorologica* II. 5. 361b.

304 *Idylls* I. 8.

305 Empousa was a hobgoblin who assumed various shapes. She was said to be sent by Hecate and was identified with Hecate. Aristophanes, *Fragment* 500. Also see Aristophanes, *Ranae* 293, *Ecclesiazusae* 1056.

306 On the midday demon see Athenaeus Epigrammaticus, *Expositio* Psalm 90:6. (Migne, *Patrologia Graeca*, XXVII. 401B). Also Tertullian, *Apol.* I. 16.

307 Psalm 90 (91):6.

308 *vero qui meridie interfecit* M

309 Psalm 118 (119):62.

310 Psalm 54 (55):18.

311 Gen. 8:1; Ex. 16:10; Psalm 17 (18):11; Ex. 15:10.

312 Psalm 134 (135):7.

regions of the sky.[313] We know by this that the power and thrust of the winds do not originate from the ordinary causes of nature.

SENAMUS: Why cannot a current of air drive a current in the same way as a wave drives a wave?

TORALBA: Indeed that is the fallacious argument of Aristotle;[314] a wave thrusts forth a wave, but only when it is driven first by air or living things or by the moon, as has been proven rather often. In like manner air can drive air, but it is necessary to have a beginning of motion from something other than from itself, namely from the sun, or from an animal
P. 63 or from a demon; otherwise, both water and air would be equally immobile, as rocks which attain a position consistent with their own gravity and nature.

OCTAVIUS: Seneca[315] records from ancient authority that a certain peculiar wind was assigned to each region. This would be impossible if wind had its origin from vapor.

CORONAEUS: I have always been influenced by this opinion that in addition to the natural order God, by a unique gift and concession, has had a special concern for particular regions and men, but demons stir up the most violent storms and gales to punish the wicked.

TORALBA: Nothing is more alien to nature than violence, so we know that storms and winds which disturb the elements cannot happen from nature.

SENAMUS: If the wind is attributed to demons agitating the air and not to warm vapors, what is the reason that the most powerful storm and violent winds are soothed by the gentlest rain? From this we see clearly that the warm and dry force is extinguished by humid and cold nature.

FRIDERICUS: It is true that the nature of the most impure demons hates the purity of waters, and those obsessed by demons curse nothing more than the sprinkling of water. There is no surer way to tell magicians than to place them in water with hands and feet bound, and from daily experience we have learned that magicians cannot sink. And so German judges were accustomed to use this proof against magicians. Since Julianus Augustus[316] had seen this done in Germany, he wrote that the spurious

[313] Ezech. 37:9.

[314] *Meteorologica* I. 3; II. 4. 360a.

[315] *Quaest. nat.* V. 17. 5.

[316] Flavius Claudius Julianus (Julian the Apostate) A.D. 332–A.D. 363. He sought as emperor to reestablish Roman reputation in the East. Educated as a Christian and baptized, he rebelled against the faith of those who had killed his relatives, and he turned to the old paganism. Although not actually a persecutor of the church, he encouraged divisions in it and attempted to improve the organization of the pagan priesthood. See below, Book III, notes 7 and 8, and Book VI, note 158.

were judged from the real by this test when there was a test of soothsayers or those who have been dedicated by their parents to demons before they were born. The people of Verona call them Acherontian boys.

TORALBA: Even more remarkable is the fact that typhoons, which are called whirlwinds by the Latins, move, not in a slanting motion, but dropping from the clouds with great violence, in a circle, often uproot tall trees but flee when vinegar is sprinkled.

OCTAVIUS: Perhaps the substance of these demons is fiery because nothing is so opposed to fire as vinegar. Indeed when we were tossed about by the storm which I mentioned, a certain fiery image stopped on the prow for a while after it had moved here and there about the ship. The sailors cursed it as a wicked demon.

FRIDERICUS: The ancients call it Helen, the surest sign of evil omen, but if a double light was seen, they considered it to be Castor and Pollux, salutary spirits.[317] Moreover, I do not doubt that the flames—the vulgar call them unwieldy fires—which move around tombs, gibbets, and swamps are demons because they misdirect men who travel at night into water or off a precipice. If summoned with words and whistles, they suddenly fly in and kill at random those who call to them lightly. P. 64

SALOMON: There is no remedy more effective for driving off airy pests of this kind than adoring God with face prostrate on the ground.

OCTAVIUS: As I question why those apparitions wander around gibbets and tombs, no truer answer occurs to me than that those demons are guardians of corpses so that I am persuaded that a demon as guardian had followed the theft of the corpse and wished to punish me by stirring up the winds. The most certain proof in this matter is that when the body was thrown overboard as Jonah was,[318] the most violent storms calmed instantly. This certainly indicates very clearly that demons have power to stir up winds.

FRIDERICUS: Physicists, so as not to seem ignorant of hidden causes, consider many things are incredible because they very mistakenly think that nothing apart from nature happens in nature. But Olaus Magnus relates that in Lapponia beyond the Swedish sea soothsayers and witches were accustomed to sell the winds in deals arranged with sailors. This would seem fantastic to me except that many sailors corroborated the story, and in fact from Homer thereafter, it has been ascertained by experience. For Homer[319] writes that King Aeolus gave Ulysses a wind

[317] See Pliny, *Hist. nat.* II. 37. 101.
[318] Jonah 1:15.
[319] *Odyss.* X. 19–27. Also see Strabo, VI. 2. 10.

enclosed in a bag so that he could sail more safely to Ithaca. Also a ship captain in Sardinia bought from a magician a rope tied with a triple knot. When he set sail from port, a gentle wind began to blow when he untied the first knot. If he wanted the ship to be carried more swiftly and with full sails, he loosed the second knot; if he wanted to stir up very strong winds, he untied the third knot.

CURTIUS: A similar story in Herodotus seemed unbelievable to me before. He writes that Persian magicians by making incisions curbed the winds and tempest when the royal fleet had invaded Greece.[320]

FRIDERICUS: The Greeks, who expressed reality in fables, used to say that Aeolus, king of the winds, kept the winds enclosed in caves. Horace[321] speaks of this in these verses:

> Thus let the powerful goddess of Cyprus,
> the brothers of Helen, bright stars,
> And the father of the winds direct you,
> After the other winds, except Iapyx, have
> been bound.

CORONAEUS: From this discussion we arrive at this conclusion, I think. Since nothing can be moved by itself, the ocean is moved by the moon
P. 65 in a peaceful movement congruent with its nature, and the air is moved by the sun. Since nothing is so alien to nature as that which happens violently and recklessly, the winds and storms are summoned by the forceful power of demons.

SENAMUS: If we grant this, by the same reasoning we shall have to attribute earthquakes, lightning, thunder, and falling stars to the actions of demons.

OCTAVIUS: Since the land is stable by its own nature, but fire may be carried upward, as a consequence falling stars, tremors and crevasses result from violence not from their own nature. If these things are not natural, it follows that they must be attributed to the actions of demons.

SENAMUS: Often heavy things are carried up, and light things are carried down in the escape of a vacuum or so that bodies not get in each other's way. So also when thunderbolts, which begin in the midst of the

320 Bodin is not completely accurate in relating the story. Herodotus, VII. 191., says that a storm lashed the Persian fleet for three days. Finally the Magicians offered victims to the winds and also sacrificed to Thetis and the Nereids because the promontory where the ships ran afoul was sacred to Thetis.

321 *Carm.* I. 3. 1–4.

clouds from warm dry vapor, cannot long endure the nature of cold, humid vapor and the middle region, at length they must break forth with a clamor and rush down with headlong fall and produce thunder and lightning.

TORALBA: Senamus thinks it is noble to safeguard the teaching received from the Peripatetics and base to desert it. And indeed I myself for a long time acquiesced in this opinion; however, the power of arguments and clearest proofs forced me to withdraw from this teaching. For how can it happen that such loud thunderings are heard from the clash of the lightest and softest clouds? Moreover, if thunder were stirred up from the clashing of clouds, it would always thunder, when clouds are broken and scattered by the wind. Besides when lightning breaks forth from a dark cloud, it would always thunder. Often, however, very dense clouds suddenly happen to be opened with a great cleft, and flashes of the brightest lightning gleam forth without any thunder. Finally, if thunder were stirred up by a crashing of clouds, it would never thunder without a crashing of clouds; very often, however, it thunders without any break in the clouds and with continuous rumblings of thunder and thunders are even heard in a serene sky without any clouds or lightning.

CURTIUS: Herennius,[322] a magistrate of the Pompeians, was struck by lightning though the sky was clear. Seneca noted this occurrence as well as Pliny and Valerius,[323] and Lucan[324] described it thus:

And the sky thunders though Jove is unaware.

FRIDERICUS: Those[325] arguments of Toralba seem to me to shatter or weaken completely Aristotle's opinion about thunder. Moreover, those who have been present when magicians assembled together agree if anyone uninitiated to demonic rites is brought there and shudders at the detestable devotions, suddenly with a clap of thunder the assemblage of demons and magicians is dissolved. Indeed there are many caves where P. 66
thunder has been heard by the inhabitants and passersby though the sky was very peaceful. You have read, I suppose, that those entering an Egyptian labyrinth were terrified by internal rumblings. And just as the assemblages of soothsayers and the dire poisons of magicians smell of

[322] Marcus Herennius, according to Pliny, *Hist. nat.* II. 52.

[323] *Ibid.* Seneca (*Quaest. nat.* II. 26. 4–7) says that we do not see lightning unless the sky is threatening. Lightning in a clear sky is a bad omen. Cf. Vergil, *Georg.* I. 487 and Lucan, *Pharsalia* I. 534–35.

[324] *Pharsalia* VI. 465; also see VI. 465–71.

[325] *illa* M

sulphur, so also those places in which lightning has struck are filled with the foulest odor of sulphur. We have observed that those fiery rocks made by demon's art smell of nothing but sulphur. Now who is so blind that he does not see the actions of demons in the flashing of lightning, though the bigger the flame is, the swifter is its upward flight. The power of demons is observed not only when lightning strikes contrary to nature but also when it moves in a circular and slanting path. The power of demons is also indicated when swords melt in an unharmed scabbard, when utensils burn in a closed and untouched cupboard, when the private parts lose hair though the skin is unblemished, when a wife recoils from the embrace of her husband. In countless actions which are most alien to nature, we must admit these things happen contrary to nature only by the force and power of demons or angels.

CURTIUS: The ancient theologians identified three thunderbolts of Jupiter, namely, white, red, black; they said the first were sent from the will of Jupiter alone, because they were harmless encouragements, as it were. According to Seneca[326] only the thunderbolt which Jupiter sends is gentle. They believed lesser gods were added for the second thunderbolt, that is, planets lower than Jupiter. Although the thunderbolt might inflict a wound, still it did not cause the death of anyone. For the third thunderbolt the higher gods were summoned, that is, the higher stars, and from it men suffered destruction. Since Pliny[327] did not comprehend this, he thought that the white lightning fell from the body of Jupiter himself, an opinion too frivolous to deserve refutation.

OCTAVIUS: I hear that Timurbecus,[328] whom our people called Tamerlan,[329] followed this method of imposing punishment. He used a white tent on the first day of siege to indicate that impunity would follow surrender; on the next day he used red to show that he would kill the princes and magistrates,[330] and on the third day black tents indicated the slaughter of all if the city were taken.

SALOMON: Into their myths the Greeks wove the truth which they received from the Hebrews. They represented Juno as presiding in the air and hurling down avenging spirits from the midst of the air to keep them from flying into heaven.[331] This indicated only that lesser spirits and

[326] *Quaest. nat.* II. 41. 1; also see II. 49. 3, II. 50.

[327] *Hist. nat.* II. 18. 82.

[328] *Temircutlum* M *Timurbecum* N

[329] *Tametclanum* M *Tamerlanem* N

[330] *principum ac magistratum* M

[331] Juno, like Jupiter, has authority over the phenomena of the atmosphere. It is she who sends clouds and storms and is mistress of thunder and lightning.

demons were enclosed by their particular boundaries to keep them from breaking out above the region of the clouds and were cast out by higher angels and powers and hurled down on the earth. By their fall they terrify mortals and warn them with the white thunderbolt first, since it is harmless. After this they chastise mortals by wounding them with the thunderbolt, and sometimes they bring death to one man or one family or one state whereby a few are punished, but all are fearful. And the harmless thunderbolts are said to be the dispensation of Jupiter to make clear the goodness of God the best and greatest; He[332] alone grants pardon, rewards, riches, knowledge, finally all good things, but He leaves judgments and punishments to be meted out by His magistrates and helpers, that is, by angels and demons. P. 67

SENAMUS: You have explained those matters elegantly and charmingly, but I do not know why demons pursue the bodies of Egyptians rather than Greeks or why they are accustomed to stir up tempests when only those bodies are stolen. Surely everyone knows that corpses are customarily carried on ships sometimes to Asia, Greece, and even to Italy without a storm.

FRIDERICUS: But those corpses were not yet buried. Theanus had come from Locris to Thebes by ship to bring back into Italy, at his friends' insistence, the corpse of Lysis, the Pythagorean, which Epaminondas had buried not long before. After he had performed the sacred rites he was warned by Lysis in a dream that he must not move the immovable, nor must he violate the tomb.

OCTAVIUS: Perhaps demons envy men[333] the salutary remedies which are recovered from those corpses of Egyptians. For they guard with unusual diligence the hidden treasures and kill those who dig them up. Philip Melanchthon wrote that while twelve magicians of Magdeburg were digging up a treasure, they were buried beneath a tower that had fallen; also many in the silver mine at Rosa had been killed by underground demons. George Agricola has many stories of this kind in which he relates that many people saw demons of pygmy size in the mines. The Pygmies hampered the digging of the ore by throwing dirt and rocks here and there, but they did not frighten away the miners provided they were not mocked. A long time ago Apuleius,[334] that greatest magician and poisoner, recalled this vexation. I find it strange, however, that no

[332] *qui* M

[333] *humano* M

[334] The reference to Pygmies throwing dirt and rocks is cited by Pliny, *Hist. nat.* VI. 22. Also see Philostratus, *Apoll.* III. 47; Herodotus, II. 32. 6.

one who had sought a treasure with a demon's help had ever found it or was enriched with the find.

Curtius: Surely by Roman law money is denied to those who search out treasures by means of detestable sacrifices or from any other forbidden art.

Fridericus: The Chaldeans say their terrestrial demons, supposedly the guardians of treasures and corpses, are more deceitful and cruel because they are farther from the purity of light and divine knowledge. Indeed
p. 68 Porphyry[335] wrote that these pant excessively with bloody breath. Ulysses under Circe's tutelage filled a ditch with the blood of victims and restrained the flying demons, which Homer calls spirits, from being sated with drinking blood before Tiresias poured a libation.[336]

Salomon: The divine law wholeheartedly curses this impiety and mischief that magicians used and those who thus feast on blood (*'al damin*) with demons.[337]

Fridericus: But if those demons are the souls of wicked men who either had placed all hope in their buried treasures secured from plunder, to be used later, or the souls of those who gave excessive attention to fattening their own bodies and filling their own lusts, always intent upon corpses which once they had earnestly loved and upon those treasures, let them pay just punishments with daily torment. Or demons may be the spirits of those who must pay the penalties for directing all their efforts to building palaces and towers with the blood of the people, who were enclosed and conquered by those same towers as if by prisons. It is not strange that voices, thunder, whispers and groans are heard when one comes to these places. Finally, I do not doubt that impure spirits wander around the foul and loathsome regions and stir up storms and winds.

Toralba: It is difficult to explain the causes of these things. A strange thing happened when I made a journey from Spain into France and observed everything, the fantastic, the ordinary, the insignificant. Passing over the Pyrenees, the highest range in all Europe, I found many secrets of nature, and most remarkable of all was a certain lake. If a rock was thrown into it, a moment later a black cloud darkened the calm sky and disturbed the whole region with lightning and heavy rains mixed with hail. On Monte Saco in the Pyrenees there is also a very ancient altar built from stones which hardly hold together. If anyone moves one of

[335] See Wolff, *Porphyry*, pp. 144–49, 218.

[336] *Odyss.* X. 516–30.

[337] Lev. 19:26; Ez. 33:25.

these stones from its place, suddenly thunder, lightning, and heavy rains are stirred up. And since this had often been ascertained with serious harm for the whole region, laws scrupulously decree that strangers be warned by the inhabitants that it is a capital offense to tamper[338] with these stones. Although I thought this was incredible, still I did not wish to test it at the risk of my life. A friend relieved me of this scruple by saying that since the crops have already been gathered you can try this without punishment. And so after tossing the altar stones here and there, we fled with no one the wiser. We had not gotten far into the next valley, however, before the most powerful thunder and lightning disturbed the whole sky with rain and hail. So it was not without cause that Thomas Aquinas, famous even among physicists, wrote that demons stir up lightning and thunder.

CURTIUS: Pliny and Strabo wrote something similar to this.[339] When the Cyrenaic rock was touched or a stone was thrown in a Dalmatian cave, the sky became disturbed with rain[340] and lightning, although I have heard these phenomena have now ceased. In like manner the oracles of Delphi and those which were customarily heard from the cave of Trophonius and Lebadius in Boeotia, became silent a long time ago. Tullius[341] wrote that nothing was more despicable than these oracles. Plutarch thought that the causes of this extended silence must be attributed to the death of demons.[342] P. 69

SENAMUS: If demons disturb the visible sky, the seas, lands, fires, if they terrify men with thunder, lightning, winds, whirlwinds, earthquakes and unexpected portents, if they hover over divine and human ambassadors, if then they regulate and overturn powers, states, cities, districts, families, finally if they are added to individual men as guardians and avengers, consider how great a multitude of demons and angels must be stationed up and down in all parts of the world and in individual places. If demons and angels are in every place on earth and heaven as overseers, vicars, and servants, we must give attention to where there would be enough store rooms to house them, since you have established that nothing is eternal and not even continual except God. Accordingly, we must provide for the marriages of angels and demons that from their unions their offspring are substituted in places for the dead and that, when magistrates resign, retire, or depart from their work as well as life,

338 *audeant* M

339 Pliny, *Hist. nat.* II. 44, Par. 115.

340 *imbribus* M

341 Cicero, *De divinat.* II. 70.

342 *De defectu oraculorum* 419B–420, 434C–F.

new officials take the places of the old. Indeed Fridericus has maintained that there were demons of each nature and sex, ephialtes and hyphialtes, in the union of witches with incubi and of magicians with succubi.

CURTIUS: Here I bring forth the authority of Plato.[343] Since he had posited that all souls had been created at the same time for immortality so that they might enter bodies at death, he said: "The number of souls will never increase or decrease, since none perishes." He even calls souls self-moving.[344] But if the mind is self-moving, it will also be self-existent and sufficient and good.[345] Toralba explained that these things were only appropriate to God alone.

TORALBA: Plato wrote the *Phaedo* when he was still a young man. When he was mature, he wrote the *Timaeus*, in which he seems to have changed his opinion. He has God speak thus: "I shall grant a begetting of souls, and I shall direct these into the body."[346] For he writes that the fixed number of immortal souls born from God are not increased or decreased by death but with a certain transmigration migrate from bodies to bodies.[347]

P 70 CORONAEUS: Senamus has proposed a very difficult but proper question. If Toralba will explain it with his usual care he will render a great service not only to Senamus but[348] to all of us.

TORALBA: Coronaeus, I have always considered it wrong to refuse you anything, and for that reason I much prefer to display my inadequacies with affability rather than refuse that burden which you have placed on my shoulders. But since a discussion of the origin of angels and demons, their place, condition and death seems far removed from positive proofs, surely we ought to seek an explanation of these things from the Hebrews, who drank divine secrets from those very fountains and sacred sources. Salomon, I believe, can surpass anyone in this matter. Although they were in different generations, Porphyry wrote to Boethius and Aristotle wrote to Callisthenes that the beginnings of all things and hidden scientific knowledge had proceeded from the Chaldeans.[349] They include under the Chaldean name the Hebrews[350] who are Chaldean in origin.[351] However, they have hidden those secrets of divine matters, treasures as it were, in

[343] *Phaedo* 77, Par. 22, 79D, 84B; also cf. *Phaedrus* 245C, Par. 24.

[344] Cf. Proclus, Prop. 20. See Dodds, *Proclus,* p. 22. Plato does not use the word *autokinētos* (self-moving).

[345] *Ibid.* Also see Proclus, Prop. 205, Prop. 16, and Prop. 40.

[346] *Timaeus* 42A; 69C, D.

[347] *Timaeus* 42B, *Phaedrus* 248D.

[348] *sed* MR

[349] Wolff, *Porphyry*, pp. 140 ff.

[350] *Hebraeos* MR

[351] Wolff, *Porphyry*, p. 185.

a certain occult discipline called Cabala which is inaccessible except to very few. The Greeks call it a recited piece[352] unless I'm mistaken.

SALOMON: I see that Toralba wishes to shake off with an honest pretext Coronaeus' suggestion which all of us eagerly anticipate. I acknowledge that the ancestors of our race were Chaldean and had migrated first into Phoenicia, which means Oriental in Hebrew. From Phoenicia Cadmus brought the alphabet into Greece.[353] After our ancestors returned to Chaldea as prisoners, they became acquainted with many things by divine communication. However, we received nothing which has not been common knowledge throughout the whole world and available to everyone.

After Salomon had said these things, the others were silent because they considered it an affront to his honor and dignity to disturb the elderly man. Coronaeus, however, broke the silence by saying: "We desire to know from you only that which your customs, your discipline, your laws allow. Since we cannot have a prolonged discussion in a limited time, it seems better to delay the matter and return better prepared for discussion." When they had entertained themselves by singing a hymn to the accompaniment of lyres and flutes, they wished each other well and departed.

[352] *akroama.* See Xenophon, *Symp.* II. 2; Aristotle, *Nicom. eth.* 1173B, Par. 18.
[353] Pliny, *Hist. nat.*, VII. 56. 57, Par. 192 ff.

BOOK III

P. 71 When Salomon had come to dinner a little late, Coronaeus looked at him and said: "Salomon, you must take care of your health and not feed your mind with so much study that you allow your body to grow weak from hunger."

Salomon: Since my age slows me down, I am afraid that I have inconvenienced you. I beg you to begin without me, Coronaeus, if I am late.

And so when they were seated, Coronaeus suggested that they pursue the reading of the *Phaedo* which they had begun on the previous days. When they came to the place where Plato wrote that souls loosed from bodies were brought to judgment by demons and their leaders and were punished according to their crimes,[1] Coronaeus requested that the passage be reread; after this the reading was concluded.

After dinner, they sang hymns and Coronaeus said: The difficulty of this passage makes me wonder why the ancient Greeks and Hebrews veiled their writings with such obscurity that even a wise man cannot really understand these precepts which are remarkably useful, first of all, and then enjoyable. For Aesop, that most ancient writer of fables, explained the universal conduct of human life with charming stories of animals. So Pythagoras,[2] by certain allegorical symbols and those songs

[1] *Phaedo*, 107D.

[2] Pythagoras was believed by his disciples to have enjoyed a closer relationship with the gods than other men. The esoteric instruction to which only his disciples were admitted probably had reference to the *orgies* or secret religious doctrines which were connected with the worship of Apollo and which held a prominent place in the Pythagorean system. For a concise account of Pythagoras, see William

which are called "golden words" because of their excellence, Orpheus, Homer, Hesiod, Trismegistus,[3] Terpander,[4] and finally the most ancient philosophers hid the principles of their wisdom under a veil of obscurity. We have observed that even sacred writings are full of allegories.

OCTAVIUS: Augustine[5] never spoke more truly than when he said a soul is miserably enslaved when it takes symbols for substance and cannot lift the mind's eye above the bodily nature to drink in the eternal light. He also said the authority of scripture is useful when it reveals different opinions.

FRIDERICUS: Since nothing is more useful than clarity, I think perhaps there is no fault in a writer worse than undue obscurity. The book of the *Apocalypse* is so involved with ambiguous[6] words and thoughts that the author, were he alive (learned men do not yet know who he was or what sort of man he was), would not even dare to state clearly what his writings mean. The emperor Julian, Porphyry, Proclus, and Celsus used this obscurity to malign the writings of Hebrews and Christians.

CORONAEUS: Since that style of writing was common to almost all the P. 72
ancients, we must be mindful not to seem to condemn the absent without a hearing. Although the emperor Julian,[7] who was called a transgressor, that is, a deserter, had defected from Christianity to paganism and dis-

Smith, *A Dictionary of Greek and Roman Biography and Mythology* (London, 1856), III, 616–25.

[3] Trismegistus is conflated with Hermes, who invented the lyre and along with his brother Apollo presided over the art of music. The earliest human cultivators of the musical art were the pupils of Apollo and even the children of Apollo and the Muses. Orpheus is the most important of Apollo's pupils and from the earliest times he is mentioned in connection with the worship of Apollo; later he is associated with Dionysus. Pherecydes mentions him as the ancestor of both Homer and Hesiod. Euripides constantly refers to Orpheus, and in *Rhesus* 943 he ascribes to him the origin of the sacred mysteries. See William Smith, *Dictionary* III, 59–62. See below, note 154.

[4] Terpander of Lesbos, who lived between 700 and 650 B.C., was the father of Greek music and hence of lyric poetry. He established the first musical school. Strabo says that he gave the lyre seven strings instead of four. Pausanias (III. 12. Par. 10), however, states that he added four strings to the existing seven.

[5] *Sancti Augustini operum tomus IV* (Paris, 1681). Enarratio in Psalmum CXXI 1384c; In Psalmum CIII. Enarratio, Sermo I 1142G.

[6] *ambiguitate* M

[7] Julian the Apostate (A.D. 331–363) abhorred Christianity mainly because he was completely devoted to Graeco-Roman civilization, and he felt compelled to rescue it from an alien uncultured Christianity. See above, Book II, note 316; see below, Book VI, note 158.

played hostility to Christianity, even he did not reject the book of Basil the Great before he had read and reread it. He said, in a letter of three words: "I examined it; I understood it; I condemned it."[8]

CURTIUS: I think that perhaps for two reasons the ancients veiled their principles of wisdom. In the first place, they did not desire to cast pearls before swine; secondly, they did not wish to cheapen most precious wisdom by its accessibility. For things commonly available, though precious, are despised. Indeed there is a letter extant in which Lysis the Pythagorean[9] severely complains that many promiscuously exposed rather secret philosophy to those who could not understand a cleansing of the mind even in a dream; these were as impious as if they had profaned the secret shrines of the Eleusinian mysteries[10] or mixed pure water with dirty. And so Porphyry wrote that Plotinus died of consumption because he had circulated the secrets of Ammonius, contrary to an oath.[11] Even Plato ordered the letters which he had written to Dion about the secrets of divine things to be burned, since things which are worthiest of admiration seem ridiculous.[12] In a letter to Archidamus in which he wrote about the nature of God, he said: "I must indicate to you an enigma."[13] Like-

[8] In letter 81 [Julian, Loeb Classics Library (abbreviated hereafter as LCL), III, 287] Julian restates his admiration for Basil; however, he says that since the Christians had destroyed three fine temples at Caesarea, they must restore the temples. Julian also confiscated the estates of the church and imposed a fine of three hundred pounds of gold.

[9] Lysis of Tarentum, a Pythagorean, after he migrated to Achaea and Thebes, became the teacher of Epaminondas. It is not certain that he wrote anything. See Hermann Diels, *Die Fragmente der Vorsokratiker*, 6th ed. (Berlin, 1954), I, 420–21.

[10] The Eleusinian mysteries, the most famous of all the old Greek mysteries are connected with the goddess Demeter. For a discussion of the mysteries, see *Oxford Classical Dictionary* (Oxford, 1961) (cited hereafter as *Ox. Class. Dict.*), pp. 313 and 593–94. Also Martin P. Nilsson, *A History of Greek Religion* (Oxford, 1949).

[11] Ammonius Saccas was born in Alexandria of Christian parents at the beginning of the third century. He was instructed in the catechetical schools of Alexandria, and under the Christian preceptors, Clement and Athenagoras, he acquired a great fondness for philosophical studies and desired to reconcile the different opinions of the philosophers. Porphyry states that he apostasized to the pagan religion, but Eusebius denies this. Ammonius founded a school with the purpose of ending the contentions of the philosophical world. He taught his select disciples, among whom was Plotinus, certain sublime doctrines and mystical practices. His disciples promised not to reveal the secrets which Ammonius taught, but rather to lodge them in their purified minds. This accounts for Longinus' statement that Ammonius left no writings. See Harry Thurston Peck, ed., *Harper's Dictionary of Classical Literature and Antiquities* (New York, 1929), pp. 66–67.

[12] Bodin is in error concerning the addressee of this epistle (*Epist.* II. 314B, C). Plato directed the letter to Dionysius, not Dion.

[13] *Epist.* II. 312D.

wise Porphyry said: "Take care not to allow yourself to communicate those things to wicked men for the danger would weigh heavier on you than on me, for the gods revealed themselves to mortals not openly but obscurely."[14]

SENAMUS: I have another opinion. Many affect obscurity in words to produce admiration for themselves. Dealers in unguents use Greek symbols, Arabic words, and Gothic letters to confuse their medicine and to keep the intelligent from mocking, for we do not easily carp at the things we do not understand. We have heard that Heraclitus wrote so obscurely about nature that Plato said there was need of a Delian swimmer.[15] For he instructed his students with one word: *skotēson* (make dark). We read that Aristotle[16] also had used this term in books of physical lectures. And although Plato wrote more clearly than the others, sometimes he wrote so obscurely that he could not possibly interpret his own writings about numbers, if he were alive. Especially difficult is the eighth book of the *Republic*. Both Theons, Plotinus, Proclus, Jamblichus, and Marsilius seemed to find it as difficult to interpret as milking a goat. What is more capricious than Egyptian deception? They concealed those absurdities in P. 73
hieroglyphs in such a way that they seemed like sacred oracles.

OCTAVIUS: Some like Lucilius[17] do not want their writings to be read by the learned or unlearned, lest some in ignorance reject the writings which they do not understand, and others malign them because they understand too well.

SALOMON: Senamus' complaint is against the sophists, not against the wise men and surely not against those who veiled the teachings of sacred wisdom in very obscure writings. Rabbi Moses, son of Maimon, implores

[14] Cf. Gustavus Wolff, ed., *Porphyrii de philosophia ex oraculis haurienda* (Hildesheim, 1962) (cited hereafter as Wolff, *Porphyry*), pp. 92–102. Also cf. Augustine, *De civ. Dei* XIX. 22–23.

[15] Aristotle called Heraclitus *ho skoteinos* in *De mundo* V. 396b. 20. Aristotle also mentions Heraclitus in a similar context in *Phys.* I. 2. 185a, 185b. Cicero, *De finibus* II. 5. 15, calls Heraclitus obscure. Also Lucretius, *De rerum nat.* I. 638–44. Heraclitus believed that knowledge is based upon perception by the senses and perfect knowledge is only given to the gods. Nature is constantly dividing and uniting herself, so that the multiplicity of opposites does not destroy the unity of the whole.

[16] See note 15.

[17] Caius Lucilius (148–103 B.C.), a Roman poet, is credited with the invention of satire. The fragments of Lucilius reveal a careless style and a fondness for obsolete and obscure words. Pierre Bayle, *A General Dictionary, Historical and Critical* (London, 1738) II, 207–12 says that Lucilius wished "his readers were neither ignorant, nor too learned." Bayle also cites the passage from Cicero (*De oratore* II. 6) in which these words of Lucilius are quoted.

his readers by his sacred writings not to allow hidden secrets to be made common or polluted by profane men.

SENAMUS: What if obscurity leads to error? Surely the works of Solomon, which[18] he wrote as allegories, seem absurd to many. What does this saying—"The evil of man is superior to the goodness of women"—accomplish? Indeed it turns many women away from the reading of the holy scripture.

SALOMON: The Hebrew word *Ra'* means evil and deformed, as *ṭov* means good and beautiful which the Academicians call *kalon kai agathon*. Thus they say that Sara was sought by kings as a concubine because she was best, that is, very beautiful.[19] Therefore a wise man signified by allegory that ugly men surpass beautiful women; also that the blandishments of women are worse than the harsh words of men; likewise souls excel bodies. Woman in an allegorical sense[20] everywhere[21] means body. Also the intellectual faculty, however base it might be, excels lust, which is called the brute and mortal soul. A passage in *Ecclesiastes*[22] is also to the point: "Among a thousand men one wise man was found, but none from all women." This description of women cannot be understood literally, since Deborah[23] in her lifetime and Hulda[24] in Josiah's time alone enjoyed the gifts of prophecy and divine wisdom among sixty thousand uninspired men. The word man indicates natural form, and woman indicates matter, which also is often called in *Proverbs*[25] *meretrix* (harlot), since as a harlot takes pleasure in a number of men, so matter delights in a number of forms. King Solomon's writings are full of allegories, which Philo,[26] following moral considerations, has energetically interpreted while Leo the Hebrew sought for natural interpretations. Although Rabbi Moses, the son of Maimon, and the writers of the Talmud clarified each interpretation, they are rather obscure; moreover, they would not have recorded their writings had they not feared loss of the books. Since that teaching is perceived only by hearing, it is called *qabbalah* (tradition). This is what Esdras[27] meant when he said:[28] "Some things you will make

[18] *quas* M [19] Gen. 12:10–15. [20] *sensu* M
[21] *ubique* M [22] Eccles. 7:28. [23] Judges 4:4–5.
[24] IV Kings (II Kings) 22:14; II Paralip. (II Chron.) 34:22.
[25] Prov. 29:3.
[26] Cf. Philo Judaeus, *Legum Allegoriae*.
[27] This quotation is from IV Esdras or the Apocalypse of Esdras (Ezra). See G. H. Box, ed., *The Ezra Apocalypse* (London, 1912) part I (Vision II) chapter 5, p. 52. It is a book of visions ascribed to Ezra the Scribe, written between A.D. 95–100. The book is composed of seven visions, the first three being in the form of dialogues

common knowledge; others you will relate to the wise." Just as the people worshipped in the courtyard of the temple separately from the Levites, P. 74 the priests but not the other Levites had access within the curtain, and only the high priest approached that most sacred place where the Ark of the Covenant was housed.[29] In like manner the sacred books were written in such a way that those things which pertained to the salvation of everyone such as the decalogue and everything connected with it are easily understood by all; namely commands, prohibitions, penalties, judgments, festivals, rites, customs are all so clearly explained in 613 chapters that no one could misinterpret them. The occult rites and sacrifices which have less to do with salvation are understood only by the learned, and the knowledge of natural mysteries, the Cabala, is understood only by the most learned. Finally the most difficult of all pertains to the chariot which is described by Ezechiel in a wondrous portrayal of the heavenly bodies and most holy matters.[30] Moses, whom we call the open eagle[31] (*aperta aquila*), was content to scratch the surface but was unwilling to explain more secret things.

SENAMUS: If these things are so sublime that they have no utility or purpose for us, we should follow the advice of the Psalmist[32] when he said: "I have not sought out miracles or matters beyond my comprehension, but I have lived humbly." But if these things are likely to be helpful for divine knowledge and wisdom, it would be the part of a spiteful mind, one contemptible because of its very envy, to snatch the hidden treasures from human use and by the ambiguity of language more and more confuse the minds of the unskilled.

---

between Ezra and the angel Uriel, dealing with the destruction of the Temple and Jerusalem and with theodicy. In the seventh vision Ezra receives the Torah, the 24 books of the Bible, and the seventy books of secret, apocalyptic lore, and then prepares for his assumption to heaven. The author is deeply concerned with how God could create man with an "evil heart," and when giving him the Torah, not remove this evil heart. After much questioning the angel can only assert that God's ways are inscrutable, that He rejoices in a few righteous ones, and that Ezra and those like him are assured of salvation. Ezra is one of the five men whose piety is especially extolled by the rabbis, and he figures in the Talmud, the Koran, and the writings of the church fathers. See *Encyclopaedia Judaica* (Jerusalem, 1971), VI, 1104–1109.

[28] *diceret* M

[29] III Kings (I Kings) 8:5–10.

[30] Ezech. 1:4–28.

[31] See Ex. 19:4; Deut. 32:11.

[32] This reference, which I could not verify in the *Psalms*, is very close to the words of the prophet Micah. See Micah 6:8.

SALOMON: In sticking to the simile of a treasure, you have read the charmingly fashioned fable of Aesop[33] in which a father on his deathbed comforted his children by saying that, although he did not have wealth and land to leave them, a treasure was hidden in his vineyard which would abundantly relieve their need. After the father's death the sons sought the treasure with the greatest eagerness and effort. Although they never found it, they made the paternal vineyard very productive by digging up the weeds and therefore reaped the fullest harvest. And so if we eagerly read divine words and think often on our reading, it will be possible to bring forth incredible treasures. For thus did that royal voice of David, in the beginning of his psalms, proclaim happiness for that man who constantly contemplates divine laws day and night.[34] Likewise he prayed that God would lift the veil from his eyes so that he could view the marvelous wisdom comprehended in divine laws.[35] Therefore we must exercise our mind on rather obscure divine words so that we may not only abstain from faults and embrace true glory but also seek health for the body, prudence and wisdom for the mind, and the closest union
P. 75 with immortal God. In praising God it is a very serious mistake to let the secrets of God grow stale in their commonness, as Solomon astutely observed. "The glory of God is to conceal the secrets; the glory of kings is to seek the secrets."[36] Tobias said it in a slightly different manner: "It is noble to conceal the secrets of kings and to praise the works of God."[37] For the works of God lie open to the eyes of all, the secrets to only a few.

SENAMUS: But obscurity seems to keep not only good men from reading but also encourages wicked men to scorn divine matters. For when Porphyry could in no way pluck the fruits from the tree of the knowledge of good and evil, he denied that fruit had any value in those gardens of delights, because it was very pleasing to see and savor but was a death-bearing pest to man whom God had placed in the gardens' cooling shade.[38] Furthermore, men ought not be kept from a knowledge of wisdom by the forbidden fruit, since sagacity alone, the guide of human life, can

[33] Collections of stories are attributed to Aesop, a figure so legendary that it is open to doubt whether he committed anything to writing. *Encyclopaedia Britannica* (11th ed.) I, 276. A valiant effort to sort out the tradition is Ben Edwin Perry, *Aesopica* (Urbana, Ill., 1952). Among Jews the "Fox Fables," compiled by Berachiah, have much in common with the "Ysopet" of Marie de France. He is thought to have lived in Provence in the 13th century. *Encyclopaedia Britannica* (11th ed.) XIII, 174.

[34] Psalm 1:1–2.

[35] Psalm 68 (69):18.

[36] Prov. 25:2.

[37] Tobias 12:7.

[38] See J. Bidez, *Vie de Porphyre* (Hildesheim, 1964), pp. 92–93.

separate the wicked from the noble. An insult to God the best and greatest is the statement that God commanded the fruit of the tree of life be snatched away from the trees of the garden so that Adam might not have eternal life if he should eat of it.[39] Finally the serpent's conversation with the woman and God's conversation with men seem ridiculous and incredible.[40]

SALOMON: In discussions of divine affairs, first we must see that nothing escapes anyone heedlessly since nothing can be more serious or damnable. This usually happens to those who, inflated with pride in human affairs and subtleties of dialectics, think they can understand all things above, below, first, and last with the sharp keenness of their own ability, although no one can attain this without divine aid. The teacher of wisdom states it succinctly:[41] "The mocker seeks wisdom, but in vain." Yet Porphyry,[42] perhaps through ignorance or impiety, maligned divine oracles, as if the law giver meant that God envied men wisdom and a blessed life. In a subsequent book he wrote that Bezaleel had been abundantly endowed by immortal God with divine spirit, wisdom, prudence, knowledge and all manner of arts, in which gifts all virtues are completely contained. Indeed, the divine spirit is granted by the gift and concession of God to illuminate the darkness of the human mind and to see into the future. Moreover, wisdom separates piety from impiety; intelligence separates the good from the evil; knowledge separates the true from the false, and art the useful from the useless. When the prince of wisdom was encouraged by immortal God to seek from Him what he wished, that one sought intelligence, so that he could separate the base from the noble and thereby urge men to the fear and worship of God.[43] He said: "Since God abundantly heaps up wisdom, knowledge and prudence are from Him alone."[44] Likewise in another place: "The reward of the just P. 76
is the tree of life";[45] he interprets this as wisdom. So far is He from keeping man from the life-giving fruit that He even challenged him by these words: "Perhaps Adam will pluck[46] the life-giving fruit so that by eating of it he may live eternally."[47] The Chaldean paraphrast in a similar vein used an elegant phrase. God turned to Isaiah and said: "Tell the people this. By hearing, hear, and by seeing, see, but still do not under-

[39] Gen. 2:16–17.
[40] Gen. 3:1–6, 9–24.
[41] Prov. 14:6.
[42] Cf. *De civ. Dei* X. 9, 11, 21, 23, 26.
[43] III Kings (I Kings) 3:5–9.
[44] Prov. 2:6.
[45] Prov. 3:18.
[46] *decerpet* MR
[47] Ex. 3:22.

stand. Render the heart of that nation dull and close their ears; besmear their eyes lest perhaps it hear, see, understand, and be restored to salvation having turned to Me."[48] The reasoning behind these words is that we always struggle against the forbidden and desire anything more eagerly when we see it snatched from us or forbidden to us. Therefore, He taught Moses and Isaiah by what arts they were to call back miserable men from their criminal and depraved lives to true honor and to restore them to salvation. "Beware of giving attention to divine laws; beware of leaning on the pursuits of wisdom lest you attain an eternal and blessed life." This speech was usually very beneficial among wicked and lustful men.

SENAMUS: Nothing has challenged me for a longer time than the allegory of the tree and the serpent.[49]

SALOMON: Greek and Latin interpreters did not know this allegory. Although a certain Hebrew[50] revealed its hidden meaning, still all his effort would be in vain unless God opened our minds for an understanding of these things.

FRIDERICUS: I think it is dangerous to interpret the sacred scriptures allegorically lest the history of the deeds vanish into fables.

OCTAVIUS: Fridericus, do you think that there was any conversation between the woman and the serpent? They contend with such implacable hatred that woman suffers abortion from only a glance of the serpent and that the serpent seeks out and pursues woman alone in a throng of men for vengeance. Nothing truer than this can be said: "The letter kills, the spirit enlivens."[51]

SALOMON: Sacred books often recount history straightforwardly—for example, a census and appointment of leaders for their own tribes.[52] History is specific, but allegory lies hidden outside history. An example is Sara's advice that her maid and son must be cast out.[53] Clever theologians explain that desire struggling against virtues, with its son the sin, must be cast aside by its master, reason; when an angel orders the maid to return home and serve Sara they explain this as the compliance of passion and the mastery of reason with the help of the agent intellect.[54] Hence,
P. 77 that voice of God spoke to Abraham: "Do whatever things Sara has spoken to you,"[55] that is, reason. When Sara said that the maid's son

[48] Isaiah 6:9–10.

[49] The allegory which perplexes Senamus is of the tree of knowledge of good and evil and the serpent's temptation of Eve. See Gen. 1:29; 2:9, 16–17; 3:1–13.

[50] Philo Judaeus in *Legum Allegoria.*

[51] II Corinth. 3:6.

[52] Cf. Numbers.

[53] Gen. 21:10.

[54] Gen. 16:9.

[55] Gen. 21:12.

would not be an heir,[56] she also signified that those who yielded to sins and lust would never claim divine rewards. Visions and divine dreams are often stated as facts. For this reason some, believing that God speaks to men who are vigilant, scuttled their ships and others even wrecked theirs. God surely spoke to no one when he was awake except Moses,[57] and then not ambiguously, because we have the witness of God's clear voice in the law itself. Therefore we should understand that the voice of the angel who spoke to Balaam or the voice of the ass came to him in a dream,[58] as[59] we should interpret all the foreknowledge given to Abraham and all the prophets, with the one exception of Moses, to whom God spoke when he was awake. Therefore, the brightest light shines to sever the darkness of the sacred scriptures. Sometimes pure allegory is not difficult to interpret—for example, when the law orders that the prepuce of the heart be circumcised.[60] Often words have a three-fold meaning; the vulgar meaning is accommodated to the understanding of the unlearned. When Solomon forbids haughtiness and arrogance to be displayed[61] before the king, in its deeper meaning, the scripture applies to God who must be approached with abject and humble mien; indeed Solomon always indicates God by the name of king[62] unless the word "God" is joined with "king," as for example—"The heart of the king is in the hand of God."[63] Moreover, God is indicated in these words: "Do not censure the king in your thought nor censure the rich man in your bedchambers; for the birds of heaven will carry the word, and a bird will make it common."[64] In these words he forbids one to think impiously about God. For in sacred allegories bed means the human body, and the voice of birds indicated demons. Birds are sometimes even[65] taken to be angels; in Isaiah angels and demons are often referred to as birds.[66] Indeed both, as guardians and lictors for men, unfold hidden thoughts and secret meanings lest any crime be unpunished or pious knowledge be unrewarded. The Chaldean paraphrast interpreted these words of Solomon about the angels Raziel and Elias who, he said, revealed all very secret crimes.[67]

SENAMUS: Salomon interprets Solomon very wisely, but who could have foretold this interpretation?

OCTAVIUS: I think this passage about birds which reveal hidden mean-

[56] Gen. 21:10.
[57] Numbers 12:6–8.
[58] Numbers 22:23–35.
[59] *ut* MR
[60] Deut. 10:16.
[61] Prov. 25:6.
[62] *regis appellatione* MR
[63] Prov. 21:1.
[64] Eccles. 10:20.
[65] *interdum etiam* MR
[66] Isaiah 46:11.
[67] Cf. Eccles. 10:20.

ings and knowledge to the king pertains to those kings who had joined themselves to demons or vice versa and thereby knew all the words, deeds, and thoughts of all as from those spies whom the ancients called the eyes of tyrants and ears of rulers, for tyrants have no secret that is more hidden.

P. 78 SENAMUS: If those birds, whether demonic or angelic, had so much power, why were they unwilling to reveal Piso's conspiracy[68] to Nero, the greatest of the profaners and tyrants, since he had joined himself to Simon the Magician and to demons, as Pliny and Irenaeus say.[69]

FRIDERICUS: Demons do nothing unless ordered, and they reveal the secret sins of no one unless by the command of God and the power of the higher angels.

CORONAEUS: Since it is in God's realm alone to search out the intimate feelings of all men and the hidden recesses of the souls,[70] as King Solomon declares openly in a dedicatory speech, why is there need for angels and demons to communicate the secret shadows of the mind?

CURTIUS: The charming speech of Thales comes to mind; when he was asked whether a man could conceal his wicked deeds from God, he said: "Not even the intention."[71] The Greeks say it even better: "If a man could escape the gods' notice doing wrong." He replied, "Not even intending to do wrong."

SALOMON: We have said before, and we ought to say more often, that God's majesty seems in some way more awesome because of the services of angels and demons than if He cared for all things in and of Himself as He is able to do. Although He alone uncovers the most hidden meanings, still individual angels acting as guardians for individual men reveal intimate meanings, not the thoughts of others. Likewise demons with whom magicians have a wicked alliance know completely their feelings. Granted that some magicians in a brief moment are turned to a proper knowledge and fear of God, then suddenly confess they are disturbed by a demon. But if a good man has turned to a wrong thought, suddenly he recognizes in the recesses of his soul a teacher and guide who leads

[68] Gaius Calpurnius Piso, scion of a wealthy and distinguished family, lived in magnificent style and was exceedingly popular in Rome because of his cultivated manners and oratorical skills. It seems strange that he should be at the head of the Pisonian conspiracy against Nero in A.D. 65. When the plot was discovered, Piso was forced to suicide. See Suetonius, *Nero* 36.

[69] Pliny, *Hist. nat.* XXX. 5–6. Irenaeus, *Adv. Haeres.* I. 20. Also cf. Justin, *Apol.* I. 26; Tertullian, *Apol.* I. 13. Irenaeus, Tertullian, and Justin.

[70] III Kings (I Kings) 8:39.

[71] Diels, *Frag. der Vorsokrat.* (6th ed.), pp. 67–81.

him away from the base thought either by the gentlest twitching and humming in his right ear or by a prick, which the poet described in these words: "Cynthius plucks my ear and advises me."[72] Socrates used to explain that this was done by a friendly demon or rather by an angel who pulled his right ear in assent and his left ear for dissent; sometimes the angel advised him with a bright disc or a fiery sign at night or by the gentlest clanking.[73] These things are very easily understood by those who allow themselves to be led by the spirit of God. If one should not obey the warnings, he is terrified by morning dreams, which are called morning reproofs by the Hebrews.[74] If he is not turned away from his wicked thoughts by this warning, an angel demands punishment. When the accusation is made, lest the innocent seem to be condemned, or any crime left unavenged unless repented, judgments are carried out by demons, as though by officials who demand their due prey which God grants to them. This statement is to the point: "The lion rises from his own bed; the robber of nations has arisen."[75] Likewise: "The lion from the forest struck them; the wolf destroyed them at evening; the panther watches above their cities."[76] Likewise: "Who gives food to the young ravens crying out to him?"[77] That is—to the executioners of divine majesty and the torturers seeking vindication of crimes. We also read: "Spirits which shake the whips of their own fury are created for vengeance."[78] Likewise: "God sent an evil spirit among Abimelech and the citizens of Sichem."[79]

P. 79

SENAMUS: The most ancient theologians say that when young ravens are deserted by their parents, they are nourished by divine goodness and care. This explains the question, "Who gives food to the young ravens?"

SALOMON: The Latin theologians were in error because they did not comprehend the Hebraic phrase which is also common to Greek. For they took sons of ravens for ravens, as sons of prophets for prophets, sons of blood and the unjust for the wicked and murderers. For thus in Hebrew *Bené 'adam* (sons of men) means men, and in Greek *paides iatrōn* (sons of physicians) means physicians. This statement illustrates the point: "Who do they say the son of man is?"[80] This is equivalent to "Who do they say man is?"

[72] Vergil, *Ec.* VI. 4.

[73] Plato, *Apol.* 19D, 31B, Plutarch, *De daemone Socratis* 588C.

[74] Cf. Athenagoras, *Expos.* Psalm 90:6 [J. P. Migne, *Patrologia Graeca* (Paris, 1857), XXVII. 4018], Cyril, Psalm 90:6 (Migne, *Patrologia Graeca* LXIX. 1220AB).

[75] Jer. 4:7.
[76] Jer. 5:6.
[77] Psalm 147:9.
[78] Psalm 78:49.
[79] Judg. 9:23.
[80] Matt. 16:13.

TORALBA: Salomon has freed me from this error, and I openly acknowledge it. However, I thought it strange why ravens were believed to desert their young if they were not completely black, since many kinds of young animals seem to have a color different from their parents, and yet the parents earnestly care for them. Indeed the swans who in old age are completely white do not drive away their black offspring, and ravens do not allow their young to starve. Aristotle and Pliny said that the hatching crow is fed by the male, but when it flies, it is fed by the mother.[81] Thus Apollonius according to Philostratus moderately censured Euripides' verse by saying that the soul resides in their children in regard to all living things, since he (Euripides) granted this only in regard to men.[82]

SALOMON: In the same vein the Psalmist wrote that God bestowed food upon the hungry lion.[83] Why did He give food to the lion, the most ferocious of animals, who eats only every four days, or at most every other day, rather than to sheep and goats, which are very useful to men?[84] Elsewhere we read about the lions' whelps.[85] "Will you prepare sufficient food for the lions whelps?"[86] If the truth be spoken about the whelps, the mother's udders provide sufficient nourishment for her whelps. And yet in another passage about ravens this common error can be easily refuted in the following passage: "Who prepares game for the raven, when its young cry to God and fly thither and yon without food?"[87] But the young recently shut out do not wander.[88] These words surely pertain to demons who seek the spoil of the wicked only with divine consent. The words of Solomon are also revealing: "The ravens at the rivers should pluck out the eye, and eagles devour him, who mocks his father
P. 80 and scorns reverence for his mother."[89] This allegory, which is beyond the

[81] Aristotle, *Hist. Anim.* VI. 6. 563b. 12; Pliny, *Hist. nat.* X. 14.

[82] Apollonius Tyaneus, a Pythagorean philosopher who was born about 4 B.C. at Tyana in Cappadocia and about whom Philostratus (Flavius Philostratus, 3rd century A.D.) wrote the romantic *Life of Apollonius of Tyana*, directed his efforts toward reestablishing the old religion on a Pythagorean basis by purifying paganism from the corruptions which he claimed the fables of the poets had introduced. See Smith, *Dictionary* (1844 ed.) I, 242-44. Philostratus, *Life of Apollonius* III. 14, relates that Apollonius says that Euripides' verse (*Andromache* 418–19) would have been truer if he had let Andromache say that for all living things life resides in their children.

[83] Psalm 103 (104):21.

[84] On the nature and habits of lions, see Pliny, *Hist. nat.* VIII. 19–21.

[85] Job 38:39.

[86] *Tune pastum sufficientem parabis catulis leonum?* MR missing in N

[87] Job 38:41.

[88] *At pulli recentes exclusi non aberrant* MR missing in N

[89] Prov. 30:17.

common interpretation means that the elementary demons of this world, which, in fact, are a torrent of flowing matter, with a blindness of soul and passion torture and blot out reason from those who insult God, the parent of all things, and do violence to the pious mother, the laws of nature. Solomon uses the word "father" as God and "mother" as nature. It is also significant that he said eye, not eyes; for in the singular eye means mind. So also Bileam[89a] the prophet was said to see very clearly with one eye, since he directed and instructed his tribes' remarkable progress for about 3,000 years, according to the Chaldean interpreter.

SENAMUS: If one may use the word "black demons" in speaking of ravens, one may also use "white demons" for swans, which live in Africa, according to Leo the African.[90] This distinguishes the Ethiopians from demons—in color, I suppose.

OCTAVIUS: Although not only contemporary writers but also the most ancient authors have maintained that demons are more often black, and the demons which Dion, Cassius of Parma,[90a] and magicians very often saw were of this sort,[91] still I do not think that for this reason demons are indicated by the word raven, but because demons hover over cadavers like ravens. This was described earlier about the Egyptian corpses and the ghosts which wander around tombs and gibbets.

FRIDERICUS: Demons also use corpses for men's ruin and for the wicked copulations with magicians. Augustine strongly confirms this and says that it is the height of folly to deny demons' copulations with human beings.[92] Sprenger also cites numerous examples of many witches who, before their execution, confessed that they copulated with demons.[93] Nay, even Franciscus Picus[93a] writes that two priests in his time were burned at the stake; one admitted[94] that he had lived with demons for more than thirty years, the other for more than forty. Before each was convicted, he confessed that he had sacrificed many infants to demons and they

89a Bileam or Balaam was one of seven gentile prophets and was considered the equal of Moses. See *Encyclopaedia Judaica* 13,1176. Also Num. 22–24.

90 *In descriptione Africae.*

90a On Dion see Plato *Epist.* VII and VIII, also Plutarch, *Dion.* Cassius of Parma was one of Caesar's murderers. Horace (*Epist.* I. 4. 3.) says that Tibullus was a better poet than Cassius.

91 Cf. Apuleius, *De deo Socratis*, Prologus 110.

92 Cf. *De civ. Dei* I. 11; XVIII. 17. *De trinitate* III.

93 Heinrich Kramer and James Sprenger, *Malleus maleficarum*, translated by Rev. Montague Summers (New York, 1971), Part I, Quest. 3; Part II, Quest. 1, Chapter 4.

93a See below, Book V, p. 282, note 224.

94 *confitebantur* MR

customarily ate the infants' flesh and drank their blood.[95] This story reminds us of what Aristotle wrote about the woman in Pontus who ate the embryos of pregnant women.[96] Horace makes a remark in the *Ars poetica* apropos of this: "Lest he draw a live boy from the womb to be dinner for a witch."[97]

CURTIUS: I recall that Pausanias[98] in Phocaea said that Cretan laws warned that the corpses of married men who had slept with these widows
p. 81 would be punished, as though alive, for a capital crime. Their heads would be pierced with a red hot sword, and their bodies would be burned; in no other way could they be kept from copulation with the living. For this reason demons have been called ravens.[99]

OCTAVIUS: Therefore it was reasonable that demons used recovered corpses for copulation, and for that reason were called ravens, because they pursued corpses and appeared black.

SALOMON: Whatever the reason may be, it is clear that the people of Ethiopia are also called demons in the scriptures,[100] for the seventy-two interpreters interpret the word *'ayyim*, demons, as Ethiopians, for the Ethiopians fall down before that one[101] and in another place: "You have broken the head of Leviathan; you have given him as a bait to the people of Ethiopia."[102] Here they interpret *'ayam*, the proper term for demons, as Ethiopians to conceal the secret by an ambiguous word. But the seventy-two interpreters translate dragon as Leviathan, who is said to be the leader of those who demand not the corpses of the wicked but the minds for punishment. Behemoth is said to be the leader of those demons who take vengeance on bodies. Each is indicated by Ezechiel[103] under the

[95] *et eorum carnibus ac sanguine vesci consuevisse* MR

[96] I cannot verify this in Aristotle, but such a charge is leveled against witches in a famous book on witchcraft. See Reginald Scot, *The Discoverie of Witchcraft* (London, 1930).

[97] *Ars. Poet.* 340.

[98] Pausanias mentions the prohibition of second marriage in Corinth (II. 21. 7); on the influence of Cretan law, through Lycurgus in Laconia (III. 2. 5–7). On widows not allowed to marry again, see Pausanias, *Description of Greece*, translated by J. G. Frazer (London, 1898) III, 198–200. On Cretan laws also see Plato, *Leges* I. 630–38d and VIII. Neither "demons" nor "ravens" are of sufficient significance to be indexed either by Frazer or by LCL.

[99] *korakinas* N var.

[100] See Isaiah 18:1–7; Ezech. 30:4–5.

[101] *Coram illo procident Aetiopes* MR. Prof. Morton Smith states that *'ayyim* is not a Hebrew word and no such form occurs in the passages cited. In Isaiah 11:15 there occurs *'ayam* which is of uncertain meaning though taken by the interpreters to mean powerful (*biaios*).

[102] Psalm 73 (74):14.

[103] Ezech. 29:3–5.

names of the kings of Egypt and Assyria in these words: "Thus the Lord said: 'Lo I am against you, Pharaoh, king of Egypt, great dragon, lying in the midst of your rivers, you who have said—This is my river, and I have made it for myself. But I shall put hooks in your jaws and I shall make the fish of your rivers cling to your scales; I shall strike you in the desert and all the fish of your rivers; you will be food for the beasts of the land and the birds of heaven.'" But Isaiah[104] speaks more clearly: "In that day God will visit with His heavy sword, sturdy as an oak, Leviathan the swift serpent and Leviathan the gliding serpent and will slay the sea monster." Esdras explained Leviathan's and Behemoth's power, which had been expressed allegorically by God's words to Job. Esdras said:[105] "Then You prepared two animals; to one You gave the name Behemoth; the other You called Leviathan and separated one from the other. You assigned Behemoth one part which became dry on the third day and habitable. But to Leviathan You granted a wet part and fashioned the beast to devour those whom You wished." For Ezechiel says: "The river is mine,"[106] which is to say, the destruction of forms in changing and fleeting matter. Nevertheless, he is said to have been created by God in the beginning. "I have created a devastator for destruction."[107] God speaks similarly to Pharaoh. "I have stirred you up to show My power against you and to spread the glory of My name throughout the P. 82
whole world."[108] Outside of historical truth, Ezechiel explains that Leviathan is signified by the name of Pharaoh who disturbed the forms of flowing matter. Nevertheless, the greatest and best parent of nature constantly repairs and renews them by his own goodness. Likewise when Leviathan sneezes, the light gleams forth and from his mouth the fiery torches originate,[109] and the sea becomes hard as mortar. He has no master on the earth nor fears anything, and he leads the king against the haughty.[110] The word sneeze here means thunder, light and fire mean lightning, the hardship of the sea means storms and hurricanes.

CURTIUS: I believe Orpheus, the father of magicians called this Leviathan the greatest snake.[111] Pherecydes[112] called him Ophyoneus, from

[104] Isaiah 27:1. [105] See Job 40:15–32. [106] Ezech. 29:3.
[107] Ezech. 32:1–12. [108] Ezech. 29:6, 16; 30:8–19; 32:15.
[109] *exoriuntur* M
[110] For this awesome description of Leviathan, see Job 41:10–26.
[111] According to legend, Orpheus' wife, Eurydice, was killed by the bite of a snake.
[112] Pherecydes of Syrus (fl. c. 550 B.C.) was a mythologist and cosmologist who wrote about the origin of the world at the instance of Zeus, Chronos, and Chthonie. Diels, *Frag. der Vorsokrat.* (6th ed.), I. 43–51.

whence developed the ancient cult of Asculapius the snake, whom many people still invoke in public[113] supplications.

SENAMUS: These examples are well and good, Salomon, provided they can be demonstrated.

OCTAVIUS: The hidden secrets of sacred philosophy and the divine oracles of the holiest prophets seem more trustworthy to me than Euclid's proofs which rely only on many postulates and concessions.

TORALBA: In matters so difficult and foreign to common understanding we ought not to seek sophisticated subtlety in our arguments but rather those things which have been handed down by wise men who have very wisely sought the secrets of God.

CORONAEUS: We are not examining the hierarchies of angels and the storehouses of demons which I am not sure have been quite sanely described by Dionysius and Wier.[114]

SALOMON: I would desire to affirm nothing in matters so obscure nor mention anything else because these matters are better known to you than to me, inasmuch as you have drunk from the same springs as I. Of course eternal God alone created not only angels but also demons. As the two chief angels, the Seraphim, are said to stand near the most powerful Creator for distributing bounty, light, rewards, and the life of the lower angels and stars,[115] so also there are two angels opposed to them, Leviathan and Behemoth,[116] chief officials of higher magistracies as it were, to inflict punishments or bring tribulations whether by damage to crops or destruction of cattle or slaughter of wars or devastation of land
P. 83 or plagues or ruin of cities or upset of the whole elementary world. Yet these misfortunes are wrought by divine decrees lest any one blame demons or fear them. The author of Proverbs says:[117] "Do not accuse the servant in the presence of his master lest by chance he malign you and cause you harm." This allegory shows that we must not accuse angels and demons who bring no calamities unless ordered and follow only the decrees ordered by God. Furthermore, each man must accuse himself and admit his own faults.[118]

FRIDERICUS: There is a district in Mainz which some demon who was posing as a stone cutter harassed for three years. Finally the demon

[113] *publicis* MR
[114] Dionysius, *De coelorum hierarchia*; Wier, *De praestigiis.*
[115] Isaiah 6:1–13; Zach. 4:1–14.
[116] See notes 105–108. Also Job 40:15–32; 41:1–26.
[117] Prov. 30:10.
[118] Sigebertus Vincentius, *In Speculo* LXXV. 38.

declared that the people were suffering because of the sins of a single man whom he named, so that this man had to leave his home. Moreover, if a home received him, that home was consumed by fire. In a short time all the homes of the district were destroyed by flames.

SALOMON: Those who fear demons commit a serious offense. Even more sinful are those who worship demons to escape a flogging, as though demons were judges for punishments which are ordained. This despicable impiety advanced because some thought Beelzebub was the prince of this world. From this came the most wicked heresy of the Manichaeans who thought there were two princes of the world. To what end did God say to Pharaoh:[119] "That you may know that I am Lord of the earth." And likewise: "That Leviathan, whom you have fashioned for mockery."[120] Thus we must believe that the mastery of the elementary world, of heavenly bodies, of angels and demons is in the hands of eternal God. Moreover, He mocks Leviathan when He renews by his continued goodness and power the things which have been corrupted or damaged by the work of demons. For the more Pharaoh in a demonic state was killing the Israelite males and forced the people to serve himself so that they would not worship God, the more the people increased with remarkable fecundity.[121] Thus, the more the manifold forms of flowing matter are corrupted by demons, the more divine fecundity shows itself in renewing and regenerating them. The prophet mocks at Leviathan in these words:[122] "How you have fallen from the sky, O Lucifer, son of morning, thrown to the earth, although you said you would climb to heaven near the region of Aquilo to become equal to all-powerful God; but you have been cast down to the depths, hurled into the lake." Likewise: "That one is He who made the earth tremble, who destroyed kingdoms, who made the world like a desert, who laid waste cities."[123] The obscurity of this passage can be illuminated if we say that the son of morning is Leviathan, who is called the founder in one place and in another the first born, or the prefect of death or corruption[124]—that is, he is called *beḵor mawet* [the first born of death]. For as privation preceded an acquired perfect
condition, so dawn preceded the sun, shadows light. Likewise it is not P. 84
consistent with divine majesty to make the earth tremble, to disturb kingdoms, and to destroy cities completely to return the world to solitude. It is rather the work of a destroyer, executioner, or lictor. The scriptures

[119] Ex. 9:29.
[120] Psalm 103 (104):26.
[121] Ex. 1:12.
[122] Isaiah 14:12–15.
[123] Isaiah 14:16–17.
[124] Job 18:13.

say that Lucifer was cast down to the lower regions.[125] Therefore Leviathan or Asmodaeus could not destroy angels and heavenly stars, because they descended into the lake, according to Isaiah,[126] or into the sea, as Job says,[127] or into the rivers, as Ezechiel says,[128] that is, in this flowing region of elements, and they were denied access to the heavens. Pertinent to this is Satan's statement. When God asked him in the council of angels whence he came, he said that he had passed over the earth;[129] he did not say heaven.

CURTIUS: Unless I am mistaken, this is what the ancient Greeks, who filled everything with fables, mean by saying that Juno, guardian of the air, kept the Furies from flying into heaven.[130] In other words, demons were cast headlong from the clouds by angels; they fell in flames[131] with a clap of thunder and destroyed or corrupted these sublunary bodies.

CORONAEUS: When then will there be a solitude of this elemental world?[132]

SALOMON: The answer lies hidden in the secrets of divine majesty, and we can only conjecture (for I think nothing should be affirmed in this matter) how tranquility and rest from agriculture are ordered by divine law for the holy earth.[133] For this reason Alexander the Great and Julius Caesar did not demand tribute from our ancestors every seventh year.[134] So the deprivation of the elementary world will happen after 6,000 years, and the elementary world will not be destroyed by floods as in the time of Noah, when the land was covered with an abyss of waters in the second month. The Chaldeans call this month Bul, that is, flood, because in that month all floods occurred and the rains which are helpful for the seeds,

[125] Isaiah 14:12.
[126] Isaiah 14:15.
[127] Job 41:23.
[128] Ezech. 29:3.
[129] Job 1:7.
[130] See Augustine, *De civ. Dei* X. 21.
[131] *inflammatos* MR
[132] *regionis* MR
[133] Lev. 25:1–6.

[134] Roman legislation concerning Jews and Judaism in the provinces allowed the Jews a high degree of equality and self-government. Responsive exponents of Roman rule repeatedly stressed the principle that the Jews were to be treated on equal footing with all other citizens. Julius Caesar, Augustus, and Claudius proclaimed this policy in various decrees. Josephus claimed that at the time of his writing (A.D. 93) many of the decrees were found engraved on bronze tablets in the Capitol. In speaking of the Jews in Alexandria, Claudius wrote in his edict of A.D. 41 that he wished that the "insanity of Gaius (Caligula) shall not deprive the Jewish population of these rights and that they continue to enjoy the same privileges as formerly, remaining faithful to their own customs." See Salo Baron, *A Social and Religious History of the Jews*, 2nd ed., revised and enlarged (Philadelphia, 1952), I, 233–46.

if they do not come in that month, predict a sterility of fruits. Moreover, as in the seventh millennium there is rest for the elementary world, so when seven times seven years have elapsed, there is a great Jubilee for all slaves. Cattle are unyoked, manors are freed from mortgage, liberty is granted, and everyone can return to his paternal possession.[135] So after seven times seven thousand years the motions and a change of all things follows, the celestial stars return to the beginnings when the greatest year has been completed. This proves that by the perpetual creation and re-creation of worlds the eternal power and goodness of God shall have been proclaimed in the continual succession of men and angels. Isaiah seems to indicate this when he said:[136] "There will be a new heaven and a new earth." Likewise, when David said that the heavens would perish when they grew old, he turned to the Builder of the worlds with these words:[137] "You, however, are the same; You are always like unto Yourself, and P. 85 Your years desert You in no ages and generations." Also note Solomon's words:[138] "There is nothing new under the sun, nor will there be anything which has not been before."

Octavius: Origen holds the same opinion in the books *About Principles* as does Caesarius,[139] especially in the discussion of the heavens: "They will perish, etc."[140] The Ismaelites also use a book in which the author writes that this world and whatever is held in the fullest embrace of the world will perish. Although that most importunate and wicked destroyer of all things has corrupted everything, he will fall at some time or other, and as Senamus says, death itself will die. Before this happens, moreover, he will witness his own destruction with the greatest crashes of thunder and with wild clamoring voices.

Fridericus: From the secrets of the Hebrews Salomon has garnered that remarkable change in all matter which seems consistent with the revolutions of the heavenly stars. For seven thousand years a motion of trepidation occurs over the heads of Aries and Libra and for seven times seven thousand years the abodes[141] of the fixed stars revolve and return

135 Lev. 25:8–22. On the Great Year or Cosmic Year, cf. Pliny, *Hist. nat.* II. 6. 36–40.

136 Isaiah 45:17; 46:22. Also cf. Rev. 21:1.

137 Psalm 101 (102):28.

138 Eccles. 1:9.

139 Saint Caesarius of Nazianzus was a physician and the younger brother of Gregory of Nazianzus. Born about A.D. 330, he studied at Caesarea in Cappadocia and later at Alexandria. He was especially adept in geometry, astronomy, and medicine. He acquired a great reputation for his medical skill.

140 *ipsi peribunt etc.* MR

141 *sedes* MR

each to their own beginnings. This proof has finally been understood in the memory of our fathers,[142] although it had been unknown to all the ancients before.

SALOMON: Indeed this had been concealed from the Chaldeans, Egyptians, and all astrologers. Obviously there are no more than ten celestial orbits, although the Pythagoreans, Plato, Aristotle, Ptolemy, that best mathematician, and Hipparchus[143] said there were eight or nine at the most. The sacred books, however, in elegant allegory show there are ten orbits, as in this verse: "The heavens are the works of Your fingers."[144] By the number of fingers they are declaring the number of heavens, which is unknown to the astrologers and Chaldeans, and also the ten curtains of the tabernacle. Hence we know that the secrets of all greatest matters are contained in the rather secret allegories of the divine books.

SENAMUS: If we should establish that Leviathan has been created by God as the prince of corruption and death at the very beginning of all things and before light itself, we must take care lest we grant that God is the author of evil. For whatever is the cause of a cause is itself[145] also the cause of the thing caused, the consequent effect.[146] Moreover, the Academicians had no more compelling argument to establish that the world was eternal than not to admit that God the best, the founder of all things, was the author of corruption and disorder.[147]

142 This reference is to the astronomical knowledge of Johann Müller (Regiomontanus), born in Königsberg in 1436. He was the pupil and protégé of the celebrated astronomer George of Peurbach. Müller and Peurbach showed how incorrect were the Alphonsine Tables and how false the Latin translations of the Greek astronomers from Arabic translations. Cardinal Bessarion's arrival in Vienna opened a new field to the two astronomers. Müller accompanied Bessarion to Italy, and in Padua he was enrolled among the Academicians and was invited to lecture. Müller's new calendar and his astronomical "Ephemerides" (1473–1474), with its positions of the sun, moon, and planets and the eclipses from 1475 to 1506, guided Columbus to America and helped him to predict the lunar eclipse of 29 February, 1504. For an account of Regiomontanus and his work, see *The Catholic Encyclopedia* (New York, 1911), X, 628–29 (hereafter abbreviated *Cath. Encycl.*).

143 Hipparchus, born 190 B.C. was the greatest of the Greek astronomers. His commentary *In Euxodi et Arati phaenomena* is extant. He adhered to the geocentric system and was the first person to make systematic use of trigonometry in his work. See Pliny, *Hist. nat.* II. 9–10.

144 Psalm 8:4.

145 *id* M

146 See Aristotle, *Phys.* II. 7. 198a; VIII. 6. 258b–259b; *Metaphys.* V. 2. 1013b–1014a. Also note E. R. Dodds, *Proclus, The Elements of Theology* (Oxford, 1963), Prop. II, p. 13.

147 See *ibid.*, Prop. LV, p. 53.

SALOMON: The erroneous opinion that the devil invented evil has been circulated for a long time, even by the theologians.[148] Nevertheless, this opinion displeased one of the Latins and one of the Greeks.

FRIDERICUS: Thus we have learned from our elders that all angels in the beginnings of their origin were most upright and holy. Certain ones, however, strayed from the path and fell from their integrity and pure light and were cast down to earth. At that time the wicked persuasion and all the calamities and plagues which happened to men emanated from them. The theologians think this opinion is indicated by the words of Isaiah and John, writing under the authority of revelation. One said that Lucifer was cast out of heaven,[149] and the other[150] wrote that a great snake with a third of the stars, that is, angels, had been cast out headlong. Likewise Christ declared that He had seen Satan,[151] as if a shining light, cast out from heaven into the earth.[152] This is the opinion of Christian theologians. P. 86

OCTAVIUS: The theologians have such a variety of opinions about the fall of demons that I would not dare assert anything. Since Augustine was so uncertain that, when he had written that the devil had fallen, he offered these words: "This cannot be stated with more certainty, and it is strange if it can."[153] Therefore when reason failed, many added the authority of Orpheus, Pherecydes, and Empedocles.[154] Those believed that the greatest of all demons, the snake Ophyoneus, and those who fell with him were called "demons fallen from heaven."[155] But when they were asked why

[148] If Salomon is referring to St. Thomas Aquinas, as the shoulder-note of M indicates, he is not accurate in expressing St. Thomas' highly complex statement. Thomas states that the devil is able to lead one, according to necessity, to do some act which is sinful, but he cannot determine the necessity of sinning. See Thomas Aquinas, *Summa Theologica* (editio altera romana, Leone XIII, Roma, n.d.) Prima Secundae Partis, Quaestio LXXX, art. 1–4, pp. 576–81.

[149] Isaiah 14:12–15.

[150] Apocal. (Rev.) 12:3–4, 9.

[151] *Sathanum* MR

[152] Luke 10:18.

[153] See *De civ. Dei* XI. 15.

[154] Orpheus was usually represented in vase and wall paintings as singing; even in the Catacombs he is depicted in this way, for the Christians related Orpheus' singing to the Prince of Peace of whom Isaiah speaks. See Aristotle, *Metaph.* XIV. 4. 5. Pherecydes of Syros, according to Theopompus, was the first to write about the nature and origin of the gods. See Diels, *Frag. der Vorsokrat.* (6th ed.), I, 43–46. See above, Book III, note 3. Empedocles acquired legendary fame because he combined the roles of philosopher, scientist, poet, orator, and statesman with those of mystagogue, miracle-worker, healer and claimant to divine honors. Tradition links him with the Pythagoreans, and Theophrastus calls him an imitator of Parmenides. He wrote two long poems, *On Nature* and *Purifications*. See Diels, *Frag. der Vorsokrat.* (6th ed.), I, 276–374.

[155] Plutarch, *Moralia* 2, 830c.

they, in almost the very moment of their creation in the highest purity and holiness,[156] rose up against their Creator with such arrogance that they equalled themselves to the Creator, or what[157] drove them to such a crime, they became silent. Manes the Persian makes two principles with equal power, one for good and heavenly things, the other for wicked and sublunary, lest evil seem to flow from the best fount of good and thereby shake the foundations of all piety and religion.[158] Although Plato clearly demonstrated that all things were brought forth from one principle, he thought it wrong to attribute the origin of evil to God.[159] Therefore he wrote that all evil was derived from matter because he thought some evil-working thing was present in it.

SALOMON: The sacred books constantly deny that evil proceeds from matter. "Neither vanity nor malice came from the earth," Job said,[160] and besides the greatest Builder of all things, after He had completed the mass of the universe, is said to have seen all things which He had made as very good.[161]

TORALBA: It is clearly proved that there is no sin in matter because in the first place the force of action is not in matter but in form, and in the second place matter has no substance at all of itself in nature.

SALOMON: The origin of all errors spread because they thought evil was something when it is nothing at all. God said: "I am making good and
P.87 creating evil, making light and creating darkness."[162] For as darkness is nothing other than the privation of light, so evil is nothing other than the privation of good. And so God said "to make good" because good is something, but He said, "to create evil," that is to say, by the privation of the good. For as a building falls when its columns are removed, so evil follows the removal of good. When God was angry with the people, He had said: "In a moment I shall destroy you."[163] A Chaldean interpreter translated it: "In a moment, I shall remove my majesty from you." For if anything were evil in the whole nature of things, surely demons, who are always said to encourage wicked deeds, would be evil; this is absurd since they are substances and participants of intelligence and life by God's gift and concession. Anything of this sort must be[164] good. Furthermore, if evil should exist or if demons were evil, assertion and nega-

[156] *sanctitate* MR [157] *quid* M
[158] See Augustine, *De civ. Dei* XI. 22; XIV. 5.
[159] *Timaeus* XXIXE–XXXD; *Leges* IX. 854B.
[160] Job 5:6. [161] Gen. 1:31. [162] Isaiah 45:7.
[163] Ex. 30:5. [164] *sit* MR

tion would be true at the same time, and they would imply a most ridiculous contradiction, because demons would be good and not good.

OCTAVIUS: Augustine[165] did not adopt this definition of evil; rather he described evil as the privation of good, lest he seem to agree with the principles of the Manichaeans in which he had acquiesced for a very long time.

SENAMUS: If evil is nothing, whoever does evil does nothing. Furthermore, he who does nothing deserves no punishment; therefore, he who does evil is worthy of no punishment.

CURTIUS: Lucilius[166] says it is better to be at leisure than to do nothing. Wherefore that argument is refuted by a contrary argument: Who does evil is worthy of punishment; who does nothing does evil; therefore, who does nothing must be worthy of punishment.

SENAMUS: If good things are opposed to evil things by privation alone, why do Aristotle and the rest with almost one accord state the contrary?

TORALBA: Aristotle errs not only in placing good things contrary to evil things but also in thinking that good is finite, evil infinite.[167] For if of contrary things one were finite, the other infinite, it would be necessary for the finite to be destroyed by the infinite. If fire were infinite, it would consume in a moment finite water with its flame, its heat, and its dryness, or infinite water would have extinguished finite fire. So infinite malice would have overwhelmed finite goodness and overturned this world. But since nothing except the first cause is actually infinite, as has been proved above, nothing can be contrary to it. It follows that nothing can be contrary to good because good alone is infinite. Moreover, evil is not only not infinite but does not even exist, and is understood in no other way than as privation.

SALOMON: Know the saying of the teacher of wisdom:[168] "Never will malice conquer[169] wisdom." P. 88

SENAMUS: If all virtue exists in the means between the extremes of vices, it is logical that virtues are conquered everywhere by vices, goods by evils, since two vices are opposed to one virtue.

TORALBA: Aristotle said nothing more trivial than that virtues abide in the midst of vices and infinite evils are contrary to finite goods.[170] If goods

165 *De civ. Dei* 11:22.

166 See above, Book III, note 17. However, this may be Lucilius Junior, a friend of Seneca, to whom he dedicated his *Quaest. nat.*, and the probable author of *Aetna*, a hexameter poem about the eruption of Vesuvius, similar in tone to Lucretius.

167 *Eth. nicom.* I. 6; II. 6. 14.

168 Wisdom 7:30.

169 *superabit* MR

170 *Eth. nicom.* I. 6; II. 6. 14.

should be finite, evils infinite, where would so many virtues be found[171] to safeguard the midst of infinite vices. Likewise, what is more alien to nature itself than to posit two vices contrary between themselves and to one virtue, since no law in all of nature is more certain[172] than for one to be contrary to one. He has decreed that evils are contrary to goods and virtues contrary to vices. Although these things are very foolish, nothing indeed is more foolish than to place a limit to evil, which he has established as infinite. For he placed evils between two extremes, although it is impossible to think of a middle or end for an infinite thing. Moreover, the extremities of vices or evils must be determined to find a middle for a thing or reason.

Senamus: If we should remove that golden mean, which always seemed most praiseworthy to all, we must dig up and tear out the roots and fibers of all virtues.

Toralba: Senamus, do you not[173] praise a man who is most wise, most prudent, most learned more than if he is moderately wise?

Senamus: Means are sought[174] for virtues and moral goods, not for intellectual goods in which extremes are very laudable. Moreover, wisdom, prudence, knowledge are intellectual goods.

Toralba: The Peripatetics sought this new medicine for old sickness, but they did not believe that all virtues were intellectual, according to the strict Stoic definition. Otherwise it would be necessary to place moral virtues in mortal and brutish lust, and rewards for good men are owed not to the immortal intellect but to mortal desire. If there were only those moral virtues, what would be more ridiculous than to consider those men who are most wise, most prudent, most learned are worthy of the greatest praise because they possess an abundance of intellectual virtues, but to condemn him who was most just, most brave, most temperate because he departed from the mean.

Fridericus: Surely it is better for a man to be moderately learned and wise than moderately just and temperate in order that we may declare, contrary to the new teaching of the Peripatetics, that the mean is more excellent in intellectual virtues than in moral virtues.

P. 89 Coronaeus: These things are indeed fitly said. However, we should not depart from the discussion[175] of goods and evils, since this question is of very great importance. We should not establish that there are two principles of the world contrary to each other or that God omnipotent and

[171] *repercantur* MR [172] *certius* MR [173] *nonne* N var.
[174] *quaeruntur* MR [175] *disputatione* M

best is the Author of evil. Although we grant that demons are good in that which they are, that is, participants of the highest good,[176] that is, essence and intelligence, nevertheless, who will not judge those are evil because[177] they bring corruption, death, calamities, wars, destruction, storms, plagues, fires, and shipwrecks? For this reason we see that spirits are called evil in sacred books.[178]

SALOMON: Who would think him wicked who diligently follows God's commands?

CORONAEUS: No one indeed, I think.

SALOMON: Why should we not judge the same thing about angels and demons, who carefully follow commands and do nothing unless ordered? For things are always just which are ordered by God, and the execution of right and justice holds no injury.[179]

FRIDERICUS: God has approved certain evils for punishment as when God harshly chides the people that there is no evil in the state which it did not commit.[180] But God curses the evils of defect, that is, adulteries, thefts, murders.

SALOMON: The Hebrew word *hiphil* indicates permission to do and to be done, to speak colloquially, rather than the very action of doing. This is clearly understood from the statement in II Kings 24: "The anger of the Lord was again kindled against Israel and aroused David to number the people." But in I Paralipomenon 21, the same history is written thus: "Moreover Satan rose up against Israel and moved David to number Israel."[181] The latter is a performance of Satan, the former the commands of God. Indeed, culpable evil is nothing other than the privation of good, or it is related to some good, as when God, the greatest and best, also directed crimes, disgraceful passions, and deceits for the punishment of the wicked. God's goodness is very apparent when one realizes that He never allows any crime to be permitted unless something better will come from it. For example, Joseph said to the brothers who sold him: "You have judged evilly against me, but God directs the evil into good."[182]

[176] *boni* MR [177] *quia* MR

[178] Cf. Matt. 8:16, 10:1; Mark 1:27; Luke 3:11, 5:13; Acts 5:16; Eph. 6:12; Apocal. (Rev.) 16:13–14.

[179] Cf. Psalms 145 (146), 148.

[180] Deut. 32:19–27; III Kings (I Kings) 9:6–9; Isaiah 104:7–8.

[181] . . . *lib II Reg. c. 24 ita scribitur. Et addidit furor Domini contra Israelem commovitque David. . . . At lib. I Paral. Cap. 21 eadem historia sic scribitur* M. II Kings (II Sam.) 24:1; I Para. (I Chron.) 21:1.

[182] Gen. 50:20.

TORALBA: Theophrastus[183] had the same opinion about God: "That which was first and most divine wishes all these things to be best." Moreover, those who[184] have fallen from the highest good are not evil, but less good and honorable the farther they depart from the highest good.[185] For God does not depart from the wicked, but the wicked depart from God who is the author of all goods, the cause of no evil, the most noble P. 90 parent of happiness, the best, the absolute, the true, as Plato[186] most divinely writes. And Porphyry[187] says: "God wishes all things to be good but nothing to be evil." Plutarch censored Chrysippus unduly. When Chrysippus had written that God had placed evil demons in charge of inflicting deaths and destruction, Plutarch chided him, saying, "Is not a charge being made against God, as if the best king would grant the reins of government to wicked ministers and allow those to cause evil against each best man."[188] Plutarch spoke harshly in this circumstance; otherwise he was a most deliberate man. Chrysippus had not written that authority was granted to evil demons, but rather they were designated as helpers, lictors, and hangmen for inflicting just punishments. Also God said to Malachi:[189] "I shall restrain the devastator to keep him from destroying the crops of your region."

SENAMUS: Why are demons and Satans called enemies and waylayers and devils called tricksters if they are not evil?

FRIDERICUS: They anxiously seek to destroy, to corrupt, and to rage, which is suited to their own nature and function.[190] Nevertheless, they do nothing without the command of the leader and the magistrates, that is, of God and the angels.[191]

SENAMUS: But Augustine[192] wrote that God himself inclined the will of men toward evil.

FRIDERICUS: We ought to interpret the writings of the theologians in good faith, since in countless instances Augustine removes the origins of

[183] This exact citation has not been located, but it seems to be from Theophrastus' *Metaphysics.* See Diels, *Frag. der Vorsokrat.* (6th ed.), I. 420. 1; I. 425. 20; I. 178. 10.

[184] *qui a* M

[185] Dionysius Areopagita, *De divin. nomin.* II.

[186] *Pol.* II. 379B–380D.

[187] Cf. Diels, *Frag. der Vorsokrat.* (6th ed.), II, 176. 7. Also see Wolff, *Porphyry,* pp. 27–33. Also see St. Thomas, *Summa Theologica,* Prima Secundae Partís, Quaestio, LXXXI, Art. I, p. 583.

[188] Cf. Plato, *Leges* IV. 713D.

[189] Malachi 3:11.

[190] Augustine, *De civ. Dei* II. 25–26.

[191] *Ibid.,* VIII. 14, 17, 19, 21.

[192] Senamus is in error here concerning Augustine's teaching. See *De libero arbitrio* III. 1.

evils as far as possible from God.[193] Therefore we must interpret this in the sense of permission.

SALOMON: It is an incurable cancer, according to Philo the Hebrew,[194] to charge God with being author of evil. For what impurity can flow from the very springs of purity? What evils can flow from the very fount of goodness? "Woe to you," Isaiah said,[195] "who[196] say good is evil and evil good." Very often He steals away famous and brave men in the prime of life lest they suffer worse conditions in this life. For example, God ordered Hulda to declare by His authority that Josiah was the best and most pious king so that wicked men would not blame God because He allowed the prince of so great virtue to be killed by Pharaoh.[197]

CURTIUS: I think Plutarch[198] surely wrote these same things under divine inspiration. "He leads out certain ones from life with foresight of the future."

CORONAEUS: Away with those who make God the author of evils not only because He does not prevent them but also because He orders and decrees them. They think that these words, "He blinded, He hardened," refer to the effectual action of God not to the permissive will. They fear that otherwise God would be idle; they even affirm that the incest of Absalom was the work of God.[199] Although they often have varying opinions, they think the words ought not to be extended to the permissive P. 91
will but should be related to the commands. Why then does the Psalmist sing this: "Since You, O God, are not willing iniquity?"[200] Moreover, when He cursed the crimes of King Manasses, He said, "Because he did that which I never commanded, and he did not ascend into My heart."[201]

OCTAVIUS: But sicker are men like Rabbi Maurus and Pliny who have numbered myriads of evils and say they can find nothing good. They scornfully call man the most unhappy of all things and nature a step-mother,[202] although God made man a little less than the angels and gave him complete power over all living creatures.[203]

CORONAEUS: I think we have said enough about the origin of good and

[193] *De civ. Dei* XI. 22.

[194] Cf. *De opificio mundi* XXIV, LIII–LXI; *Legum allegoria* III. 21–24, Par. 65–75.

[195] Isaiah 5:20.

[196] *qui* MR

[197] IV Kings (II Kings) 22:14–20.

[198] Cf. Plutarch, *Consolatio ad Apollonium*, 106E–107.

[199] II Kings (II Sam.) 16:21–22.

[200] Psalm 5:5.

[201] IV Kings (II Kings) 23:26, 24:3.

[202] Pliny, *Hist. nat.* 7:1.

[203] Psalm 8:6–7.

evil. Still we do not yet seem to have answered the question posed by Senamus. Namely, what is the origin of so many angels and demons, since they are mortal in their own nature, unless God sustains them by His goodness? Or whence are they substituted in the place and order of the dead?

SALOMON: Granted there is nothing more excellent in nature than the proper order, there is no doubt that dominion and sovereignty exist in each order of angels and demons. For when God spoke about Leviathan saying, how great is his strength; with what great splendor has he marshalled his forces, He is speaking of the army of demons.[204] Moreover, Daniel, writing about angels, said: "The prince of the Persian kingdom resisted me; yet Michael, one of the supreme princes, brought me aid."[205] I believe that it is not given to the human mind to affirm whence and when they were born, and when they will die.

CURTIUS: The creation of the angels is not mentioned in scripture, but some divine interpreters of those sacred oracles include them in the creation of the stars and heavens.

FRIDERICUS: If they are right, you would think that the stars and the heavens would have to have an angelic and animal nature.

TORALBA: Why not? To be sure, both Theophrastus and Alexander of Aphrodisias,[206] the leader of the Peripatetics, stated that heavenly bodies excelled not only in the intelligible faculty but also in the sensible; otherwise they would be very inferior to animals in dignity and excellence of nature. And so Plato[207] calls the sun an everlasting living animal.

SENAMUS: Why then did they divide animal nature into man and brute if heavenly stars are animals?

TORALBA: What forbids one from using clear arguments to establish a dual animal nature, namely intelligent and brute? The intelligent nature is also dual, heavenly and sublunary, and some of the heavenly animals are visible, as stars, and some invisible as angels. Likewise there are two orders of sublunary animals. Men are contained in one which
P. 92 is visible; immortal minds which enter the nature of either angels or demons are contained in the other which is invisible.

[204] Cf. Isaiah 14:12.

[205] Dan. 10:13.

[206] On Theophrastus, see Diels, *Frag. der Vorsokrat.* (6th ed.), II. 15–16; on Alexander see Diels II. 106, Par. 92.

[207] *Timaeus* 30B. It is the cosmos rather than the sun which Plato calls living, etc. But in *Leges* 886D he speaks of the sun and moon as gods and divine beings.

SENAMUS: But what sensation will there be for such animals, what food, what drink, what life?

SALOMON: Reason, understanding, contemplation, and action for they are possessed not only by angels, but also by the stars themselves; as this statement proves: "The heavens declare the glory of God."[208] Indeed Abraham Aben-Esra and Moses Rambam teach that the word *Shamayīm* [heavens] is applicable only to a rational nature, and to this refer the words of God himself:[209] "When the morning stars rejoiced and all the sons of God exulted." Likewise this statement:[210] "There was a war in the heavens, and the stars themselves waged wars against Sisara." Daniel also wrote very openly that those who taught others excelling in integrity would be as illustrious as the glory of heaven, but those who led many to the honor of true justice would have eternal splendor like the stars and a home in heaven.[211] And so the containers in the sanctuary are decorated with the images of angels so that we may know that the stars bear the angelic nature in themselves. The temple is an example of the world, but the world is the exemplar.[212]

OCTAVIUS: Ibn Farid,[213] a most famous theologian of the Ismaelites, writes that the planets and stars are lesser gods; also Alexander of Aphrodisias, Origen, Diodorus, and Johannes Picus[214] say that as fish live in the waters, wild beasts in the forests, cows in the pastures, so animated stars live in the heavens and are arranged in their own[215] abodes and positions. Hipparchus[216] thoughtfully said that human minds were particles of heaven because the power of understanding was present in each. But do you think, Senamus, that one should ask whether celestial beings have to have food and drink to sustain life or do you think that even God cannot live without food?

SENAMUS: I'm not so stupid as to believe God eats food. After all Toralba has shown Him to be incorporeal. Posidonius, however, easily the leader

208 Psalm 18 (19):2.

209 Job 38:7.

210 Judges 5:20.

211 Dan. 12:3.

212 Philo, *De specialibus legibus* I. 12. 66–67.

213 *Ibim* M Ibn Farid (1181–1235) was a great mystic poet whose poems were said to have been written when he was in ecstasies.

214 In Gen. 1 is a Hebrew expression of an idea developed by the ancient Greeks of a universe of order, more specifically a place for everything and everything in its place.

215 *in suis quaeque locis ac sedibus* MR

216 See note 143. Also Pliny, *Hist. nat.* II. 24.

of the Stoics in his time, confirmed that heavenly bodies, constellations, stars, and meteors need sustenance and said that the world would burn up at the time when all the moisture of the elements had been consumed as continual maintenance for the stars.[217]

P. 93 OCTAVIUS:[218] Why do we not see the moisture of the waters lessened or consumed by the heat of the stars in so many centuries that have progressed since Posidonius' time?

SALOMON: There is in the scriptures a marvelous secret hidden from all astrologers and physicists—namely, the aqueous heaven, which is as far distant from the convex vault of heaven as the ocean is from the concave arch of this same heaven. Moreover, both Hebraic and Arabic astrologers confirm that it is 17,000 earth diameters distant. The following saying illustrates this: "He divided the waters from waters and established the heavens between each."[219] Hence the deluges of waters which poured from the open waterfalls of heaven filled up the lands; otherwise there would never have been any floods despite the opinion of the theologians and naturalists of all peoples. If the whole ocean and all rivers vanish into vapors and clouds, hardly a thousandth part of such a deluge would have resulted. The force of the waters did not pour over the earth from the ocean's shore, but rained from heaven for forty days so that the waters rose fifteen cubits above the peaks of the highest mountains.

SENAMUS: I do not know whether or not those living constellations feed on the heavenly waters above; yet I do not see why constellations need waters or why those globular lights are called living beings.

CURTIUS: The best teacher of speech is usage. Not only did the Academicians and Peripatetics call the heavens and constellations living rational beings,[220] but also Augustine, Jerome, Thomas Aquinas, and Scotus called this world a living being.[221]

SENAMUS: If the sun and sky are living beings, they must have parts of body and soul, matter and form, as it were, to be united in one and the same substance. However, a group of Peripatetic and Arabic philosophers said that intelligences are severed and separated from heavenly bodies.[222] Therefore, how will they be joined to living beings?

[217] Pliny, *Hist. nat.* II. 28. 94.

[218] *Curtius* MR

[219] Gen. 1:9.

[220] Plato, *Timaeus*, 34. Aristotle, *De caelo* II. 12. 292a. Pseudo-Aristotle, *De mundo*, 2; Aristotle, *Metaphys.* XII. 7. 5–8.

[221] Cf. Augustine, *De civ. Dei* XI. 4–6.

[222] See paragraph above and below.

TORALBA: To be sure, Thomas Aquinas, following Aristotle's opinion, admitted that heavenly intelligences are joined to heavenly bodies whether they are called angels or separated minds.[223] Therefore, an alternative is necessary concerning these two; either there is complete union in substance of one living body, or there is utter separation from heavenly bodies. But if heavenly intelligences are joined to animate nature, it must be either rational or irrational; not the latter, hence the former. If, however, heaven is not the same substance of this living body nor the same natural body consisting of intelligence and the heavenly body, surely the courses of the heavenly orbits must be violent and not natural, and im- P. 94
pelled by an external mover. In respect to mobility they are as angels to a star or builders to a machine. In other words, an abstract incorporeal substance which is not joined to heaven moves the natural and lifeless heavenly body around, since no union of a natural body exists without conjunction. Moreover, since nothing is more consistent than the remarkable movement of heavenly orbs, it follows that heavenly movements are not violent—that is, from an external mover, but natural—that is, from an intrinsic and coessential form. Indeed what violent motion can be lasting for a long time in the nature of things? How strange it is that Aristotle made heavenly natures lifeless and driven by separated minds as wheels are moved by artisans,[224] yet he did not hesitate to call God the supreme everlasting living being,[225] and he states everywhere that living being consists of soul and body.

SALOMON: Toralba has clearly proved that heavenly bodies and the stars themselves are living, and even divine authority bears witness to this fact. When Ezechiel in a vision of divine majesty said that the wheels, which Hebraic and Chaldaic commentators interpret as heavens, are moved by themselves, he adds these words: "Because the spirit of life was in them."[226] And there Aristotle is clearly proved wrong. For Aristotle believed that the heavens were moved from the outside and by an external mover.[227] Beyond the heavens, in which he said a spirit dwelled, he noted there were living beings also around the heavens, that is, angels. Then above the heavens was a kind of Saphiric stone which he called

[223] *Summa Theologica*, Prima Secundae Partis, Quaestio XVIII, Art. II, p. 401. Cf. also Augustine, *Conf.* III. 6; *De civ. Dei* XXI. 5.

[224] Toralba's statement is not accurate, for Aristotle says in *De caelo* II. 12. 292a that we are inclined to think of the stars as lifeless, but indeed we should think of them as partaking of life and initiative.

[225] *Metaphys.* XII. 7. 9.

[226] Ezech. 1:21.

[227] *Metaphys.* XII. 7. 1–7.

chrystallus, namely the great aqueous heaven, like a chrystallus, the firm abode of all powerful God.[228] He also explained how the springs and rivers are produced from the sea and flow back again into the seas, except that which is absorbed by the earth and living creatures or evaporates.[229] In this way, he said, the souls which are of celestial origin fly back into that intelligent and heavenly ocean where the stars gleam, except those who, defiled by the terrestrial stain, attach to the earth a particle of divine air, as the Epicurean poet described.[230] Among those who seek again the heavenly realms after the fall from heaven there is this difference that those who instruct many in time have been or will be like the splendor of the heaven and those who teach true piety and divine wisdom will be like the stars themselves. The prophet Daniel wrote clearly about this.[231] Philo the Hebrew[232] interpreted these words—"Your seed will be as numerous as the stars"[233]—not only to indicate the future increase of the race but also the future happiness and[234] the celestial nature of souls.[235]

OCTAVIUS: Surely this teaching received from antiquity came to the
P. 95 Greeks from the Chaldeans and Hebrews. Hipparchus[236] wrote that the minds of men were part of heaven and returned into the celestial nature; he also noted that a new star came into being in his lifetime, and he recorded on which day it gleamed forth. He also doubted that this happened very often. Aristotle confirms that most ancient teaching which has been handed down through succeeding generations, namely, that those who had distinguished themselves in praiseworthy virtues at length became angels; however, there were few whom Jupiter justly loved or zealous virtue carried to the heavens.[237]

228 This statement is a Platonic idea, not Aristotelian. See *Phaedo*, 109–110B.

229 Aristotle does not say that rivers are produced from the sea; rather he says (*Meteorologica* I. 13. 350a) that the sources of rivers flow from mountains. In Plato's *Phaedo* 111e–113d, the description of the rivers which flow into a chasm under the earth and out again is very similar to the statement attributed to Aristotle.

230 Cf. Lucretius, *De rerum natura* II. 73.

231 Dan. 12:3.

232 *Quaest. et solutiones in genesim* III. 1. 2.

233 Ex. 32:13; Gen. 15:5.

234 *ac* MR

235 See *Legum allegoria* III. 13. 37–40; *Quis rerum divinarum heres sit* 76, 86.

236 This reference is from Pliny, *Hist. nat.* II. 24, Par. 95.

237 This statement cannot be verified in Aristotle; Plato, however, states that souls which have lived virtuous and holy lives will find gods as companions and guides. See *Phaedo*, 108c and 114c.

SENAMUS: Still good men are not so scarce that[238] the stars would not increase in number if good men's spirits returned to them. There are no more than 1025 stars in the sky, or if we believe some Hebrew astrologers, there are 1095.

FRIDERICUS: Not only do God's words "count the stars"[239] show the infinity of stars, but also the Milky Way proves the multitude of innumerable stars in its own radiance. Indeed, if the smallest star of the eighth sphere, which is barely visible, is twelve times larger than the earth, according to some astrologers, who doubts there are infinite stars, smaller than the earth, which are invisible?

SALOMON: But when the spirits of the good and noble reach heaven because of their unusual virtue, only divine majesty knows in secret what duties they will first perform, what they will do first after having left the earthly bodies or in what places or regions or peoples or offices they must be located. When Moses in a canticle said:[240] "When the Highest divided the nations according to the number of Israelites," many Hebraic and Chaldaic interpreters read "according to the number of God's angels," because powers are granted over regions and peoples to the blessed spirits, that is angels. Ezechiel's words also illustrate this point:[241] "I shall raise up a shepherd for My sheep to feed them, My servant David. But I am also God to them, and My servant David is in their midst." He said servant twice, lest any one think the words of Jeremiah and Ezechiel pertain to the Son of God; however, David died 420 years before Ezechiel wrote.

CURTIUS: Indeed Plato seems to confirm this when he said: "God gave kings and princes for our cities, not men, but He appointed demons of a better and more divine order."[242] This agrees with Daniel's words who wrote that the chief angel of the Persian kingdom had resisted the angel of Daniel.[243]

SENAMUS: I agree with Pliny that it is foolish to say that man believes he will be a god when he dies.[244]

FRIDERICUS: It is ridiculous to think that God comes into being from a human mind. However, earlier arguments and the convincing remarks of the evangelists whom no one doubts make clear that man puts on the nature of an angel.[245] Pliny ought to recall in that same contemplation of P. 96

[238] *quin* MR [239] Gen. 15:5. [240] Deut. 32:8.
[241] Ezech. 34:23, 37:24; Jer. 30:21; Psalm 88 (89):4, 21, 36–38.
[242] *Leges* IV. 713D. [243] Dan. 10:13. [244] *Hist. nat.* II. 5. 22–26.
[245] Matt. 22:30; Mark 12:25; Luke 10:19.

nature that a chrysalis rather often comes from a caterpillar and from a chrysalis comes a butterfly, which flies with a much purer essence and does not feed on leaves and foliage but on the fragrance of flowers and honeysweet dews.[246] And more remarkable is the fact that when a caterpillar is changed into a butterfly, it brings those same colors painted on its wings; in like manner do those spirits which can exist after the bodies are dead resume those pristine customs and characteristics. For example, the most illustrious men have the purest and most refined bodies, completely different from those who were crafty and sly.

TORALBA: The active intellect which Aristotle said came "from outside"[247] this is, as I think, "from God, from on high, from heaven," is, I have always believed, nothing other than an angel granted by God to each man as a leader. Aristotle's opinion about the nature of souls has been rejected in earlier explanations because he thought that the intellect of man was likewise active and passive.[248]

SALOMON: If anyone should wish to understand the force of the passive intellect on the active intellect, which Rabbi Moses calls an angel, he must consider nature as the guide for the sun and moon. For as mankind (*anthrōpos*) is called a microcosm by the ancients, so also a macrocosm (*makrokosmos*) can be properly called great mankind (*meganthrōpos*). Moreover, as the moon is illuminated and derives its light in conjunction with the sun, it is obscured when it is separated from the sun's orbit. So the human mind is enlightened by the attendance of an angel, as if by the sun's light, but languishes and grows dull without the angel's presence. Just as when the moon, deserted by the sun, sends forth to the earth's shadows the reflected light of the sun, and as long as the sun and moon shine, the enemies of Joshua, that is, demons, the enemies of human salvation, are driven into flight. For this reason Joshua, the counsellor of salvation, ordered the sun and moon to stand still so that he might utterly destroy the Moabites.[249] We should not cling to a literal interpretation of this passage, for the meaning is allegorical. And yet by divine power the sun and moon and similar stars illuminated that night for an easier destruction of the enemy. Still I prefer the allegorical interpretation. Many theologians have disagreed over interpretations and have comprehended divine secrets in a rather dull manner. "Night," said Micah,[250] "rushes upon us in place of vision and darkness in place of

[246] Pliny, *Hist. nat.* 11:32. 37. Par. 112; 11:35. 41. Par. 117.
[247] *De anima* III. 4; also see *Metaphys.* XII. 6. 1–9; 7. 7–9.
[248] *De anima* III. 5. [249] Joshua 10:12–13. [250] Micah 3:6.

divination, and the sun sets over those prophets and the day will darken." These words have been subject to untold errors of interpretation. Many think they must imply the visible sun and the final day of judgment. This interpretation is as absurd as to defer the judgment of the dead until the second millennium, since these words refer to the angelic sun, or the active intellect, which the teacher of wisdom calls the sun of understanding.[251] This statement is apropos: "The sun will grow dark in its rising, and the moon will not shine."[252] Also: "The sun will become bashful, and the moon will blush."[253] These words refer to the punishment of the wicked, but the following statement applies to the reward of the good. "You will have sun no more in the daylight, and the brightness of the moon will not shine, but the Lord will be your perpetual light."[254] Or in other words, such a bright light will shine on your soul from immortal God that even the light of the agent intellect will be obscured or dimmed as the light of the moon and stars is obscured by the sun's rise or does not appear. Philo the Hebrew said clearly:[255] "When the divine light rises, the human light sets; when the divine light sets, the human light rises." The prophets experienced this: that their mind seemed to depart with the importation of the divine spirit. And so Isaiah said: "Your sun will not set too far away, nor will your moon be clouded, since God is your eternal light."[256] Indeed very properly does the Psalmist call God the sun. In this place—"God loves mercy and truth," the Hebraic reading has *shemesh wemagen* YHWH, that is, God is the sun and shield.[257] Thus it becomes clear that the light of the passive intellect flows from the active intellect, but the light of the active intellect flows from a higher and holier light. Let no one think that the active intellect is God or worship it as God. This statement illustrates the point. "After the third watch the sun will suddenly receive light at night and the moon three times during the day."[258] If anyone should wish to interpret this as a reference to the visible sun, surely he makes himself a laughing stock for the learned and unlearned alike. Therefore, the statement indicates that the active intellect is joined with the passive intellect after the third watch, that is, after the third hour of night. With that in mind the prophets Bileam[258a] and Hulda had ordered the legates of the kings consulting them about the

P. 97

[251] Wisdom 5:6.
[252] Isaiah 13:10. [253] Isaiah 24:23. [254] Isaiah 60:19.
[255] Cf. *Quis rerum divinarum heres* I.
[256] Isaiah 60:20.
[257] Cf. Psalms 46 (47):11; 24 (25):10; 97 (98):3.
[258] Cf. Isaiah 30:26. [258a] See pp. 103 and 181.

future to wait so that they might receive divine oracles in dreams during the next night.[259]

CURTIUS: I think Salomon's explanation of the secrets of the Hebrews really illuminates the difficult questions about acquired intellect. Moreover, the Greeks also said that truer and clearer dreams came after dawn, that is, after the third watch.[260] They also believed that Morpheus, the god of dreams, appeared to them at dawn in sleep.[261]

SALOMON: Sometimes the passive intellect received inspiration from divine light during the day when the prophet was awake; however, I do not think this happened except to the most divine prophets such as Elias, Elisha, Samuel, and Ahijah the Shilonite.[262] Without reference to allegory Themistius calls the celestial and visible sun the active intellect of this world.[263] Pico della Mirandola in this vein interprets Plato's world-soul as the moon, which is the mistress of the liver and blood in man and
P. 98 of the waters in the elementary world; however, the Hebrews made the sun the mistress of the heart and spirit in man and the moderator of the air.

CURTIUS: Perhaps this confusion among the ancients forced the Chaldeans and Greeks as well as the Palestinians to think that the sun, which the Chaldeans and Greeks called Apollo, the Palestinians Bahal, the Persians Mithra, being the ruler of nature, was the chief leader of divination.

SALOMON: From this, one gathers the kindling wood of impiety. For when king Ahaziah was seriously injured in a fall from the roof and had sent a messenger to the oracle of Apollo to find any misfortune that might happen in the future, Elias said to the messengers: "Since king

[259] IV Kings (II Kings) 22:14; II Paralip. (II Chron.) 34:22.

[260] Cf. Aristotle, *De somniis* and *De divinatione per somnum.*

[261] See Ovid, *Metamorph.* XI. 633 ff.

[262] *Aiah Silonites* MR. Ahijah II Paralip. (II Chron.) 9:29, 12:5, 13:22) was a Levite at Shiloh. He was the sixth of seven men whose lifetimes following one another encompass all time. He is given a life span of more than five hundred years. Maimonides makes him an important link in the early tradition of the oral law. Ahijah was reputed to be a great master of the secret lore (Cabala). Cf. *Encyclopaedia Judaica* II, 459.

[263] *hujus mundi* MR. Themistius was a distinguished philosopher who flourished first at Constantinople and later at Rome in the reigns of Constantius, Julian, Jovian, Valens, Gratian and Theodosius, and enjoyed the favor of all of them, notwithstanding their diversities of opinion and the fact that he was not a Christian. He claimed full liberty of conscience both for the Christian and the heathen, and he persuaded Valens to cease his persecution of the Catholic party. His philosophical writings were voluminous, and he wrote commentaries on all the works of Aristotle. See Smith, *Dictionary* (1856), III, 1024–26.

Ahaziah consulted Bahal in place of God, tell him that the day of his destruction will be near."[264] Other equally wicked men believed that angels were the leaders of human life in place of gods and consequently established Lares and Familiares.[265] They ought to have realized all things are from one all-powerful God by whose powerful ways good angels are granted to men. Thus God said to Moses: "I shall send My angel before you."[266] Likewise God distributed the spirit which hovered over Moses and granted it to seventy elders, and they prophesied.[267] God sends not only good spirits, but He also sends bad spirits to punish the wicked. God sent the very bad spirit to the inhabitants of Sichem;[268] likewise, an evil spirit of God took possession of Saul.[269] The actions of angels as well as demons are attributed to God so that all may know that man must confess to eternal God alone, that He alone must be worshipped and feared. Demons should not be feared by man, as if they through themselves bring calamities, fires, wars, slaughter of men and flocks, since they dare nothing unordered, nor can they, if they wish. God said: "In the destruction of the Egyptians I shall not allow the demon to visit your homes as devastator, as is said to have befallen the Egyptians everywhere."[270] Likewise, this statement: "I shall rebuke the devastator lest he destroy your crops."[271] All these things explain that demons must not be feared or angels worshipped. Although demons have power in the imagination and intellect, God alone claims the highest power for Himself over the imagination, intellect, and will, and demons have no power without God.

CORONAEUS: Apuleius, a very wicked man, wrote a little book, *About the God of Socrates*, to draw men to the worship of demons. Although Plutarch had written a book, *About the Demon of Socrates*, that is, about the angel of Socrates who always called him away from evils to good, he never said that Socrates worshipped him as God, but rather considered him as the most faithful and wisest advisor.

SALOMON: The seventy-two interpreters of the Bible, whom Ptolemy[272] P. 99

264 IV Kings (II Kings) I. 2–3.

265 The Lares are ghosts of the dead, according to Samter, but Wissowa points out that the Roman dead are honored not in the house but at their graves. The hearth is the place for Vesta and the *di Penates*, the Lar (familiaris) being a late intruder. See article "Lares" in *Ox. Class. Dict.*, pp. 479–80. The Lar familiaris or lares is used by metonymy for house or home.

266 Ex. 23:20. 267 Num. 11:25. 268 Judges 9:23.

269 I Kings (I Sam.) 18:10.

270 Ex. 12:23. 271 Malachi 3:11. 272 *Ptolomao* MR

Philadelphus, King of Egypt, had requested to translate the sacred letters from Hebrew to Greek, read *daemonium* everywhere for *cacodaemon*. For example, the angel Raphael is said to have bound the demon in upper Egypt.[273] This statement is similar: "The gods of the Gentiles are demons."[274]

SENAMUS: I shall gladly learn by what chains demons are bound, in what prisons they are restrained, with what rods they are flogged, and what punishments they suffer.

TORALBA: If demons consist of corporeal union, as was shown above, who would doubt that they suffer strictures, force, and those same things which animated bodies suffer.

CURTIUS: When I was at Toulouse, I remember that a demon flying down in a clap of thunder had stood for seven days on a cobbler's table and had grievously disturbed the household with a continual barrage of rocks, yet he did not draw blood or kill anyone. However, the demon could not be routed until swords and spears were brandished through the empty spaces of the bedroom.

SALOMON: Indeed I think that demons cannot be routed by any sword, by any force, by any weapon; in short, there is nothing in the elements that terrify them. The voice of God said to Job: "He holds iron as a straw and brass as rotten wood."[275] Therefore if a demon is said to have been routed by the liver and heart of a fish or by smoke,[276] we ought to understand that he is put to flight only by divine power, and the divine voice witnesses to this: "Whoever established that one, He moves a sword against him."[277] For when Saul had decided to destroy David and had come to Samuel in torment from an evil demon, the evil demon left Saul, who at the same moment began to sing praises to God and to prophesy. When Saul had departed from Samuel, however, he was again tortured by an evil demon.[278]

FRIDERICUS: Good and bad men alike put evil demons to flight. We often see some very wicked magicians free with no difficulty those possessed by demons. Some whisper in the ears; others make circles and symbols on the middle of the forehead, as is customary in Africa for magicians whom they call *mahazini*. Finally, some feign devotions and

[273] Tobias 8:3.
[274] Cf. Deut. 32:16–21; II Paralip. (II Chron.) 32:15.
[275] Job 41:19.
[276] Tobias 6:1–19.
[277] Job 40:19, 21–32; 41:18.
[278] Cf. I Kings (I Sam.) 19:9, 24; 20:31.

prayers by which they are accustomed to soothe quietly the chief demon and gain the praise of piety and holiness from the unlearned common people. And so Polycrates[279] said: "Evil demons do these things willingly, but they seem to do them reluctantly and pretend that they have been driven out by the power of exorcisms which they fashion in the name of the Trinity. They transmit these to men as long as they can involve men in sacrileges and the punishment of God's displeasure." While these P. 100 considerations were leading me on in wonder, I toyed in verse of Sapphic measure:

Who can easily tell of the strength, the numbers,
The honors, the right, the power,
The duty, the appearance, the
order, the feeling of demons.

For the essence of good spirits is said to be
purer than the essence of evil spirits,
and it has a lighter motion.
Indeed the evil are pressed down by a heavier body.

But man exists alone in the midst of the good and
evil spirits, the last of the gods and supreme
over all things living in the whole
world.

A guardian angel and a wicked genius
lead us now here, now there
until the time when one of the two draws
stern triumphs from the hated enemy.

The supreme guardianship of cities is entrusted
to spirits as custodians and, with
God's approval, the care of everyone's
home is ordered.

There are some who are granted rule over nature,
to add form to fleeting
circumstances and powerful honor
to flowing matter.

[279] Polycrates, bishop of Ephesus, second century A.D., attested to the death of St. John the apostle at Ephesus, as did St. Irenaeus and Clement of Alexandria. See *Cath. Encycl.* V, 491.

The angels who dedicate their minds, souls and
prayers to God with like countenance
Enjoy fully the face of the divine
and shining light.

But nothing has been ordained more nobly than for the
wicked to obey the good;
the sacred right of power is granted
to the just by eternal law.

P. 101 SENAMUS[280]: Indeed I acknowledge that power has been handed down to each best man who is skilled in governing. Still I do not understand the origin of such a multitude of demons and angels as seems necessary in our judgment for so many provinces, powers, states, and for so many thousands of men, even if[281] we grant that the souls of good men depart into the nature of angels. However, good men are so scarce that we hardly find one among many thousands, and not even one who does not stray from the straight path; yet the number of wicked men is almost infinite. Since we have pointed out in our discussion of the immortality of the soul that the souls of men survive the corpses, it follows that the number of angels would be remarkably small and the number of demons innumerable, provided it is true that the souls of the wicked are changed into the nature of demons as the souls of the pious and excellent are changed into angels. For one thing follows another according to the nature of opposites.

OCTAVIUS: Indeed Plato,[282] using Hesiod and the ancients as authority, wrote in the *Cratylus* that good men, snatched from this corporeal ruin, become demons.

FRIDERICUS: Tertullian[283] had the same opinion, and he only differed from Plato in that he used[284] the word bad demon in place of Plato's demon.

CORONAEUS: Since Salomon can easily clarify the greatest difficulties of the secret shrines of the Hebrews, he will settle Senamus' complex and difficult question.

SALOMON: I satisfied your wishes, Coronaeus. I do not know how wisely, yet in good faith I have revealed the things which I know and

[280] *Senamus* MR *Toralba* N [281] *etiamsi* MR

[282] *Cratylus* 398A–B. See also Apuleius, *De deo Socratis* III. 123; XV. 1; Augustine, *De civ. Dei* IX. 11. 283.

[283] *Apol.* I. 22–23. [284] *usurpavit* M

all the things which I do not know, and I fear that I may seem to have poured out too much, to probe the innermost meanings. However, nothing could satisfy Senamus. He even demands proofs of matters hidden from all human senses, although they have no value for salvation; but everybody may think as he pleases.

Coronaeus: Although these questions may not pertain to salvation, still they do pertain to better knowledge, to the understanding of divine matters, to the delight of the soul which is calmed by the recognition of truth. Indeed, I pledge the matter will be explained sufficiently for Senamus with arguments as credible as the nature of those matters can tolerate.

Salomon: Once I heard from a most learned man that the souls of those who had surrendered themselves completely to lusts and, in their filth, had no concern for virtues and honorable teachings, perished along with the bodies. This is clearly confirmed in sacred books. "Hear," the Psalmist says,[285] "hear all peoples; pay attention to the greatest and most serious matters of all which I have decided to reveal to high and low alike." We have read repeatedly that those who have placed their hopes in wealth and human rewards or have established the foundations of their own name and power in the substructures of haughty buildings will perish just as the beasts. Likewise, when Isaiah had said that tyrants would never live again, he added: "But Your dead, oh Lord, will rise up and live."[286] Nevertheless, all the souls of the wicked will not perish completely with the death of the body, as some have thought from this passage from David,[287] that is, *lo'yaqumu*,[288] they will not stand, but as dust is scattered by the gentlest gust of wind, so also will the wicked be scattered from the sight of God. Daniel also bears witness to this. He said: "Many who are sleeping in the dusty earth will rise; indeed these for eternal life, but those for reproach and eternal dishonors."[289] Were this not so, death would be profitable for the wicked, as Trypho the Hebrew says in Justin.[290] Still Daniel did not promise that all would rise up, but many. For those whose souls God has crushed (moreover, God alone can crush souls and bodies)[291] are without hope and are appropriately called dead. The following words are applicable: "Will any man live again, after he has died?"[292] Others are properly called sleeping. "As long as

P. 102

[285] Psalm 48 (49):1–3.

[286] Isaiah 26:19.

[287] Psalm 1:5.

[288] *lo'yaqumu* M

[289] Dan. 12:2.

[290] *In dialogo cum Tryphone.*

[291] Cf. Matt. 10:28.

[292] Job 14:10.

one sleeps, will he not rise again?"[293] And also: "Ruben may live and not die with a second death."[294] In Ezechiel also we read: "Moreover, they will outrage Me for My people in order to kill their souls which do not die and to promise life to souls which do not live."[295] But those who have, in addition, abandoned God know that they will die, after they have paid the penalty for a defiled life.[296] Thus Isaiah also said: "They will see the bodies of those who have wickedly departed from Me, since this worm will not die, and their fire will not be extinguished."[297] This proves that the end of life for good and bad men will not be the same. Far removed are those who have contaminated themselves with every disgrace and have felt no remorse from those who do not differ in judgment from the beasts since they had been subjected to appetite and gluttony alone. These will die along with their bodies. Yet the others will pay justly for their enormous crimes before they die. For the Chaldean interpreter, who clearly interprets obscure passages, wrote that the wicked would rise up again for the sole purpose of suffering the harshest torments. There is also another ugly kind of these men who have associated with demons and made a very wicked agreement with them. Demons use the help of these men to inflict punishment. Many think that these dead souls always follow their leaders, the demons, and take on their nature and assume
P. 103 their most depraved duties with extreme torment. To others who, though still unrepentant, were not wicked to the end, less severe punishments have been decreed, until they are admitted into the association of angels after their souls have been cleansed. A certain Hebrew had a slightly different interpretation. He said: "I would like you to know that God created men inferior to the image of higher beings and placed two appetites in him, good and bad, and just as many angels. If he has lived well, he is changed into a good angel, if badly, into a bad angel."[298] The neat and succinct interpretation of Paul Riccius[298a] speaks to this point. To these words, "He formed man from the mire of the earth,"[299] he adds, not only did He fashion him in the shape of a human body from clay and dirt, but also He made for him a passive intellect which became active, that is, an angel from the human mind.[300]

[293] Psalm 40 (41):9.
[294] Deut. 33:6.
[295] Ezech. 13:19.
[296] Eccles. 9:4–6.
[297] Isaiah 66:24.
[298] Cf. Psalm 139 (140).
[298a] Paul Riccius, a 16th century Hebraist, was a great influence on Guillaume Postel in Biblical exegesis and Cabalistic studies. A detailed study on the relationship of Postel, Bodin, and the *Colloquium* has recently been completed by this author.
[299] Gen. 2:7.
[300] *De agricultura coelesti.*

TORALBA: I do not see how one can know by reason how long the life of angels and demons is to be, since no definition of life for living men can be perceived.

SALOMON: Certain boundaries for the life of each man have been established and decreed by God,[301] and these can be extended according to the excellence of unusual virtues in each man. But the wicked diminish and contract the boundaries of their lives. The sacred books speak often of the contraction and propagation of time and life.[302] This concerns not only the life which we live in misery but also the future life, because God often draws to himself the most holy and upright in the very flower of youth; witness Abel, who was dearest to Him and Josiah, the glory of princes.[303] And God indeed told him that he would die in a short time lest he be overwhelmed by the lamentable ruins of punishments. Isaiah said: "The just man perishes; yet there is no one who will recall that he has been snatched from imminent perils."[304] An angel told Esdras that "almost all perish, and they are most wretched. But whoever shall have escaped perils will conquer, and he will see My salvation; then they will lament for themselves who have scorned my orders and have left no room for virtues or repentance. They must be tormented after their ruin. But do not seek out of curiosity how the wicked must be punished, but how the just must be saved."[305]

CORONAEUS: Indeed I agree with everything Salomon says except when he states that the souls of those who have lived their lives as beasts will perish together with the body. Nor does he think that eternal torments have been decreed to the wicked, but after long punishment they will perish completely although he wished to affirm nothing. We trust the sacred writings which state that all the souls of all men will be immortal P. 104
and at length will live again when they have left the bodies.

CURTIUS: That the dead will rise again is also the hope and trust of the Hebrews in the last chapter of the symbol.[306]

SENAMUS: Indeed I pass over all those things which the crowd marvels at as if they were divine oracles; however, the resurrection of bodies is

[301] Job 10:14; I Kings (I Sam.) 26:23; Deut. 31:17–21.

[302] Psalms 53 (54); 108 (109):6–20; Job 20:4–29.

[303] Gen. 4:4–12; II Paralip. (II Chron.) 35:20–24.

[304] Isaiah 57:1.

[305] G. H. Box, ed., *The Ezra-Apocalypse* (London, 1912) IV Esdras, Chap. 8, Part I (Vision III), Chap. 1, pp. 198–211.

[306] Cf. Dan. 12.

most difficult for me to believe. I do not find it surprising that the Athenians laughed[307] at Paul when he spoke about the resurrection of bodies.[308]

FRIDERICUS: There was a philosopher, Athenagoras,[309] who wrote an elegant speech to Marcus Aurelius the emperor, *About Resurrection.* Also Justin Martyr excelled in the teachings of philosophy under the same prince and refuted the arguments of the Sophists about resurrection most accurately.[310] In addition to these Democritus, easily the leading philosopher of his time, believed in the resurrection of bodies.[311]

TORALBA: Pliny[312] made fun of the empty promises of Democritus who affirmed resurrections, although he himself was not resurrected. Is it not madness and evil to repeat life and death?

SENAMUS: I would gladly hear those arguments of Justin which Fridericus has mentioned.

FRIDERICUS: I am reluctant to relate everything; still I am not reluctant to discuss one thing or another, lest I seem inept. Justin said if things are from elements, they again become elements, although it is foolish for the same things to exist again which have existed from elements. Likewise, if it is in God's power that men are made and destroyed, is it not also in His power that we are made a second time and are destroyed?[313] Toralba showed earlier that the state and condition of all things depend on God's will alone. Why then can God, who created matter from nothing and men from dust, not create again the same from dust?

OCTAVIUS: No one doubts that God can do this. The question is, however, whether He wants to or not.

CURTIUS: If it is wrong to be in doubt about power, surely it is wicked to be undecided about will, since in countless places in sacred scripture we have clear evidence of divine will.[314]

307 *non sine risu* R

308 Acts 17:32.

309 Athenian philosopher (2nd cent. A.D.) who converted to Christianity and defended Christian doctrine against paganism.

310 *Apol.* I. 19–20.

311 Democritus (c. 460–370 B.C.) adopted the atomic theory of his master, Leucippus. Concerning Democritus' belief in the resurrection of bodies, Proclus cites Democritus in his book *About Hades* as one who wrote about those who seemed to die yet lived again. Indeed death was not an extinction of all the life of the body. See Diels, *Frag. der Vorsokrat.* (6th ed.), II, Demokritos, B I, 130.

312 See *ibid.*, II, 68, Par. 76, p. 103. Also cf. *ibid.*, I, Herakleitos, B. Frag. 63, p. 164.

313 Justin, *Apol.* I. 19.

314 Matt. 12:22; Luke 22:19; John 20:17; I Cor. 15:20–28, 38–40; Dan. 12.

OCTAVIUS: The Ismaelites believe there will be a resurrection as the books of the *Koran* prove. Mohammed, in *Azora* 48, 10, said: "At the sound of the trumpet the dead surrender everything, unless the right hand of God shall have saved them; with the second sound of the trumpet all things shall rise up." Moreover, he states that those who will be resur- P. 105
rected will have the stature of Adam, the learning of Mohammed, the beauty of Christ; moreover, God will arouse the dead with the same facility as He created them. Still, some among the Ismaelite theologians and philosophers who reverence sacred allegories hope there is no resurrection of bodies but only of souls. And surely there are two tenets of the Christian faith, namely resurrection and deification of men, which have kept countless people from the Christian religion; I mention in particular, Origen Adamantius,[315] Synesius[316] a bishop, the Phereonites,[317] Barbonians,[318] Zachaeans.[319]

CORONAEUS: Indeed we should rejoice that there is an agreement among Hebrews, Ismaelites, and Christians about the resurrection of the dead.

SALOMON: Rabbi Jochanan, explaining God's words—"I shall destroy man whom I have created," according to the view of Simon Jozadach said that bone of the vertebra, called *netz*, which was to have been the means of resurrection for those who perished in the flood, at that time had disappeared. He writes that this bone is not crushed under pressure, does not burn when subjected to fire and does not dissolve when placed in water.[320] It is not weakened in any part when forged with anvil and hammer; however, the anvils and hammers break. Indeed, no bones are harder than teeth, which according to Pliny,[321] resisted fire and burned only after constant application of flames. The Hebrews recounted these

[315] Although Origen made a journey to Arabia to refute certain heretics who denied the resurrection (Eusebius, *Hist. Eccl.* VI. 37), he was criticized after his death for his views about resurrection. Among the critics was Methodius, who wrote several works against Origen, one being a treatise, *On the Resurrection.* Origen's own book *On the Resurrection* has been lost.

[316] Synesius of Cyrene, before he became bishop, declared in a letter to Euoptius that the duties of a bishop were incompatible with his way of life. He also stated that he did not consider the soul to be posterior to the body, and he expressed a belief in the resurrection of all nature. In spite of these unorthodox opinions he was consecrated bishop of Ptolomais in 409 A.D. See below, Book IV, note 186.

[317] *Phibionitas* M [318] A Gnostic sect. [319] A Gnostic sect.

[320] *nec in aquam conjectum dissolvi* MR. Prof. Morton Smith explains that the reading *netz* (*Bereshit rabba* XXVIII. 3, edited by J. Theodore) means flower, but here perhaps base of the spinal column. There is no such word as *Lutz.*

[321] *Hist. nat.* VII. 16. 70.

things allegorically to indicate the resurrection of souls. Rabbi Juda, Moses Rambam, and Cynaeus say that no chapter of sacred scripture is free from affirmation of resurrection. "Those who have fallen from heaven will return into heaven," Cynaeus said. "Those who have fallen from the earth will die completely." And so the Hebrews call a wicked man *beli ya' al*, that is, one who does not ascend; the unlearned call him Belial. For when the teacher of wisdom had written that there would be the same end for man and beast,[322] a Chaldean commentator interpreted it thus: "For the wicked who have not repented and for beasts of burden there will be the same ruin and destruction." Moreover, in Sacred Scripture men who live as cattle are frequently referred to as beasts of burden. The psalmist says this: "Sheep, cows, and flocks of the field."[323] Jerome interprets: "Cattle, brute animals or brute men who are no different from the beasts." When a fast had been proclaimed by royal decree for men and beasts that they might invoke God,[324] they explain the word beasts as men who live as beasts; they think their souls die with the bodies, but they say the souls of the just will remain beyond the bodies, that is, they will rise again.

P. 106 CURTIUS: But Isaiah[325] confirmed there would be a resurrection of bodies in these words: "Your dead will live and will rise again just as My body."

SALOMON: This is the place which has deceived many interpreters who read for the word *nevelati* (of my corpse) another word because of the similarity of the letters. And indeed my soul clothed in body will rise, but with a subtle body, that is, with an airy or lighter one, as Toralba earlier explained that all the minds of all men have corporeal substance. Now if air is not visible, for this reason it is still a body. In like manner the mind, whether airy or fiery, will not be called incorporeal because it cannot be seen. The preceding words of this same chapter show this interpretation agrees with Isaiah's words. He[326] said: "The dead will not live, and the violent tyrants will not rise again." But it is much truer and more reasonable that the soul in the manner of angels is clothed with some heavenly and delicate essence rather than with a heavy and impure body. The Jerusalem interpretation confirms this. For when Esau had sold the rights of primogeniture,[327] this interpreter adds: "Because when he denied the resurrection, he scorned the future life." Stili human minds will live without bodies. Therefore, the true resurrection is not of body but of the soul leaping from this tomb. For this reason, it is called *sōma* (body), that is, *sēma* (tomb), as Plato explains.[328]

322 Eccles. 3:19. 323 Psalm 8:8. 324 Jonah 3:7. 325 Isaiah 26:19.
326 Isaiah 26:14. 327 Gen. 25:34. 328 *Cratylus* 400B; *Gorgias* 493A.

Toralba: Therefore, this interpretation explains the countless absurdities, which Senamus hates, and the empty opinions of those who think that angels and separated souls are free from body. For if they think that souls will be happier with a covering of bones and flesh and will fly to heaven along with their bodies, surely they think the condition of angels is much worse than the human condition, although this is much lower. Nevertheless, this opinion of Salomon seems consistent with the writings of Paul:[329] "A living body is sown; a spiritual body will rise." Likewise: "We have worn the image of a terrestrial body; we will wear the image of a heavenly body."[330] Also these words are clearer: "When this mortal body has put on immortality, already it will not be flesh or blood, but a heavenly body."[331] It is sufficiently clear from these words that bodies which will rise will be free of flesh and bones; still they will be spiritual[332] and heavenly bodies. But now what can we say about the ascent of bodies to heaven? For from earth to the heaven of stars the distance is at least 74,697,600 miles, as the Arabs say; from the starry heaven all the way to the Chrystallinum,[333] where they say the abode of God and the saints is, the distance is the same, according to Hebrew theologians and philosophers. Consequently, if the bodies were borne in a straight line upward in the swiftest flight—that is, if they travel 50,000 miles every day, it is logical that they could not arrive at the blessed abode in 80,000 years; indeed neither bodily mass nor even the fleetest swallows are carried with such swiftness. Besides, when they believe that the wicked and the good P. 107 will rise again with the same members as before, it is reasonable that the wicked, by sheer numbers, would overcome the number of good men. Nevertheless, they have affirmed that the wicked will suffer in the depths of the earth the eternal misfortune of punishment. Obviously these ideas seem not only incredible but also absurd; since, if all the bodies of all men who have died up to this time will rise again, they cannot be confined in the very narrow confines and prisons of the earth nor even in the most ample bosom of heaven. For bodies cannot penetrate bodies. But if they become phantoms, true bodies will not rise, but empty forms and fleeting images of shades.

Curtius: We have been told that bodies which will rise again will be penetrable for this reason because they will be glorified; furthermore, Christ passed through closed doors in the gathering of his disciples.[334]

[329] I Cor. 15:44. [330] I Cor. 15:49. [331] I Cor. 15:54. [332] *spiritualia* MR
[333] Cf. Seneca, *Quaest. nat.* III. 25. 12.
[334] John 20:19, 26.

Toralba: Then one must admit that rotted bodies become glorified with the resurrection. This is absurd; still more absurd is it to admit that bodies of whatever sort they will finally be are penetrable. For fire and air, the thinnest bodies, can indeed be rarefied, but then they must break forth and exist in a different place when they are rarefied to the utmost degree.

Fridericus: This is to do violence to our faith, since the most sacred testimonies of the evangelists have confirmed that Christ, clothed in skin, flesh and bones, rose up with the same body as before, ate roasted fish, and ascended to heaven in this state.[335] This testimony leaves no room for doubt. Augustine[336] wrote that all sects which claim some religion admit a final resurrection of souls. But if Salomon puts less credibility in our books because of his religion, I think he will not repudiate Isaiah and Ezechiel. Isaiah affirmed clearly that the body would rise again.[337] Ezechiel had a vision about bones moving in a field and coming together to their own place. Then they were covered with ligaments, nerves, fibers, flesh, and skin; later the winds breathed on these bodies and enlivened them.[338] Ezechiel thought this indicated that the resurrection was very true.[339] When the Spanish rushed into Peru and snatched gold from all the temples and treasures, the Indians thought nothing more repulsive than that they threw bones from the tombs in their search for gold, since they believed this would prevent a resurrection of bodies. Augustine said, to allay doubt, that not only would men of ripe age rise again in perfect bodies, but even those abortive and imperfect conceptions, dead in the womb, would have a resurrection into perfect bodies.[340]

P. 108 Salomon: We seem to have explained a passage in Isaiah which was incorrectly interpreted before. Moreover, the vision of Ezechiel would have no meaning unless it indicated more than it seemed to. If any one thinks that Jacob's ladder[341] which extended from earth to the summit of heaven was a ladder, he completely misses the true meaning. And so the prophet explaining the vision that was received said: "These the bones are the Israelites who complain that their bones have dried up and their hope has perished, since they have been led away as exiles by the enemy."[342]

Coronaeus: If there is no destruction of souls in a dead body, how can it happen that resurrection is understood to refer to minds? For we say that something rises again, which is again raised up after a collapse because

335 John 21:9–14.
336 *De civ. Dei* 22:5.
337 Isaiah 26:19.
338 Ezech. 37:1–14.
339 Ezech. 37:12.
340 *De civ. Dei* 22:12, 13.
341 Gen. 28:12.
342 Ezech. 37:11.

of its destructible nature. The human mind does not die, since it survives the body, nor does it fall. Therefore it will not even rise again. But if according to certain hidden judgments of God certain minds of wicked men perish completely and have no hope of a resurrection, still it seems that we must understand a resurrection of bodies in each case.

Octavius: More probable would be the opinion of those who explain the resurrection of the wicked as a change from impiety to piety, from sins to virtue, according to these words of Christ: "Who shall have believed in Me has passed from death to life."[343] The Pythagoreans were accustomed to erect tombs for the wicked as if for the dead.

Fridericus: Tertullian[344] refuted this heresy with these words: "Certain people say that a resurrection has already been accomplished; they malign a future resurrection of the dead as imaginary and feigned. They think there is no other resurrection than that which has already happened, and happens daily, when one rises up to God, after he has left the tomb of death, that is, the tomb of damnation in which he lay dead, and acquires a knowledge of God which leads the soul back into life. Hymenaeus and Philaetus were leaders of this heresy; Paul rebuked them in his Epistle to Timothy,[345] and Augustine[346] refuted them in these words: "Let us not hear those who deny a resurrection of the flesh, since they do not understand the apostle when he says that it is necessary for the corruptible to put on incorruption[347] and the mortal to put on immortality. When this will happen, there will be no flesh and blood, but a heavenly body."

Octavius: If the body will be celestial, there will be no flesh, no blood; the invisible body, just as heaven, will be something intellectual without skin, without flesh, without bones, without solid flesh, without entrails, without teeth. For if the corpses themselves did rise, it would have been written in vain that the souls of the blessed will be like angels, since angels are clothed in human form with a certain celestial essence. For when certain Epicurean Sadducees asked Christ whose wife was the woman who had married seven husbands in turn, Christ, cursing the corporeal pleasures of marriage, said the blessed would be like to angels.[348] He strengthened P. 109
his argument by saying: "Moses showed that truly the dead will rise when he said: 'The God of Abraham, the God of Isaac, the God of Jacob

[343] John 5:24.
[344] *De praeser. haer.* XIV. 33; also cf. *Apol.* I. 48.
[345] II Tim. II. 17.
[346] *De civ. Dei* 22:21.
[347] *incorruptionem* MR
[348] Matt. 22:23–30; Mark 12:18–25; Luke 20:27–36.

is not the God of the dead but of the living.' "[349] From this passage it is clear that there is not a resurrection of bodies but of souls, since He says that Abraham and his son and grandson had risen again and live.

FRIDERICUS: Epiphanius writes that these words about Abraham and Isaac were lacking in the text of Marcion.[350]

OCTAVIUS: Still we see these were repeated by three of the gospel writers in the very same words.

SALOMON: If you accept the text of Marcion, you will find innumerable passages in all the books of the New Testament have been cut out;[351] an example of this is: "You seek the living; He rose from the dead."[352] This statement is lacking in the text of Marcion.

CURTIUS: Let us omit Marcion the corruptor of the prophets and let us use the books which are yours[353] as well as ours,[354] that is, the books of the Old Testament. For no one can deny that Elias brought forth the son of the widow of Sarepta, and restored him to his mother.[355] Likewise a corpse tossed into the tomb of Elisha revived at the same moment.[356]

SALOMON: I do not doubt that the recent and inviolate corpses of the prophets had revived because of prayers and virtue; but we have never read that the ashes of burned corpses or defiled bones or those corpses which before had been food for wild beasts and fish had been revived. Indeed from the book of David,[357] in which he denies that divine praises are celebrated by the dead, the Chaldean interpreter changes it thus: "Will bodies recovered from dust rise again?"

SENAMUS: Pliny said that often when recent corpses, which were thought to be completely lifeless, were placed on burning pyres or carried to the fire, they revived from the warmth.[358] Although Pope Julius II had lain lifeless for two days, his revived spirit returned to him without fires. Nay even John Duns, who used the name Scotus, revived after he was let down in the grave and covered with dirt. But, when he had bashed his head on the bier[359] although his spirit was buried, he was raised up, bloody but still breathing. Indeed we have read from the most ancient writers that souls follow their corpses for a while.[360]

[349] Matt. 22:31–32; Mark 12:26–27; Luke 20:37–38.

[350] *Contra haeres*; also cf. Tertullian, *De praeser. haer.* XIV. 33.

[351] See Tertullian, *De praeser. haer.* XIV. 16–17; Origen, *Contra celsum* II. 27; Irenaeus, *Adv. Haeres* I. 28 (29). 4.

[352] Luke 24:5–6.

[353] *vestris* MR

[354] *nostris* MR

[355] III Kings (I Kings) 17:21–22.

[356] IV Kings (II Kings) 13:21.

[357] Psalm 88:11–12.

[358] *Hist. nat.* VII. 52. 174–79.

[359] *ferculo* MR

[360] Plato, *Phaedo* LVII. 107E–108B.

FRIDERICUS: We read that not only Lazarus,[361] who had been in the tomb for four days, but also many corpses of saints who had already become dust so many centuries before had revived at the sound of Christ's voice and had risen up with the dying Christ.[362]

OCTAVIUS: I remember that a clever theologian[363] was accustomed to recall the opinion of those who said that those corpses of saints, which were said to have revived, had lived for three days, then disappeared. "Why," he said, "did those saints rather than others rise up again?" Then he denies that those who had lived again were dead, since Paul[364] clearly wrote that the resurrection would be life eternal. He also believes the same about Lazarus whom John[365] alone of all the gospel writers says lived again. Surely it would seem that no kindness had been granted to Lazarus but rather punishment, if he were forced to return into a defiled and rotten corpse from the heavenly company of angels. When Pompey's followers in the *Pharsalia* asked the Thessalian Erichtho about future victory, the witch, summoning the shades from the dark, misty shadows of the underworld promised that, if she were rewarded, the soul which she had called forth would never return into the corpse, even with songs or sacrifices: "No words or herbs will dare loose your long sleep of forgetfulness."[366] And the Platonists[367] thought that as the souls were sent down into these corpses on account of some great crime, so also the souls of most holy men which returned into corpses at Christ's death would necessarily have committed some inexplicable disgrace, to be subjected again to the most foul prisons, since death was defined by the theologians as punishment for the wicked. Or if we grant that those saints who had come to life again could not die, where in the world have they hidden themselves? For it was not right for them to ascend to heaven before Christ, with the original body recovered. For example, when Christ at the point of death had promised to the robber that He would be with him on that very day in paradise,[368] where He is said to have arrived only after forty days, obviously He meant He would be with him in spirit not in body. P. 110

TORALBA: Surely no one can prove the vulgar resurrection of bodies without openly admitting the Pythagorean *paliggenesian*, regeneration

[361] John 11:39–44.

[362] Matt. 27:52–53.

[363] Calvin.

[364] I Cor. 15:53-54.

[365] John 11:39–44.

[366] Lucan, *Phars.* VI. 768–69.

[367] Cf. Plotinus, *Enneads* III. 4. 2–4. Plato, *Phaedo* 107D. See Gustavus Wolff, ed., *Porphyrii de philosophia ex oraculis hauriende* (Hildesheim, 1962), p. 216. (Cited hereafter as Wolff, *Porphyry*.)

[368] Luke 23:43.

as Marcus Varro[369] calls it, or *metempsychōsin* transmutation, as Plotinus[370] says, or *metensōmatōsin*, corporeal change, according to Justin,[371] or *metaggismous tōn psychōn*, transferring of souls, as Epiphanius[372] said, or according to the Hebrews, a change of souls. This return of souls into bodies was indeed pleasing to the Pythagoreans, but was also distasteful to all others. But now those who hope for a resurrection of bodies hope not for the deaf and dumb, not for the deformed, nor the leprous, or those misshapen in any part, but for the alert, the strong, and the handsome, with a certain acquired and constant health and strength of bodies. Nay even Scotus, the theologian, wrote that women would rise again as
P. 111 men. Augustine[373] held this opinion because Paul himself wrote that we as perfect men would finally meet Christ face to face, and he knew well enough that there would be no need for that sex. A resurrection of this kind formerly would have been desired for the wicked who were leprous, dumb, or deformed. How much better was the opinion of the Academicians[374] who believed that the souls of depraved men would return not into human bodies but into the bodies of wolves or ravenous beasts.

CURTIUS: But Theopompus,[375] Aeneas Gazaeus,[376] and Seneca[377] in their writings acknowledged a resurrection that was popular and consistent with the Christian and Israelite faith.

TORALBA: Since it has been stated previously that the souls of noble and brave men would pass into angelic natures, surely a fall of souls

369 Servius, on Vergil, *Aen.* III. 68, says: "non me sed *paliggenesian* esse dicit (Pythagoras)."

370 Cf. Alexander Aphrodisias, *De anima* XXVII. 18; Wolff, *Porphyry, De abstinentia* IV. 16; Dodds, *Proclus, In Platonis rempublicam commentarii* in R II. 340 K. Pherecydes is said to be the first to use the word. See Diels, *Frag. der Vorsokrat.* (6th ed.), I. 44. 20; also I. 99. 28 ff.

371 *Apol.* I. 18–19, *Dial. Tryph.* 80. Empedocles said that all souls change into all living things. See Diels, *Frag. der Vorsokrat.* (6th ed.), I. 289. 3. Origen, *Contra celsum.* V. 49, speaks of the Pythagorean myth about corporeal change. See Diels, *Frag. der Vorsokrat.* (6th ed.), I. 367. 14.

372 *metaggismous* means transmigrations, which is a metaphor from literal pouring from one vessel to another.

373 *De civ. Dei* XXII. 17.

374 *Academici* MR

375 Theopompus of Chios was a famous historian and orator of the 4th century B.C. None of his works are extant; however, he wrote a book *About Holiness* (*Peri eusebias*). Cf. Porphyry, *De abstin.* II. 16. See Smith, *Dictionary* (1880 ed.), III.

376 Aeneas Gazaeus (fl. A.D. 487), was at first a Platonist and Sophist, later a Christian. When a Christian, he composed a dialogue on the immortality of the soul and the resurrection of the body, called *Theophrastus*. See Smith, *Dictionary*, I, 32.

377 *Quaest. nat.* II. 58. 3–7; VI. 32. 6–8.

from those heavenly abodes into the hovels of corpses would make completely wretched a life which had formerly been blessed. Moreover, when misfortune supplants happiness, this is the most unhappy misfortune. In short, if human souls became more blessed with a resurrection of bodies, the condition of angels would be worse than that of men, whereas the status of angels is promised by Christ as the highest happiness to good men.[378] Also it would follow from this that eternal incorporeal God would be much lower than corporeal creatures, and this is the most dangerous consideration. The glory of Roman wisdom, Cato,[379] used to say that he did not want to be a boy again, even if someone should cook him as they cooked that old man Pelias. Finally, if resurrection is granted as a kindness, the wicked would thus secure reward indeed of punishments.

FRIDERICUS: Justin[380] wrote that the final end of resurrection was merely rewards for the good and punishment for the wicked.

OCTAVIUS: As if the good may not secure rewards without bodies nor the wicked punishments. Why had the happiness of a heavenly paradise been promised to a robber who had not yet risen again, if those corpses are necessary for happiness? Or why would an evil rich man be said to be tormented in Hell if there were need of corpses for dispensing punishments?

CORONAEUS: I beg you by immortal God and for the right of our piety and friendship that we not allow ourselves to be pulled away by any enticing arguments from the established and accepted opinion of faith. And since we have strayed from physical questions to metaphysical ones, we must take care not to mingle the sacred with the profane. Tomorrow we must decide whether it is proper for a good man to talk about religion.

With these words each departed after his customary farewell.

378 Luke 20:36.

379 Marcus Porcius Cato "Censorius" (234-149 B.C.) fought as a youth in the Second Punic War. Throughout his long career in public service, he distinguished himself by stern traditional morality. His conservatism was associated with his hatred of things Greek entering into Roman life. He wrote, among many things, an encyclopedia for his first son and letters, *apophthegmata.* His best known work seems to have been *De agri cultura,* which inspired historical study and founded prose style. See *Ox. Class. Dict.*, pp. 173–74.

380 *Apol.* I. 52.

BOOK IV

ON the following day Octavius brought Coronaeus a tragedy that he
P. 112 had written about the parricide of three children of Prince Solimannus; Coronaeus asked me to read it because of the erudition of the author and because of the merit of the theme. After I had completed the reading at lunch, all congratulated Octavius. Coronaeus praised him profusely and said that tragedy had been elegantly composed in regard to the choice of words, the seriousness of the sentences, the arrangement of the topic and the variety of verses.

When they had given thanks to God according to their custom, they sang hymns of praise to their soul's delight. CORONAEUS said: Often I have wondered why there is such sweetness in a tone that has the full octave, the fifth and the fourth blended at the same time;[1] just now you have heard the sweetest harmony with the full system of the highest tone blended with the lowest, with the fourth and fifth interspersed; although the highest tone is opposite to the lowest, why is it that harmonies in unison, in which no tone is opposite, are not pleasing to the trained ear?

FRIDERICUS: Many think that the harmony is more pleasing when the ratios of numbers correspond.[2]

CURTIUS: I am amazed that the most learned men approve of this, since no ratios seem to combine more aptly than geometric progressions; the last members accord with the first, the middle with each, all with all, and also positions and orders are related, as 2, 4, 8, 16. Still in these systems that most pleasing harmony fails. When the numbers are arranged in this manner, 2, 3, 4, 6, and the ratios have been separated, we delight

[1] Cf. Pliny, *Hist. nat.* II. 20. 85.

[2] Cf. Philo, *De opificio mundi* XXXVII. 107–110.

in this harmony. Indeed, what is the reason that the interval of the pure fifth (3/2) is most pleasing, but the apotome (9/8) is heavily offensive?

OCTAVIUS: I think harmony is produced when many sounds can be blended; but when they cannot be blended, one conquers the other as the sound enters the ears, and the dissonance offends the delicate senses of wiser men.

SENAMUS: I do not think a ratio of numbers or a blending of tones produce this sweetness, since a variety of colors presented to the eyes is more pleasing than if all are mingled simultaneously. Likewise, the flavor of fresh oil and vinegar is very pleasing, but it cannot be mingled by any force. Also the most dissimilar songs of birds, blended by no ratio, produce a most pleasing delight for the ears. Plato thought it strange that no dissonance is perceived in the song of birds,[3] however much it is joined with men's voices or lyres.

TORALBA: Indeed I think that pleasing delight of colors, tastes, odors, and harmonies depends on the harmony of the nature of each, a harmony which depends on the blended union of opposites. For example, something too hot or too cold offends the touch; likewise too much brightness or too much darkness offends the sight, and too much sweetness and too much bitterness offends the taste. But if these are blended by nature or art, they seem most pleasing. I find it hard to agree with Seneca's opinion,[4] based on the Stoics, that nothing bad can touch a good man, since, he says, opposites are not[5] blended. If boiling water is mixed with the coldest and driest dust, the greatest blending of opposites exists, tempered by art and pleasing to touch. We also see elementary bodies, which are joined together in nature herself, blended from opposing qualities and elements which Galen[6] thought could not be united by any craft. And so we can defend Seneca and vindicate him from censure if we say that he spoke about substances, not about qualities and accidents. Indeed nothing can be so easily united as water with wine; still they are not blended among themselves as things which are mingled by nature, because wine is separated from water by soaking it in a sponge which has been saturated with oil. Likewise gold is blended by design with silver, and bronze infused with silver; they are separated by gold water, yet they P. 113

[3] On Plato and music, see *Res pub.* III. 10–12; IV. 4. Also cf. Aristotle, *Polit.* VIII. 4–7.

[4] *fistulis* M

[5] *Quaest. nat.* IVA. 19–20; VI. 2.

[6] Hermann Diels, *Die Fragmente der Vorsokratiker*, 6th ed. (Berlin, 1954) [cited hereafter as *Frag. der Vorsokrat.* (6th ed.)], II. 97. 49.

would never be drawn apart if they had been blended by nature herself. An example is amber, which nature herself tempered with equal portions of gold and silver.

SENAMUS: If there is no contrariety in substances, how is it possible that contrary substances are blended?

TORALBA: Aristotle believed that nothing was contrary to substance.[7] However, since there is opposition of form with form, as the form of fire to the form of water, and since the contrariety of accidents, for example, extreme dryness and humidity, severest heat and cold, could happen only from the contrariety of the forms of fire and water, which differ in their whole nature, who can doubt that forms of each, that is, substances[8] are contrary among themselves? Indeed that most certain decree in nature is proclaimed, not as plainly as appropriately for the question. On account of this one each thing is of such a kind, and that the more.[9] If accidents of fire and water are opposite because of the power of forms, forms must be much more[10] contrary among themselves. Therefore, things which are contrary to each other in nature herself cannot be mingled by design, but only blended, joined, or united so that they seem to be one. For example, oxymel is very pleasing to taste; it is made from vinegar and honey; and from the bitter with a light burning of sweet meats[11] it becomes bittersweet,[12] a flavor most pleasing to the palate.

FRIDERICUS: In musical modulations that contrariety does not seem to be destroyed, but extreme opposites are brought together by intermingling of the middle tones. For the simple sound of the hypaton produces a
P. 114 sweet harmony with the highest sound of the hyperbolaion or the whole octave since from opposites it is united in the whole diameter. If you shall join the middle voice to these, with one it will produce a full octave, with another a fifth, from which comes the most pleasing harmony of all modulation from the proper union of opposites.

TORALBA: This is very apparent in all of nature. Opposites when united by the interpolation of certain middle links present a remarkable harmony of the whole which otherwise would perish completely if this whole world were fire or moisture. In like manner tones[13] in unison would take away all sweetness of harmony.

[7] *Metaphys.* V. 8. 10.
[8] *id est, substantias* MR
[9] *Propter unum quodque tale: et illud magis* MR
[10] *multo magis* MR
[11] *carnium* MR
[12] Cf. Diels, *Frag. der Vorsokrat.* (6th ed.), II. 114. 134.
[13] *duo* missing in MR

FRIDERICUS: Surely heavenly revolutions, though contrary and moving in an agitated pattern, are held in check, and the contrary force of Mars and Saturn is restrained by the intermediate light of Jupiter.

SENAMUS: How then does it happen that we see that salutary mean always confounded by some hindrance, as health with sickness, pleasure with pain, peace of mind with anxiety?

CURTIUS: That impediment is as useful as a drainage ditch is in a city. The poisonous toad in the garden or the spider in the house are as necessary for gathering poisons as the hangman in the state. Even that keenest sweetness of harmony which we have heard most eagerly just now would not have been so[14] pleasing unless the musician had contrived some dissonant or harsh note for our sensitive ears, since the pleasure is not perceived without a pain that precedes it and produces boredom when continued too long. We have attempted to imitate in these verses this contrariety in all things which has been tempered by immortal God with remarkable wisdom:

Creator of the world three times greatest of all,
Three times best parent of the heaven,
Who tempers the changes of the world,
Giving proper weight to all things,
And who measures each thing from His own ladle
In number, ratio, time,
Who with eternal chain joins with remarkable wisdom two things
opposite in every way, preparing protection for each,
Who, moderating melody with different sounds and P. 115
voices yet most satisfying to sensitive ears,
heals sickness, has mingled cold with heat and moisture
with dryness,
The rough with the smooth, sweetness with pain,
shadows with light, quiet with motion,
tribulation with prosperity
Who directs the fixed courses of the heavenly
stars from east to west,
West to east with contrary revolutions,
Who joins hatred with agreement,
A friend to hateful enemies.
This greatest harmony of the universe
though discordant contains our safety.

[14] *tam* MR

Toralba: In a state of illustrious men justice, integrity, or virtue would not even be perceived unless wicked men mingled with the good, sane with the mad, brave with the cowardly, rich with poor, low with the noble, were contained within the same walls, provided that evils, if evils are anywhere, are weaker than good. Indeed, these discussions which Coronaeus began would offer no purpose or pleasure unless they took lustre from opposing arguments and reasons.

Senamus: I do not understand why a state, which drove out all wicked men, would not be happier than one which preferred for some wicked ones to remain? Or how can dissension be harmonious when there can be no firmer bond for the eternal harmony of citizens and friends than supreme agreement and will in the mutual love of human and divine matters.

Curtius: Indeed Marcus Tullius[15] expressed this opinion in words which were at variance with his actions, so that one must seek less what he thinks, since it is evident, than what he did.

For who cherished Epicurus[16] more than Atticus?[17] Still has one ever been a more devoted friend than Cicero was to Atticus? Nonetheless Cicero followed the philosophy of the Academicians, and for as long as he lived he scathed the Epicureans with his writings because nothing is more difficult than to refrain from speaking ill about the wicked, as Theophrastus used to say.[18]

P. 116 Toralba: To be sure the Academicians, Stoics, Peripatetics, Epicureans, and Cynics used to fight about their philosophy, but they easily protected the harmony in the same state because the opposite camps of Epicureans and Stoics were joined, as if by certain bonds, midway by the Academicians and Peripatetics. Otherwise, if one opposite were joined to another opposite with no middle ground between, there would necessarily be continual battle.

Fridericus: It has always seemed to me a very difficult matter to cherish friendship and preserve harmony when there is such a variety of differing opinions about human and divine matters.

Curtius: It is one thing to cherish friendship, another to preserve

[15] *De amicitia.* 6.20 [16] *Epicurum* MR

[17] Titus Pomponius Atticus (109–32 B.C.) was an intimate friend of Cicero and a great patron of the arts. Because he took the middle course and was a friend to conservatives and Caesarians alike, he survived the civil wars. Whether his neutral policy was a result of calculation or his Epicureanism is difficult to decide.

[18] Cf. Pliny, *Hist. nat.*, Pref. 28–29.

harmony. For as the variant natures[19] of individual things combine for the harmony of one universe, so also do the hostilities of individual citizens foster the harmony of all peoples. The Roman state flourished when the patricians blocked the plebs and the tribunician power thwarted the consular greed.[20] For this reason Marcus Cato the Censor used to sow strife among the slaves and discord among the magistrates lest they agree in a wicked conspiracy for the former to plunder private property and the latter to plunder the state. Lycurgus[21] decided on a similar plan when he summoned for the same duties magistrates and legates who he knew were divided by civil strife.

CORONAEUS: To be sure, we admit this consideration in this state if there are many colleagues of the same charge and office. For a third party forces two opposing factions toward harmony, when the others have allied themselves. Otherwise it seems dangerous to entrust the same office to two of opposite views. As long as Marcus Crassus lived there was no disagreement of will between Pompey and Caesar, since Crassus, a middle voice as it were, easily reconciled Caesar to Pompey;[22] however, when Crassus was killed in Chaldaea, the other two rushed to arms.[23] Likewise, when Marcus Lepidus was toppled from the triumvirate, Antony and Augustus engaged in civil war.[24]

[19] *naturae discrepantes* MR

[20] The citizens of Rome were divided into two classes, patricians and plebeians. When the plebeians suffered grievances, they brought pressure by seceding and virtually creating a new state. During this struggle the plebeians established their own officers, tribunals and aediles. Landmarks in the struggle are the *Lex Publilia Valeronia* (471 B.C.), the appointment of the *Decemviri* and the codification of the Twelve Tables, and the *Lex Hortensia*, which gave *plebiscita* the force of laws binding on the whole community. As the patricians tried to thwart the plebeian assault, new magistracies were created. The plebeians gradually gained admissions to the major magistracies. See Sir Ronald Syme, *The Roman Revolution* (Oxford, 1939), and T.R.S. Broughton, *Magistrates of the Roman Republic* (New York, 1951–52) for illumination on the republic and office holding. Also helpful is Lily Ross Taylor, *Party Politics in the Age of Caesar* (Berkeley, 1961).

[21] Lycurgus was the traditional founder of the Spartan constitution. See Herodotus I. 65–66.

[22] Crassus, Pompey, and Caesar engaged in an alliance in 60 B.C., known as the "First Triumvirate" (Dio Cassius XXXVII. 56).

[23] While on a Parthian campaign, Crassus was killed in 53 B.C. Relations between Pompey and Caesar were disintegrating by 50 B.C., and the result was Pompey's defeat by Caesar at Pharsalus in 48 B.C. Pompey fled to Egypt but was stabbed to death as he disembarked.

[24] After Philippi (42 B.C.) Marcus Lepidus was deprived of his provinces by Antony and Octavian Augustus, who were planning to oust him from the triumvirate.

SALOMON: I agree this is true in a state balanced between the nobility and the people, but in a royal tyranny nothing prevents two adversaries from joining in the same office, since they are easily bound by royal power; for example, Alexander the Great reconciled Hephaestion[25] to Craterus with only a nod. Indeed this becomes more obvious in nature herself, which is the most ancient exemplar for a well-ordered state. Not only the contrary elements, but even the stars themselves, and also the powers of angels are subject to the power of one divine majesty. And so God alone is said to reconcile peace in the lofty abodes.

SENAMUS: Are civil wars also waged among the angels?

SALOMON: I believe the intelligible or angelic world is governed by the power of God alone, the heavenly world by the angelic, the elementary by the heavenly; moreover I think the higher orders are exemplars for the
P. 117 lower orders. But if a conflict of virtue often exists among the best leaders and officers, if the elements war among themselves, if we see contrary motions of the heavenly stars, who can doubt that strife also happens among the angels? The voice of the angel speaking to Daniel is applicable here: "The prince of the Persian kingdom resisted me for twenty days, but Michael was at my side among the princes."[26] Similar was that word of God to Pharaoh, whom[27] we have interpreted in a more secret meaning to indicate the prince of demons: "I have raised you up to exercise My power against you,[28] so that the glory of My name might be sowed in every part of the world."[29] Therefore among angels there exists no conflict except the conflict of virtues and noble souls. Among men virtues seldom vie with virtues, but often vices struggle with virtues. Also vices struggle with vices, opinion with opinion, piety with impiety, superstition with religion.[30] Still superstition itself most often contends with superstition.

FRIDERICUS: I am amazed that any harmony could exist in a state with such a variety and multitude of sects; Epiphanius and Tertullian said

---

However, his support of Octavian in the Perusine War won for him Africa and Numidia. After 36 B.C. Octavian won over his army and forced him to retire. Octavian defeated Antony at Actium in 31 B.C.

[25] Hephaestion was the closest friend of Alexander from childhood. Although a competent commander, his great value to Alexander lay in his understanding of his plans for empire. Hephaestion's death in 324 B.C. brought great grief to Alexander.

[26] Dan. 10:13. [27] *quem* MR [28] *in te* MR [29] Ex. 9:16.

[30] *superstitio cum religione* MR

there were more than 120, though Themistius numbered more than 300.[31] In this age many and great wars and revolutions result from the disagreement among Christians of two religions.

CURTIUS: Nothing is more destructive in a state than for citizens to be split into two factions, whether the conflict is about laws, honors, or religion. If, however, there are many factions, there is no danger of civil war, since the groups, each acting as a check on the other, protect the stability and harmony of the state.

TORALBA: This system has been most aptly obtained from musical modulations. The natural is more elevated[32] because obviously, there is only one contrary to one; many things cannot be opposite by nature to the same thing.

OCTAVIUS: For this reason, I think, the kings of the Turks and Persians admit every kind of religion in the state, and in a remarkable harmony they reconcile all citizens and foreigners who differ in religions among themselves and with the state.

FRIDERICUS: I think nothing more desirable can happen to the greatest kingdoms and states than that all citizens be joined in the same sacred rites and in the same worship of the divine will. In no affair was Aratus[33] more praiseworthy than when he accustomed the Achaean federation, which embraced more than three hundred cities, to the same laws, the same religions, the same institutions, the same culture, the same jurisdiction, the same weights and measures; in short nothing was missing P. 118 except that so many cities were not surrounded by the same walls. And so this is, in my opinion, the stable foundation of friendship which Tullius placed in the supreme harmony of divine and human affairs.

[31] See Tertullian, *Apol.* I. 13–16. He says that Varro introduced more than 300 Jupiters. Themistius, a deacon in Alexandria about A.D. 537, belonged to the Monophysite group. Themistians denied completeness of knowledge to the human nature of Christ. The sixth century A.D. was one of strife for the church because of the Monophysite and Eutychian controversies, whose adherents were reacting against the Nestorians who taught that there is in Christ a human hypostasis as well as a divine. See *The Catholic Encyclopedia* (New York, 1911), V, 16, 533–638. This reference is quite apropos to Fridericus' next remark. The theologians of the sixth as well as the sixteenth centuries were straining at gnats.

[32] *sublimior* MR

[33] Aratus (271–213 B.C.) was a Sicyonian statesman who sought refuge at Argos after his father's murder in 264 B.C. He recovered Sicyon in 251 B.C., and united it to the Achaean League; he received subsidies for his defense against Macedon from Ptolemy Philadelphus. See *Oxford Classical Dictionary* (Oxford, 1961) (hereafter cited as *Ox. Class. Dict.*), p. 77.

OCTAVIUS: Fridericus, do you think that the Achaeans, who worshipped 36,000 gods, could agree on one and the same religion? Could the Bacchanalia be compatible with the Eleusinian mysteries?[34]

CORONAEUS: Indeed we ought to desire and to pray to immortal God, rather than hope, that there be one and the same harmony of citizens, indeed of all mortals[35] about divine matters, and one religion, provided it is the true religion.

SALOMON: Let there be no religion unless we shall grant[36] it to be the true religion.

SENAMUS:[37] Since the leaders of religions and the priests whom the ancient Greeks call *mystagogous* (one who initiates into mysteries), have had so many conflicts among themselves that no one could decide which is true among all the religions, is it not better to admit publicly all religions of all peoples in the state, as in the kingdom of the Turks and Persians, rather than to exclude one? For if we seek the reason why the Greeks, Latins, and barbarians formerly had no controversy about religions, we will find no other cause, I think, than a concord and harmony of all in all religions.

SALOMON: An exception must be made in regard to the Hebrews, who, alone separated in a unique way from all people, worshipped God eternal and cursed other divinities. Likewise the Chaldeans overturned all the temples of the gods because they thought it a sacrilege to wish to enclose gods in the confines of temples.

SENAMUS: Yet the Hebrews alone among all other people seem to me to have upset the harmony of states and kingdoms. When Antiochus Nobilis,[38] after the conquest of Jerusalem, made sacrifices to the gods,

[34] The Bacchanalia were orgiastic rites held in honor of Bacchus or Dionysus. They were frenzied in character and had many oriental elements and were celebrated only by women. The Eleusinian mysteries were celebrated at Eleusis in honor of Demeter and Persephone. The Eleusinian mysteries had no fixed doctrine, and the rites had various interpretations which could conform to the religious needs of every age. For the most complete account of these mystery religions see Lewis R. Farnell, *The Cults of the Greek States* (Oxford, 1896–1909), III and V; also see M. P. Nilsson, *A History of Greek Religion* (Oxford, 1949).

[35] *civium imo etiam mortalium omnium* MR

[36] *demus* MR

[37] *Senamus* MR *Salomon* N

[38] Antiochus IV Epiphanes ruled the Seleucid kingdom from 176–164 B.C. Thinking that the Jews in Jerusalem intended to defect to Egypt, he despoiled the Temple, and after 168 B.C. he tried forcibly to suppress the practices of Judaism, which act caused the Maccabean rebellion. Antiochus tried to hellenize the Jews, and he favored hellenization in general.

Ptolemy, son of Lagus, was one of Alexander the Great's most trusted generals.

the Jews cursed the prince. Now that prince was overcome with anger because they thought him impious. He forced the Jews to accept the sacred rites of the gentile gods, after he had inflicted severe punishments. Then they stirred up so much hatred in many nations against themselves that all nations seemed to have sworn to the destruction of one race. Celsus[39] wrote that Christians and Jews deciding too arrogantly about their own gods scorned all the divinities of the people.

FRIDERICUS: Whoever admits a variety of religious differences seems to bestir an upheaval of the true religion. Proclus[40] writes appropriately that ignorance destroys God and polytheism is no different from atheism. For who can worship God and a demon at the same time, since one is so opposite to the other?

SENAMUS: Toralba has shown that nothing can be contrary to God P. 119 because even demons are the most compliant ministers of the divine majesty. For why does one refuse to reverence the servant, not indeed as lord but as legate and messenger of the lord? Why does one likewise refuse to pray[41] to two divinities, to one that it should not harm, and to the other that it should help? For this reason the Opuntians had two high priests, one who made sacrifices to gods, the other to the demons. The Romans worshipped with supreme veneration not only those beneficent gods, as Jupiter, Mars, Diana, but also those who were said to cause harm—for example, Robigus, Febris, Paventia, Occasio, Invidia, and the other gods who avert evils or mischief.[42]

SALOMON: In this matter I surely desire the prudence of the Greeks and Latins. The Greeks gave their gods masculine names as malice, advan-

---

After Alexander's death, Ptolemy's first object was to hold Egypt, possess Cyrenaica, Cyprus, and Palestine. He occupied Palestine in 318 B.C. and was said to have conciliated the native population. Bodin seems to be in error in attributing to Ptolemy, son of Lagus, the crime of feeding Jewish infants to the soldiers.

The Ptolemy here referred to could be either Ptolemy II or Ptolemy III, under whose reigns vivisection was said to have been practiced on criminals. However, the reference seems more descriptive of Ptolemy IV, a debauchee under whom the decline of the Ptolemaic kingdom began. He was devoted to orgiastic forms of religion, and he built a temple to Homer. See below, Book V, p. 272, note 183.

[39] Origen, *Contra Celsum* III.

[40] See E. R. Dodds, *Proclus, The Elements of Theology* (Oxford, 1963), p. 101 ff. Note especially Prop. 113: "The whole number of the gods has the character of unity."

[41] *obsecrare* MR

[42] *Pliny, Hist. nat.* II. 5. 15–16. Cf. Varro, *De re rust.* I. 1. 4–6; *De ling. Lat.* VI. 16. Also Tertullian, *De cor.* XV.

tage,[43] fear, but the Latins made them feminine in sex and habit, as envy, opportunity, fear.[44] Moreover, we see that divine law places a holy injunction against the worship of foreign gods, since they can neither harm nor help anyone. For this reason we have very often read that no calamity weighs upon mortals except from the one immortal God.

SENAMUS: With such a large number of religions before us, perhaps it is possible that none of these is the true religion; on the other hand, it is not possible that more than one of these is true. Since the priests of all religions are disagreeing among themselves so violently, it is safer to admit all religions than to choose one from many, which may, perhaps, be false or to exclude this one which may be the truest of all.

OCTAVIUS: It is not safe for princes or magistrates to try to uproot religions which have been received harmoniously for a long time and whose roots are deep. For when the Greek emperors, Thomas and Constantine VI, rashly threw out the statues from all the temples, they were very cruelly killed, one by his mother, the other by the populace in the temple of Sophia itself.[45] And so Valens, Theodosius, Valentinian, Jovian, and Theodoric not only were unwilling to prohibit the sect of the Arians which had spread far and wide but even permitted it in public edicts.[46]

[43] *phthonon, kairon, phobon.* These nouns are masculine in gender.

[44] *invidiam, occasionem, paventiam.* These nouns are feminine in gender.

[45] Constantine VI (780–797) became emperor at the age of ten, but his mother Irene was his guardian and the real ruler. The Arabs and Bulgarians made devastating attacks against Constantine, and Irene used these disasters to turn the populace against her son. As he tried to escape to the Asiatic coast he was brought back and blinded. The hatred of the people seemed to stem from his poor war record rather than the question of the statues.

[46] Valens was emperor of the Eastern Roman Empire from A.D. 364 to 378. His brother, Valentinian I, chose him to be his associate in the empire and the formal division into East and West was arranged. In A.D. 366 Valens was baptized by Eudoyus, leader of the Arian party and bishop of Constantinople. After concluding a peace with the Goths which established the Danube as a boundary between Goths and Romans, he began the persecution of his orthodox and Catholic subjects. In A.D. 378 the Roman army, under Valens, was slaughtered at Adrianople.

Valentinian's reign in the West (A.D. 364 to 375) was, for the most part, able and honest. Although he was constantly occupied with the defense of the frontiers, he established schools and medical services. Unlike his brother, Valens, he was an orthodox Catholic who permitted absolute religious freedom for all his subjects. Theodosius II (A.D. 401–450), emperor of the East, summoned the Council of Ephesus (A.D. 431) which heard the charges brought against Nestorius, bishop of Constantinople, who was accused of heresy concerning the divine nature. Theodosius championed Nestorius who was finally, however, declared a heretic by the council.

The Robber Council of Ephesus was summoned by Theodosius in A.D. 449 to de-

FRIDERICUS: If according to the ancient[47] decree of the senate[48] the task had been given to the holy aediles of the Romans to keep foreign religions from the city and to permit only the worship of paternal gods, how much greater must this be the concern of Christian princes?

SENAMUS: Even the Romans could not safeguard the constancy of their own edicts when they received into the city the sacred rites of Isis, Osiris, Anubis, Apis, Asculapius, Cybele, mother of the gods.[49] Finally, Marcus Agrippa called the temple which he had constructed the Pantheon because he had dedicated it to the divinity of all the gods.[50] This is the only P. 120 temple which remains from all the ancient shrines at Rome, and Pope Boniface III[51] consecrated it to all the gods. The Athenians established

cide whether Flavian had justly deposed the archimandrite Eutyches for refusing to admit two natures in Christ. Eutyches was absolved by a small margin.

Jovian (A.D. 332–364) was a Roman emperor for one year only (A.D. 363–364). Although he established Christianity as the state religion, he is said to have passed an edict of toleration which insured full liberty of conscience, although the evidence for this is not certain.

Theodoric, king of the Ostrogoths (A.D. 454–526) was the greatest of the Gothic rulers. His reign brought an era of exceptional prosperity and progress to Italy. Taxes were reduced, marshes drained, harbors formed, and the state of agriculture vastly improved. Theodoric's tomb is one of the gems of Ravenna. Theodoric was an Arian, yet his reign was distinguished by its completely impartial attitude in matters of religion.

The one characteristic which four of these emperors had in common was a tolerance toward religion and a lack of dogmatism in religious questions. It is interesting to note that two of the five were Arian, and Theodosius was sympathetic to the Arian cause. Indeed, the Arian controversy, though never specifically identified, is apparent in many of the remarks of Bodin's speakers. In Book V Salomon, Toralba, and Octavius, who follow an Arian line of argument, are not countered sufficiently by the Protestants, and even Coronaeus is at times inclined to agree with them.

47 *veteri* N var.

48 *senatus consulto* MR

49 As early as the second century B.C., Marcus Porcius Cato warned against the "demoralizing" effects of Greek culture, and these eastern religions would fall in that class. Also see Augustine, *De civ. Dei* VII. 24–26.

50 The Pantheon was built in 27 B.C., by Marcus Agrippa, son-in-law of Augustus. Along with the adjacent baths of Agrippa it was one of the most impressive structures of ancient Rome. The existing building was completed by Hadrian. The Pantheon has been commonly assumed to have been dedicated to all the gods, but Mommsen's conjecture that, because of the seven interior niches, it was dedicated to the seven planetary deities is appealing. See S. B. Platner and T. Ashby, *A Topographical Dictionary of Ancient Rome* (London, 1929), p. 382.

51 Boniface IV, not Boniface III, secured permission from Emperor Phocas in A.D. 609 to dedicate the pagan temple to Santa Maria and all the martyrs. Because of its circular shape, it was also commonly known as Santa Maria Rotunda.

so many altars for unknown gods as Pausanias[52] in *Attica* and Paul[53]
P. 120 himself in the speech to the Athenian people attested, that they sacrificed in some way to the true God whom they did not know. Thus the ancients maintained that this world was very full of gods, since they saw admirable divine beings in all places, so they did not hesitate to exclaim: "All things are full of Jupiter!"[54] Indeed the skies and the earth are full of the majesty of divine glory. When Seneca was asking what God is, he answered by saying God is all that you see, and all that you do not see.[55] Pliny called the whole universe itself the eternal divinity.[56] For this reason I think that when these men in ages past dedicated the temples to virtues, that is, to justice, courage, peace, hope, faith, chastity, harmony, safety, piety, honor, truth, foresight, reason, clemency, sympathy, happiness, generosity, fame, eternity, they set forth the virtues of immortal God for men everywhere to view and imitate, so that they might turn from sins.[57]

CURTIUS: Cleverly spoken, Senamus. But why did they take higher vices for gods? Why was there a temple to money, to food, to drink, to pleasure, to debauchery, to Venus, and Priapus, unless they used food, drink, pleasure, lust, debauchery with greater license as though the gods were granting it.[58] I omit Febris (fever), Furina (thievery), Laverna (roguery), Risus (mockery), Luxuria (luxury), Impudentia (rashness) and the goddess Memphitis with her foul stench.[59] I pass over the gods which were consecrated to all parts of the homes[60] and to all places and the three hundred Jupiters whose names depend upon the will of each, and the hoards of countless gods, even serpent gods.[61] All these gods and goddesses Marcus Agrippa enshrined in one and the same abode.[62]

SALOMON: It would have been better to separate eternal God completely

[52] *Attica* XXIV.

[53] Acts 17:22. Cf. Augustine, *De civ. Dei* IV. 25.

[54] "Zeus is air, Zeus is earth, Zeus is sky, Zeus in truth is all things, and whatever is higher than these." Aeschylus, *Ap.* 70 N². "All things are full of Jupiter," Vergil, *Eclog.* III. 60. Also cf. Augustine, *De civ. Dei* IV. 9–10. In addition, cf. Pseudo-Aristotle, *De mundo* V. 397b.

[55] *Quaest. nat.* I. Pref. 13.

[56] *Hist. nat.* II. 1.

[57] Cf. Augustine, *De civ. Dei* IV. 16–24.

[58] Augustine, *De civ. Dei* VI. 9. Venus and Priapus were associated at an early time with gardens and productivity.

[59] See Pliny, *Hist. nat.* II. 5. 15–20.

[60] Curtius is referring to the Penates, who were guardians of the home and were worshipped in conjunction with Vesta, and the Lares, deities of the farm and, then of the home and crossroads. *Omnibus aedium partibus ac locis consecratos* MR

[61] Erectheus and Asculapius.

[62] See note 50.

from that alliance of empty gods rather than to add Him to their numbers. For what is this except a pollution of most sacred things with profane? For this reason the people of God, sent into a holier land into the possession of plenty, as it were, according to the Twelve Tables, ordered the shrines, the statues, altars, and groves of all empty and worthless gods, to be leveled to the ground.[63] Moreover, God Himself did not suffer the ark of the covenant to be contaminated by the defilement of Dagon's statue; indeed the priests of Palestine twice saw the statue cast down and broken when they had placed it near the ark.[64] P. 121

Curtius: Surely both these priests and Marcus Agrippa were violating sacred rites; indeed it was a sacrilege to consecrate the same shrine to two gods. When Marcus Marcellus[65] had simultaneously dedicated a temple to Honor and Virtue, the Roman priests interceded lest the sacred rites of each god be confused. And so they ordered that temple to be divided in the middle by a wall, so that one could not enter the sanctuary of the temple of Honor before he had passed through the door of Virtue. How much less should one allow this mingling in the worship of eternal God!

Octavius: Truly we ought to despise the blending of sacred rites. However, the kings of the Turks and Persians and also the kings of upper Asia and of Africa were instructed and influenced so much by Homarus II and the legate of Homarus I, the high priest among the Ismaelites, and also by Elhari[66] the famous theologian, that they believed all men would be pleasing to immortal God if each one reverenced his God with a pure spirit although he would not know which God he should have, since they believe the fountain of all action must be placed in the force of the will and the mind itself, whose integrity and purity the most just God always regards. I see that the theologians not only of the Ismaelites but also of the Christians held this opinion. Thus Thomas Aquinas said: "When errant reason has established something as a precept of God, then

[63] Ex. 20:2–6.

[64] I Kings (I Sam.) 5:2–5.

[65] Marcus Claudius Marcellus was the son of the most illustrious of the Marcelli, celebrated as consul five times and the conqueror of Syracuse. The son accompanied his father on many campaigns and received his father's ashes from Hannibal. He dedicated the temple of Virtus near the Porta Capena in 205 B.C. This temple had been dedicated by his father but was unfinished at his death. (Livy XXVII. 27). See William Smith, *Dictionary of Greek and Roman Biography and Mythology*, II (London, 1846), p. 931.

[66] *Helhari* M. The theologian is Elhari Ibim Esed of Bagdad. See Roger Chauviré, *Jean Bodin, auteur de la république* (Paris, 1914), p. 12.

it is the same thing to scorn the dictate of reason and the commands of God." Divine Augustine had confirmed this before.[67]

Curtius: I agree that there is such power in the will itself for judging men's actions that whoever kills someone unwillingly is innocent of that murder, and whoever could not kill the one whom he tried to kill is considered a murderer. Still for this reason we shall not establish, shall we, that all actions which proceed from an upright and sincere will are good? Surely the greatest confusion of true piety and impiety would follow.

Senamus: Do you think that Scaevola,[68] who tried to kill king Porsenna but instead destroyed his legate, should be regarded in the same manner as if he had killed the king?

Curtius: Indeed no one can doubt it.

Senamus: Then if Scaevola had presented royal honors in good faith to the legate as if to the king and indeed with the king observing, would he merit the same honors as if he had offered them to the king himself?

P. 122 Curtius:[69] So it would be if the cause of his error had been just.

Senamus: If he did the same with the legates and messengers of God, and conferred the honors, which he owed to the Creator, to His servant without feigning an error, why would he not be in full right and deserve the same reward as if he had bestowed honor upon immortal God? We have read that the Egyptian midwives had obtained the greatest rewards when they had eluded the cruel orders of Pharaoh with beneficial lies, because they had feared God.[70] But they were not fearing or worshipping any god except Apis the bull, which not even the Israelites with their encompassing law could forget. For when Pharaoh ordered the Israelites to worship their God in Egypt, Moses answered that sacrifices could not be offered to God, whom the Egyptians cursed. The Israelites would be in danger of being stoned by the Egyptians. Therefore God had pity on the midwives who were worshipping a bull.

Salomon: It is one thing to grant rewards for noble deeds, another to excuse sins committed by error. Rewards are bestowed upon him who

[67] See Thomas Aquinas, *Summa Theologica* (Editio altera romana, Leone XIII, Roma, n.d.) Prima secundae partis, Quaest. LVIII, Art. 2., p. 401. Also see Augustine, *Conf.* III. 6; *De civ. Dei* XXI. 6.

[68] Gaius Mucius Scaevola was, according to legend, the brave Roman who, having failed to kill Porsenna, an Etruscan king, held his right hand in the fire, being indifferent to pain. Cf. *Ox. Class. Dict.*, pp. 720 and 798.

[69] *Curtius: ita quidem si justam erroris causam habuisset* MR. There is a typographical error in N at this point. *Idem . . . debuit* should be deleted. These words appear in their proper place after Curtius' speech.

[70] Ex. 1:15–20.

worships God, although no reward is owed for a duty. Whoever worships the sun is guided by a just error (if an error can be just) so that not only may he be excused but even merit rewards, since before God it is enough to have willed to obtain rewards, although you could not fulfill that which you desired. Therefore God the highest rewards an upright will and a fear of the divine, yet he who worships a statue is not therefore said to have acted uprightly, since the piety of nations is[71] impiety towards God, as Solomon wisely wrote. Indeed the Ismaelites, who allow all religions in the state with separate temples, do not, for this reason, desert their own religion. No one can practice without impiety many religions which are different from each other.

SENAMUS: Alexander Severus is said to have been a brave and most religious emperor.[72] Still he worshipped Abraham, Orpheus, Hercules, and Christ in the chapel of the Lares in place of the Penates and indeed in good faith, since in the opinion of all writers he obtained the highest praise for integrity. When, therefore, he realized that Jews, pagans, and Christians were divided on religious principles, he chose to embrace all the religions of all groups rather than, by repudiating one, to arouse any one to the contempt of divinity. With this reasoning he joined not only individual men but all men in the state to the greatest harmony of piety and love.

CURTIUS: Surely that is praise of integrity and wisdom, not of piety. Nevertheless, without piety virtues have no place.

OCTAVIUS: If virtue has no place without true religion, why was Jonas, sent as a representative from God to the Ninevites, ordered[73] not to proclaim the true religion?[74] He did not order them to stop worshipping the stars or statues or to accept divine laws after the idols were rejected, but he said there would be a destruction of so great a city in a short time. Since the magistrates and princes were terrified at this warning, they P. 123
fasted, offered supplications, and repented. "And God saw," the prophet said, "that they were refraining from their sins, and He pitied them lest He bring the destruction which He had decreed upon them."[75] It is worthy to notice what the prince said in an edict: "Who," he said, "would dare to state that God does not have pity on us?"[76] Although they were worshipping Mithra or Bahal for god, they still prevailed upon eternal God.

[71] *pietas gentium, impietas est erga Deum* MR
[72] Alexander was emperor in A.D. 222–235.
[73] *jussus est* M
[74] Jonas 1:1–2; 3:2.
[75] Jonas 3:4–10.
[76] Jonas 3:9.

FRIDERICUS: They had the creator propitious for their repentance for past crimes and for their fasting, not for their worship of the sun.

SENAMUS: If the sacred rites of nations had not been pleasing to eternal God, why were the people beset with crop failure, sickness, and horrors of war when sacred rites were neglected? Why do we see those who perform the rites of the gods with the greatest care, that is,[77] those who cherish dead men and statues, laden with power, honors, victories, and the greatest affluence in everything? Polybius[78] wrote that Roman power increased more through religion than through any other thing. Marcus Tullius skillfully confirming this opinion said: "Our elders did not conquer the Gauls by strength nor the Spanish by number nor the Greeks by culture nor the Carthaginians by cunning nor the Italians by sensitivity, but they conquered because they relied on the fear of religion and the gods and the practice of sacred rites."[79] Papinianus,[80] the god of the jurists, says that the highest reason is that which acts in behalf of religion. When the Christian religion was beginning, the sacred rites of the gods had been put aside and the states and republics throughout the world began to struggle with violent upheavals. Justin wrote that for this reason the Greeks and Latins offered serious objections to the Christian deity.[81] Indeed Augustine is said to have written his books about the city of God to remove this charge and for no other reason than to vindicate Christians from that insult whether true or false, since they were accused of being scorners of all gods.[82]

SALOMON: These were the same complaints of the Israelites who under Jeroboam had forsaken the worship of eternal God.[83] From the time when we ceased making sacrifices to the stars and those heavenly lights, we bore the penalty of calamities and great miseries. Also more important

[77] *id est* MR

[78] Polybius (c. 203–120 B.C.) was the Greek historian of Rome who considered the Roman constitution the ideal mixed constitution.

[79] *De haruspicum responso* 19.

[80] Aemilius Papinianus was one of the greatest classical jurists. He had a brilliant career, and in A.D. 203, he became Praefectus Praetorio. Caracalla ordered his execution in 212 because Papinianus disapproved of the murder of Geta, the emperor's brother. Papinianus' chief works are *Quaestiones* and *Responsa*. In the *Law of Citations* (426) his opinions were so highly valued that, failing a majority of jurists, Papinianus' view would be decisive. See *Ox. Class. Dict.*, p. 644.

[81] *Apol.* I. 6.

[82] Cf. *De civ. Dei* I. 15; II. 3. Also see Tertullian, *Apol.* I. 40.

[83] III Kings (I Kings) 13:33; 14:7–10.

is the statement that those who had destroyed the shrines of the gods always had violent deaths. Lucius Flaccus,[84] Antiochus Nobilis,[85] Menelaus,[86] Marcus Crassus,[87] the Herodes,[88] Gabinius,[89] who had plundered the gold of Jerusalem which was consecrated to eternal God, were not the only ones who died most violently, but also Quintus Caepio the consul,[90] Brennus,[91] the sacrilegious Phocians,[92] Ahab,[93] and the others who de-

[84] Lucius Valerius Flaccus was curule Aedile in 98 B.C., praetor from 96 to 89 B.C., and consul suffectus to replace Marius in 86 B.C. Sent to relieve Sulla of his command against Mithridates, Flaccus crossed to Greece, but his troops began deserting to Sulla. He was killed in Bithynia by his legate.

[85] See above, note 38. Antiochus met his death in Egypt.

[86] Bodin obviously means Agamemnon, the brother of Menelaus, who despoiled the temples in Troy and on his return home met a violent death at the hands of his wife, Clytemnestra. See Aeschylus, *Agamemnon.*

[87] Marcus Licinius Crassus, called Dives (rich), was a member of the First Triumvirate in 60 B.C., along with Julius Caesar and Crassus' long-standing rival, Pompey. In 53 B.C., while conducting a campaign against the Parthians, he suffered a disastrous defeat at Carrhae and during the disorderly retreat he died through treachery. See Plutarch, *Crassus.*

[88] Herod, the son of Antipater, was a ruler of Galilee whom Antony and Octavian had nominated king of Hyrcanus' ethnarchy together with Idumaea. He was hated by the Jews because of his hellenization program and his establishment of a subservient priesthood. His family life was filled with intrigues. On his death bed he found that his son, Antipater, had plotted against him, and he secured permission from Augustus to have him put to death. Two other sons of his were strangled. Herod's father, Antipater, also was murdered. See Josephus, *Antiq.* XV, XVI, XVII.

[89] Aulus Gabinius served Pompey as a legate in the East. He administered the province of Syria competently but he had to face three bribery charges when he returned to Rome in 58 B.C. Sent into exile, he was recalled by Caesar in 48 B.C. to fight for him in Illyricum, but he was beseiged by barbarians in Salonae and died there. See *Ox. Class. Dict.*, p. 374.

[90] Quintus Servilius Caepio was consul in 106 B.C., during Marius' rise to power. He struck at Marius' partisans by the law which transferred the jury courts to the Senate. He plundered Tolosa in Gaul (see below, note 94) but was defeated by the Cimbri. He lost his *imperium* and was condemned in 103 B.C. *Ox. Class. Dict.*, p. 152.

[91] Brennus, leader of the Galatian invasion in 279 B.C., overran Macedonia and then attacked Delphi. Brennus was wounded at Delphi and during the retreat was attacked by the Thessalians; thereupon Brennus committed suicide. *Ox. Class. Dict.*, p. 145.

[92] The district of Phocis is in central Greece and its chief city is Delphi. The Phocians are called sacrilegious because they attacked Delphi in 357 B.C., seized the sanctuary, and for ten years fought the Sacred War. See Pausanias, X. 2. 1–7.

[93] Ahab was the most evil of all men in God's sight. See III Kings (I Kings) 16:30—20:39.

stroyed the temples of demons. Thereafter the gold of Tolosa[94] was employed as a byword by the ancients.[95]

P. 124 Senamus: The divine law warns under penalty of death against molesting anything that has been dedicated to idols, either because the dedication was made to the idol as if to the true God, or because demons as avengers vindicate their property from robbers everywhere, or because they sometimes commit the thefts of idols so that they may be worshipped instead of the gods of the Lares.

Octavius: Indeed I think that the man who scorns the true religion and false divinities, which are believed to be true, is guilty of the greatest impiety. For example, Caligula Augustus whispered insults into the ear of Jupiter Stator, yet whenever it thundered, he was accustomed to hide in a cave in terror.[96] When he demanded to kiss the statue of Vesta, it fell to the ground.

Fridericus: This is customary for all magicians. They trample underfoot consecrated hosts with ritualistic words, feed toads with this food, or strike with arrows the images of Christ, whom they think is also God, as if they were about to violate God. They say that they do this and have done this under the persuasion of demons. Demons would not urge this unless they clearly knew that the magician thought those hosts were gods.

Senamus: Who can then doubt that the religion of the pagans is also pleasing to God if demons try to encourage contempt for it and strive to overthrow all religions.

Coronaeus: I believe that all are convinced it is much better to have a false religion than no religion. Thus there is no superstition so great that it cannot keep wicked men in their duty through the fear of divine power and somehow preserve the law of nature,[97] since rewards for the good and punishment for the wicked are considered part of divine judgment. In regard to this Epicurus committed an unpardonable sin because in trying to uproot the fear of divinity he seems to have opened[98] freely all the approaches to sin. Of all the categories of public consideration[99] nothing is more destructive than anarchy in which no one rules, no one obeys,

[94] Tolosa, a town in Gallia Narbonensis, modern Toulouse, was sacked by Caepio in 106 B.C. Before he was condemned in 103 B.C., there had been a *quaestio extraordinaria* about the "gold of Tolosa" which had been largely lost in transit.

[95] *veteribus proverbio* R

[96] Suetonius, *Caligula* XXII.

[97] *naturae legum* MR

[98] *aperuisse* MR

[99] *de omnibus rerum publicarum generibus* M

no rewards are granted to good men, no punishments for the wicked.[100] And so the Indian priests of Narsingae are accustomed to place in their temple statues of gods and demons which are most terrifying and monstrous in appearance so that the wicked will be restrained by fear of divinity from a guilty and wicked life.

FRIDERICUS: If we grant that those who cherish false religion are excused because of a just error, who, pray, can rightly plead a just cause of error for impiety when a cowardly servant is about to be flogged because he, just as consciously, neglected the commands of his master. P. 125

SENAMUS: Indeed this is so, if we agree with the words of Luke. But who will be so unfair a judge, so cruel a tyrant who wishes to kill those who violate the prince's edicts which have been secretly hidden?

CURTIUS: If we are all obligated to obey human laws and are not excused because of ignorance of the law, who will excuse ignorance of divine law which has been manifested so often and so long throughout the world?

SENAMUS: But if there are laws contrary to laws and lawgivers hostile to lawgivers, religion opposed to religion, priests warring with priests, what will the poor subjects do when they are pulled here and there into the sects?

TORALBA: In such a variety of different laws and religions one must decide what is the true religion. When one finds the true religion, will he also find out who can excuse ignorance and sickness of mind?

FRIDERICUS: Who can doubt that the Christian religion is the true religion or rather the only one?

OCTAVIUS: Almost all the world—Asia, large as it is, most of Africa, a great part of Europe—has an infinite variety[101] of sects, and each group thinks the religion which he especially loves is the most beautiful and noble.

CURTIUS: The best kind of religion is not determined by numbers of people, but by the weight of truth which God himself has commanded. It is characteristic of man to believe; it is characteristic of God to know.

CORONAEUS: Before we stray too far in our discussion about religions, we must consider the question that was presented yesterday; namely, is it proper for a good man to discuss religions?

[100] This sentence was copied twice in the MS. It appears as the second sentence in the paragraph as well as in this position, in which I prefer to read it.

[101] *varietate* MR

Toralba: I think Plato[102] was wise in saying that it is difficult to find the parent of the universe and wrong to spread it abroad when you find him. Tullius,[103] the interpreter of Plato, did not wish to convey, as many think, that it was wicked, but he wished to give a more Latin interpretation than "impossible" (*to adynaton*). In the same vein Horace[104] said: "Do not question—it is wrong to know—what ends the gods have given to you and to me." The common herd whose eyes are covered with mist cannot comprehend the splendor of sublime kings. If anyone should see more clearly, still no one has the eloquence to describe the secrets of divine majesty; moreover many things are necessarily in error. For this reason, Plato[105] in answering the question about angels, whom he everywhere
P. 126 calls gods, said: "By the gods let us restrain the investigation about gods, for I am afraid to speak about them." And so it is better to be silent altogether than to speak rashly about the holiest matters and without the proper dignity.

Salomon: Conversation about religion has always seemed dangerous to me. In the first place, it is a serious offense to speak about God in any way other than with dignity. Next, it is wrong to uproot anyone's opinion of piety, of whatever sort it may be, or to cast doubt by arguments on anyone's religion unless you believe you will persuade him of something better. Many have fallen into the deadly trap of trying to disturb others in their accepted religion but were not able to accomplish this. There are many examples of this, but the case of Florus,[106] governor of Judea, was especially grave. When the high priest of our race tried in friendship to draw Florus to the worship of one eternal God and turn him from the worship of empty idols, he was unsuccessful, and he caused deadly hostilities with a powerful enemy. As a result, our race began to be afflicted

[102] Plato, *Timaeus* XXVIIIC; also see Apuleius, *De dogmate Platonis* I. 5; Tertullian, *Apol.* I. 46.

[103] Cicero, *De nat. deorum* I. 12.

[104] *Car.* I. 11. 1.

[105] The same passage is quoted by Apuleius, *De dogmate Platonis* I. 5. The original reference is Plato, *Timaeus* XXVIIIC.

[106] Gessius Florus (A.D. 64–66) was credited along with his predecessors, Porcius Festus and Albinus, with the deterioration of relations between Romans and Jews preceding the civil war. He attempted to collect arrears of tribute, which the revolutionaries were convinced were for himself and not for Caesar. Hence they went among the people with baskets, begging coppers for their destitute and miserable governor. This led to the Roman sack of the upper city of Jerusalem and the death of 630 persons. He even crucified Jews who belonged to the Roman Order of Knights. *Encyclopaedia Britannica* (11th ed.), XV, 401.

with so many and so great wars that we lost our freedom and ancestral homes and became slaves to the Romans.

SENAMUS: Even if a new religion is better or truer than an old religion I think it should not be proclaimed. I think a new religion offers not so great an advantage, as its novelty may draw men away from old piety and necessary fear of deity. If anyone should wish to change the cornerstones of a building shaking with age, he would be acting foolishly. A change in religion has more dangerous consequences, namely, upheaval in public affairs, destructive wars, even more deadly calamities from plagues and torments of demons.

CORONAEUS: I do not understand clearly the reasons for the public upheavals that follow upon religious changes.

OCTAVIUS: Is it because men are wont to waver between the true and the false and to uproot all piety from their souls when the old religion is cast aside and the new religion, not yet accepted, is held in contempt? At that time they are accustomed to be tormented by demons.

SALOMON: In this period of doubt the most effectual amulet is to beg from immortal God in continual prayers that we may be directed on the right path.

FRIDERICUS: It is both dangerous and destructive for the masses to engage in discussions about the accepted and approved religion unless one can control the resisting common people by divine power, as Moses did, or by arms, as Mohammed did. However, I have always considered a private discussion about divine matters among educated men to be most fruitful. Often before, I have tried to draw out our Salomon into this
discussion but have been unsuccessful. Perhaps he feared that he might P. 127
be forced to abandon his acknowledged religion. They say that vipers block both their ears from the enticement of magicians.

Everyone hoped that Salomon would reply to these remarks, but he answered nothing; TORALBA broke the silence by saying: It is quite reasonable that Salomon shies away from discussion about religions[107] both for the reasons he gave, lest he seem to abandon the religion of his ancestors if he does not defend it, or to cause offense to anyone if he defends it too strongly.

CORONAEUS: In such a harmonious gathering of wills and spirits as we have here, who can give or receive offense in this discussion?[108] I pledge to Salomon that he will bring to all of us the greatest knowledge and de-

[107] *a disputatione de religionibus* MR [108] *disserendo* MR

light through his speech, and nothing will be more gratifying to me than for each among us to enjoy the greatest freedom in speaking about religion. Come then, Salomon; freely reveal what is in your mind.

SALOMON: Indeed that is pressure. For it does not matter how you force me. Either I am ungrateful if I doubt your kindness toward me or unfair if I am afraid to change[109] my opinion because of the force of arguments. Moreover, according to our laws and customs we are prohibited from discussing religion. Our elders established public synagogues and schools of religion in which they are accustomed to read the divine laws and interpret them to people of all ages and both sexes. In an ancient commentary we read that Jerusalem once had 481 schools.[110] Still no discussion about religion was allowed lest divine laws seemed to be called into doubt. Conjecture follows upon discussion; moreover, opinion wavers between the true and the false; doubt produces the opinion of impiety. Nothing is more foolish than for geometricians to advise or for orators[111] to try to demonstrate by eloquence. Likewise, nothing seems to me more destructive than to try to disturb by doubtful discussion things which ought to be more certain than all demonstrations and upon which the foundations of our salvation rest. I remember reading a dialogue of Justin Martyr with Trypho the Jew, whom he presents so untutored and foolish that I was annoyed with the work and the foolishness of the writer. Indeed the author decrees victory, just as the braggart warrior standing in the theater. In one place he presents Trypho rebuking himself because he [Trypho] argued with him about religion contrary to the custom of Trypho's elders.[112] I ought to thank you, Fridericus, since you wish with pious intent to change my mind. However, since I am already old, I could scarcely uproot from my heart my religion of long standing. Indeed the
P. 128 decrees of your priests and ours forbid me to lead you away from your religion. What then will be the fruit of this discussion? Or how will you suffer me to say freely what I think, as the method of discussion demands. Or how could I hope for God's kindness toward me if I wish to abandon His prophecies by concealing the truth?

[109] *decedere* MR

[110] "At the time of the destruction of Jerusalem (A.D. 70) there were in the city itself 394 synagogues, according to the Babylonian Talmud (Kethub, 105a); 480, according to the Jerusalem Talmud (Megilla 73d). Besides these synagogues for the Palestinian Jews, each group of the Hellenistic Jews in Jerusalem had its own synagogue—the Libertines, the Alexandrians, the Cyrenians, the Cilicians, etc. (Acts 6:9)." *Cath. Encycl.* XIV, 380.

[111] *oratores* MR

[112] Justin Martyr, *Dial. Tryph.* XXXVIII.

FRIDERICUS: If the evident truth of divine matters is so clear to you, Salomon, I do not see why you ought to be afraid to yield to true and evident arguments.

SALOMON: I have always yielded to the truth, but in whatever way you force me, it will be an unfair war if I wish to oppose all of you. Nothing can cause me more pain than if I allow your affection for me to be diminished by these disputations.

CORONAEUS: I beg you, my Salomon, to toss aside this fear. Whether you shall conquer or be conquered, I promise, on behalf of all the rest, that nothing will be lessened in our unusual love for you.

As Salomon hesitated, SENAMUS looked at him and said: At Siena the Senate for a long time permitted academies, but the condition was stipulated that there would be no discussions about divine matters and the decrees of the popes. Although one man foolishly violated this edict and suffered capital punishment, there have been no uprisings in that city up to this day.

OCTAVIUS: The edicts of the Persians and the Turks also warned that no discussions about religion be carried on. Also the kings of the Moscovites and the princes of the Germans at a great assembly at Augsburg,[113] after destructive and lengthy wars, proclaimed that there would be no more discussion about religion among Catholics and priests of the Augsburg confession. When one man rashly violated this edict, he was put to death, and the uprisings in that city were quelled up to the present.[114]

FRIDERICUS: Still discussions in the public schools of the Academies are not prohibited, but these discussions customarily were held among theologians of the same religions.

CURTIUS: I can say that when Mohammed, with the greatest cunning or impiety, saw that the foundations of his religion would easily be disturbed by discussion, if it were attacked by arguments as though by machines of war, he placed anyone who discussed the laws given by him under penalty of death.

OCTAVIUS: Similarly we have the interdict of Justinian Augustus, who prohibited public contention about the Trinity and the Catholic faith.[115]

[113] After many years of religious turmoil a religious peace of Augsburg was concluded at the Diet of Augsburg in 1555. See *Cath. Encycl.* II, 75.

[114] *quo edicto unius hominis temeritate violato, ea capitali poena secuta, seditiones in illa urbe ad haec usque tempora conquierunt* MR missing in N

[115] Justinian's *Corpus Juris* is full of laws against pagans, Jews, Samaritans, Manichaeans, and other heretics. There was no room for toleration.

SALOMON: I think a discussion, either public or private, about the established and accepted religion is more dangerous among those who are satisfied with their religion than among those who have resolved to consider various sects, since every one fights very ardently for his own religion; p. 129 but he who deserts his own religion[116] tries to attack it and to subvert it by doubts.

SENAMUS: I remember a certain crafty chief of Lyons who wished the bickering Lutherans would tear themselves to pieces. Consequently, he used to pit one group against the other as though gladiators, so they could kill each other by their own sword.[117] Similarly, the ancient priests of Mars after execrations used to give the signal for battle by tossing flaming fire-brands between each battle line.[118] Yet those same priests, who were called "fire-bearers," suddenly withdrew because of the dangers of war. Thus many fires of war were stirred up from those discussions for the enjoyment of the spectacle. Julian Augustus[119] did the same thing when he recalled the Arians to break the power of the Catholics. Not only did he encourage the Jews to weaken or destroy the strength of the Christians, whom he violently hated, but he also reinstated the priests of Jupiter and Apollo and the almost defunct rites of the pagans. He linked the statues of the gods with the statue of Caesar in such a way that danger could not be avoided, while honor due to the emperor was joined to the worship of demons or a charge of treason threatened if the prince was held in contempt.

TORALBA: Marcus Tullius[120] recognized that a discussion about the gods was a wicked custom whether done sincerely or insincerely, because one must never act insincerely, much less frivolously, about so important a

116 *suam ipsius religionem deserit* N var.

117 Cf. Guillaume Postel, *Apologie de Guill*[*aum*]*e Postel aulx calumnies d'un qui se dict docteur en loix nommé Matthieu d'Antoine (qui est fils d'un souverain marchant de Lyon) avec naturele et rationale preuve des catholiques vérités, qui par le susdict et ses adherents sont oppugnées.* Bibliothèque Nationale fonds latin 3402. fol. 1–29v.

118 The Salii or leaping priests (from *salire*, to leap or dance) were members of one of the minor priesthoods at Rome. They were associated with the war god Mars and were active in their rites in March and October, the opening and closing of the campaign season. On their origin see Ovid, *Fasti* III. 365–92; on their dress see Dion. Hal. II. 70.

119 Among the last writings of Julian the Apostate was an attack on the Christian Church whose every weakness or unsound teaching and practice, as he judged them, he exposed.

120 Cicero, *De nat. deorum* I. 1–5.

matter. If you shall have engaged in a serious discussion contrary to your belief, it is necessary that you strive to overthrow your religion.

FRIDERICUS: But what if the reason is for teaching or learning?

TORALBA: Even this is not free from danger because religion will be grounded either in knowledge or opinion or faith. If religion depends on opinion, that ambiguous opinion wavers between truth and falsehood and totters during hostile discussion. If religion abides in knowledge, there must be proof based upon the surest principles and fortified by necessary conclusions which admit no discussion of this kind. Moreover, there is no one, in my opinion, who has devoted himself to the proofs of each religion. Although several tried to accomplish this, they did not succeed, because faith is destroyed if it must rely on proof and science. Science (*scientia*) is called knowledge (*epistēmē*) in Greek from *apo tou* P. 130 *epistanein ton noun*, "to attend to the mind," because knowledge alone can check the mind drawn here and there in different directions. Here I am speaking of faith according to the interpretation of the theologians, not the logicians who illustrate the dubious truth of a dubious[121] thing by necessary arguments that produce faith. The theologians believe that faith is pure assent without proof. Of the things of which we have faith as long as we live here, celestial minds attain knowledge. Moreover, they have said that faith is either infused or obtained by effort and study, for example, that which is acquired by reading or listening, when we agree with one whom we think is good and scholarly. But if we reject this opinion of his uprightness or erudition, we lose faith. If, however, we continue to agree, the discussion is empty, because we found pleasure in believing this or that, whether true or false. Indeed, whoever agrees with a teacher of geometrical theories and does not understand geometry has faith, not knowledge. But if he understands geometry, he obtains knowledge, but at the same moment loses faith. The theologians call infused faith a theological virtue which has God as its only proof and object. This faith, however, is granted by divine gift and concession. If, however, it is inevitable and fixed so that it cannot be lost, this is force, not faith. If faith is based on free assent, it is the greatest impiety to try to tear away from anyone by human arguments the instruction which God has bestowed from his bountiful goodness. Since these things are so, we must abstain altogether from discussions about religion.

OCTAVIUS: The Florentine republic allowed no discussion about laws

[121] *dubiae* M

already passed, and Lycurgus[122] long ago gave the same law. But if it is not permissible to argue about human laws so that there will be no approach for breaking the laws through disputation, how much less should this be done about divine laws. It is dangerous enough in private but even more so in public.

CURTIUS: According to the ancient prophets it is indeed laudable to abstain from discussions of divine matters, but this must be understood by each man with reference to his own religion. Christians should not cast doubt on the articles of their own faith, nor should Jews among each other or Mohammedans among each other. Yet Mohammedans are not only not allowed to discuss their religion with other Mohammedans, but not even with Jews or Christians, and this is absurd and wrong. Indeed, if their religion or superstition is true, persuasion is easier the truer the religion. If they do not wish to communicate such a great good to Christians and Jews, surely this indicates an envious and malevolent attitude. But it is truer that Mohammedans and Jews refrain from discussions about religion[123] because they cannot see the clear light of Christian truth with bleary eyes.

P. 131 CORONAEUS: I think Curtius' opinion is rather commendable, for it keeps Christians either privately or publicly from arguing about the tenets of our religion or faith and from becoming hopelessly entangled by doubtful considerations and involved in various errors. Yet the divine laws are set forth for both sexes, for all orders, all ages, all places to read and contemplate according to the provision of divine law.[124] Still, there has always been and will always be debate among the various branches of sects about the best kind of religion, and it will always be permitted to lead into the proper pathway of salvation the converts, catechumens, the demoniacs, the Ismaelites, Jews, Pagans, and Epicureans who have wandered from the straight path. This is done by reason, authority, tradition, knowledge, and clear proofs make this possible and in the interest of the union of humanity and love that man has with man.

SENAMUS: I think those discussions about religion will come to nothing. For who will be the arbiter of such a controversy?

[122] Lycurgus was the traditional founder of the Spartan constitution and military system. He is first mentioned by Herodotus I. 65–66. The dates of his life are uncertain (1100 to 600 B.C.), and some scholars even doubt that Lycurgus was an historical figure.

[123] *de religione* MR missing in N

[124] Joshua 1:7–9; 8:35.

FRIDERICUS: Christ the Lord! For He said that if three were gathered together in His name He would be in their midst.

SENAMUS: But the point of disagreement among Christians and Jews as well as among Mohammedans and Christians is whether or not Christ is God.

CURTIUS: We need to use suitable witnesses and references to confirm this.

SENAMUS: It is doubtful what witnesses are reliable, what records are trustworthy, what bondsmen are secure in determining a certain and sure faith.

CORONAEUS: The church will be the judge. Augustine[125] said: "I would not believe the Gospel unless the church also confirmed it."

SENAMUS: An even more serious problem is what is the true church? The Jews say their church is the true one, and the Mohammedans deny it. On the other hand, the Christian makes a claim for his church, and the pagans in India say their church ought to have preference over all others because of its age. And so the very learned Cardinal Nicholas of Cusa wrote he must represent nothing about the Christian church, but by positing the foundation that the church rests on its union with Christ, he assumes that which is the chief point of debate.

SALOMON: Christians and Mohammedans agree with the Hebrews that the one true church of God has been in the tribe of the Israelites, which nation alone of all the world safeguarded the true worship of the one eternal God; this nation was the only preserver of the eternal covenant, incised by God's finger on stone tablets and made holy by blood, the only P. 132
guardian of the eternal law and sacred writings.

FRIDERICUS: So it was up to Christ's time.

OCTAVIUS: The Jews and Mohammedans reject the New Testament as corrupted by Christians, although Mohammed did not hesitate to cite the gospel writings especially in *Alcoran Elmeidis* and in the twelfth *Azora*; however, not in the text that is available to the Christians.

TORALBA: If the foundation of true religion resides in the sole authority of writers, the ancient maxim of the Pythagoreans, "he said," will be right. But if the words are obscure and allow various meanings, then arbiters, that is, wise men, must consider the problem.

SENAMUS: But it is still doubtful who is wise? If they are considered

[125] *Sancti Augustini Operum Tomus VIII–IX* (Paris, 1688) *Contra epistolam Manichaei* 154a.

wise by the judgment of others, that is, of fools, they are fools by their own judgment.

TORALBA: We usually consult a specialist in a particular skill, and even artisans do not want to be believed without experience and strong arguments. Yet they can be deceived if there is no proof. Moreover, faith in divine matters depends upon the authority of God alone, and He cannot be deceived nor deceive. This authority has by far more weight than all the proofs, arguments, writings, and witnesses.

SENAMUS: Necessarily, the religion which has God as its author is the true religion, but the difficulty is in discerning whether He is the author of this religion or that religion.[126] This is the task and difficulty.[127]

SALOMON: When the priests of Apollo[128] proposed that he, whom the Chaldeans called Bahal,[129] be worshipped[130] as God, Elias the prophet suggested to King Ahab the test that the god whose sacrifice a heavenly flame consumed be considered the true God.[131] This test was carried out in a large gathering of people,[132] when the priests of Apollo, the Camarim,[133] moaned their prayers in the blazing heat of the sun and drew blood from their faces and veins. Elias told them in elegant irony that they should cry out more loudly. Then at sunset with three words he

126 *religionis* MR

127 Senamus' remark has a Vergilian ring. Cf. Vergil, *Aen.* VI. 129, *hoc opus, hic labor est.*

128 *Apollinis* MR

129 Bahal, a Semitic word meaning "lord" or "owner," was sometimes applied to the Israelite Yahweh. But for the prophets there were many repugnancies involved in this identification. The bahals were many; Yahweh was one; the bahals were nature deities, identified with springs, trees, mountains, stones, and various sacred places; Yahweh was beyond nature; the bahals were associated with goddesses of fertility; Yahweh was a model of chaste indifference to sex. One of the bahals was the bahal of the heavens. The late Greek writers identified this bahal with the sky god. The characterization of Bahal as Apollo is an aspect of Alexandrian syncretism. The bahal of Heliopolis was identified with Helios and Sol. More frequently, Bahal was identified as the supreme god, with Zeus or Jupiter. *Encyclopaedia Britannica* (11th ed.) III, 88–89; James Hastings, ed., *Encyclopedia of Religion and Ethics* (Edinburgh, 1909) II, 283.

130 *colendum* MR

131 III Kings (I Kings) 18.

132 *acta res est ingenti concursu multitudinis* MR missing in N.

133 The worship of Melkart, bahal of Tyre, was introduced into Israel in the time of Ahab. After Ahab formed an alliance with Phoenicia and married Jezebel, daughter of the king of Tyre, he was compelled to establish the cult of Melkart in Samaria. The fullest accounts of his worship are derived from the Old Testament accounts. There were prophets of the bahal and also *Chemarim* or priests of the bahal. IV Kings (II Kings) 23:5, *Sophonias* (*Zeph*) I. 4. See Hastings, *Encycl. of Rel. and Eth.* II, 292–93.

drew down from heaven the flame which suddenly consumed the sacrifice, the altar, the stones, and even dried up the waters that had been poured on the stones. The king was so astonished by this miracle that he worshipped the eternal God, and Elias ordered the 450 priests of the sun to be killed. After a while the drought of three years and six months, which Elias had invoked, ceased, and the rains fell in abundance in compliance with this contrary prayer.

FRIDERICUS: Would that now a certain Elias in sight of kings and people would prove by a heavenly sign which religion from so many is best.[134]

SALOMON: Divine law forbade anyone to inquire who or what God is. P. 133
Elias performed the miracle because God ordered it. No miracles and signs move the wicked. Even with that great portent Elias accomplished nothing, for after a little while King Ahab and the people fell back into the worship of Bahal, and Elias would have been killed by Jezebel had he not fled. The Hebrew nation witnessed more signs than any other peoples. Can there be any more certain approbation of the true religion than this?

CURTIUS: I think that the true religion must be approved by the authority of the church, the truth of sacred Scripture, by its antiquity, divine pronouncements, heavenly portents, and clear reasons.

SALOMON: Rabbi Moses Rambam put the matter more briefly and said that we must believe only three things, namely, proof, sense experience, and the words of the prophets. We can believe other things, but are not forced to.

SENAMUS: If there is any faith in oracles, consider the ancient oracle of Apollo.[135] When he was asked what was the best religion from the countless variety of religions, he replied in one word—the oldest. Since it was not clear what was the oldest religion, the oracle replied the best.

TORALBA: I am also convinced that, even without the oracle's witness, the best religion is the oldest. So great is the faith in antiquity that it can easily sustain itself by its own authority. New religions, new sacrifices, new sacraments, new rites, new laws, new methods, new churches, new decrees, new customs have completely disrupted some of the most prosperous states.

[134] Is this a humorous reference to Bodin himself, who signed one of his books, *Sapientiae moralis epitome* (Paris, 1588), Elias Bodin? Or is it a more cryptic reference to Elias Pandocheus (Elias Who-Reveals-All) who was, in fact, Guillaume Postel?

[135] Cf. Augustine, *De civ. Dei* 19:23.

CORONAEUS: This is a strong argument for the Roman Catholic church against the creators of new religion. For this reason let us decide, if you agree, what is the most ancient religion, so that then it will be obvious which is the best. Indeed one point depends on the other.

SALOMON: I beg that we proceed not by the path by which we see but by the one we should go. For divine law which Christians and Jews uphold forbids that we consult demons or seek prophecies of empty[136] gods or have any faith in them. Elias told King Ahaziah, who was sick, that he would die because he had consulted Bahal, whom the Greeks call Apollo,[137] about his health and safety. It was customary for the best rulers to consult God if they were hesitant about anything or if they were about to engage in a serious undertaking; if they had the gift of prophecy, God answered them in dreams or visions. If the prophetic gift was lacking, God spoke through his prophets, and if there were no prophets, He spoke through priests. A prophet was accustomed to answer his questioners with a clear
P. 134 speech, saying what he had received from God. The priest, however, clothed in sacred garments, made conjectures about the future from a golden table in which twelve jewels were encrusted, inscribed with the names of the twelve tribes. From the brightness of the jewels he predicted a favorable outcome, from their obscurity an unfavorable one, or he inferred a positive or negative statement from the letters.[138] For this reason the prophet Balaam said that the Israelites would be blessed because they were not contaminated by demons or magicians but listened to their oracles inspired by God.[139] If it is wrong to consult the demon Apollo, how much more wicked is it to accept him as arbiter of religion, since he struggles to overthrow all religions?

SENAMUS: Indeed, Salomon, he approved your religion as the best one. When he was consulted about the best kind of religion, he also said: "The Chaldeans alone have secured wisdom, but the Hebrews piously worship the eternal God."[140] Likewise when consulted about the Jewish race, he answered thus: "That race worships God the King omnipotent before whom the sea, vast earth, starry heavens, the genii tremble and whom the abyss of the sea fears."[141]

SALOMON: These are the inventions of Christian leaders or Christ's disciples who were also considered Jews and were commonly thought to

[136] *inanium* MR. Biblical reference is Deut. 18:9–13. Levit. 20:1–8.

[137] See above, note 129. Also see IV Kings (II Kings) 1:1–6.

[138] See Ex. 28.

[139] Num. 23:7–11.

[140] See Augustine, *De civ. Dei* 19:23.

[141] *Ibid.*

profess the religion of the Jews, made in order to add an appearance of antiquity to the Christian religion. Still we would not have any faith if a thousand Apollos had judged the Jewish religion the best of all.

FRIDERICUS: Indeed, it is truer that Apollo the demon confounded[142] the religion and wisdom of the Hebrews and Chaldeans to destroy both by his ambiguity. A while back among the Julianists[143] in the village of Laemus a priest, making bad use of his leisure, asked a demon why he urged forward so eagerly to mass a girl whom he possessed, or whether he thought that sacrifice was salutary for men? The demon said to the priest that he must think about it some more. For if he had answered that the mass was salutary, the Lutherans would have decided it must be rejected for this reason. If the demon had rejected the mass, the Catholics would have said it was salutary. And so with an ambiguous answer he deceived both. Likewise, another[144] priest asked the demon, who was harassing a monk, who he was. The demon said: "I am Matthias Durensis Abbas, and I shall not cease my possession until the monk goes to Treves and appeases the Virgin Mary because he did not amply satisfy the painter of a statue of the Virgin." P. 135

OCTAVIUS: In order not to confuse the oracles of Apollo with the replies of the possessed, I have always thought that the oracles of the Christian religion were invented in large part by the Greeks according as anyone approved or disapproved this or that religion. For example, we have read things in Porphyry contrary to things which Eusebius and Lactantius[145] mention. This is an example. When the Jews[146] were asking of what sort the Messiah would be, Apollo is said to have replied that He

142 *confudisse* MR

143 The Julianists were so called from Julian, bishop of Halicarnassus (6th century), who held that the earthly body of Christ was incorruptible, insensible to the weakness of the flesh. The doctrine was known as Aphthartodocetism.

144 *alius item* MR

145 Eusebius (A.D. 260–339), bishop of Caesarea, was primarily an apologist for Christianity, and among his apologies was his *Against Porphyry*, which was directed to the vindication of Christianity against heathens and heretics in his own time. This work contained twenty-five books but is now lost. See *New Catholic Encyclopedia* (New York, 1967), V, 633–36.

Lactantius (A.D. 240–320) was first a pagan and then a Christian apologist. He wrote the *Divinae institutiones* to refute attacks on Christianity. His goal was to show that the union of true wisdom and true religion was possible only in Christianity. Scarcely using the Scripture to accomplish his purpose, he relied on pagan prophets such as the Sibylline oracles and Hermes Trismegistus. See *New Cath. Encycl.*, VIII, 308.

146 *Judaeis* MR

will be mortal according to the flesh. There is also a similar oracle which they say was spoken to father Augustus. "A boy," it said, "the Hebrew God king forces me to be silent."[147] But surely Suetonius, Dio, and Tacitus, who recorded the slightest dreams of Augustus, would not have omitted an oracle of such importance. Also Marcus Tullius, who was consul when Augustus was born,[148] writes that the oracles of Apollo had been silent for a long time so that now nothing would be more despised.[149] If Apollo was so silent for many generations[150] before Tullius, who[151] could have poured out so many oracles which we read were reported[152] 300 years later.[153]

CURTIUS: Plutarch thought that the long silence was caused by the death of the demons.[154] Porphyry[155] did not relate Apollo's oracle about the cause of his silence to that boy,[156] the Hebrew God and King, but to Jupiter. He said: "Apollo goes, he goes upon the flame, and Zeus restrains him; Zeus is light." Moreover, who, except one completely mad, would want to ask about the future from a woman possessed by a demon, foaming at the mouth, and babbling ambiguously, as Plutarch, Heraclitus, and Basil recorded.[157] It was very often necessary to move the ears close to the private parts of the women in order to hear the replies. Coelius of Rovigo wrote that in the town of Reggio he had seen a witch who spoke from her private parts. About past events she spoke clearly, but about future events obscurely. Yet madness[158] compelled not only unlearned men to sell the responses of such witches as divine oracles, but even men who were considered to be wise, as Justin, Eusebius, Lactantius, and

[147] *tacere* MR

[148] 63 B.C. Also the year of the Catilinarian conspiracy.

[149] Cicero, *De divinatione* I. 19.

[150] *multis temporibus* MR

[151] *quis* MR

[152] *prodita* MR

[153] The oracle of Apollo at Delphi lost its importance in the second century A.D. One of its last responses led Diocletian to decide to persecute the Christians. The oracle of Apollo at Claros was very famous, and the priest, relying on telepathy, gave his responses in verse. From the first century A.D. questions could be submitted in writing, and even "speaking" statues of the god were sent into various regions and could be questioned directly. In the later imperial age there is evidence that questions were presented at the oracle itself even from distant Britain. See *New Cath. Encycl.*, X, 710.

[154] *Moralia, De defectu oraculorum* XV. 418D.

[155] See Gustavus Wolff, ed., *Porphyrii de philosophia ex oraculis hauriende* (Hildesheim, 1962), p. 30. Cited hereafter as Wolff, *Porphyry.*

[156] *puerum* MR

[157] Plutarch, *Moralia, De defectu oraculorum* XLVI. 435D; Heraclitus, see Diels, *Frag. der Vorsokrat.* (6th ed.), I. B93; also Plutarch, *Moralia, De Pythiae oraculis* XXI. 404E.

[158] *amentia* MR

Porphyry.[159] Justin[160] said: "Believe the most ancient Sibyl of Erythrea whose books are preserved in the whole world." He did not hesitate to ✗ translate the responses of the Sibyls from Greek into Latin, and not long ago Castalion[161] decided to publish them, in which biblical history has been very briefly summarized.

OCTAVIUS: I do not doubt that all Sibyls are notorious for their con- P. 136 cubinage with demons. I think the strongest evidence for the wicked superstition is the fact that it is supported by the oracles of the Sibyls as if by the fates. Indeed, I think Tertullian was in grave error when he attempted to secure approval for the Christian religion from the fact that demons in persons possessed spoke certain secrets to Christians and praised the wisdom and virtue of Christ, but answered nothing to the pagan priests.[162] In those same replies of the Sibyls the name of God is declared to be a four-syllable word. It is not the sacred four-letter word appropriate to eternal God in Hebrew, for this four-syllable word has three syllables of two letters first and finally a syllable of three letters. There are four vowels and five consonants, and it agrees with the number MDCCXI [1711] which Cardan thought was *arsenikon*[163] (masculine). Cardan was justly mocked for this because the numbers of the letters do not correspond, although other points coincide. Others have discussed this more carefully, and they have judged the word to be *phaosphoros*, which contains four syllables, the same number of vowels, five consonants, the first three syllables of two letters, the fourth syllable of three letters. The demon Apollo himself said through the oracle that the light-bearing sun—that is, *phaosphoron*, or Apollo, ought to be worshipped by miserable men as though God.

SENAMUS: I really consider the name of *phaosphoros*, or Lucifer, appropriate for the creator of all light, who alone can dispel the shadows and mists from human minds.

CURTIUS: This is a trick of demons to confound the false with the true so that they can more easily deceive the unlearned and arouse admiration

[159] See above, note 145.

[160] *Apol.* I. 20, 45.

[161] Sébastien Castellio (Castalion), 1515–1563, was a scholar of distinction and a teacher in Geneva. He was excluded from the preaching ministry by Calvin because he had criticized the inspiration of the *Song of Solomon* and the Genevan interpretation of the clause "he descended into hell." See *Encycl. Brit.* (11th ed.) V, 74d, 214c. See below, Book VI, p. 462, note 674.

[162] Tertullian, *Apol.* I. 23.

[163] Cardan published a celebrated treatise on astrology; he also had a strong belief in dreams and omens and claimed to have a guardian demon. He was sharply criticized by Gabriel Naudé.

✗ Nach dem lat. Text Castellio, nicht Justin

for themselves, yet they speak as madmen. You have read that in the cave of Trophonius in Lebadea[164] the Mopsitani, while terrified by dreams in sleep and similar to madmen, had poured out oracles.[165]

SENAMUS: When certain Epicureans made fun of the oracles of Mopsus in the presence of the proconsul of Asia, they sent a certain farmer to Mopsus with a sealed letter in which nothing else was written except whether Mopsus wanted a black or white cow to be sacrificed to him. The farmer slept in the shrine and had a vision. When he returned to
P. 137 the Epicureans with the sealed letter, he said he had heard nothing except a voice which whispered the word, black.[166] When the proconsul heard this, he accused the Epicureans of impiety and did not cease afterwards making sacrifices to Mopsus. But let us listen to the words of Herodotus, during whose lifetime all oracles of Apollo were most loquacious. He wrote: "When the Cnidians were trying to dig the Isthmus of Halicarnassus with little success because of stones flying into their eyes and the workmen wounding themselves, they asked Pythia for advice. They received this reply: 'Do not fill up nor dig the Isthmus, for if Jupiter had willed it, he would have made an island himself!' Consequently, they stopped the work."[167] That this was God's decree is argued from the fact that Demosthenes, Demetrius Poliorcetes, Caligula, Nero, and Domitian, who tried to dig the Isthmus of Corinth, were either killed, captured, or defeated by the enemy because they scorned divine oracles or tried to upset the balance of nature.[168] Now what about this? When the Athenians consulted Apollo because they were oppressed by numerous defeats and plagues, Apollo told them that his altar should be made double. Now the altar was cubical, and the carpenters ignorantly added a cube to the cube. When the plague became worse than before, the Athenians again consulted Apollo who answered that his altar had not been made double. And so geometers from all of Greece were summoned to double the cubical altar. Finally Plato accomplished this with the mesolabe, and the plague abated, although many citizens had died.[169] I beg you to notice that the "geometer" demon had proposed the most difficult task of all for the

[164] *Lebadio* MR

[165] Pausanius, IX. 37. 4. Also see Apuleius, *De deo Socratis* XV. 154.

[166] Plutarch, *Moralia, De defectu oraculorum* XLV. 434D–F.

[167] Herodotus I. 174.

[168] Pausanius, *Corinth.* I. 5. Suetonius, *Julius Caesar* XLIV, *Caligula* XXI, *Nero* XIX. Also see Pausanius, *Attica* VIII. 3 about Demosthenes.

[169] Eratosthenes of Cyrene (275–194 B.C.) used the mesolabe to find mean proportional lines. In addition to his investigations on arithmetical and geometrical problems, he wrote *Platonicus,* which dealt with mathematical definitions, and he

Athenians, namely, to double the cube. No mortal hitherto could attain this by proof but only by physical reasoning. For it would have been necessary to find two mean proportions for two given lines, and no one could do this as yet. Nicholas[169a] of Cusa tried it; Orontius boasted that he attained it, and from this proved a quadrature of the circle which was completely unknown.[170] Yet, Nonius Lusitanus and Buteo Delphinas clearly explained his paralogism. Thus Apollo aroused much greater admiration for himself than before. Plato in good faith increased this admiration, when he with his Egyptian learning declared that Apollo by this response wished to recall the Athenians from luxury, lust, intoxication, and plunder to the honorable pursuits of the liberal arts.[171]

TORALBA: If the builders had made a cubical mass of clay equal to the cubical altar and had added just as much to the weight, and then had fashioned each mass joined together at the same time, with the figure of a cube, the matter would have been accomplished with no difficulty by physical reasoning.

SALOMON: There can be no doubt to anyone who thinks seriously about this matter that the oracles of Apollo as well as of Bahal, whether true or false, had been inspired by demons. Indeed the Pythian priestess never P. 138

wrote on principles of music and geometrical works in *On Means* and *Duplication of the Cube*. If Plato used the mesolabe, I can find no verification of it. The error possibly arose because of the title of Eratosthenes' book *Platonicus*. A possible link between Plato and the problem of squaring the circle is through Hippias of Elis. Hippias discovered the *quadratrix*, the first curve other than the circle recognized by Greek geometers. It was used in trying to trisect the angle and subsequently in trying to square the circle.

169a Cusanus wrote *Dialogus de Circuli Quadratura*. Msg. José Ruysschaert called this to my attention. See also Paul Lawrence Rose, "Humanist Culture and Renaissance Mathematus: The Italian Libraries of the *Quattrocento*," *Studies in the Renaissance* 20 (1973), 73.

170 "Squaring the circle" is the attempt to find a square whose area is equal to that of a given circle. In early attempts there are fallacies evident to us, which still escaped the attention of such an amateur as Thomas Hobbes (born 1588). In the sixteenth century the Italian mathematician Vieta is given credit for making excellent progress in reducing the problem of trisecting the angle to that of cubic equation, and stating the problem of squaring the circle in an equation. See James R. Newman, *The World of Mathematics* (New York, 1956), I, 90–91, 120–21. Cf. Hippocrates George Apostle, *Aristotle's Philosophy of Mathematics* (Chicago, 1952), p. 76.

171 Plutarch tells the story but Bodin was careless in relaying the details. Plutarch does not say that Plato doubled the cube but that he interpreted what the oracle meant about doubling his altar namely, a need to study geometry which was required to find two mean proportionals, that being the only way to double a cube. This would be done by Eudoxus of Cnidus or Helicon of Cyzicus. For the complete story see Plutarch, *Moralia, De genio Socratis* VII. 578f–579d.

made an utterance except in a manic state, with foaming mouth, swollen neck, and staring eyes; often she even prophesied from her private parts or from the depths of her heart even though her mouth was closed. I have read that before the arrival of the Spanish there had been Indian priests in this state who fostered the worship of demons, witchcraft, and human sacrifice. However, divine law[172] clearly teaches that divine oracles are only granted to prophets as a gift of God and the prophets do not give them with a raging mind but with a tranquil, steady soul. Divine law clearly shows that God appeared among immortals only to Moses when he was awake.[173] He appeared to the other prophets only when they were sleeping, in dreams and nocturnal visions. Moses Rambam listed ten classes of these dreams or nocturnal visions. To very few, such as Samuel, Elias, Elisha, and Isaiah, was divine light poured out for the whole course of life. As often as God or an angel of the Lord spoke in Scripture, His prophecy was revealed by a dream or by a vision in sleep; such are the visions of Abraham[174] and the conversations of God with him and all others except Moses. If one does not comprehend this secret, he becomes involved in various delusions. Sometimes what to do is suggested to persons awake, but this is done through the inner senses of the soul, through a guardian angel.[175] Often divine voices are heard by persons asleep, or their ears are twitched, or they are beset with nightmares.[176] Elihu said to Job: "God speaks one time, and then He speaks again; if man does not heed Him in dreams and nocturnal visions when sleep has overtaken him, then He twitches his ear and gives divine utterance as if by the imprint of a seal, so that He may snatch away depravity[177] from the poor and haughtiness from the powerful."[178] Isaiah spoke in the same vein: "God twitched my ear at daybreak so that I could hear; He opened my ear, and I yielded to His voice."[179] No one understands this twitching of the ear unless he has had experience. Indeed our prophets have been favored with remarkable gifts for many centuries, and they have predicted carnage of the masses, destructions of cities, overthrow of empires, and deaths of princes that have been confirmed in their own time and in succeeding ages. Therefore we must seek oracles from the words and writings of the prophets and also testimonies of the true religion from them alone.

[172] Num. 12:6. [173] Num. 12:7–8. [174] Gen. 15:1.

[175] See Plutarch, *Moralia, De Pythiae oraculis* VII. 397c, *De genio Socratis.* Also III Kings (I Kings) 13:18.

[176] Philo, *De somniis* I. 26. 164, 33–34; II. 1–8.

[177] *pravitatem* MR [178] Job 33:14–17. [179] Isaiah 1:4–5.

CURTIUS: Surely we must consider Abraham and the Israelites as the chief prophets, but there are others also. Bileam[180] a Chaldean was divinely inspired and prophesied a revolution in public affairs 2,000 years before it happened. Also Job, Elias, Elisha and the Arabs excelled through divine oracles before the promulgation of the law. P. 139

SENAMUS: If true dreams of present and future occurrences are called prophecies, there will be innumerable prophets. Has not everyone learned something true in a dream or nocturnal vision which he could not have known otherwise? Why, even very wicked men have very true dreams. A little while before Pisistratus[181] the tyrant was killed, he dreamed that he was thrown headlong out of heaven by Jupiter.[182] Likewise, on the day before the emperor Caracalla was killed, he had a dream that he was struck with a dagger[183] by his father, Severus, and heard his father's voice upbraiding him with these words, "Lo, the reward for a brother's murder," for Caracalla had ordered Geta's death.[184] Artemidorus[185] and other historians frequently attest to such dreams as these. Also that Christian bishop, Synesius,[186] wrote a book *About Dreams* in which he said that prophecies were communicated not only to men but even to animals.

SALOMON: Certain dreams are true, yet many are false such as those which result from a soul upset with cares. Dreams follow worry, according to a wise teacher,[187] and when there are many dreams, there are many deceptions. Dreams often come after a heavy meal. Yet when a sober

[180] Num. 23–24. See above, p. 103. [181] Pisistratus M

[182] Pisistratus, tyrant of Athens 560–527 B.C., died of sickness. However, compare Cicero, *De nat. deorum* III. 33.

[183] *sica* MR

[184] Marcus Antoninus Aurelius (A.D. 188–217), commonly called Caracalla, became sole emperor in 212 after the death of his father, Septimius Severus, and after Caracalla had assassinated his brother Geta because of the latter's popularity. See *Ox. Class. Dict.*, pp. 125, 387.

[185] Artemidorus of Ephesus (late second century) traveled extensively to collect dreams and wrote a treatise, *Oneirokritika*, on their interpretation. See *Ox. Class. Dict.*, p. 104.

[186] Synesius of Cyrene was Bishop of Ptolomais and a Neoplatonist. In Alexandria he was a devoted disciple of Hypatia, to whom he expresses gratitude, as to "a mother, a sister, and a teacher." He led a rich and many-sided life that included the love of animals. In commenting on the puritan restrictions forced upon him by the episcopal office, he regretted amusements, as his "darling dogs no longer allowed to hunt." He wrote not only of animals in his *De insomniis* but contributed *Cynogetics*, a treatise on breeding dogs, which posterity unfortunately did not preserve. The significance philosophically of his claim that revelation is to animals is that all parts of the universe are in sympathy. See *Cath. Encycl.*, XIV, 386–87. See above, Book III, note 316.

[187] Eccles. 5:2.

man whose soul is free from baseness, lust, idle cares, and greed sleeps soberly he often has true dreams and excellent visions. He is taught to avoid base things, to preserve honest ones, and to know the future, and these can generally be called prophecies. Indeed, prophecy is a divine power granted by a gift of God for seeing and announcing the future, and this gift has been bestowed not only to men of old but also to men of our times. We have read in the commentaries of the Hebrews that prophecy ceased after their return from exile. This, however, does not mean that the Hebrews afterwards had no divine dreams, but only indicates that God did no longer speak through prophets but revealed His commands and laws to the rulers and to the people. To be sure, there are very many who receive divine commands in dreams regarding their own salvation or that of others or in order that they may escape the enemies' snares, refrain from evils, turn from impiety and superstition to the true religion, or become firmer in doubtful matters. Indeed, true dreams and nocturnal visions are more powerful than those very actions of men wide
P. 140 awake. For example, Abraham in sleep prayed for the salvation of Sodom and Gomorrah and spoke freely with God;[188] that prayer was no less effective than if he had prayed while awake, and perhaps it was more effective. Likewise, Solomon in dreams beseeched God for wisdom, and his prayer was so efficacious that God answered him in a dream that He had heard his prayers and had inspired him with such wisdom as no mortal before or since possessed.[189]

FRIDERICUS: If we reduce the apex of our religion and salvation to idle dreams, religions are done for. A long time ago Paul warned against false prophets. He said that, even if an angel came down from heaven and taught something other than what he had related, we should not believe the angel.[190] Paul meant by this that we should not seek new seers or Apollos or any oracles in determining the best kind of religion, since he clearly taught that the best religion was the Christian religion.

SENAMUS: Since the Jews repudiate not only Paul but also all the books of the New Testament, and the Mohammedans do not accept any Christian writings, we must use other witnesses. I think nothing will be a better proof than to decide which is the oldest religion, for this will be a strong argument that it is the best.

TORALBA: If we measure the best kind of religion by its antiquity, we must seek its origin from the parent of the whole human race. For he

188 Gen. 18:23–33.
189 III Kings (I Kings) 3:5–15.
190 Gal. 1:8.

must have been supplied with the best habits, the best training, the best knowledge, and finally the best spiritual virtues by God since he had learned the holiest language from the same God. He would never have been able to speak for himself or could have learned and expressed the natures of all living creatures to whom he is said to have given names according to their inherent power, if he had not been influenced by the best Parent and Teacher.[191] It is consistent with his nature that he should endow his beloved sons with such unusual virtues and especially with true religion so that they would adore the eternal God and worship Him, first by offering prayers, then with offerings from the crops, and then from the flocks, which were consumed by the sacrificial flames, because they did not eat flesh before the floods.

SALOMON: I can readily agree with you for the most part, Toralba, but I have no doubt that men lived from the flesh of the flocks as well as from the milk. Otherwise why were there so many herds? If men had not been allowed to eat the very savory flesh of the cows, would not the stench from so many dead herds have been harmful? Divine law permitted eating of flesh provided the blood was poured on the ground. From this it is clear that no longer could the people fatten themselves with blood as had formerly been permitted. Indeed nothing is more impure or more harmful than eating blood, nor is anything more likely to cause leprosy and elephantiasis.[192] P. 141

TORALBA: I shall have no quarrel with you, Salomon, about diet. I only conclude that Adam and his son Abel had been instructed in the best religion, and after them Seth, Enoch, Methusaleh up to Noah who worshipped in great holiness, to the exclusion of all others, that eternal and only true God, the Builder and Parent of all things and the great Architect of the whole world. Therefore I believe this religion is not only the oldest but also the best of all, and those who have departed from that most ancient and best religion have fallen into an irreconcilable labyrinth of errors.

SALOMON: I agree with you, Toralba, when you say that religion which has been handed down from the best Parent of the human race is the most ancient; this religion devotes itself to the purest worship of one eternal God, shunning the throng of gods and divinities and all created things. When it was written that during Seth's time God began to be worshipped,[193] the ambiguity of the word *huḥal* deceived many, because

[191] Cf. Philo, *Legum allegoria* XXX. 92–96.
[192] See Philo, *Quaestiones et solutiones in Genesin* II. 59. (Gen. 9:4).
[193] Gen. 4:26.

the word means to begin and to desecrate. Jonathan, a Chaldean interpreter, translated it from the Hebrew thus: "Then man began to pray in the name of the Lord." But Onkelos, whom the Latins call Aquila, translated it from the Hebrew into Chaldean as: "Then men began not to pray in the name of God." That is, since they had begun to turn to the worship of creatures and of objects of the senses. This opinion is truer, since it is apparent that Abel and Cain worshipped God alone; also, Enoch distinguished himself with such religious piety that while still alive and breathing he was taken by divine goodness from the sight of men.[194] This sign of divine pleasure happened besides him only to Elias.[195] Noah practiced this same religion, and he alone of all mortals was called righteous and just by the testimony and judgment of God himself.[196] In like manner Shem, Noah's son, a priest of most noble God and a most just king of Jerusalem, embraced his paternal religion with the same piety which flourished up to Abraham's time—that is, 345 years from the flood. At this time, Abraham left Ur, a city of the Chaldeans, because, according to tradition, the Chaldeans turned from the true God to the worship of the sun and stars.[197] I think the reason for the Chaldeans' apostasy was that while they were offering sacrifices to eternal God, they
P. 142 looked heavenward and allowed themselves to be drawn, as if by hands, to the worship of the stars which they perceived. Abraham placed his life in danger by openly cursing the worship of the stars.[198] A Chaldean interpreter wrote that Nimrod,[199] who first imposed tyranny upon free men, had ordered Abraham to be cast into the furnace because he was unwilling to be turned from the worship of immortal God to created things. Nevertheless, God rescued him by an amazing sign and sent him into Syria,[200] where he and his offspring found repose in that purest religion of their elders until they yielded to the tricks of the Egyptians and turned from their hereditary religion to the worship not only of the stars, but also the elements, animals, statues, and demons, thus deserting the founder of the universe. Then God took pity on his people 400 years after the covenant with Abraham and inspired Moses to call the people back to their natural and God-inspired religion which had almost become obliterated from their souls.[201] Although Numa Pompilius[202] forbade statues to be built,

[194] Gen. 5:24. [195] IV Kings (II Kings) 2:11.
[196] Gen. 6:9. [197] Gen. 12:1–6. [198] Deut. 4:19–24.
[199] Gen. 10:8–9. [200] Mich. 5:6. [201] Ex. 3:4–22.
[202] Numa, the second king of Rome (715–673 B.C.), is probably a historical figure. Numa is credited with organizing the priestly colleges and building the

Zeno the Stoic and the most holy Persian kings did not allow temples to the gods to be erected lest they seem to confine God's majesty which is not bound by vast limits of the world to a small dwelling.[203] Moses, nevertheless, ordered a tent,[204] then a temple to be constructed so that he could lead the people from the view and worship of the heavenly stars when they were offering sacrifices.[205]

TORALBA: Thence it is certain that the best and most ancient religion of all was implanted in the human minds with right reasons by eternal God, and this religion proposes the one eternal God as the object of man's worship. Already we have shown that God, who is most alien to every contact of bodies, is the founder and preserver of all things; and since He is the best and the highest, supreme worship is due to Him. If anyone prefers or joins to Him in worship of other divinities which were created by God, he will suffer great punishment. If anyone has followed in his life the pure worship of God and the laws of nature, can he doubt that he will enjoy the same happiness which Abel, Enoch, Noah, Shem, Abraham, Job, and the rest enjoyed, because God Himself declared with laudable testimony that they were most pleasing and holy to Him? Indeed, Plato[206] could have said nothing truer than that the most ancient parents of the human race were better than their posterity because they were not so far removed from a union of gods, from whom flowed the ancient vestiges of the golden age to posterity.[207] Indeed Simplicius,[208] an adversary of Christians and Jews alike, defined the consummate perfection of the human mind as a turning to the Lord. He also states that as long as the human soul shall cling with deepest roots to its originator, he shall easily safeguard this integrity in which it was created; but if the soul is P. 143

Regia, the home of the *pontifex maximus*. See *Ox. Class. Dict.*, p. 613. For a full account see Plutarch, *Numa*; also Augustine, *De civ. Dei* III. 9–10; VII. 34–35.

[203] *gurgustiis* MR [204] *tentorium* MR [205] Ex. 25:8–9.

[206] *Leges* III. 677–79.

[207] *ad posteros aurei vestigia prisca dimanarunt* M R adds *secuti.*

[208] Simplicius was one of the last seven philosophers of Plato's Academy when it was closed by Justinian in A.D. 529. Together they sought protection of the king of Persia, but although welcomed, they could not live among the barbarians. Returning to Greece, they were allowed by Justinian "to return to their own homes, and to live henceforward in the enjoyment of liberty of conscience." The end of pagan Neoplatonism left commentaries of prodigious learning. Henceforth, Neoplatonism lived only under the guise of Christian theology. In Christianity this philosophy was often a mysticism stressing the kinship of man and god. See *Encycl. Brit.* (11th ed.), XXV, 134-35; XIX, 372–78.

torn away from its source, it will languish and wither until it turns itself again to its origin and founder.

SENAMUS: If this best and most ancient religion of nature, which is the simplest of all, is sufficient for a blessed life, why did the Mosaic law order so many sacrifices, ceremonies, and rites? Indeed, we have read of animal sacrifices as well as human sacrifices. Jepthah,[209] a prince of that race, sacrificed his daughter at almost the same time as King Agamemnon sacrificed his daughter Iphigenia.[210]

SALOMON: Abel at first and then the others seem to have practiced animal sacrifice according to the very law of nature,[211] but almost all people—the Chaldeans, Persians, Amorrhaeans, Greeks, Italians, Gauls, Carthaginians, Indians—were acquainted with the very wicked custom of human sacrifice. Still Jeptha did not sacrifice his daughter, as almost all think, but promised that she would be forever chaste. This interpretation of a Chaldean, Rabbi Levi Ben Gerson, and David Kimchi is better and more accurate than the charge of a most cruel murder by a parent. This interpretation is feasible because every year maidens visited her and offered consolations. The Hebrew word, *letannot*, which produced the ambiguity in this place, does not mean to mourn as much as to console; indeed Jeptha sacrificed those things which were properly sacrificed according to divine law.

TORALBA: If the law of nature and natural religion which has been implanted in men's souls is sufficient for attaining salvation, I do not see why the Mosaic rites and ceremonies are necessary.

SALOMON: There is nothing more ancient or sacred in the majesty of the Bible than the divine law which has a threefold division. Aside from the books of histories, the foremost is the moral law, second the ritual law, third the political law. The moral law has two parts; one part oversees the worship of God; the other part oversees the mutual duties of men among themselves. The worship of God is contained in the first four headings of the decalogue; the other six headings pertain to the protection of faith and society of man with his fellow men. The political laws give a fuller account of the same things which the second table briefly contains, namely the judicial laws, marriage laws, and the prediatory[212]

[209] Judg. 11:30–40.

[210] Agamemnon, son of Atreus and brother of Menelaus, king of Mycenae, sacrificed his daughter, Iphigenia, at Aulis to secure favorable winds to carry him to Troy to avenge the rape of his brother's wife, Helen. See Aeschylus, *Agamemnon* and Euripides, *Iphigenia at Aulis*.

[211] Gen. 8:20.

[212] *praediatorias* MR

laws on which the Hebrew state was founded. Even without these laws a good man can attain salvation in the most isolated solitude or anywhere in the world. Rites and sacrifices, however, were instituted by God so that the Israelites, who had learned from the Egyptians and neighboring peoples to make sacrifices to demons and animal statues, might henceforth abstain from these practices. This would not have been possible because of the ancient custom of sacrificing to demons unless they were ordered to make the same sacrifices to God. And so for this reason that more se- P. 144
rious and many times unjust charge was made against the Israelites that they feasted on blood, as wicked Circe taught Ulysses[213] and his companions to feed the Shades with the blood of many animals poured in a trench. When all kinds of sacrifices were set forth, finally the lawgiver proposed that one, lest they then sacrifice to satyrs and demons with whom they had been accustomed to harlot.[214] Clearly, God is not at all pleased by sacrifices because He refused for animals to be sacrificed to Him in any place except the one which He had chosen for sacrificing,[215] although He allowed his people to have synagogues and shrines anywhere for proclaiming praises and divine laws. That temple of Sion, where animal sacrifices were allowed, was burned by the emperor Vespasian[216] according to God's goodness and care, so that all might know that sins were not removed or guilt expiated by sacrificing flocks, and salvation was not attained from this sacrifice. According to Jeremiah, God spoke to His people in a loud voice against this practice: "Heap up your burnt offerings with victims and consume flesh to satiety; indeed I commanded nothing of this sort to your elders when I led them out of Egypt."[217] And God surely ordered nothing in a loud voice except the decalogue;[218] moreover the decalogue, which is called everywhere a covenant struck with the people, contains no sacrifice. The prophets repeated many times that God was offended by the sacrifice of flocks, that the temple was burned, and God's people seemed to be cast out from Palestine for no other reason than that they might not from that time on place the hope of salvation in the blood of cattle.[219] "Take away the iniquity from us, and we shall

[213] Homer, *Odys.* X. 516–30. [214] Lev. 17:8–12.

[215] Deut. 15:19–20.

[216] Vespasian (Roman emperor A.D. 69–79) delegated the task of subduing Palestine to his son Titus, who captured Jerusalem in A.D. 70.

[217] Jer. 7:21–23.

[218] Deut. 4:1–8.

[219] Psalm 39 (40):7; Josh. 22:26–29; Psalm 50 (51):18–19; Psalm 49 (50); Prov. 21:3; Jer. 33:11, 18; Hosea 6:6; Amos 4:5.

render the cattle of our lips," said Hosea.[220] And likewise: "I shall not come, shall I, into the sight of God with burnt offerings, with calves and lambs? A thousand rams and 10,000 flames of oil do not please God, do they? I shall not give my first-born as an expiation of my sin, shall I? I have shown to you, O man, what is good and what God requires from you; namely to use judgment, to choose goodness and be humble before your God."[221] When Saul excused sacrifices, in disobedience to God's command, Samuel, rebuking him sharply, said, "Obedience is more excellent than sacrifices."[222] Also, according to Isaiah, God more sharply reprimanded those who thought their sins were washed away by sacrifices.[223] Therefore, salvation must be established in the execution of the decalogue, not in sacrifices. "Do this," he said, "and you will live!"[224] Indeed, when King Solomon had ordered a golden ark to be built and placed it in the holy of holies, he put nothing in it except the two stone tablets of the decalogue.[225] Moreover, he protected the ark, where God was said to dwell between each angel, as a place of atonement, so that all might
P. 145 know that God would be propitious to mortals if they followed the sacred covenant of the decalogue. Likewise, when Solomon represented God speaking, he said: "Keep My commandments so that you may live!"[226] He indicated by these words of what sort these commandments were: "Bind these upon your fingers; write them upon the tablets of your hearts!"[227] In this neat allegory of ten fingers He indicated the ten headings of the decalogue, and by the double tablet of the heart He meant that the first tablet of the decalogue pertains to the higher faculty of the soul which is the mind itself, to which the laws of the first tablet about divine worship are related; the second tablet is related to the lower part of the soul by which we are taught to control anger,[228] to restrain passion, to master desire,[229] to keep our minds, eyes, and hands from another's possessions. For the 613 headings of the laws[230] which are contained in the book of law refer partly to judgments, partly to customs, partly to rites, partly to a fuller explanation of the decalogue. With one word of the decalogue fornication is prohibited, for the Hebrew word *na'oth* means fornication, whether with demons, or with statues and other things, or

[220] Hosea 14:3.
[221] Mich. 6:6–8.
[222] I Kings (I Sam.) 15:22.
[223] Isaiah 1:13–16.
[224] Isaiah 55:3.
[225] III Kings (I Kings) 6:19; 8:9.
[226] Prov. 7:2.
[227] Prov. 7:3.
[228] *iram* MR
[229] *domitas habere cupiditates* MR
[230] *capita legum* MR

with close relatives with whom incest is committed, or with another's wife. Finally that law forbids all vagrant copulations, defilements, pederasty,[231] and wicked uniting with animals. Moses explained these more fully in the book of laws than the tablets revealed. Rabbi Moses Rambam divided universal law into fourteen parts. The first part referred to a turning away from sins and a turning toward God; the second part contained a prohibition of idolatry, and the third an uprightness of morals; the fourth part discussed love toward individuals, and the fifth pecuniary fines; the sixth referred to rights of contracts and inheritances; the seventh pertained to court days, days on which judgments were not pronounced, and feast days, and the eighth dealt with fastings; the ninth concerned prayers and praises, the tenth the sanctuary, and the eleventh sacrificial rites; the twelfth pollutions and expiations; the thirteenth described foods that were forbidden and lusts that must be destroyed, and the fourteenth pleasures that were forbidden. All these matters are elaborately contained in the sixty-one books of the Hebraic Pandects[232] and in 532 headings. Penalties are added to the prohibitive laws and rewards to the prescriptive laws. For example, when we are enjoined to open the founts of kindness to the weak, these words are added: "It will also be well for you, or I will heap riches upon you, if you shall have done this." For always prosperity of goods follows the largess to the weak; although no reward is owed from this duty, nonetheless, to those who have abstained from things that were prohibited and to those who have followed the things commanded, God has decreed a great reward.

OCTAVIUS: Since the Jews everywhere in the world abstain from the sacrifices of flocks, those laws of sacrifices are useless.

SALOMON: There is no sacrifice, no sacred vessels, no rites which do not contain the most beautiful secrets of things hidden in the treasure chests of nature, as Philo the Hebrew, Abraham Aben Esra, King Solomon, Leo P. 146 the Hebrew very ingeniously interpret.[233] We are also taught by these first to confess sins, next to avert harsher punishments and imminent dangers by earnest prayers, then to give thanks for so many kindnesses with which we are constantly blessed, then to glorify God with praises, and finally to sacrifice our pure minds to God.

[231] *paederastiam* MR

[232] See below, Book VI, p. 451, note 627.

[233] A sixteenth-century author who shared the belief that secrets are contained in sacred vessels, rites, and sacrifices is Guillaume Postel; note especially his *Candelabra of Moses.*

TORALBA: Indeed I learned from a Jewish astrologer that those ten headings of the decalogue correspond to the ten celestial orbs in the proper order of nature. The first head is granted to God Himself as the supreme author of universal nature; the second to the second orb which is called by the Hebrews desert-place because no star is contained in this heaven; so also are statues most scrupulously forbidden. The third heading in which we are forbidden to take God's name in vain is compatible with the third orb, lest we swear an oath by Jupiter and the other stars. The fourth heading about the holiness of the Sabbath is related to the orb of Saturn to whom also the seventh day of Saturn is vowed, just as the day of the Hebrews' Sabbath. The fifth heading about the worship of parents is agreeable with the fifth orb or the orb of Jupiter, who was called the parent of the gods by the Greeks, Jupiter by the Latins, a helping father, as it were. The sixth heading about murders is appropriate to the orb of Mars, whom Homer[234] called a man-slayer and destroyer of cities. The seventh heading about adulteries and lust is fitting to Venus' orb. The eighth about thefts is in the sphere of Mercury whom the ancients made the god of traders and the originator of gain. The college of merchants in Rome was called that of the Mercurials. The ninth heading about forbidden lies and the crime of falsehood is attributed to the sun about which Vergil said:[235] "Who can say that the sun lies?" The Hebrews also used the sun to indicate truth; for example, in this passage, "God loves compassion and truth,"[236] the Hebraic text has also "because God is the sun and shield." The seventy-two interpreters render this as "because he loves mercy and truth, the Lord." The Greeks made Apollo the parent of oracles and divination of hidden things, even the ruler who makes all things clear by sundering the clouds. The tenth heading is related to the orb of the moon, to whom they grant the same power in the macrocosm as to the lover in the microcosm, where the power of desire especially resides; also in the tenth heading we are ordered to restrain our desires.

FRIDERICUS: I think the conformity of the decalogue with the heavenly orbs which Toralba brought to light from the hidden secrets of the Hebrews is very acute and admirable. This conformity seems not only to be agreeable to the whole universe of nature but also to confirm the order of the planets according to the tradition of the ancients. Ptolemy[237] was

[234] *Iliad* V. 31.
[235] Cf. Vergil, *Ec.* IV. 42. "Nor does the wool teach the various colors to lie."
[236] Psalm 25:10.
[237] Ptolemy (Claudius Ptolemaeus) of Alexandria, born at Ptolemaïs, made ob-

the first to depart from the opinion of the ancients by placing Venus and Mercury beneath the sun, and he reasoned that the apogee of the sun was 604½ terrestrial diameters distant from the earth; moreover, he thought it incongruous to leave a vast space free of planets, since the earth was 570 diameters distant from the apogee[238] of the moon. The Arabian and almost all the other astrologers were more mistaken because they thought that between the apse of the Sun and Mars a space of 3815 ter- P. 147 restrial diameters intervened, which is seven times greater than the distance of sun and moon.

SALOMON: From these matters you can know, if any one should wish to investigate them in more detail, that all the secrets of the highest matters and the hidden treasures of nature are concealed in the divine laws, that is, even in the records and books of our elders. Abraham Aben Esra considered this decalogue to be the epitome of natural law. Since the latter seemed to be obliterated and violated by the great sins and crimes of men, the best and greatest God, having pity on the ruin of man, renewed the laws and prohibitions of nature with solemn covenant in the greatest assemblies of His people and incised on stone tablets with the clang of trumpets, with thunder, lightning and flames striking on Mount Horeb even to the midst of the heaven. When the mountain was trembling from that awesome blow, He sanctified that eternal covenant of the decalogue with the people after the tablets were sprinkled with blood, as was customary in making covenants.[239] When I placed these things before my eyes and contemplated more deeply the appearance of so great a spectacle, I sang these words briefly, struck as if by a divine madness:

> Indeed who, O one to be feared, has heard your thundering voice and been unafraid,
> when you commanded laws to be made sacred and from the top of trembling Mt. Sinai gave covenants that must not be violated?
> Who was not stunned by the clang of trumpets resounding through the empty airs?[240]

---

servations between A.D. 121–151. His great work, originally called *Mathēmatikē syntaxis*, became known as *Megalē syntaxis* (*Great Collection*) to distinguish it from the *Mikros astronomoumenos* (*Little Astronomy*). The Arabs changed *megistē* into *al-Majistii*, whence *Almagest*. It details the Greek achievement in astronomy with some additions of Ptolemy. See *Ox. Class. Dict.*, pp. 746–47.

[238] *auge* MR

[239] Ex. 19–20; Deut. 6.

[240] *auras* MR

Or what wicked man could endure the harsh anger of your sacred divine will,
as often as you, armed against the enemy, brandish flaming thunderbolts with your great right hand?
Surely you press down the swollen necks of haughty kings, and as victor you repel the violent sceptres with your brave hand, striking the crown of the cruel tyrant.
You crumble great peoples, and you diminish with your powerful arm kingdoms which seem unconquered.
Moreover, as deliverer you always raise up your anointed from the lowly dust and without exception you overturn the indomitable battle lines,
and under your command the unarmed is victorious!

Toralba: What is this covenant which was perceived on two tablets and under ten headings except the very law of nature? Indeed we have snatched this law from nature; we have drunk it in, we have imitated it. In consequence of this law we were not instructed but made, not taught but imbued with the knowledge that eternal God, the first cause, is not only the effector of all things but also the preserver. Because of His majority He must be feared and revered. Because of His incredible goodness
P. 148 to us He must be loved and honored with the complete power of our soul. Although there is no law which is not weakened by some limitation of time or place or person, still this one law is eternal. With no exception is it violable and it applies to all places, times and persons: namely that God must be solely loved and followed.[241] Moreover, to steal away the veneration and worship due God is a sacrilege, and to grant that honor to created and fleeting things and to place the rewards of salvation and trust in those things is a wicked crime. Likewise, in the second heading of the decalogue we are forbidden to render any statue or image of God. Nature also implanted this concept in us because by natural and evident reason we have shown that God is incorporeal. For this reason Numa Pompilius[242] by his own law forbade any statues of the gods to be made. And surely if it is wrong to worship the sky, the stars, and the sun, how much more wicked is it to venerate the images of men? I have often

[241] *et cum nulla omnino lex sit, quae non aliqua temporum aut locorum aut personarum exceptione minuatur, haec tamen una lex est aeterna, nec ulla exceptione violabilis quin omnibus locis temporibus ac personis conveniat, scilicet Deum unice amandum ac prosequendum* M Missing in R and N

[242] See above, p. 184, note 202.

thought it strange that so many people in such learned times cherished statues in their eagerness for piety, since Heraclitus, the most ancient of philosophers, said that the worshippers of statues were acting just as if they were speaking with doors.[243]

CURTIUS: The Persians, Scythians, Africans, and ancient Romans must be excepted from these peoples, for Marcus Varro[244] wrote that they worshipped gods[245] without images for more than 130 years.

SALOMON: Why do you need proof in a matter so apparent? It is sufficient to describe a statue with one detestable and most loathsome word *kopros* that is, dung. Indeed with this word our elders were accustomed to curse idols.

TORALBA: The other headings of the decalogue are common to almost all nations because there is sufficient proof that divine law is altogether consistent with nature. I make an exception to the fourth heading of the decalogue, namely, rest on the Sabbath. Indeed I do not see what it is or why the Jews keep the seventh day as a day of rest rather than the sixth, as indeed the Mohammedans do, or the first, as the Christians do. To be sure, that which is unjust[246] by nature cannot be made just by the passage of time, or vice versa. If, therefore, before the law was handed down by Moses, it was not a sin to be involved in work on the seventh day, why did it become sinful afterwards?

When Salomon was silent at this point, contrary to their hope, FRIDERICUS said: "The matter is safe; Salomon has lost his voice."

SALOMON: I do not see why I ought to speak, since it is a capital offense to betray the token of the emperor.

CORONAEUS: So it is among enemies, but not among friends and acquaintances whom you[247] see here. Explain then, Salomon, what you call here a token, lest Toralba seems to report a bloodless victory.

SALOMON: Surely the Sabbath is a token between God and his chosen people.[248] Other people cannot understand this, and if they could, they would not want to. A long time ago Justin Martyr had reproached Trypho[249] with the proof proposed by Toralba. But I ask you this, Toralba. Does it seem just or unjust, according to nature, to bear arms?

TORALBA: It seems indifferent. P. 149

[243] Cf. Plutarch, *Moralia, De Pythiae oraculis* XXI. 404E–F.
[244] Augustine, *De civ. Dei* IV. 31. Plutarch, *Numa* VIII.
[245] *deos* MR
[246] *injustum* MR
[247] *vides* MR
[248] Ex. 31:17; Ezech. 20:12.
[249] Justin, *Dial. Tryph.* 20–24.

SALOMON: What if a prince, with a rebellion threatening, should prohibit bearing arms? Would not a citizen seem unjust, criminal and evil, if he would advance in arms contrary to the edict?

TORALBA: Indeed I agree.

SALOMON: Why so, since it was not unjust before?

TORALBA: Because it is the law of nature that we should obey the magistrate issuing the orders, and whoever does otherwise is considered unjust.

SALOMON: How much more unjust is he who, when God was forbidding that which was not forbidden before, did not obey the interdict, whether he thinks it just or unjust; yet it is not possible that God orders anything unjust.

CURTIUS: The lawyers say the chief difference between natural and civil laws is that civil laws are concerned with those matters which cannot be called just and unjust before they are ordered or forbidden, but natural laws have a justice forever binding without any decrees or edicts.

FRIDERICUS: Why then before Moses do we read that nothing was decreed about rest on the seventh day?

SALOMON: Who can affirm that nothing had been spoken before about the sacred rest of that day? Notwithstanding, in their ancient piety[250] men were accustomed to devote almost all their leisure to honorable pursuits and a contemplation of sublime matters, so that every day seemed to be a day of rest and a continued Sabbath. Afterwards, however, when the meaner age, intent on the pleasures of empty skills, on merriment, lust, wars, and plunder, scorned the study of heavenly and divine matters, was anything as necessary as to call men back to this law of nature, that is,[251] to the honest pursuits of virtue, to peace of mind, to meditation on divine matters, and to his own salvation? It was pleasing, moreover, to sanctify this by the solemn rest of the seventh day.

SENAMUS: But why the seventh rather than the first? Nor do I see why in the final heading of the decalogue we are forbidden to strive after another's possessions, since it is enough not to defraud anyone and not to practice those things which disturb the public peace. Who, moreover, can have the power to command the human mind or to bare his thoughts?

SALOMON: One thing at a time. In the first place, it is a sin to demand from God a reason for His own laws;[252] it is wrong to doubt. The fact that divine law forbids us to desire another's possessions is alien to all human laws, and in this especially, the excellence of divine law is mani-

[250] *pietate* MR [251] *id est* MR [252] *legum* MR

fest; divine law applies the ax not only to the trunk and branches but also to the roots and fibres of all sins. Whoever can hold back rampant desires will surely merit praise of the invincible commander. He who desires another's possessions already has committed sin, although he could not fulfill his depraved desires, since he will try everything that he can; P. 150 yet he will never try if his lust is cut away. In no way is it strange if men have not established laws for the lusts of men because they could not impose rewards nor punishments for those deserving them. To be sure, since senses of souls are not seen, this is in the power of God alone who searches out the hidden darkness of the souls and, for this reason, is called *kardiognōstēs* [the one who knows the heart].[253] Indeed, He does not order the prepuce of actions and words to be destroyed before those of thoughts. Just as God is accustomed to carry over credits and distribute rewards for the noble wills of men,[254] so also does He consider him like a murderer who could not kill, although he was very desirous of killing. This is true because he sinned more in his soul, which found delight in depravity, than in the execution of the crime, which concerns the senses, the agents of the soul, as if the attendants of a prince.

Coronaeus: But let us return to the quiet of the seventh day. What reason can exist for this?

Salomon: That lawgiver submitted the reason of his own law, which happened very rarely. He said: "Since God created the heaven, the seas, the earth, and all things contained therein in six days and on the seventh day He rested, He blessed this day and made it holy."[255] And to allay doubt, He proclaimed that principle in more words than the chapters of the whole decalogue, nor have we ever read that He blessed other days or consecrated them for Himself. When all the people were very busy in building a tabernacle for God and securing the provisions for the tabernacle, God, excepting expressly the seventh day, said:[256] "Nevertheless, honor My Sabbaths, since those are, as it were, rather secret tokens and mysteries between Me and you and your posterity, so that you may know that I am eternal God who sanctifies you. Therefore, rest from work on the Sabbath since it is sacred to you. Whoever shall have violated this Sabbath, let him be put to death.[257] Whoever shall have done any work on the day of the Sabbath, let him be cut off from the assembly of people. Six days should suffice for carrying on business; let the seventh day be a

[253] Jer. 12:3. [254] Deut. 11. [255] Ex. 20:11.
[256] Ex. 20:8–11; 31:17; 34:21.
[257] *Quisquis violaverit ipsum capite puniatur* MR missing in N

day of rest sanctified to eternal God. Whoever shall have done any work, let him die. Therefore let the sons of Israel rest on the seventh day so that they may honor the Sabbath with an eternal covenant, since that is the secret and the token between Me and the sons of Israel, an eternal token, I say, since in six days God created the heaven and the earth; on the seventh day He rested." These things God said. You see when He had ordered men, children, slaves, and cattle to rest on that most holy day, He impresses them again and again with as great a supply of words as with remarkable reason. Not content with this, He ordered all the people to be called together again; then in the assembly the lawgiver, as if about to bring forth a new law, said: "These are the things which God com-
P. 151 manded. Six days are allotted for transacting business and for work; let the seventh day be sacred to you because the Sabbath is a day of rest for God. Whoever shall have done any work on this day, let him die lest you kindle a fire on your houses."[258] And in another place he said: "Advise the people of Israel that they honor the Sabbath in a most holy way."[259] We have read this oft-repeated account. When a certain man dishonored the day of rest by gathering wood on the seventh day, Moses, although the law had already been handed down, thought a judgment should not be rendered before he summoned God as judge. God commanded that the defendant[260] be condemned of a capital offense and stoned.[261] It is rather remarkable that although fleeting manna rained down every day, nevertheless, on the seventh day it was not accustomed to fall.[262] When certain men had gone out from their tents on the seventh day as if about to gather manna, God burned with anger[263] and He rebuked them in harsh language, saying: "How far will you try Me? I have given the Sabbath to you for rest, so that you must gather double portions of food on the sixth day; therefore, remain in your tents on the seventh day, and let no one after this go outdoors."[264] Likewise, when the city of Jerusalem was besieged and seemed about to fall, Jeremiah under God's orders promised complete liberation if the people would honor the holy Sabbath.[265] And so God crying out to Isaiah said: "O blessed is that one who calls My Sabbath his delight!"[266] And a little later in like manner: "Whoever has feared to desecrate My Sabbath and has honored that covenant of most holy quiet, I shall carry him aloft onto my sacred mountain"[267]—

[258] Ex. 35:1–3.
[259] Ex. 31:13; Levit. 19:3, 30; 26:2.
[260] *reum* MR
[261] Num. 15:32–36.
[262] Ex. 16:4–6, 23–26.
[263] *ira* MR
[264] Ex. 16:28–30.
[265] Jer. 7:2–3.
[266] Isaiah 56:2.
[267] Isaiah 56:6–7.

that is, into heaven. What about Ezechiel? He called the Sabbath a sacrament of God and a more secret token between God and the people of Israel.[268] For this reason the theologians very eagerly endorsed the rules and laws of the sabbaths in the second book of the Pandects, in twenty-four chapters.[269]

Curtius: I think this was the reason why a certain very sagacious theologian[270] is amazed even to astonishment that the leisure of the Sabbath is impressed in so many chapters of divine laws and prophecies as if, he says, the main points of divine law and our salvation are contained in the honor and rest of this day. The same man also denies that the Sabbath or the law had been abrogated by Christ, and he censures those who think otherwise.

Octavius: I think the Mohammedans had no other reason for resting on the sixth day instead of the seventh than to be separated from Christians as well as from Jews on their day of rest; likewise the Christians established the first day instead of the seventh for honor so that they might withdraw from the Jews. On the other hand, if the Mohammedans rightly made the sixth day a day of rest because of the flight of Mohammed, who was harassed and wounded by his enemies on the sixth day, surely it was more propitious for Christians to make the sixth day, on which Christ was overcome with death, a day of rest than the first, on P. 152
which He is said to have risen.

Toralba: I am amazed that the Mohammedans and Christians agree with the Jews that the decalogue, proclaimed by divine word, held eternal authority, as if the law of nature, yet they changed the day of rest, "make sacred the seventh day in Jewish worship," to use the words of the poet.[271]

Fridericus: May the Christians not[272] be bound by any religious superstitions of the Jews?

Salomon: If the fourth chapter of the decalogue is sacrosanct, the others are also sacrosanct. However, if it is a certain profane superstition, it is necessary that the other laws of the decalogue, which they admit are eternal and immutable with no exception, also perish.

268 Ezech. 20:12.

269 *libro secundo pandectarum, capitibus quatuor et vaginti sabbatorum.* MR Missing in N

270 The theologian is John Calvin. For a discussion of Calvin and Judaism, see Salo W. Baron, *A Social and Religious History of the Jews* (New York, 1969), XIII, 279–96.

271 Ovid, *Ars Am.* I. 76.

272 *ne* MR

TORALBA: Nature herself asserts the other chapters of the decalogue, but not the fourth, as Abraham Aben Esra frankly admits.

SALOMON: When God had ordered him who had gathered wood on the Sabbath to be stoned, turning to Moses He said:[273] "Tell the people to sew fringes and fillets dyed in purple on the hem of their garments to remind them to become accustomed to remember all the commands of God and follow them. Do not search out too diligently among you nor look behind for those with whom you used to be wanton."

FRIDERICUS: Why can one not honor the day of rest, cherish the creation of the universe, acknowledge God's kindnesses as the Parent of nature with continuous praises on the first day as well as the seventh? In no way does it seem to refer to holiness which day it is practiced.

SALOMON: If it does not matter whether we honor the first day or the seventh day, why do you think the first day ought to be chosen more than the seventh, contrary to the clear orders of God, unless you wish intentionally to trample down the laws of the true God? You are accustomed to celebrate very pleasurably your birthday, not the day before, with feasting. Why do you reject the seventh day, the birthday of the world, to make a holiday on the day before or the day after? God blessed no day except the seventh and made no day holy except the seventh. He did not hallow the sixth nor the first. Yet the pagans with their ancient impiety make holy the day of the sun. So do the Christians with an imperial edict order the day of the sun to be made holy with only the name abandoned.[274] Is anything more wicked than this?

CURTIUS: The law was written in this way not because sacred rites were offered to the sun, as you know well, Salomon, but because in enacting laws, in order to make them clear it is necessary to speak in regard to the people's comprehension.

SALOMON: Then, leaving out the popular error, when God foresaw that
P. 153 because of the ignorance of unlearned men or of impiety, the memory of creation would be removed from men's minds, he ordered the birthday of the world to be celebrated with solemn honor. Aristotle and Epicurus had either such impiety or ignorance or both, that they thought the world had been and would be eternal,[275] and the opposite has been clearly demon-

[273] Num. 15:37–41.

[274] *Quamquam ista vetus paganorum impietas est diem solis feriare, sic enim Christiani legibus imperialibus diem solis appellatione deserta feriari jubent.* MR

[275] See Aristotle, *De mundo* II. 391b ff. To Epicurus this perishable world, men and gods, and all other worlds are due to atoms which are imperishable because in

strated above. He commanded to posterity by the glorious recollection of many holy days not only the seventh day, but also the seventh month in which the world was created; also He ordered a reading of the divine laws to begin on this month and day on which the creation of the world was completed. In the seventh year agriculture was ordered to be abandoned. Likewise on this day and month on which the creation of the universe was completed, the priests themselves begin to interpret for all the people the divine laws point by point, with a great display of torches and lights; Herodotus[276] wrote that this custom was observed by the Egyptians. This most ancient observance, the sign of the earth's creation, has not yet passed from view. The Chaldeans call this month of creation the month[277] of *Ethanim*, that is, the month of the illustrious men, since especially in this month in which the world was established, the births and deaths of famous men and unusual changes in public affairs were accustomed to happen. The day of creation, moreover, is so famous and so remarkable before others in all of nature that no one ought to doubt that the law about the rest on the Sabbath is most natural and consistent with universal nature. But enough!

CORONAEUS: Why enough? Why do you break the thread of your conversation at this point which we especially seek, namely, that the quiet of the seventh day is just as natural as the other points of the decalogue?

SALOMON: Because I am afraid to profane by conversation these things which lie hidden in divine secrets. I would not have said so much had I not known you were very fond of divine matters.

CORONAEUS: Then do not begrudge us these secrets since we are the venerators of sublime and divine matters.

SALOMON: Then I shall say a few things about many matters. On the seventh day strength and power is especially increased in our bodies, and also the wisdom of good men is especially increased on that day, as our elders learned from the prophets. Moreover, on this day, especially, vengeance against the wicked by the powers of the air is allowed. This has been often observed but never more clearly[278] than in the awesome destruction in Egypt in which all the first-born of men and beasts throughout the whole kingdom perished in the middle of the night of the seventh day

---

all destruction there must be one last imperishable element. See *Diogenes Laërtius* X. 26 ff.; also Diels, *Frag. der Vorsokrat.* (6th ed.), II. 97. 21.

[276] Herodotus, II. 58–64. [277] *mensem* MR

[278] *planius* MR

at the same moment when the demons were killing.[279] Wherefore divine law orders the circumcision of an infant to be performed on the eighth day, so that the holy Sabbath intervening may add strength to the infant.[280] Even physicians are not accustomed to diagnose anything about sickness or a wound before the eighth day because of the power of the seventh day. All antiquity has shown that harmful demons disturbed the wicked at the
P. 154 beginning of the seventh day, that is, after sunset on the sixth day, but were banished to a distance by the chosen of God. A saying of a certain Rabbinic theologian[281] must be interpreted in this way; he said that on the seventh day harmful demons were restrained by angels to keep them from being troublesome to good men. From this one realizes that the whole nature of things so feels the power of that most holy day that it is accustomed to be mentioned even in a popular proverb. "No Sabbath day has ever passed in which the sun did not offer itself to men's view." Unless the obliquity of the horizon beyond the sixtieth part of a great circle, with the earth intervening toward each pole, removes the sun's appearance, the sun customarily appears brighter on the seventh day; or if the humidity of the sky is changed, and the sky is overcome with excessive heat for six days, on the day of the Sabbath, rosy clouds and northerly winds cool the sky in some way. Even if for six whole days rain and black clouds have appeared, the Sabbath day dawns serene with the sun shining. Likewise, those who are beset with illness and constant fever, unless hope has been lost, become better on the seventh day. On this point, the old question of that Greek philosopher regarding why the air is changed on the seventh day has a bearing. Since antiquity man has searched for this answer. The soul of a good and God-fearing man is nourished on the sacred day by the contemplation of heavenly matters and by divine praises, as if by the choicest banquets. These lead him away from himself, and better prepare him for absorbing the brightness of divine light which gleams more fully on the seventh day than[282] all the others.[283] This rapture of the human soul into God David calls a precious death,[284] and Solomon says it is a kiss from the divine mouth.[285] What of this? Jo-

[279] Ex. 11.
[280] Gen. 17:11–12.
[281] In the margin of M the scribe adds *in symbolum Judaeorum c.* 4.
[282] *quam* MR
[283] For a lengthy discussion of the significance of the number seven, see Philo, *De opificio mundi* XXX–XLIV.
[284] Psalm 115 (116B):15.
[285] Cant. 1:1.

sephus,[286] the famous antiquarian, said that a river in Syria is thus called "Sabbathicus" because only on that day was it accustomed to flow.

Toralba: Indeed I admit that the exceedingly wondrous secrets of the seventh day had been hitherto unknown to me.

Curtius: I do not doubt that contemplation of the soul and meditation greatly sharpen ability. I even grant this, that man can do nothing more noble than contemplate the kindnesses of God, the greatest and best, His laws, actions, and works and from these bring forth and proclaim His praises. However, when those first parents of the human race, before the law, did not distinguish the seventh day as a day of honor or an aid for contemplation, I did not see why we ought to seek out more accurately a conformity of time, or why we should proclaim the seventh day as holier than the others.

Fridericus: There is no distinction of days in Heaven and not even everywhere on earth. There is so great a variety of light and darkness beyond the sixtieth part of the great circle that to those approaching each P. 155 pole beneath the seventieth part of the sky the day is a month long. Nearer to the pole a day is two, three, or four months, where instead of twenty-four hours, a day has 2880[287] continuous hours without seeing the sun above the horizon. Moreover, under each pole one day is six months long without a sunrise; likewise one night continues six months without sunset. Although other places have 365 days as the year progresses, those who live under the pole have one day and one night, each six months long.

Salomon: Beyond the seventieth part of the midday circle toward the pole, no abode is accessible for any mortals; and should any be accessible, who is so stupid that he[288] is not able to observe the sun's revolution of twenty-four hours whether above or below the horizon.

Fridericus: Perhaps more learned men can observe this when the sun is above the horizon, but who could mark that distinction in six months of night? But to return from each pole to the middle regions, it is not possible in any way for the same day to be the seventh in every part of the world, because when the noble Sabbath begins at sunset in the month of April with the sixth afternoon hour in Jerusalem, at that same moment

[286] Josephus says that for six days the river Sabbaticus is dry; on the seventh day it flows. See *Bellum Judaicum* VII. 96–99. Pliny (*Hist. nat.* XXXI. 11) says exactly the opposite. It flows for six days and is dry on the Sabbath.

[287] *2880* M; *duo mille octingentas octoginta* R; *bis mille octigentas* N

[288] *qui* MR

in the Brazilian regions of the Indies it is midday. From this consideration it is necessary that, with an interval of six hours, the seventh day begins more quickly for the people of Jerusalem than for the Brazilian people.

SALOMON: Clever point, Fridericus, but who, in such a vast space of ocean and lands from farthest Syria to the American region, that is, more than 6060 miles distant, would think that the seventh day can be uniform? Therefore, let us pass over the subtleties and admit that the seventh day, which has been illustrated by so many proofs and clear demonstrations of nature, pertains to divine laws as well as to the laws of nature.

FRIDERICUS: If the seventh day alone is sacred, why is the new moon cherished by you on each thirtieth day?

SALOMON: No day is removed from divine praises or honorable actions, but the seventh day is ordered to be a joyous sign of the world's creation and the thirtieth day a sign of divine care, because the foundation of the world was not sufficient unless God provided for His creation and protected the condition of the world—the increases, decreases, and changes in all things.[289]

OCTAVIUS: This is, I believe, what Horace had in mind when he calls the Jewish thirtieth day the thirtieth Sabbath.[290] Yet not only the Jews but even the Greeks and Latins cherished the new moon as a holy day, as Juvenal indicated in this verse:[291]

When the kings keep the Sabbath holy
with a bare foot . . .

See also Plutarch in the book,[292] *About Superstition*.[293]

P. 156 CURTIUS: With excessive religious fear the Jews allowed Jerusalem to be besieged by Pompey[294] with scaling ladders and all the citizens to be caught, as if in a net or snare; some of them even were cruelly murdered, and the city opulent with wealth was plundered on the day of the Sabbath, which the historian Dio wrote had been made sacred to Saturn in this expedition when Vegetius as well as Plutarch mocked the Jews.

SALOMON: Divine law has blessed those who have not sat in the seats of the scorners.[295] Strabo wrote that this conquest of Jerusalem took place

[289] I Kings (I Sam.) 20:5; IV Kings (II Kings) 4:23.

[290] *Sat.* I. 9. 68–70. [291] Juvenal VI. 159. [292] *in libro* MR

[293] *De superstitione* VIII. 169C.

[294] Pompey captured Jerusalem in 63 B.C. See Dio Cassius XXXVII. 16; Josephus, *Bellum Judaicum* I. 128–56.

[295] Psalm 1:1.

on a fast day of the Jews, although we are still prohibited from fasting on the Sabbath;[296] Josephus, however, disagreed not only with Strabo, but also with Dio and Eusebius. He wrote that the city was captured by Pompey on the day of Tammuz, when Marcus Tullius Cicero and Marcus Antonius were consuls.[297] The fact that the attack occurred on the seventh day ought to merit praise rather than mockery for the Jewish religion and its fear of the holy.[298]

FRIDERICUS: Agatharchides of Cnidos scorned the laws and religion of the Jews chiefly because they had allowed Ptolemaeus, the son of Lagus, to invade Jerusalem at leisure on the holy day.[299]

SALOMON: Still the situation turned out advantageously for the Jews. For Ptolemaeus Philadelphus,[300] the son of Lagus, adorned that city and its temple with great gifts and tributes; he freed a hundred thousand captives of our race with ransom from his own funds; he brought a solid gold panel of two and a half cubits into the holy of holies. He rewarded seventy-two theologians with bountiful gifts for translating the sacred books from Hebrew into Greek, and nothing more excellent or greater than this could have been done by any prince.

FRIDERICUS: It cannot be denied that thoughtless negligence, or shall I say folly, was surely a capital offense, in that the Jews preferred for the city, flourishing with resources, towers, and youth, to be conquered at will and their children, wives and holy temples to be exposed to the plundering of the soldiers rather than to protect them on the Sabbath day. For what is this but trying and tempting the goodness of God? Where did He forbid us to cast away danger from our head, our children, our family on the

[296] It was a mistaken idea in the Graeco-Roman world that the Jews fasted on the Sabbath.

[297] Josephus (*Bellum Judaicum I.* 149) said the temple was taken in the third month of siege.

[298] Josephus (*Bellum Judaicum* I. 148, 152) says that Pompey admired the Jews' bravery and their observations of their religious practices in the midst of battle. Although Pompey penetrated to the interior of the sanctuary, he did not plunder the gold vessels, but rather ordered the custodians to purify it and resume sacrifices.

[299] Agatharchides, Greek grammarian and Peripatetic of Cnidos, became guardian to a young Ptolemy (Soter II) of Egypt about 116 B.C. See *Ox. Class. Dict.*, p. 20. The Ptolemaeus here referred to is Ptolemy I Soter (376–283 B.C.), son of the Macedonian Lagus and a certain Arsinoë. He conquered Palestine, Cyprus and many places in the Aegean and in Asia Minor from 301–286 B.C. See Josephus, *Antiq.* XII. 5–7.

[300] Ptolemy II Philadelphus (308–246 B.C.) was the son of Ptolemy I Soter, who was the son of Lagus. Philadelphus, in addition to his commissioning the seventy-two theologians to translate the scriptures into Greek, built the museum and the library.

Sabbath day? First Agamemnon ordered each one to prepare arms; then he begs Jupiter for victory with these words: "Allow me to overthrow the lofty abode of Priam."[301] Although once the Romans, because of their religious scruples, distinguished battle days from holy days, as Marcus Varro described,[302] finally they removed the battle days from the holy days, after constant attacks by the enemy, lest any one use religion as an occasion for commencing war on holy days.

P. 157 SENAMUS: Long ago the Jews repudiated the rite of battle days. When Judas Maccabaeus, an energetic commander, had heard that Jerusalem was attacked on the Sabbath by Antiochus Nobilis and a part of the Jews were burned in caves, a part sacrificed, a part strangled without defending themselves, he openly declared to the army which he had gathered from the fugitive citizens that he would fight for the shrines, the altars,[303] the law, the safety of citizens, and for liberty even on Sabbath days;[304] from that time he gained great victories from the enemies and with a small band often conquered and laid low the legions of Antiochus.

FRIDERICUS: Not religion, but superstition is the reason that the Jews think they must abstain from all affairs, even necessary ones, on the Sabbath. So steadfast are they in this superstition that a son would not even snatch his parent from the waters or flames[305] or wish to bind the wounds to stop bleeding. When a priest had deserted a wounded traveller on the Sabbath, Christ shuddered at this superstitious cruelty, but He praised the kindness of the farmer because he had ordered the sick man to be brought home in a carriage to have his wounds bound.[306] Moreover, when the priests rebuked Christ sharply because He had healed on the seventh day and had ordered a bed to be brought to another place, He cast aside their objections with a word, saying, "the Sabbath was made for man, not man for the Sabbath; moreover, the Son of Man is Lord of the Sabbath."[307] And so He very often on the Sabbath day marvelously displayed remarkable cures for the multitude which was sick with many diseases.

CURTIUS: That Jewish skipper was raging under a similar superstition; Synesius wrote that on the Sabbath he deserted his ship's helm in the deepest waves and could not be recalled to his position under any fear of death, or torture, or loss of ship and cargo.

301 Homer, *Iliad* II. 414.
302 See Augustine, *De civ. Dei* VI. 3.
303 *pro aris* MR
304 I Maccabees 3:43.
305 *flammis* R
306 Luke 10:31–34.
307 Mark 2:27–28.

SALOMON: We also think that laws were made not for the safety of the laws but for the safety of men. We do not think that he did anything against the law, if he did anything forbidden on the Sabbath under the pressure of necessity, which is not bound by any laws or obligation. Still, if we grant that it is lawful to cure on the Sabbath, it is not therefore lawful to move a bed. The fact that Christ had ordered a bed to be carried was especially censured. Why, even the priest when conscious of the deed rebuked the people with these words: "Six days are for activities; therefore on these days attend to a cure, but not on the Sabbath."[308]

FRIDERICUS: The words of the priest do not mean that he considered it a crime to cure on the seventh day, but that he anticipated every opportunity for reproach from the envious disparagers.

CORONAEUS: If the illness is so severe that a delay would endanger life, P. 158
I do not doubt it is permissible and has always been permissible to administer treatment even on holy days. But if the sick person can suffer a delay of one day, I think the cure should be deferred until the holy quiet has passed which we called *domenica*, because the day is sacred to the Lord, as we are taught by the holiest ordinances of the Christian church. I admit that I am satisfied with these ordinances, and I bear witness to them. I shall not allow myself to be carried away by the arguments of any one or to be separated from the accepted religion of the Roman pontiffs. Indeed Solomon spoke allegorically when he said: "My son, guard the commands of your father and do not loose the law of your mother."[309] I interpret this as the commands of God and the church. Likewise: "Do not move the boundary-mark which your elders have fixed."[310]

SALOMON: God seems to me to be indicated under the name of father and nature under the name of mother. Nevertheless, I do not doubt that it can also be transferred to the church which had flourished 2,000 years before Jesus, the Son of Joseph and Mary, was born. Still He very often ordered the Sabbath to be cherished, and Paul himself wrote that the Sabbath was given to the people of God,[311] by which words he openly distinguished the people of God from Christians and barbarians. Although the rising church of the Christians kept holy[312] the first day, which you call *domenica*, the Lord's day,[313] the Sabbath was also honored during Tertullian's time. His words were: "We hold back two weeks in the year

[308] Luke 13:14. [309] Prov. 6:20. [310] Prov. 22:28.

[311] Hebrews 4:9. [312] *feriaret* MR

[313] *Dominus* means lord in Latin. In Italian the Lord's day is *domenica.*

from eating meat with the exception of Sabbaths and Sundays."[314] Likewise: "He who shall have heard[315] will find God on all Sabbaths."[316]

CURTIUS: Justin, who lived in the same age as Tertullian, wrote an apology to Marcus Aurelius Augustus[317] on behalf of the Christians; he stated that Christians were accustomed to come to prayers and communion of the eucharist on the Lord's day,[318] yet he said nothing about the Sabbath. Although in the early days of the Christian church many were circumcised, as the Ethiopian Christians are even today, and kept the Sabbath,[319] nonetheless, Paul frequently chided Peter when the disciples were gathered together and persuaded him that the legal rites of the elders ought to be repealed by a common decree.[320] And so when he wrote to the Colossians, he said: "Let no one judge you in regard to food or drink or festival or a new moon or Sabbaths; these are as a shadow of future things."[321]

CORONAEUS: It is possible that the first and the seventh day were holy days for Christians; however, when the observance of both days seriously handicapped business, the Roman pope Victor, in the year of Christ 196, ordered the quiet of the Sabbath to be in force and *domenica* to be observed as holy day in place of the Sabbath.

P. 159

SALOMON: Do not think, Coronaeus, that I wish to persuade you Christians to accept the Sabbath in place of *domenica.* The greatest spiritual grief seizes me when I see the holiest day of the Sabbath as well as *domenica* defiled in a loathsome way by shameful dances, intoxication, wantonness, hunts, games, and finally by filthy fornications. It is better to spend that day in transacting business affairs than to violate it with the most loathsome disgraces.

SENAMUS: You sad and gloomy Jews do not seem to honor as festive the days which all the ancients, first the Greeks, then the Latins, wished to be more joyful because of public games, banquets, choruses, songs, dances and therefore more pleasing to the immortal gods.

SALOMON: Our nation is not averse to choruses and dances; we even call the holy day *ḥag* from the dance and meditation, so that holy days may be given up not only to divine choruses but also to meditations. And

[314] Tertullian, *De corona* III.

[315] *audierit* MR

[316] Tertullian, *De idol.* VII, XIV.

[317] *The Apologies* of Justin Martyr were addressed to Antoninus Pius, not Marcus Aurelius.

[318] Justin, *Apol.* I. 67.

[319] *feriarent* MR

[320] Acts 15:1–12.

[321] Col. 2:16–17.

so at the new moon we enjoy every kind of delight, which is not base, and nothing is more often enjoined to us than to rejoice in the depths of our souls. Although we abstain from common dances on the holiest day of the Sabbath, still we are accustomed to make that day most happy and joyous by mingling the sweetness of voices and strings in songs of divine praises.[322] At festive meals in the presence of immortal God we bear witness that we feed on the best food of sacrifices with the greatest joy, as we are ordered by divine law; nevertheless, for several hours we feed our soul with the lesson of divine laws, and we have practiced this from the most ancient teachings of the prophets even to these times.[323] In regard to this we have read about a Sunamite woman who came to Elisha: "Why," her husband said, "do you come to the prophet since it is neither new moon nor Sabbath?"[324] It is allowed to depart two miles from home but no farther, in order that learned theologians may drink from divine oracles. Senamus complains that we seem sadder and more melancholy than other nations; the chief reason for this is that we grieve[325] because not only the Sabbath, but also all of the headings of the decalogues are violated without fear of punishment. For in the first heading the worship of one eternal God is advocated, but nevertheless, we see that 600,000 and many more gods are worshipped everywhere. The ancient pagans worshipped three hundred Jupiters, which that one mentioned with hyperbole, "He (the priest) thunders three hundred gods from his mouth, Erebus and Chaos,"[326] and they increased that to thirty-six thousand. Still we see that Christians worship as many gods as they consider to be angels or blessed souls (and these are legion), with the addition of those whom the popes have written in the registry of gods, invoking demons by magic art and with a certain detestable apotheosis. Although in the second heading of P. 160
the decalogue we are prohibited from falling before statues or any images and from worshipping them at the risk of capital punishment,[327] still we see all the shrines and every nook and cranny of the temples overflowing with sculptured idols which are made from every material, from every kind of metals, stones, woods, earth, wax, and flour. Amid blazing tapers they kiss decayed corpses, flesh preserved with acid and salt, and bones and ashes; they think by touching these the body becomes healthy and

[322] Psalm 97 (98):4–5.

[323] Cf. Deut. 26:10–11. 2 Esdras (Nehemiah) 8:5–12; Isaiah 56:18–19; Sophonias 3:14–17.

[324] IV Kings (II Kings) 4:23.

[325] *dolemus* MR

[326] Vergil, *Aen.* IV. 510.

[327] Ex. 20:4–5.

the soul sanctified and saved. Even more abominable is the fact that in all the hourly prayers they have blotted out and erased completely from the decalogue the second heading in which the worship of statues is forbidden. This has been done not only in Italy, France, and Spain, but even in Germany itself. I have always thought it strange that Martin Luther believed that divine law prohibits only images of God and does not prohibit images of the cross and the apostles. Then he added: "We do not wish to hear or see Moses; commands about statues and the Sabbath are ceremonies that have been removed."[328] Who can bear these things calmly, especially in one who admits that he is a critic of religions? The third heading of the decalogue, in which we are forbidden to use the Lord's name in vain, is much more seriously violated than the preceding. Not only is the most sacred name of God sworn falsely but is even torn apart by insults. In place of the name of eternal God foreign names of gods and demons are sworn by, although we have been repeatedly prohibited from making an oath on anything other than the name and divinity of eternal God.[329] I omit the headings of the second table especially those that deal with fornications, adulteries, lewdness and homosexuality in the sacred orders, basely indulged in under the guise of chastity.

When Salomon had spoken more vehemently than was customary for one of his advanced age, silence followed. The reason for the silence was that his speech had pricked Coronaeus, who was a most stalwart defender of the Roman rites. Although Coronaeus, with all eyes upon him, seemed about to answer Salomon at any moment, he restrained his words. Then he broke the silence and said: "I thought I would remove the charges and complaints of Salomon, but I think I should defer to another time, lest I seem to have hampered anyone's liberty of speaking."

Octavius: I also am weighing whether I should speak or be silent.

Coronaeus: Why should you be silent, when such a full seed for conversation has been cast forth, or if indeed you wish to refute Salomon?

Octavius: When I compare the religion and the institutions of the Mohammedans with the customs and rites of Christians, I seem to have fallen from heaven to earth. For the Mohammedans, with the greatest

[328] Luther's attitude respecting the use of images was rather indefinite. "The images of saints, crucifixes, etc., are not to be abolished on their own account, but only to serve God. Because of the harmful abuse to which they have been put, they do not deserve to be retained. If people once find out that images are worthless, they will disappear." See Hartmann Grisar, *Martin Luther, His Life and Work* (Westminster, Md., 1961), p. 218.

[329] Josh. 23:7.

veneration, worship eternal God and no more gods than the One; moreover, they call Jesus Isaiah himself, and they recognize that he was not only the word of God but also the spirit and messenger of God and that he was snatched from the hands of the enemy so as not to be put to death by the wicked. Yet they do not think this one was God nor the Son of God, and for this reason they most conscientiously refuse to worship him. P. 161 They admit that they uphold the law of Abraham and worship the same God whom Jesus worshipped while he was alive. They are so greatly offended by the adoration of statues that not only do they not allow any embossed, sculptured, molded, or painted images in their temples and shrines, but not even any of those things which nature has produced—whether plants or living things. The laws make a man subject to the death penalty if he ever looks at these for enjoyment. Although I excused Christian statues which were erected for the imitation of virtue, as it were, a certain Paracadius[330] told me that those very persons whose statues we worship enjoy heavenly bliss because they had cast aside the images of the gods in order to worship God eternal. They customarily accompanied the Psalms of David, which they say were given to men by God, with voices and strings and even prayed publicly sometimes four times a day and likewise privately at night. When I had shared a bedroom with an African guest, I remember that he, getting up from bed in the middle of the night, sang praises to immortal God, and complained bitterly because I was silent. In Arabic, he said: "I was wont to rise up in the middle of the night to declare glory to Your name."[331] Then he quoted from the book of Job: "Many complain that they are oppressed by tyranny and afflicted with calamities; yet there is no one who honors God at night with hymns of praise."[332]

Coronaeus: It has been the practice of the Roman church since the time of Pope Pelagius[333] to worship God with praises seven times a day and with prayers and songs day and night. We have learned this and imitated it from David himself who said: "I have glorified You seven times a day."[334] The Jews do not do this, nor do the Lutherans and the Zwinglians, who have so pared their public worship (I except the Anglicans, who have been separated from the Puritans) that they allow prayers to be offered publicly only twice in the whole week.

[330] *Paracadius* MR *Pracadius* N

[331] Psalm 118 (119):55, 62.

[332] See Job 8.

[333] Pelagius and Pelagius II were popes during the sixth century A.D.

[334] Psalm 118 (119):164.

SALOMON: Divine law orders priests and Levites to sing praises to God morning and evening, and Rabbi David writes that there was a morning sacrifice of four hours and an evening sacrifice of one hour; moreover, it is most praiseworthy for each one constantly to offer divine praises in private at every moment. For to praise God seven times a day, as David says, does not refer to a definite number, as the Roman church thinks, but almost always means an infinite or uncertain number. Samuel's mother spoke thus, when she thanked God, saying, "A sterile woman has brought forth seven."[335] Our elders wished for nighttime prayers to be spoken privately according to each man's desire, and nothing can be more effectual and pleasing than this.

OCTAVIUS: The entreaties of the Mohammedans are indeed brief, but
P. 162 very efficacious: "Praise to God the compassionate and flexible King of the last judgment! O mortals, lovers of piety, let us worship that One and obtain His aid. Grant us, eternal God, the most certain knowledge of those whom You have chosen, so that I may never depart from Your favor because of offending those. Amen." They call this prayer the Lassala, which means common to all; except for this prayer there are various and almost innumerable prayers which each one makes according to his own will.

CORONAEUS: I do not see why the Pater Noster of Christians[336] ought to yield to the Lassala of the Mohammedans or the Shema of the Hebrews.

SALOMON: That Shema of ours which all Jews use daily is not a prayer, but a reminder that we should never depart from the eternal worship of God. Even Moses in the assembly of all the people thus expressed these same words, which do not seem to be rendered suitably by the Latins and the Greeks. I think this is much better: "Hear O Israel! He who is our God eternal is the one eternal God; therefore, you will love your God eternal with your whole heart and with your whole soul and with the

[335] I Kings (I Sam.) 1:20, 26. See also Augustine, *De civ. Dei* XVII. 4.

[336] *Christianorum* MR. The Pater Noster is the "Our Father" which Jesus Himself taught (Matt. 6:9–13). The Lassala (Salāt) is the ritual prayer of Muslims, the most important part of Muslim liturgy. Mohammed's intention in prescribing the Salāt as a religious duty was doubtless in imitation of the ritual prayer of Christians and Jews in the Orient. In the generation after Mohammed's death five daily salāts were obligatory. The Shema at first was prayer only in the form of several important sections of the Torah which were repeated by the people as a sort of confession. Gradually the Shema was provided with introductory and concluding pieces which were no longer taken from the Torah but were original compositions. For a full discussion of the above-mentioned prayers, see Hastings, *Encycl. of Rel. and Eth.*, X, 177–80, 191–98.

whole power of your strengths. And these words which I order will cling in your heart, and you will rather often instill them in your children whether you sit at home or walk about or lie down or rise up, and you will bind them on your hand, and they will be as if signs before your eyes; nay even write them on the door posts of your homes and in front of your doors."[337] This is our Shema which, written on veal parchments and placed in boxes, we indeed bind on our left arm and between the hair of the head and the brow; the Chaldaic word *tephilin*, from *tafal* which means to bind or hang, indicates this. Others interpret from the Hebraic word *tefilhin*, which means entreaty, since they cherish these things daily as if the holiest prayers. Also on these same parchments they write the sentence from the thirteenth chapter of Exodus, which begins: "Remember this day, on which you departed from Egypt," up to these words "from days unto days,"[338] and from the same chapter, a little after the sentence, which begins: "And it will be, when he shall bring you forward," up to these words, "because of his powerful hand our God has led us from Egypt."[339] Likewise the sentence from the second chapter of Deuteronomy which begins: "And so he goes out if by hearing," up to these words, "the heaven above the earth."[340]

FRIDERICUS: The Jews are so superstitious that they think that carrying around these parchments is sufficient for attaining salvation; similarly some[341] Catholics bind the beginning of John's Gospel on their necks in P. 163 the faithful hope that they may be safe from all calamities and sicknesses. Augustine calls these accursed amulets.[342]

SALOMON: If any one of our race was led on by this hope and faith that a carrying of these things alone would be beneficial for salvation, I judge this man—I think there is no one—to be mad. Our elders wished these four[343] most important chapters to be carried around by everyone so that as often as they see the boxes or the Mezuzah[344] on the posts, they would be mindful of the first heading and the divine law and abstain from all worship of foreign gods and become accustomed to direct their life to the true God.

OCTAVIUS: The Mohammedans abhor all those amulets and feigned[345] images, so that they may embrace true piety.[346] This is also very clearly

[337] Deut. 6:4–9. [338] Ex. 13:3–7. [339] Ex. 13:8–9.
[340] Deut. 2:1; 11:21. [341] *quidam* MR
[342] *Sancti Augustini Operum Tomus I* (Paris, 1679), Epistola CCXLV. 2.
[343] *quatuor* MR [344] *Mezuza* MR [345] *fictis* MR
[346] *ut . . . amplectantur* MR

the reason that they build mosques or shrines in such a way that the women and men cannot look at each other; moreover they have places for each, separated by a partition in the middle.

SALOMON: The Mohammedans have borrowed[347] these things, as everything that is best, from our race and imitated them so that men could not see the women in the temples or synagogues. This is done so that there may be no occasion for arousing wicked desire or any lewd enticements.

CURTIUS: Would that this practice would come into our men's minds! Why do we not imitate praiseworthy practices, wherever they may be? Indeed, we can surely say that almost no Christian temples are free from enticement.

SALOMON: I think nothing more disgraceful than to conceal lust in the appearance of piety. For this reason our elders removed the custom of the women keeping watch before the doors of the holy tabernacle because the priests, the sons of the high priest and leader Eli, did not hesitate to bring disgrace on them.[348] It was always a great concern of our elders to remove completely from the sacred temples not only lewdness but also the suspicion of lewdness. Why, even harlots from the farthest recollection of our elders did not ever go outdoors unless their faces were veiled. Afterwards, even in Arabia, all Hebrew women's heads were completely covered except for their eyes whenever they went out in public. Finally they found it fitting not only to be veiled in the temples but also to be separated by walls from men's sight, a practice which the Ismaelites wisely imitated by having partitions for each sex.

FRIDERICUS: There was no accusation against the ancient Christians more serious than that they dishonored the nocturnal holy services with lewdness and disgraces under the pretense of religion; indeed the apologies of Origen, Justin, Athenagoras, and Tertullian were written to dispel this charge; Tertullian even, in the book about veiling virgins, strongly censured the Christian custom of embraces and kisses of charity between men
P. 164 and women, which practice, he said, aroused[349] the women, although these acts took place in the temples themselves.[350]

[347] *hauserunt* MR

[348] I Kings (I Sam.) 2:22.

[349] *incaluisse* MR

[350] Tertullian speaks of the veiling of virgins in *De orat.* XVIII and the kiss of love or peace in *Ad uxorem* II. 4. Athenagoras (*Legat.*, Par. 32) cautions against the kiss of peace. "The kiss of love or rather of reverence must be given with such great care, as that if it be ever so little defiled by thought, it excludes us from eternal life." The church was very careful to guard against abuses, and so the women

CORONAEUS: The Roman popes will change this at some time or other, as I desire and hope, even as they have removed those kisses of piety.

OCTAVIUS: I acknowledge that the Jews and Mohammedans hold in common almost everything which pertains to religion. Each believes in the worship of one eternal God, curses idols, and practices circumcision, and each derives his origin from Abraham. Each abstains from eating blood and pork, and finally each has frequent washings[351] which Tertullian not very cleverly censures in the case of the Jews. He writes that they washed themselves daily because they defiled themselves daily,[352] as if indeed Christians, circumcised inwardly, were purer, although David cursed Goliath because he had been uncircumcised and unclean.[353] The Ethiopian Christians had practiced circumcision.[354] Herodotus wrote that the ancient Egyptians also were accustomed to perform it.[355] Indeed in these times not only are males circumcised, but even females.

CURTIUS: Indeed that was the sign of the covenant concluded with Abraham,[356] yet I do not see that there has been any advantage in circumcision.

SALOMON: What advantage can be greater or holier than the secret of a divine covenant? Although some who view those things rather cautiously, say there are very great advantages in circumcision. In the first place, it was helpful for easier procreation of children, next for removing the infection of tumors, then for restraining the power of violent lust, which Rabbi Moses thinks was the main reason for circumcision.

OCTAVIUS:[357] Still the Jews differ from the Mohammedans in that

---

were separated from the men so that only women kissed women, etc. In the 12th or 13th century the *osculatorium*, a small plaque of metal, ivory or wood was used. Gradually even this practice died out. Now after Vatican II the kiss of peace is again a part of the mass, but a hand clasp is given rather than a kiss.

351 *lotiones* MR

352 *De bapt.* VIII. 15.

353 I Kings (I Sam.) XVII. 26.

354 The rite of circumcision is not only spread throughout the Muslim world but also is practiced by the Christian Ethiopians and Copts. The Ethiopian church has kept a visible imprint of the Jewish religion, reflected not only in circumcision but also in keeping the Sabbath and dietary laws. Ethiopian children are circumcised two weeks after birth. See *Cath. Encycl.*, I, 78–79.

355 Herodotus (II. 36) indicates that the Egyptians were the first people to practice circumcision. It is not generally considered probable that the Hebrews derived the rite directly from the Egyptians. See article "circumcision," in *Encycl. Brit.* (11th ed.), VI, 389–90. Also see James Hastings, *A Dictionary of the Bible* (New York, 1900), I, pp. 442 ff.

356 Gen. 17:10–14.

357 *Octavius* MR

the Mohammedans do not observe the feasts of unleavened bread and the passover nor the holy quiet of the Sabbath. They do not turn to the west to pray, nor do they await a Messiah, as the Jews. I except those who follow the sect of 'Alī whom they call Imamites.[358] Although they admit that prayers can be directed to all the temples of heaven, still very often they turn their faces to Mecca, as once Daniel, an exile in the city of Babylon, fell on his knees and began his prayer facing to Jerusalem.[359]

SENAMUS: Mercurius Trismegistus ordered those who would worship first to turn to the east, in the middle of the day to the south, in the evening to the west.[360] Moreover, numerous Greeks made sacrifice to the gods facing the east, but they made sacrifices to the heroes toward the west, and to all others toward the east. This custom flowed from the Chaldeans and especially the magi of the Persians to almost all peoples. They were accustomed to worship turned to the dawn and especially the
P. 165 rising sun whom they called Mithras.[361] Hence Maro said: "Those turned to the light of the rising sun."[362] Vitruvius wrote that the statues were placed in western regions, facing east.[363] Porphyry ordered the worshippers to be face to face with the statues facing east and to turn themselves to the west.[364] Contrary to this practice the Christians were accustomed to arrange their statues facing west, so that they could worship them with their faces turned to the east.

FRIDERICUS: When the Christians of old were asked why they turned to the east to say their prayers, they answered that this was their practice because the rising was more noble than the setting.[365] Thus Pompey is said to have remarked to Cornelius Sulla that more people worship the

[358] A party of city Arabs, influenced by Persian ideas about the divinity of the ruler, regarded 'Alī and his descendants as the only legitimate caliphs and came to be known as Shi'ites. The Imamites were one of the chief divisions of the Shi'ites. See *Encycl. Brit.* (11th ed.), XVII, 422–23 for a listing of the sects; also see pp. 417–424.

[359] Dan. 6:11.

[360] *Hemetica*, edited by Walter Scott (London, 1968), Vol. I, *Asclepius* III, 40d, 41a, p. 372.

[361] Mithras was an ancient Indo-Iranian god who in Zoroastrianism was one of the good powers and closely associated with light; therefore, it is easily seen why Mithras was called a sun god, whatever his original character may have been. See *Ox. Class. Dict.*, pp. 575–76. See Plutarch, *Moralia. De Iside et Osiridi* XLVI. 369E–F.

[362] Vergil, *Aen.* XII. 172.

[363] See below, note 370.

[364] Wolff, *Porphyry*, pp. 31–34, 164–65, 206–13.

[365] Cf. Justin Martyr, *Dial. Tryph.* 121.

rising sun than the setting sun.[366] Moreover, I do not see why the Jews, differing from all people, turn to the west to worship.

SALOMON: Many think that we do this lest we seem to worship the sun and the rising stars. They are deceived, however, since the sun looks on each region, and we worship at each time. Our lawgiver built a tent for holy objects after the exemplar of the universe.[367] There is, moreover, the most rapid change of the heavenly orbs from east to west, and whoever wishes to comprehend the course of nature must proceed with the stars to the west, not return to the east. From this the most beautiful secrets of nature are drawn out so that we may know that fitting custom harmonious with nature, namely which part of the universe is called the right, which part the left.

TORALBA: This discussion especially exercised all writers, and still they did not bring forth a probable cause about the position of the universe. For Pythagoras, Homer, Plato, Aristotle, Galen, Averroës placed the right side of the universe in the east, but Pliny and Varro the left.[368] The Roman augur, dividing the sacred objects of the temples with his wand before God, turned his face to the south so that he might have east on his left side and the west on his right.[369] Empedocles, Cleomenes, Lucan, Solinus, and Philo the Hebrew granted the right section of the universe to the north.[370]

[366] Marginal note in M attributes this to Plutarch. However, see Josephus, *Contra Apionem* II. 265.

[367] Cf. Ex. 25:8; 40:1–8, 34–38.

[368] See below, note 370.

[369] Roman augurs had as their business the observation of signs, *auguria*, which would indicate whether the gods approved or disapproved an action. Birds or chickens were often observed. In observing wild birds the augur marked out a *templum* or boundary within which he would look for signs. The *templum* was divided into right, left, front, and back; the significance of the flight or cry of the bird varied according to the part of the *templum* in which it was heard or seen. The augur faced south or east. See *Ox. Class. Dict.*, pp. 120, 292–93; also consult H. J. Rose, "The Inauguration of Numa," *Journal of Roman Studies*, XIII (1923), 82–90.

[370] Literally, the "orient" refers to the rising sun, and the basic literal meaning of "orientation" is to place a thing so that it faces east. The discussion in the *Heptaplomeres* is peculiarly valuable because those who are in the tradition of Gothic cathedrals feel the larger axis of a church properly must go from west to east, the chancel or chief altar at the eastern end. And it is easy to presume that all churches must be so oriented, and even that temples of all religions must be also faced east. Northern Christians not only feel it only right to say the Creed and celebrate the Eucharist facing east, but bury the corpse with the feet towards the east. (See *Oxford English Dictionary*, VIII, 199–201.)

The Fathers and Doctors of the church substituted for the primeval pagan natural

SALOMON: When the priest of the Hebrews offers sacrifice with his face turned to the west, he places his right side opposite to the north and the left to the south, which position is harmonious to universal nature. For the right is stronger and more vigorous than the left; as the right foot and right arm are larger than the left, they are more vigorous and stronger. "The heart of the wise man," Solomon said, "is on his right side, but that of the foolish man on the left."[371] This is true because fools are not able, as wise men are, to master their passions because of the power of their lust. Thus northerly men are stronger and more robust than southerly men. In almost all the regions near Aquilo men have more outstanding physiques but less ability.[372] The liver, the laboratory for the blood, is on the right side, while the spleen, the receptacle of black bile, is on the left.[373] Thus, near the northern region men are ruddy and robust, for the Latins
P. 166 derive the word robust from red, but near the south they are dark; yet men who live near the southwest have greater abilities and melancholy natures.[374] On the right side the liver holds the power of desire, the maintaining element of faults, and for this reason, victims are ordered to be

---

orientation towards the sun the historical explanation that man's original home was in the east, that here was paradise, here Jesus Christ lived, and from the east He shall come to judge mankind. Yet the great Roman basilicas and others have the apse in the western extremity, and this excited wonder and provoked speculation. (*Cath. Encycl.*, XI, 305.)

This sacred orientation lies behind the secular orientation when we represent the earth's surface. We now expect the north to be "up," the south "down," the east "right," the west "left." How to draw a map was by no means a closed and settled question even in the sixteenth century, after the great century of exploration (the century between Columbus and the *Heptaplomeres*). A crucial rediscovery was that of Ptolemy's map about 1410. Henceforth the north-orientation of the Greek tradition prevailed over that of the Roman and the Hebrew. Each is a convention, and they do not exhaust the possibilities, yet only one has come to be the accepted and "correct" way. "Orientation" loses its literal meaning: by extension it is to arrange the parts of any structure or to determine one's "bearings," to find out "where one is." Hence, an informed reflection upon orientation is most fitting to the discussion of toleration. See G. R. Croe, *Maps and Their Makers: An Introduction to the History of Cartography* (London, 1953), and Lloyd A. Brown, *The Story of Maps* (Boston, 1949).

It lies in the range of possibilities not only to think of east as "right" (Greek) or "left" (Roman) or "down" (Hebrew), but also to consider east as "up." We find this scheme was used, with church approval, by Isidore of Seville.

371 Eccles. 10:2.

372 Cf. Aristotle, *Physiognomonica* II. 806b. 16; *Politica* VII. 1327b. 20–32.

373 Aristotle, *Hist. animal.* I. 17. 496b. 16.

374 Cf. Pliny, *Hist. nat.* II. 80. 189.

killed looking to Aquilo.[375] On the left the strength of black bile from the spleen itself causes men to be dedicated to contemplation and meditation of heavenly matters.[376] Thus, in the sacred writings wars, calamities, and armies are rather often indicated by Aquilo,[377] and the great power of Leviathan is indicated as Aquilo,[378] who is also called Aquilonaris for this reason. On the other hand, God is said to come from the south (auster) and Abraham's departure was toward the south (auster). Apropos to this is the statement—"I shall say to the north, yield, and to the south, do not prohibit"[379]—because the power of prohibiting is greater than the power of yielding. It ought not to seem strange that all the regions of all peoples—I say, Chaldeans, Jews, Ismaelites, Christians—are derived from *auster*. The armies of Goths, Vandals, Herulians, Hungarians, Turks, Tartars, Franks,[380] and Anglo-Saxons were led from the north to the south. Likewise, the movement of all animals is from the right to the left side, and the rotation of the trembling orb is from north to south with a remarkable harmony of nature.[381] From this one realizes that the temples of the Jews face west and priests also face west when making sacrifices because this position is consistent with the universe of nature.[382] From this not only are the errors of Homer corrected but also those of Pythagoras, Plato, Aristotle, Averroes, Galen, Pliny, and Varro; moreover, the wonderful secrets of nature are known, although prayers to all temples of heaven and divine praises in every place and region have always been most pleasing to God.

Octavius: I do not believe that the Mohammedans are so keenly philosophical. However, those who live on this side of the Tropic of Cancer turn toward Mecca or Jezecat or Medina Alnabi, near the state of the Prophet and Mount Moriah, where Abraham was ordered to sacrifice his son; namely they face south. Those who live beyond the tropic turn to the north. Nevertheless, it is unique that the Ismaelites, as often as they pray, kiss the ground and both hands twice with heads bowed, but the Christians seldom do this.

Curtius: From ancient times worshippers kissed the hand, as Job himself witnesses, not that they might think about the kiss, but that they

375 Lev. 1:11.
376 Cf. Aristotle, *Problemata* XXX. 953a. 10–955a. 40.
377 Jer. 46:10. 378 Joel 2:20. 379 Isaiah 43:6.
380 *Francorum* MR
381 Aristotle, *De motu animal.* II. 698a. 1–714b. 24. Also cf. Pliny, *Hist. nat.* II. 2–3.
382 Ezech. 46:19–20.

might put silence on the tongue from which sin often comes.[383] Even now when many confess their sins, they are accustomed to beat the breast where the heart resides, the originator of wicked thoughts. Others strike the forehead with the palm of[384] the hand because they think the abode of the soul is here, as if they could demand punishments from the originators
P. 167 of crimes by that blow. But no one can kiss the ground without a crime;[385] indeed this recalls the ancient idolatry of those who were worshipping the land as parent of the gods and all things, calling on great Cybele in the wicked song: "O eternal creatrix, of men, flocks, and gods!"[386]

SALOMON: We stand erect to praise God.[387] We pray for favorable things on bended knees.[388] We pray against adverse circumstances, sometimes standing, as Ezechias,[389] turned toward the wall, but never sitting, much less lying down,[390] unless sickness or weakness forces us. For example, Moses, with his hands extended to heaven for a very long time, had stood erect as long as the battle was being fought against the Amalecites; when his strength failed, he sat down but still with his hands outstretched to the west.[391] Moreover, Plutarch[392] was wrong when he wrote that Numa had ordered that those who were about to worship should sit down, because this was not practiced by the Latins and was foreign to Pythagorean decrees with which Numa is said to have been imbued. The Pythagorean symbol says *peripheromenon proskunein*, that is, to fall forward having rolled around. We in confessing our sins show our humility by touching the ground with our forehead, which Plutarch calls a falling upon the face. In the most earnest prayers we imitate the position of Elias. Although he by his own prayer had kept rain or dew from falling for three and a half years, he prayed seven times for rain, until he was listened to by God,

[383] Job 31:27.

[384] *manus* MR

[385] *terram vero sine scelere* MR

[386] Statius, *Thebais* VIII. 303. Cf. Hastings, *Encycl. of Rel. and Eth.*, IV, 377.

[387] 2 Esdras (Neh.) 9:2–3; I Kings (I Sam.) 1:26. Also cf. Matt. 6:5; Mark 11:25; Luke 18:11.

[388] III Kings (I Kings) 8:54; Dan. 6:10.

[389] II Paralip. (II Chron.) 29:1–11, 20–36. Also see Sirach 48:17–25.

[390] *accubantes* MR

[391] Ex. 18:9–12.

[392] *De superstitione* VIII. 169E. See "Numa" in Plutarch, *The Lives of the Noble Grecians and Romans*, Modern Library (New York, n.d.), p. 86. Numa advised that the worshippers sit after worship, after the completion of what they had done, and after intervals of rest to seek favor for new undertakings. Worship was not to be hurried in any way. See *Ox. Class. Dict.*, p. 613; to say that Numa was a disciple of Pythagoras is an anachronism.

with his head between his knees and lying on the ground,[393] which is the humble position of the infant in the uterus. Indeed a sitting position is the very opposite of a worshipping attitude.

Octavius: It is far afield to say that the Ismaelites by kissing the ground wish to worship Cybele,[394] for no nation is any farther removed from the suspicion of idolatry. They think it is a crime to speak or make conversations in the temple or to walk about. On holy days at the sixth hour there is a regular gathering of people, and they do not eat before noon on the holy day. At Passover, which is cherished as the holiest of all days, after the monthly fast they celebrate the feast of Elmeide. They lovingly forgive offenses, exchange kisses of the hands, and recall the loves of their ancestors, not with pretense but with good faith. If anyone avenged an injury after accepting the kissing of hands, he would go unpunished but would be condemned by severe judgment. If anyone shall have refused to be present for public gatherings and prayers, he will be treated to fines, disgrace, prison.[395] They by far surpass all people not only in the purest worship of one eternal God but also in humanity and kindness. They are amazed that Christian men are able to bear with equanimity so great a multitude of needy people, such want and poverty of their own people, since among Mohammedans there are more homes for the needy and P. 168 strangers than people who need them. Often you could see Turks in this city throwing coins freely to the poor who were chasing everywhere after the money. Indeed they cherish no law as holier than *Al-zāt*,[396] that is, to pay what is owed and to give generously to the needy, and so rather often the *chorabitae*, whom the Greeks call hermits, run up to travellers and beg them to lodge with them. After they have favored the travellers with exquisite dishes, baths, and beds, not only do they ask no price but even give thanks with these words: "May this be granted to my soul that God loves you!" Also educated men have provided numerous homes near the shrines and very ample provisions for food. There is hardly any rich man

393 III Kings (I Kings) 17:1; 18:36–42.

394 Cybele was the great mother goddess of Anatolia. She was primarily a goddess of fertility and also mistress of wild nature, symbolized by the lions that attended her. Ecstatic states and wild frenzy were characteristic of her worship. Cf. Catullus, *Car.* LXIII. Also see Augustine, *De civ. Dei* II. 4–5, 7.

395 There are five acts of worship required by Islam: (1) the recital of the creed; (2) the observance of five daily prayers; (3) the fast in the month of Ramadhān; (4) giving of the legal alms; (5) the pilgrimage to Mecca.

396 *Alzache* MR. The legal and determined aims were the *zakāt*; the voluntary alms were the *ṣadagāt*.

who is not responsible for consecrating either a temple or public lodging. However, we see numerous Christians who do not delight in doing good, but in seeming to have done good to foster their ambition more than need. And when very few open the founts of kindness to those in need, then they do this either for the expiation of thefts or evil deeds (for water does not check fire more quickly than largess to the needy checks sin)[397] or for the increase of their property. Indeed, Basil the Great[398] could say nothing truer than that the most profitable art of all is alms-giving. Muslims do not look to the profit of their domestic situation, but distribute their goods because of respect for God alone. Their preachers instruct them very diligently in this so that they seem to me able by right to oppose to Christians what once a certain Spartan said when he stood up in the theater for an older man, so that he did not have to stand up while the young were sitting, namely that the Athenians had honorable arts and disciplines for ostentation and arrogance but not for use. Indeed, it is remarkable that Ismaelites abstain from wine and dice since their laws forbid, although many Christians think they have been freed from the laws, whether they follow the luxury of wine and dice, or adulteries, harlotries, rapes, injuries, blows, murders, blindness of soul in everything, and, that which is more loathsome than all the rest, deadly insults against God. Moreover, they [Muslims] very carefully instruct the pliable and impressionable years of youth in the divine laws, and they do not allow them to hear fables or see games of lust. However, they fill their minds so constantly with the divine precepts of the Koran that before puberty they remember them faithfully. Also no impure songs are heard. Finally, when I compare their religion, justice, laws, customs, institutions with yours, I very truly judge the Ismaelites of all people to be "Musulmanni," that is, faithful, not only because the law of Mohammed is harmonious with nature, as Agazel[399] and Avicenna wrote, but also because others have the appear-

[397] Tobias 12:9.

[398] Although Basil (*Ep.* 150) favored almsgiving, it was Gregory the Great who insisted that the bishop enforce the rule which divided church revenues into four parts, at least one of which should be devoted to almsgiving. See article "Charity," Hastings, *Encycl. of Rel. and Eth.*, III, 382–84.

[399] Avicenna (980–1037), Arabian philosopher famous for his prodigious learning, was the guide of medical studies in European universities from the 12th to the 17th century. His best known work is the *Canon of Medicine*; his *Logic, Metaphysics, Physics*, and *About Heaven and Earth* reveal a synoptic view of Aristotelian doctrine.

ance and the semblance of true religion, but Muslims seem to me not only to have religion itself, but also to possess it. P. 169

The others were silent during this speech and were amazed that Octavius had defected from the Christians to the Ismaelites. When no one contradicted Octavius' speech, finally FRIDERICUS broke the silence by saying: I did not intend to refute the discourse of Octavius, and I think you were silent for the reason that there was little need of refutation. I am not inclined to argue about the customs and religion of Mohammedans because I had no opportunity to examine their cities and states; nevertheless, I do not think that Octavius, a very religious[400] man, approves their religion, but said these things only for the sake of speaking. I assume you have read books about the doctrine of Mohammed, also about his customs and the whole course of his life, and especially that this most ingenious originator of religions was called Mohammed on the earth,[401] but Almad in heaven. Thus Homer says that the river which flows by Troy is called Xanthus by men, Scamander by the gods.[402] When Mohammed was born, the winds, birds, clouds, and angels came together to nourish him; the winds came with sweet perfumes, the birds with fruit, the clouds with waters. Since nothing remained for the angels to offer the infant, they departed angrily. They say that this same one was taken into heaven by Gabriel himself, and after his return became a prophet and held public gatherings. Yet, since he could not persuade by any eloquence or reasons the things he wished, he decided to use the force of armor. They say that he was routed by the enemy on the day of Venus and fled; from this flight they count the beginning of years. Afterwards he attacked Mecca with a stronger band and gave the city for plunder to the soldier-disciples. From these beginnings they became wealthy from booty, and little by little they increased their power, since they had gathered together the thiefs of Arabia and the slaves[403] by offering liberty and the hope of plunder. He is said to have died in old age of epilepsy. Although he had promised that he would rise again on the third day, he lay unburied for so long that he was thrown into the sewers of the city by the people because of the most loathsome smell. Many say that he was seized and killed with Garuffa, wife of Mazuchi, since he said that the Prophet could take by right those wives that he wished. Also some say that he had ordered Abdallah and

400 *religiosissimo* MR
401 *terris* MR
402 *Iliad* XX. 74.
403 *ac servitia* MR

Machilius killed because they denied he was a prophet. Although he had married seventeen wives, still he is said to have seized the wife of his friend Zaid.[404] He also devised a very pleasing story not only to remove the abuse of wine but to prohibit its necessary use. He pretended that two angels were sent to earth from heaven to administer justice and became so enthralled with drunkenness and the charms of a beautiful prostitute that one carried her to heaven and the other brought her back to
P. 170 earth. For this reason the use of wine was forbidden to mortals. The story of Mohammed's paradise is the most copious fable of all. In this paradise they promised there would be exotic dishes of food, flowing streams of wine, milk, and honey, also hoards of beautiful women and fish; one could use or misuse these pleasures for 70,000 years after the feast, which also ended after 70,000 years. When Averroës,[405] the chief Arabic philosopher, had read the story, he said this was a paradise for pigs, so that it ought not to seem strange if that despicable impiety with such numerous rewards proposed invaded almost the whole world.

CURTIUS: So great is the power of wicked opinion that once placed in men's minds, its conquest is more powerful than nature herself. Indeed it is a custom among the Narsingae, a people of India, for women to be burned alive on the pyre with the bodies of their dead husbands. Ancient and contemporary writers say that their friends help them in this so that they may enjoy the eternal pleasures of their husbands. Moreover, the Ismaelites very childishly think that sins are removed by constant washings, just as the Indians of Hispaniola thought that sins were overcome by vomiting from the pit of the stomach before the altars and statues.

OCTAVIUS: It is not strange that Averroës desired the religion of the Ismaelites to prevail, since he despised all the laws of Christians and Jews.

[404] Mohammed had fourteen wives and three concubines. There was a scandal when the Prophet took Ayesha as his wife, for she was the wife of his adopted son, Zaid. During Mohammed's final illness he was taken to the home of his favorite wife, the youthful Ayesha, and he is said to have died in her arms. See *Encycl. Brit.* (11th ed.) XVII, 408; also pp. 399–423. Also see Hastings, *Encycl. of Rel. and Eth.* VII, 871–907.

Abdallah, mentioned in the preceding sentence, was the name of Mohammed's father, although the name Abdallah, which means "slave of Allah," is used at a later period as a substitute for an unknown name.

[405] Averroës (1126–1198) declared that the ultimate aspiration of the human soul was rational knowledge. In regard to immortality, he maintained that immortality does not imply the eternal separate existence of the individual soul, but that the active principle common to all men alone survives. For concepts of immortality which influenced Renaissance thought, see Paul Oskar Kristeller, *Renaissance Concepts of Man and Other Essays* (New York, 1972), pp. 22–42.

Avicenna, however, leader in every branch of philosophy and most famous for medicine, wrote that the law of Mohammed set forth the miseries and joy of supreme bodily pleasures, but held another happiness, by far more[406] excellent in the soul. Fridericus recounted these things from the books, *Ta*[407] *Elimel Nebi*, that is, *About Life of the Prophet and his Teaching*, and *Edit el Nebi*, that is, *History of the Prophet*. These are apocryphal works of the Ismaelites, and the theologians never approved them. Indeed, they rejected them as writings by unlearned men, as the stories which are circulated by the theologian Bonaventura[408] about the life of Christ are rejected. For example, the fruit trees had bent gently down so that it would be possible for the infant Christ to eat the fruit to satiety. Christian theologians do not approve these or innumerable stories of this sort which we have read in the golden, or should I say, the iron book of the saints which I do not wish to relate lest we be disgusted with the absurdities. *Alcoran*, which is so called from its collection, or *Alphurcanus*[409] from the distinction of its 123 headings, has no absurdities, no contradictions, no offensiveness, as Dionysius Carthusianus[410] and the Cardinal of S. Sixtus[411] believed, who wrote against the law of Mohammed. Richard, a Dominican who was instructed in Arabic letters and discipline, was more kindly disposed even if in certain places he pretended the false and

406 *longe* MR 407 *Ta* MR

408 Bonaventura, a saint and doctor of the church (1221–1274) aroused hostile criticism when in 1266 he convened a general chapter in Paris which decreed that all the "legends" of St. Francis, written before that of Bonaventura, should be destroyed. Octavius' statement concerning Bonaventura may also refer to the violent outbursts of opposition against the public teaching of the Franciscans and Dominicans by the lay professors at the University of Paris. Bonaventura received the right to teach publicly in 1248 as *Magister regens* and continued to lecture with great success at the university until 1255, when he was forced to discontinue his teaching because of the hostile opposition. Guillaume de Saint-Amour's book, *The Perils of the Last Times* (1255) bitterly denounced the Friars and was the catalyst for opposition in the universities. See *Cath. Encycl.* II (1907), 648–54.

409 *Alcoran*, or the Koran, was not revealed by God all at once, but gradually. Mohammed issued his revelations in fly leaves of varying lengths. A single piece was called, like the entire collection, *ḳor'ān*, "recitation" or *ḳitāb*, "writing," or *sūra*, "series." In the lifetime of Mohammed the sūra became the designation of the individual sections and accordingly the name given to the separate chapters of the Koran. See *Encycl. Brit.* (11th ed.) XV, pp. 898–906. *Alphurcanus* M. See Chauviré, *Jean Bodin*, pp. 12–13.

410 Dionysius Cathusianus is Denis the Carthusian (d. 1471), the *Doctor Ecstaticus* who was a prolific author. See *Cath. Encycl.* III, 391.

411 Sanctus Sixtus is Sixtus IV (Francesco della Rovere, 1414–1484) who was energetic in the prosecution of the war against the Turks. The cardinal of Sixtus was his nephew, Rafael Riario, who planned the famous conspiracy of the Pazzi in 1478. See *Cath. Encycl.* XIV, 32–33.

P. 171 concealed the true. Those who have mocked at the paradise and the wicked pleasures are sufficiently refuted by those things which are written in the 75th and 77th *Azora*, namely, that adulterers and perjurers would burn in the eternal fires of hell, as the lawgiver Mohammed clearly witnesses. Moreover, women are not allowed to be seen by men while sacred rites are being performed, and the faces of those who are bound by the laws of Mohammed are not allowed to be shown in public. Even though Christians mention that Mohammed had said that he would rise again, you will never find those things in the writings of the Ismaelites. On this very point Christians disagree among themselves, because some say he had promised the resurrection on the third day, others say after the eightieth year, as if another Lycurgus,[412] about to consult Apollo, would bind citizens to his own laws until the time of his return. Therefore, when one omits all the empty fables and carefully reads the Koran, he will find nothing in it, as far as I can judge, except the purest religion toward God, piety toward parents, love for relatives, kindness toward the weak, and justice for all constantly instilled.

FRIDERICUS: It is strange that the Agareni of Mohammed could not fashion an ascent into heaven without a mule. Why did they not use a ladder rather than a mule, unless they thought that the ascent of mules into heaven would be more likely.

OCTAVIUS: Nothing of this sort has been set forth in the sacred writings of Mohammedans. These stories are no more incredible than those of Numerius Atticus, a Roman praetor, who confirmed on oath that Augustus had ascended into heaven after he received 10,000 gold pieces from Livia.[413] However, when another confirmed Drusilla's ascent which was celebrated because of incest[414] with her brother Caligula, the people mocked at him.

[412] Lycurgus was, according to tradition, the founder of the Spartan constitution and military system. Lycurgus' legislation was said to have been suggested or at least approved by the oracle at Delphi. There is considerable doubt whether he was an historical figure, and if he was, what his dates were. Estimates range between 1100 B.C. and 600 B.C. See *Ox. Class. Dict.*, p. 521. Also cf. Tertullian, *Apol.* I. 4, 46.

[413] Suetonius relates that a Roman praetor swore that he saw Augustus' spirit ascend from the funeral pyre to heaven but he does not mention Livia or the gold. See Suetonius, *Caesar Augustus*, XCVIII.

[414] *incestibus* MR. Julia Drusilla (A.D. 16–38) was the favorite sister of her brother Gaius (Caligula). Rumors were rampant that their relations were incestuous. Drusilla was named Gaius' heir, but she died in A.D. 38. Public mourning for her was enforced throughout the empire, and she was consecrated as Panthea. See *Ox. Class. Dict.*, p. 301.

CORONAEUS: I wonder that Octavius could approve the superstitions of the Agareni,[415] which are more worthy[416] of pity than mockery, since he is[417] a man of acute judgment and excellent doctrine. His opinion is the more unique the longer he is oppressed with their harsh servitude.

OCTAVIUS: God the best and greatest suffered me to be seized by pirates on the shore of Sicily and sold to a Syrian merchant. He in turn gave me to Paracadius. Since he noted that I was very religious and studious, he began to question me about my religion, because I spoke Arabic after three years as a captive. While I was explaining each heading and was trying to lead him to my opinion (since I thought immortal God would desire no act more than this), he on the other side was pressing with so many arguments that I was brought to a standstill by arguments as if stuck in a shoal. At length he showed me a little book in defense of the Moham- P. 172 medan faith, written in the Arabic tongue by a certain Dominican who had deserted the Christian faith. As I read and reread the book, confused by various opinions, I was amazed that this could be written by a Christian man, and indeed a Dominican, who had rejected the religion of his elders. At last convinced by the arguments, I gave in. When the master had noticed this, he granted me my liberty. Many are accustomed to embrace Mohammed and allow themselves to be circumcised in order to obtain freedom.

FRIDERICUS: Once I heard those who went into the cave of Trophonius were accustomed to leap about as if they were driven into madness by the demon.[418] When their friends tried to call them back and had entered the cave, they joined the dancing. We see the same thing has happened to Octavius.

OCTAVIUS: I pass over the insults by which the dignity of Mohammed is torn to bits by the disparagements of his adversaries. I stick to the substance, that is, the true and sincere worship of the one eternal God.

TORALBA: If true religion is contained in the pure worship of eternal God, I believe the law of nature is sufficient for man's salvation. We see that the oldest leaders and parents of the human race had no other religion. They left the memory of the golden age to posterity, not taught, but wrought, not instituted but imbued by nature herself. From nature they drank the streams of piety, religion, integrity, and all virtues and imitated them. We see that this has been approved not only by all the opinions of

[415] Yet Coronaeus, in Book V, p. 239, says that superstition is better than atheism.
[416] *dignas* MR [417] *cum sit ipse* R [418] Pausanias, IX. 37. 4–8.

all philosophers, but also confirmed by oracles, if there is any faith in oracles. For when Marcus Tullius[419] asked what course of life he should follow, the answer was that he should follow nature as his guide.[420] Paul, writing to the Romans, says this not obscurely or ambiguously but openly:[421] "Nations which are free from law live legally by nature herself, because even though they have no tablets of laws, none the less they bring forth edicts entrusted to their minds with their conscience as witness." By these words he taught that right reason and the law of nature were sufficient for man's salvation. Since these things are so, why do Jews, Christians, Saracens, and Pagans need so many rites and superstitions?[422] Indeed I think that this religion is the oldest and the best of all.

After Toralba had spoken briefly, silence followed. Nor had anyone revealed up to this point what he felt about religions, with the exception of SALOMON, who, supported by common consent, finally broke the silence: My feelings are entirely agreeable with yours, Toralba; for example, all the things which pertain to salvation are contained in the laws of nature. By these laws of nature Abel, Enoch, Noah, Abraham, Job, Isaac,
P. 173 and Jacob lived; what men! Surely they secured the highest praise of piety and integrity according to the testimony of immortal God, than which nothing greater nor more awesome can be imagined. Indeed circumcision, which was granted to Abraham and posterity, as if a sign of the covenant, was not necessary for salvation, but we are ordered to be circumcised for this very reason that we may seem to be chosen and separated from other people by God. Moreover, God himself seemed to indicate this law of nature when he said:[423] "All nations will be blessed in the seed of Abraham for the reason that he obeyed My voice and never violated My edicts and My laws." No law was brought forth by Moses except after the four hundred thirtieth year. The others, which were contained in the ritual and judicial laws, were antiquated when the temple of God was destroyed,[424] and the republic of the Hebrews was overturned. We are expressly prohibited ever from sacrificing flocks except in this place which God designated by name.[425] Only the decalogue and circumcision are employed by us with the paschal lamb as an eternal memorial to the kindnesses that have been received. Moreover, I am persuaded that no religion can exist completely without rites and ceremonies. I believe the Roman religion has no greater secret for its so great duration than every imaginable vari-

[419] A common Stoic principle. Also see Tertullian, *De corona* VI–VII.
[420] *ducem* MR
[421] Rom. 2:12–15.
[422] *ac superstitionibus* R
[423] Gen. 27:4–5.
[424] A.D. 70.
[425] Deut. 12:13–14.

ety of rites and ceremonies. Also the sweetness of songs with organ accompaniment[426] and the splendor of vestments and sacred and costly furniture, hold the people in awe, as if in a wondrous spectacle. For why had immortal[427] God made the vestment of the high priest Aaron venerable in its noble appearance?[428] Or why had He ordered so many rites of sacrifices, so many washings, so many excellent expiations if He did not think that the minds of the unlearned people could be bound more fittingly in the worship of religion? Indeed the Roman church has received many things from the Jews and a great part of the rites from the ancient Greeks and Latins. Even now we see that the practice of the priest covering his head with the skins of sacrificial animals was taken from the Canons. Perhaps shaving one's head had its origin from the time when Isis shaved her head together with her priests when she heard of the death of Osiris. Then also consider the dismissals of the people after the end of the sacred ceremony, which they called *tou dēmou apheseis*, the lustral waters, choruses,[429] impudences, theophanies, carriages for carrying the gods, biers, dances, and couches of the gods.

CURTIUS: This pomp of the Roman religion is more suitable to the theatrical games and spectacles of the ancient pagans than to true piety which scorns deceit and hates pretense and show. Nothing is more deceitful than that which appears beautiful on the outside, as painted wares, embellished walls, painted faces. Moreover, in like manner, the Tulis fish and the tiger have a skin that has a marvelous variety of colors, although no living creature is more cruel. So we must also judge about religions which concern themselves only with rites and ceremonies.

SALOMON: Surely one is dependent upon the other. P. 174

OCTAVIUS: The Mohammedans differ not at all with Toralba, even little with Salomon. The lawgiver in the Koran very often calls all people to witness the confession and pursuit of the law of Abraham, that is, the pure worship of one eternal God, completely alien to all idolatry, showing kind-

[426] In the 13th century the use of the organ in divine service was considered profane by the Greek and Latin clergy, just as in the 17th century the Puritans called it a "squeaking abomination." However, in the 14th century an organ was built in Germany for the Venetian patrician Narinus Sanutus and was installed in St. Raphael's in Venice. The Venetians greatly admired this instrument, and organ music was a regular part of the divine service in the 15th and 16th centuries. See J. A. Fuller Maitland, ed., *Grove's Dictionary of Music and Musicians*, III (Philadelphia, 1926), pp. 513–35. See below, Book VI, pp. 322–23, notes 65 and 66.

[427] *immortalis* MR

[428] Ex. 28:2–43; Lev. 8:1–13.

[429] At this point R abruptly ends.

ness toward the weak, and in every situation justice toward all. I think the only difference is that when the lawgiver of the Hebrews proposes rewards for his worshippers, he absolves the matter in two words—"Do this and you will live."[430] The lawgiver of the Ismaelites, however, has built his paradise with so many delights and the hope of enjoying pleasures so as to hold those unwilling in their duty by such enticements and call back the wicked from a harmful and wicked life by proposing great punishments. Moreover, we have only necessary rites and ceremonies, none useless. We have no spectacles, no pictures or sculptures which can divert the people from the worship and contemplation of divine matters. We also use frequent washings so that we may learn to wash away more often the inner filth.

TORALBA: Those who press the people with a multitude of rites turn religion into superstition; however, those who completely remove all rites overturn all religions from the root, as the pruner who, taught by his neighbor to cut the superfluous stalks from the vines so that the vines might regrow more abundantly, cuts his own vines down to the ground. We see the same thing happened to those who were displeased with the ancient religion of the Romans: they also will be displeased with the new religion in a short time, unless they try to hold the best and learned man with necessary rites and ceremonies and also with the greater hope of rewards promised by pontiffs and priests. Nothing is enjoined more carefully by divine law than that the tenth of all goods, the best fruits and a right portion of sacrifices be granted under all circumstances to priests and Levites.[431] For thus the wise men of the Hebrews say that sterility of crops, destruction of herds, and extreme poverty follow those who take their own from the priests and lie about the tithe. God said to the prophet:[432] "Carry all the tithes into My dwelling so that from thence bounty can come, and in this very thing take the risk and try Me, if I shall not have opened all the windows of heaven so that I may fill my treasures for you and the abundance of all goods; I shall rebuke the devastator from bringing calamity and sterility to your fields." Surely there can be nothing greater than this mystery for gathering wealth.

OCTAVIUS: The Mohammedans take special care that the high priests of the sacred rites abound in wealth, and Mohammed wisely provided for this lest the poverty of priests bring contempt on divine things and religion.

[430] Ex. 15:26; Deut. 5:17–19.
[431] Num. 18:21–32.
[432] Mal. 3:10–11.

X Noack vermerkt: Alius [codex]: Coronaeus. In der Tat paßt die Bemerkung nicht so gut zu Toralba

CURTIUS: Was it fitting for Mohammed, who was presenting himself as a prophet, to entice the untutored minds of the common people with dishes of lies by saying untruthfully that the law was given to him by Gabriel? When he had written in the Koran that the Virgin Mary, the mother of Jesus, was the sister of Moses and Aaron, he lied about history like a school boy. Mary, the sister of Moses, died 2,000 years before Mary, the mother of Jesus, was born. The Agareni have departed from their own law when they say that they worship and adore God eternal whom once Abraham worshipped, for they often praise God and Mohammed; they scrupulously honor the tombs of Mohammed and Nabissa and bestow lavish gifts upon them. Indeed what is more destructive than the fact that Mohammed tried in every way to entice wicked men to the worship of his religion by the foulness of the basest pleasures? Or what public corruptor does not persuade himself that this which the lawgiver taught was honorable in paradise was noble and honorable on the earth? Moreover, Leo Afer,[433] who embraced the Roman religion after abandoning the Mohammedan religion, wrote that a certain follower of Ibn Farid[434] in the city of Cairo publicly raped a woman with a crowd of people looking on, and after the embrace citizens began to kiss the garments of that woman, after they had touched them with the tips of their fingers, as if they had gained divinity by contact with dishonor. Indeed, the husband not only thanked his wife and the adulturer but even celebrated joyous feasts and games for all his friends. This ought not to seem strange, since Mohammed promised such rewards to the worshippers of his religion. But if Pythagoras said that Homer, Orpheus, and Hesiod were rightfully tormented in the lower world by serpents and suspended from trees,[435] and Plato cast Homer out of his state because he had wickedly fashioned the quarrels of the gods, the tricks, the panderings, disgraces, murders, and incests,[436] Mohammed is worthy of how much greater punishment because he said P. 175

[433] Leo Afer (1494–1552), known among the Moors as Al Hassan Ibn Mahommed Al Wezaz Al Fasi, was long known as the best authority on Muslim Africa because of his travels and his *Descrizione dell' Affrica.* He was captured by pirates soon after the Turkish conquest of Egypt and presented as a slave to Leo X. The pope, impressed with his abilities, persuaded him to profess the Christian faith, was his sponsor at his baptism, and gave him his own names, Leo and Johannes. Leo Afer lived in Rome for some years but returned to Tunis before his death. Some say he renounced his Christianity and returned to Islam, but this cannot be verified. See *Encycl. Brit.* (11th ed.), XVI, 441.

[434] *Ibuni farida* M

[435] Cf. Tertullian, *Apol.* I. 14. 23.

[436] *Res pub.* II. 31. 383B; III. Also cf. Augustine, *De civ. Dei* II. 14.

that he was a prophet and lawgiver and teacher of piety and censor of religions.

SALOMON: I think it is loathsome to mention these things and dangerous to offer men wicked pleasures in place of virtue and piety and to draw the unlearned by false promises beyond what is right, since God the best and greatest not only bestows promises but gives even more generously than promised; imposters, however, always promise more than they can or wish to accomplish. For when God had promised that the twig which He had granted to his priest would sprout, soon the same twig brought forth buds, flowers, branches, fruits; also when He promised the earth to worshippers of his law, He bestowed heavenly rewards; when He promises life, He not only grants this but a much better one in the future. Onkelos the Chaldean interprets this passage, "Who follows My
P. 176 covenants and judgments will live,"[437] to mean eternal life. More dangerous is the fact that those who know those rewards of pleasures are fairy tales also believe punishments are fables, and they rush headlong into every disgrace.

OCTAVIUS: I greatly admire the sentiment of Xenophon and Plato, namely, that it is justifiable and has always been justifiable for magistrates and physicians, as well as nurses of infants, to lie to the people for the sake of the bodies' health and for the sake of the republic.[438] How much more should the souls' salvation be cared for in every way? To be sure, let us grant that Mohammed promised bodily pleasures in the afterlife to those who cherished chastity which the lawgiver himself commended, in the case of the Virgin Mary, Zacharias, and John, with supreme praises in many places of the Koran, but he cursed adulterers to the eternal fires of hell. Moreover, who does not see these things had been written by him so that all might understand that those who had given themselves over to the enticements of base pleasures would be deprived of eternal rewards and a blessed life? The Prophet made this quite clear. Since, however, people of the southern regions are most of all inclined toward Venus,[439] Mohammed thought up those rewards so that he might draw men though unwilling to true honor. Since he sanctioned those pleasures to preserve souls from destruction, what error was there then in this not to merit pardon? Did not Christ declare that those who had lived with the greatest integrity would attain the most blessed life by enjoying eternal pleasures?[440] And yet good and wise men are not very

[437] Ex. 15:26; Deut. 5:17–19.
[438] Cf. *Res pub.* II. 21D.
[439] See above, notes 372–74.
[440] Cf. Luke 23:43.

anxious about how great the rewards for virtue and piety will be, since virtue in itself is the greatest reward to them, nor[441] does it seem[442] that the man who does nothing good ought to be praised greatly, although no reward is proposed. Therefore, if one omits the rewards of virtues, inquire into all the religions of all nations to see if any nation exists or has ever existed before which teaches a purer worship of eternal God than the Mohammedan religion or one which is farther removed not only from the worship of idols and creatures but even from their appearance and design.

SALOMON: The fact that the Ismaelites worship eternal God and Him alone is derived from divine law. It was not proper for Mohammed, under the guise of a new law which he untruthfully said was given to him by the angel Gabriel, to mingle truths with lies and base acts with honorable ones.

OCTAVIUS: Events have proven that the law of Mohammed was necessary, for in no other way could the peoples of Asia and Africa have been pulled away from that opinion of deity which they had conceived about Jupiter and Christ, unless Mohammed had taken this task upon himself with divine aid. He hoped to keep men from placing any hope or safeguard for salvation in the life of that one or in the death of this one whom he denied was dead but was snatched from the enemies' hands by the power of God. After he had laid these foundations, he added two powerful defenses for stabilizing religion. First, he summoned those in servitude to freedom and proposed liberty for all who followed him and P. 177
his teaching. Second, he refused that there be any discussion about his law; moreover, he ordered those who criticized his commands to be taken to task by the devastation of wars and the terrors of punishments. And Homarus, Mohammed's legate, with a large army of slaves crushed by force of arms the governors and prefects of the cities of Arabia, Syria, and Egypt; in a short time they invaded the territories of Chaldea and Persia and burned all the books of the pagans and Christians.[443] Still, he employed that mystery which drew even Christians to him when he called Christ a prophet, and he won over to his side Jews, Arians,

[441] *nec* M [442] *videtur* M

[443] Mohammed seems originally to have set about to convert only Mecca. After his exile to Taif, however, he began the conquest of Arabia and excluded paganism there. Disputes with Christians occurred later than those with Jews. "The Prophet's policy was to give Christians lighter terms than Jews, and though the Koran reflects the gradual adoption by the Prophet of an attitude of extreme hostility to both systems, its tone is on the whole far more friendly to the former than to the latter." See *Encycl. Brit.* (11th ed.), XVII, 407.

Nestorians, and Sabellians when he denied that Christ was God.[444] Indeed, the opinion of the Arians is the foundation of the Mohammedan religion, since both admit that Christ is the son and creature of a virgin, but still they deny that He is God. This opinion of the Arians has been confirmed by eight councils, namely, those which were held at Tyre, Sardes, Smyrna, Milan, Seleucia, Nicaea, Tarsus, and especially at the synod of Rimini, where six hundred bishops harmoniously approved the Arian religion. More renowned is Nestorius who openly denied that Mary was the Mother of God.

CURTIUS: If a multitude of heretics conspiring together ought to be called synod, what hinders a crowd of Epicureans from being called churches or councils? Even lawyers do not allow any league for crimes or any society of wicked men to meet, how much less ought the wicked conspiracies of the Nestorians, the Sabellians, and the Arians against God be called councils, since they denied the supreme point of faith, namely, the deity of Christ and the Trinity of three Persons in the essence of One. We ought to safeguard this doctrine which has been strengthened by the firmest foundations of countless councils and especially of the Nicene synod.

OCTAVIUS: The antiquity of the Christian religion. . . .

At this point, when Coronaeus saw that Octavius was prepared to reply, and since he realized that the discussion about the most serious matters would have been drawn out too long, he dismissed the gathering and said that they would continue the discussion after dinner, so as not to seem to deny Octavius the right to speak. At that time the discussion would be concerned with whether it is right for a good man to feel otherwise about religion than he confesses publicly. And so, after greeting each other in turn, they left with the keenest anticipation of the future discussion.

[444] Arianism was a fourth-century heresy which denied the divinity of Christ. It described the Son as a second or inferior God standing midway between the First Cause and creatures. The Arians denied that the Son is of one essence, nature, or substance with God; He is not consubstantial with the Father nor coeternal nor within the real sphere of Deity.

The Nestorians insisted upon the completeness of the humanity which the Word assumed. They represented Jesus' human nature as a complete man and the Incarnation as the assumption of a man by the Word.

Sabellius was the leader of the Monarchians in Rome. The Monarchians were heretics of the second and third centuries who stressed the unity of God as a first principle and denied the Trinity. The Monarchians, properly called Modalists, claimed oneness of the Father and Son as to person; therefore, the distinctions in the Holy Trinity are energies or modes, not Persons. On these heresies, see *Cath. Encycl.* I, 707–10; X, 755–59, 448–51. See below, Book V, pp. 255–56, note 112.

BOOK V

WHEN each one had returned for dinner, I was asked to continue to read the tragedy of Octavius. I came to the place in which Soliman, king of the Turks, ordered the neck of his first born, Mustapha, to be broken in his bed, and then for him to be exposed to the great army assembled near Brussa, as the voice of a herald cried out this song in a loud voice after[1] the sound of the trumpet: P. 178

> Let there be one greatest commander
> for heaven;
> Let there be one all powerful
> commander for earth.

At this point Coronaeus ordered me to stop; for the second dish he had mingled artificial apples with real so skillfully that even the shrewdest could not tell the difference. When Fridericus, good man that he was, bit into an artificial apple, being deceived by its appearance, he said: "I do not see how any one of you could have not been deceived." After the others looked more closely at the apples which were so cleverly fashioned that they seemed freshly plucked, Coronaeus said: "If the eyes which are the keenest of the senses are so irrationally deceived in insignificant matters, how can it happen that the mind, which gathers everything from the senses, attains certain knowledge of difficult and sublime matters?"

SENAMUS: I learned from Aristotle that the senses were never deceived, but the mind of men was.

TORALBA: I believe the Academicians err when they say that the senses are always deceived and can know nothing;[2] also Aristotle, who thinks

[1] *post* M

[2] Cf. Plato, *Theaet.* XXXVI. 202B–C.

that the senses are never deceived.[3] Still, Aristotle made a more serious error than the Academicians because they [the Academicians] say there is nothing present in the mind except that which the mind draws from the senses. However, since we have discussed this matter in the question on the soul rather fully, there is no need for repetition.

CURTIUS: Art in the making of this fruit (which he was viewing intently) seems to have surpassed nature or surely to have equaled it.

SALOMON: Indeed, art is the ray of man, but nature is the ray of God; moreover, art is so far from conquering or equaling nature that it cannot even imitate it. Although art objects, statues, and paintings often deceive men's eyes, still, in this regard, it is remarkable that animals cannot ever be deceived. And so when the queen of Sheba tried to deceive King Solomon by placing a real and an artificial flower side by side and asked which was the real flower, the very wise ruler asked that bees be brought in; immediately they flew to the real flower and passed over the artificial one.[4]

And when they had spoken a little along this line, they thanked immortal God with a hymn.

P. 179 FRIDERICUS, who was vexed by the fictitious fruit, said: Would that these men[5] who know very keenly how to simulate the false and conceal the true with such happiness be exposed.

CORONAEUS: Fridericus desires the greatest power of all, which we ought not to seek, for it is proper to God alone. For if every wish and thought of all men were exposed to all, good men would not be able to protect their innocence against the power of wicked men nor could just punishments be meted out for the wicked, because according to human laws, wicked thoughts do not merit punishment. For this reason wicked men, if their thoughts were revealed, would always try to trap good men, but good men would never try to trap the wicked. So Momus deserved ridicule when he rashly slandered nature by contending that a window should be made in the breast so that the secret darkness and the inner recesses of the soul might be unfolded.[6] But as the proverb says: "It is easier to find fault than to emulate."[7] For although he should have admired and praised the parent of nature, he wickedly abused her.

[3] *De anima* III. 3. Par. 428a.

[4] Cf. III Kings (I Kings) 10:1–10; II Paralip. (II Chron.) 9:1.

[5] *hi homines* M

[6] Cf. Plato, *Conviv.* XXXII. 3. 215a–b.

[7] Attributed to Hippocrates, *De arte* I. 1.

CURTIUS: But how important is it that crimes would be detected in advance if plans were revealed?

SENAMUS: Not even God, who understands all the thoughts of men and foresees intended murders, establishes punishment before the completion of these acts, contrary to what Isocrates and Tullius Tiro thought,[8] lest repentance of the evil thought prevent punishment.

TORALBA: If I could, I would not wish to lay bare the feelings of others. However, I would desire that no one should feel something and say something else unless it was advantageous for another. For Octavius said earlier that it was always praiseworthy to use helpful lies.

FRIDERICUS: Men for the sake of men make decisions about public and private matters. However, since God looks very deeply into individual souls, it is strange that many go to the temples, make sacrifices, and make prayers contrary to what they feel or desire. About these God said in Isaiah: "These people praise Me with their tongues, but their hearts are far from Me."[9]

SENAMUS: Since Fridericus has led us into a more accurate consideration of the question posed by Coronaeus, whether it is right for a good man to feel otherwise about religion than he professes publicly, I believe a distinction is necessary. For in the opinion of almost all the theologians, religion is nothing other than a turning away from created beings to the pure worship of one God, while impiety is a turning from the worship of the Creator to the created. This is a truer statement, I believe, than that of Aristotle who defined religion as a concern for things divine.[10] A few are still found who worship eternal God publicly and privately wherever they are, without any fear for their possessions, reputation, or life, and we can place these in the first order. There is a second class of those who privately worship eternal God and flee the public temples of idols. The third class is composed of those who as captives of enemies come to the temples of idols and demons from fear of punishment; nevertheless, they say that they worship eternal God in the

P. 180

[8] Isocrates (436–338 B.C.), Athenian orator, is reported to have been a friend of Socrates. See *Oxford Classical Dictionary* (Oxford, 1961) (cited hereafter as *Ox. Class. Dict.*), pp. 460–61, for a discussion of his life and works. Marcus Tullius Tiro was the freedman friend and secretary of Cicero who wrote a biography of him. He also published several original works. He invented a system of shorthand (*notae Tironicanae*). See *Ox. Class. Dict.*, pp. 876, 912.

[9] Isaiah 29:13.

[10] Aristotle, *Fragments* 12a, 12b, 13. *Works of Aristotle*, XII, translated by Sir David Ross (Oxford, 1952).

intimate senses of their souls and that they keep their souls free and pure of all idolatry. Jeremiah gave this advice in the letter that he wrote to the citizens who were brought to Babylon. He strongly urged them to worship eternal God in their souls and minds although they were forced to fall before idols.[11] In the fourth group are those who are neither captives of enemies nor forced to approach dangers of death but who, having attained wealth, honors, and children, come to the public shrines of idols so as not to lose their wealth or become exiles. Nevertheless, they worship eternal God with private prayers and vows, and falling before the statues, they summon him as a witness of their purity, and they beg immortal God that force may not deceive them. The fifth class is composed of those who are deeply involved in a false religion which they think is true. They shun the temples of others as profane and serve private and domestic gods. In the sixth class are those who privately and publicly without fear worship private gods and a false religion, which they honor as true. The seventh group consists of those who doubt whether the opinion which they hold is true or false, yet because they have been brought up in this opinion, they give assent to it in public and private, although their hope of salvation is doubtful. The eighth class consists of those who follow whatever religion they think is true only to deceive more safely with a reputation of piety. The ninth class contains magicians and sorcerers who, although they fall down in adoration in the temples, wickedly curse with silent souls and mouths that God whom they think is true and privately offer human sacrifices to demons. If they have the opportunity to stipulate anything about religions, they defile the majesty and worship of sacred things with every kind of shamelessness; for example, those who founded the sacred rites of Bahal Peor[12] were forced to expose very shamefully their private parts and defile the appearance of religion with excrements. Equally base were those who listened for oracles by placing their ears near the private parts of the Pythian soothsayers.[13] The tenth group consists of those who have no concern for religion at all, not even in appearance, but follow like animals their lustful desires. The most loathsome of all[14] are those who consider it insufficient to cast all religion from their souls and to have destroyed the appearance of religion, but also in public and in private mock

[11] Baruch 6:1–6.

[12] Cf. Num. 25:3; Psalm 105 (196):28–29.

[13] The Pythia was the priestess of Apollo through whom his oracular responses were delivered at his temple at Delphi. See Lewis R. Farnell, *The Cults of the Greek States* (Oxford, 1896–1909), IV, 179 ff.

[14] *omnium* M

at everyone's religion. From this it is clear that there are seven classes of religious men whom I am accustomed to discuss; however, there are four groups we can call atheists, some worse than others.

OCTAVIUS: If it is not possible for a man to worship eternal God without fear for life and goods, Jeremiah judged that this one could worship God with a pure heart, although he bows before the altars of demons and idols.[15] Who can dare or desire or be able to reject his opinion? P. 181

CURTIUS: I surely cannot approve the hypocrisy of those who think they can worship statues with their body and God with their mind. If this had been possible, why did Paul indicate otherwise by saying: "One believes in his heart in justice, but confesses with his mouth salvation."[16] Tertullian, calling those foreign who do otherwise, said "Whoever conceals denies."[17]

OCTAVIUS: Many things are approved, many more rejected; some are neither approved nor rejected but in some way are excused as those things which happen from force and fear.

CURTIUS: Thus perhaps before judges the fear of blows or more painful tortures is excused.

OCTAVIUS: Curtius, do you think, then, that God is more severe than human judges?

FRIDERICUS: Granted that there may be an excuse, from fear[18] of torture, for not professing eternal God with a clear voice. Still I do not see that anyone should be excused because he falls before the statue of Diana[19] or another virgin lest he lose his riches and positions, provided that he is permitted to leave his country, as Abraham did by divine command so as not to be forced to worship the stars.[20] Otherwise, I do not see how we can flee that prophecy of the divine voice: "Who confesses Me before men, I also shall confess him before My Father who is in heaven."[21] And so those ancient Christians, who had sacrificed to demons because of the trickery of Julian Augustus, were warned by their priests, and touched by repentance, they cried out publicly: "We are Christians in our souls and we have been, O Christ our Savior; we have not broken faith in You."[22]

[15] Baruch 6:5. [16] Rom. 10:10. [17] Cf. *De poenit.* X.

[18] *metu* M

[19] Diana is the goddess of the hunt and a woodland goddess. At an early period she was associated with Artemis. Diana was largely a goddess of women, and though herself a virgin, one of her central functions seems to have been fertility.

[20] Gen. 12. [21] Matt. 10:32.

[22] See Athenagoras, *Apol.* XXVII. Also see Tertullian, *Apol.* I. 31.

Octavius: If they had not broken faith for that reason but were deceived by error, there was no reason why they should curse their error and beg forgiveness, since those who err offer no assent.

Curtius: Origen harshly reprimands those who deny verbally what they perceive in their souls about Christ.[23] God rebuked such hypocrites to Elias with this statement:[24] "I have the remnant of seven thousand men, who have not bent their knees before Bahal and have not kissed him."[25] Who does not see that these words do not refer to soul but to bodies? If the ancient priests of Apollo, Diana, and Jupiter loudly urged the atheists and Epicureans (Lucian even adds the Christians)[26] to leave their temples, how much truer is it that this must be done in God's temple?

p. 182 Octavius: When two wrongs are proposed, the greater must be avoided, as all wise men agree. Indeed, it is a serious mistake for a man who is prudent and religious to fall before empty images, to kiss them, and embellish them with gifts, although the heart of the worshipper has been united with eternal God. Still, it is a more serious offense to subject one's self to the everlasting stigma of impiety and seem to be deserted by all religion if you desert public worship. The most serious offense is to summon others to every kind of impiety by setting a wicked example of scorn for public religion. Therefore, these latter wrongs must be avoided before those. Not everybody is at liberty to lead away his wife, children, parents and family, and even if it were possible, one must wander to the most remote regions to find people practicing true religion. Indeed, Moses and Jeremiah perceived the Israelites' impending punishments.[27] They saw that in the future they, as captives to the enemy, would reluctantly worship stones and trees. Because they preferred idols to the true God, each man would be punished in accordance with his sins. Nevertheless, God Himself had bestowed this unique amulet against idolatry:

[23] Discordance between what one intends and what one does is called "hypocrisy." As a Christian sin, see *The Catholic Encyclopedia* (New York, 1911), VII, 610. Also see Justin, *Apol.* I. 7, 39.

[24] III Kings (I Kings) 19:18.

[25] *qui non curvaverunt genua ante Bahal nec illum osculati sunt. M* missing in N

[26] It is fitting that Lucian (A.D. 120–180) should be mentioned—or is this St. Lucian, martyred in A.D. 312? The pagan satyrist was caught between conflicting claims of philosophies and religions setting out to destroy each other. Although he could not decide upon the truth in a philosophic sense, his stories are a protest in name of personal integrity. See *Encyclopaedia Britannica* (11th ed.), XVII, 100–103. See above, Book II, p. 22, note 24.

[27] Deut. 28:36–37; Jer. 16.

that they should direct their thoughts to Him when they were forced to worship statues; and He witnessed that He would be propitious to them.

Curtius: This discussion concerns slaves and captives or those who are driven to wicked practices because of imprisonment and torture. For example, Albuguerius, Viceroy of the eastern Indians, is noted for his extraordinary cruelty because he ordered the amputation of the right hands and left thumbs, the noses and ears of the Christians who had turned to Mohammed, though unwillingly. But these things do not pertain to those who have the opportunity to emigrate elsewhere.

Octavius: Yet prince Naaman could have left, but he did not choose to. Nevertheless, the prophet Elisha excused him, because after he was cured of leprosy, he vowed that he would from then on sacrifice to eternal God.[28] "If, however," he said, "the king of Syria, my oppressor, should sacrifice to the god Rimmon, may you be propitious to me." Elisha said to him: "Go in peace!"[29] From these words it is clear that Elisha excused him who, because of his resources, could have gone safely to Palestine, which borders on Syria, to make sacrifices freely to God. In fact, I do not think that God ordered Abraham to leave his country lest he be compelled to worship the stars, but to free him from the plots of his enemies.

Fridericus: I hold that the one who publicly prostrates himself before the altars and statues of the dead, even if he worships God with a pure heart, sins as much as if he were really an atheist who deserted every religion, since he leads the ignorant away from the true worship of God.

Coronaeus: However great superstition may be, it is more tolerable than atheism. For the one who is bound by some superstition is kept by this awe of the divine in a certain way within the bounds of duty and of the laws of nature. The atheist, on the other hand, who fears nothing except a witness or a judge, necessarily rushes headlong toward every crime.[30] P. 183
Although every man who is truly wise measures the excellence of human actions not only by the ends themselves, but also by all parts and causes, namely, the efficient, the material, the formal, the end, still he determines the principal cause of all actions by the end itself.[31]

[28] IV Kings (II Kings) 5:11–19. [29] IV Kings (II Kings) 5:18–19.

[30] Cf. Plutarch, *Moralia, De superstitione*, V. 167 b.

[31] Aristotle discusses formal, efficient, and final causes in the context of choice (*proairesis*). "Now the cause of action (the efficient not the final cause) is choice, and the cause of choice is desire and reasoning directed to some end." *Eth. Nicom.* VI. ii. 4.

Curtius: What then will happen to the Scriptures which so many times deprecate hypocrisy?[32]

Octavius: The Scriptures deprecate those who worship God with their lips not with their hearts because they put on an appearance of piety and justice as an excuse for their great faults. But he who falls on his knees and prostrates himself before idols and nevertheless worships God with a sincere heart is far removed from the deadly pretense of the hypocrites.

Salomon: Coronaeus uses an argument that is certainly credible. He is a man who is not only an excellent statesman, but also a most religious person, and he believes that superstition, no matter how great, is more tolerable than any atheism. Still an atheist who has completely foresworn God and cast Him from his soul seems to sin less than the man who unites Him with created things in the same worship. In like manner a runaway slave or a military deserter sins less than the man who contemptuously defers to his lord or commander. To be sure, those who join the eternal and true God with false honor of worship by sharing His worship, sin more seriously than those who separate the one worship from the other but desert the worship of the true God and serve those whom they have fashioned as gods for themselves because of an erroneous opinion. Similarly, the wife who has defiled her legitimate marriage by committing adultery is condemned to death; such is not the case with the harlot, who cannot deceive a husband whom she does not have. Thus, two classes of superstitious men are proposed; some are the ungrateful ones who do not search out the true God; others are the insolent ones who know the only and eternal God yet do not hesitate to defile Him with signal abuse by attendance upon most wicked demons and statues. However, those who have any[33] concern for their own dignity and glory customarily take insults more harshly than injuries. Still, that witness of Isaiah shows how important to immortal God is the honor of His own glory. He said: "To whom have you made me equal or in whose likeness have you made me? Do I live if I import my honors to anyone?"[34] Moreover, God often curses those impious men; more often, when He is aroused by excessive jealousy, He curses those who have joined Him to foreign gods in the common service of sacred rites.[35] And how often does He act according to the right of His own majesty, and He thus acts
P. 184 most frequently, placed above men, above the gods feigned by the empty

[32] Job 13:4–12, 15:1–6, 20:12–22, 27:1–4; Prov. 30:7–14; Isaiah 9:17, 33:14; Matt. 6:42, 7:5, 15:7, 16:3, 22:18, 23:13; Luke 6:42, 11:44, 13:15.

[33] *ullam* M

[34] Isaiah 46:5.

[35] *sacrorum* M

opinion[36] of men, and above whatever there is which we see comprehended by this world. As His station is on the loftiest peak of power and honor, He despises other things as very fleeting and changing and far below Himself, and He witnesses that these things have been created for nothing and from nothing and will perish into nothing.[37]

Octavius: I do not doubt that the one who, though knowledgeable and wise, imparts honor equally to the creator and the creature is bound by a more deadly crime than the one who completely casts out the feigned gods together with the true God. And indeed, I would prefer you to say that Octavius had never existed or was rejected by you, Coronaeus, you, who have displayed unusual affection toward me, rather than that I was furious, petulant, irascible, wicked, and an associate of such men. It is also better to lie that there is no God rather than to think He is mortal or corporeal or to hallow Him and the saints in the same worship, the same rites, and at the same altar. Although those who hold statues and stars in the same esteem as gods or join angels and the souls of saints to the eternal God by the same rites, do not act rightly. Still they deserved to be excused in some way because, with pure heart and soul and an upright conscience, they were thus instructed and trained by the priests and thus worship the divinity that was known to them and related to them.

Salomon: I acknowledge that an upright conscience is pleasing to God. Proof of this is that in a chapter of the divine law both he who offended with a word him whom he considered as God and he who pronounced less clearly the eternal name of God should be punished by death.[38] For He distinguished the word *'elohek̲a*, that is, your God, from the most holy name *YHWH*, by which God eternal is indicated. Each chapter[39] is separated from the other, which secret lies hidden to those who are unskilled in the holy language. Consequently, even worship which is offered in good faith to a clay god is not unpleasing to eternal God. Hence we see that when Abraham, Isaac, Jacob, and Joshua made covenants with the pagan worshippers of idols,[40] they bound those by the oath of their own gods, so that those who[41] profaned the clay gods by perjury sinned no less than those who profaned God eternal.[42]

[36] *inani opinione* M

[37] Cf. Persius, *Sat.* III. 83: "Nothing can come from nothing; nothing return to nothing." Also cf. Lucretius, *De rerum nat.* I. 242: "Nothing therefore returns to nothing."

[38] Lev. 24:14–16.

[39] *caput* M

[40] See Gen. 37:31.

[41] *qui* M

[42] Gen. 31:45–54; Josh. 24:16–28.

Octavius: Aristotle recounts a remarkable story.[43] If anyone had written on oath on a paper and had thrown that paper into the fountain of the Palici, the paper fell to the bottom if the oath was false, and the one who had perjured himself died after a short time.

Salomon: If he sins who offends by perjury him whom he considers as one God although he is not God, it is reasonable that honors which are offered to clay gods in a just error and in good faith are not displeasing to God.

P. 185 Curtius: Who can defend himself by a just error when in his worship he prefers and compares the slave to the master, the subject to the king, the creature to the creator?[44]

Octavius: The ancients, with few exceptions, either worshipped foreign divinities or joined them with God. Even those who had come into Samaria on the order of the king of the Assyrians, customarily sacrificed to God eternal at the same time as they sacrificed to the paternal gods.[45] Indeed, this was done by just error, since they had been so instructed and trained by their own priests, that[46] they would seem to be guilty of impiety if they had disobeyed their priests. For everywhere priests are judges of religion, as Lucius Lucullus, the pontifex, said in the Senate.[47] The divine law did not grant judgments of religious matters to anyone except the priests and the Levitical order,[48] although it also stipulated that the punishment for violated religious duty be imposed also by[49] others.

Fridericus: What then did Christ mean when he said that the "one who perceived the commands of the Lord in his mind and understood them thoroughly and did not follow them would be afflicted with severest blows, but the one who was completely ignorant would be beaten but would suffer less, and the ignorant would perish along with his ignorance."[50]

Octavius: Surely, not only is the man who scorned his master's commands which he could have followed worthy of punishment, but also worthy of punishment is he who did not follow them. Still, he who could

[43] *De mirabilibus auscultationibus* LVII. 834b. 8–18.

[44] *creatorem creaturae* M

[45] IV Kings (II Kings) 17:6–18.

[46] *ut* M

[47] Cicero, *Epist. ad Att.* IV. 2. Lucullus was the conqueror of Mithridates. He was also famous for his elegant life-style.

[48] Num. 18:1–2; Deut. 12:12; 18.

[49] *a* M

[50] Luke 12:47–48.

not know them and who was driven into error by the fault of his priests is not worthy of punishment, since he very diligently sought the will and commands of his own God.[51]

Moreover, pontiffs, priests, bishops, teachers of religion and interpreters of religious rites say to the ignorant and unlearned that this is God's will, and they persuade them to offer sacrifices not only to eternal God, but also to Apollo, Diana the virgin, Pallas, angels, demons, statues of men and beasts, corpses, and ashes. Therefore, who can censure this ignorance of illiterate and uncultivated men? Or who can believe they deserve punishments? Who may not rather rebuke the stubbornness and pride of those who have not given assent to the pontiffs and priests, since divine law most solemnly decrees that those who have not obeyed the decrees of the high priests must suffer death.[52]

SENAMUS: This is what I think. Those who have relied on the authority of their pontiffs and follow their commands by worshipping, in good faith, statues and rotten bones in place of God are always excused.

SALOMON: Divine law wished the pontiffs and priests to be of so great erudition and wisdom that they did not provide any excuse for error as often as there was a question about the divine law, although the divine law always excuses the masses and individuals and the ruler of all the people who sin from error.[53] P. 186

TORALBA: I do not doubt that a just error is erased by a just excuse; also that those who have no knowledge or education and who yield to the teachings of their elders and the decrees of their priests have a just cause of error. Still, there is no just cause of error for those educated and especially for those who have been imbued with a knowledge of natural things, from which they could have drawn the clearest ideas about the nature, power, and goodness of one God, as Paul himself openly declares.[54]

SALOMON: Indeed there is a remarkable power of nature inserted in the minds of men which awakens them to piety, justice, and all virtues. Still it is no more possible for man to attain divine knowledge[55] without God's inspiration than for a picture in a dark place to seem distinct without a clear light, even though painted by a skilled hand and with an elegant variety of color. To an assembly of the people Moses spoke to the point when he said: "God had not given you hitherto a heart to understand, or eyes to see, or ears to hear; yet after forty years He had led

[51] I Corinth. 12:1–3. [52] Deut. 17:12. [53] Lev. 5
[54] Rom. 2:14–16. [55] *scientiam* M

back the people from Egypt through the vastest wildernesses into Palestine with great and amazing portents and signs of remarkable wonders."[56] Sometimes, God allows men thus to be so blinded that, even if they acquire knowledge of all great matters, they never enjoy the knowledge of God and true religion, since, elated by the cleverness and subtlety of their mind and arrogant in their pride, they believe that they can grasp divine wisdom by their own effort. Indeed, Job openly confesses that wisdom does not reside in waters nor lands nor demons, whom he calls birds, but is granted by the gift and concession of immortal God alone and the divine lamp enabled him to attain it.[57]

TORALBA: Indeed, I agree that the power of nature is not so great that a man may attain the consummate wisdom of divine affairs without the aid of divine light. We see that Aristotle, who had drunk from the founts of all the ancient philosophers, wrote many things in a clever and logical order but had no knowledge of divine matters, as the discussion has already clearly proved. But Plato, whom Aristotle surpasses by the subtlety of his arguments, had much more sure understanding about God and about the power of immortal[58] souls, which he never could have attained without divine light. For when he wrote the *Phaedo* in the very flower of his early age he said: "Gladly would I have become acquainted with the excellence and nature of that eternal mind, but I could never understand it through myself nor hear it from another; however, there will be
P. 187 no one who can explain by what rites man must worship God unless God Himself offers Himself as leader."[59] He calls this the greatest and most excellent matter of all. The statement of Arrian[60] to Epictetus is consistent with this: "We are advised by God through an angel about the greatest and most noble matters." He expresses the same idea a little later: "Remember eternal God and call on Him as helper." What about Iamblichus? "It is certain that we must do only those things which delight God Himself, and no one can attain them unless he either has heard God Himself or by a certain divine art has obtained this for himself."[61]

SALOMON: The nearer each man comes to God and the more passionately he loves and fears Him, the more fully the light of salvation gleams for

[56] Deut. 29:3–5. [57] Job 28:27–28. [58] *immortalium* M

[59] *Phaedo* VII. 62d; also cf. *Timaeus* 28c.

[60] Arrian (2nd cent. A.D.) governed Cappadocia under Hadrian. He was the pupil of Epictetus, and he preserved Epictetus' *Discourses*. His chief work was the *Anabasis*, his history of Alexander. See *Ox. Class. Dict.*, p. 101.

[61] Iamblichus, *On the Mysteries*, translated by Thomas Taylor (London, 1908), pp. 85–88.

him. How can anyone wonder that this light had failed Aristotle, since he hardly ever is mindful of God; he also mocks Him when he calls Him "animal" or denies that He is just, brave, prudent and wise because of his reliance upon very empty subtleties of the sophists. Indeed, what is more deadly than to think that He from whom wisdom, prudence, justice, and all virtues spring lacks these same qualities?[62] Likewise in the fourteenth book of the *Metaphysics* (the two last books were translated into Latin by the efforts of the Arabs) where there was the chief discussion of God, nothing is ever said except in the final chapter of the eleventh book, and this discussion is so brief that it seems to have bypassed the matter rather than to have touched on it. Plato very often writes about the true God and always with the greatest reverence and fear of the divine, and he glows with anger against the scorners of God; indeed he frequently is accustomed to say: "If God should will, or when it shall have pleased God." Finally he is persuaded that God alone is good and in Him all virtues are contained as examples and causes.[63] Therefore, who can doubt that there was great wisdom and perspicacity of the divine in him who was so dear to God and to whom God was so dear?

SENAMUS: Although Plato wrote and felt so admirably about God, we see that he sacrificed to Apollo, Pallas, and the other gods and attended sacred rites; nevertheless in rather secret letters he urged his friends to the worship and knowledge of the one eternal God.[64]

SALOMON: No one ought to think it strange if the divine light shone more abundantly for Plato than for the other philosophers, since he pursued God in all his writings with such reverence that Numenius the Academician[65] did not hesitate to call him the Attic Moses. Still our lawgiver, as well as Solomon, did not at any time indicate that God is found by those who are driven with all the power of the mind to a searching and reverence of Him.[66] Indeed, fear overtakes me as I speak about God and realize that nothing which can correspond to so great a majesty can

[62] These remarks about Aristotle seem groundless and unfair. When Aristotle speaks of God as "animal" (living) he indicates God's life-giving nature to the universe and his immortality. These remarks seem out of character to Salomon.

[63] Cf. *Epinomis*, 977a; *Leges* X. 886–899b; *Res pub.* II. 379C ff.

[64] Epist. 2:314.

[65] Numenius of Apamea (c. A.D. 150–200) is the immediate precursor of Neoplatonism and treated the philosophies of Plato and Pythagoras as identical. He had great interest in eastern religions and Judaism. Numenius maintained that there were three gods—the Father, the Creator, and the Created World. See *Ox. Class. Dict.*, p. 614.

[66] See Deut. 29:3.

proceed from the speech and mind of men, whether the question is measured by the weight of thoughts or words. Moreover, granted that someone
P. 188 is endowed with this religion and goodness of nature, that he is moved with all the effort of his soul to the love of God, that the richness of his speech and the light of his word can extol the praises of God, that he embraces with the fullness of his speech all His deeds, judgments, laws, His remarkable concern for all things, that he can comprehend the infinite power and wisdom of that One by his thought, words, and writings, finally that he displays the majesty of so great a divinity for all to view, nevertheless he may strive in vain unless God himself has inspired the ears and minds of his hearers.

CORONAEUS: As we seem to be one and the same in the love and necessity of our pursuits, let us see to it that we feel one and the same about divine matters and that we feel rightly[67] and become at length similar to that all-powerful and best Founder of all things. Indeed, in this similarity Plato seems to have placed the highest and final good for men.

CURTIUS: This is the same opinion of Christ and of a certain most astute theologian. He said: "We shall be like Him, when He shall have appeared."[68]

SALOMON: I do not see why we ought to place the greatest good of man in this, since nothing can be completely similar and common to the Creator and the created, as Rabbi Moses often said. Moreover, it is truer that the final good for man rests in the enjoyment of eternal God. David said: "I shall be satisfied when Your glory shall have appeared."[69]

SENAMUS: I had learned from Aristotle that the highest good of man resides in the action[70] of virtue.

TORALBA: But Aristotle does not uphold the consistencies of his principles, since in other cases he has established the highest good to be in the action of the mind. Indeed, he used this manner of speaking lest he seem to say the same things as his teacher, Plato, whose entire principles he tried to overturn although he still thought the same way. No one doubts that this very action of the mind is contemplation which he improperly calls action. Neither one seems to have touched on the true good of man because, although work is related to leisure, motion to repose, action to

[67] *et recte sentiamus* M

[68] I John 3:2; also cf. John 3:3, 7:16–17, 28–29, 38; Heb. 2:17.

[69] Psalm 16 (17):15.

[70] *actione* M. See *Eth. nic.* I. 7. 1098a. 15; VII. 12. 115 3a. 10; X. 7. 1177a. 12; *Polit.* IV. 2. 1295a. 35.

contemplation, that very contemplation can still be of mean and vile things; and even if that contemplation be about the greatest and best thing of all, since it is related to another, it cannot be said to be the final good. In this matter Aristotle again slipped into a serious error because he confused the end of man with his highest good.[71]

SENAMUS: Can there be one end for man but another final good?

TORALBA: Why not? The ends of all created things are outside the things themselves. Indeed, nothing happens on account of itself. The good of each thing depends upon itself and is sought solely for its advantage, not for that of another since each man loves himself more than that good which he seeks for his own happiness. Grass grows to feed the flock; cattle to serve as food for men; beasts of burden to aid men and die for P. 189
them. Still no one has said that this end of the beasts is their final good, since the good that is common to all things is to be well according to the nature of each thing. So also the end of man is to have served the glory of God. That One said: "I have made all things on account of Myself, also the wicked for the day of vengeance."[72] The wicked man is undoubtedly consumed by the flames or submerged in the sea; for example, Pharaoh had this end with his legions, and for this end they had been born, made, and brought forth. For thus God said to Pharaoh: "I have beset you for this reason—to show My power in you and to scatter the glory of My name everywhere."[73] Yet no one could have said that Pharaoh had attained his highest good. From this it also follows that those are undoubtedly in error who say that the content or subject of moral philosophy is the highest good. God of Himself is this, and nothing else can be considered the highest good.

SENAMUS: Then what will be the subject of moral wisdom?

TORALBA: A man that is to be happy.

SENAMUS: Why so?

TORALBA: Since every discipline which is related to action has as subject that for which the good of the action itself is acquired in the first place. However, it does not have as subject the good itself; for example, health is not sought for itself but for man. Another error of Aristotle is discovered in the fact that he placed the highest good in that thing for the sake of which you desire[74] other things; but that thing itself you desire for itself, not for the sake of another thing.[75] This statement is in error because the

[71] *Eth. nic.* X. 7. 1177a 12–1178a 8; I. 7. 1097b–1098a 15.
[72] Prov. 16:4.
[73] Ex. 19:4.
[74] *concupias* M
[75] See above, notes 69–71.

enjoyment of God, in which the psalmist and Solomon place supreme human happiness,[76] is sought by man on account of man, not on account of enjoyment itself. When these errors have been removed, the other things which pertain to that happiness become easier. Indeed, since the divine law urged man to pursue noble deeds and avoid base goals,[77] it adds that thus you will be well because nothing can be added to God, nothing subtracted from Him. Therefore, the action of virtue is not the final good for man; since it is related to contemplation as motion is related to repose, contemplation is related to the recognition of the best, that is, to the recognition of God; recognition is related to the love of Him; extraordinary love is related to enjoyment. Indeed, for what purpose do you love except that you enjoy the thing loved? Moreover, in this enjoyment the highest pleasure of the soul abides in reflected motion, that is, in the clearest effusion of the light and love of God toward us, which we obtain by suffering, not by acting.

SENAMUS: But since this happiness of divine enjoyment touches no mortal as long as the soul is confined in the squalid hovel of the body,[78] who will ever be happy?

SALOMON: Yet surely that happiness happened only to a few; for example, to Moses alone when awake,[79] to the other prophets when sleeping;
P. 190 yet not to all did it happen. Isaiah said: "I see God on the sublime seat of majesty, and my eyes have seen God, the King of the armies."[80] Likewise Ezechiel in a longer speech boasts that he has attained this blessedness.[81] The stage of prophecy nearest to this happiness is when the divine light, with an intervening angel joined to the human mind, illuminates during sleep.

SENAMUS: What will become of Aristotle who taught that a happy life consists therefore in the action of virtue lest the sleeping seem to be happy?[82]

SALOMON: That one was so far from the understanding of the true and highest good that he confused the ends of good and evil with the final good and evil, as Toralba explained. Why, he even thought the duty of man, his end, and happiness were one and the same because it is man's duty to live according to virtue which he calls the highest good.

FRIDERICUS: I believe that the highest good of man finds its goal in the

76 Psalm 15 (16).
77 Cf. Prov. 4.
78 *squallenti corporis gurgustio* M
79 Ex. 3:2–6.
80 Isaiah 6:1.
81 Ezech. 1:1–28; 2:1–9.
82 See above, note 69.

knowledge of God through Christ. That one said: "This is life eternal, that they recognize You as true God and the One whom You have sent, Jesus Christ."[83]

SALOMON: About Christ is another matter. But the knowledge of God is the nearest step to that happiness which we seek. Indeed the Teacher of Wisdom spoke thus: "To have known God is consummate justice; and the recognition of your power is the root of immortality."[84] Still that knowledge leads to worship, worship to love, love to enjoyment which produces the highest pleasure of the soul, or rather is the very enjoyment of pleasure.

TORALBA: Therefore, it is my opinion that those first parents of the golden age, whom we have mentioned earlier, Abel, Enoch and Job without the law and Moses had without Christ secured most purely that true enjoyment of divine pleasure by the law of nature.

SALOMON: I do not disagree with you. For when we read that Abraham cherished the law of the most high,[85] what does this mean except that he followed the example of the law of nature? And indeed Philo the Hebrew said: "The commands of the two tables in no way differ from nature, and there is no need to endeavor to spend one's life according to the precepts of divine laws, since these laws contain nothing other than the law of nature and the life of our elders."[86] However, in Moses' time the law of nature had been so defiled by the shameful crimes of men that it seemed to be completely obliterated from men's souls and antiquated, as it were, because of its duration. For this reason, God, the greatest and best, pitying the vicissitude of men, wished to renew the same law of nature by His own word and decalogue which He had incised on stone tablets; and especially the prohibitions which prevent us from violating nature. Therefore, when men had become deaf to the law of nature, the divine P. 191
voice was necessary so that those who had scorned nature might hear the parent of nature resounding his own words.

OCTAVIUS: Mohammed imitates Moses. When he realized that natural laws, that is, divine laws, had fallen into ruin and dead men were worshipped in place of eternal God, he renewed the law of nature concerning the worship of one eternal God and removed the most harmful sacred rites for the dead. Thus the fourth *Azora*[87] clearly witnesses that he worships the God of Abraham and recalls the life of Abraham for use, but he

[83] John 17:3.
[84] Wisdom 15:3.
[85] Gen. 22; Sirach 44.
[86] Cf. *De vita Mosis* III. 14.
[87] *Azoara quarta* M

says that he is only a messenger and servant of God and also inferior to the other prophets.

CURTIUS: We have the best interpreter of the divine law, Christ, and we cannot desire any one greater or better. He is none other than God himself born from time eternal who took the form of man only to save the human race from eternal death and destruction.

FRIDERICUS: I am of the same mind, and my idea about religion is not different from that of Curtius, except that he favors, I believe, the Swiss view. I, however, favor the Lutheran notion which approves of aural confession, but not an enumeration of every single fault. Likewise, I believe that the true body of Christ is present in the appearance of bread with the mystical utterance of words, which belief the Swiss church rejects. I also think that statues ought to be allowed for imitation but not for worship, although the Swiss teachers of the new religion completely reject statues.

CORONAEUS: I promise that you will approve of the Catholic religion of the Roman church, in which I was born and educated, and to which I have always given assent, if you will have any faith, which has always been greatest through sacred Scripture,[88] the decrees of the councils, and the spirits and opinions of the most holy fathers which have been harmonious for fifteen centuries.

Indeed, its firmest foundations have been established by Christ Himself, the Head of the whole church. Then the church was built with walls, as it were, by the apostles and disciples, and roofed and completed by the Roman pontiffs. Thirty-three of these pontiffs are remembered as having been killed for the name of Christ,[89] and innumerable bishops and pontiffs of all nations have supported this same church by their conduct, by miracles, and by divine writings. I call to mind Irenaeus of Lyon who proclaimed the apostolic faith from the Roman succession; Augustine of Hippo, who writes that the preeminence of the apostolic church flourished in the Roman church; Ignatius and Chrysostom of Antioch, Petrus Alexander, Athanasius, Theophilus of Alexandria, Macarius and Cyril of Jerusalem, Gregory and Basil of Cappadocia, Polycarp of Smyrna, Justin of Athens, Dionysius of Corinth, Gregory of Nyssa, Methodius of Tyre, Epiphanius in Cyprus. But to mention all would be an endless task.

P. 192 At this point SENAMUS, who had hesitated for a while, but had wanted

[88] *scripturis sacris* M

[89] Since both lists of popes and of martyrs are to a degree legendary, that thirty-three popes died for their faith is unverifiable. See *Cath. Encycl.*, IX, 741–42.

to speak, said: I believe that all the religions of all people, the natural religion which Toralba loves, the religion of Jupiter and the gentile gods, whom the Indians of the Orient and the Tartars cherish, the religion of Moses, the religion of Christ, the religion of Mohammed, which everyone pursues not with faked pretense but with a pure mind, are not unpleasing to eternal God and are excused as just errors. Still that religion which is the best is the most pleasing to Him of all. Hence I was accustomed to go eagerly to all the shrines, temples, and little chapels of all religions, wherever they are, so as not to be considered an atheist by wicked example and also that others may hold in awe the divine. I trust that this endeavor of mine will be approved by each best man, not only from those things which have been mentioned before, but especially from the fact that the eternal God seems to me to have blessed with virtues, power, empire, wealth, and victory the people who are most religious, whatever superstition of fictile gods they employ. But those who had deserted the worship of their own religion and also the worship of empty gods in which they thought some divinity resided always were disturbed by unusual misfortunes of war, sickness, poor crops, unproductive flocks, and internal strife. All the historians plainly agree on this statement.

Toralba: If true religion is natural religion, and this is settled by positive proofs, as not only Octavius but also Salomon himself confesses, what is the need for Jupiter, Christ, Mohammed, mortal and fictile gods? Who of all the theologians can unfold the majesty, power, goodness, wisdom, and the remarkable judgment of God, and finally His greatest concern for all things better or more accurately than Job? Who likewise entwined more secrets of natural and divine things in allegory than he? Who of mortal men has worshipped eternal God more purely? Nevertheless, that Arab[90] who was more ancient than Moses lived by no other law than the law of nature, the law of Abel. Still, God, the fairest judge of integrity and piety, praised Job's justice, religion and purity more than any other mortal's. Job neither hoped nor ever thought that Christ, who was born two thousand years afterwards, would come—much less Mohammed. Moreover, when he comprehended the remarkable size of the sun and the stars, their height and swiftness, he said: "May I perish if, when viewing the splendor and beauty of the sun and stars, I should fall down and worship them; this is a sin to be punished by death for I should have foresworn God the most high."[91]

[90] Job was from the Land of Uz, which was somewhere in Edom or Arabia.
[91] Job. 31:26–28.

FRIDERICUS: Because Toralba uses this very book of Job and its authority (and no book is more divine than this) and honors the more sacred majesty of letters, does he really think that he ought to be separated from the groups of philosophers?

P. 193 TORALBA: I do not disapprove of the more holy books of better merits, yet I do not agree with them on account of the authority of the documents. Indeed, I cannot do this, and I would not even want to if I could. But because I am led by sure reasons and since I have often disputed with the Epicureans who consider the sacred writings to be fables, I wish to crush the Epicureans not by the authority of books but by clear arguments. Also I want approbation to be stripped from them, as it were, when an examination has been applied. As a result, fact may contend with fact, cause with cause, reason with reason. Indeed he who believes that God is Three and One since this has been revealed by God Himself must establish by necessary proofs that this has been revealed by God, for we give assent to this more readily as to a conclusion on account of its principles. If these principles shall not be more certain than the conclusion, nothing will be accomplished because the conclusion would be resolved into the principles. Likewise, these are equally as uncertain as the others.

CURTIUS: In divine matters which are most removed from demonstration, we ought to use St. Luke's words: "Lord, add to my faith."[92]

SALOMON: We have said earlier that all faith depends upon clear arguments or blameless perceptions or divine oracles and that faith is not infused unless through the divine voice of prophecy given by God to man, which is more certain than any knowledge. However, since divine prophecies are very rare now, we must rely on the divine responses of the prophets which our forefathers left to posterity with supreme faith, since Christians reject the Koran, the Ismaelites the New Testament, and the Hebrews both.

OCTAVIUS: Indeed, the Ismaelites reject these books of the Gospels as completely corrupted by heretics, while Christian hands wear them thin. The Ismaelites think the true Gospels, which, nevertheless, they themselves do not have, have perished completely.

FRIDERICUS: Why, therefore, does Mohammed show Gabriel speaking thus: "If you have any doubt concerning the laws and edicts which have been sent to you, read the books of your elders, and you will hesitate no more." Likewise the *Azora* which begins thus: "Destiny has given you

[92] Luke 17:5.

the *amr*; God the merciful, living, highest, has given you first the Old Testament, next the New Testament, finally the true *Fātiha*,[93] the confirmer of your law." Therefore, each of the testaments, the old and new, either must be completely accepted or completely rejected. Notwithstanding, nothing has been expressed in the New Testament writings which we deem inconsistent with divine laws and prophetic inspirations.

SALOMON: The Ismaelites, Christians, and Jews approve the ancient writings of our elders. However, when the reliability of the Koran and the new writings are considered dubious, we must use the old writings, and witnesses greater than any exception must be employed. Moreover, we must search out these witnesses from the true church whose authority is so great that, if the records of all the Scriptures and letters should perish, P. 194 the truth and memory of things done by the church still existent would reside forever with posterity. For this reason Moses said in a gathering of the peoples: "You will tell these things to your sons, lest anyone think that the divine law will perish with the Scriptures."[94] Likewise God witnesses thus to Israelites through Isaiah: "I summon you as witnesses of My deeds."[95] God did not say this because He needed witnesses to make firm the honor of His majesty but to make clear the church of the Hebrews had been established and chosen[96] by immortal God. He was rousing the Israelites still living to witness that they might bring to light for all nations the acts, deeds, and laws not only from written laws but also from the glorious voice of God, even if the writings perished completely. Yet God, the most wise, provided that the sacred Scriptures would not be destroyed since He ordered them to be cut in stone and flint and to be unfolded and explained to every generation and to every sex.[97] Hence, it may seem incredible though it is true, in so many calamities, exiles, changes and final overthrow of the state itself, the books of divine law remain unimpaired and indeed have been translated into languages of all people. Even the Christians and Ismaelites lay the foundations of their religions in them.

FRIDERICUS: Indeed there was a church of God among the people of Israel before Christ, and this church has now been transferred to the Christians; moreover, divine law[98] is nothing other than a prototype of the Gospel, as Origen says. But when the Jews not only repudiated the

[93] *Fatiha* M. *Amr*, the "word," is one of the mediate beings between God and man. From *amr* comes *rūh*, the "spirit."

[94] Deut. 4:9–10. [95] Isaiah 55:4. [96] *selectamque* M

[97] Ex. 24:12–18. [98] *lex* M

Messiah,[99] the preserver of the human seed, even the head of the whole church sent from heaven from Abraham's seed, but also afflicted Him with disgrace and shameful death, God also rejected them and cast them away deservedly so that the other nations might enjoy the benefit of divine salvation.

SALOMON: We surely do not envy other nations their salvation, but we desire it with eager entreaties, and we pray continually for them.

FRIDERICUS: We can easily do without your prayers and entreaties. Indeed we even think that the entreaties of Jews would be harmful rather than helpful to Christians.[100] Did you not read in Isaiah that there would be a time when it would be said: "Blessed My people of Egypt, the work of My hands, Assyria."[101] Likewise in the last chapter: "I shall gather together all nations and tongues which will come and see My glory, and I shall send to them so that My name can be proclaimed and My praise made known everywhere. And from their number I shall choose My Levites and priests."[102]

SALOMON: It is worthwhile to add this which Fridericus passed over
P. 195 in those prophecies of Isaiah: "Blessed, My people of Egypt, and the work of My hands, Assyria, and My inheritance, Israel."[103] God said this because He is the Creator and common Parent of the peoples. And so He wished the same law to exist for citizens and foreigners, and He wished both to consult the law.[104] Nevertheless, by a certain unique selection He received unto Himself the Israelites who were chosen from all people, and He bestowed upon them the name of His own property and inheritance and His first-born and a certain singular honor before others. He said: "My first-born son is Israel, a holy tribe, a priestly nation."[105] Since these things are true, who could think that immortal God would ever be unmindful of His people, His flocks,[106] His inheritance and desert His own tribe, His own church? When long ago the neighbors of the Israelites saw the cities of our elders leveled to the ground by the enemy, the temple plundered and burned, and the remnants of the people led into slavery by the Chaldeans, they charged with haughty reproach that Israel had been rejected by God. Yet God confirms to Jeremiah with every

[99] *Messiam* M

[100] Fridericus is the only scholar at Coronaeus' home who displays feelings that appear personally hostile to Jews.

[101] Isaiah 19:25.

[102] Isaiah 67:18, 21.

[103] Isaiah 19:25. Fridericus did indeed omit "my inheritance, Israel."

[104] Ex. 4:23.

[105] Ex. 19:5–6.

[106] *sui populi, sui peculi* M

assurance that the fixed courses of the heavenly orbs and the swift revolutions of the stars would stop before He would forget Israel.[107] Likewise, He said if the vast breadth of heaven shall be able to be measured or the depth of the earth plumbed, I shall also cast away My people Israel.[108] And although He threatens severe and harsh calamities upon His people if they depart from His law, still He confirmed by solemn oath that He would never forget His people and His covenant with Abraham.[109] And in truth, He never was unmindful of His own nation; moreover, wherever it has been scattered, we[110] are disciplined in this same divine law in which our elders have reposed for about four thousand years, and sacred and profane writers testify to this fact. Indeed Tacitus says: "The Jews worship one God, one Spirit eternal, unutterable, everlasting, and they hold profane those who worship and reverence images." And although the Hebrews, Ismaelites, and Christians do not hesitate to believe that Abraham is the father of their church, yet the Hebrews alone have always cherished the same law and religion. The Christians and Ismaelites have always fostered numerous sects—the Arians, Nestorians, Sabellians,[111] Manichaeans, Donatists, Ebionites, Novatianites, and Nazarenes.[112] But

[107] Jer. 31:36. [108] Jer. 31:37. [109] Lev. 26:44–45.

[110] *qui* M

[111] For these heresies see Book IV, p. 232, note 444.

[112] The Manichaeans were so called from their founder, the Persian Mani, in the 3rd century A.D. They claimed to be the synthesizers of all religions then known, and Manichaeism consisted of Zoroastrian dualism, Babylonian folklore, Buddhist ethics, and some elements of Christianity. They believed that before the existence of heaven and earth, there were two Principles, the Good and the Bad. See *Cath. Encycl.*, IX, 591–96. The Manichaeans are out of place in this list of sects of the Christians and Ismaelites, for they never belonged to either group.

The Donatists were a powerful sect that arose in the Christian church in Africa in the 4th century A.D. The Donatists held that the validity of all sacerdotal acts depended upon the character of the agent; from this belief came their insistence that those who had handed over their copies of the Scriptures under the compulsion of the Diocletian persecution were not eligible to perform sacerdotal acts. See *Encycl. Brit.* (11th ed.), VIII, 410–11.

The Ebionites were the ultra-Jewish party in the early Christian church and called themselves "Poor Men," perhaps claiming to be the true representatives of those who had been blessed in the Sermon on the Mount. Although they admitted the world to have been made by the true God, they did not accept the preexistence of Jesus as Logos and Sophia. They kept both the Jewish Sabbath and the Christian Lord's day, but they rejected both Paul, as an apostate from the Mosaic law, and his epistles, and used only the Gospel of Matthew. When the old church of Jerusalem was scattered in A.D. 135 by the edict of Hadrian, the more conservative element, the Ebionites, became more and more isolated and exclusive.

The Ebionites closely resembled the Nazarenes, also an obscure Jewish-Christian

why should I mention the almost hundred twenty sects which Tertullian[113] recorded and the even greater number which Epiphanius[114] enumerated in the beginning of the young church of Christ? Indeed, Themistius,[115] a noble Peripatetic, did not present a more forceful argument to restrain Valens Augustus from killing and proscribing the Christians than to state that Christians cherished more than three hundred sects, each differing from the other. Now what church could consist of so great a variety of opinions differing among themselves? Why, even in this time,
P. 196 the Swiss church refutes the Roman church, the Lutheran opposes both. The Catholics oppose the Anabaptists; the Puritans oppose the superstitious, and the Abyssinians the Greeks, the Greeks the Latins, and in turn, all are refuted by all. Among the Ismaelites there is no less variety of sects. When Mohammed died, 'Alī, the son of Mohammed's sister and Habital, proclaiming himself a prophet, established a very powerful sect which was most hostile to the followers of Mohammed. These two sects gradually were increased by the disciples, Lesharion and Imanian, who rival each other in deadly hatreds; moreover, in addition to both these sects sixty-two other sects are counted. Elhesiba Abilaben[116] abrogated many things from the laws[117] of Mohammed. After eighty years Elhari Ibim founded a new sect, which after the hundredth year was suppressed

---

sect, existing at the time of Epiphanius (4th century A.D.). Indeed there is insufficient evidence for dividing the Ebionites into two separate communities, namely, the Ebionites and the Nazarenes, although there were grades of Christological thought among them.

The Novatianites were founded in the beginning of the 3rd century by Novatianus, a Roman presbyter and one of the earliest antipopes. During the Decian persecution Novatianus maintained the view that those who had sacrificed to idols after baptism should be excluded from ecclesiastical communion. He allowed himself to be consecrated bishop, in opposition to Cornelius, by a minority opinion, but he was excommunicated along with his followers by the synod held at Rome in A.D. 251. After his death as a martyr under Valerian, the Novatianites spread rapidly over the empire. They called themselves Puritans and rebaptized their converts from the Catholic view. However, because of the liberal spirit prevailing in the Council of Nicaea, the clergy of the "Puritans" were readmitted to the Catholic church and the sect finally disappeared two centuries after its origin. See *Encycl. Brit.* (11th ed.), VIII, 842–43; XIX, 319, 832.

113 *De bapt.* XV. Library of the Fathers, Tertullian, I (Oxford, 1842), note G, pp. 280–297.

114 In the middle of the 4th century Epiphanius wrote a book on heresies, but its accuracy is difficult to determine because he did not quote his authorities by name.

115 Themistius was a Neoplatonist who lived at Constantinople in the 4th century A.D. He was one of the followers of Iamblicus.

116 *Elhesibu Abilaben* M

117 *legibus* M

by capital decrees and punishments of priests and caliphs. Then after the fiftieth year the sect was reinstated, and after twenty years it was again rejected. The discords could not be quelled in any way except that the theologian Elgazuli as arbiter in seven books called the priests interpreters of the laws, but sectarian castigators of the Mohammedan law.[118] Nevertheless, the common people were not allowed to follow this sect, but only the educated.[119] Why only the educated? Or if the law of Mohammed had been given by the angel Gabriel, as indeed that one falsely declares, what need was there for human castigators? Esseh Renardus also established one sect, and Ibn Farid[120] another. Ibn Farid wrote that all religions of all peoples are pleasing to God, if any one thinks there is some God and worships him with a sincere heart. Moreover, he calls the stars, heavens, and elements gods. But let me not go on forever. I will become tedious if I try to be able to enumerate all the sects of the Ismaelites which Eleofanus the theologian clearly seems to explain in seven books as best he could. It is clear from this that neither the Ismaelites nor Christians have any established religion which they follow, much less an established church amidst such variety.

FRIDERICUS: The surest proofs of the church and true religion are first in the teaching of Christ, which is consistent with divine laws, then in the legitimate use of the sacraments, and in the continuous multitude of the elect, establishing one and the same teaching of Christ. Almost all people except the Jews, pagans, and Epicureans, believe that Christ fulfilled Abraham's covenant and by His benefit all nations would secure the happiness promised from on high. The church, that is to say, the Roman, Zwinglian, Lutheran, Greek, Abyssinian—not only these—but also the Arians, Manicheans, Donatists, Nestorians, Sabellians, Eutychians, Pelagians—not only these, but also the Saracens, founded by Mohammed, witness that Christ is Messiah. In addition to those is also a good part of the Jews, the Apostles, disciples of Christ, and founders of the Christian church. And indeed, if any Jew has given himself for adoption into the [Christian] P. 197
community, he must first confess that Christ, the son of the Virgin Mary, is the true Messiah. Even if Christians disagree among themselves, for this reason I say that the church, undisturbed and stable, which consists of the invisible community of the elect, must not ever[121] be overturned.

118 *legum interpretes, sectarios vero legis* M

119 For a concise article on the various sects see *Encycl. Brit.* (11th ed.), XVIII, 421–24.

120 *Ibim Faridus* M

121 *unquam* M

Curtius: We shall find no church at all if we wish to count all the divisions of lesser opinions. Moreover, that old multitude of Israelites also would not deserve the name of church, since it also had its sects, namely, the Nazarenes, Pharisees, Sadducees, Essenes, Samaritans, Herodians, and Hemerobaptists.

Salomon: We must separate the sectarians from the heretics. The heretics are completely separated from the church, but not so the sectarians. Rather they are separated from the filth of the people by living a purer life. For example, the divine law designates them as Nazarenes, that is, separated, because they vowed constant abstinence from wine for some days or months or years or forever, in which time they were not allowed to cut their beard or hair. And so this one sect has been instituted by immortal God, whose members are holier than the rest; indeed the Pharisees, that is, the separated ones, and the Essenes, that is, the workers, imitated this sect, and they [Essenes] led the holiest life of all people, not in feigned action, but in works themselves. The Essenes established communities apart and enjoyed the same mode of living as the monks, without any change of attire. The Hemorobaptists differed from the rest only in that they washed their bodies daily. The name of the Sadducees is from *tzedeq*, which means just, because the Sadducees wanted to be considered more just than the rest. Many people, however, thought this was ironic, as in the case of the kings of Egypt who had killed their brother or father or mother and called themselves *Philadelphi, Philopatres*, and *Philomatri*.[122] Therefore, you know that all those men differed in the holiness of their life, not in the variety of religions. Otherwise if those must be called heretics, one must brand with the name of heresy the orders of innumerable monks who differ in mode of living and dress. The Samaritans are not Jews in race or religion, nor are they a part of the assembly of the Ismaelites. For indeed, they join a throng of gods to the worship of eternal God, as do the Roman Catholics, who have added angels and hierarchies of saints to the worship of eternal God and even, prostrating themselves, kiss statues and have crusts of bread for gods. The Zwinglians consider this the greatest impiety. The Roman Catholics pursue the Zwinglians, Lutherans, and Greeks with decrees of death at the stake. Therefore, these or those are responsible for impiety.[123] But the purest and simplest religion of the Hebrews has no mingling of the impure, no heresies added; it recognizes nothing except the worship of one God.

[122] The three words mean brotherly love, fatherly love, motherly love.
[123] *sunt igitur hi, aut illi impietatis rei* M

CURTIUS: Let us grant that boast of Salomon, that the Israelites had been chosen by a certain unique kindness of God. However, they fell away of their own will from that heavenly gift when they oppressed Christ, God and man, who had offered himself to them as savior of the human race, with false witnesses and lies and gave him the most disgraceful punishment. And in no way is it surprising that God, moved by the enormity of so great a crime, allowed more than a million Jews to be killed in the passage of one year when Vespasian besieged and conquered Jerusalem.[124] At that time the cities of Palestine and the temple itself fell to sword and fire; the city was leveled, and the remnants of the people were led into slavery and scattered throughout the world. The very greatest proof of divine wrath is the fact that they had been not only cut off from the holiest religion and utterly destroyed, but also were forbidden by the agreement of almost all rulers to possess any plot of land anywhere in the world. Wherefore, who can doubt that great calamities had befallen them because of Christ's death? P. 198

SALOMON: More than five hundred years before Christ was born, our elders had suffered much graver injuries from the Chaldeans who had brought death and flames to the temple, the cities, and towns, and had laid waste the whole region and led the people into slavery.[125] But afterwards, we returned little by little and rebuilt the towns, the city, and the temple itself. After he had captured and destroyed Jerusalem, Antiochus, whose cognomen was Epiphanes, slaughtered ninety thousand Jews in three days. Likewise Ptolemy, the son of Lagus, king of Egypt, displayed such great cruelty against our elders that he even forced his soldiers to eat Jewish babies. These things happened two hundred years before Christ was born.[126] However, if a religion must be rejected on account of calamities of this sort, no religion ought to be rejected more deservedly than the Christian religion, since for more than three hundred years continual

[124] A.D. 70.

[125] Jer. 39:8; IV Kings (II Sam.) 25:1–26.

[126] Concerning Epiphanes and Ptolemy, see Book IV, note 38. Also see Josephus, *De bello Jud.* I. Anti-Semitism is indeed more than two thousand years old. Cf. Esther 3:6: "for he heard that he [Mordecai] was of the nation of the Jews, and he chose rather to destroy all the nation of the Jews that were in the kingdom of Assuerus." Leaving this passage out of account, we may say that Egypt, especially Alexandria, was the seat of anti-Semitism. The earliest anti-Semitic author was the Egyptian priest, Manetho (270–250 B.C.). For a discussion of anti-Semitism, see James Hastings, ed., *Encyclopedia of Religion and Ethics* (Edinburgh, 1909), I, 593–99.

deaths, punishments, torments, proscriptions, and intolerable cruelties were decreed against the Christians throughout the whole world.[127]

FRIDERICUS: Indeed, they give credit for this to the Jews, whose synagogues Augustine called the rabble of Christian persecutions.[128]

SALOMON: How can this be possible, since the Jews were judged to be enemies of the Romans by a senate decree, first under Claudius, next under Trajan, afterwards even under the emperor Hadrian?[129]

CURTIUS: Salomon, if faith in your religion was stable or sure, or if the religion of Christians was not the surest of all, why did the apostles of Jewish seed and blood and the disciples and those first bishops, the founders of the Christian religion, embrace Christ with the most burning love?
P. 199 Why have innumerable men of your race and name in times past and also in these times allowed themselves to be adopted by Christian priests and with the highest praise confess Christ publicly in words and writings?

SALOMON: Indeed it ought to seem more strange why so few fall away from us or rather from God, since they are beset by so many insults and poverty. Moreover, we admit that those travails were imposed upon our nation in the first place by the Chaldeans for the reason that many had fallen away from the true worship of God, and we have witness of this from the words and writings of the prophets. Thus we also think that our elders suffered the dire slavery of the Romans because they had, with few exceptions, turned away from immortal God to the worship and adoration of a mortal man.

CURTIUS: But why did the Jewish nation alone of all suffer so many and so great calamities?

SALOMON: God Himself, unfolding the reason, said: "Sons of Israel, I have known you of all peoples, and for this reason I shall punish in you

[127] The Edict of Milan in A.D. 313 issued certain regulations in favor of the Christians, and they were allowed for the most part to worship without persecution. Between A.D. 325 and 330, the Christian capital of the East, new Rome, was built and called Constantinople after its founder.

[128] Cf. *Sancti Augustini Operum Tomus V-VI.* (Paris, 1683); *Sermo LXXXIX de verbis Evang. Matt.* 483b, 484c–e.

[129] The Roman government, notably Caesar and Augustus, upheld the privileges of the Jews and protected them and their synagogues from violence. Gaius, however, disliked the Jews because they refused to worship him, and he took away many of their former privileges, but Claudius reaffirmed these. Bodin's reference should have been to Gaius rather than to Claudius. In A.D. 115–116 the Jews of Cyprus, Cyrenaica, and Egypt rebelled. Hadrian then imposed harsh penal laws prohibiting circumcision, but these were allowed to lapse by Pius, and thereafter the Jews enjoyed toleration.

the crimes of all."[130] The worship of God has led us to be separated from those nations. Balaam, the Chaldean prophet, had comprehended this a long time ago when he said: "This people will live alone and will not be counted among the other nations."[131] Likewise, although God had made the other nations subject to the strength[132] and powers of the heavenly stars, still He released the Israelites. He said: "Lest you worship the sun, moon, and stars which God indeed prepared for other peoples, who are restrained by the most ample protection of heaven, He has joined you to Himself and has snatched you from the fiery furnace for you to be an hereditary and select people."[133]

Coronaeus: I have always stumbled at this point. I did not know what God willed when He said that the heavenly stars had been granted to other peoples but that Israel had been chosen by Him with a certain unique prerogative.

Salomon: The Hebrew theologians interpret that passage to indicate that other peoples are governed by the laws and powers of the heavenly stars. The Israelites alone and those who wish to be enrolled in their assemblage are freed from the laws of the heavenly stars that they may have God alone as the Author of life and happiness and not fear those phenomena with which the astrologers threaten—the oppositions and conjunctions of the planets. Indeed it is a pleasure to mention in a certain way in verse those kindnesses that have been received:

I have often borne easy triumphs, since I have been
saved from the cruel enemy and in no way did the stars
execute their power against me.
Good men must not fear harsh fates. The wrath of the P. 200
awesome prince did not terrify the undaunted, nor did the
robbers' conspiring hands, thirsty for fresh blood,
    harm me.
The legion, which was spreading a bloodbath throughout
the great city and was slaughtering citizens everywhere,
    caused me no fear.
Already an armed cohort, seeking an entrance, had
    surrounded me when the divine will from the shining
    citadel snatched away the enemies' senses and con-
    founded their minds,

[130] Amos 3:2. [131] Num. 23:9. [132] *viribus* M [133] Deut. 4:19–20.

And protected me with a heavenly shield and heavenly weapons
and abundantly filled me with its own wealth.
Why should I mention every single thing?
The divine will filled my heart with a holy breath and
explained the secrets and hidden recesses of the law in
which is the human hope for eternal salvation.
With my winged teacher as constant guide
We renew eternal honors for this.

CORONAEUS: You have elegantly sung heroic kindnesses in heroic verses. But since the favors of divine goodness toward the Israelites are so great, the punishments remain harsher and more severe.

SALOMON: As soon as we sin, at that moment God punishes us, and the punishment customarily begins with the priests. When He had sent angels as avengers of crimes, He said: "Begin with My holy ones."[134] The fact that He constantly chides and continuously punishes us is the very greatest proof of divine love toward us. The Psalmist says: "O blessed one whom God punishes!"[135] But against those who have become insensible to the blows and have drawn on their thick skin,[136] He uses stronger force and at length says that He will desert them and will punish them no more. He said: "I shall no longer correct your daughters when they shall have prostituted their chastity nor your wives when they shall have submitted to adulterers."[137] The Teacher of Wisdom could say nothing truer or better than to say that prudence is obtained by punishments and griefs. Indeed who would think that God had punished the Israelites so much that on account of their sins He infected not only their bodies with leprosy, but also their clothes and door posts? The interpreter of divine law says that nowhere had leprosy contaminated garments and door posts except in Palestine.[138] This would have seemed to be extremely strange to all the Jews and incredible to the other people unless long experience had proved it. And yet, the punishments and disasters of our elders produced
P. 201 the greatest services to all people. For from those came the overthrow of idols in the beginning of the young church of Christ; and when in almost all parts of the world, stars, demons, elements, fruits, and animals were worshipped everywhere for gods, at length after almost three thousand years they ceased to be worshipped because of the assemblies and teaching of the Jews who had absorbed the Christian religion with their own.

[134] On angels as ministers of god see *Cath. Encycl.* I, 476–81.
[135] Psalm 94:12. [136] *callum* M [137] Hos. 4:14. [138] Lev. 13, 14.

Finally by the command of Constantine the temples of the old gods were closed.[139] Then the books of Moses and the prophets, which we have in common with the Christians, began to be made known from all orders and peoples so that Chrysostom deservedly called Judea the mother of nations who had produced salvation for all other people by a divine gift and concession.

SENAMUS: The lyric poet spoke more truly: "Captured Judea captured the savage conqueror."[140]

SALOMON: In this one can surely see the remarkable goodness and wisdom of God. While He was demanding just punishments of sins from His own people and was sending them far from their paternal homes and was justly casting them down, He led groups of Israelites everywhere in the world to call foreign nations away from the worship of empty gods and demons, to instruct them in divine laws and institutions, then to accustom them to the worship and fear of one eternal God. For this reason, the divine law[141] calls the Israelites a priestly kingdom and a holy people.[142] Therefore, by the prayers and entreaties of this people, a priest, as it were, for all nations, God not only preserved all the most excellent empires from destruction but also blessed them and sprinkled them with the salt of wisdom lest they perish completely. Thus God said to Isaiah: "I have given you as a witness to the nations, a leader and teacher for the people."[143] That covenant struck with Abraham is also relevant here. "In your seed, that is, in your posterity, all nations will be blessed."[144] For through this people God was made known to all the world, and by the prayers of this people He was more pleasing to others. Indeed God promised Abraham that the tribe of Ismael would be illustrious, since, as God said, he is your seed.[145] And so Rabbi Johannes proclaims that the nations which were dedicated to idols did not know how great a loss they were bringing upon themselves when they burned that temple at Jerusalem,[146]

139 In A.D. 313 Constantine issued the Edict of Milan, which granted tolerance to the Christians; however, he showed favor to the pagan as well as the Christian religions. He did suppress divination and magic, but shortly before his death he confirmed the privileges of the priests of the ancient gods. On the other hand, as he favored the Christians more and more, he forbade the repair of temples that had fallen into decay and suppressed offensive forms of worship. He did not, however, close all the pagan temples. See *Cath. Encycl.*, IV, 295–301.

140 Horace, *Epist.* II. I. 156. "Graecia capta ferum victorem cepit."

141 *lex* M

142 Ex. 19:6; Lev. 11:44–45; Num. 16:3.

143 Isaiah 55:4. 144 Gen. 12:3. 145 Gen. 17:20.

146 The Temple was destroyed in 586 B.C.

in which the sins of all nations were being expiated. On festive days, which they customarily celebrated in tents, seventy animals are ordered to be sacrificed; the interpreters say that this was done for seventy people. Indeed Curtius thinks that our ejection from our ancestral homes and the holy land and our dispersion and wandering, banished and homeless, as it were, is proof of divine anger. We think this is the surest proof of divine goodness since we were never allowed to possess a little bit of land. For this reason God calls the Israelites His inheritance, because those to whom P. 202 heaven has fallen as an inheritance do not need land. They are called by the Greeks, appropriately and elegantly, holy, *hagioi*, that is, without land, *aneu tēs gēs*. Indeed God spoke thus about the tribe of the Levites, which He endowed with pontifical and priestly privilege and with the administration of the sanctuary: "Let the Levites hold no part of the earth because they are My inheritance."[147] That which He declared about the Levites among the Israelites, He likewise declared among all peoples about the Israelites when He said: "Blessed be My people Egypt and the work of My hands Assyria, and indeed My inheritance Israel."[148] Therefore, those who think this exile of ours and our poverty of land are a sign of divine vengeance against us are mistaken. How much more correctly did wise men state that just men initially suffer travails, but in the end are prosperous and happy. On the contrary, wicked men have prosperous beginnings but very unhappy ends. This is clearly illustrated by the fact that when the Israelites were rich and affluent before their proscriptions and exiles, they worshipped eternal God less than was fitting. Afterwards, when they were driven far away from their paternal homes and were cast into slavery, they loved God so deeply that they could not be torn away from their proclaimed religion by huge rewards nor terrified by harsh punishments from adoring the Founder of the universe in purest worship in the midst of their enemies. Moreover, they retained the most unerring antiquity of their race among all people and preserved the inviolable majesty of the sacred language. This language alone has been granted to the race of men by a divine gift. The other languages, as we see, are illegitimate and fashioned by the will of men. This language alone is the language of nature and is said to have given names to things according to the nature of each. Since these things are so, who can doubt that the people, herein chosen by God, are the most true church of God, the most faithful witness of the deeds wrought by God, God's custodian of the holy law and prophecies, from whom salvation flowed to all people?

[147] Num. 18:20.

[148] Isaiah 19:25.

CURTIUS: To be sure, I willingly assent to the praises of your elders, the prophets, and illustrious men. However, I cannot bear to praise those who killed the prophets, the apostles, and Christ Himself with bloody hands and who dishonored His holy teaching with all insults, much less grant to them the holy name of the church, since the true church of God consists in the assembly of the elect. And although all are called, few, nevertheless, are chosen. Moreover, they must be chosen through faith by Christ Himself, who is the Head of the church. Since they [the elect] are unknown to men, for this reason we regard the church as invisible. The others, who reject the faith of Christ, have completely separated themselves of their own accord from the roll of the church—I mean, the Jews, P. 203
Romans, Ismaelites, pagans and Epicureans.

SALOMON: A coming together is indicated by the word for church, and the acceptance of this is twofold. One comprehends the people of Israel as chosen by God, as when the Moabites and Ammonites are prevented from being counted in the church of the people of God, that is, from enjoying marriage with an Israelite woman. The other acceptance has greater latitude. That is to say, when the Ammonites, Moabites, Idumeans[148a] and all foreigners wished to embrace God's covenant struck with the people and come into the covenant relation, they represent a part of the church; the others are banished.

Indeed we are not able to approve the invisible church of the elect—for example, those who have defected from the Roman church—but only the visible church from which no one is separated except by his own will; that is, the one who rejects eternal God in order to embrace the things created or join the Creator with those things.[149]

OCTAVIUS: One can be easily convinced that the true church of God is the church of the Ismaelites, whether because of the expanse of its infinite territories or because of its multitude of people, who are innumerable,[150] or because of the origin of Abraham from whom Mohammed the Ismaelite derived his race, or because of the worship of eternal God whom alone they worship most purely, or because of the execration of idols and images which they detest both publicly and privately, or because of the purity of doctrine which by its own splendor removes the shadows of inex-

[148a] Although the Edomites (or Idumeans), who were forced to live in the desert south of Judea, had been forced into Judaism by John Hyrcanus, they became fanatically devoted to Judaism, and could not be recalled to the old national cult of Kose. See *Ox. Class. Dict.* p. 449.

[149] This sentence is spoken by Salomon in M, by Curtius in N

[150] *sive multitudine popularum qui sunt innumerabiles* M

plicable questions by which the other religions are miserably confounded, or because of the exceptional ease to abide by the law.

Coronaeus: If we measure the true church by landed properties, the church of Satan[151] will be far superior, first in its antiquity, next in the multitude of its people, and then in the concord of almost all the princes. Indeed, Seneca said nothing more truly than that the multitude was a very bad proof;[152] for this reason Pythagoras refused to follow the popular path, that is, he urged us to walk off the beaten path.[153] And surely, that the royal road and the widest path led to hell was never seen truer or clearer than in the age of Noah when the church of God clearly resided in the family of this one man. Moreover, since the true church has been founded by the blood of Christ, has flourished in an unbroken line of apostles, martyrs, confessors, and priests for fifteen centuries, and has maintained the extraordinary authority of the Roman see, who can rightly doubt that this church which the Roman pontiffs oversee is the truest and holiest church? Luther himself did not even doubt this, but openly admitted it. And yet I do not see why the Saracens ought to boast about the multitude of their people and territories, since the Christian religion has been extended in our century into all the vastest regions of
p. 204 eastern and western India, three times larger than Europe, and has spread to regions of the world hitherto unknown.

Fridericus: Of the four kinds of religions, namely, those of the Jews, Christians, Ismaelites, and pagans, more than one cannot be the true religion. The pagan religion refutes itself. But the religion of the Ismaelites which customarily recognizes Mohammed as its founder is too foolish to merit refutation by proofs. And so our chief contention is with the Jews, who boast about the holiness of their books and their ancient origin. In the first place, Salomon, I ask if you will admit that the Christian church, whose head is Christ, is the true church if it can be proven by most certain evidence and very reliable witnesses that Christ is the true God.

Salomon: Why not? But this is the task; this is the labor.[154]

Fridericus: Indeed, nothing is easier.

Salomon: I do not seek a proof but some probable argument.

Fridericus: Then I ask you this. Can you think that the Messiah has come before or that He will come at some time?

[151] *Satanae* M

[152] *De vita beata* II. 1.

[153] Porphyry, *Vita Pythagorae*, edited by Ludovicus Nauck, *Porphyrii Opuscula* (Hildesheim, 1963), p. 42.

[154] Vergil, *Aen.* VI. 129.

SALOMON: I believe that he will come.

FRIDERICUS: Indeed you do not hesitate to admit that a Messiah must be awaited, a teaching which Rabbi Moses communicated to the people, since it was written in the last chapter of the symbol of the Jews.[155] Moreover, this was done by the most adroit stratagem. Since they, in emulation of the Christians, had fashioned the symbol of faith in the same number of chapters as the Christians, they substituted the last chapter, namely, that a Messiah would come, lest any one should believe that Christ Jesus was the Messiah. But if He has not yet come, when do you think that He finally will come? Your Abraham, whom you called leader, was very skilled in astrology, and he had promised that your Messiah would come in the year of Christ 1464. Nevertheless, he disappointed everyone's conjecture. Not many years ago a certain Jew thought he was the Messiah, and for this so great sin he was burned at the stake by the prefect of Boulogne. Another man in Judea, whose cognomen was Barcochab, that is, son of the star, claimed he was the Messiah and persecuted many Christians.[156] I do not doubt that when we ask why your Messiah delays so long, you are accustomed to use the sins of the people as an excuse as indeed we read in the books of the Talmud. However, when the more experienced men of your race realized that they were rejoicing in empty hope, they not only withdrew from the Jewish sect, but even wrote books supporting the Christian religion. The book on the faith of the Jew who came to Christ is a witness. The Hebraic catechism of Emmanuel Tremellius[157] with its elegant letter to his He-

[155] On Jewish symbolism see *Encyclopaedia Judaica* (Jerusalem, 1971) X, 390–450; XV, 567–78. On symbolism in the prophetic books, see XIII, 1150–79, esp. pp. 1174–75. See above, Book IV, p. 200, note 281.

[156] Barcochab was the name given in Christian sources (Eusebius, *Hist. Evang.* IV. 6) to Simeon, the leader in the Jewish revolt against Rome in the time of Hadrian (A.D. 132–135). He was recognized as Messiah by Rabbi Aquiba, who applied Num. 24:17 to him, reading not Cochab ("a star") but Cosiba ("goes forth from Jacob"); thus Barcochab is a Messianic title of the "man of Cozeba." At first the Romans paid little attention to the rebels, who were able to strike coins in the name of Simeon, prince of Israel, and Eleabar, the priest, and to persecute Christians who refused to join in the revolt. The end came, however, with the fall of Beth-thar in A.D. 135.

Barcochab or Bar Kokhba in Hebrew, was a general midrashic designation for the "king messiah," and the messianic hopes which were cherished by the nation centered around Bar Kokhba. See *Encycl. Brit.* (11th ed.) III. 395; XV. 402. Also *Encycl. Judaic.* II, 227–39.

[157] Tremellius produced a Latin version of the Old Testament (Frankfort, 1579). The daughter of Tremellius married Franz (Franciscus) Junius, who translated Bodin's *La démonomanie des sorciers* into Latin in 1581.

P. 205 brew brothers is a witness. A third witness is Isaac of Cologne, a most erudite man. Paul Paradisus, royal professor of Hebrew in the University of Paris, is a witness, and also Paul of Burgos. Nicolas Lyranus, the most astute interpreter of the Bible, and countless men of your race, who even now in this age embrace Christ as Messiah, true God and [true] man, are witnesses.[158]

SALOMON: If the Pythagoreans are justly praised because they build empty tombs for those who have fallen away from their teaching, as though they were dead, how much more just is it to erect monuments for the deserters of the divine law? Still, I am amazed, Fridericus, that you bring forth proofs of the true religion and church from those who have fallen away from their own; indeed with this reasoning we shall say that both the Arians and the Ismaelites uphold the true religion. If this is absurd to us, then that ought to seem absurd. When our elders in the desert erected a calf wrought from gold and worshipped it as God, God, addressing Moses, said: "Your people have turned from Me by violating the covenants."[159] He had always said before, "My people," which is sufficient proof that those who have completely deserted the worship of eternal God to serve the dead are completely excluded from the church of God.

CURTIUS: Therefore, with this same argument let us conclude that the Jews who have deserted Christ, true God, savior of mankind, and surrendered Him to the most harsh sufferings on the cross have separated themselves from the true church. For the first time then, the true church resided in the group of apostles and disciples.

SALOMON: We must be cautious lest we assume as proof that which must be demonstrated; namely, that Jesus, whom you worship as God, is God. In the first place, a lack of understanding of the Hebrew language[160] confounded the early Christian theologians, and because of this ignorance one cannot easily say how many mistakes they made in the interpretation of divine laws. As a proof, when a Jew asked Justin Martyr what the Christians meant when they sing "halleluia" and "hosianna," he replied that it meant "to praise fitly" and "outstanding greatness." Is

[158] There was considerable doubt that Nicolaus Lyranus was Jewish. According to Scharbau, Paul of Burgos tells of his conversion and says that he is an adversary of Nicolaus Lyranus, but Paul makes no reference to the fact that Nicolaus converted from Judaism to Christianity, and therefore he doubts that Nicolaus is Jewish. Scharbau did, however, present other evidence that Nicolaus was Jewish. See M. Henrico Scharbau, *Judaismus detectus* (Lübeck, 1722), pp. 80–86. (See p. 298, note 306, below.)

[159] Ex. 32:7.

[160] *linguae* M

anything more inept than this answer? For the word hallelu means "praise Jah, God," and the word hosia means "save nah, I beg."

CURTIUS: But when the Jews mocked Saint Jerome because he did not know the meaning of hosianna, he went all the way into Judea and easily excelled the Jews themselves in this respect.[161]

SALOMON: I think I must advise you that the ancient Latins and Greeks did not sufficiently comprehend what the word for Messiah indicated. Indeed a Messiah is nothing other than an anointed one, and since kings and princes were by custom anointed, they were called Messiahs. The seventy-two interpreters translate this word *Christon*, not *Chrēston*, as P. 206 the Greeks once thought. As a result, the opponents, in an assault on Christ, made a statue of a man clad in a toga, lame in one foot, with ears like an ass, and holding in his hand a book with this inscription—"Christus." That the word for Messiah means prince [leader] of the people is known from David's complaint against Saul's attendants. He said: "Why have you deserted the garrison of our lord Messiah?"[162] Likewise, angered with the one who had cut off the head of Saul when slain by his enemies, he said: "Are you not afraid to lay violent hands on the Messiah?"[163] In the same vein, when Samuel saw Eliab, the elder brother of David, he said: "Surely this is the Messiah of God."[164] Both Samuel and David even call themselves Messiahs. Moreover, Nehemiah explained in the assembly after the return from exile how very many Messiahs there had been when he said: "You have given more Messiahs to your people to free them from their enemies."[165] Indeed the word *mashiaḥ*, which the seventy-two interpreters translate *christos*, is used in the same way in this verse: "Do not touch my Christs (anointed ones), my Messiahs."[166] Moreover, Samuel explains this in the full assembly of the people before he announced the king designated: "The Lord sent Messiahs to the people—Jerubahal, Jepthah, and Samuel."[167] Therefore, those who think that there is or will be only one Messiah are mistaken. Still of all the errors none is more dangerous than the error of those who think that this Messiah, who we hope will come, will be God. Yet I think

[161] When St. Jerome began to work actively on exegesis (A.D. 382–390), the opposition of the ecclesiastics of Rome caused him to retire to Bethlehem. He translated the Old Testament from the Hebrew and wrote numerous commentaries on the Old Testament prophets.

[162] I Kings (I Sam.) 26:16.

[163] I Kings (I Sam.) 26:9.

[164] I Kings (I Sam.) 16:6.

[165] Cf. II Esdras (Neh.) 9.

[166] Psalm 105:15.

[167] I Kings (I Sam.) 12:11.

those make a more serious mistake who call the Messiah—whoever he shall be or whoever will come—the savior of the human race. For our expectation hopes only for a man from man, a strong leader in war who will lead back the Israelites, scattered here and there, into Palestine and their ancestral homes and free them from the high-handed domination of others. Such men were Moses, Joshua, the Maccabees, and all the leaders granted by God's gift to our elders. There are some who think that the Messiah will be anointed by Elias. So far was your Jesus from freeing our elders from Roman servitude that he suffered a servile death at the hands of the prefect of the province after his case was tried.

CURTIUS: It is the mark of a stupid mind to wish to refer the secret of the Messiah to princes and tyrants, because no one will ever perceive a distinctly divine secret unless this be granted to him by divine will. Christ said: "No one comes to Me unless the Father shall have drawn him."[168]

FRIDERICUS: If the word for Messiah pertained to princes and tyrants, why does it have to do[169] with the promised Messiah? Why would Moses
P. 207 Hardusa write that the great and unspeakable name of God YHWH was nothing other than Messiah if the Messiah were not God?

SALOMON: Because many of our race understand Messiah in a more secret meaning, as immortal king, not a dead leader or one that would die.

CURTIUS: I receive this answer very coldly. But let us come to the parent of your race. He, now about to die and having prayed for favor on his children, turns to Judah and prophesies: "The sceptre will not be carried away from Judah, nor the scribe from his heirs until King Messiah comes, under whose power the nations are made subject."[170] If he thought that the kings and leaders would all be Messiahs and did not indicate that Messiah, as savior of the human race, by a unique sign, this would have been ridiculous and completely contrary to sense; namely, that the scepter would not be removed from the tribe of Judah before the Messiah would come, in whose power the kingdom of people would be. Onkelos, the Chaldean, changed the word *shevet* (scepter) to *sultan* (ruler). Not only Chaldean, but also Arabian and Syrian rulers are accustomed to be indicated by this word. Moreover, for the word *shiloh* the Chaldean translates *meshiha'*, Messiah, to settle the ambiguity. This is the same interpretation of the Jerusalem *Targum* which Rabbi Salomon follows, and he writes that in the meantime the powers will reside in the tribe of

[168] John 6:44.

[169] *agitur* M

[170] *neque scriba de nepotibus eius, donec veniat Rex Messias sub cuius imperium gentes subiungantur* M. See Gen. 49:10.

David until the Messiah shall come. And when he was asked where the kingdom of David was, he answered "in Babylonia," where he imagines the chiefs from his tribe who rule those exiles still reside. Ridiculous, I say, or a wicked fiction. But this was the stupidity of the age. He lived in the year of Christ 1200, so that he could not easily be convicted of lying, since France was separated by the farthest expanse of seas and lands from Babylonia, which was then held under the cruelly powerful domination of the Arabs. Later others, repudiating this interpretation, say that in place of a scepter (authority), there will be greatness and excellence in the tribe of Judah until he who was to be sent had come, namely, King David. At that time they think that excellence[171] will then give place to royal authority.[172] Others relate the word Shiloh to the place where the ark of the covenant was,[173] and which David had brought from that place. Others have related it to Saul's anointing in Shiloh.[174] This interpretation is completely contrary to sacred history because the ark had already been brought from Shiloh into the city of Cariatharīm[175] and Saul was not even anointed in Shiloh. The Talmudists say that the name of the future Messiah will be Shiloh; more recently the Talmudists say that these things pertain to King Nebuchadnezzar of the Chaldeans because he killed King Zedekiah,[176] and no one afterwards secured the kingdom from the line of Judah. This is false, since Zorobabel from the royal line[177] led his tribe back again to their ancestral homes.[178] Thereafter, the Sanhedrin, from the line of David, maintained a form of
aristocracy under the Asmonaean princes. Herod removed this assembly P. 208
(Sanhedrin), slaying the fathers except for Semea.[179] At almost the same time Jesus Christ, God and Son of God, was born of the Virgin Mary. The seventy-two interpreters translate for the word Shiloh reserved for that one, as if Shiloh[180] on account of the small letter *sh*, indicates [the

[171] *dignitatem* M [172] *potestatem* M [173] I Kings (I Sam.) 4:3.

[174] I Kings (I Sam.) 10:1.

[175] *Caris tharim* M. See I Kings (I Sam.) 7:1.

[176] Jer. 32:4. [177] *de gente regia* M [178] Matt. 1:12.

[179] Herod, who endeavored to promote hellenization, crushed the old aristocracy and built up a new nobility of service, many of whom were Greeks, and a subservient priesthood from which he filled the Sanhedrin. Cf. Josephus, *De bell. Jud.* I. 203–673.

[180] *Shilo* M; missing in N. The problems related to the interpretation of the word Shiloh are manifold. The seventy-two interpreters render *heōs elthē ta apoḳeimena auto*, i.e., "until the things reserved for him come." For a concise analysis of the problem, see James Hastings, ed., *A Dictionary of the Bible* (New York, 1902), IV, 499–501.

relative pronoun] which (quod or quae) and *lh* has been written for *lk*, since the letters Echeri[181] are interchangeable. Moreover, force has been applied to the holy scripture. Finally, David Kimchi, to seem more clever than the others, tries to derive Shiloh from Schiliath, which word means the afterbirth in which the embryo rests; as if to say *beno*, that is, the son of that one, namely the mother. I am amazed that Galatinus could follow this interpretation.

SALOMON: You see that the obscurity of this passage is so great that no acceptable argument can be elicited for the Messiah to come at the time when Jesus was born. Indeed the last king of the Jewish nation was Zedekiah.[182] Although Zorobabel from the line of David was in command of the Jewish people under the king of the Persians, in the year of the world 3432, still he had no descendants. But the sovereignty truly was in power of the priests from the tribe of Aaron. Indeed, the Maccabees even from this same Aaron maintained power in the state together with the priesthood for 126 years up to the time of Antigonus, the last of the Hasmonaeans. Herod, called king of the Jews by the Senate and the Roman people, ordered him to be killed in the year 3840. Antigonus was called by a double name—Christ, that is, anointed, because he was king and high priest.[183] In the fortieth year after this time Jesus was born. This proves that for about six hundred years before Christ no one from the tribe of Judah held the sovereignty of the Jews and that prophecy cannot pertain to Jesus. I pass over many things which Galatinus misrepresents by completely changing the meaning of the Talmudic books. For example, he writes that the Messiah was born at the time when the temple of Jerusalem was burned and that this Messiah was hiding at Rome and

[181] *Echeri* N *Eheni* M

[182] Zedekiah was blinded, his sons were slain, and he was carried off to Babylon. Nebuzaradan was sent to take vengeance on the city, and Jerusalem was destroyed in 586 B.C. The Temple was burned, as well as the palace and public buildings; the chief priest and other leaders were killed, and a large group of people was again carried away.

[183] The Maccabees were a distinguished Jewish family dominant in Jerusalem in the second century B.C. The Maccabees are more correctly designated as Hasmonaeans. Judas Maccabaeus led the revolt against Antiochus Epiphanes; following the rebellion, in 164 B.C., the Jewish religion was no longer proscribed, and the Temple was restored. The Maccabaean struggle gave fresh life to the Jewish nation. Cf. Book IV, p. 152, note 38.

Antigonus was the son of Aristobulus. In 41 B.C., the Parthians established Antigonus as king, but with the help of the Romans Herod seated himself on the throne of Judea in 37 B.C. Mark Antony effected the execution of Antigonus the same year, and his death saw the demise of the Hasmonaean dynasty.

would appear at an appointed time. These things have confused the unlearned, since they do not understand that manner of speaking which is filled with allegories.

CURTIUS: Then it is plain that here you have clung to the prophecy of your ancestor so much that no one of you could untangle himself in treating the Hebrew and Chaldaic texts, which are clear when related to Jesus. Let us proceed to other matters lest the Jews seem to have clung to only one point; to this, I believe, that prophecy of Isaiah refers: "Behold, a virgin will conceive and bear a son, and she will call his name Immanuel."[183a] Luke explains that this pertains to Christ.

SALOMON: Isaiah did not ever suppose anything about Jesus, much less P. 209
about his mother, Mary. He uses these words: *Hinneh ha'almah*, that is, "Behold, a young girl!" for *ha'almah* does not mean a virgin, but one whose love a man [husband] enjoys. Even Christian theologians who know Hebrew now are forced to admit this. This word is used by Solomon in the love canticles about those things concerning which it would have been unsuitable to speak in the presence of virgins. Therefore, he means sweetheart or young girl. Additional proof lies in the fact that they call a widow *halmanah*, one who was separated from a husband, as it were, or who lost a husband. As many times as virgins are mentioned in the sacred scriptures, and this is often the case, very wisely the appropriate word is always used, namely, *beṭulah* (virgin) or *ne'arah* (young woman) or each one in turn.

CURTIUS: Why, then, would the word *ha'almah* be used concerning Rebecca before she had been married, for she was a most chaste maiden?

SALOMON: But in the same chapter, *beṭulah*, that is, a virgin, is added for clarity. Moreover, it would have been absurd for Isaiah to have wished to indicate the parturition of a virgin contrary to the laws of nature and to have used, in so great and awesome portent, the ambiguous word *ha'almah* which rather often means single [uncommon]. Indeed history itself clearly reveals that Isaiah had written about the wife of King Ahaz. For when the army of the two kings, namely, Samaria and lower Syria, had overrun all Judea, the prophet says that the young wife of the king would bear a son and after a little while each king would leave Judea, as it happened. Two years later Abia, the wife of the king (for so Josephus calls her), bore Ezechias, the most religious and brave leader of all after David; after a little while the siege of the city was lifted. Moreover, that

[183a] Isaiah 7:14.

hope of liberation from the enemy who was devastating the region would have been empty if it had been delayed until the birth of Jesus, that is, for eight hundred years.

CURTIUS: Why, then does Isaiah promise a sign or portent? Or what portent would there have been for a woman to give birth?

SALOMON: The prophet did not say a portent, but that there would be a sign before the liberation of the country that the queen would bring forth a male child. For in three chapters he includes the history of the little boy who would be born; in the seventh chapter he writes that a boy would be born and would be called Immanuel, that is, God is with us. In the following chapter he writes these things: "The prophets Uriah and Zacharias having been received as most earnest witnesses," he says, "I have gone to the daughter of Zacharias (for Queen Abia was the daughter of Zacharias and wife of King Ahaz) who had conceived and borne a son. And God said to me: Call his name Lamaher, *schalal chusch bas*, that is, hasten the spoil, hurry the plundering, because, before he can say 'Abi, Imi,' that is, my father, my mother, the riches of Da-
P. 210 mascus and Samaria[184] will be carried away before the king of the Assyrians,[185] since Immanuel, God, is with us."[186] In the ninth chapter, when the boy Ezechias was now two years old and the citizens had been freed from siege, he said: "A boy was born to us, and his name will be called wonderful, Counsellor, brave, Father of the future age, Prince of peace."[187] From these words it is clearly fitting that all these things pertain to King Ezechias and in no way to Jesus, who the elders complained ought to be called Immanuel according to the prophecy. Many Christians have stood firm on this point, although that which the evangelists say is impossible: that Jesus had been called the Nazarene[188] to fulfill what was written in the prophets, "He will be called a Nazarene," since no prophet has ever written these words.

CURTIUS: Each name—Jesus and Immanuel—is most appropriate, for Christ Jesus means savior, because He was to save the human race, as the evangelist wrote. Let no one be confounded by the fact that Jerome and Chrysostom find nothing written by the prophets about the name Nazarene; they think that some prophets had disappeared because of trickery of the Jews. Nothing should be suspect in this matter, since Nazarene is the name of the domicile where he was educated.

[184] *Samariae* M
[185] *ante regem Assyriorum* M
[186] Isaiah 8:1–4.
[187] Isaiah 9:6.
[188] Matt. 2:23.

Fridericus: I think Osiander wished to derive the name Jesus not from the word *yasha'* which means to save, but from the most holy name of God YHWH joined with the salutary letter *sh* in this way *Yehoshuah*, to show that the divine nature had been joined with human nature at the time when Jesus was born.

Coronaeus: Although Salomon maintains that the meaning of the prophecy pertains to Ezechias, still I do not see that Ezechias had been called Immanuel, much less that the following words are applicable to him: "Wonderful, Counsellor, strong God, Father of the future age to strengthen David's kingdom forever." These words most truly are suitable to Christ, the God, as also are these: "The branch from the line of Jesse will shoot forth, and a flower will come from its branches, over which the spirit of God, the spirit of wisdom, courage, knowledge, prudence will reside."[189] These words relate so clearly to Jesus that Isaiah seems to have pin-pointed not future things but present, not a shadow but the thing itself.

Salomon: We see that the words which Isaiah had spoken in chapter seven[190]—"A son would be born to the king"—happened two years after according to the words of the prophet himself which follow in chapter nine.[191] He says: "A boy has been born to us, and a son has been given to us. . . ." Indeed the Hebrew language does not allow the past [tense] to P. 211
take the meaning of the future, and all Hebrew grammarians proclaim this.

Coronaeus: Why then would he call the boy Ezechias by the name of God?

Salomon: The Hebrew word *'el* means nothing other than strong and powerful. Therefore, Isaiah means that Ezechias would be not only a great, powerful, peacemaking and wise hero in governing the state, but also that he would be pious and religious; and indeed he was the leader, after David, who was the most famous of all for his piety, prudence, council, and all virtues.

Fridericus: It ought not to seem strange if the Jews distort prophecies, which are somewhat obscure, to another sense, since they try to becloud those very prophecies which are not obscure, but quite clear, with dark subtleties and hide the splendor of the sun itself. Notwithstanding, there are many prophecies of this kind by which that prophecy of Jeremiah is

[189] Isaiah 11:1–2.

[190] *cap. 7* M

[191] *quae sequuntur in cap. 9* M

confirmed:[192] "Behold," the Lord said, "the day will come that I bring forth a just seed for David; the king will reign wisely and rule justly, in his days Judah will be saved and Israel will flower in security, and this is his name by which they will address him—eternal God, our justice."[193] He uses, in addition, the most holy name YHWH which is communicable to no creature. A certain very astute theologian[194] concludes from this passage in Jeremiah that the Messiah would be God. These words cannot in any way be related to Ezechias since he would have been dead before Jeremiah was born.

SALOMON: They evidently pertain to Zorobabel, a prince of the royal line, since he led the people from Babylonian captivity back into Judea. Moreover, the passage which Fridericus cites from Jeremiah—"They will call Him God eternal"—is never read in any exemplars as "they will call Him," but the Hebrew word *yiqre'u*, that is, they will cry out or the people will say with a loud voice, "God is our justice." This Hebrew phrase is often found in sacred letters, and Jeremiah used it a little later. "In those days," he says, "Judah will be saved; Jerusalem will cherish peace and will be called God eternal, our justice."[195] In each place the name Jehovah has been added. But who is so foolish that he grant the name of God to a city? This passage is similar: "And Jacob called the altar 'the brave God of Israel.' "[196] Likewise in Ezechiel: "And Jerusalem will be called God eternal,"[197] his name, that is, YHWH, for Mappik in *h*, which sounds feminine not masculine. You see into what errors the deplorable ignorance of the sacred language has driven the Christian theologians.

P. 212 FRIDERICUS: The Jews stir up amazing subtleties not as much out of ignorance as out of obstinacy so that they may color the clear passages of sacred scripture with inky darkness as it were. Let us look to other things.

CURTIUS: A passage in the book of Psalms says: "The Lord said to my lord, sit at My right hand."[198] Christ Himself with this statement aptly refutes the unyielding stubbornness of the Jews in order to teach that the Messiah is God. He said: "If David calls Christ Lord, how would he be His son?"[199] Matthew[200] writes that they were then silent.[201]

[192] *confirmatur* M [193] Jer. 23:5–6.
[194] The "very astute theologian" is always, in the *Colloquium*, a reference to John Calvin.
[195] Jer. 33:16. [196] Gen. 33:20. [197] Ezech. 48:35.
[198] Psalm 109 (110):1. [199] Matt. 22:42. [200] *Matthaeus* M
[201] Matt. 22:46.

Salomon: Probably those were silent so as not to seem foolish in a subject so futile, because in the first place this is not a Psalm of David. There are ten authors of the Psalms whom Rabbi David Kimchi lists in his Hebraic commentaries on the first Psalm. Moreover, this Psalm is number 109, and at the end of Psalm 72 these words are added: "The end of David's prayers." We know from this that the following are not David's Psalms. Their argument was based on the fact that they thought these were David's words.

Fridericus: Why then was this inscribed as a "Psalm of David?"

Salomon: All the Hebraic exemplars are free from this notation, as the 137th Psalm, although it is inscribed a "Psalm of David" by the Latin writers, nevertheless was written almost 500 years later, that is, after the return from the Babylonian exile, as those words declare—"over the rivers of Babylonia." Since David surpassed the other nine authors of the Psalms in dignity, the inscription of the whole book is granted to him, although no more than eighteen of the 150 Psalms are considered to have been written by David. Moreover, if that were a Psalm of David, still the Christian theologians feebly hand down that proof for Christ because they say it was possible that Christ Jesus, the future Messiah, would have surpassed David by far in resources and power.

Curtius: Everyone ought to approve on every occasion[202] those who[203] approve the authority[204] of Christian theologians. If they are approved,[205] they assert the deity of Christ in all the passages and prove in this Psalm of David that the word *Adonai* befits God alone, so that this must be an interpretation about the Messiah who is to come.

Salomon: The word *Adonai* with *kamez* is granted to the Creator, but with *patach* to the created, as the grammarians have noted. But in this Psalm neither *patach* nor *kamez* is written, but only *la'adoni*, which word is never attributed to the Creator. Although the Psalms were written in Hebrew without vowel points, when the Greek translation appeared, as is known from numerous passages and especially from the thirtieth and forty-sixth Psalms, neither *kamez* nor *patach* can be understood on P. 213
the penult, by pronunciation.

Coronaeus: Who could interpret or know the Psalm better than Christ Himself?

Salomon: How many places in Sacred Scriptures do we see ignorantly distorted into another meaning. For example, the statement—"Their

[202] *usquequaque* M [203] *qui* M [204] *auctoritatem* M
[205] *si probantur* M

sound has gone out into all the world."[206]—is assigned to the apostles, although the meaning in that passage is about the stars and the heavens. And also they relate the statement—"You have made him a little less than an angel."[207]—to Christ, who, if he had been less than angels, in no way could have been God.

Curtius: The word *me'elohim* means from God. The significance of the passage is that Christ, although equal to the Father in regard to His divinity, still had to be lower in regard to His humanity.[208]

Salomon: Both Chaldean translators completely overturn this interpretation. They render the Hebrew word in Chaldean *me'elohim*, that is, from the angels, and the seventy-two interpreters render it by the angels, so that the ambiguity of *'elohim*, which is appropriate for God and the angels, might be completely removed. Indeed the consideration is about the worth and excellence of man, to whom God had subjected all things; still He made man a little lower than the angels. Similar is this statement—"They cut My hands and My feet"[209]—which does not appear in the Hebrew. For the Hebrew was written thus: *'Adat mere'im hiqqifuni ki sevavuni kelavim ka'ari yadai weraglai*; that is, the "assembly of the wicked offends Me, just as a lion My hands and My feet." The Chaldean interpreter Jonathan translates it in this way: "The assembly of the wicked besets Me, just as lions biting My hands and My feet." The word *ka'ari* (as a lion) has been changed into *ka'aru* (they bound) as David Kimchi very fully explains, in order to adjust crucifixion[210] (crucifixionem) to the cutting (confixionem) of hands and feet.

Fridericus: Indeed it is truer that the word *k'ru* has been corrupted[211] to *k'ry* by the younger Massoretes because of the similarity of the letters. Let the proof be the fact that the seventy-two interpreters, who translated the Bible into Greek from the Hebrew at the behest of King Ptolemy Philadelphus, would not have inserted the Greek word *ōruxan*, that is, they cut, for the words *hōsper leōn* which have no similarity among themselves.[212]

[206] Psalm 18:5.
[207] Psalm 8:6. Cf. Heb. 2:7.
[208] *eo tamen fuisse inferiorem quoad humanitatem* M
[209] Psalm 21 (22):17.
[210] *crucifixionem* N var.
[211] *corruptum* M
[212] The Hebrew text of the Old Testament was established by the Massoretes in the 6th century A.D. Many textual corruptions, additions, or transpositions must have crept into the Hebrew text between the third and second centuries B.C., and the sixth and seventh centuries A.D. The manuscripts which the Seventy had at their disposal may have been better than the Massoretic manuscripts. It is difficult

Salomon: I know that the old interpretation of the seventy-two has an advantage in that what is possible to change in one language is not possible in another because of the difference between the Hebrew and Greek languages. For example, when Moses had written that the Israelites had spent 430 years in Egypt, the seventy-two interpreters rendered this same number. However, because the word *tetrakosiōn* is like the word *triakosiōn,* many think three hundred (trecentos) must be emended because they seemed to have spent hardly 140 years in Egypt, if you consider the ages of each. Still it happens that nothing must be changed, since pure Hebrew expressions allow no shortening. Moreover, in accordance with the covenant struck with Abraham and God's promise made him up to the departure from Egypt, the number is fitting, so that all may understand that Egypt stands for a terrestrial home in a more secret sense. Therefore, it is necessary to return to the springs of the Hebrews if there is any ambiguity in the Greeks. And so from this we know with how great faith, integrity, and diligence[213] our elders left the sacred writings uncorrupted for us. For although the scripture at first was free from vowels, points, accents and distractions of lines, the theologians, after the last destruction of the Temple, and especially Ben Asser and Ben Naphthali, leaders of the Massoretes, marked the individual[214] books by chapters, the chapters by verses, the verses by sections, the sections by syllables, the syllables by vowels and accents. Still not content with this, they numbered all the verses and indicated the middle of each book so that nothing ever could be added or subtracted. For example, they noted that the book of Genesis contained 1534 verses, and the words, "You will live on your sword," marked the middle of the book. We see they did the same thing in other books, and in the Psalms more accurately. They divided the Psalms into four books and then into chapters, and they specified the verse which is in the middle of all the books. Moreover, there are 5845 verses in the five books of Moses, 9294 verses in the prophets, and 8664[215] in the Hagiographers. In order that nothing could seem to have been added or taken out, Ptolomaeus Philadelphus ordered the sacred books of the Hebrews to be translated into the Greek language although the project was very expensive. This happened more than 300 years before

P. 214

---

to determine the exact date for the translations, but if Ptolemy II Philadelphus (284–247 B.C.) did indeed commission the translations, it is reasonable to assume that most of the books were completed by 130 B.C. See *Cath. Encycl.*, XIII, 722–24.

213 *diligentia* M 214 *singulas* M 215 *8064* M

Jesus was born, and for accomplishing the task Ptolemy did not hesitate to summon seventy-two of the most learned men from the twelve tribes. A triple Chaldaic interpretation followed: one by Onkelos, called Aquila by the Latins, who lived before the destruction of the second Temple;[216] another by Jonathan, called Theodotius by the Greeks because this name has the same meaning as Jonathan, who lived forty-two years before Jesus. The third is the Jerusalem interpretation which appeared after the destruction of the Temple; this edition is fuller and has paraphrases so that that which had been expressed obscurely or ambiguously in the scriptures might be more clearly understood. Thus Jerome complains unjustly that some passages of the Bible that contained the divinity of Jesus were omitted by the seventy-two translators to make their translation more agreeable than the older one from which they borrowed everything. However, these passages that pertain to history for example, the last eight
P. 215 verses of the books of Moses, are said to have been written by Joshua; the last twelve verses of the book of Joshua by Samuel, who also compiled the book of Judges from the ancient writings of the elders and the first book of Samuel up to the twenty-fifth chapter. Moreover, they say that Jeremiah had written the books of the Kings in large part on his own, namely, the later books, as he had received the collection from the elders; that Esdras had written the book Paralipomenon, in which the books of the prophets Hanania, Nathan, and Gadus are contained.

Fridericus: When Salomon speaks about sacred literature, he says nothing about the books of the New Testament. Yet the Old Testament is designated as having its validity in the books of the New Testament, as we see that old things have always yielded to new contracts, new laws, new covenants.

Salomon: Let us grant this about testaments and covenants, provided the author of the later and earlier testament is the same and the books are not false or suspect. But the New Testament of the Christians is not the testament of him who wrote and promulgated the first tables of the laws,[217] the first covenants on Mount Horeb, not in the presence of seven

[216] The name Onkelos, by which the official Targum to the Pentateuch is designated, has been confused with the name of Aquila, the translator of the Bible into Greek. It seems that in Babylonia, although there was correct knowledge of Aquila's Greek translation, Aquila was erroneously considered the author of the anonymous Aramaic translation; Onkelos instead of Akylas is a corrupted form of Aquila. Thus it is not known who wrote the Targum named after Onkelos. See *Cath. Encycl.*, XIV, 454–57.

[217] *primas legum tabulas* M

young men as witnesses, but in the presence of six-hundred thousand witnesses not counting the women, slaves, and foreigners. No one can say of what kind or whose writing the New Testament is. Yet in the New Testament we see so many things have been deleted and added, uncertain, and changed that it has more than three hundred variant readings, not only in letters or syllables or phrases, but also in additions, changes, and deletions of sentences and whole chapters. As proof, Epiphanius writes that the first two chapters of Luke were missing in the original of Marcion, John's disciple. Still these chapters contained things which have never been recorded by other writers: namely, the visit of the angel to Mary, the amazing birth from a virgin, the journey of the wise men from distant shores into Judea, the star preceding them to the stables in which the virgin had given birth. Moreover, Marcion was a disciple of John, the evangelist, and a most eager man among the early Christians in as much as he lavished four hundred sesterces on the Christian church. The closer he was to the principles of the Christian republic the less he could depart from the truth of the events. Therefore, he rejected the whole gospel of Luke as completely corrupt, as indeed Tertullian writes.[218]

CORONAEUS: All confidence in Marcion, the greatest of the heretics, is rightfully removed, since the fountains and rivers of Manichaean error flooded the whole world from that corrupter of the gospels. Not without merit did Tertullian write that one epistle of Paul to Philemon had escaped the falsifying hands of Marcion on account of its brevity;[219] Epiphanius complained this letter also had been corrupted by the same.

SALOMON: In no way do those first two chapters of Luke have power P. 216
to confirm the opinion of Marcion; nor is it likely that the other evangelists would have omitted that heavenly visit, the virgin birth, the guiding star of the wise men, finally the most important events, since they include the most insignificant things and often repeat the same, even to the cure for dysentery and hemorrhage. There is also another proof that those first two chapters had been added to the writings of Luke because the third chapter, as if a preface for the whole history, begins thus: "In the fifteenth year of the rule of Tiberius Caesar, when Pontius Pilate was governor of Judea, Herod the tetrarch of Galilee, and his brother Philip[220] tetrarch of Iturea[221] and Lysanias tetrarch of Abilene,[222] in the priesthood of Anna and Caiphas the word of the Lord came to John. . . ." Almost

[218] *De praescr. haer.* XIV. 17.
[219] *De praescr. haer.* XIV. 22.
[220] *Philippo* M
[221] *Ituraea* M
[222] *Lysania Abilenes tetrach* M

all the beginnings of the prophets and historians begin this way. Indeed Daniel, Ezechiel, Hosea, Micah, Zephaniah, Zacharias, and Esdras, begin in this fashion. Luke, imitating them, began his future history this way, so that it is clear enough that the two first chapters are from one other than the author.

FRIDERICUS: However, the particle *de*, placed in the beginning, indicates well enough that it relates to the part preceding.

OCTAVIUS: I have nothing which I can establish about this matter, but I remember that I read in the sacred books of *Alcoran* that the visit of the angel to the Virgin Mary and the things which are told about the virgin birth reveal the greatest discrepancy from the writings of Luke. For Gabriel is thus introduced to Mary, according to Mohammed: "Oh Mary, more glorious than all women and men, purer and more pleasing, I report to you the joy of the highest. A man, best and wise, is sent by the Creator of the universe with the Word of God, and His name is Jesus Christ." She said to him: "I have not touched a man, God eternal; how shall I bear?" The angel replied to her: "All things are easy for God. He Himself will strengthen your Son with divine virtue; He will teach the book of the law, the true Gospel; He will heal the blind and deaf; He will cleanse the lepers, raise the dead, and confirm the Old Testament."

SALOMON: Indeed, I admit that Mohammed had perhaps read those suspicious chapters of Luke in a form different from those that have been recorded. But as to the particle *autem* at the beginning of the third chapter, it was easier for the one who had supplied the two chapters to insert it than to persuade philosophers of virgin conceptions and birth, since this is incompatible to nature.

TORALBA: A virgin birth does not seem as remarkable to me as the multitudes of fish, birds, and reptiles, which earlier have been shown to be born suddenly without a father. You have heard Fridericus telling about the copulations of demons and women and their fruitful embraces, which were so customary that not only did Augustine say that those who
P. 217 doubt this were shameless,[223] but also Thomas Aquinas and almost all the theologians held the same opinion by stating, as a most certain fact, that women became pregnant by demons. John and Franciscus Picus,[224] the

[223] Cf. *De civ. Dei* IX. 16, 18; X. 9. Also note Justin Martyr, *Apol.* II. 5; he says that angels had intercourse with women and produced those who are called demons. See below, p. 284, note 234.

[224] Johannes Picus was Giovanni Pico della Mirandola, and his father was Giovanni Francesco Pico, prince of Mirandola.

most learned philosophers of their century, confirmed these statements. If these things are true, why is it surprising if a virgin became pregnant from the favor of an angel without intercourse with a man and gave birth? Add to this the fact that not only plants and many animals spring forth from the innermost womb of the earth without any seed, but also men came forth from the rich soil warmed by heavenly fire, as Anaximander, Empedocles, Anaxagoras, Plato and the whole Arabian school, according to Avicenna, confirm.[225] Among the historians Diodorus Siculus, Pausanias, Justin, Strabo, and finally Aristotle himself seem to have held the same opinion;[226] I pass over the poets who mentioned nothing more frequently. Even Maro, Varro, Pliny, Solinus, Justin, Strabo, Columella and Silius Italicus say that mares rather often conceive and bear without the males, but the foals born this way live only three years.[227] According to Varro, in Portugal there is an incredible, but still true, breeding and conceiving of horses by the wind, about which Maro says:

> All stand on the lofty cliffs on the shore facing the west wind, and they receive[228] the gentle breezes and often without any mates become pregnant from the wind, a thing remarkable to tell about.[229]

Homer had written this before about the horses of Achilles. Therefore, the virgin birth ought not to seem so remarkable.

SENAMUS: Let us grant that these things can happen in accordance with nature, although they happen rather infrequently. However, it is contrary to nature that Christ was born from the completely closed womb of a virgin. On the contrary Tertullian writes that the virgin had given birth in accordance with the law of the opened body.[230] All the schools of theologians did not hesitate to refute this because they had loosed the nature of God and man united in Christ from the law of nature.

OCTAVIUS: The Ismaelites state that Christ was neither God nor the Son of God. For thus it is written in the sacred books of the Koran: "Many

[225] For the statement of Anaximander, see Hermann Diels, *Die Fragmente der Vorsokratiker*, 6th ed. (Berlin, 1954) [cited hereafter as *Frag. der Vorsokr.* (6th ed.)], I. 30, p. 88; Empedocles in *ibid.*, I. 62, p. 335; Anaxogoras in *ibid.*, II. 42, p. 17.

[226] Aristotle (*Phys.* II. 2. 13) says that man is begotten by man and by the sun. Also cf. *De plantis* I. 2. Justin (*Apol.* I. 59–60.) states that Plato borrowed his doctrine of creation from Moses.

[227] Augustine (*De civ. Dei* XXI. 5) makes this statement when he is discussing things in nature for which reason cannot account.

[228] *exceptantque* M

[229] Vergil, *Georg.* III. 273–75. Also see Varro, *De re rust.* II. 1. 18–20.

[230] *De praeser. haer.* XIV. 13.

lie in saying that God has a son." Likewise: *Azora* 121:[231] "Constantly tell those that God is one and incorporeal, and He neither begat nor was born, nor does He have anyone like unto Himself. Moreover,[232] Jesus is the best man and the configuration of all people," who is also called Ruella; whom[233] they interpret as the spirit and breath of God. Still, they admit that Christ was born of a virgin, and they think there are many of this kind whom, in common language, the Ogli call Nephlis, the Britons call Merlins, the Germans call *Wechselkinder*. Why, even
P. 218 in Hispaniola in the West Indies they believed that the god Concoto lay with women and those who were born from this union were marked with a double crown. This seems to have been the most ancient opinion of the elders, as Toralba previously explained. Thus Josephus said: "Many angels of God who have lain with women have borne quarrelsome sons."[234]

Fridericus: Why do the Ismaelites call Christ, born from a virgin, the word and spirit of God, if they only think He was an excellent man?

Octavius: Indeed the Ismaelites recognize that Christ is by far superior to all the prophets and Mohammed. For thus it is written in *Azora* 12[235] that God said to the Jews that Christ was the Son of Mary to whom I gave the Gospel, the light and confirmation of the testament and the proper path, for the God-fearing, for the complete and consummate perfection of your law. Likewise in the chapter Elmeide: "We have indicated men's pathways through Jesus, the truest Son of Mary, and we have given the good news to Him in whom there is light and clear truth."

Curtius: If the Ismaelites admit that there was clear truth in Him, why do they deny that He is God, since Christ said openly: "I who speak to you am the beginning"?[236]

Octavius: They deny that these words were spoken by Christ but were added by the forgers who corrupted the Gospels.

Salomon: When Jesus was asked in the synagogue of the elders why He presented himself as the Son of God, He said: "Has it not been written, I said, you are all gods and sons of the exalted [God]?"[237] By these words he clearly declared, and indeed from lawful impulse, that He thought that He, as Son of God, was no different from other men. And yet the

[231] *Azoara CXXI* M [232] *autem* M [233] *quem* M

[234] See Gen. 4:4. Philo, not Josephus, comments on this passage. See Philo, *Quaest. et Solut, in Genesin* I. 92. The emperor Julian also refers to it. See *Contra Galil.* 290B–D. See above, p. 282, note 223.

[235] *Azoara XII* M [236] John 8:24–25. [237] Psalm 81 (82):6.

Chaldean interpreter changes that statement of David *'elohim 'atem* (you are gods) to *'ahen mal'akaya'*, that is, you are angels. Afterwards the same interpreter used the corrupted Greek word *'angeli* namely: "You magistrates and judges think you are no lower than the angels; still it is necessary that all prostrate themselves without exception." These things have been said for the punishment of princes and tyrants, not for praise, as the evangelist thought.

CURTIUS: The statement of Christ to the Pharisees is just, in that He took away from them the opportunity to accuse, but to the apostles He said: "It has been given you to know the secrets of God, but to others in parables."[238] He spoke thus in order to lessen the accusation which came mainly from the fact that He presented Himself as a Son of God. If this had been a common term by which anyone acknowledges God as the parent common to all, the charge against him was meaningless. Therefore, there was in Him a certain more sublime and divine begetting of a son who was born from eternal time. Indeed, He was rather often called this to distinguish the term from Son of man,[239] which He called Himself P. 219
because He was true man and of man, that is, son of a virgin, and true God born from God from eternity.

SALOMON: If He was born from eternity, His origin must not have been corporeal.

CURTIUS: Indeed, He was born from eternity from an incorporeal begetting without a mother, but later He was born in the womb of a virgin by the favor of the Holy Spirit without a father.

SALOMON: Why then is He everywhere called the son of David and the son of Joseph? For Matthew and Luke would have derived the lineage of Jesus from David all the way to Joseph in vain, unless he had been the son of Joseph. Here both historical accounts show that they taught that He descended from the tribe of Judah and indeed from the royal line of David. Otherwise He would not be the Messiah according to the prophets for the Messiah had to be from the tribe and lineage of David. Why, even in the *Talmud* the Messiah is called David, since he would be born from the house of David.

FRIDERICUS: Suidas[240] surely gives a memorable account; namely, that

[238] Matt. 13:11. [239] *hominis* M

[240] Suidas was a Greek lexicographer who lived in the latter part of the 10th century. Suidas' lexicon is an encyclopedia and dictionary and includes many quotations from ancient writers. The work deals with scriptural as well as pagan subjects. In the shoulder note in M, there is inserted "Suidas, on the word, Jesus."

Jesus had been chosen as priest by the college of priests because of His excellent erudition and piety. When they sought His origin and found, first from his mother, then from the attending midwives, that He was conceived from the Holy Spirit by a virgin and that an angel had revealed that the Son of God would be the one who would be born, the priests related this publicly. Yet marriages were rather often contracted legally with kinsmen and relatives. Thus it was enough to say that the lineage of Joseph was from David, in order to indicate that the tribe of his wife Mary sprang from the same lineage. Notwithstanding, it is pleasing to many that the tribe of Mary belongs to the Levitical and Davidic line.

SALOMON: It is surely an innovation that women propagate their line when the families die out. Moreover, that law about marriage contracts in the same tribe had been antiquated for a long time by the consent and practice of almost all. For example, we see that David's grandfather had betrothed to himself a Moabite woman, the widow of a kinsman, and Jojada the high priest of the tribe of the Levites married a woman from the tribe of Judah's royal line, because the law prohibiting it was amply satisfied if the estate were not transferred from one tribe into another, which was the only reason for the law. Who can think that a carpenter brought home a wife of the royal line?

FRIDERICUS: Also who can doubt that grandsons of kings and their descendants who are penniless pursue mechanical trades? When the tyrant Dionysius[241] lost his imperial throne, he was not ashamed that he was a school teacher; nor was the son of Perseus,[242] king of Macedon, or the
P. 220 king of Juba[243] ashamed that they were listed among the servants of scribes. Thus it ought not to seem strange if David's descendants, led as exiles into Chaldea, manifested servile obedience to the victors.

SALOMON: But when David's descendants returned home again, they

[241] Dionysius II succeeded his father in 367–366 B.C. as tyrant of Syracuse. Weak and inexperienced as a ruler, he was cultured, wrote poems and philosophical dissertations, and entertained Plato, Aeschines, and other philosophers. Plato and Dion tried to transform Dionysius into a model monarch of a philosophic state, but they were unsuccessful. In 345 B.C. Dionysius was granted safe passage to Corinth after he surrendered to Timoleon, the Corinthian general who freed Syracuse.

[242] Alexander was the son of Perseus, king of Macedon, who was defeated by Lucius Aemilius Paulus at Pydna in 168 B.C.

[243] Juba II, son of Juba I, king of Numidia, was carried to Rome in 46 B.C., as an adornment of Caesar's triumph. Augustus transferred him from Numidia to Mauretania in 25 B.C. He wrote many books in Greek, now lost; also a history of Rome and works about Libya, Arabia, and Assyria. He is often mentioned by Pliny and also by Tertullian, *Apol.* I. 19.

obtained senatorial honors. And yet Matthew and Luke show discrepancies not only with history, but also with themselves. For example, one traces Jesus' genealogy from Solomon, the other from Nathan with a limitless variety of names.[244] Each is very different, first from Philo the Hebrew,[245] the best author of antiquity, then even from sacred history. Since a clever theologian could not tolerate this, he wrote openly that from the writings of Matthew and Luke it could not be proven in any way that Jesus seemed to have descended from David. Of the two things, one is possible: either theogony or genealogy is false; it is impossible that there is more than one that is true, since each has altogether different lineages, namely, the brothers Solomon and Nathan. Each evangelist reported numerous contradictions; for example, Boas, Solomon's son, is the great-grandfather of David, although 368[246] years separate them. Also of no consequence is the fact that Justin Martyr, contrary to others' opinions, writes that Eli was the adopted father of Joseph.[247] Suidas' *History* is not even approved by any Christian except Suidas, since it clearly contradicts all the writers of the gospels. Indeed, it is unheard of that among the Jews there was an election of priests, much less from the royal line. When King Uzziah tried to abolish this law[248] and take the honors away from the resisting priests, he suddenly contracted leprosy because divine law had granted the priestly privilege to the tribe of Aaron,[249] and this was without lot or vote, since the other tribes were excluded from access to the priesthood.

CURTIUS: Those who do not see that particular names are often changed in sacred Scripture are in error. For the man who is said to be Azarias, king of the Jews, in one[250] place, is called Ozias in another place.[251] Likewise Esdras is called Athiarsatha, then Nehemias, then Malachias,[252] and he who is often called Artaxerxes is sometimes spoken of as Ahasuerus and Asverus.[253] Wherefore, we must not especially labor over names,

[244] Cf. Matt. 1:1–16; Luke 3:23–28.

[245] Of the discrepancies between different genealogies of Jesus, see the *Cath. Encycl.*, VI, 408–12 and Hastings, *Dict. of the Bible*, II, 137–41. However, among many early sources, Philo's authority is not invoked.

[246] *CCCLXVIII* M

[247] Justin Martyr (*Dial. Tryph.* XLIX) refers to Elias and his relationship to John and Jesus. However, Augustine (*De civ. Dei* XVII. 5.) refers to the new priesthood of Eli and the transfer of this to Jesus.

[248] *legi* M

[249] IV Kings (II Kings) 15:1–5.

[250] *uno* M

[251] Isaiah 6:1.

[252] II Esd. (Nem.) 8:9; I Esd. 2:63.

[253] I Esd. 4:6; Esth. I. 1; II. 16, 21; III. X. 3; Dan. 9:1.

provided that we agree that Christ stems from David's line whether He is descended from Solomon or Nathan, since each was a son of David.

SALOMON: Granted that these are lapses of memory of Matthew and Luke, but they present more serious problems. Either Joseph is the father of Jesus, or another one is. If Joseph is not the father, that description of
P. 221 the genealogy from David is useless or even that traced from Adam. But if he is a natural father, Mary would not be a virgin and his origin would be no different from that of other men. But if they think Mary was from David's line, the proof about her marriage to Joseph is very uncertain, first because the law had been long since outmoded from contrary usage, and furthermore, because Mary is called the kinswoman of Elizabeth of the tribe of Levites.

CURTIUS: Salomon, your arguments refute you. For if the law was out of use about marriage orders, who can doubt that Mary was descended from the tribe of Levites on her father's side, but from David on her mother's side.

SALOMON: However, if we leave out these points, it was necessary, according to the prophecies, that the Messiah be born in the town of Bethlehem. But Jesus was born in the village of Nazareth in the district of Galilee, which was divided from Judea by rivers and rule. Hence that reproach when there was a discussion about Jesus: "Can anything good be from Nazareth?"[254] He also confirms this reproach in Acts by saying: "I am Jesus of Nazareth, whom you persecute."[255]

CORONAEUS: That old objection has for a long time been refuted by the theologians. Who does not know that Joseph and Mary had gone from Galilee to the town of Bethlehem to be enrolled in the census and there Mary gave birth? Still He was called a Nazarene because He was raised in the place where His mother had her home. Even Origen, in his work *Contra Celsus*, and Justin Martyr say that the stable in which Christ was born in the grotto in Bethlehem was often visited by pilgrims in his own age.[256]

SALOMON: Indeed they believe this, but the account of the time does not coincide with the history of Augustus' census. Augustus took a census of the whole Roman Empire in the second last year of his reign, as Dio states, when Jesus was fourteen years old.[257]

[254] John 1:46. [255] Acts 9:5.

[256] Justin, *Dial. Tryph.* LXXVIII.

[257] The last year of Augustus' reign was A.D. 14; therefore, the census took place in A.D. 13.

CURTIUS: Augustus had two enrollments. For thus Luke says: "The first when Cyrenius was governor of Syria."[258] Since it was necessary that each one be registered in his own district, for this reason Joseph from the tribe of Judah with his wife Mary went to the town of Bethlehem.

SALOMON: This could not have happened, since, according to Josephus' history, Quintilius Varus was governor in this year, not Cyrenius.[259] Likewise, Josephus writes that Cyrenius had taken a census only of Judea, and this was nine years after Herod's death. Moreover, Christian theologians who[260] seek out those things more accurately infer from Jesus' age that He was born when Quintilius Varus was governor. To this must be added that Augustus' order contained a census of Roman citizens, not[261] also of foreigners, or[262] allies, or[263] taxpayers. Eusebius makes it clear in his writing that a census of Roman citizens was taken after the Egyptian victory, in the city and in the provinces. Moreover, the number of citizens was 6,560,000, and at Christ's birth 15,820,000. Now Joseph was not a Roman citizen; otherwise, Pontius,[264] governor of the province, would have sent Joseph's son Jesus, who was accused of treason and impiety, to Rome, as afterwards Festus,[265] governor of the same province, sent Saul, a Roman citizen whose father had bought the right of citizenship, to Rome. If the taxpayers had been recorded with the allies who lived in the boundaries of the Roman Empire, it is unbelievable that there would be so few men as Eusebius recorded in his history from the census lists. Although the historians disagree, if[266] we grant that taxpaying people also had been enrolled, what censor is so harsh and senseless that he even forced the subjects to go out from the cities and provinces into other cities and provinces[267] for the sake of a census? But if this had ever been done,[268] who would have forced pregnant women to do this? It is untrue P. 222

[258] *Syriae* M. See Luke 2:1–3. Another census is mentioned (Acts 5:37) which took place A.D. 5–6, after the deposition of Archelaus.

[259] See Josephus, *Bell. Jud.* I. 20, 617–18. Varus was *legatus* of Syria, 6–4 B.C.

[260] *qui* M [261] *non* M [262] *aut* M [263] *aut* M

[264] Pontius Pilate was procurator of Judea A.D. 26–36. According to Philo (*Leg. ad Gaium* XXXVIII) he was merciless and inflexible. Tertullian (*Apol.* I. 5. 21) calls him a Christian according to his own conscience. Justin Martyr (*Apol.* I. 35. 48) also mentions that Pilate sent an official account of Jesus' death and miracles. Also see Matt. 27:2. 24; Luke 3:1.

[265] Porcius Festus was procurator of Judea about A.D. 60; he carried on the trial against Paul, whom he sent to Rome. See Acts 25 and 26.

[266] *si* M

[267] *in alias civitates ac provincias* M

[268] *factum esset* M

that they made this necessary for pregnant women, for women were not even enrolled, as we can see from Livy;[269] as often as he recorded the number of citizens, according to the census, he usually added these words —"except for women." For example, in the seventh book he said: "Of the citizens who were adult men, the number was more than 110,000; however, the number of women, boys, slaves, merchants, and those who practice base occupations, if indeed it is not lawful for a Roman citizen to engage in handicrafts, is three times greater than the civil body." Neither Moses, in the two censuses that he took, nor David, when he had ordered the people to be enrolled, included women or minors below twenty years of age.[270] Then surely, if the census had caused the people to move, it would have been necessary for the inhabitants of Africa who were Roman subjects to go with their wives, children, and all the family to Europe where they had been born, and those from Asia to go to Africa. We have never read that any ordinances of the Romans or any people demanded this unbearable trouble and expense; rather, each person was enrolled where he had his dwelling and the censors had been accustomed to send to Rome the censors' lists of the colonists, as Livy writes. Even the dictator Caesar himself went to the individual homes of the citizens of the city of Rome to take the census, as Tranquillus writes in his *Caesar*.[271] Therefore, it is not strange if the shrewder Christian theologians cut that knot which they could not loose.

FRIDERICUS: This discussion is very subtle, or should I say futile. Whatever occasion compelled Mary to go to the town of Bethlehem, it is clear enough that Christ had been born there, since also the wise men from the east came to that place to worship the babe to fulfill the ancient prophecies. "The Kings of Arabia and Sabaea will bring gifts and be led by the star to the stable where the virgin was said to have given birth."[272]

P. 223 OCTAVIUS: I believe it must seem impossible to all mathematicians for a star to be directly over the roof of one stable; rather it must illuminate

[269] A national register of citizens was prepared at Rome from the regal period on for taxation and military service. A census was normally taken every five years. The citizens were required to state their full name, age, and amount of property. The names of women and children were not included. See Dionysius Halicarnassus, *Ant. Rom.* IV. 15. Under the republic the census was taken irregularly, but Augustus revived the procedure and took the census every three years. The provincial towns took the census at the same time that it was taken in Rome. See Livy, XXIX. 15.

[270] Num. 1:1–2; II Kings (II Sam.) 24:1–4.

[271] Suetonius, *Caesar Augustus* XL.

[272] Isaiah 60:6.

very many towns and regions, because all Christian theologians say it was not a comet, but they say it was a star. And yet, a comet, which is distant[273] from the fixed stars by a huge distance, could not even shine directly over one city, however large, without also illuminating a very broad expanse of territory.

SALOMON: How could it happen that God brought forth a new star, since it is said that He rested from all labor after the creation of this world? This would be to say that He did not have the help of angels to guide the kings or that He had brought forth a star to show the way which is useless during the day and least suitable and subject to perishing in a moment.

FRIDERICUS: Although God led His people through the desert, nonetheless, He made a column of fire to go before the people always as a guide for the journey.

CURTIUS: We know that the wise men came to this place because Herod, fearing a future king from the line of David, ordered the babies to be sought out and killed. When he demanded the death of the baby boys, he killed all the leaders of the royal line and the rest except Semea.[274] And so Joseph, according to Luke, after being warned in dreams, took the boy into Egypt to fulfill the old prophecy: "I have called My son out of Egypt."[275]

SALOMON: In this passage the prophet Hosea is not speaking of the future but of things that happened two thousand years before Christ was born; namely, God wished to summon Israel to its ancestral home. For Israel is spoken of thus in the sacred Scriptures: "The first-born, My son Israel."[276] Nevertheless it is foolish that a future event follows a prediction because it has been predicted; rather it is foreseen and predicted because it is future, as Julian Augustus very often taunted the Galileans and Celsus the Christians.

[273] *abest* M

[274] There is no Semea (Semaeus in M) in Biblical literature or indexed in *Cath. Encycl.* The famous *Testimonium Flavianum*, the passages about Jesus Christ in Josephus *Antiq.* XVIII, 63–64, was first suspected in the sixteenth century by Scaliger. This famous section does not mention the hatred and envy of Herod, though elsewhere Josephus goes into the greatest detail about this Nero of the Jews. See footnote in Josephus, *Antiq.*, Loeb Classical Library, IX, p. 49. See above, Book IV, note 88.

[275] The correct reference is Matt. 2:13–15, not Luke, as the text states. Also from the Old Testament, see Hosea 11:1.

[276] Ex. 4:22.

CURTIUS: Now for a long time the authority of Augustine, Jerome, Theophilus, Chrysostom, and Cyril have broken all these fallacies of the old heretics so that in no way can the clear light of the Gospel's truth be obscured by the darkness of such subtleties.[277] But truly it is easier for a star to be created to lead kings than for the course of the sun and moon to be stopped at the will of the commander Joshua.[278]

SALOMON: The written tablets of the Old Testament are most certain; their testimonies are most authentic according to the consensus of not only Hebrews but also Christians and Ismaelites. But what faith can there be in the Gospels which the Hebrews and Ismaelites rightly reject?

P. 224 CORONAEUS: If you reject the evangelical testimonies, it is as if you denied the principles of the sciences, without which not even the geometricians will have any proof.

OCTAVIUS: The principles or postulates of the sciences lie open to all the understanding of all men and are clear to the minds of the unlearned. But on what principles do these things which are contrary to nature rely? The Gospel writers vary so much among themselves and in so many places that it is an endless task to pursue these. It is impossible that there is more than one thing which is true; therefore, the others are false. For so Augustine said: "If the Scripture does not contain ineffable truth and if any part proves to be false, there is no firm faith in it for belief. Moreover, because of the falsity that has been found in one part, the whole is considered suspect."[279] Why even[280] in conducting the actions and accounts of men among men, a record which contains a falsity in one part is completely rejected.

CURTIUS: The Gospel writers are so far from disagreeing with each other that the truth of sacred Scripture is amended from their harmony. Ambrose said: "If you are asking what Matthew wrote, it is that which Luke, Mark, and John wrote. What did Luke write? The same as Mark, John, and Matthew. What did Mark write? That which John, Matthew, and Luke wrote. What did John write? That which Mark, Matthew, and Luke wrote. As a result, no one is so like himself as all resemble all."[281]

[277] The only authority on orthodoxy not previously mentioned is Theophilus, Patriarch of Alexandria (385–412). His nephew was Cyril. He is asociated historically with the decay of paganism in Egypt, the Origenistic controversy, and the deposition and banishment of St. John Chrysostom. See *Cath. Encycl.* XIV, pp. 625–26.

[278] Josh. 10:12–13.

[279] Cf. *De moribus eccl. Cath.* XXIX; *Conf.* XII. 16. 18; *De trinit.* I. 1.

[280] *quin* M

[281] Cf. above, Book I, p. 4.

Augustine said: "If there is anything which seems to be contradictory, I think that the fault lies only in a false manuscript or in an interpreter who did not follow the text closely enough or did not understand what was written."[282] We see that Chrysostom made the same judgment about the sacred Scriptures. Moreover, as the foolish think that a twin sun and a triple Thebes appear,[283] and the unlearned believe the fixed course of the heavens change, though they themselves are buried in the depths of darkness, so also does it happen to them who have turned from the true way that they think that others err.

Octavius: How can the accord of the evangelists and the New Testament be as great as you think? Since the emperor Julian, if any renegade is acknowledged, had no greater proof for refuting the Christians than the fact that he explained their books were full of contradictions. The Christians, to escape this censure, decided to approve only the four Gospels and to repudiate all the others. Indeed, according to the book which is entitled *Orthodoxographia* and on the authority of Origen, Epiphanius, Jerome, and Ambrose, we call fifteen Gospels sacred: namely, the Gospel according to Mark, Paul, Basilides, Matthew, Bartholomew, Luke, Thomas, Nicodemus, John, Matthias, Cerinthus, Hebrews, Egyptians, Nazarenes, and P. 225 according to all the apostles. The same applies to the Acts of Saint Andrew. If there had been so many true Gospels, least of all should they have been rejected. However, if they were false or showed discrepancies, what faith is held in either, since we see all these authors, except Cerinthus and Basilides, considered divine by the Christians?[284] If the authors are proven to be untrustworthy and impious, why are they worshipped as saints? If they are truthful and holy, why are their writings rejected as false?

Senamus: We see that the Ismaelites were wiser in their deliberations in this matter than the Christians. When many books varied in their readings, a certain Caliph, the high priest of Asia, having summoned two hundred

[282] Cf. *Epist. XXVIII and XL ad Hieronym. Sancti Augustini Operum,* Tomus I. II (Paris, 1679), pp. 46, 84–86.

[283] Pentheus, king of Thebes, after he is completely in Dionysus' power, says that he seems to see two suns and two (not three, as the text says) Thebes. See Euripides, *Bacchae,* 918–19.

[284] Cerinthus, a Gnostic-Ebionite heretic, contemporary with St. John, admitted one Supreme Being; however, the world was produced by an inferior power and this Creator is not identified with Jehovah of the Old Testament. Basilides was the earliest of the Alexandrian Gnostics; he lived in the first half of the second century A.D. According to Basilides, "God is Not-Being, even He, who made the world out of what was not; Not-Being made Not-Being." See *Cath. Encycl.,* II, 326–28; III, 539.

theologians to Damascus, collected the sacred books with the exception of the Koran. (It took two hundred camels to transport them, as we have read.) Then from these, six theologians who were of the same mind gathered together the sacred books into one volume, which they call *Zuna*. From this the Book of Flowers was selected, and nothing could be added or deleted later. He ordered all the other copies except the amended one to be thrown into the lake of Damascus; it was a capital offense if anywhere a [copy] other than from the exemplar or the example of the archetype was considered to have been written. I think that the priests of the Saracens had nothing greater than this secret for stabilizing religion. But many think that Merba, son of Elhequem, is the author[285] of the Koran which is worn by hands. Even[286] Elgag is said to have taken out eighty maxims from the true Koran, and substituted the same number. The first successor of Homarus gathered up and separated the *Azoras* of the Koran which began to be called *Alphurcanus* to distinguish it. Lest it seem to have been written by human thought, they did not hesitate to consider God as the first author of the *Azora* and to say that it was given to Mohammed by Gabriel, written in verse. And lest any letter be changed, the later authorities prohibited that it should be printed.[287] This edict was enforced with such severity that when a certain merchant of this city had arranged for the Koran to be printed in this city and carried to Constantinople, he was sentenced to death. And unless an ambassador of the Venetians who were allied by treaty with the ruler of the Turks had pled ignorance for the printer, since it was abounding in numerous errors, he would have been put to death. Still, he did not escape until all his books were burned and his right hand was cut off.

FRIDERICUS: Since that Koran is not the work of Mohammed, who did not have so much leisure from his own affairs to write divine laws in verse but the fables of Merba[288] or rather metrical rhapsody (for the Arabic word *ḳor'an* is said to mean this), why do the Agareni hold it in such authority?

OCTAVIUS: I do not see why the Koran should be called the work of any
P. 226 other than Mohammed because it was purged from the errors of the copyists or written in verses, since almost all the ancient lawgivers wrote in

[285] *Merbam filium Elhequem authorem esse plerique putant* M

[286] *quin* M

[287] For a concise but highly informative discussion of the Koran and its transmission, see *Encycl. Brit.* (11th ed.), XV, 898–906.

[288] *Merbae* M

verses so that nothing could be easily added or deleted. Indeed Draco, Solon, Terpander,[289] and the Decemviri for proposing laws, who composed the Twelve Tables[290] which Tullius calls the twelve songs,[291] wrote in verse so that all could memorize them with greater ease and sing them with pleasure. In fact, song is derived from singing. Why, in ancient times even history and science used to be written in verses; for example, the words of Orpheus, Hesiod, Linus, Musaeus, Parmenides, Homer, Empedocles, Xenophanes, Pherecydes, Thales, David, the Sibyls, and Apollo, and especially divine praise were written in verses.[292] And although Moses alone of the lawgivers did not write in verse lest he make the most serious considerations depend on rhythm, nevertheless, he utilized all songs in poetry.

Curtius: Because the more pleasant stories are customarily written in verse, Mohammed wrote his stories in verse and compiled them in only one volume so that there would be no variation among them. However, it was fitting that the Gospels and the faith of Christ's deeds not be written in verses nor by one person, but by many. Would that the Gospels according to all the apostles and the same Gospels which Octavius mentioned just now, according to the Egyptians, according to Thomas, because of whose doubt his faith had to depend upon his senses, according to Nicodemus, according to Matthias, according to the Nazarenes—would that all these Gospels were extant so that truth would be more and more manifest, and the same harmony of all the evangelists which has always existed would be perceived.

289 Draco, an Athenian lawgiver, drew up a code of laws with fixed penalties (621 B.C.) which were extremely severe. Solon (c. 640–561 B.C.) was an Athenian statesman who reformed the constitution and issued a new humane code of law, abolishing all of Draco's laws except those of homicide. Terpander (fl. 647 B.C.) wrote Nomes in which he set his own or Homer's lines to lyre music.

290 *Decemviri* was the name given to several magistracies held by ten men. There were *decemviri* to decide suits whether a man was free or a slave, *decemviri* to keep the Sibylline books, and *decemviri* to prepare a code of laws. In 451 B.C., the latter group prepared ten tables of law, and a new board was appointed in 450 B.C., to complete the work. The Twelve Tables represent a compromise between patricians and plebeians and contained rules from all spheres of law: private and criminal law and procedure, sacral and public law. The Twelve Tables were never abolished, and even in Cicero's day they were learned by heart. See *Ox. Class. Dict.*, pp. 257, 929.

291 Cicero, *De re pub.* II. 17. 36 ff.

292 All the men mentioned except Parmenides and Xenophanes have been referred to in other notes. Parmenides' account of the ways of thought is treated in a long didactic poem written in hexameters. For the fragments, see Diels, *Frag. der Vorsokr.* (6th ed.), I. 217–46.

SALOMON: If the Christian theologians cannot reconcile a harmony among only four of the Gospel writers, how much harmony do you think there would be if those fifteen Gospels which you have mentioned were extant? For those who wrote harmonies of the Gospels are as different as four voices which would produce no harmony unless they were opposite to each other.

CURTIUS: We often see the false joined to true with such similarity that the inexperienced have no guide for agreement or disagreement; still to one more observant nothing will be seen to be inharmonious in the sacred letters.

SALOMON: The documents of the Old Testament show no discrepancies, but they disagree so much with the new laws that seldom are similar passages found in each. The variance of the New Testament is easily perceived by anyone reading it for the first time; so as not to bore you with specific instances, one author is not consistent with himself when he is writing about the same things or when he tells the same story twice.
P. 227 Luke writes that Paul's companions stood amazed when Paul fell, although they saw no one but only heard this voice saying: "I am Jesus of Nazareth whom you have persecuted."[293] In a later passage he writes that Paul's companions saw a gleaming light, although they heard no voice.[294] No interpreters[295] could yet reconcile these passages.

CURTIUS: The Acts of the Apostles were written in Greek; moreover, the similarity of the words, *phōs* and *phōnē*, that is, light and voice, could have occasioned the use of one word in place of another because of the carelessness of the scribes who had copied from the archetype. For example, this happened to the ancient Greeks who misinterpreted the oracle of Apollo. When the oracle said that light, that is *phōs*, was pleasing to him, they thought for *phōs* was said *oxutonōs*, that is, man, and from this the custom of sacrificing men is said to have grown among the Greeks.

SENAMUS: With so great a variety of writers and sects as there was in the beginning of the Christian republic and indeed in the very foundation of the church, I would consider it miraculous if nothing contrary were found in the writings of the apostles and disciples, since Epiphanius writes that the Catholic priests used to complain that sacred Scripture was distorted by the Arians. For example, Tertullian bitterly complained that the Arians were speaking in a contrary fashion and said that all the Gospel writings were being corrupted by their adversaries.[296] To be sure,

[293] Acts 9:5. [294] Acts 22:9. [295] *interpretes* M
[296] *De praeser. haer.* XIV. 16–19.

Origen did not hesitate to demonstrate the error in the Gospel of Mark. Moreover, Jerome called Origen the patriarch and light of the churches.[297] Rufinus himself writes in the *Apology for Origen* that Apelles and Marcion used to boast how their zeal and labor had expurgated the Gospels of many errors.[298] Likewise, Marcion, the companion and disciple of John the apostle, rejected the Acts of the Apostles, the Apocalypse, and the Epistles of Paul, with the exception of very few, as falsified, as indeed Tertullian writes.[299]

Octavius: For this reason the Ismaelites completely rejected the New Testament as entirely corrupted by the sects of early Christians. And yet there are even many historical errors. For example, Christ said that Zacharias, the son of Barachiah, was slain in the temple.[300] Now this Zacharias was not killed, but Zacharias, the son of Jehojada, the high priest, who lived about four hundred years before Zacharias the prophet. The writings of the prophet are extant, and he is called the son of Barachiah, the son of Iddo, contemporary with the prophet Haggai. He returned again to Jerusalem with Zorobabel before the restoration of the temple had begun.[301] Isaiah also cites the other Zacharias, the son of Barachiah.[302] In
this particular, the theologians disagree in their effort to reconcile things P. 228
which cannot be reconciled. Clement of Alexandria, who lived shortly after Christ, says that Christ spoke in public for only one year. Epiphanius rebukes Clement and claims that for two years Jesus spoke in public.[303] Later theologians, according to the Gospels, reckon five years from His baptism to His death. Tertullian and Africanus think He died in His thirtieth year;[304] others in His fortieth, but Augustine refutes these. Whatever things the evangelists have written about the supper come to naught,

[297] *De viris illust.* LX.

[298] After Origen's death (253 or 254) Eusebius and St. Pamphilus composed an *Apology for Origen* in six books, but only the first book has been preserved in a Latin translation by Rufinus. Cf. *Cath. Encycl.*, XI, 306–12.

[299] *De praeser. haer.* XIV. 16–19, 37.

[300] Matt. 23:35. [301] Zach. 1:7. [302] Isaiah 8:2.

[303] There are two extreme views regarding the duration of Jesus' public ministry. St. Irenaeus suggests a period of fifteen years. On the other hand, the prophetic phrases, "the year of recompenses" and the "year of my redemption" (Isaiah 34:8; 63:4) seemed to have persuaded Clement, Julius Africanus, Philastrius, Hilarion, and others that the duration of Jesus' public ministry was one year. Epiphanius diverges from Clement's opinion not only concerning the length of the public ministry but also the day of the crucifixion, which Epiphanius places on Tuesday. Cf. *Cath. Encycl.*, VIII, 375–85.

[304] Cf. Tertullian, *Apol.* I. 21. Julius Africanus (c. A.D. 160–240) is the father of Christian chronography.

since all the evangelists share the opinion that Christ had died on the sixth week day at the ninth hour. However, the paschal supper was held after sunset at the beginning of the seventh day, as had always been the custom, to say nothing of the fact that it was a capital offense to do otherwise, since the law forbad[305] it. Therefore, we know that Christ did not eat the paschal supper and could not have eaten if He had wanted to, since He was seized before sunrise on the sixth day and was put to death when daylight came. Nonetheless, Christians think that the very substance of their religion and salvation resided in that rite which institutes the supper. Likewise, they say that Christ rose on the Sabbath after He had lain for three days and nights in the tomb. Thus, Christian theologians disagree not only individually but also collectively. In an effort to unite them in thought, Paul of Burgos,[306] a Jew by birth, wrote that the Passover was held on the fifth week day, in contradiction to the evidence of the Gospels. From that time the custom of renewing the supper on the fifth day became fixed in the Roman church. This belief is refuted not only by the testimony of the evangelists, but also by very persuasive arguments of recent theologians who say the disciples ate[307] the paschal lamb on the very day on which he was crucified, in the year 1, Olympiad 203, on the fourth of April, the fourteenth day of the moon, sixth week day. On the other hand, Mercator, learned in history and chronology, says he died in the year 4, Olympiad 202, on the thirteenth of March, the sixth week day of festival, and the fifteenth day of the moon; Lucidus says it was on the sixth week day of April.

Fridericus: Trifling critics and those who split hairs find everywhere an infinite variety of readings and times. However, those who come with clean hands and a pure heart see no contradiction. Yet, the year, the month,[308] the day, the hour in which each thing happened have no relevance to salvation.

Octavius: Therefore, let us pass over the things which are considered

[305] *vetantibus sacris legibus* M

[306] Paul of Burgos, also called Pablo de Santa Maria, whose Jewish name was Solomon Ha-Levi, was the most influential and wealthy Jew of Burgos, a scholar in Talmudic and rabbinical literature, and a rabbi. He converted to Christianity, persuaded in part by the logic of St. Thomas Aquinas, and was baptized in 1390. In 1415 he became archbishop of Burgos. After the death of King Henry of Castile, Paul was a member of the council which ruled Castile in the name of the regent Doña Catalina. See *Cath. Encycl.*, XI, 588. Also see M. Henrico Scharbau, *Judaismus detectus* (Lübeck, 1722), pp. 84–86. (See above, p. 268, note 158)

[307] *edisse* N var.

[308] *quo mense* M

rather unimportant. But how can we excuse what we read in John, which, I believe, is of utmost importance. He said: "There are Three in heaven who bear witness, the Father, the Word, and the Holy Spirit, and these Three are One."[309] The most reliable interpreters complain that in all the ancient exemplars this sentence is missing, and they use Cyril, the most ancient priest of Jerusalem, as their authority.

FRIDERICUS: Indeed they are missing in certain exemplars. Nevertheless, an Hispanic codex has the same words in Greek. And these words are held to be true by the consent of all Catholics. P. 229

OCTAVIUS: Who can believe that Cyril, Hilary, Ambrose, Augustine, Jerome, and so many priests would have omitted this passage of such momentous impact, when they refuted the Arians, since we see they examined the most insignificant conjectures, yes, even the syllables and points of this argument? Not even John, the author of that letter, would have omitted it, since he did not begin writing the "good news" before Cerinthus and Ebio declared that Jesus had been only a man, as Epiphanius writes.

FRIDERICUS: Then that fact is the strongest proof. John had written these things with special clarity to anticipate every occasion for doubting.

SALOMON: John, who is said to have surpassed as an eagle the other Gospel writers, seems many times to forget his own words but especially in the passage where he has Jesus speaking thus before He died: "No one ascended into heaven unless He descended from heaven, the Son of man, who is in heaven."[310] However, Jesus had not yet ascended into heaven (if indeed He did ascend) since He had not even died.

CORONAEUS: A certain distinguished theologian[311] explains it thus: he attributes to each nature at the same time that which separately is not appropriate to either. Others imagine a twofold ascent, one visible and one invisible, of which this passage speaks.

TORALBA: But an ascent into heaven befits neither God nor man.

CURTIUS: It befits both natures, although it does not befit one of them separately.

CORONAEUS: And so this explanation applies widely to Christ's wondrous actions which cannot occur in man alone or in God alone.

SALOMON: John likewise presents Jesus speaking thus: "If I bear witness about Myself, My witness is not true."[312] Nevertheless, another time

[309] I John 5:7.
[310] John 3:13.
[311] A note in M says that the "distinguished theologian" is Calvin.
[312] John 5:31.

He says exactly the opposite: "Yet if I bear witness about Myself, My witness is true, because I know whence I came."[313] Likewise, writing about Christ, we read: "My doctrine is not Mine, but His who sent Me."[314] Why does He call it His, if it is another's? Indeed, here He seems to have cast aside all deity from Himself.

CURTIUS: Christ spoke one way to the apostles, another way to the Scribes and Pharisees who customarily maligned his words. When He spoke to them, He said He was nothing other than man, that is, in the Hebrew and Greek phrase, *ton huion tou anthrōpou*, the Son of man.
P. 230 However, in the company of the apostles, He affirmed openly that He was the Son of God and had come from Him.

SALOMON: Likewise John says: "He upon whom you see the spirit descend, He has been baptized by the Holy Spirit."[315] But Matthew on the other hand writes that Jesus had been recognized by John the Baptist who said: "Rather I ought to be baptized by you."[316]

FRIDERICUS: Jesus was known as a prophet, not, however, as the eternal Son of God, because the voice of God had not yet been heard to say: "You are my beloved Son."[317]

SALOMON: Since both Johns have been mentioned, even Christian theologians rightly wonder why Luke maintains that Elizabeth, who was speaking with Mary, felt the baby leap in her womb at the very moment of Mary's visitation, although John had been born before Mary's visit. To avoid this absurdity, the Greeks removed the day of that visitation[318] from their calendars; however, on this day they celebrate the feast day for the veneration of the Virgin Mary's garment in the *Blachernae*.[318a] The Syrians say that both the Greeks and Latins are in error, and for this reason they have established the feast of visitation seven days before the birth of John the Baptist and this seven days before the birth of Christ.

CURTIUS: As if the ancients followed so carefully the feast days which we celebrate and which were not yet established!

OCTAVIUS: More troublesome is the passage in which John writes that Christ had imparted the Holy Spirit to His apostles before He ascended into heaven;[319] still He bears witness that the spirit will not come before He should go to the Father.

[313] John 3:13. [314] John 7:16. [315] John 1:33. [316] Matt. 3:14.
[317] Matt. 3:17.
[318] The earliest evidence of the existence of the Feast of the Visitation is its adoption by the Franciscans in 1263 on the advice of St. Bonaventure.
[318a] *Blachernis* M. See p. 440, note 589. [319] John 20:22.

FRIDERICUS: This was written thus, that we may know the Spirit proceeds from the Father and Son, contrary to the opinion of the Greeks.

SALOMON: I do not hinder those solutions. However, I am amazed that the apostles err so many times, when they customarily summoned the prophets as witnesses. For example, Matthew writes that Christ had been betrayed for thirty silver coins to fulfill the prophecy of Jeremiah. He says: "They appraised Me for thirty silver pieces."[320] These words are not found in Jeremiah or any other Old Testament writers.[321] Likewise, they seized from the Psalms—"Tell among the nations, God reigned from the tree"[322] —to show that the Messiah God would be hung from a tree; indeed Justin Martyr, Lactantius, Augustine, Cassiodorus Theodulphus, each following the others' mistakes, recorded this.[323] We see that the words "from the tree" are missing in the Hebrew, Chaldean, Greek, and Latin interpretations of the Old Testament, not only in the books of Psalms, but also in the books of the Paralipomena. For thus we read in Hebrew: *baggoyim* YHWH *malak̠* (say among the peoples, YHWH is King), which P. 231 the Seventy-two translate accordingly: "Tell among the nations, God reigned." Moreover, John described spectacular miracles which the other writers passed over. For example, when the praetorian guards tried to seize Jesus, they fell to the ground in terror at only the sound of His voice.[324] Likewise, we see that the remarkable resurrection of Lazarus[325] resides in the testimony of John alone, although the other authors noted even the most insignificant cures of fevers.

CORONAEUS: Everything could not be written by everyone nor surely ought they to be written,[326] since all the evangelic writers were not present when the events happened, and had they been present, they could not have recorded everything. If they had recorded everything, the world could not have understood these things, as John himself writes. However, he knew the things which either had been omitted by the others or were said to be rather obscure, since he undertook his writing last of all the authors and started from the very divinity of Christ in this time when Cerinthus and Ebio proclaimed Christ is a Friend of man. Epiphanius said: "At that time John began to proclaim the good news."

[320] Matt. 27:9.

[321] Thirty pieces of silver are referred to in Zach. 11:12.

[322] Psalm 95 (96):3.

[323] See Justin, *Dial. Tryph.* LXXIII. The Latin Fathers often used this passage, but the Greek Fathers did not.

[324] John 18:6. [325] John 11. [326] *nec certe debuerunt* M

SALOMON: I do not understand what divinity there could be in Christ. For if He began to be filled with the Holy Spirit after baptism, as indeed Luke asserted,[327] how was He tormented by demons so that He was carried above the pinnacle of the temple and then to the summit of the mountain?[328] This is similar to John's statement that after Judas the apostle received Christ's body in the feast, he was seized by evil demons.[329] But a good and evil demon could not exist in the same man at the same time. For when Saul was consecrated and anointed king by Samuel, he began to be blessed and inspired by an angel.[330] Moreover, after he had scorned God's orders, the angel deserted him, and an evil demon began to torment him.[331] Now why did Christ begin to be inspired by the Holy Spirit only in His thirtieth year? Surely it is clear from this that the Holy Spirit had been lacking before in Him who they, nevertheless, affirm was God.

CURTIUS: It is possible that each stands: that the same man can be disturbed by a good demon and by an evil demon.[332] It may serve as a proof that Job, the most upright of mortals, when he was tortured by an evil demon, was nevertheless not deserted for that reason by the good demon. Rather, power to torment him was granted for a brief time to Satan, prince of this world, in order that he be chastened.

SALOMON: What is more alien to divine power than for God to be tormented by a demon? What likewise is more absurd or dangerous than to call Satan the prince of this world, as Jesus said,[333] or prince of this air,[334] as Paul writes. Indeed this is the most wicked error of the Manichaeans, who tried to make Satan the prince of elements and bodies. To be sure, in sacred Scripture angels are said to be princes of provinces and
P. 232 custodians and guardians of cities, but Satan is their hangman and accomplice.

CURTIUS: When we read that the Holy Spirit filled Christ after His baptism, it does not mean that we think He was deprived of the divine Spirit[335] before, since He was God, but because especially at this time the divine virtue, which before had been hidden[336] and contained by the appearance of humanity, began to pour forth and involve itself in actions plainly divine.

327 Luke 3:22. 328 Luke 4:1. 329 John 13:27.
330 I Kings (I Sam.) 10:6.
331 I Kings (I Sam.) 16:14.
332 *scilicet a calodaemone et cacodaemone eundem exerceri posse* M
333 John 14:30. 334 Eph. 2:2. 335 *divino flatu* M
336 *contecta* M

SALOMON: If He thus had been deprived of the Holy Spirit, as is thought, why did He use these words: "The Holy Spirit, when it shall have come, will teach you all things?"[337] One knows from this that the things which were known to the Holy Spirit were unknown to Him, or He would not or could not teach the most beloved disciples these things. In no way can these things be consistent with God.

CORONAEUS: Yet in this the divinity of Christ shines forth. He bestowed the deepest love upon the apostles and taught things which they could comprehend. Still, the more divine and loftier secrets, unless God had inspired them with His spirit, could not have been understood any more than colors could be seen without light. Therefore, He delayed this benefit until after His ascension into heaven. And so, similar to this is the elegant allegory which King Solomon fashioned about the girl who was calling her lover, that is, about the mind most eager for wisdom. He said: "Draw me after you, and we shall run after you."[338] Thus Christ spoke not obscurely or ambiguously but openly: "No one comes to me unless the Father shall have drawn him."[339]

SALOMON: Unless the Gospel is strongly distorted, one cannot deny that Christ did not know many things. He said: "Not even the angels know the day and hour of judgment, but only the Father himself."[340] On this account a more divine spirit of Christ had to be summoned from heaven. If Jesus was the very selfsame wisdom of the eternal Father, how was it possible that He would be ignorant of anything, since the theologians think that ignorance is derived from base origins and sins?

FRIDERICUS: This ambiguity can be removed in two ways: namely, the Son did not know the day of judgment to spread it abroad. For it is one thing not to know negatively, another to ignore privatively, to use the scholastic terminology, or as man He did not know, not as God. Those words belong here: "He was advancing in age and wisdom."[341] Likewise, He learned through His suffering the things which are related to the human mind. Still I do not approve Ambrose's view that He began to be filled with knowledge and wisdom according to the flesh.

SALOMON: Hunger, thirst, grief, sadness, fear, horror, alarm, with which Christ was afflicted, are common to the body and lower soul. Although we say these things are alien to a wise and brave man, still we admit they are human because they show a certain contact of the body with the lower P. 233

[337] John 14:26.
[338] Cant. (Song of Sol.) 1:4.
[339] John 6:44.
[340] Matt. 24:36.
[341] Luke 2:52.

soul. However, knowledge, prudence, and wisdom are characteristic of the mind alone, and this mind, if it were joined to divinity, could in no way be unknowing of anything. Notwithstanding that, they grant human feeling to that one of such a kind that He suffered nothing unless voluntary. If this indeed were true, to what end would He have said: "My soul has been disturbed"?[342] Likewise, why did He sweat blood mingled with water in the garden[343] when He was praying to avert His punishment? Why did He hurl forth these words?: "Father! If it is possible, may that cup pass from Me."[344] Now is that the voice of God? Or rather, is it not the voice of a man broken by grief and desperation? What of that final cry: "My God, My God, why have You forsaken Me?"[345] Do these statements not indicate sufficiently the voice of a man most abject and confessing that God is one other than himself?

TORALBA: Zeno of Elea and Anaxarchus, each at different times, were pounded in a mortar-trough with iron hammers at the tyrants' command.[346] They endured the harshest pains with a great braveness of spirit, and also by the majesty of words they scorned all the cruelties and conquered them. Therefore, who thinks that Christ, whom they call the fountain of all divine wisdom, was so abject and broken in spirit?

SALOMON: Josephus records a memorable story of seven Hebrew brothers, *About Free Reason*, whom the most cruel tyrant Antiochus ordered to be tortured on the rack and their limbs burned with flames lest they violate the divine law, because they were contaminated from eating pork. The story goes that they did not cry, nor sigh deeply or change expression, but they endured all torments by the unconquered strength of their soul.[347]

TORALBA: There was in Christ a necessary fear of His future death, or there was no fear, because He pretends to fear who fears willingly. If He was not terrified by the fear of death, since He cried out with so great passion and force, He surely feigned fear, since it was in His power not to fear, not to be troubled, not to grieve, not to die, not to be crucified; and with a certain pretense He poured out those empty requests that the

342 Matt. 26:38.
343 Luke 22:44.
344 *transeat a me calix iste* M. Cf. Matt. 26:42; Luke 22:42.
345 Matt. 27:46.
346 Zeno (fl. 5th century B.C.) is said to have been tortured when he was implicated in a plot against a tyrant. See Diels, *Frag. der Vorsokr.* (6th ed.), I, 249, fr. 9.
Anaxarchus (fl. 4th century B.C.) was a philosopher of the school of Democritus. It was he who was pounded to death in a stone mortar by Niceron, king of Cyprus. See Cicero, *Tusc. Disput.* II. 21; *De nat. deor.* III. 33.
347 Cf. IV Maccab. 7:6 ff. Also Eusibius, *Hist. eccles.* III. 10.

Father free Him from the most cruel punishment, since He suffered nothing.

CORONAEUS: The fear was not feigned in pretense, but was a true fear, true crucifixion, true grief, true death. Otherwise, we would admit that so many places of Scripture about the most severe griefs of Christ, about His death, about His crucifixion for the salvation of the human race were false. Christ would have had no humanity, as it were, if He at that time suffered nothing, "But nevertheless He was sacrificed," Paul[348] said, "because He willed it."[349]

CURTIUS: The question hinges only on whether He was afflicted with true fear or was completely free from fear. Many think He was free from fear. For thus Paul says: "When in the days of His flesh He poured out all prayers and supplications to that One who could save Him from death, with a strong cry and tears He was heard from His fear."[350] For thus P. 234 they interpret those words, *apo eulabeias*, from the Hebrew phrase and preposition *be'ad*, since the letter was first written in Hebrew.

SALOMON: Surely He prayed for crucifixion and death to be averted in these words: "If it is possible, may that cup pass from Me";[351] that is, crucifixion and death itself which followed crucifixion. If He was heard, He escaped punishment without crucifixion and death. If He knew grief and death, He was not heard.

OCTAVIUS: The Ismaelites constantly affirm that He was heard and was snatched from the hands of the enemies by the goodness of God. According to the second *Azora* of the Koran a certain Simeon was fastened to the cross. In this opinion we cite Hilary, Simon Magus, Celsus, and Marcion who indeed admit that He was fastened to the cross, but still endured no griefs. Hilary said: "Christ had a body capable of suffering but not of grieving, as a weapon penetrating fire and water." But, neither Christians nor Ismaelites believe that Christ had a body of different form and phantom-like. Indeed, He would not have been a true man if He had had the passionless body of a ghost.

FRIDERICUS: Indeed, that is the most destructive fiction of that most filthy Mohammed: namely, that Christ was snatched from the punishment of death, lest men place trust and hope in the saving death of Christ, true God and man. It would be fitting to bring to mind all the writings of all the saints in one word. Paul said: "He died for our sins, and He

[348] *Paulus* M

[349] Heb. 10:8–10.

[350] Heb. 5:7.

[351] Matt. 26:42; 27:46; Luke 22:42.

rose for our justification."[352] Who can doubt that He was mortal and who admits that He was man? For, rising He received a true body. And so at that time He showed Himself to the apostles to explain that His body was real. He said: "A spirit does not have flesh and bones. Touch and see the places where the nails were and the scars from the wounds."[353]

Octavius: This Celsus, who wrote seven books against the Christians, used to say that the resurrection of Christ was quite like the resurrection of Cleomedes Astypalaeus; the ancients recorded that he had risen again according to the oracle of Apollo, and his body was not found in the tomb afterwards. Likewise Celsus writes that it seems completely absurd to him that the belief in Jesus' resurrection rests on the testimony of one harlot, although many were witnesses to his death on the cross the day before.[354]

Fridericus: This is consistent with Celsus' Epicureanism. Moreover, there is no better sign of piety than to be mocked by the Epicureans.

Senamus: If Christ was born from a virgin womb, as all Christians say, if He disappeared from His enemies who wished to stone Him as we find in the eighth chapter of John,[355] if He was seen in a gathering
P. 235 of His disciples, although the doors were closed[356] and rather often fled the sight of men,[357] as Gyges,[358] if He walked on the sea with a dry foot,[359] surely we must admit that He was a ghost or had an empty body, because a true body, whether of stone or air, allows no penetration.

Salomon: Let us grant that bodies allow no penetration of bodies. Nevertheless, we see angels have adopted true bodies. Indeed magicians, having been transported, have rather often appeared and disappeared, and also when put to the water test they could not be immersed by any whirlpools, as all the judges found out. Nevertheless, it is established that they were clothed with true bodies. So we must also admit that Jesus had a true body and endured in grief the most cruel crucifixion and the harshness of death itself. But this worries me. Why would He entreat the remission of death and punishment with so ardent a supplication

[352] Rom. 5:10. [353] Luke 24:39.

[354] Origen, *Contra celsum* III. Cleomedes (c. A.D. 150–200) was an astronomer who wrote *De motu circulari corporum caelestium.*

[355] John 8:59. [356] John 20:26.

[357] Cf. Matt. 14:13, 23; John 10:39.

[358] Plato (*Res pub.* II. 3. 358–60) recounts the story of the ancestor of Gyges the Lydian who had a magic ring which, when turned around, made him invisible.

[359] John 6:19.

when, if He were God, he could have obtained this with no effort from Himself?

CURTIUS: So that all could know that Christ was not only true God but also true man, nor had each nature been mingled in Him.

OCTAVIUS: The Ismaelites constantly deny that Christ claimed divinity for Himself. Paul said: "He did not think it robbery that He was equal to God."[360] And so we see the eternal testimony of this matter in the Gospels. When a certain one addressed Christ with these words, "Good teacher,"[361] that one then said: "Why do you say that I am good, since no one is good except God alone?"[362] He not only cast divinity far away from Himself but even confessed that He was a sinner. Likewise, when He was asked why He called Himself a Son of God, He answered this: "Is it not written: I have said, you are gods and all sons of the Most High?"[363] In the same vein: "I go to My Father and to your Father, to My God and your God."[364] Not only did He associate Himself in the same origin with the rest of mankind, but also recognized with the others that one God was common to all. Suggesting this and also the cause of His return, He said: "Because the Father is greater than I."[365] In this passage against Praxeas Tertullian said: "The Father is different from the Son because He is greater."[366] And also: "This is life eternal that they may know that you are the one true God and the one whom you sent, Jesus Christ."[367] Here He divests himself completely from all divinity, as is pleasing to certain very sagacious theologians. Likewise: "He who believes in Me does not believe in Me but in Him who sent Me."[368] Likewise: "Father, into Your hands I commend My spirit."[369] Likewise: "Father, because You have hidden this from the wise."[370] Yet, Paul in every place calls Christ Lord (*dominum*), but he always separates Him from the name of God. He says: "Blessed is the God of our Lord Jesus Christ."[371] Although he had written many things to Timothy about Christ, he adds P. 236 these words with a particle of contrast: "To the King of the ages, immortal and invisible, to God alone is honor and glory!"[372] Likewise: "There is

360 Philip. 2:6–7. 361 Mark 10:17. 362 Mark 10:18. 363 John 10:34.
364 *Deum meum et Deum vestrum* M. John 20:17.
365 John 14:28.
366 Tertullian devoted a great part of his life to combating the Gnostic heresy. His book *Against Praxeas* is one of his anti-Gnostic works.
367 John 17:3. 368 John 12:44. 369 Luke 23:46. 370 Matt. 11:25.
371 II Cor. 1:3. 372 I Tim. 6:15–16.

one Lord, one baptism, one faith, one God."[373] He also calls Christ the image of God,[374] as Moses in the beginning of the book of Genesis writes that man was created in the image of God; however, the thing differs from the image in its whole nature. Likewise: "The God of peace, moreover, who brought back from the dead our Lord Jesus Christ."[375] Likewise: "You believe in God who raised up our Lord Jesus Christ."[376] Likewise: "May grace be increased in you through the recognition of God and our Lord Jesus."[377] Also: "There is one God from whom all things are and one Christ through whom all things are."[378] Also: "Let every assemblage know that God makes this Jesus the Christ."[379] Likewise: "Those who guard the commands of God and the faith of Jesus."[380] Moreover, the word for lord means nothing more in Hebrew than an instructor, a leader, and teacher. And so Lucian, having professed the Christian religion, calls Christ great Wise Man for the sake of honor, as Plato calls Protagoras.[381]

CURTIUS: What is strange if Lucian, thrice greatest of the atheists, tries to snatch divinity from Christ whom he basely and impiously rejected? Moreover, those who say that Paul only called Christ Lord and not God have not read the following, I believe: "Christ is from the Jews, according to the flesh, who must be praised as God in all places."[382]

OCTAVIUS: The writings of Cyril and Epiphanius witness that these words were missing in the ancient exemplars; for example this: "Christ was the rock." Epiphanius has noted the greatest number of these almost infinite references. Moreover, how could it be that the one who is God credits His own wisdom, holiness, and renown[383] to another. He says: "Father, glorify the Son!"[384]

FRIDERICUS: It is necessary for you in good faith to add the rest, Octavius. "Glorify the Son with the glory which He had before this world was made!"[385] Moreover, who existed before this world was made except God Himself? By this passage, therefore, the previous statements, which the ancients extended to the distinction of persons, are easily weakened.

373 Eph. 4:5–6.
374 Col. 1:15.
375 I Pet. 1:3.
376 *Item qui creditis Deo qui suscitavit Dominum nostrum Jesum Christum* M I Pet. 1:21.
377 I Pet. 1:2; II Pet. 1:2.
378 I Cor. 8:6.
379 Eph. 3:9–11.
380 Apoc. (Rev.) 14:12.
381 Lucian, *De morte peregrini* XIII; Plato, *Protag.* 313c.
382 Rom. 9:5.
383 *claritatem* M
384 John 17:1.
385 John 17:5.

Octavius: But the younger theologians refute the words of the ancient theologians; an example of which is the following: "I who am the beginning even I speak to you." The ancients say this must be related to divinity. Also the words of Isaiah: "Who will tell of His generation?"[386] The old theologians think these pertain to deity. Calvin says they must be content with the clearer passages of Scripture lest they offer themselves as mockery to the Jews. There was an exception at hand that the prophet was not thinking about Christ. Also, there was a refutation of Peter's speech in which he said that the words, "God will raise up a prophet for you from your brothers, like unto Me; hear Him,"[387] pertain to Christ. P. 237
When Peter says that Christ was like Moses, he takes away His divinity. Mohammed, the lawgiver, in the third[388] *Azora* has God speaking thus: "O Jesus, Son of Mary, You persuade men that they hold and worship You and Your mother as gods in place of God." To these words Jesus answers thus: "Be it far from Me that I lie that I am God. You know that I have always persuaded men that they worship You, My God and theirs."

Fridericus: It is one thing to take away Christ's divinity, another to deny that Christ acted as God. To be sure He publicly rejected the name of God. However, among His own He openly declared who He was and of what sort He was; still in such a way that He refused the honor of that divine majesty because of the weakness of human nature. But since many things come to mind about Christ's divinity, two of the most important are words of God the Father Himself witnessing from heaven: "This is My beloved Son in whom I am well pleased; hear Him!"[389] Also: "And I have glorified [Him] and I shall glorify Him."[390] Likewise, the words of Thomas confessing with a clear voice: "My Lord and My God!"[391] For he united each in the person of Christ. Yet nothing can be clearer than the testimony of John himself, who described the divine wisdom from the depth of Christ's heart. For thus the Holy Spirit begins that Gospel: "In the beginning was the Word, and the Word was with God, and God was the Word."[392]

Salomon: Although the church has no more, even less, influence among us than among the Israelites, nevertheless we see that the passages which Christians consider the firmest foundations of Christ's divinity are lack-

[386] Isaiah 53:8.
[387] Deut. 18:15.
[388] *Azora tertia* N; *Azoara XIII* M
[389] Matt. 3:17; Matt. 17:5.
[390] John 12:28.
[391] John 20:28.
[392] John 1:1.

ing in the old exemplars. For Epiphanius writes that these words: "A voice was heard from heaven: you are My Son,[393] etc.," are missing in the archetype of Marcion. And also the following are missing: "At the death of Christ, the sun was obscured."[394] And also: "Today you will be with Me in paradise."[395] And also: "Christ was a rock."[396] And also: "The end of the law is Christ to all believing in salvation."[397] And also: "Do you seek the living? He has risen from the dead and is the total principle of resurrection."[398] And also: "That you may know that the Son of man has power for releasing sins."[399] Why, I could mention about two hundred places which Epiphanius noted as missing in Marcion's exemplar.

CURTIUS: If anything has been cut out by the heresiarch Marcion, if anything has been deleted, added, changed, transposed, and corrupted by the Arians, on that account does faith in the gospel writers come to be disparaged? "For Christ's divinity is especially concluded from the fact that He pardoned sinners, but it was fitting for God alone to take away the sin," said Theophylactus.[400]

P. 238 SALOMON: Indeed I agree with that, and it is so proper to God that the immortal One did not even grant so great power to the angels, as Rabbi Joseph noted. However, among all kinds of impiety—and there are many—none is more detestable than the assumption that man's sin against God is pardoned by man.

CURTIUS: Yet nothing occurs more often in sacred Scripture than that formula of Christ in healing the sick: "Your sins are forgiven you."[401] And is the judgment of the world characteristic of anyone save God alone? Still it is established that the judgment of the world has been given to Christ. Therefore, who can doubt His divinity? Since these things are so, and since not only all proofs but even all sophistic subtleties are very easily destroyed by divine revelations, it is necessary that we with constant and immutable accord hold to the divinity of Christ, true God and man, confirmed so many times and in so many ages, in such a way that we never allow ourselves to be separated from the acknowledged faith.

393 Matt. 3:17; 17:5.
394 Matt. 24:29.
395 Luke 23:43.
396 I Cor. 10:4.
397 Rom. 10:4.
398 See I Cor. 15:20; Matt. 28:5.
399 Matt. 9:6.

400 Theophylactus of Achrida (1078) was one of the most famous of the medieval Greek exegetes. He was archbishop in Bulgaria. See *Cath. Encycl.* I. 104a; IV. 160a.

401 Psalm 129 (130):3–4. In regard to the previous speech of Salomon, cf. Matt. 16:19; II Cor. 2:10.

Coronaeus: Indeed you have spoken most correctly, Curtius. However, it is not enough to have explained that Christ is true God and man, as we are persuaded, unless we know what is the unity of each nature and of what sort it is. This topic we must leave for the next discussion.

After Coronaeus made these remarks, they departed one by one, after they gave their customary thanks.[402]

[402] *cum solita gratulatione* M

BOOK VI

P. 238 On the following day they had come together a little later than usual because it was a Friday sanctioned by fasting; on this day Coronaeus' home took only one meal. Although he ate very frugally because of the fast, still he extended the dinner a little longer so that I could finish reading the tragedy which I had begun, in which Muphtes, the chief high priest and interpreter of divine law, atoned for the death of three leaders by begging remission from God. And when they had given thanks to God by singing a Psalm of David, as was their custom, Coronaeus said: "I would have received you with more elegant fare, if papal laws had allowed us to eat meat."

P. 239 SENAMUS: I never enjoy a dinner more than on fast days when elegant courses of fish are served us; for the forgiveness of sins we eat food which once kings enjoyed with the greatest pleasure, that is, fish. Almost no course of meat then graced the tables of princes, unless someone perhaps had brought thrushes or hares or a full-grown wild boar full of the most delicious birds, which they used to call a Trojan horse and a wild boar.[1] Even Caligula Augustus, to celebrate magnificently his birthday at the beginning of his reign, ordered the whole Mediterranean sea to be fished so that the roe of the best fish could be brought into the city, especially red mullets, turbots, murenas, and sheat-fish which were accustomed to be placed on the tables with triumph.[2]

OCTAVIUS: Those are proofs of a mad greed. When Marcus Cato the Censor observed these things many generations before, he said that no state in which fish were more costly than beef could endure very long.

[1] *aschidōron* M

[2] On the extravagance of Caligula see Suetonius, *Caligula* XXXVII.

For the ancients ate cattle and also used them for sacrifices, and there are almost no sacrifices of fish.

CURTIUS: The ancients made offerings to the gods from their plenty, and very often they offered grains of spelt (*mola*) which, as Homer tells us, is made from barley mixed with salt and water from whence the word for sacrificing (*immolandi*) comes.[3] Later pigs and other cattle were acceptable for sacrifice, but seldom birds. Athenaeus writes that coastal dwellers, sailors, and fishermen used to sacrifice the largest tuna to Neptune, the mullet to Diana, the cytharus to Apollo, the sea fish[4] to Mercury, the anchovy[5] to Venus, and the rudder-fish to Mars.[6] Moreover, Caligula went so far in his madness that he ordered pheasants, rhinoceroses, and peacocks to be sacrificed to him as if he were a god.

TORALBA: If anything[7] most excellent is most pleasing to God, the more excellent the gift is, the more pleasing it is. Therefore, nothing among living creatures ought to be more pleasing than a sacrifice of fish, whether[8] you are considering the purity, that is,[9] holiness of that species, or bodies free from all diseases or their longevity, in which fish excel other creatures.[10]

FRIDERICUS: Indeed, I think fish are purer than other animals: first, because they live in the purest element; second, because all impurities not only of bodies but also of souls are thought to be washed away and expiated by the purity of the sea. However, I can hardly believe that sea creatures live longer than land creatures, since we learn from King Juba, the fiercest hunter of natural things, that elephants lived more than one hundred and twenty years.[11]

OCTAVIUS: To be sure, Philostratus records that Apollonius Tyanaeus saw an elephant in India who had lived from the time of Alexander the Great to his own time, a period of three hundred years.[12] This, in a cer- P. 240

[3] Spelt was called *mola salsa* and was spread on victims at sacrifices. Cf. Vergil, *Eclog*. VIII. 82; Cicero, *De div*. II. 16. 37; Plautus, *Amph*. II. 2. 109; Pliny, *Hist. nat.* XVIII. 2. 2, Par. 7.

[4] *bocas* M. This fish is mentioned in Pliny, *Hist. nat.* XXXII. 11. 53, Par. 145, but what kind it is is not known.

[5] *apuas* M

[6] Cf. Horace, *Carm*. I. 5. 16.

[7] *quicquam* M

[8] *seu* M

[9] *id est* M

[10] Pliny, *Hist. nat.* XXXII. 10, relates that immediately after the foundation of Rome Numa ordained that scaleless fish should not be provided at sacrificial meals, for reasons of economy.

[11] Juba II (d. between A.D. 19 and 24), to whom Pliny constantly refers, has been called the African Varro. He wrote many historical and geographical works.

[12] Philostratus, *Apollonius of Tyana*, I. 12. XII.

tain way, agrees with Aristotle's opinion; he says that no animal is more long-lived than man except the elephant.[13]

FRIDERICUS: To be sure, sacred Scripture verifies that man is the most long-lived of all animals: namely, those first creatures of the human race lived more than nine hundred years, and some lived very nearly a thousand years.[14]

SENAMUS: What is the reason, then, that a long life was concluded by such a brief span that even Moses, who wrote the books of beginnings and longer lives, complained that the life span of strong men scarcely, or not even scarcely, passed the eightieth year?[15]

FRIDERICUS: I know that the books of beginnings seemed incredible to many Epicureans and especially the things which detailed the long life of men. Still, in order to confirm Moses' statements, Josephus, the best interpreter of antiquity, did not hesitate to summon as witnesses twelve histories of greatest authority and antiquity from almost all peoples: namely, Berosus the Chaldean, Mochus, Aestiaeus,[16] Jerome the Aegyptian, Nicolaus of Damascus, Homer, Hesiod, Hecataeus, Hellanicus, Ephorus, Theopompus, Acesilaus, and Xenophon, who confirmed that several men had exceeded not only 400 or 600 years but also 900.[17] Why, even in the time of our elders a certain[18] soldier became renowned in history because he had lived 369 years; he is called John of the Times. But in our age, that is, in 1519, Francisco Alvarez[19] wrote in the *Ethiopian History* that Marcus Abuna,[20] high priest of the Abyssinians, did not show any senility at age 150. We know from this that those are wrong who think that after the flood the longest life span for a man had been limited to 120 years, since God had given[21] this time to man before the flood for repentance.[22]

[13] *Hist. anim.* VIII. 9. 596a. 12; IX. 46. 630b. 22.

[14] Gen. 5:27.

[15] Cf. Psalm 89 (90), which is attributed to Moses.

[16] *Aestiaeus* M

[17] Josephus, *Antiq.* I. 105–108.

[18] *quidam* M

[19] Alvarez (1465–1541?) was a Portuguese missionary and explorer who was sent in 1519 as secretary to Duarte Galvão and Rodrigo da Lima on an embassy to Ethiopia. In 1540 at Lisbon he published an account of his travels, entitled *Verdadera Informaçam das terras do Preste Joam.* This work was translated into Italian (Venice, 1550), Spanish (Antwerp, 1557), French (Antwerp, 1558), German (Eisleben, 1566) and English (London, 1625). See *Encyclopaedia Britannica* (11th ed.), I, 774, 89–95.

[20] *Abuna* M The title Abuna is equivalent to Metropolitan.

[21] *datum esset* M

[22] Gen. 6:3.

Salomon: The philosophers have established among themselves that not only has the time of life for all living things been fixed by the Founder Himself but even the years, months, days, hours, and minutes are defined for each man. The sacred writings say that at some time these are increased because of virtues; at another time they are limited because of faults,[23] whether in this hovel of a dead body or snatched away from dead bodies. Nevertheless, I interpret it to mean that the life of breathing man does not exceed 969 years, since Methuselah, who lived the longest of all mortals, did not live longer than this.

Toralba: I think that this long life span was granted to the first men P. 241 not by the force of nature but by divine care for establishing the arts and sciences and especially for the understanding of the heavenly motions.

Curtius: I think that in the beginning long life was granted to men for the propagation of the human race rather than for the investigation of sciences and arts. But afterwards, when the race of men was scattered far and wide, the life span became shorter, otherwise the population would have outstripped the land area, great as it is.[24] Moreover, nature has so arranged that for those creatures whose life span is shorter, propagation is most frequent, and few are the offspring of those who enjoy longer lives. We see that the life of the sea-polypus is limited to two years, but no kind of fish is more fertile. Likewise, rabbits are the most fertile of all land animals, and their life span is only seven years.

Toralba: These things are partly true and partly conjecture. So great fertility has not been granted to rabbits and sea-polypuses because their life span is brief, but because God in His greatest care supplied these as food for ravenous fish, the others as game and provision for land beasts and men. A shortness of life follows fertility and the pouring out of seed. Moreover, we see that birds of prey and wild beasts of land and sea are unfruitful; yet they vanquish other animals because of their long life span, and especially is this true of aquatic animals. That huge bulk of whales and Mysticetus,[25] which is sometimes eight jugers, could not have increased to such size except through many generations. For instance, King Juba in the *Commentaries* writes to Augustus about the capture of a whale of such great size that it was 300 feet wide and 600 feet long.[26]

[23] III Kings (I Kings) 3:14; Joshua 14:10–12; Psalm 60 (61):6–7.

[24] Cf. Aristotle, *De long. et brev. vitae* I.

[25] *Mysticeti* M. See Pliny, *Hist. nat.* IX. 6. Mysticetus was a fabulous sea monster.

[26] See Pliny, *Hist. nat.* XXXII. 4.

No proof of their longevity is stronger than the fact that fish, especially sea fish, are not attacked by any diseases.

FRIDERICUS: Frederick II, the German emperor had a ring put in the gills of the fish Lucius to indicate his age before he was thrown into Lake Helpruntius. This fish was caught in 1497, which was 267 years after he had been put into the lake in his true size. Nevertheless, this fish was very active and would have lived longer had not a violent death overtaken him.[27]

And in our lifetime our grandfathers told about carp that were more than 120 years old, to say nothing of what Seneca[28] wrote about the fish who died sixty years after this huge fish was brought by Pollio[29] into the fish pond; two others of the same age survived. We know from this that sea animals live the most abundant lives of all living creatures in salt water which is purer and healthier. I shall gladly disagree with the opinion P. 242 of Aristotle and Theophrastus, for they wrote that sea creatures had briefer lives than terrestrial or flying creatures.[30]

TORALBA: I look askance at the 800 talents that Alexander the Great paid Aristotle as wages when he made so serious a mistake in a matter so obvious.[31]

CORONAEUS: Since we have discussed the longevity and health of fish, it seems that they are more beneficial than land animals for man's sustenance. However, meat provides a more solid food. It is for this reason, I think, that the Roman popes in their decrees gave attention to the choice of foods, both for the food's purity and for restraint of passions on fast days and especially on Good Friday, so that we may abstain from animal food whether of land creatures or winged ones. Those who are more religious also abstain from fish and sleep; indeed, some stand on one foot for twenty hours as they view the heaven. The most religious not only abstain from these things which I have mentioned, but also they spend the day of the fast in water up to their necks to keep them more alert and drive

[27] The European pike is *Esox lucius*. Pike often weigh 40 to 50 pounds, and captures of larger ones are on record. Large specimens will attack foxes and small dogs.

[28] Seneca does not seem to be the source for this story of Pollio's sixty-year-old fish. See Pliny, *Hist. nat.* XXXII, for a rich collection of fish stories.

[29] *a Pollione* M

[30] Aristotle, *De long. et brev. vitae* V. 467a; Theophrastus, *De causis plantarum* IV. 19.

[31] Aristotle received liberal support from Philip and Alexander for his researches into natural science and zoological investigations. See Pliny, *Hist. nat.* VIII. 7. Also see article, "Aristotle," in William Smith, *Dictionary of Greek and Roman Biography and Mythology*, I (London, 1844), 319–20.

sleep away. Likewise, Francisco Alvarez writes that the same thing was customary for Ethiopian Christians, and especially on the sixth day for expiation.[32]

SENAMUS: A fast on the sixth day is more appropriate for Christians than for Mohammedans, who honor the same day in solemn fast, since on this day Mohammed was severely wounded by his enemies and fled. It is better that Christians fast on the same day on which Christ is said to have risen from the dead.

CURTIUS: In the early church Christians were accustomed to fast on the day of resurrection. Tertullian said: "On the paschal day which is a public religious fast, we[33] justly lay aside the kiss of peace,"[34] yet later on fast was prohibited on this day.

SALOMON: If all must rejoice about the freedom and salvation of the human race, surely Christians should be joyful on that very day when they believe that freedom and salvation for their souls have been secured for them. The divine law thus admonishes that we should honor most joyfully in festive banquets of the paschal lamb that day on which the first born of all animals were slain throughout Egypt, except[35] the Israelites and their flocks, since we, surviving death, were freed from harshest Egyptian slavery. We are ordered to observe no fast day except on the tenth day of the seventh month for execration and expiation of the grievous sin of our elders who had built a calf to worship.[36]

Moreover, we observe that fast from sundown to sundown of the following day,[37] and we neither eat nor drink nor have sexual relations nor engage in any work or business; moreover, we are ordered to repent of our sins, and then with our body prostrate[38] and face touching the ground we are ordered to confess our sins to merciful God and to prostrate P. 243
ourselves. For the Hebrew word *taʿanīt* means suffering and sadness. In addition to that lawful fast for expiation, twenty-five fasts are appointed, partly on account of the devastation that had been received,[39] partly for the deaths of the illustrious prophets, Moses, Aaron, Joshua, and Samuel, partly for the destruction of the city and the revolt of the people;[40] these are explained in the little book, *Tahamith*. Some people fast for forty days, following the example of Moses and Elias.[41] Very holy men, in

[32] See above, note 19.
[33] *deponimus* M
[34] *De orat.* IX. 18.
[35] *praeter* M
[36] Lev. 23:27–32.
[37] *diei* M
[38] *prostrato* M
[39] *partim propter clades acceptas* M
[40] Josh. 7:10–15; Judg. 20:25; I Kings (I Sam.) 7:6; II Kings (II Sam.) 12:16.
[41] Moses fasted forty days on Mt. Horeb (Ex. 34:28), and Elias fasted an equal number [III Kings (I Kings) 19:8].

addition to the Sabbath and new moon fasts, take food only once a day throughout their lives, as the Book of Judith records.[42]

CURTIUS: Origen writes in the *Contra Celsum* that the ancient Christians fasted on the fourth and sixth days, but they were not allowed to fast on the Sabbath or the Lord's Day.[43]

OCTAVIUS: The Ismaelites were accustomed to apply the dictum of Empedocles: namely, one must abstain from sins.[44] Still they celebrate most piously the fasts of Elmeide and the monthly pascal fasts, and they take no food until after sunset. There are some who set aside three fast days every month when the moon is in its thirteenth, fourteenth, and fifteenth day. They call these days "bright" because on these days the moon is full and makes men's bodies more vigorous and most suitable for fasting. The Mohammedans have almost the same scruple about foods as the Jews, for both refrain from eating blood or pork, as the divine law commands.[45]

FRIDERICUS: Many people have many religious scruples which are considered very profane or wicked or superstitious to others. Jews and Mohammedans as well as the ancient pagans offer sacrifices with heads veiled, as these words indicate: "Having begun to veil the hair with a purple shawl."[46] But the flamens piously dwelled under the open sky with uncovered head. Saturn, because he had been veiled, was worshipped with a bare head.[47] Nevertheless, one prays to Christ with head uncovered.

SALOMON: Indeed at sunrise Sabaean and Arabian women danced in the nude to give thanks to that God. Those who were performing sacred rites to Bahal Peor shamelessly displayed their sexual organs. No idol is execrated in divine law as more detestable than this one.[48] Indeed divine law commands the priest to veil his head when sacrificing.[49]

[42] Judith 4:7–9.

[43] *Contra Celsum* V.

[44] See Hermann Diels, *Die Fragmente der Vorsokratiker*, 6th ed. (Berlin, 1954) [cited hereafter as *Frag. der Vorsokrat.* (6th ed.)], I. 369. 17.

[45] Muslims are required to fast during the month of Ramadhān, in which month the Koran was revealed. The fast is severe, and no food or drink is taken from sunrise to sunset each day of the month. See *Encycl. Brit.* (11th ed.), XVII, 417–20. Also James Hastings, ed., *Encyclopedia of Religion and Ethics* (Edinburgh, 1909) (cited hereafter as Hastings, *Encyl. of Rel. and Eth.*), V, 763–64; II, 99–102.

[46] Vergil, *Aen.* III. 405.

[47] Saturn was sacrificed to in Greek fashion with head uncovered. There is no evidence that he was ever worshipped in any other manner. See *Oxford Classical Dictionary* (Oxford, 1961) (cited hereafter as *Ox. Class. Dict.*), p. 797.

[48] See Num. 25:1–5. For an excellent account of Bahal worship, over which Yahweh finally triumphed not by avoiding or destroying the bahalim, but by absorbing them, see Hastings, *Encycl. of Rel. and Eth.*, II, 283–98.

[49] Lev. 21:10.

Octavius: This was a common custom for all people who scrupulously worshipped. On the other hand, Prusias,[50] king of Bithynia, with head uncovered, is said to have offered divine honors to the senate by worshipping the doors of the Curia. Lucius, some flatterer or other, in the act of worshipping Caligula, who considered himself a god,[51] tossed his veiled head around like a dog and threw himself before the feet of the emperor.

Salomon: What about Moses? When he heard the voice of God for the first time, he covered not only his head but also his face, because he was afraid, the sacred scripture says, to look upon God.[52] Likewise, when P. 244 Elias had heard God's voice on the same mountain where Moses heard it, he covered his head and face with a cloak.[53]

Curtius: We often come to the same place by different routes. The people of Asia consider it a grave wrong to look upon their ruler, and they walk backwards from his sight so as not to turn their backs on him; in addition they veil their heads and bow to the ground when they speak to him. On the other hand, it is reprehensible in Europe to cover the head in the ruler's presence. According to the edicts of the king of Abyssinia, one must not only uncover the head but also bare the body even to the private parts. Formerly, dancing was a common part in the worship of almost all people; now this is practiced nowhere.[54] Moreover, to dance in the sanctuary would be a capital offense among the Genevans and the Swiss, a practice which the Jews most scrupulously observed. We read that when David brought up the Ark, he leaped to the sound of the lyre higher than seemed proper to Michal, his wife.[55] If anyone should come to bring any gift before the sacred altars, it was customary for him to leap for joy.

Senamus: Dancing and solemn choruses were established in the worship of all people. Not only were the priests of Mars called Salian from their

[50] In 169 B.C. Prusias II sent an embassy to Rome to offer his good offices in favor of Perseus. His intervention was rejected, and since fortune had favored the Romans, he tried to avert any offense he might have given by the most sordid flatteries. He received the Roman emissaries dressed in the garb of a slave, and the next year when he came to Rome, he sought the goodwill of the Senate by his slavish adulation. See William Smith, *Dictionary of Greek and Roman Biography and Mythology*, III (London, 1850), 559–60.

[51] See Suetonius, *Caligula* XXII.

[52] Ex. 3:6.

[53] III Kings (I Kings) 19:13.

[54] The marginal note of M indicates that this is discussed by Francisco Alvarez in his *Ethiopian History*.

[55] II Kings (II Sam.) 6:14–16, 20.

leaping,[56] but also a public dancer was leading a chorus in rhythmic measure at the games of Jupiter himself. Moreover, although Jupiter appeared in dreams to a certain Senator and ordered the games to be renewed, the Senator had neglected the fact that the public dancer had danced unskillfully, even though he had been warned three times about the matter. At the death of two sons he was terrified and revealed the matter to the Senate who ordered the games to be renewed. From this it is clear what we have said before: even sacred rites of pagans performed carelessly were displeasing to immortal God and brought death and destruction to the people.

CORONAEUS: I think our buffoons who leap with swords and shields are only imitating the Salii of old or even that dancer who was called Bouphonos (cow-sacrificing) because he sacrificed a cow to Jupiter at Athens.

CURTIUS: When the church was young, Christians at first omitted sacred dances, as Justin Martyr writes, since they were forced to go to the sacred rites by night for fear of punishments.[57] When Constantine the Great was emperor, he took away their fear, and they began to engage frequently in dances and choruses. This custom has not yet been entirely abandoned by the Roman church.[58] Although they were called processions, the processions were danced, not walked. Not so long ago two singers who began a song in the middle of the chorus danced from night till morning, then from morning till night. Next, in the middle of the chorus they stood motionless for quite a while, as one looked to the south, and the other looked to the north. This procedure was observed
P. 245 from antiquity by the *citharoedus* in the sacred games to imitate the motions of the heavenly bodies and the gods leading their choruses in the sky and to imitate the position of Earth herself, mother of the gods.[59]

[56] The verb *salire*, from which Salian is derived, means to leap. The Salian priests were connected with the war god. On certain days during the months of March and October, which marked the opening and closing of the campaigning season, the Salians went in procession through the city, stopping at certain points to perform elaborate ritual dances. See *Ox. Class. Dict.*, pp. 789 and 846.

[57] See below, note 58.

[58] In early Christianity bishops led the worshippers in sacred dances both in the churches and before the tombs of martyrs. The Council of 692 forbade the practice, but the prohibition was ineffective. Centuries later the Liturgy of Paris included the rubric, *le chanoine ballera au premier psaume*. See Hastings, *Encycl. of Rel. and Eth.*, X, 356–62.

[59] Music was an integral part of many public religious observances and other festivals in ancient Greece. At the Pythian games musical contests were held along with

Nevertheless, unique among Christians was the fact that two singers in the chorus, lest they seem to be rejoicing in the wicked gods or idols by their dance, as the pagans did, used to raise their right hand to heaven. Because it was difficult to keep the hand raised too long, they began to carry silver staffs which had a silver hand on the end and to move on tiptoes, so as to dance more modestly. However, when they had granted priesthoods and benefices to those unskilled in this sort of thing, they began not to dance any more but to walk. After that, there was a proverb about the unskilled who learned neither to sing nor dance. And so we see that walking was gradually acknowledged by the Roman church, and dancing was abandoned.

SALOMON: Dancing in moderation always seemed to us most effectual to divine praises. The Psalmist wished this when he danced and sang publicly before God: "Cherish God with fear; exult in Him with trembling!"[60] To exult is to leap higher, because as one leaps and exults with a certain eagerness of spirit toward God, it is impossible that he not be seized also with the most ardent love of God. In truth, it is wrong to praise God with a sad spirit. For this reason, when Aaron the priest was sick because of the untimely death of his sons, he refused to go to a sacred feast and said: "How could I please God with a sad spirit?"[61] Moreover, whoever is graced with a joyful spirit toward God must not only hate all sins but also live with the greatest integrity and innocence. So the word Selah rather often occurs in the Psalms, which Symmachus and Theodotion[62] translate[63] *diapsalma* (a musical interlude). The Latins have omitted an interpretation. The Chaldean interpreter thinks that the word Selah means eternal, and Origen and Jerome agree. However, Abraham Aben Esra translates it as *'amen* that is, verily. I think *diapsalma* truly means a change in modulation and a certain variety with silence interposed. David Kimchi thinks that Selah means a raising of the voice. I see there was, in fact, a leap of the voice and the whole body, which we are accustomed even now to use in holy canticles to show delight

---

the athletic competitions. Prizes were offered for singing to the accompaniment of the cithara, and victors in these contests were honored as much as the athletes. See Pindar, *Pyth.* XII.

[60] Psalm 2:11. [61] Lev. 10:19.

[62] The second century A.D. Greek versions of the Psalms by Symmachus and Theodotion remain only in fragments, which are witnesses to a text very similar to the Massoretic.

[63] *vertunt* M

toward God and joy in our innermost heart. Indeed, the most eminent testimonies of Nathan and Gadus declare that divine praises had been instituted by immortal God not only with dancing and song but also with every kind of instrument.[64] At their advice David summoned 285 singers of the tribe of Levi who were most skilled in modulations of divine praises; he allotted some parts to the voice, some to the lyre, some to the reed. This is easily understood from the beginning of each Psalm; for *Mizmor* (Psalm) indicated the use of lyres, *shir* (song) the voice alone; when both notations were there, voices were mingled with lyres. Sometimes a trumpet of horn, which is a Sophar, or a metal trumpet, which is a Halsopherat, was used, and the metaltaim or cymbal and
P. 246 mahol or flute. Because Jews, just as southern people, prefer the lyre, and northerners the sound of trumpets and flutes, they called the songs of David Psalms. For as you know, a *psalmos* (Psalm) is a song accompanied by lyres; however, the psaltery is an instrument in the shape of a square shield, fitted with ten strings. Still the Hebrews appropriately call the songs of David *tehillim* (praises) so that all may understand that they must be attentive to very short prayers but constant praises. Moreover, nothing occurs more frequently in the Psalms than the word *halleluyah*, that is, praise God.

CORONAEUS: I think that the instruments of the Roman church which were invented at Constantinople about A.D. 700 and which use lead pipes by far surpass all ancient musical instruments,[65] and I am amazed that those who have deserted the rites of the Roman church have completely abandoned that kind of instrument, since nothing could be more melodious.

CURTIUS: I think this was done so that the people would not forget divine praises because of the enticements of the modulations. For this reason, Justin Martyr thought those musical instruments were for boys and ought to be taken out of the sanctuary, and Bishop Theodoret agreed.[66]

[64] I Paralip. (I Chron.) 25:1. II Esd. (Neh.) 12:44–46.

[65] The organ has its prototype in the syrinx or Pan's pipe, a little instrument consisting of several pipes of differing length tied together in a row. Ctesibius, who lived in Alexandria about 300 B.C., is credited with the application of the mechanism. In 826 a Venetian priest named Georgius built an organ at Pachen. In building his organ he probably used Vitruvius' instructions, which detailed the construction of Ctesibius' organ. See *The Catholic Encyclopedia*, XI (New York, 1911), 297–301. Also *Enciclopedia della Musica*, III (Milan, 1964), 328–35.

[66] Clement of Alexandria condemned the use of instruments even at Christian banquets (*Patres Graeci*, VIII. 440, edited by J. P. Migne). When the organ came

And more than this, I think nothing is more ridiculous than for priests to use a foreign language which the unlearned do not understand; nothing is more absurd, and no people except those of the Roman [churches] approve of this custom.

CORONAEUS: Surely this happened by chance. Although the Hebrews, Greeks, Latins, and also other nations worshipped the gods in the popular language, still there was a long-standing custom that the ancient songs of sacred works, at the time of Polybius,[67] could no longer be understood, due to a change of the Latin language. Moreover, it was not allowed to change the accustomed songs on account of the veneration of antiquity and religion. Therefore, the songs of the Roman church at that time were established by Gregory in Latin,[68] when everyone understood everything [in this language]. Little by little the Latin language began to be changed and corrupted because strangers from everywhere flocked into Italy. Nevertheless, the customary songs cannot be changed without serious detriment.

CURTIUS: I do not see what disadvantage can follow the use of David's most beautiful songs of praise in all languages. Still, if we must also use sacred musical instruments, as indeed we are ordered according to the divine prophecy of Nathan and Gadus, it would be better to use stringed instruments rather than lead pipes, for when voices are confounded with the sound from the pipes, they break forth with such force that no words are understood. The Britons alone, I think, were accustomed to mingle instruments of lead pipes with voices. Still, nothing is as necessary as that all understand Psalms and divine praises so that all may be instructed.

SENAMUS: I have often thought it strange that Jews, Christians, Ismael-

---

into use in the church in Carolingian times, it was used solely for the accompaniment of the chant, which practice continued until the 16th century. See *Cath. Encyl.*, X, 648–58. Theodoret was bishop of Cyrus (Cyrrhus) from A.D. 423–57. Cyrus is a small city between Antioch and the Euphrates. See above, p. 227, note 426.

67 This was the period of Silver Latin, broadly from A.D. 17 to 130. Polybius was one of Claudius' freedmen and his secretary, especially for literary matters. He translated Homer into Latin and Vergil into Greek. For an excellent work on age of Silver Latin, see J. Wight Duff, *A Literary History of Rome* (3rd ed., N.Y., 1953), II.

68 The Gregorian chant alludes to Gregory the Great, pope from 590 to 604; in a strict sense Gregorian chant means the Roman form of early plain chant, as distinguished from the Ambrosian, Gallican, and Mozarabic chants. John the Deacon, Gregory's biographer, also names Gregory as the founder of the most famous song school of history, the Roman *schola cantorum*, most of whose singing boys came from orphanages. See *Cath. Encycl.*, VI, 779–87; III, 693–94; XIII, 547.

P. 247 ites, Swiss, Romans, and Germans disagree because of the great variety of religions, but on the Psalms of David all agree completely and every day, everywhere in the world, thank immortal God with these Psalms.

SALOMON: This ought not to seem strange, since all these people acknowledge that they worship the name and the divinity of one eternal God, and they confess there is one God alone. Moreover, the praises of David refer to eternal God, not to the divinites of Jupiter, Apollo, Diana, Mars, Hercules, Saturn; they say nothing about Venus and Bacchus, nothing about Jesus of Nazareth, nothing about Mohammed or the Virgin Mary; nothing about the countless myriads of saints which Christians had chosen, not as much for imitation as for devotion. However, they remind us of the praises and acts of one eternal Builder of all things.

TORALBA: What, then, is the reason that in so great a multitude of countless peoples, Christians alone praise, invoke, and adore Christ as God with an infinite multitude of saints, yet they say that God alone is founder of the universe.

FRIDERICUS: Because Christ is no other than God Himself, the eternal Son of God.

OCTAVIUS: If Christ is the same as God eternal, why does Peter in the sermon to the people use these words: "Let the whole house of Israel know that God has made this Jesus, Lord and Christ."[69]

FRIDERICUS: By this speech Peter distinguished human nature from divine nature: how Jesus was made man by God and how as God He was begat from eternity by the Father. Each nature came together in one Jesus in such a way that He was the mediator of God and men, because there can be no mediator for one. God, however, is one.

TORALBA: Indeed, in universal nature often from two natures that are incompatible a certain third thing, different from each of the two, is produced, and each nature perishes on account of the conflation of forms. Therefore, if the human as well as the divine form unites in the one nature of Christ, each of the two must perish and a certain third thing must be produced from both and different from both; for example, we see that hydromel is formed from water and honey, although the nature of each is forfeited.

CORONAEUS: The double nature is united in Christ in such a way that it is not mingled; it is separated in such a way that it is not divided.

OCTAVIUS: Why then does Athanasius in the book about incarnation recognize not two natures in Christ but only one?

[69] Acts 2:36.

CORONAEUS: Let no one think that the divine nature of Christ was worthy of adoration, but not also the human nature. For this reason Gregory Nazianzus and Cyril recognize two natures in Christ. However, because no division [in His nature] occurred after His assumption of humanity, [His nature] is said to be one and the same. P. 248

CURTIUS: It is not proper for those discussing metaphysics to draw the conversation to physics, as Toralba did when he transferred the discussion from natural form to divine form.

TORALBA: Christ, to the extent that He is man, is a subject for physics, but God is the true and indeed appropriate topic for metaphysics, that is, for theology. Therefore, if we must discuss God with no reference to natural matters, surely there is nothing in universal nature which can be affirmed about God, but everything can be duly denied because whatever there is except God must be either substance or accident. However, God is neither; nor is there any conception of nature common to God and creature, because nothing can be said with one word about the finite or the infinite; nor is any species infinite or indifferent to the finite and infinite. Hence, although concerning all things one is accustomed to ask what they are;[70] concerning God one asks what He is not. It follows from this that all theologians who grant substance or hypostasis or person to God speak improperly. This matter drove Simplicius[71] to say that the first cause of all things was without name. Proclus the Academician writes that God, for this reason, is ineffable[72] because He is one, or as Parmenides says, unwritten.[73] And although many things are said improperly about God, still He cannot be spoken of nor even imagined. However, those who speak of Him less ineptly call Him the eternal essence, one, pure, simple, and free from all contact of bodies, of infinite goodness, wisdom, and power. And in this the Academicians, Stoics, Peripatetics agree with the Hebrews and Ismaelites; in a certain way this [concept] seems to have been planted, as it were, by nature herself in the hearts and minds of all men.

SALOMON: The Hebrews have ten names which are granted to God in

[70] *sint* M

[71] Simplicius was one of the chief Neoplatonic commentators on Aristotle and was teaching in Athens in A.D. 529, when Emperor Justinian ordered the philosophical schools to be closed. See *Cath. Encycl.*, I, 717–18; IX, 325–26; X, 744.

[72] See E. R. Dodds, *Proclus, The Elements of Theology* (Oxford, 1963), p. 142, Prop. 162.

[73] Cf. Diels, *Frag. der Vorsokr.* (6th ed.), I. 222. 28.

sacred literature,[74] and seventy-two epithets all are common in a certain manner to the creator with the creatures, except the most sacred name, the Tetragrammaton, which He said was appropriate for Himself, namely, YHWH, that is eternal, because nothing is eternal except God. We maintain that each one ought to worship this One alone after all others have been cast aside.[75] We think it is wrong to worship and honor with any prayers and reverence the other things which we see, not only in the heavens, but also in the elements and in the structure of the whole world; in addition, we think it wrong to honor the blessed spirits which survive from corpses and the angels of each nature, hidden from men's senses. And much more wrong it is to join the incorporeal God to any creature.

SENAMUS: I believe the ancients derived Jove from the Tetragrammaton because of the likeness of both names.

P. 249 SALOMON: Those who pronounce Jova or Jehova for the sacred name YHWH do not understand this language. Indeed the system of the Hebrew language does not allow that name to be pronounced thus. Although we rather often read *Yehowah* with the vowels written subscript, still those err who think it must be read thus. Nor do they know that our elders, who first added vowels to the letters, represented that mystery by a variety of writing, sometimes *Yehowah*, sometimes *Yeheweh*. The reason why they concealed that mystery is the fact that divine law enjoins capital punishment on him who clearly spoke this name. And so we never have that name on our tongue but are accustomed to use the name Elohim or Adonai as often as it occurs to those reading the Sacred Scripture.

CURTIUS: My feelings are in harmony with yours, Salomon, and my heart is the same, except that I am persuaded that God, the Builder and Ruler of all things, assumed human nature that He might expiate man's sins by His death. I do not value the other empty things of gods and the divinities of saints, and I do not even wish angels, who come closest to the divinity of immortal God, to be worshipped with any prayers or reverence.

[74] The names of God fall into several classes; names expressing the general notion of Deity, e.g., El, Elohim; descriptive titles, e.g., El Shaddai, El Elyon; personal names of the God of Israel, Yahweh. The latter acquired such sacredness that, in reading, the name Adonai, lord, was substituted for it. Yahweh was also called Sebāōth (Lord of Hosts), 'ēsh Yahweh (fire of Yahweh), and kōl Yahweh (voice of Yahweh). See James Hastings, *A Dictionary of the Bible* (New York, 1900), II, 196–205; Hastings, *Encycl. of Rel. and Eth.*, VI, 253–55.

[75] Lev. 21:6; 24:11–16.

CORONAEUS: Indeed, with Curtius I cherish the twelve articles of Christian faith and beyond this the atoning sacrifice of the body and blood of Christ. Also I think that we ought to elicit in sacred petitions the souls of angels and saints so that God may be propitious to us, and likewise the fires of purgatory, by which the sins of our souls are cleansed.

OCTAVIUS: By that reasoning it is necessary that a host of innumerable gods be admitted along with the immortal God.

CORONAEUS: Indeed, for the rest, each in its own place. But before that, Salomon must be persuaded about the divinity of Christ. If he will be persuaded, he will easily bring Octavius and Toralba to his own opinion.

SALOMON: I see that Toralba will be more difficult to persuade than my people, since we firmly believe uniformly many things which philosophers reject altogether. For example, that lyric poet speaks about us: "Let a Jewish Apella believe, not I."[76]

TORALBA: It is the mark of a stubborn mind to be unwilling to yield to convincing arguments and also the mark of greatest folly to agree rashly with everyone on everything. Also there are those who try to overwhelm us with a multitude of theological mites. However, I do not believe them, or, to use the words of that Sicilian shepherd, "I am not one soon persuaded."[77] Indeed, is any one so limited in his mental capacities that he agrees that God eternal, who had been incorporeal for 600,000 centuries, indeed from infinite time, came down from heaven not so long ago and hid himself in the womb of a young woman for nine months; then clothed with flesh, bones, and blood, and born from a virgin womb, after a little while he suffered a shameful punishment, was buried, and P. 250
rose again, and took to heaven that bodily mass which was unknown there before? All Hebrew and Ismaelite people and all groups of philosophers uniformly deny that this so new and unusual change befits God. Indeed that awesome, heavenly word stands in the way: "I am God eternal, and I am not changed."[78] These words not only pertain to essence but also to those things which are thought to happen to that essence.

SENAMUS: I agree with Salomon on the other things, but I do not understand this: if God even in the nature of His mind is unchangeable, why is He said to become angry and to be placated so many times, and to regret His actions?

SALOMON: Indeed that is like the word of a best parent, as it were, stammering with babies; as when God had said to Samuel that He felt

[76] Horace, *Sat.* I. 5. 100.
[77] Theocritus, VII. 38.
[78] Isaiah 44:6.

annoyance with Saul in that He had renounced him as king;[79] moreover, in the same chapter He added these words: "God will never repent the deed, because He is not man that He should repent any deed."[80] To be sure, either that so great change of God toward man or the assumption of mankind makes God better or worse. It is a sin to say the one; it is wrong to think the other. For from the infinite eternity of time He was the best and greatest. He could not become better or more blessed than Himself; otherwise He would not have been best and most blessed before. It must be admitted that He became worse through so great a change of His state and nature, and nothing more dangerous than this can be imagined.

CORONAEUS: He became neither better nor worse, and He was not even changed from that One who had always existed before and as He will always exist. In similar argument Proclus established that the world was eternal, lest, if it should have a beginning, God would seem to have been aroused from deep rest to motion, from inactivity to activity.[81]

SALOMON: To be sure this is consistent with the hidden secrets of divine laws that God rejoices in the perpetual creation and recreation of worlds, and there is nothing new under the sun which shall not have been before, nor had been which will not be. For this reason God does not allow any change or conversion of His own state. However, for the same One to have joined Himself with human nature and flesh not so long ago, that is, a little more than fifteen centuries, is not only contrary to the nature and essence of God but also contrary to the honor of His majesty.

FRIDERICUS: Indeed unbelievers think this is incredible, but those on whom the divine mind has breathed can very easily be persuaded.

P. 251 OCTAVIUS: Surely it was not difficult to convince the Greeks and Latins[82] in the beginning of the early Christian church that man became God, for they believed so much in the embraces of gods and men and their children that not only by rustic and untutored men was this held to be most certain and established, as it were, but also by the Greeks and Romans[83] who flourished in the praise of all disciplines. Let the trustworthy story about Mundus, a Roman citizen, be a proof.[84] Mundus, with the greatest show of piety and with the detestable pandering of the priests, seduced a most chaste matron who was persuaded, along with her husband, that

79 I Kings (I Sam.) 15:11.

80 I Kings (I Sam.) 15:29.

81 Dodds, *Proclus*, pp. 37–38, Prop. 33–35; also cf. p. 53, Prop. 55.

82 *Graecis ac Latinis* M

83 *Graecis ac Romanis* M

84 Josephus, *Antiq.* XVIII. 67–77.

Hercules himself had lain with her in the temple for the propagation of a divine offspring. When the fraud, which Mundus could not conceal, was found out, Tiberius Augustus ordered the temple to be levelled and the priests to be burned with avenging flames. And so, it is not strange if the pagans were persuaded to believe that Christ, who had been famous for the integrity of his life and the number of his miracles, was born from God and a virgin, since they had already been imbued with a similar generation of gods.

SENAMUS: Surely the childbirths of gods and goddesses introduced not only theogony but also remarkable apotheoses for the Roman emperors and popes. When Cardinal Bessarion had seen these apotheoses happen at Rome, he said that the stories of the old saints had become strongly suspect to him.

TORALBA: I do not doubt that the unlearned could be persuaded[85] of those things, but I am amazed that the learned could be persuaded. For if, extremes having been known, the intermediate things are not therefore known, even if they were connected by an essential order of causes, who can comprehend Christ, who, they say, is of a human and divine nature, since God can be connected by no order of nature with man, and even less than the sky can be united to the earth?

CORONAEUS: The old Academicians say that man is a link between the heavenly and elementary world, and therefore he alone of every living species has been fashioned to the likeness and image of God.[86] Since these things are so, who can think that the order of nature has been disturbed if God is united to man in Christ?

TORALBA: The comprehension of an infinite matter is a certain infinite thing which cannot be compatible with finite nature. Nor is there truth in that which I see has pleased certain theologians: namely, that the human mind is capable of infinite intelligible successions which would necessitate that the mind be eternal in men or surely everlasting by its own nature. This has been proven otherwise before. But if the human mind cannot even comprehend infinite God in thought, how is it possible that it can comprehend the infinite essence of God and be united to Him in action and in substance itself?

FRIDERICUS: The remarkable acts of Christ and His wondrous deeds furnish that which the weakness of the human mind cannot grasp.

[85] *imperitis ista persuaderi non dubito* M

[86] Cf. Plato, *Tim.* 42E. Also see Dodds, *Proclus*, pp. 29–31, Prop. 25–26; also commentary, pp. 213–16.

P. 252 OCTAVIUS: If miracles make gods, what hinders each greatest magician making himself a god? What indeed do soothsayers not undertake? What does a throng of witches not accomplish? Is not anyone's clear vision dulled? The magicians of Pharaoh, the followers of Orpheus, Medea, Circe, Cleomedes Astypalaeus, Apollonius of Tyana are examples.[87] This Apollonius[88] caused such wonder with so great a variety of portents, that the ancients preferred him not only to Christ himself but also to all the gods of Christians. Indeed, he is said to have aroused many from the dead, checked common diseases, often cured the dying, rather often predicted future events, often caused demons to flee by his presence. He always abstained from eating living things as long as he lived; he was most famous for his erudition and wisdom; he was most divine in his precepts of wisdom. He drove away hordes of witches with a word; he freed Ephesus from a deadly plague. He ordered an old man wearing a mantle to be covered over with stones; when buried, the man was uncovered; he revealed a dead lion had been uncovered. He lived 140 years, and he ascended into heaven, snatched from the very temple of Diana and was greeted by the trees themselves speaking from the curved summit with a learned voice. Finally, all Greece and Asia considered him a god. Surely he was received by the ancients with such praise that oracles were sought from his statues as if from Apollo himself. He was famous and admirable not only to pagans but also to Christians, and especially to Jerome and Justin Martyr, who[89] say that storms at sea, violent winds, hordes of mice, and attacks of wild beasts were prevented by the dictates of that Apollonius.[90]

FRIDERICUS: Indeed Philostratus says many things about Apollonius,

[87] Cleomedes Astypalaeus was considered a magician and worshipped as a god. In 492 B.C. he killed Iccus in a boxing match at the Olympic games. The judges, concluding that he was guilty of unfair play, took away his prize. He returned to Astypalaea and in anger shook down the roof of a boys' school. When the people prepared to stone him, he fled to the temple of Athena and hid in a box. When the box was opened, it was empty. The people consulted the Delphic oracle, who said: "Cleomedes the Astypalaean, the last of the heroes whom you honor with sacrifices, is now no longer a mortal." See Smith, *Dictionary* (London, 1844), I, 791–92. Also Pausanias, VI. 9. Also see Homer, *Ody.* X. 210 ff.; Ovid, *Metamorph.* VII. 162 ff.; Pindar, *Pyth.* IV. 250; Apollonius Rhodius, *Argonautica* IV. 410 ff.

[88] See Philostratus, *Life of Apollonius of Tyana.* Note especially IV. 40–41.

[89] *qui* M

[90] According to Philostratus' account, Apollonius did not lay claim to divine powers. He believed that the virtue he possessed was to be attributed to his knowledge of Pythagorean philosophy and his asceticism. Cf. Justin, *Ad orthod.* 245 and Jerome, *Ad rufinum.*

but only the things which he had heard from Damis; Damis likewise heard from Apollonius other things. Nevertheless these things were refuted as incredible in eight books by Eusebius of Caesarea. However, he was more famous for his magic than his learning, since he was accustomed to veil himself in the manner of magicians and to break iron chains with the help of demons. Therefore, his hair was plucked out by the order of Domitian Augustus, and he was forced to defend himself naked when charged with the impiety of witchcraft.

Octavius: Still you see that the miracles of that magician had so much power that for several generations he was worshipped as a god, and it was objected to the Christians that the miraculous deeds of Apollonius were far superior to those of Christ. Indeed he was almost the same age as Christ, or not much younger.

Salomon: To be sure, that age was most productive in its rich supply of magicians; in addition to Apollonius it brought forth Dositheus, P. 253
Theudas, Judas Galilaeus, and Simon Magus, who claimed for themselves the names and reputation of divinity.[91] Why, even when a certain magician in Arabia who claimed to be the Messiah had enticed as many as possible to himself by remarkable signs, the king of the Arabs asked by what miracle he wished to show that he was the Messiah. He said: "Order my head to be cut off; then if I do not come back to life, do not think that I am the Messiah." The king accepted this condition and ordered the man's head to be cut off as the people watched; and he did not come back to life.

Curtius: The madness, or shall I say, impiety of many was so great that they not only claimed divinity for themselves but also tried to cast God Himself headlong from heaven, as formerly the brothers sworn to ascend to heaven. Even Heraclides Ponticus did not hesitate to bribe the Pythian priests with money so that they would proclaim that he was God, and he ordered a serpent to be placed on a bier on which he was carried. However, when the fraud was disclosed, he was judged not as he wished himself to be, but as he was.[92] Also they say that Psapho the African was

[91] See Acts 5:34–38. On Judas the Galilean, see *Encyclopedia Judaica* (Jerusalem, 1970), X, 354; on Theudas, see *ibid.*, XV, p. 111; on Dositheus (Samar.) see *ibid.*, VI, 313.

[92] Heraclides of Heraclea, who was called Ponticus, was an Academic philosopher, a disciple of Pythagoras, and writer (390–310 B.C.). He was left in charge of the school during Plato's third Sicilian journey. After Xenocrates was elected master of the Academy, Heraclides returned to Heraclea. His most important contributions to science were his molecular theory and his astronomical discoveries. He even

of this kind, who had taught divining birds[93] to say these words: "Psapho is a god."[94] Next he flew. However, Simon Magus seemed to surpass all the tricks of everyone.[95] He was famous for his portents and signs; he not only raised many from the dead but also raised himself on the third day after he had been cut into pieces and was thus carried on high into the air in the sight of the Roman people and a crowd of nobles. The impudence of that man was so great that he called himself God. Moreover, he said that he had come into the world to correct those things which[96] had been corrupted by angels and to save those who believed in him from eternal destruction, not according to their merits but according to his grace.

FRIDERICUS: What sort of end did he have except that he crashed headlong with a clatter as he was cast from the lofty air!

SENAMUS: If he had crashed with a clatter, why would the Senate and the Roman people, why would the college of priests, with the emperor's approval, have erected statues to him with divine inscriptions? Indeed Claudius Augustus ordered his statue to be placed between the two bridges of the Tiber and inscribed to "Simon Magus a god." Justin Martyr says that he saw this statue.[97] No one could be enrolled in the number of gods without the decree of the Senate. For example, Tertullian in writing about Christ says that the emperor Tiberius had written to the Senate about Christ who in his opinion should be listed among the gods.[98] The Senate was unwilling, either because it did not approve or because it was reluctant for a Jew, who had been condemned to death, to be inscribed in the list of gods. According to Tertullian, Tiberius, nevertheless, kept his opinion. We know from this that Simon Magus seemed more famous than Christ in the number of his remarkable deeds and miracles.

OCTAVIUS: No one doubts that that magician surpassed the rest in the deception of his tricks. Still who does not see that all these were done with
P. 254 the help of demons? Nothing seemed more remarkable than to be aroused

---

hypothesized that the sun is in the center of the universe and the earth revolves around it. However, he was not a scientist in the strict sense; he believed strongly in occult and supernatural knowledge. Diogenes Laërtius (V. 86–90) refers to Heraclides. See *Ox. Class. Dict.*, pp. 414–15.

[93] *oscines* M

[94] Cannot be identified. This may be from Leo Afer.

[95] See Justin Martyr, *Apol.* I. 26, 56; *Dial. Tryph.* 120. Also Tertullian, *Apol.* I. 13.

[96] *Quae . . . corrupta* M

[97] *Apol.* I. 26, 56.

[98] *Apol.* I. 5.

from the dead and to be carried on high, yet each of these feats is very common to necromancers. Apollonius from farthest Ethiopia and the sources of the Nile was borne to Rome in a second where he knew he was summoned by the decree of the emperor Domitian; then in a moment he went to Corinth, and from Smyrna to Ephesus. Likewise, Pythagoras flew from Thurii to Metapontum,[99] and Romulus was numbered among the gods for no other reason than that he was carried from the sight of men and disappeared into heaven as the army and Senate looked on.[100] The ancient writers have said that the same thing happened to Aristaeus Proconnesus[101] and to Cleomedes Astypalaeus.[102] It is certain that all these magicians had been found guilty of the crime of impiety.

CURTIUS: This happened if they gave themselves over to demons of their own free will. However, sometimes men of outstanding piety and integrity are tormented and tortured with divine consent, as is said about Job. The same is true of Christ, who, although He was the exemplar of all piety and divinity was nevertheless carried by a demon up to the pinnacles of the temple and then to the mountain to test His virtue and excellence. However, when Christ's steadfastness, piety and divinity were discovered, the evil demon was crushed, and he departed. And so Christ at this time said: "The prince of this world will be cast out; he will bear no triumph from Me."[103]

CORONAEUS: As a monkey is a monkey, though clothed in purple, so a magician, however he presents himself, will always be like himself. The emperor Vespasian is said to have been always most devoted to the art of magic, and with a crowd of Alexandrians watching he wished to imitate Christ in the miracle of the man blind from birth to whom He gave sight by placing clay mixed with spittle on his eye. Tranquillus and

[99] There were a multitude of fictions connected with the life of Pythagoras: namely, that Apollo was his father; that he gleamed with a supernatural brightness; that he displayed a golden thigh; that Abaris flew to him on a golden arrow; that he was seen in different places at the same time. See Herodotus, IV. 94.

[100] As Romulus was reviewing his people in the Campus Martius, darkness came over the earth, and a terrible storm scattered the people. When daylight came, Romulus had disappeared, for Mars had carried him up to heaven in a fiery chariot. See Horace, *Carm.* III. 3; also Ovid, *Fast.* II. 496.

[101] Aristaeus, who was once a mortal, became a god because of the benefits he had bestowed upon mankind. He was worshipped as the protector of flocks and shepherds, of vines and olives. He also taught men the art of bee-keeping. See Pausanias, X. 17. 3. and Vergil, *Georg.* I. 14; IV. 283 ff.

[102] See above, p. 330, note 87.

[103] John 12:31.

Tacitus, the most authoritative historians recorded this.[104] Pliny writes that Nero had been addicted to these skills. But to judge true religion no proof is more certain than that which Gamaliel wrote. When the Christian apostles were charged with impiety by the magistrate and priests because they had granted some divinity to Christ, Gamaliel addressed the assembly. "Turn your attention to these things which you are about to decree. In the past a certain Theudas lived who claimed many things about himself and drew about 400 disciples to himself; yet not much later he was killed with all his followers. Likewise another impostor was Judas Galilaeus, who had seduced the people for a time; at length he was vanquished with all his associates. Therefore be unwilling to rage against those men. For if this teaching is from men, it will be destroyed in a short time; if it is from God, we would block His will in vain."[105] Persuaded by this speech the priests freed the apostles from the fear of dangers. What
P. 255 did it benefit Apollonius, Simon Magus and Cleomedes Astypalaea that they raised themselves from the dead? What benefit was there for Empedocles and Romulus that they are said to have been taken up into heaven? Since the teaching of Christ has been spread throughout the world now for more than fifteen centuries, it has planted its roots very deeply, in spite of the opposition of people and princes; death and cruel tortures could not destroy it nor the utterances of countless heretics. Who can doubt that it is the best and most divine of all religions?

SALOMON: If God opposes, I admit that nothing can happen; nor do I doubt that all religions which do not have God as their founder will perish sooner or later. For thus our elders, as if with one voice, testified.

SENAMUS: Against immortal God nothing can be commanded for any length of time, as once Themistocles the Athenian and Marcus Cato the Censor before the assembly of the Roman people are said to have said.[106] Now on the other hand, those who measure the excellence of a religion by its duration alone say that the religion of the pagans was best, since for almost four thousand years from the time of Belus and Nimrod it flourished throughout the world and even in this age among the orientals of India, who worship the sun, moon, stars, fires, cows, elephants, and statues of dead men for gods. Not so long ago, the American Indians sacrificed men on the altars of demons. And indeed our grandfathers remembered that in Mexico[107] more than twenty thousand men were sacrificed in one

[104] Suetonius, *Vespasian* VII; Tacitus, *Hist.* IV. 82. 2.

[105] Acts 5:34–39.

[106] Plutarch, *Themist.* and *Cato cens.*

[107] *Messica regione* M

year. We read that sacrifice was very common not only to the Amorites and the Ammonites, but also to the Latins, Greeks, Germans, Gauls, and Africans.[108] Yet Darius, king of the Persians, in a decree had forbidden the Carthaginians to eat human flesh and to sacrifice human victims. Likewise, one article of the treaty which Gelon struck with the Carthaginians near Himera forbade the Carthaginians to sacrifice human victims.[109] Nonetheless, when they had been ordered by Agathocles to make the gods propitious to them, they sacrificed to the gods two hundred children of the nobles.[110] And before the consulship of Cornelius Lentulus and Publius Crassus, the Romans themselves did not even abstain from human sacrifices. These consuls decreed that no longer were sacrifices to be offered with human blood. The Gauls, however, did not stop this practice before the rule of Tiberius, who was the first to forbid this.[111] If so great impiety throughout the world for so many centuries was considered most religious, who can think that the truth of a religion can be approved by its duration?

CORONAEUS: Gradually all this impiety was removed, and the Christian religion was spread far and wide into both Indies, so that now its boundaries are the same as the course of the sun. And this is the greatest proof of the true religion, that is, the Roman Catholic church, which both Indies accepted of their own accord. P. 256

CURTIUS: We have established proofs of the best religion in the true church, in true records, in true prophecies, true reasons, and in true piety,

[108] See Pliny, *Hist. nat.* VII. 2. 11–14.

[109] Gelon was the son of Deinomenes, tyrant of Gela and afterwards of Syracuse. His family was one of the most illustrious in his native city, having been among the original founders. See Herodotus VII. 158–66 and Diodorus XI. 26. The forbidding of human sacrifice is most likely a fiction of later times.

[110] Agathocles (361–289 B.C.), a tyrant of Syracuse, was noted for his cruelty. See *Cambridge Ancient History* (New York, 1930), VIII. 19.

[111] The offering of a human victim in Greece is attested by Homer, *Iliad* XXIII. 171 ff. Human sacrifice was not a regular practice at Rome; in the third century B.C., however, two pairs of Gaulish and Greek men and women were buried alive in the Forum Boarium in accordance with Sibylline oracles. At an early stage human sacrifice was abolished from the official religion. Under foreign influence and especially under the influence of the Sibylline oracles it again surfaced and survived in sacrificial transactions outside the state religion till the close of the Imperial period. Pliny (*Hist. nat.* XXX. 12 ff.) refers to the Senate's decree of 97 B.C. against human sacrifice. Tiberius prohibited the immolation of the Druids and also human sacrifice in the worship of Saturn in Africa. See Tertullian, *Apol.* IX. Claudius re-enacted the decree against the Druids, and Hadrian stopped human sacrifice in the cult of the Cyprian Jupiter. See Hastings, *Encycl. of Rel. and Eth.*, VI, 858–62.

not in its duration, its vast boundaries, or in the number of ceremonies or gods. And perhaps both Indies would have profited more if the Spanish had brought them the simplest and purest religion of the Christian sects —and there are many—that is, the Swiss. Indeed the Spanish were outstanding in that they removed the most loathsome sacrifices of men, because they forbade the most cruel eating of human flesh, because they refused that sacrifices be performed to demons, and they destroyed the statues of demons. However, I cannot approve the fact that they exchanged idols for idols.

Octavius: When Francisco Pizarro in our age had penetrated the innermost recesses of Peru, the inhabitants were worshipping almost no god except the sun.[112] Moreover, when a certain Franciscan tried to convert King Athabaliba to Christ and call him away from the worship of the sun by telling him rather often that Christ had died for the salvation of the human race, this Athabaliba said: "Do you thus worship a mortal god who died on the cross? I worship that God, immortal and eternal (pointing to the sun) and not hung." And since nothing is more admirable in this universe than the sun, nothing more excellent, nothing more divine except eternal God's majesty, it is not strange if all peoples everywhere in the world have not yet completely stopped worshipping the sun. And if there is any excuse for idolatry, those surely sin less who worship the most beautiful image of divine majesty than those who worship a dead man as the Christians do. Moreover, almost all Asia and Africa and a great part of Europe have withdrawn from this superstition by accepting the saner and better teaching of Mohammed, which flourishes now for about a thousand years and will flourish forever. The most ancient pagan religion showed how great a debt Christians owe to ancient religions. For who in this time cannot wonder that Jupiter, some one or other of the Cretan tyrants,[113] a man who took part in parricides, incests, and adulteries, was believed to be a god and was worshipped for so many thousands of years in the whole world.

Salomon: The Israelites must always be excepted. They cursed not only that monster of evils, Jupiter, I mean, but also felt sympathy for those who had found pleasure in so great superstition. Out of pity they atoned

[112] Sun worship dominated not only the Inca life of Peru and the Aztec life of Mexico but of all Indians of the Americas. The dances imitated the orderly movement of the sun, and the ball in games represented the sun. See "Sun, Moon, and Stars (American)," Hastings, *Encycl. of Rel. and Eth.*, XII, 65–71.

[113] Jupiter was said to have been born on Mt. Ida in Crete.

for them as much as they could in the most holy temple before immortal God, whom alone from the foundation of the world up to the present our elders declared we must worship.

From this one knows that the religion of the Israelites is by far superior to all others in its antiquity, truth, and constancy, and it has neither Jupiter nor Christ nor Mohammed as its founder, but God eternal. Indeed all people will some day embrace this religion; God Himself says to Isaiah that at some time all nations will make sacrifices to the God of Israel. P. 257

FRIDERICUS: Do you think, Salomon, that immortal God would have allowed Christ to be worshipped as God by all for so many thousands of years if He were not God?

SALOMON: With that same reasoning and argument the worship of demons and dead men must be directed to God, if it were right to measure the truth of religion by its duration and course of years. But with a clear voice God cursed that impiety. "Your destruction is from you; however, salvation is from Me, oh Israel!"[114]

TORALBA: I think men's destruction must be attributed to men themselves, not to the Creator, because they, of their own accord, departed from the law of nature which contains the worship of one eternal God; and when their error was recognized, they did not allow themselves to be recalled to its service. Indeed as I view the almost infinite variety of sects, Christians differing with Ismaelites and pagans differing among themselves, no standard of truth seems more certain than right reason, that is, the supreme law of nature, planted in men's minds by immortal God, than which nothing more stable, nothing more ancient, nothing better can be made or even imagined. Moreover, with this law of nature and religion Abel, Seth, Enoch, Noah, Job, Abraham, Isaac and Jacob lived, and they reaped the highest praise of piety, integrity, and justice from the most awesome testimony of God eternal, the only One whom they worshipped. I see that no religion is better or more ancient than this.

CURTIUS: If we follow the laws of nature, the Christian religion ought to seem especially compatible with the nature of all things because it proclaims that we ought not to worship and emulate anyone except that eternal God, Parent of the universe, who took on the nature of man for man's salvation.

CORONAEUS: I see that we have gradually slipped into the question which we had proposed yesterday about the union and mingling of both natures,

[114] Hos. 13:9.

namely, divine and human, which we must diligently unfold because of the merit of the argument.

TORALBA: But before we talk about the union of both natures, divine and human, we must explain whether it was necessary for the salvation of the human race that God eternal be clothed in flesh. For if it was in no way necessary, a completion of the discussion about the union of both natures will be far easier.

P. 258 FRIDERICUS: Why easier?

TORALBA: Because nothing must be established in the nature of the universe if without its establishment no perfection is lacking the universe and the supreme happiness. No perfection was lacking either the highest good or the universe before God became man, as you wish. Therefore, God would have assumed the bodily nature of man in vain, because it was not necessary. A plurality ought never to be permitted by nature, unless necessary. Moreover, it is a constant in universal nature that necessary things are not lacking nor do superfluous things abound.

CORONAEUS: Previously Toralba has proven that divine power is so free that it is subjected to no necessity. Therefore, God could do things which were not necessary, and so the question would remain whether God willed that which He could.

TORALBA: That God did not will to produce a divine person is obvious from the most powerful proof: namely, that a creature alone is able to be and not to be, not so the divine person, who was from time eternal, before all this which could be. Therefore, the will of God was to produce only a creature, not also a person divine and uncreated. The theologians agreed that only two persons were produced from one producing as from a creator. To steer clear of this argument as if of a rock,[115] each of the keenest theologians held that producing was necessary in God.[116]

CURTIUS: Indeed those questions are too craftily and subtly posed; since the secrets of God can be sought out, still they cannot be found except by him to whom God Himself has made them clear. However, from the Builder's works one knows well enough what He willed. And so the Master of the Sentences said: "The Father in His divine sanction produced a Son not from necessity, since necessity or coaction is not in accordance with God, nor from will, since change is not suitable to God. Nevertheless, God is said to have produced a Son by a previous or ante-

[115] *scopulum* M

[116] Marginal note in M indicates Scotus, *Quaest. VI in prolegom, sentent, 1. 1.*

cedent will, as if He willed first and[117] afterwards produced, as the heretics claimed."[118] That one said these things.

TORALBA: Still one of the two is necessary because there is no third, and it cannot even be conceived that a producing of persons by a certain divine will or necessity has happened. But if neither existed, it follows that there could be no producing of persons in a divine essence, which is most simple in its own nature.

FRIDERICUS: If we lay aside a discussion of divine power and will which exceeds weak human intelligence, let us use these reasons which come nearer to human understanding. If anyone happened to do the things P. 259 which are only suitable to God alone, let us admit that this one surely is God. But to one mortal alone, Christ, did power equal to God, the same essence, the highest holiness, remarkable wisdom, and infinite goodness, befall. Therefore, we must confess that this One is God.

TORALBA: If the antecedent is true, the consequent will be a necessary consequence. But that is an assumption which must be demonstrated. And so if the antecedent is destroyed, the consequence topples. Since the creature cannot be the creator, then Christ, since He was a true man and a true creature, could not be creator of Himself. For nature does not allow, nor reason admit, that he who is from another is himself the same one from whom he is. Christ is a creature, first, by reason of the flesh because He was conceived in the womb of a woman; next, by reason of the created soul, as the Christian theologians admit; next, by reason of the producing of a second person which necessarily follows the first. Therefore, the same one who is a creature cannot be a creator. Just as other things which are light have splendor and light from the very light of the sun, still, none of these can be either light or the sun. So also are angels, stars, and human minds participants of goodness and the intellectual light, yet in no way can they become gods because they have another principle of their origin. So the divine Plato judged most correctly that from a likeness of the sun—Dionysius says from the likeness of fire—[one] is guided in a certain way to the recognition of God.[119]

FRIDERICUS: Who doubts that God, insofar as He is Creator, cannot be creature. But, since in one Christ there is a dual nature, also in Him it is necessary that contradictions be true at the same time, since the rationale

[117] *ac* M

[118] Marginal note in M indicates Lombard, *Lib. III. distinct. 6.*

[119] Plato, *Res pub.* VI. 19.

is different. Damascenus said that Christ is created and uncreated, passible and impassible, creator and creature by reason of a communication of idioms.[120]

CORONAEUS: I see that we have entered an inextricable labyrinth, and I would almost say a deep gorge. One can learn who Christ was and of what sort He was better from His actions than from subtle discourse; that is, from the purpose of His life, from His holiness, His teaching, the multitude of His remarkable miracles, and from the voice of immortal God Himself witnessing. And we see that these things have happened to no other mortal.

SALOMON: Who can affirm what holiness of life there was in Christ, since it appears from the writings of the apostles that he was on good terms with criminals and harlots? And indeed Origen writes that Celsus seized this opportunity for writing against the Christians because Barnabas, a disciple of Christ, said in a certain letter to the Catholics that Christ had received to Himself the most wicked disciples and those worse than vileness itself.[121] Yet all wise men acknowledge that no advice is more important than to stay as far as possible from the association, companionship, and intimacy of wicked men.[122] In the beginning of the Psalms the
P. 260 Psalmist says: "O happiness of that man who does not go to the counsel of the wicked and does not stand in the path of sinners and does not sit in the seat of the scornful."[123]

CURTIUS: When Christ was charged with the crime of speaking with the shameful and with sinners, He refuted the charge with an honest remark: "I came not to call the just, but sinners."[124] Pontius Pilate, the governor, sufficiently showed how innocently He lived when he said that he had found no reason for the charge for which he should condemn Him.[125] Nevertheless, he is said to have given Him over to the people to be scourged for their enjoyment of the spectacle so that by some reckoning he might arouse the accusers to pity. When he was not able to accomplish

[120] Johannes Damascenus is noted for his resolution of the problem of how the divine Logos can also be man. The former is controlling and formative agency, the latter a potential human individual (neither humanity in general nor a developed person). This personal Logos acquires concrete reality, which is substance only through the Logos. Thus he speaks of the interchange of divine and human attributes, a communication between the active and the passive. The drift is thus towards the Monophysite position. *Encycl. Brit.* (11th ed.), XV, 448–49.

[121] *Contra Celsum* I, 63; *Ep. Barn*, 9.

[122] Eph. 5:7. [123] Psalm 1:1. [124] Matt. 9:13.

[125] John 18:38; 19:4, 12.

this, he feared the charge of treason which was being brought against him because of Christ, and at length he sentenced Him to death.[126]

OCTAVIUS: So the Christian theologians think, but they err in this because they do not understand that no one was sentenced to death according to Roman law without first being beaten with scourges and ropes.[127] In truth, the miracles of Christ are limited to about three kinds: namely, the resurrection of two women (for only John bears witness to Lazarus' resurrection), the banishment of demons, and the cure of some diseases. Finally, there is the fact that He is said to have walked on the waters and to have been carried up into the sky.[128]

SENAMUS: You overlook, Octavius, the first miracle of all and a solemn sign, the changing of water into wine, when no wine was left in the empty jars.[129]

SALOMON: It seems to me that he would have acted more fittingly if he had inured the guests to sobriety. Simon Magus, Apollonius, and countless others did this kind [of miracle] and very often from dry trees drew wine in form, color, smell, and taste. When Galen deals with hermetic medication, he wonders how many cannot cure[130] unless the one who wishes[131] to be cured has[132] most certain faith in the cure.[133] Indeed magicians use these words: "Believe and you will be healed; your faith has made you well."[134]

CURTIUS: With the most powerful proofs, Christ refuted the idle and shameful calumnies of the Jews who accused Christ of using the help and work of a demon. He said: "If demons were cast out by demons, you would see the power and force of demons collapse in a short time."[135] In the same way families and empires collapse from civil strifes and are scattered.

[126] John 19:12–13.

[127] Suetonius, *Nero* XV. The profession of Christianity was classified as *crimen maiestatis,* which included all offenses against the security, independence, or honor of the Roman people. The penalty was always death. See *Ox. Class. Dict.,* pp. 484–91, 663.

[128] The division of miracles into three kinds is not uncommon. For example, miracles worked upon man, miracles worked upon nature, and events that might be explained by coincidence but not by themselves *praeter naturam.* Hastings, *Dictionary of the Bible,* III, 390 uses this and refers to other schemes.

[129] John 2:1–11. [130] *curare* M [131] *cupit* M [132] *habeat* M

[133] See Book II, p. 31, note 90; p. 48, note 186.

[134] Matt. 9:22; Mark 5:34; 10:52; Luke 7:50; 8:48; 17:19; 18:42.

[135] Matt. 9:33–38.

SALOMON: Long experience has very often proved that argument to be most insignificant. Quite often those obsessed by demons are freed by the words of magicians or by a light touch, or a circle drawn on the forehead
P. 261 or a whisper in the ear. But rather often demons pretend to struggle or resist. Polycrates, however, refutes this pretense by saying: "Evil demons do willingly what they seem to do unwillingly, and they pretend that they are driven by the power of exorcisms which they form in the name of the Trinity, and in this way they mock at men until they involve them in a crime of witchcraft and[136] the punishment of condemnation."[137] Likewise, Leo Afer writes about African magicians that very often demons were driven out by magicians by drawing[138] a circle on the forehead. And yet we see that the banishment of demons caused more harm than good. For example, when demons left bodies, Jesus sent them into a flock of pigs which the demons immediately drove headlong into the water with great harm to the home and community.[139] There is a similar story about a certain rich soothsayer-nobleman in England. When he freed a Spanish demoniac in Belgium and sent the demon into a herd of cows, the cows mangled each other and killed the shepherds. Then the magician disappeared while the magistrate sought him for punishment.

FRIDERICUS: However, Christ easily refuted all the charges by the holiness of His life and His marvelous integrity. And yet the accusers cannot reject Josephus, the son of Mathatias, witness by far above any objection.[140] He writes about Christ "as if about a man most eager for wisdom, if it is right to call Him a man."

SALOMON: That chapter has been attributed to Josephus, but its brevity and the manner of writing shows it is an addition. However, Josephus, son of Gorio, who wrote the same history as that one and at the same time, did not write one word about Christ because he wrote in Hebrew;[141] and the Latins and Greeks could not violate the faith of the Hebrew truth because they did not know the Hebrew language.

TORALBA: Since magicians make use of cures of disease, casting out of demons, resurrection of the dead, airy flights and other things of this kind,

[136] *ac* M

[137] The Polycrates referred to may be the Athenian rhetorician and sophist who was a contemporary of Socrates and Isocrates. He wrote an accusation of Socrates. It is uncertain whether Polycrates the rhetorician is the same as the Polycrates who wrote a work on Laconia, referred to by Athenaeus.

[138] *descripto* M

[139] Matt. 8:32; Mark 5:13; Luke 8:33.

[140] Josephus, *Bellum Jud.*, I. 3.

[141] Josephus, *Antiq.*, XVIII. 63.

they hold a strong argument not only for the proof of deity but also for the conjecture of impiety.

Octavius: The Ismaelites attribute to Christ not deity but divinity, as to Moses, Elias, and Samuel, and they even admit that He was greater than all these and Mohammed and lived in the highest holiness of life, with a unique teaching and piety.

Curtius: Then what sort of stubbornness is this to take deity away from Him who distinguished Himself with so many virtues and so much divinity and who, they finally admit, was the Messiah. I think I could say most truthfully that Christ would have explained the edicts, decrees, and laws of the princes and magistrates by the briefest saying of all: "Do not do to another that which you are unwilling to be done to you." Alexander Severus considered this statement of such importance that he ordered it to be published as a perpetual edict. He indeed was the first who P. 262
proposed that Christ be worshipped as a god in the chapel of the Lares.[142]

Coronaeus: That emperor showed how great was the power of Christ's teaching. Although he had been educated along with his cousin Heliogabalus and had grown up with him, still Heliogabalus was the dregs of all disgraces and filth, but that one was singular in all heroic virtues.

Senamus: If Alexander had obeyed this decree, he would have allowed no one to suffer deserved punishments, and the lictors would not have executed the judgments because neither judges nor lictors wanted to be crucified or even scourged. Another simliar saying of Christ is: "Whatever you wish that men do to you, do the same to them."[143] All wish for wealth and honors to be granted for themselves and to indulge in their own pleasures, which no one can satisfy without shame and crime.

Curtius: The laws forbid one to perpetrate a fraud by laws and to distort the meaning of words into an opposite opinion and to change to faults the things which are meant to be virtues.

Fridericus: It is of great importance that Christ alone among so many

[142] Alexander Severus was Roman Emperor from A.D. 222–235. During his reign he improved the morals and condition of the people. His advisers were men like Ulpian, Dio Cassius, and sixteen well-chosen senators. Alexander's reign was noteworthy for its encouragement of literature, art, and science; decrease of taxes, moderate loan rates, and lessening of extravagance at the court. He was broadminded in religious matters. In his private chapel he had busts of Orpheus, Abraham, Apollonius of Tyana, and Jesus. He was dissuaded by the pagan priests from erecting a chapel to Jesus. See Dio Cassius LXXVIII. 30; LXXIX. 17; LXXX. 1; Lampridius, *Alexander Severus.*

[143] Matt. 7:12.

legislators, princes, and philosophers persuaded [men] not only to abstain from all revenge for injuries but also to pray for their enemies.[144]

SENAMUS: Still we see that David in every place and the prophets themselves prayed for all evils to come to their enemies. Therefore, either Christ made a very serious mistake or those did who fashion decrees so contrary that no theologians can reconcile them. However, who can accuse so many prophets of impiety? David spoke thus against his enemy: "Stand over this sinner, and let the devil stand on his right. When he is judged, let him go out condemned, and let his word become a shame. Let his sons become orphans and his wife a widow, and may no one pity his children, and may his name be cut out in one generation!"[145] And at the end [of the Psalm] he added: "This is the penalty for those who scorn me."[146]

SALOMON: Surely we see that David and the prophets are begging vengeance concerning the enemies of God rather than about their own enemies. "Rise up, O Lord," Moses said, "and your enemies will be routed."[147]

SENAMUS: David is indeed speaking openly against the enemies of God, but in almost innumerable places the prophets most eagerly seek the destruction of their own enemies. For example, in the aforementioned Psalm,[148] after he cursed his enemies in an execrable way, he said: "This is the penalty for those who scorn me."[149] He did not say[150] those who scorn God or Christ, but me.

SALOMON: No one doubts that the holiest prophets and men of the greatest piety and integrity wish and pray for destruction upon their own
P. 263 enemies, for no other reason than to teach that they must abstain from all injury and revenge, and vengeance must be left to God alone. The divine law forbids one to avenge private injuries, but God himself demands revenge for them. The advantage of this plea by which we seek vengeance from God is that we have Him as witness of our integrity and innocence and that we abstain from bringing injury in the appearance of vengeance. Jeremiah said: "Since vengeance is God's."[151] However, one must not support Luke's words which seem to defraud divine law. "It has been said of old that you will love your neighbor and hate your enemies."[152] These last words are never found in divine law or any prophets, but the contrary

[144] Matt. 5:44; Luke 6:27.
[145] Psalm 108 (109):6–10.
[146] Psalm 108 (109):20.
[147] Num. 10:35. Also cf. Psalm 67 (68).
[148] Psalm 108 (109).
[149] *mihi* M
[150] *non dixit* M
[151] Jer. 1:15.
[152] These words are from Matt. 5:43, not from Luke.

is plainly enjoined. The law says: "Do not hate anyone with a hidden hatred, but openly accuse him."[153] Likewise:[154] "Do not be mindful of injuries lest you bring vengeance on yourself but love everyone as you love yourself."[155] Indeed there is no greater or better antidote against the lust of raging vengeance and the desire for revenge than to pour it all into the bosom of God Himself who would receive no vengeance except the most just. Still the new lawgiver, to detract from the divine laws, said: "If any one strikes your right cheek with his hand, turn the left cheek to him, and to him who has stolen your tunic, give him also your cloak. Do not ward off force with force."[156] Still all divine and human laws have always allowed and will always allow one to repel an unjust blow from his head in an honorable manner. This ought to be tolerated even less: "Who shall have called his brother a fool, let him be in danger of the fire of Gehenna."[157] These utterances seem so absurd not only to wise men but also to Julian the emperor who attacked the Christian religion after he had deserted it that he completely repudiated them after the books.[158] For if there had been any power in those laws which the Christian princes and magistrates upheld for a long time, there would be no place for innocence against the power of the wicked. The wicked would be allowed to do everything against the good, and the good would be allowed to do nothing against the wicked.

Senamus: Aristotle's opinion is far removed from that of Christ, for he writes that those who do not claim vengeance bring injury on themselves.[159]

Fridericus: Julian the Apostate very wickedly and shamelessly maligned Christ's teaching when he said that Christ gave impunity to robbers and murderers and did not allow anyone to ward off any attacks of enemies.[160] It is one thing to speak of complete duties, another thing to defend meanness of duties. For who would say that he is innocent in

[153] Lev. 19:17. [154] Lev. 19:18.

[155] sed *unumquemque ames aeque ac te ipsum* M

[156] Matt. 5:39–41; Luke 6:29–30.

[157] Matt. 5:22.

[158] After a visit to the schools of Athens in A.D. 355, Julian became completely hellenized and was initiated into Eleusinian mysteries. In 362–363 at Antioch he wrote his books against the Christians. See above, Book II, note 316; Book III, notes 7 and 8.

[159] Cf. *Eud. eth.* III. 1. 1229b. 32. Senamus enlarges upon Aristotle's statement; indeed Aristotle says (*De virt. et vitiis* 1250b. 41) that a magnanimous man is one who can be injured and is not eager to take vengeance.

[160] Julian, *Contra Galil.* 238E, 245B.

respect to all laws? But granted that there is some one who claims to be good in relation to law, how honorable is his innocence, how much piety, humanity, justice, and faith apply to the things which are outside public laws. To ward off force with force and to be unable to control one's
P. 264 anger are characteristics of wild beasts; but to bear injury patiently and to pray for one's enemies are characteristics of consummate and perfect justice which Christ in His superiority to David and all the prophets revealed to mankind. Moreover, Job makes this clear by his speech. After he had spoken many things about his justice, he also added this remark: "If I have felt joy at the misfortune of my enemy, and if I have exulted when evil had come upon him; but not even by a word have I prayed evil for him."[161] This is that highest praise of perfect justice which God granted to Job by the most awesome testimony.

CORONAEUS: Surely this teaching of Plato agrees somewhat with that principle, for he says: "It is better to be wronged than to wrong."[162] It is a well-worn saying that the Academicians were not far away from becoming Christians. Still if anyone did not give his cloak to the one snatching his tunic, the lawgiver, Christ, would have thought him worthy of censure, because His teaching, not His decrees, have been preserved. However, a most upright man will suffer a blow before he will fight or quarrel. We know from this that the teaching of Christ was not the teaching of ordinary philosophers or lawgivers, but was the true archetype of perfect wisdom and integrity.

OCTAVIUS: Let us grant this which Salomon does not concede: that the teaching of Christ was extraordinary, that His life was most holy, that His reputation was most famous, finally that His miracles[163] were not magic but plainly divine. Let us also grant this which is written in the fourth *Azora*: that Christ had a spirit most famous and divine before all other prophets. Nevertheless, since all these things can be true of a man, I do not see why we ought to confess that he is God. And indeed, Moses, Elias, Samuel, and Joshua were much more famous, first, in their teaching, next in the holiness of their lives, next in their miracles. They did not perform these terrestrial miracles of Christ which were almost like the miracles of magicians, but they divided the seas, they checked the courses of rivers, they kept the heaven from raining, they secured rains by prayers, they made the sun and moon stand still. Likewise, Elias and Enoch were

[161] Job 31:29.
[162] Plato, *Gorgias* 474c.
[163] *miracula* M

not carried away from the sight of men after death according to the dubious faith of witnesses but before death by divine power from the view of man.[164] Nevertheless, Christians think it an impiety to have them for gods or worship them.

CURTIUS: The principal proof that Christ far surpassed those prophets is the fact that all the prophecies of all the prophets are directed to Christ as if to a target; nor did He lack the heavenly signs more than Moses, Joshua, or Elias. Even in that vision on Mt. Tabor Moses and Elias were speaking to the triumphant Christ, and those present heard God's voice from the sky, saying: "This is My beloved Son in whom I am well pleased. Hear Him!"[165] When God orders Elias and Moses to hear Christ, did He think that Christ was to be made equal or compared with them? Truly, at P. 265
no other mortal's death except Christ's did the sun seem to vanish and lose its splendor. This could not have happened through nature, since at high noon, when the event occurred, the moon is opposite the diameter of the sun. As Dionysius, a Senator of the Areopagites, said most truthfully, either the God of nature suffers or He threatens the destruction of nature. Moreover, Phlegon Trallianus,[166] a freedman of Hadrian Caesar, writes that the signs of this eclipse occurred in the fourth year of the 210th[167] Olympiad, that is, in the 18th year of Tiberius Augustus.[168] The following men confirmed this in their writings about that eclipse of the sun: Matthew, in the 27th chapter; Mark, in the 15th chapter; Dionysius the Areopagite, in his letters; the historian Eusebius in his *Evangelical Demonstratio* (in the 19th *Demonstratio*); Origen, *Contra Celsum*; Suidas in the article on Dionysius; and Tertullian in the *Apologeticus*.

SALOMON: I shall pass over that transfiguration on Mt. Tabor as unworthy of refutation. Those authors made a serious mistake in their record of the solar eclipse. The fourth year of the 210th Olympiad which Phlegon recorded is the next to last year of Nero's reign,[169] when Silius Nerva and Julius Atticus were consuls, about thirty-two years after Christ's crucifixion. This date accords with the Roman *fasti* and the *Olympiads*[170]

164 II Kings (II Sam.) 2:11; Gen. 5:24.

165 Matt. 17:1–5.

166 Phlegon wrote *Olympiades*, a history reaching from the first Olympiad to A.D. 140.

167 *ducentesimae decimae* M

168 Tiberius' reign was from A.D. 14 to his death in A.D. 37.

169 The dates of Nero's reign are A.D. 54–68.

170 The *fasti* were the *dies fasti* and *dies nefasti* for legal and public business, according to the old calendar, which received definite publication by Cn. Flavius

which Marcus Varro, Dionysius Halicarnassus, Cuspinianus,[171] Sigonius, Onuphrius, Mercator, and Funccius[172] have recorded with such care and detail that no one can doubt them. Moreover, this eclipse of Phlegon which happened thirty-two years after Christ's death was ordinary and natural, in the conjunction of sun and moon, not in the opposition, which those wish, and it followed the murders of the illustrious nobles whom Nero ordered to be killed—Thrasea,[173] Seneca, Piso, and others;[174] and also the murders of his mother and both of his wives.[175] This happened a little after the civil wars and after three Roman emperors in the same year.[176] Also add this to overcome their error, the fact that they say the sun was at that time in the sign of the Fish. This is impossible since no paschal victim was ever sacrificed unless the moon was in the fourteenth [day] of the month of Nisan, when the sun is accustomed to enter the sign of the Ram.[177]

---

in 304 B.C. The Olympiads were so designated from the Olympic games which were held once every four years. The Olympic games began in 776 B.C., hence the first Olympiad was dated 776 B.C.

[171] *Cuspinianus* M

[172] Carolus Sigonius (1524–1584), an Italian humanist, attended the philosophical schools of Bologna and Pavia, was elected professor of Greek at Modena in 1545. Sigonius achieved renown by his publications on Greek and Roman antiquities. The work to which Bodin refers is most like *Fasti consulares* (1550), a history of Rome based on some fragments of bronze tablets dug up in 1547 on the site of the Forum Romanum. See *Encycl. Brit.* (11th ed.), XXV, 82; also J. E. Sandys, *History of Classical Scholarship* (Cambridge, 1908), II, 143. Gerardus Mercator (1512–1594) was a very important geographer and cartographer. He was instrumental in freeing the geography of the 16th century from the tyranny of Ptolemy. In 1587 he completed his world map, *Orbis terrarum compendiosa descriptio.* See *Encycl. Brit.* (11th ed.), XVIII, 149–50.

[173] Thrasea Paetus, a noble Stoic, was renowned for his uprightness and republican sympathies. Nero condemned him to death in A.D. 66, and Thrasea ended his life with characteristic nobility. See Tacitus, *Ann.* XIV. 12; XV. 20–22; XVI. 21–35.

[174] Although the evidence was tenuous, Seneca was named as one of those involved in the conspiracy of Gaius Calpurnius Piso against Nero, along with Faenius Rufus and Lucan. Seneca and Piso were compelled to commit suicide in A.D. 65.

[175] In A.D. 59, Nero had his mother Agrippina murdered. In A.D. 62, he divorced Octavia and had her murdered. He then married Poppaea, but she was murdered in A.D. 66.

[176] The year of the three emperors was A.D. 68–69. Galba was named emperor after Nero's suicide in June, A.D. 68. Galba was murdered by Otho in January, A.D. 69, and he in turn committed suicide in April, A.D. 69, after his army was defeated by Vitellius, who was named emperor.

[177] Ex. 12:6.

CURTIUS: Why then did Dionysius the Areopagite, writing to Polycarp, refute Apollophanes the Sophist with these words: "I do not know by what spirit you have turned your inspiration to divination, Apollophanes, because when you and I were looking at the eclipse of the sun, which was contrary to the order of nature, at the time of Christ's passion, you said to me: 'These are wondrous changes of divine things.' "[178]

TORALBA: Leaving off the controversies of writers of those times, let us seek by clear methods whether or not Christ is God. For if He is the founder and Saviour of the human race, surely, He must be God. But if He is not God, He cannot even be a Saviour of men.

CURTIUS: Surely a necessary proof is that by which the Arians are cleverly refuted. They admitted that He was the Savior of the human race, still they denied that the same one was God. P. 266

SALOMON: Sacred Scripture warns us of nothing more often than that the salvation of all depends on the power of eternal God. "I am God eternal Saviour, holy."[179] Likewise:[180] "I am God eternal,[181] and there is no other one except Me." In like manner: "Our Redeemer is Jehovah, His name is Zebaoth."[182] Likewise: "I am God eternal, the only Savior, who alone is able to bring death and alone can snatch one from death, nor is there another but Me."[183] Likewise: "I am God eternal who removes your iniquities through Myself."[184] He did not say through His Son Jesus, who was crucified or through the future Messiah. Moreover, the theologians of each religion admit that this ineffable and most sacred name YHWH, that is,[185] eternal, is communicable to no creature. If, indeed, the merit of Savior is fitting for him to whom that most sacred name has been granted by divine law, how could it be appropriate for a mortal man?

FRIDERICUS: That very name Jesus or Jehovah means Savior, and it was given specially to Him because He would save mankind. And indeed Paul did not write obscurely or ambiguously that the name, Jesus, was given to Christ alone, and when this name is heard all creatures of heaven, earth, and hell bow.[186] Likewise: "There is no other name under heaven given to men in which we must be saved."[187] Likewise: "As He is higher than the angels, He has secured a more excellent name."[188]

[178] *Epistula* VII, according to marginal note in M
[179] *servator, sanctus* M Isaiah 43:11.
[180] *item* M
[181] *Ego Deus aeternus* M Cf. Isaiah 45:22; 46:9.
[182] Isaiah 47:4.
[183] Cf. Psalm 62:7; 64:12; 118:27.
[184] Ezek. 36:33.
[185] *id est* M
[186] Phil. 2:9–10.
[187] Acts 4:12.
[188] Heb. 1:4.

Salomon: But what are those names? Since the name Jesus or Jehovah is an ordinary and common name, it is never the ineffable name YHWH. Indeed a certain clever theologian[189] rightly refuted the old Christian teachers because they interpret those words—"There is no other name under heaven, etc."—in such a way that the majesty of salvation among mortals was fitting to Christ alone. He said: "Since men cannot ascend into heaven." This reproof is commendable, yet the explanation does not fit the reproof, because it is inconsistent to think that power and excellence can be communicated to any creature of the human race, since this is appropriate only to God alone. However, Peter in an assembly of the people proclaimed that Christ was made by God.[190] Also, Clement, the next successor to Peter in the same priesthood, about whom Paul himself bore praiseworthy testimony, published a book following Eunonius, which is entitled *Recognitions* in which he writes that Jesus had been created.[191]

Curtius: We also admit that Jesus was a creature in regard to His body and mind; that He was conceived in the womb of a virgin, born, was
P. 267 educated, died, was buried. Nor is He called Saviour as a man, but as a Creator. Although He used the human body for producing salvation for men, He was both God and man at the same time; still the divine essence was not mingled with the human mind; nor was the one nature united or blended with the other nature, nor yet altogether divided from the other[192] but in some way each was united with the other under one and the same hypostasis of Christ.

Senamus: I have often been uncertain for what reason this was declared a truth in the time of Peter Lombard: God put on human nature as a garment. Nonetheless, this began to be considered false and heretical afterward, because a garment is not united with the body.[193] Still they believe that human nature is united with divine nature.

189 Calvin.

190 Acts 2:36.

191 Pope Clement I, called Clemens Romanus, is the first successor of St. Peter of whom anything is known. Tertullian (*De praescript.* XXXII) states that the Roman church claimed that Clement was ordained by St. Peter, as also does Jerome (*De viris illust.* XV). However, Jerome correctly states that Clement was the fourth pope after Peter Linus and Cletus. Origen identifies Pope Clement with St. Paul's fellow-laborer, mentioned in Philip. 4:3, and so do Eusebius, Epiphanius, and Jerome; but this Clement was probably a Philippian. The book entitled *Recognitions* is a pseudo-Clementine work, as are many other writings attributed to him. His one genuine writing is a letter to the Church of Corinth. See *Cath. Encycl.*, IV, 12–17.

192 *nec tamen omnino ab altera divulsa* M

193 Duns Scotus, according to the marginalia in M, said the statement was declared heretical after the time of Lombard.

TORALBA: Dionysius says that no duality can be a principle, but a unity is the beginning of duality.[194] But if each nature, namely, divine and human, is not united into one and the same, and one is not separated completely from the other, surely a duality will be united. For this there is need of a certain bond or interlocking, since those two natures are mutually more distant from each other than opposites which are contained under the same species. Still, infinite and finite cannot be encompassed in the same species and cannot be joined by any union. For there is a certain proportion of things which are joined, but there is no proportion of the infinite to the finite. From this it follows that each nature is separated from the other. For if each nature were mingled, both would have to perish for[195] a certain third nature to be established from both. But if divine nature is most simple, it can allow no compounding at all. Otherwise, affirmation and negation about one and the same thing would be necessary to be true at the same time and at the same time to be false.

FRIDERICUS: Christ taught that both natures were united when he said: "I and the Father are one."

OCTAVIUS: The Arians used to contend that that saying pertained to the harmony and mutual consent of each, as also this: "Father, grant that just as You and I are one, so may those be one in Us."[196] Otherwise the apostles themselves would have been gods. In like manner is this: "The One who plants and the One who waters are One."[197] Likewise: "The One who clings to the Lord is one Spirit."[198] Even Christian theologians approve this interpretation of the Arians.

SENAMUS: But Hilary says that we ourselves are one and the same with Christ, not only by adoption and consent, but also by nature.

CURTIUS: By the judgment of all, this opinion is refuted. For we all would be gods and sinless if we were of the same nature and essence with Christ.

CORONAEUS: Many think this happens when one takes Christ's body P. 268
with the help of the sacrament, when His flesh and blood are mingled with ours, and even His mind and divinity are communicated to those who believe.

TORALBA: I do not understand what union of Creator with creature can

[194] Dionysius, called "the Areopagite," stressed unity in his metaphysics: God the One transcends all quality and predication, all affirmation and negation. All things come from him as from one source of light. On this basis he can defend, in theology, a form of Monophysitism (cf. the conciliation of extreme groups that used the Heneticon of Emperor Zeno, A.D. 482). *Cath. Encycl.*, V, 14.

[195] *ad* M [196] John 17:21. [197] I Cor. 3:8. [198] I Cor. 6:17.

take place, since the nature of God is simple and incorporeal, not many nor manifold nor changeable. But if[199] it is not manifold, how will it be three-fold? For whatever is perceived numerically[200] must be divided. Evagrius[201] said: "Either the nature of the Father, Son, and Holy Spirit is simple, or it is composite. Since it is not composite, it is simple. If it is simple, it is also devoid of number."[202]

CORONAEUS: No one thinks God is three-fold. Indeed we admit three in a Unity and one in a Trinity; we deny that He is three-fold or two-fold.

TORALBA: If there is a trinity in divinity, there is a plurality in deity. A numerical distinction is not essential, because when two are established, a third does not follow. Therefore, when a numerical division is separated from a unity, it produces a division of deity, and a manifold arrangement destroys the simplicity of deity. An even more absurd consequence is that the power of God, which is infinite, is changed and weakened by a division in numbers. For the force and power of any thing is greater, the more it is united into itself, and it is weaker, the farther it withdraws from that most simple union. Wherefore, since unity alone is omnipotent, and nothing is simply or absolutely one except God, consequently, the trinity is not omnipotent.

CURTIUS: Number is not related to essence, but to the hypostasis of persons, and divine essence is not divided because of the division of the hypostasis of each person.

SALOMON: If God were three, why does Moses address the assembly of the people thus: "Hear Israel, our God is one God!"[203] Why, in a matter of such great seriousness and importance, would he have omitted that necessary epithet, Three and One? And lest any one doubt that he was looking to the future, he placed larger letters at the end of the first and last word, contrary to the custom of writing. For what does this mean if not to make it clear to all that gods are not infinite nor can they be more than one, in whom no number is suitable.

CURTIUS: Arguments drawn from denials are quite fallacious. He did not say He is three; therefore, He is not three. Nothing follows from this.

[199] *quod si* M [200] *in numerum* M

[201] Evagrius Scholasticus, an ecclesiastical historian of the sixth century, was the last of the writers who continued Eusebius' work. Evagrius' history begins with the Council of Ephesus (431) and ends with the twelfth year of the reign of the Emperor Maurice (593–594). His works shed light on the religious controversies of the fifth and sixth centuries, Nestorianism, Eutychianism, and Monophysitism. See *Cath. Encycl.*, V, 639–40.

[202] *etiam numeri* M [203] Deut. 6:4.

Toralba: There seems to be no fallacy of proof since when one is posited, another is necessarily excluded. For whoever calls him One, excludes three; otherwise, opposites are true at the same time in the order of one and the same thing; namely, God is one; God is not one. All Christian theologians are familiar with the fact that God cannot bring it about that opposites in the same order are true at the same time. This is not to say there is any weakness in God, but because a subject is incapable of affirmation and negation at the same time. Plato does not seem to have meant the contrary when in the *Parmenides* he speaks very fully about Being p. 269 and One, except to explain that the One is that most simple principle of nature and cannot receive anything except unity.[204] Likewise, Xenophanes and Melissus, who also wrote books about Being and One, wished only to prove that the principle of all things is the most simple unity.[205] The Pythagoreans agreed. Iamblichus said that the end of all contemplation is to lift the mind from the multitude to the unity.[206] And so when the Academicians seek an appropriate name for God, they call Him the One, the good, true, simple,[207] which Proclus calls the one foundation of divine unities.[208]

Coronaeus: I see no contradiction in these pronouncements: God is one, God is not one, because they are not in the same order. The first is in the order of essence; the second is in the order of persons. Indeed in the order of persons the Trinity is nothing other than a unity, omnipotent, not divisible, not compounded, not numerable, but most simple in its own nature. Even if in the order of essence it is one, in the order of persons it is threefold.

Toralba: Therefore two hypostases must be concealed in it since one cannot say about one and the same subject that it is creator and creature, mortal and immortal, eternal and changing, stable and fleeting, born and

[204] *Parmenides* 142c–143.

[205] Xenophanes (6th century B.C.) became the poet in Magna Graecia of the Ionian intellectual enlightenment. He criticized Homer and Hesiod by denying that the gods have human shape or understanding. He maintained there was a single supreme Deity who directs the universe through thought. See Diels, *Frag. der Vorsokrat.* (6th ed.), I. 113–39.

Melissus (5th century B.C.) was the last member of the Eleatic school of philosophy. He differed from Parmenides in maintaining the spatial infinity of the universe. For the fragments of his work, *About Nature or About Being*, see Diels, *Frag. der Vorsokrat.* (6th ed.), I. 258–76.

[206] *On the Mysteries*, translated by Thomas Taylor (London, 1968), p. 348.

[207] See Plato, *Parm.* 128, *Soph.* 244b, *Theaet.* 180e.

[208] Dodds, *Proclus*, Prop. XXV, p. 29.

unborn. For it is needful that movement, connection, quality, quantity, and finally body be joined to eternal God.

FRIDERICUS: The union of a human body with a divine nature does not happen, rather the union of a divine nature with a human mind.

TORALBA: It is not possible that things which are united to one third thing are not[209] united among themselves, and things which are to one thing the same among themselves[210] are the same, according to the very principles and decrees of philosophy. Therefore, if the divine mind is united with the human mind and the human mind to body, it is necessary that there will be the same union of divine mind and body. This is ridiculous; therefore, the former is. Yet it is altogether impossible that the human mind combine[211] with eternal God into a unity, to which the human mind is not of one and the same essence nor even of like essence, nor infinite. How much less will we think that the divine nature is mingled with a human body?

SALOMON: To be sure, Moses Rambam thinks that he who believes there is anything corporeal in God is guilty of a more serious blasphemy than he who worships idols.

FRIDERICUS: Why do you cite those Talmudic theologians, subverters of the Christian religion, who try by every means to snatch deity away from Christ, and reason, memory, and will[212] which He shares in a certain way with man from God?

CURTIUS: I see that the aim of Salomon and Toralba is to pursue the nature of God and the mysteries of the Trinity by reasons and proofs.
P. 270 Faith is needed. If you apply reason and proof to the things which depend on faith alone, you will accomplish no more than if you wish to be mad with reason. And so since Plato, a divine man, feared to write anything about God which was alien to His majesty, he orders the things which have been handed down by the elders to be believed without proof.[213] Aristotle also says this in these words: "The undemonstrated sayings and opinions of the experienced and the elders or the wise have no less [value] than from proofs."[214] Wherefore I cannot approve the writings of Eusebius, Galatinus, Augustine, and Eugubinus from which Mornay tries to draw out evangelical proofs.[215] For they did not see that knowledge and

[209] *non* M

[210] *quae uni sunt eadem inter se* M.

[211] *coeat* M

[212] *voluntatem* M

[213] *Leg.* V. 738c.

[214] Cf. *De anima* III. 3. 428a. 20 ff. Also *Rhet. ad Alexandrum* XIV. 1431b 9–19.

[215] Philippe de Mornay (1549–1623) was a French Protestant who was a supporter of Henry of Navarre. His influence was so great that after the death of Condé in 1588 he was popularly called "the Huguenot pope." When Henry IV

faith, which they call imparted, could not exist together.

TORALBA: Indeed, that may be valid among Christians. However, we must consider what one can answer to the philosophers, pagans, and Epicureans, who scorn imparted faith or the "good news," lest they have the same objection as formerly the emperor Julian had against the Galileans: namely, that for all arguments, principles,[216] and demonstrations they had nothing to say[217] except this—believe.[218] Therefore, it is better to put reason to the test with the philosophers rather than to seem to have "skipped bail." For if essence or that substance which is the Father, is the Son, the Father is the same to Himself and the Son, the same is born and unborn.

FRIDERICUS: There is one Father, unborn, and one Son, born from time eternal.

TORALBA: If the same thing is not born and unborn, the substance of the Father and Son is different.

FRIDERICUS: In essence, one and the same, not in hypostasis.

OCTAVIUS: Why then did the Council of Toledo[219] decree that only the Word was made flesh and became man? For it follows from this that the essence of the Father is not the same as the essence of the Son.

FRIDERICUS: We must be advised that hypostasis is different from essence; the unlearned confuse this and this confusion has cast the darkest cloud on this discussion.

TORALBA: If the Father begat God, either He begat Himself, God, or another God from Himself.[220] There is no third. But nothing begets itself nor can be the cause of itself. Although the Platonists[221] rather often use

---

abjured Protestantism in 1593, he became despondent and gradually withdrew from court life and devoted himself to writing. The work to which Bodin refers is *De L'institution, usage et doctrine du saint sacrement de l'eucharistie en l'église ancienne*, which contained about 5000 citations from the scriptures, fathers, and schoolmen. He was accused of misquoting at least 500 and a public disputation was held in 1600. See *Encycl. Brit.* (11th ed.), XVIII, 848–49, for a concise article with full bibliography.

216 *principia* M

217 *in ore habuisse* M

218 See Augustine, *De civ. Dei* XVIII. 52.

219 For the many Councils of Toledo, see *Cath. Encycl.*, XIV, 758–59. The reference in Bodin probably refers to the council held in 589 in which King Reccared, prelates, and nobles abjured the Arian heresy and professed their faith according to the doctrine of the Council of Nicaea. In the council of 650 the heresy of the Monothelites, who denied that Christ had two wills, was condemned.

220 *a se* M

221 Proclus (see Dodds, *Proclus,* pp. 60, 102, 134, 180) uses the terms *autotelēs* and *autophuēs.*

those terms about God—self-produced, complete in Himself, self-grown—still they only mean that God is eternal; namely content in His own power, nature, majesty, and goodness,[222] in need of nothing from another's resources. However, we must not think that anything is produced by itself. Because of this, Plutarch writes that God is most ancient because He was unborn.[223] From this, it follows that that which is born cannot be eternal. And indeed Hilary writes that this which is born did not exist before it was born.

P. 271 CURTIUS: As proof from contradictions it follows that this always existed which was born from time eternal, as we believe about the Son.

TORALBA: If anything had begotten or made itself, this which was begotten and which begat would be incomplete, since it would be necessary that it was whole to beget itself[224] and that it was not whole in order that it might be begotten from itself. For if it were, it would not become because it would already be. If it were not existent, it would not beget because it would not be. Therefore, God did not beget from Himself the Son Himself. From which it happens that He is different from the Father, not in the respect of persons but in the whole order of substance. Christ openly acknowledged this by these words: "The Father who sent Me is of another kind."[225] This cannot be said about a man who was not yet man when he was sent.

FRIDERICUS: Your argument is clever and subtle, but Augustine and Lombard deny each part of the argument,[226] and rightly. For Scotus says: "It does not follow that if the sun produces a mouse, the sun produces itself as a mouse, or a mouse different from itself, but another thing which is a mouse.

OCTAVIUS: Then Augustine forgot himself. He said: "In order that the Father might have a Son from Himself, He did not lessen Himself but produces another from Himself in such a way that He would remain complete in Himself; He would be as much in the Son as He is alone."[227] Surely these statements involve a contradiction with the previous ones,

[222] *bonitate* M

[223] Cf. Plutarch, *Moralia, De animae procreatione in Timaeo.* 1015b.

[224] *totum esse ut gigneret semetipsum* M

[225] Cf. John 14:24.

[226] Augustine, *Sancti Augustini operum tomus* VIII (Paris, 1688). *De trinit.* VII. 3–8, pp. 855–60. Lombard I, dist. 4. Scotus, I. dest. 4.

[227] Cf. *Sancti Augustini operum tomus* II (Paris, 1679). *Sex quaestiones contra paganos expositae seu Epist. CII, Quaestio Quinta.*, p. 283.

since in all nature the same and different are contrary. Elsewhere he said: "When God begat the Word, He begat this which is."[228] Basil said: "Moreover, God is not begotten from Himself nor from another."

FRIDERICUS: In this very matter Lombard refuted Augustine when he writes that the substance of God had begotten the Son. Lombard said: "The Son is produced either from the substance of the Father or from nothing. This is not true; therefore the former is. Or God is altogether of another nature."[229]

OCTAVIUS: Lombard added these words to this argument: "Those things which are understood in some way strongly inspire us. I would prefer to hear from others than to propose."[230] Still it is necessary to admit one or the other. If we say that the Son is begotten from the substance of the Father, God will be the same or God will be different, and each is absurd. In fact there are not two "sonships," to use the theological term, but one sonship of God eternal: first, a Son to God, then a Son to man. And so the later theologians refute Lombard because he denied that substance was begotten from substance, although the old theologians think so. Tertullian says: "The Father is wholly substance; moreover, the Son is a part and portion of the whole."[231]

TORALBA: Nothing is so alien to God as to grant a part to Him or to take away a part, since His own nature cannot have parts; otherwise [His nature] would be body and indeed divisible, and this has been proved wrong already. Absurdity is the most certain judge of the true and the false. We are led by this to admit that which cannot happen through P. 272
nature, or we are forced to give up the suspected opinion.

CORONAEUS: Therefore, all the many things which happen outside the course and uniformity of nature which Toralba has presented must also seem absurd.

TORALBA: Many things are not considered in the ordinary or accustomed course of nature, yet they do not war with the divine nature.

CURTIUS: Since one can say nothing accurately and suitably about God but can skillfully deny everything, Toralba uses these propositions in vain. God is substance because God is united with and underlies no accidents, which is very characteristic of substance.

[228] Augustine, *Sancti Augustini operum tomus* VIII (Paris, 1688). *De trinit.* IV. 3, pp. 811–12.

[229] *Quatuor libri sententiarum* III. dist. 8.

[230] *Ibid.*

[231] *Apol.* I. 21.

TORALBA: The Father is a name for essence or for act. If act, surely the Son has been created; if He is a name for essence, the Son in His whole substance is different from the Father.

CURTIUS: The argument of Aetius is different. Although Basil does not respond to him, still each argument is overturned by denial, because the word for Father indicates only a relation.

OCTAVIUS: Epiphanius writes that Aetius had gathered three hundred arguments against the deity of Christ, part of which are extant.[232] Nevertheless, none is more persuasive than the one by which the younger [theologians] concluded against Hilary and Athanasius. When they said that God was born from God and light received from light, he said that Christ is God from Himself, not from another. For if it means that He is God from another, He cannot be God. I do not see what answer one can give to this.

FRIDERICUS: It has been stated earlier that God who was born from the Father is not another. For in divinity the Father is not the efficient cause of the Son, but the essential cause, which is very different[233] from the efficient cause.

TORALBA: If Christ the Son of God is of His same essence,[234] He must have been born at some time or other. If He was born at some time or other, there was that time in which He not yet was, which indeed He declares had a beginning of origin and time.[235]

CORONAEUS: Augustine and Hilary impair this argument by acknowledging the Father is[236] eternal without a progenitor and the Son also eternal but with a progenitor, as warmth from fire and light from the sun.[237] "Christ," Tertullian said, "comes forth from the Father as a ray from the sun, a stream from a fountain, and shrub from a seed."[238]

232 See Epiphanias, *Contra Haer.*, LXXIII. 23–27, in J. P. Migne, *Patrologia Graeca* (Paris, 1857), XLII. Aetius was the founder of the Anomoean party when in the 4th century the church was burdened with the problem of the relationship of the Father and the Son. Much of the argument centered in the use of the terms *ousia* (essence or substance), *homoousion* (identical in essence) and *homoiousion* (similar in essence). Aetius maintained that since the Divine Nature is simple, the various terms and names applied to God are to be considered synonymous. If not, they would imply composition in God. (See below, note 315.)

233 *differt* M

234 *Christus Dei filius est eiusdem essentiae* M

235 *Originis ac temporis principium* M

236 *esse* M

237 See Augustine, *Sancti Augustini operum tomus* III (Paris, 1680). *De genesi ad litteram* IV. 32, p. 174.

238 *Apol.* I. 21.

TORALBA: Often an effect is concurrent with the cause; for example, light itself, is neither prior nor posterior to the sun. However, they are never the same, since the sun is substance but light is accident, which can in no way be said of the Father and Son. For if anything is born, there must be a time antecedent to it in which it not yet was. From this it follows that the Son either had not yet been born or if He was born, He was not able to be eternal.[239]

FRIDERICUS: We have already said that the Father is the essential cause of the Son and the beginning,[240] as Augustine, Hilary, Gregory Nazianzus, and Basil declare;[241] the eternal beginning[242] of a certain eternal effect. I do not see why we ought to be stuck on this point. P. 273

OCTAVIUS: Why then was the Master of the Sentences so bogged down that he speaks of this in this manner: "This exceeds human understanding and knowledge of the world, which reason does not comprehend."[243]

TORALBA: Indeed reason, which is divine light, innate to the mind of each man, sees, feels, and judges that which is right, that which is wrong, that which is true, that which is false.

FRIDERICUS: Yes, indeed, for those things of which reason is capable. But God, eternal and infinite, cannot be comprehended in the hovel of the human mind, because He is incomprehensible, most divine, supreme; that is, to use Theophrastus' more elegant words, not perceptible, most excellent, most high.

SALOMON: Theophrastus was speaking there of God, but we have been speaking about the man Jesus, and we must not assume as proof that which must be demonstrated: namely, that Jesus is God. For God declared who He was in no ambiguous or obscure manner when He said: "There is not a God before Me nor will there be one after Me."[244] Likewise: "I have existed first, and I shall be last."[245] Moreover, the Christian theologians admit that a person was created and had the person of Son before He became man in the womb of woman. If the person of Son was created,[246] who can doubt that a Son is a creature? Therefore, He is not a creator. He is not God.

OCTAVIUS: The Master of the Sentences denies that the person of Son consists of God and man, as of parts; then he adds: "The order of that

[239] *esse non posse* M
[240] *principium* M
[241] *In eunom.*, in Migne, *Patrologia Graeca*, XLV.
[242] *principium* M
[243] Peter Lombard, *Quatuor libri sententiarum* I. dist. 4.
[244] Isaiah 43:13.
[245] Isaiah 48:12.
[246] *si creata est persona filii* M

union is unexplainable."[247] Still he denies that each nature is mingled and calls it idolatry to worship the body and soul of Christ since, he said, the body and soul of Christ are creatures. Philip Melanchthon had the same opinion.

CURTIUS: Each was right, since the Synod of Ephesus[248] decreed that Christ must be worshipped in one adoration.

OCTAVIUS: If each nature is not blended in a hypostatic union in Christ, the worship ought not to be blended in order that the creature be blended with the Creator as well as worshipped, since it is very near sacrilege to think that the Father and Son are a singular God; for example, Hilary says it is impious to believe there are two in the Father and Son, and there is no third.

FRIDERICUS: If there is anyone who more cleverly seeks out those things and still does not understand them completely, let him realize that those matters more often still cannot be understood, even if they depend upon the most certain proofs. All the theologians and philosophers except Au-
P. 274 gustine and Lactantius agree there are Antipodes. Although one may examine this with clear and positive proof and also with long experimental knowledge, still no one can explain it by reason. For example, Moses Rambam, a most clear-sighted philosopher, says that it ought not to seem strange if Lactantius and Augustine mocked at astrologers as unlearned and mad who believed those things. Impelled by the power of Augustine's authority, many theologians judged those to be heretics who thought there were Antipodes. Among these Virgilius, a certain bishop of Salzburg, was condemned by the pope as a heretic because he held this belief in A.D. 745.[249] Therefore, how much less shall we perceive the union of the divine

[247] Lombard, *Quat. lib. sent.*, II. dist. 9.

[248] The Third Ecumenical Council was held at Ephesus in 431. The council condemned the heresy of Nestorius, and defined that Mary was mother "in the flesh of God's Word made Flesh. It anathematized all who deny that the Word of God the Father was united with the Flesh in one hypostasis; all who deny that there is only one Christ with Flesh that is His own; all who deny that the same Christ is God at the same time and man." See *Cath. Encycl.*, VIII, 713; also V, 491 ff. See below, note 403.

[249] Geographical questions caused grave differences of opinion among the early Church Fathers. Many declared the earth was flat, and Cosmas Indicopleustes even declared that the earth was constructed in the shape of the Tabernacle of the Covenant. Augustine, however, declared that the doctrine of the sphericity of the earth did not conflict with the Scriptures. The question of the Antipodes caused controversy for a considerable period. Lactantius and others denied it on religious grounds, since the people of the Antipodes could not have been saved. The learned Irishman, Virgilius, patron saint of Salzburg, was the first to declare openly that he believed men lived beyond the ocean. See *Cath. Encycl.*, VI, 447–53.

nature with the human. And so Hilary himself, who was very famous for his eloquence and learning, said: "That which is completed is beyond talk and beyond understanding. It is not articulated, it is not reached, it is not comprehended." He says a little later: "There is a defect in my understanding, a sluggishness in my intelligence, a silence in my talk." Also: "God is from One, not through a part, a section, diminution, derivation, and extension but through an incomprehensible mode."[250] What of the statements of Justin Martyr? "Unity is born in the Trinity, and the Trinity in Unity. I cannot satisfy myself how this is, nor would I wish others to examine it, since I think it is wrong to speak out sublime words in base language."[251] Therefore, if such men found this shameful, why should we think that we must scratch the surface of the most sacred matter of all?

Octavius: I do not know whether there is less[252] or greater obscurity about the Holy Spirit, which Athanasius and Chrysostom wrote is proceeding from the Father and Son, although the Greek councils still declare anathema upon him who shall believe this. And indeed, Damascenus said: "We say that the Holy Spirit proceeds from the Father and finds rest in the Son." When John, whose surname was Scotus, could not reconcile this opinion with the variety of different opinions, he said: "Who could condemn Damascenus, Basil, Gregory Nazianzus, Gregory the Theologian, Justin Martyr, and Cyril as heretics? Also who could prove Jerome, Augustine, Hilary, Ambrose, and all the Latins guilty of error?" Still it is necessary that one or the other, or even both, are notably mistaken and deceived.[253]

Fridericus: The western Catholic church which followed the creed of Athanasius acknowledges that the Holy Spirit proceeds from each one, "Because it is neither born nor unborn," Augustine said. "Neither can there be two Sons, if born, or two Fathers of a Son,[254] if unborn. Consequently, there are two principles if[255] two are unborn"—to use their words.

250 *De trinit.* I.

251 *Apol.* I. 13; *Dial. Tryph.* LXI.

252 *minor* M

253 Athanasius witnessed that the Holy Spirit is united to the Son in the manner in which the Son is united to the Father, and the Son is the source of the Spirit. Cyril stated that the Spirit has His "nature" from the Son. Basil stressed the traditional order in mentioning the Divine Persons because "as the Son is to the Father, so is the Spirit to the Son, in accordance with the ancient order of the names in the formula of baptism." Epiphanius said that the Paraclete is from the Father and the Son. The Latin writers say that the Holy Spirit proceeds from the Father and from the Son, while the Eastern writers say that the Spirit proceeds from the Father through the Son. In reality the thought is the same; the difference is semantical. See *Cath. Encycl.*, VII, 409–15.

254 *filii* M

255 *si* M

Octavius: The Master of the Sentences, refuting this opinion of Augus-
P. 275 tine, said: "Who can explain this? For if the Spirit is unborn, it will be without principle. And there will be two principles: if He is born, there will be two Sons and Brothers among themselves; if the Spirit is born of the Son, already there will be a Grandson to the Father from the Son.

Fridericus: Therefore to avoid that ambiguity, the Latins say that the Spirit proceeds more properly from both.[256]

Toralba: That procession of the Spirit from the Son, who has the Father as cause and principle of birth,[257] is very dissimilar and unequal to that procession which is from the Father who has no begetter. Moreover, why is there a procession of the Spirit rather than a generation? Or why is there a generation of the Son rather than a procession, since there is one and the same essence of the three? Surely similar are those subtleties of Scotus, when he writes that the Father and Son are one breather, still not One breathing but Two.

Coronaeus: Hilary opened an approach for understanding these things in one way or another, when he compared the Trinity to the sun, the ray, and the light.

Toralba: That comparison is in no way suitable for the proposed matter, since the ray and light are accidents, and the sun is a body consisting of substance. Still, those say that the three Persons are of the same essence. Besides it is impossible to add or subtract anything from God. Finally, if we should say that the Son and Holy Spirit are born, or proceed, or are derived from the Father we will have to admit that an infinite emanates from an infinite, which is the greatest absurdity of all. When one asks why God cannot make God, there can be no other answer than that the infinite cannot be plucked from the infinite. And so, Anselm is praised because, when asked by a pupil why God had not made man sinless, he said: "Since He could not make God." From this it follows that the statement, "God became man," is absurd, because God would be changed into man and man into God; for on both sides there is action and passion. In truth, the conclusion of such statements is impossible: deity or eternity is unborn *qua* Father, but born *qua* Son, and neither born nor unborn *qua* Holy Spirit. This cannot be stated about one and the same essence.

Coronaeus: If things which are compared among themselves were everywhere harmonious, there would not be likeness of things, but the

[256] See above, note 253.

[257] *generis principium* M

thing itself. Wherefore, Basil, differing from Hilary, compares the Trinity to three suns in order to be nearer the thing itself.

OCTAVIUS: Jerome calls it a sacrilege to place three substances in God, although Hilary rather frequently states this and surprises the younger theologians because of this. Why, the younger theologians even rebuked Hilary when he had written that there was eternity in God. "Did Hilary say this," one said, "to snatch away Christ's deity?"

FRIDERICUS: That frequent repetition in Hilary's writings shows that he did not wish this—that Christ is God; however, the Greeks use more P. 276 appropriately the word hypostasis in regard to the distinction of persons.

OCTAVIUS: Jerome thinks that danger lurks in the word hypostasis. And indeed Paul seems to use this word in another sense when he calls the Holy Spirit a characteristic of the Father's hypostasis.[258]

TORALBA: Hypostasis is an accident or a substance; there is no third. Moreover, it is impossible to add anything to God; therefore, it must be substance. But if we accept hypostasis for essence, there will be three essences or three substances in God, because they grant their own individual hypostasis to each person.

CURTIUS: Accident or substance is indicated by the word for essence. Indeed, the Schoolmen did not accept this statement—"The Son is of the essence of the Father"—in the same way as that statement—"The Son[259] is of the substance of the Father"—because in the latter statement the Son is represented as consubstantial to the Father, but not in the former. In addition, hypostasis is attributed to Persons, lest three Persons seem to be confounded in one and the same Person, since there is a certain property of each Person which is not communicable to the other.

OCTAVIUS: Why, then, in the first chapter of the Augsburg Confession, is the word for Person denied to mean any part or quality, but that which remains strictly for itself. For the property of Persons is this: that the Father has power from Himself, not from another, as Augustine wished, but the Son does not have power from Himself, but from the Father. Likewise he says that the Father is without principle and without progenitor, but the Son is not without principle but has His essence from the Father. Moreover, who can seriously think that He is God who owes the principle of His origin, His essence, and power to another. And lest anyone think that this had escaped Augustine, pondering another [mat-

[258] Rom. 8:11; Gal. 4:6; note especially II Cor. 13:14.
[259] *filius* M

ter], he repeats it more openly and says: "The Father possesses from no one that He is God, but the Son possesses from the Father that He is God."[260] Basil also writes the same thing.

Toralba: If the Son owes to the Father the beginnings of His origin, He cannot be eternal. For if the Father brought into being a Son, He made an end of begetting once and for all, or He always begets. If He always begets,[261] as it seems to those who relate these words to Christ, "Today I have begotten You," the begetting of the Son is always unfinished. But if He ceased to beget, He also began [to beget] at some time or other. But if the Son began to be begotten, He is not eternal; He is not infinite; He is not God.

Coronaeus: We are spinning in the same place. Indeed we must consider not three eternal, not three infinite, not three gods, but one God, eternal and infinite, yet distinguished by a variety of Persons and having a certain property appropriate to each Person, as when Lombard denies that the spirit is a principle except in regard to creatures.

Salomon: Therefore, there was in no way a principle of the Holy Spirit before six thousand years, since nothing created existed up to this time.
P. 277 And so because of this the Macedonians used to call the Spirit a creature, which the Christians, according to their creed, had asserted was coeternal to God and was God.

Fridericus: The words of the Master of the Sentences have reference to the relationship and naming of Persons, not to essence.

Octavius: If the Spirit has its beginning from the Father and the Son, why do Athanasius, Chrysostom, and Augustine affirm that the three are coequal and coeternal?

Curtius: Indeed those speak rightly because essence is coeternal; but in the relationship of Persons the Father is called prior in nature to the Son and greater, to which this statement refers: "The Father is greater than I."[262]

Salomon: Indeed, Matthew, Mark, and Luke make the Spirit superior to the Father and the Son by affirming that the things which are sinned against the Father and the Son are pardoned, but they deny that the things which are sinned against the Holy Spirit are pardoned.[263] Still when Moses tried to reconcile God lest he be abolished from the book of life, lo, the divine voice said to him: "Whoever sinned against me, I shall abol-

[260] *De trinit.* VI. 10.

[261] *si semper gignit* M

[262] John 14:28.

[263] Matt. 12:31–32; Mark 3:29; Luke 12:10.

ish from the book of life."[264] Would He have passed over the Son and the Holy Spirit, if they had been coequal to the Father? Also there is no proof of the Trinity in the divine law, and not even any trace of it in the prophets.

CURTIUS: What are you saying, Salomon? Is[265] there any chapter and page of the ancient covenant of the prophets where some trace of the holy Trinity does not appear?

OCTAVIUS: To be sure, Martin Luther did not hesitate to abolish not only many things from the Roman prayers but also this popular song, "Holy Trinity, one God, have pity on us," because the Trinity cannot be God, since the Word is feminine, of the second intention, as the dialecticians say, or of a collegium, as the lawyers say who define the collegium by three Persons. Moreover, the things which are said about the whole collegium are not valid in one colleague. Thus Origen, whom Jerome calls the teacher of the churches, curses exceedingly the word for Trinity and censures most harshly the sect of the three names. Even Rufinus, his interpreter, writes that he corrected many things which had been written by Origen against the Trinity.[266] But with the good leave of Rufinus, let it be said that it was not fitting that a translator should act as corrector; nor should it seem strange if Origen, because of [textual] corruption, seems to write the same things as Athanasius sometimes did or to use the word *homoousios*, about the Son which had not yet been heard of. With the same license the book of Tertullian about the Trinity was inserted in Cyprian's letters, as Rufinus warned.

CORONAEUS: Although we do not see the word for Trinity or triad used in sacred scripture, nevertheless we read that one must be baptized in the name of the Father, Son, and Holy Spirit, and indeed Justin Martyr, who was nearest to the apostles, wrote a book about the holy and consubstantial Trinity. P. 278

OCTAVIUS: A clear consideration of the times convinces one that this little book is not genuine. He flourished when Marcus Aurelius was em-

264 Psalm 68 (69):29.

265 *an est* M

266 Rufinus Tyrannius (A.D. 345–410?) was an Italian who, after he was baptized at age 25, developed a great admiration for Origen and began his labors as a translator of Origen with a Latin version of Pamphilus' *Apology for Origen.* Rufinus' concept of his role as translator was to omit and rectify the falsification of Origen by heretics, making his emendations from what Origen had said elsewhere. He also praised St. Jerome's earlier zeal for Origen and this led to a renewal of the Origenist controversy and a final break with Jerome. Jerome attacked Rufinus, who replied with an *Apology.* See *Cath. Encycl.*, XIII, 222.

peror, and the apology was addressed to him. Yet in one hundred twenty-four questions to the orthodox the author of that book asks why the superstition of the pagans has been uprooted and destroyed, although it was still quite flourishing in the age of Justin.[267] For the first time under the emperor Constantine they began to make use of the word *homoousios*, about two hundred years after Justin's time. With the same license the mass of St. James written in Greek appeared, in which words for Trinity, apostles, confessors, and virgins are quite often heaped up, although this James, with the exception of Stephen, was the first to suffer martyrdom.[268] Similar is the mass of Chrysostom in which Chrysostom extends entreaties to Chrysostom. What is more foolish than this?

CORONAEUS: Would that all the books of all might labor with this same sickness! But lest I seem to rely only on the New Testament or its interpreters or other theologians, many mysteries of the holy Trinity lie hidden in the Old Testament. I shall touch very briefly on those things which have been fully discussed by others;[269] for example, the statement in Deuteronomy: "What is the nation which has heard the word of living gods,"[270] that is, *'elohim hahayyim*, where one God is indicated by a plural word. Likewise, in Joshua:[271] *'elohim qedoshim*, that is, "holy gods" in place of holy God. Likewise: "If I am the Master, where is My fear?"[272] Also: "Let Us make men in Our image."[273] And a little after: "We shall make a helper like to Us."[274]

SALOMON: The word *'elohim* [gods, pl.] is very often used for *'eloah* [god, sing.]. Moreover, the Chaldean interpreter Jonathan, as often as he refers to one God, explains it for the most part by a singular word. For example, in the writings of Malachi he used the Chaldaic word *ribbon* [master] so that it is clear that the prophet was never thinking about the Trinity. The statement, "Let Us make man," is a transfer to the angels, for it was pleasing for these to be added as helpers for human creation so

[267] Marcus Aurelius was emperor A.D. 161–180. Justin was born about A.D. 114, lived during the reign of Antonius Pius, and suffered martyrdom in the reign of Marcus Aurelius, probably in the year A.D. 165.

[268] The liturgies originally used in the Patriarchate of Antioch begin with the Apostolic Constitution, then the liturgy of St. James in Greek, the Syrian Liturgy of St. James, and the other Syrian *Anaphoras*. The oldest, and the one from which the other liturgies derive, is the Greek Liturgy of St. James. The earliest reference to it is Canon XXXII of the Quinisextum Council which quotes it as composed by James, the brother of Jesus. See *Cath. Encycl.*, I, 571–74; XIV, 417–19.

[269] The marginal note of M indicates Peter Galatinus and Eugubinus.

[270] Deut. 5:26. [271] Josh. 24:19. [272] Malach. 1:6. [273] Gen. 1:26.

[274] Gen. 2:18.

that they might use the elements and elementary things, from which the divine nature is free, for strengthening man.

CURTIUS: Why then did three appear to Abraham in the valley of Mamre,[275] yet the conversation is of one [man] to one.

SALOMON: There is a hidden meaning. God is said to sit between or above the Cherubim, since He guides the world by the functions and services of two angels who stand nearest to His majesty. Zacharias proclaims this in an elegant vision,[276] and from this comes that old saying about Abraham: "He saw three and adored one." All the things which are spoken about God by a plural word can be easily explained from this passage.

FRIDERICUS: Why then does Rabbi Simeon, son of Johai, in the book of the *Zohar* which they call the storehouse of secrets, affirm that these words, "Hear Israel, the Lord our God is One," indicate the mystery of the Trinity? Indeed he attributed the name *'elohim* to the Son, the name YHWH doubled, to the Father and the Holy Spirit.[277] P. 279

SALOMON: This passage has been torn to pieces by Galatinus[278] and the younger [theologians] to whom it offered the opportunity of substituting the words for Son and Holy Spirit. Why indeed would the most holy name YHWH be granted to the Spirit, but not to the Son who is superior in honor? Or why would that passage in the Old Testament where the nature of God is said to be of the most simple unity be confounded with the addition of three Gods or Persons?

CURTIUS: Isaiah confirms this by repeating that word *qadosh* three times —holy, holy, holy. Likewise, the Psalmist says *el, 'elohim*, YHWH, that is, God, God in a variety of words indicating to the Hebrews almost the same thing. Likewise in another passage: "May God bless us; may our God bless us, may God bless us."[279] What else is this but the mystery of the Trinity? Why, even the ancient Egyptians, naming the principle of things, used a three-fold repetition, as Damascenus the Platonist writes.

SALOMON: Then it would have been necessary to worship a "sextility"

275 Gen. 13:14–18.

276 Zach. 4:1–5.

277 *patri et spiritui sancto* M

278 Peter Galatinus (1460–1540), Franciscan friar, Hebraist, and Orientalist, believed that he was the "Angel Pope," first prophesied by the followers of Joachim of Fiore. He published in 1518 *De arcanis Catholicae veritatis*, a work of Christian mysticism. Although anti-Jewish in tone, it defended the German humanist Johann Reuchlin and promoted in large measure Christian Hebraism. See *Encycl. Judaica*, VII, 262–263; also *Cath. Encycl.*, VI, 340.

279 Psalm 66 (67):7–8.

rather[280] than a trinity, because in addition to those three—holy, holy, holy, three names of God also follow—God, Lord, Zebaoth. But on the other hand, one should worship a duality as often as the two names of God occur—God Zebaoth or Eloha Zebaoth.

FRIDERICUS: But let us hasten to uproot Salomon with the force of arguments! Joseph of Castile and Nehemiah, son of Halcana, explain that the word of twelve letters, *'av ben ruaḥ haqqadosh*, that is, Father, Son, Holy Spirit comprise Three in One and One in Three.[281]

SALOMON: It is easy to publish books with another's name added, as, for example, the books of the wise men published under the name of Solomon. Why even the defenders of the Trinity did not hesitate to summon from hell Zoroaster and Orpheus, parents of the magi, and even Iamblichus himself, who, conscious of the impiety, drained off the poison, lest he suffer capital punishment. The book of Galatinus is full of these authors, and Augustinus Eugubinus [also uses them].[282] Indeed Galatinus drew partly from Mishna,[283] partly from the sacred literature, partly from the books of the Talmud, and partly from that gate of darkness rather than of light.[284] These writings were not translated but perverted, not corrected but distorted, and they were received in earnest, though written in irony of the Trinity. Let this be a proof, the fact that when the Hebrew theologians write in earnest about Jesus, they do not even dignify him by calling him by name but scornfully refer to him as the one that was hanged.

CURTIUS: Let us add Philo the Hebrew, who was most famous for his praise of philosophy and knowledge of divine things. For he speaks thus about the mystery of the Trinity: "There are two things; first God
P. 280 and the Word, the beginning and end of the will."[285] What can be said more clearly?

[280] *potius* M

[281] Joseph of Castile (d. 1480), son of Shem Tōbh ibn Tōbh, the Cabalist and anti-Maimonist, was a commentator with cabalistic tendencies but also versed in Aristotle and Christian doctrine.

Nehemiah (the reading of M) is difficult to identify, but I suggest that the reference is to R. Nehemiah ha-Navi, one of the Hasidim who attained the highest spiritual levels and were considered to be masters of the Holy Spirit. The attainment by the Hasidim of spiritual heights was connected not only with their behavior on the ethical plane but also with the distinction they received in the area of esoteric theosophy. Number mysticism held an important place in the "ascent to heaven" as well as meditation, prayer, and the mysteries of prayer. See *Encycl. Judaica* X, 514.

[282] See above, notes 269 and 278. [283] *partim ex Misna* M

[284] *Porta lucis* (Gate of Light) is the name of a book written by Nehemiah, son of Halcana, as indicated by the marginal note in M. See above, note 281.

[285] Cf. *De opific. mundi* VI–VII.

SALOMON: Granted there is the Word, granted there is will in God. What does this have to do with three Persons? The same Philo calls the world the son of God, born second, but first born, the exemplar of the world itself, that is, the archetype.[286] Still it would be no more foolish to call the exemplar God than to call the example or Word of God God. For example, when John writes that the Word of God is God,[287] he is no less incongruous than those who think that the wisdom of God is God. Those same men, nevertheless, say that He has been created because of the statement in Solomon, "I was created from the beginning and before the centuries."[288] They do not see that it follows from this that the Son or wisdom is said to be created. To be sure Tertullian, in order to explain that Jesus was created, said: "You hear that wisdom has been created." In like manner: "The law of God is nothing other than the Word brought forth from the mouth of God and created, which ought to be called, by the same analogy, the Son of God and God."[289] Moreover, the Valentinians[290] used to say that the Word of God, or the Son, was born from the utterance of the Father; likewise, they call the Holy Spirit at one time the love of God, at another time the will of God, which precedes the Word in essence, nature, and time. From this one understands that the Word is not coequal or coessential to the Father. And since Augustinus Eugubinus was displeased that the Word of God was called the Son, he amended or rather corrupted the passage of Philo and wrote instead the word of law, contrary to all typed copies. Similarly they speak of knowing (*intelligens*), known (*intellectum*) and understanding (*intellectionem*), that is, *sekel, mesakkel, moskal,* as a trinity, as loving (*amantem*), love (*amorem*) and loved (*amatum*). Still in no way is it possible that a horse which is known and loved is the same as the man who perceives and knows him, unless accidents are mingled with substances, heavenly things with terrestrial, higher with lower.

FRIDERICUS: Whatever is in God, this wholly is the essence of that very One. Nothing happens to this One, nothing disappears, and for that reason John calls the Son of God[291] most rightly the Word and the thought of God, and God.

[286] *Ibid.*, V. [287] John 1:1. [288] Prov. 8:22.

[289] Tertullian, while contending against the heretic Praxeas, expressed himself in such a way on the doctrine of the Trinity that he fell into suspicion of heresy. See *Contra Praxeas,* VIII Proverb.

[290] As regards the Christology of the Valentinians, their teaching was that a body was brought down from Heaven.

[291] *Dei* M

TORALBA: Who would be so foolish as to say that he thinks the ordinances, the laws, the actions, and words which proceed from out of the man are the essence of the man? Also if these things are the same as the Creator, there must be no distinction between the Creator and the created, for the things which are the same to one are the same among themselves.

CURTIUS: When John says that the word of God is the son, he understands not an utterance but His intimate essence, wisdom, and mind. These words speak to the point: "And the Word was with God."[292] Tertullian fell in error when he said that the Son of God was created, because he thought that the wisdom of God, which they call the Son of God, was created.[293] But Basil said: "The wisdom[294] of God has always been, nor has it ever been born." For if wisdom had been created, there would have been a time in which wisdom not yet was; contrary to this,[295] Solomon
P. 281 writes that it had been before the ages. And so discarding the interpreters from whom the errors usually flow, let us listen to Solomon's own words: "These things have been ordained from eternity, from the beginning, from the ancient days of the earth."[296] Otherwise, if wisdom had been created, it would follow that God had existed before without wisdom which is no less absurd or wicked than to imagine the Father without the Son.

CORONAEUS: Therefore, although the mysteries of the holy Trinity are clear in so many passages of Scripture, let us also, for the instruction of the philosophers, cite the most ancient decrees of the philosophers.

FRIDERICUS: Although Proclus the Academician wrote twenty-two books against the Christians, nonetheless he admits to three principles: the good, mind, and soul. Numenius[297] calls the first the Father, the second the Creator, the third the Builder. Amelius[298] makes the Builder also threefold, whether three minds or three kings; namely, the one who is, who has, who sees. Still Trismegistus surpassed the others in his antiquity as well as in his clarity. He said: "God, who is intellect, life, light, man-woman, gave birth to the word, which is another intellect and builder of

[292] John 1:1.

[293] See above, note 289.

[294] *sapientia* M See *Contra Eunom.*

[295] *contra quam* M

[296] Prov. 8:23.

[297] Numenius was a Platonist who lived at the end of the second century A.D., and had a direct influence on Plotinus, the first systematic Neoplatonist. Numenius taught that there were three gods: the Father, the Maker, and the World. See *Cath. Encycl.*, X, 742.

[298] Amelius, an eminent pupil of Plotinus, modified his teachings on certain points; he also put some value on the prologue to the Gospel of John. See *Encycl. Brit.* (11th ed.), XIX, 374.

all things, and along with the word he gave birth to the spirit, a fiery god."[299] Plotinus spoke similarly in the book about the three principal substances. He said: "There are three hypostases, the one or the good, the intellect, and the soul of the world. About these one must not speak before sacred rites have been performed properly, and the mind is tranquil."[300] Even Theophrastus in the book about the world [written] for Alexander, which is falsely attributed to Aristotle, noted the secret of the Trinity, when he placed the beginning, middle, and end in eternal God.[301]

CURTIUS: Of all the monuments of the pagans which can be related to the mystery of the Trinity, there is none more outstanding or noble than the oracle which Heraclides Ponticus[302] says was inscribed on the temple of Serapis with these words: "In the beginning is God, then the Word, and the Spirit is together with these." These three are congenital; all these unite into One.

OCTAVIUS: I do not doubt that that oracle came from the same Christian workshop as other similar utterances which have been cited yesterday from Apollo.

TORALBA: I pass over the other writings of the Academicians which need less refutation, because they have no relevance to our subject. However, whoever that Trismegistus shall have been, the inscription on the statue of Isis and an understanding of the time forces one to admit that he was both a teacher of Isis and the Egyptian writer most ancient of all after Moses. Those books which are circulated under the name of Trismegistus clearly did not exist except in Greek, when they were translated into Latin. It is clear that the author borrowed from the younger Academicians many of Plato's statements.[303] Indeed those who are less given to exaggeration attribute to him 36,525 books, but Iamblichus grants 110,000.[304] Moreover, the excerpts which Iamblichus, Plotinus, Proclus, and Cyril took from P. 282 those books are very different in every way from the writings in the

[299] *Hermetica*, edited by Walter Scott (London, 1968), I. 2. 13–17b; 3. 1a.

[300] Plotinus held that all modes of being are constituted by the expansion of a single immaterial force, the One. Rather than persons of a trinity, which are on the same level, Plotinus has descending grades of reality: The World-mind, the World-soul, and Nature. Thus the resemblance of Neoplatonism to Trinitarianism is incomplete.

[301] Theophrastus joined Aristotle, probably in Mitylene and Assos, and became his most faithful pupil. The work mentioned here is not extant.

[302] Heraclides is referred to as "joint editor" of Plato's lectures on the Good. He was left in charge of the school during Plato's third Sicilian journey.

[303] See Scott's introduction to *Hermetica*, pp. 1–111.

[304] *110,000* M.

Poimandres and *Poëma*.[305] In addition, those statements which Fridericus brought forth as a proof of the Trinity seem, to the word, to have been transcribed not so much from Trismegistus as from a letter of Plato to Hermias and Dionysius,[306] in which he posits God the ruler of the universe, then a second intelligence created from the first, that is, the mind of the whole world, and a third intelligence created from the second which all Platonists interpret as the soul of the world; a fourth from the third and thus successively to the final mind. But the Peripatetics say that all minds are derived at the same time from the same principle. However, whichever opinion we follow, it is necessary that all other things originate from one principle and for this reason are considered compounded, created, changeable, and fleeting. For Plotinus said: "Everything which is not first is not simple."[307]

FRIDERICUS: What then? Nothing in the Trinity is before or after in time, but only in the order of relation; nor is the Creator less Son than Father, or less the Holy Spirit than either. Moreover, this is indicated by the first word of Genesis, *bereshit bara'* (in the beginning He created), that is, in the beginning the Father, Son, and Holy Spirit created; for the word of three letters, *bara'*, signifies three Persons, namely, *av, ben, ruaḥ*, Father, Son, Holy Spirit. Salomon will not deny that this is drawn forth from the holy secrets of the Hebrews and the holier Cabala and from the word *bereshit*, with the letters changed, transposed, composed, and divided, these words are produced: the Father through the Son created the beginning, the end, head, fire, the foundation of a great man in a good covenant. *Lev* [heart] is often taken for *ṭov* [good]. For it helps to silence the Hebrews with their own daggers and swords.

SALOMON: Who does not see that very diverse sentences can be fashioned from those same letters? Indeed our elders never strongly approved of that kind of Cabala. It would be much more likely to contrive a quaternity from the same Tetragrammaton than a trinity, as did Basilides the evan-

305 *Poimandres* and *Poëma* are headings in the *Corpus Hermeticum*.

306 This seems to be a reference to Epistle II, which is a reply to an inquiry from Dionysius. The famous passage in 312e is much discussed. "Upon the king of all do all things turn; he is the end of all things and the cause of all good." There is no explicit reference to "the creator," nor are the second and third principles identified as "intelligence" and "soul of the world." Does the "fourth" refer to the "soul of man," which according to the Epistle, seeks to understand these superior principles? See Glenn R. Morrow, *Plato's Epistles* (Indianapolis, 1962), pp. 115–16, 196. Morrow judges that "the vagueness of the passage and its rhetorical coloring indicate the hand of an imitator."

307 Cf. *Ennead* III. 9. 9.

gelist,[308] whose opinion the Noëtians[309] and Lombard himself, the Master of the Sentences, seem to follow, as Abbot Joachim[310] wrote, because in addition to three persons, they substituted a fourth which they called "power."[311] The Pythagoreans seem to have held this opinion. They had been accustomed to swear to a holy quaternity. Timaeus Locrensis[312] indicated that by means of a tetragonal pyramid this quaternity held many thousands of worlds together. The powerfully sagacious reasoning of the Master of the Sentences concerning the quaternity either established the quaternity or overturned the Trinity, because he opposed the two relations of things produced to the two relations of things producing, namely, the thing begetting, the thing begotten, the thing breathing, the thing neither begotten nor begetting nor breathing. The four wheels would be appropriate to this opinion, and also the four animals of divine vision,[313] and

[308] Basilides was an Alexandrian Gnostic who lived during the reigns of Hadrian and Antoninus Pius. Almost nothing remains of Basilides' writing; his teachings, however, are discussed by St. Irenaeus, Clement of Alexandria, Hippolytus of Rome, and Pseudo-Tertullian. According to St. Irenaeus, Basilides taught that *Nous* (Mind) was first to be born from the Unborn Father, from *Nous* was born *Logos* (Reason); from *Logos, Phronesis* (Prudence); from *Phronesis, Sophia* (Wisdom) and *Dynamis* (Strength). Basilides is referred to as the evangelist because Basilides, according to Origen, had dared to write a gospel according to Basilides. See *Cath. Encycl.*, II, 326–29.

[309] The mention of the Noëtians in regard to Basilides seems inappropriate because Noëtus and his school denied categorically that the unity of the Godhead is compatible with a distinction of Persons. Hence the Noëtians should not be associated with Basilides and his "Quaternity."

[310] *Joachimus Abbas* M. Joachim of Fiore was a Cistercian abbot and mystic. After his return from a pilgrimage to the Holy Land, he retired to the Cistercian Abbey in 1159. He was ordained priest in 1168 and now applied himself entirely to Biblical study, with a special view to the interpretation of the hidden meaning of the Scriptures. The mystical basis of his teaching is the doctrine of the "Eternal Gospel": there were three states of the world corresponding to the three Persons of the Blessed Trinity. In the third epoch there would be some cataclysm, calculated to be in 1260, after which Latins and Greeks would be united, Jews would be converted, and the Eternal Gospel would abide to the end of the world. Joachim inveighed against Peter Lombard after his death, perhaps because of his proposition on "Christological nihilism." See *Cath. Encycl.*, VIII, 406–407; XI, 768–69.

[311] For a discussion of Joachim, Galatinus, and Postel on the quaternity, see François Secret, "L'Emithologie de Guillaume Postel," *Archivio di Filosofia, Umanesmo e Esoterismo*, nos. 2–3 (1960), 381–437.

[312] Timaeus Locrensis was one of the chief professors, besides Plato and Pythagoras, of the doctrine of metempsychosis. This Pythagorean is the chief speaker in Plato's *Timaeus.* Nothing else is known of him. For testimonia, see Diels, *Frag. der Vorsokr.* (6th ed.), I. 441.

[313] Ezech. 1:15.

that voice of God repeating to Moses the four divine names, namely, the
P. 283 God of your father, the God of Abraham, the God of Isaac, the God of Jacob.[314]

OCTAVIUS: When the old pagan gods were being deprived of their ancient divinity, in the beginning of the young Christian church, only one God was worshipped by Christians. However, when Emperor Constantine the Great had ordered the temples of the gods to be closed, deity was granted to Christ in the Synod of Nicaea, but with the bitterest strife of the bishops, who were differing among themselves.[315] Still nothing up to this time had been decreed about the deity of the Holy Spirit, and there was not even any mention of it in the creed, nor was it believed to be God, as Gregory of Nazianzus wrote.[316] Even the opinion of the Arians, which placed Christ among the creatures, held so much validity that it was confirmed by the eight councils which were held at Tyre, Sardes, Milan, Smyrna, Seleucia, Nicaea, Tarsus, and Rimini, and especially by the Synod of Rimini in which six hundred bishops had gathered.[317] Although the deity of Christ was restored by the Council of Constantinople after twenty years, still concerning the third Person no one had supposed that he should fabricate a new god; nor was there any word about the Trinity. However, at length in the year of Christ 430, the Holy Spirit was brought into the number of gods at the Synod of Ephesus and in the subsequent synods in which some chapters about the Holy Spirit were substituted in the Nicene creed; namely, I believe in the Holy Spirit without any mention of God, so that the mention of the new god would be less offensive to religious ears. One knows from this that Athanasius, who lived during the time of Julian, could not have been the author of the common creed unless he had lived one hundred and thirty years. I pass over the fact that a Greek man, the lone dissenter, said that the Spirit proceeded from both, namely, the Father and Son, contrary to the penalty of anathema affixed by the Greek

[314] Ex. 3:6.

[315] Constantine met with the prelates of the entire Catholic world in council at Nicaea in 324, in hopes of putting an end to the quarrels that were disturbing the peace of the church. At Nicaea the term *homoousion* was adopted to indicate the orthodox belief in the Person of the historic Christ who was defined as identical in substance or coessential with the Father. See *Cath. Encycl.*, II, 37; IV, 425; XI, 266. See above, note 232.

[316] Gregory of Nazianzus wrote his fifth discourse against the Macedonian heresy, which denied the Divinity of the Holy Spirit—which, the Macedonians claimed, was mere impersonal energy of the Father. See *Cath. Encycl.*, VII, 10–14.

[317] See *Cath. Encycl.*, IV, 425.

councils, because he thought that the Spirit was derived otherwise than from the Father.[318]

FRIDERICUS: Nevertheless, Christ did not begin nor cease to be God because of the assemblies or disputations of men, nor likewise the Holy Spirit. But the things which were called doubtful by heretics have been confirmed by the most certain[319] decrees of wise men. And surely memorable is that which we have read recorded in church histories about two bishops who had been unwilling to subscribe to the decrees of the Nicene Council. When they were raised from the dead, they subscribed to the decrees after the matter was more clearly understood.

OCTAVIUS: "Sacred Scripture," Chrysostom said, "must be believed more than angels from heaven or men rising again." Moreover, who can be found to be so stupid or demented that he thinks demons, enticed by magic art, and shades, summoned by necromantic impiety, must be believed, since the impieties of that magic are forbidden as a capital crime not only by divine but also by human laws. And if there were any deity in Christ, which cannot be possible in any way, it would be completely uprooted by the assertion of such profaners and demons. When the Roman P. 284
pontiffs wish someone to be enrolled in the number of saints, they have been accustomed to call forth shadows with the help of necromancy, whence follow the remarkable apotheoses and the feats of demons by which they confirm the opinion of polytheism to the ignorant.

CORONAEUS: We ought to interpret in good faith the things which the Roman pontiffs piously do.

CURTIUS: Even if demons were summoned and appeared, I do not doubt that they would reverence the name and divinity of Christ as true God, since they feared Him and held Him in awe when He was alive on the earth. However, the most ancient prophecies of the Sibyls declared most openly that Jesus was the Son of God omnipotent and the Virgin Mary many generations before he was born; Eusebius and Lactantius Firmianus record these testimonies—lest I spend an infinite time in enumerating them.[320]

318 Epiphanius said that the Holy Spirit proceeds from the Father and the Son. See above, note 253. Also see article "*Filioque*" in *Cath. Encycl.*, VI, 73–74. Also Augustine, *De trinit.* VI. 1–10.

319 *certissimis* M

320 The prophecies of the Sibyls had been famous from antiquity. Their sayings were carefully collected and guarded in the temple of Jupiter Capitolinus in Rome. Because of the influence of these oracles in shaping religious opinions, the Hellenistic Jews in Alexandria in the second century B.C. composed verses in the same

Octavius: What is remarkable about this, since Proba Falconia[321] left for posterity a life of Christ made from a patchwork of verses transcribed from Maro himself? However, it is wicked for the majesty of the sacred books to be defiled loathsomely by the verses of the Sibyls and the Orphics, since rather often it has been proven that Sibyls were and had always been infamous for their concubinage with demons.

Coronaeus: If one can be satisfied by evidence, proofs, and authority, I think it has been done abundantly to prove that Jesus, the Son of God, born from eternity, is God, and together with the Father and Holy Spirit preserves His deity in the unity of His essence and His unity in the Trinity of Persons.

Senamus: Indeed, it is sufficient and even more than sufficient to me, who gives assent to all in regard to all things concerning divine matters. Yet a much more difficult question still remains. Even if we grant that fifteen centuries ago the Person of the Son was coequal and coeternal to the Father, for what reason did He assume human flesh? Then if we grant that the divine essence wished to enter the womb of a woman, why was this necessary for the redemption of the human race? For if God could save the human race and expiate it from all sins without the help of men or human flesh, without the death and blood of anyone, it was in no way necessary for the Son to come down to earth from those heavenly abodes and enter the womb of a woman; then to be born and in the flower of His youth to be tormented and crucified, when by only a nod He could easily have washed away all the sins of all men. For it is vain to attempt a thing by many things which can be accomplished by fewer things.

Octavius: Augustine said: "God did not lack another method for redeeming mankind; although one may think that God decreed it thus, still no necessity forced Him to follow His own decrees."[322] Hence, there was

---

form and attributed them to the Sibyls. These Jews circulated the oracles among the pagans as a means of spreading Jewish doctrines. The Christians continued this custom, and a new class of oracles from Christian sources came into being. Hence, the Sibylline Oracles can be thought of as pagan, Jewish, Christian prophecies. See *Cath. Encycl.*, XIII, 770; XIV, 598; XV, 460.

321 Proba Falconia, sometimes called Proba Faltonia, was a Christian poetess of the fourth century. She was a Roman aristocrat who was at first a pagan, but when she became a Christian, she also persuaded her husband to abjure paganism. She wrote an epic, no longer extant, which celebrated the wars between Constantine and Magnentius. She also wrote a cento in hexameters in which she relates sacred history in terms borrowed from Vergil. See *Cath. Encycl.*, XII, 440.

322 *De trinit.* III. 1.

no necessity antecedent or consequent why God put on the vilest flesh of man that He might die by a base death, since either an angel or another P. 285 man could make reparation by offering a sacrifice which God would have considered pleasing, because an offering is no more than as it pleases God to estimate it.[323] But if anyone should say that no one was sinless from the fall, God could also take this upon Himself so that someone could be born pure from all the contagion of sins; the more recent theologians proclaim this purity for the mother of Christ, and they had decreed this in the Council of Trent,[324] contrary to the opinion of the old theologians,—namely, Anselm, Bernard, the Master of the Sentences, Thomas Aquinas, Augustine, and Jerome.

TORALBA: Indeed I think it very strange that the most blessed minds of so many and such men are now condemned by the Roman church for impiety and are considered heretics.

CORONAEUS: The church cannot err because in the age of Bernard and Lombard this was not yet a heresy.

TORALBA: That which is true cannot be false because of the passage of time.

OCTAVIUS: Let us not be bogged down in these matters! Adam could merit pardon because of his singular love toward God, because love toward God is much more excellent than all the offerings and sacrifices which He could receive from creatures. Therefore, why was there need of so great a change, so cruel a punishment for a most innocent man?

CURTIUS: Even if no necessity forced God to act, still it pleased Him to do so. Moreover, it is a sin to examine and wrong to discuss, why it pleased Him to do so.

CORONAEUS: Ambrose denies that we should search out the profound immeasurableness of God's secrets. Still I must always search out the will of God, not why He willed this or that. However, if it is right to make any conjecture about the divine will, the most likely reason as to what

[323] *illam* M

[324] The doctrine of the Immaculate Conception had been debated for centuries before Pope Pius IX, on Dec. 8, 1854, pronounced and defined that the Blessed Virgin Mary "in the first instant of her conception, by a singular privilege and grace granted by God, in view of the merits of Jesus Christ, the Saviour of the human race was preserved exempt from all stain of original sin." The Council of Trent in 1546, when the question was touched upon, declared that "it was not the intention of this Holy Synod to include in the decree which concerns original sin the Blessed and Immaculate Virgin Mary, Mother of God." However, since this decree did not define the doctrine, the controversies continued. See *Cath. Encycl.*, VII, 674–80.

impelled Him to assume human nature and die a most shameful death seems to be to recall us from the defilement of faults to virtues, for we know how much He abhors sins. And next, to inflame more ardently with love of Him men whom He filled with greater dignity and excellence than the angels.

TORALBA: I think that Christians and ignorant men—certainly no philosphers—can be easily persuaded of this: that eternal God had always existed from the infinite myriads of ages with an immutable nature, yet this same One was not so long ago disturbed from the sublime excellence of His nature, assumed the concreteness of human blood and a new form in order to endure the harshest torments and vilest death from the executioners of iniquity, to rise again, and to bear a bodily mass of bones, flesh, ligaments, humors, and marrow into heaven, where a body had never before been seen.

FRIDERICUS: Yet Justin Martyr, Athenagoras, Basil, Origen, both Greg-
P. 286 ories,[325] Cyril, and Augustine, all most renowned in the pursuits and training of philosophy, also Boëthius, the glory of the Latin philosophers who also wrote books about the Trinity, and countless others in subsequent ages—Albertus Magnus,[326] Philoponus,[327] as well as both [men named] Pico della Mirandola, Scotus, Thomas Aquinas, who far surpassed the ancient Peripatetics in the subtlety of discussion—esteemed the symbol of the Christian[328] Trinity. No theologian ever thought that the divine mind also shall have suffered, with the exception of Eutyches, who was condemned for heresy.

OCTAVIUS: If God suffered and died, one must admit that the divine nature suffered and died. Even Tertullian used these words: "Did not God truly die?"[329]

CURTIUS: It does not follow that divinity suffers, because the divine mind is something abstract, but God the Christ, something concrete. Indeed, when Sabellius declared that God the Father began to be called

[325] Gregory of Nazianzus and Gregory of Nyssa.

[326] Albertus Magnus (1206–1280), scientist, philosopher, and theologian, was the teacher of St. Thomas Aquinas.

[327] John Philoponus (6th century), an Alexandrian philosopher, taught that there were three natures in the Holy Trinity, the three Persons being individuals of a species. His followers were called Tritheites and were excommunicated by Damian, Jacobite Patriarch of Alexandria. See article, "Eustychianism," *Cath. Encycl.*, V, 633–38.

[328] *Christianae* M.

[329] *Apol.* I. 21.

the Son, when He assumed man's appearance, and the Holy Spirit, when He descended into the gathering of apostles (lest one should believe otherwise, he thought the divine nature was divided into three parts), he was condemned for heresy, because he made no distinction of Persons.[330] Nestorius completely separated the divine nature from human nature when he addressed the assemblies thus: "Do not boast, Judea, for you did not fasten God to the cross." And he very fiercely defended this opinion in the Council of Ephesus. His adherents threw out Flavianus, the pontiff of Constantinople, and felled him with blows. And yet the manner of speaking was changed in the Council of Chalcedon lest anyone say henceforth that the divine nature suffered or died; rather God was born, suffered, and died so that one might say in concrete terms that which would be fitting only to one nature in abstract terms. They called this figure of speech a communicating of idioms, and in turn they called Jesus immortal, eternal, and omnipotent because of the joining together of deity with humanity. But they defined the name of mediator or king or priest in such a way as to signify nothing other than duties. Thus both sides were dissuaded from their opinion: those who completely separated the divine nature from the human and those who blended both natures. Still we admit that the union of both natures takes place in Christ, but in a way that is incomprehensible to human minds.

TORALBA: Nothing is more alien to divine nature, which is free from the world's contagion, than concreteness. But if we grant that a third nature comes from those two natures, God will thus be concrete. But if we grant that each nature has been completely separated from the other, that is, the divine mind has not mingled with the human mind, Christ will be nothing other than man.

FRIDERICUS: Thus if God shall have been wholly separated from the man Christ, no joining will exist; however, it is one thing for one to be mingled and blended, another to be joined and united. P. 287

TORALBA: Concrete things always produce one, but joined things no more unite into one than oil and water when poured into the same vessel. The debates[331] of the Lutherans whom they call Ubiquitarians, and the

[330] Sabellius emphasized the unity of God (Monarchians) and saw in the concepts of the Father and the Son merely manifestations of the Divine Nature. He was excommunicated by St. Callistus shortly after A.D. 220. See *Cath. Encycl.*, VII, 359 ff.; X, 449; XV, 50, 756. Nestorius has been discussed in preceding notes.

[331] *disputationes* M

Swiss who are called Sacramentarians, and the Catholics whom they call Papists, often cause amazement.[332] The Ubiquitarians say that a property does not depart from a subject; to speak more fully, omnipotence, omniscience, and omnipresence are appropriate to human nature not through themselves, not essentially, not formally, not subjectively (for they use these words); that is, they are not from the essence of flesh or accidents. Still they say those same divine properties are appropriate really to flesh. Indeed, can things more contrary than these be imagined? For whatever is said about anything is either substance or accident; there is no third. The Sacramentarians say that the man Christ is everywhere through His deity; His flesh, however, is not, neither through itself nor through deity. I would gladly learn from them what deity of human flesh can be imagined? The Ubiquitarians say that the man Christ and His humanity are omnipotent, but that the man and not His humanity are eternal. Yet eternal things will be much more appropriate to abstract things than to concrete things. This statement is even more absurd. Brentius said that the body of Christ which was hanging from the cross at Jerusalem in view of all was also present at the same time at Rome with deity. What does this mean? For if the flesh of Christ in itself is everywhere omnipotent and omniscient, surely the flesh is God eternal. Yet it will not be true flesh, that is, human flesh, a thing which both deny, with the exception of Eutyches and Schwenkfeld.[333] Differently, the Catholics, who deny that

[332] The Ubiquitarians were a Protestant sect, started by John Brenz at the Lutheran synod of Stuttgart. Melanchthon maintained that Christ's body was not in the Eucharist, for, he contended, a body could not be everywhere at the same time, and the Eucharist was everywhere. Brenz argues that the attributes of the Divine Nature had been communicated to Christ's humanity. If Christ was divine and possessed this Divine Nature, it was everywhere, ubiquitous, and therefore really present in the Eucharist.

The Sacramentarians, who were Zwingli's disciples at Zürich and elsewhere, opposed the Real Presence, and contrary to their name tended toward a Christianity without mysteries. Calvin was committed to a struggle with the Sacramentarians. In 1553, when the German Lutherans were in controversy about the Lord's Supper, Calvin declared his agreement with Melanchthon.

The "Papists" were so called by some members of the Church of England who protested the "usurpation" of the name Catholic by the Church of Rome. The Anglicans also called them "Romish." This protest in Protestant England against the use of "Catholic" to indicate the Church of Rome has raged off and on since the middle of the sixteenth century. See *Cath. Encycl.*, III, 198, 450; V, 575; XV, 117.

[333] Kaspar Schwenkfeld, one of the early disciples of Luther in Silesia, assailed Luther's teaching on the doctrine of justification and the Eucharist. Schwenkfeld denied the presence of Christ in the Eucharist. Schwenkfeld wandered from place

the body of Christ is everywhere, say, nevertheless, that it can be in many places simultaneously and at the same moment. But not to be everywhere and to be in many places at the same time and simultaneously are contradictory, and Christ cannot be in two places any more than in all places simultaneously. But if Christ ascended into heaven, He is not everywhere, and He is not even in many places. Or if He was everywhere, He did not ever ascend nor descend. They do not wish that human nature also be extended everywhere. Christ's body is everywhere complete, not having parts beyond parts, but all parts in all, that is—to state it more plainly—feet in the head, hands in the stomach. Still, they nevertheless deny that humanity is everywhere. However, humanity is an abstract idea; man is truly a concrete idea. Why then do they make these conclusions? Because they fear that those two natures, divine and human, would be separated unless the body of Christ were everywhere. Then the body must be, at one and the same time in the womb, on the cross, in heaven, in the stable, visible and invisible, a real and a phantastic body. Who can endure these ideas calmly and listen to them patiently? They admit that an atheist does not partake of divinity in the consecrated host, even if the atheist consumes the body of Christ and digests it. Therefore, they admit that in the atheist each nature is divided. The Ubiquitarians say that not only the soul of Christ but also the flesh is united with deity, but the Sacramentarians P. 288 deny this. The Ubiquitarians imagine that the properties of deity are in fact communicated to humanity, but the properties of humanity are not communicated to deity. Why such a variation, since they say there is one and the same foundation, indeed one and the same hypostasis, which must admit either both or neither.

CORONAEUS: All those ambiguities are removed if we understand what Marcus Tullius Cicero wrote: nothing in souls is concrete, nothing mingled.[334] Therefore, how much more must concreteness be sundered from the divine nature? Sometimes, nevertheless, concreteness is spoken of in Christ as a relation because of the marvelous union of the dual nature, which is incomprehensible to the human mind, in one and the same hypostasis, which Hilary writes, is similar in a certain way to the union

---

to place because of persecution against him by Lutheran ministers who condemned his writings in a meeting held at Schmalkalden in 1540. See *Cath. Encycl.*, IX, 40; XIII, 597–98.

[334] See the article "Soul (Roman)," in Hastings, *Encycl. of Rel. and Eth.*, XI, 748, on the revival in Cicero of the Pythagorean belief in the soul, especially in *Sommium Scipionis* and *Tusc. Disp.*, Book I.

of the human mind with the body. Still the Academicians, Stoics, and Peripatetics say that the soul is separated from the body and is not united to the body.

TORALBA: Then if the human mind is simple and is completely abstracted from the body, it is wrong to think that there is any concreteness in the divine nature. If each nature is separated and divided from each nature, that is, the divine mind joined with the human mind, so that they never come together into one and the same, Christ is nothing other than a man who will cling to God, as the mind of each best man, most upright and loving toward God, clings to God. This statement is pertinent: "It is good for me to cling to God."[335]

FRIDERICUS: Toralba thinks that divine matters must be verified by the scales of philosophers, and he does not believe that Christ is God. Even if he knew the clear truth of the matter, he would still oppose it by subtle arguments, as Paul says, excusing the Jews, his countrymen: "If they had known God, they would never have crucified the Lord of Glory."[336]

SALOMON: I seem to remember that Caligula Augustus excused the legates of the Jews in an urbane manner, when he said that they seemed to him good and very simple men, for they did not think that Caligula was God.[337] And so Fridericus also excuses the simplicity of our people because we do not think that the son of a carpenter was God.

OCTAVIUS: I do not see why we ought to be angry with the Ismaelites because they deny that Christ died and because they think He was snatched from the hands of His enemies, since Christians say that deity cannot suffer anything.

CURTIUS: Mohammed could think of no better trick to take away the belief in Christ's divinity and His concern for human salvation than to deny that He died, so that no one would place any hope of salvation in His death or seem to have any merit towards the human race.

P. 289 TORALBA: To speak of the merit of Christ's death is vain, if it could merit nothing. Moreover, Christ could not merit, since He was always established on the summit of happiness and attached to the best end, that is, to eternal deity, as indeed they say. We do not even say that angels or blessed souls merit, because a reward given to them would be less than their merit, although God has always granted rewards greater than the merits themselves. Moreover, no one can obtain a greater reward than the

[335] Psalm 72 (73):28. [336] I Cor. 2:8.
[337] Philo, *De legatione ad Gaium* XXVIII. 178–83.

heavenly kingdom and the enjoyment of God which are given to them. So Christ, who was joined to the best end, could merit nothing. If He were able to merit, He also would have been able to err, sin, and fall, because no one is able to merit who is always in the situation that if he should wish to sin, he could not. They say further that Christ, if He especially wanted to sin, still in no way could sin. Finally, infinite rewards would be given to the finite merit of Christ, because the merit of Christ, whatever it is, must be finite. Although His body died, not only the human mind of Christ, but also His divine nature shall have suffered nothing. Moreover, sins are as infinite as the number of men. But if sin could be washed away only by the punishment of a man, it was in no way necessary for Christ to die.

FRIDERICUS: Indeed, it has been said that God, from no necessity, put on human nature to expiate man's sins. However, since He has so decreed, it was necessary that it happen thus, not indeed in respect to God, but in respect to man himself, for Christ as man could merit. And so the words which often occur in sacred Scripture are pertinent here: "It was necessary that Christ suffer." Also: "It was necessary for these things to happen." "It is expedient that one man die."[338]

SALOMON: If it was necessary that Jesus die, what is the reason that Christians blame our elders for the cruelty which, nevertheless, produced salvation for the human race?

FRIDERICUS: Certain evils are spoken of badly; certain goods are well spoken of; certain evils are well spoken of. But this good is spoken of badly by the Jews, for at that time especially they were unwilling to do good, since they wickedly willed to do harm.

TORALBA: Indeed, that is, as I think, the point of beginning, since that very hypothesis which was in question is taken as proof. It must first be discussed whether that had been decreed by God.

CURTIUS: If faith, which ought to be supreme, should be granted to evangelical writings and the writings of the apostles, nothing would be found more frequently than the statement that God will become clothed in the weak raiment of man to free mankind from eternal destruction. The authority of the New Testament and of the Gospel depend upon the most certain and most divine revelations of the Old Testament and the prophets.

SALOMON: But where have so many revelations hidden for so long a time?

[338] Mark 8:31; Matt. 16:21; Luke 9:22, 17:25.

P. 290 CURTIUS: Indeed many revelations have been scattered here and there. Yet no revelation is as clear as Daniel's.[339] With divine inspiration he not only said that the Messiah must be killed, but he also noted the years, months, days, and hours in such a way that he seemed not to have written a tragedy with a reed as much as he seemed to have painted a picture with a brush and to have illustrated in bright colors the prophecies which Isaiah had outlined three hundred years before. Isaiah said: "A man contemptible in appearance, who bore our sicknesses and weaknesses, whom we think has been smitten and afflicted by God. He was gravely wounded on account of our faults and weakened on account of our crimes; the punishments which had been proper for us to pay were placed on Him, and we have been healed by His stripes. Like a sheep led to slaughter He did not open his mouth, but was snatched away for punishment. Who will tell of His generation? He will justify many by knowledge of Him; my just servant, whose crimes He will sustain."[340] These prophecies are confirmed by Zachariah's words and the verses of Jeremiah, who said: "The spirit of our mouth, Christ the Lord, has been captured in our sins."

SALOMON: Surely this passage, which Christians push forward before all others and in which many have remained firm, pertains in no way to the Messiah, in no way to the Son of God, much less to Jesus; nor does Isaiah call this person the Son of God but the servant. The statement which the Roman pontiffs proclaim in solemn song on the day before Easter would indeed be false and absurd. "O marvelous thing! You have handed over a son that you might redeem a servant." Isaiah calls him a servant, not a son. Therefore, how will those remarks be consistent? We see in sacred Scripture many Messiahs—namely, Moses, Joshua, Jephthah, Gideon, Samuel, David, and Saul. All of these are called Messiah, yet no one of these was killed as an expiation for the people.[341] Nevertheless, I do not doubt that God sometimes wishes to absolve the whole state and region because of the virtues of one most upright and innocent man. Perhaps the saying of Isaiah has reference to this, and also Solomon's statement which is similar. He said: "The town is small, and few people inhabit it because a most powerful king has it under siege, and foundations and great towers surround it on all sides for its storming. Yet in this city there was one who was very poor and very wise, and he saved the town from destruction, and no one of the citizens knew [him]."[342] That is, sometimes the integ-

[339] Dan. 9:25–26.
[340] Isaiah 53:3–8.
[341] Zach. 12:10; Jer. 23:6–7.
[342] Eccl. 9:13–15.

rity and outstanding virtue and probity of one citizen, although unknown and lowly, preserved the whole state from the vengeance and wrath of God, the most powerful King, from war, from famine, and from common plagues. The common translation differs a great deal from the Hebraic text[343] in regard to the line in Jeremiah. For it is literally thus: "By the breath[344] of our nostrils, the anointed of the lord[345] has been captured in their nets." And these words do not pertain to Jesus. P. 291

FRIDERICUS: We see how well these prophecies have been distorted. Nevertheless, this interpretation of Salomon differs in its whole concept from that of Rabbi David Kimchi, who thinks this passage must not be related to the Messiah, but to the people of Israel, as if the people of Israel might expiate for the sins of other people, as it were. These words do not allow this interpretation: "He was wounded for the sins of the people of God."[346] For how might the people of God be slain for the people of God?

SENAMUS: In order to weaken the atoning death of Christ, Julian Augustus writes that Asculapius, the son of Jupiter, took on human nature to cure diseases of the body just as Plato cured the sickness of the souls, not to die for the salvation of the human race. Moreover, God certainly was accustomed to avenge the slaughter of good men with a great calamity, but to preserve the whole region from destruction with the destruction of the wicked. And so the Athenians on the seventh of April used to lead the two most wicked men of the whole region throughout the city; having beaten them with branches of seven unhappy trees and with clubs, they burned them with this same wood and threw their ashes into the sea. And since this happened every year as a solemn vow for expiating the sins of the citizens, they called that day the purification day.[347] In like manner up to the time of Tiberius the ancient Gauls, near Arae Laetae (a town of this name exists even up to our time), enclosed criminals and wicked men in wood statues and colossi of huge dimensions and burned them to expiate the sins of the others.[348]

[343] *dictione* M [344] *spiritu* M [345] *Domini* M

[346] Isaiah 53:5.

[347] The Thargelia was a primitive vegetation rite. The *pharmakoi* in the Thargelia were actually put to death, according to some authorities. Tsetzes, our chief authority, says that a man chosen for his ugliness was led to sacrifice, and after several rites intended to indicate his connection with a fertility vegetation deity, was burned and his ashes scattered to the sea and winds as a purification.

[348] On appeasing angry gods by human sacrifice, see the article "Scapegoat (Greek)" in Hastings, *Encycl. of Rel. and Eth.*, II, 218–21. On the widespread notion of purification by sacrifice see the articles under "Purification," *ibid.*, 10, 445–505.

TORALBA: It was fairer for each man to pay the penalty for his own sin, as Herodotus writes that the ancient Egyptians did. While a cow was being sacrificed, a multitude of the people with bared backs was being beaten.[349] This custom spread from the Egyptians and Amorites to the Jesuits[350] and the Hieronymites. Also, while the Camarim,[351] priests of Bahal, clothed in sooty garments, sacrificed a victim, they lacerated themselves with swords and daggers. Xenophanes did not sufficiently understand this custom of the Egyptians, and when he was observing those punishments he said: "If you believe these are gods, why are you weeping? But if you think they were men, why do you perform sacrifices to them?"[352] This occurred for the expiation of each man's sin. Nevertheless, he subtly castigated the insane madness of men because they worshipped dead men as gods.

SALOMON: It happens almost universally that wicked men atone for their own sins and often also for the sins of good men, but it is entirely unheard of that good men are sacrificed for wicked men. Indeed, every year in
P. 292 February we honor the day of the sacred lots, which the Latins call the day of atonement and cleansing, as if a lot had been cast by God, to determine whether it would seem fairer for Haman, a most wicked and haughty man, or Mordecai, an excellent man, to die with the whole tribe of Israelites. When the lots were drawn from the urn, with God Himself moving the urns, Haman, whose lot was drawn, was put to death and atonement was made for the Israelites.[353] Thus Solomon writes that a wicked man will atone for the just. When a Moabite harlot had enticed the people of God and led them astray to the worship of Bahal Peor, a great plague overcame the people. The plague was not checked until the priest Phineas brandished a spear and ran it through an Israelite as he

349 Herodotus II. 61.

350 *Jesuitas* M. As late as the sixteenth and seventeenth centuries flagellation was used as a punishment for blasphemy, concubinage, and simony. The Hieronymites, hermits of St. Jerome, flourished in Spain and Italy during the sixteenth and seventeenth centuries and were noted for their almsgiving and piety. The Jesuits were noteworthy, among many other things, for their strict discipline and piety.

351 See above, p. 172, notes 129 and 133.

352 Cf. Diels, *Frag. der Vorsokr.* (6th ed.), I. 116.

353 See Esther 3–4; II Mac. 15:36–37. This is the festival of Purim, which commemorates the vengeance taken by Mordecai and the Jews on their enemies. Purim means "lots" and refers to the lots cast by their enemies to destroy them. Purim may originally have been a Persian or Babylonian institution adopted as a secular feast by the Jews and invested with a religious character in a later time. See Hastings, *Encycl. of Rel. and Eth.*, V, 866.

was joined in love with the Moabite woman. God witnessed that the descendants of Phineas would hold an eternal priesthood because he had assuaged His anger by the murder of the offending ones. For this reason the law orders a parricide to be snatched from the sacred altars and openly strangled lest the whole state be destroyed, since often the sins of all are punished because of the unpunished impiety of one man. Indeed, when Ahaz had seized the cursed booty, the enemy routed the army of God, with God Himself witnessing that this had happened because of the shameful act of one man.[354] From this it is clear that God is appeased by the punishment of the wicked, but He is stirred up with anger[355] to avenge the death of the good. Since this is true, who can believe that God, the best and greatest, was delighted with the punishment of the best and most upright man?

FRIDERICUS: When Salomon attacks us with divine laws, with laws we ought to restrain him. The divine law forbids that an animal sacrifice be offered, if the animals are spotted or mangy or weak or lame, or damaged in the eyes or any other part.[356] Therefore, if just punishments of the wicked are pleasing to God, still He is not pleased with sacrifices of the wicked.

SALOMON: The divine law means this: God is not pleased with the offerings of those who waver in following God's law, who are blind to the want of the poor, who are deaf to the voices of the afflicted.

CURTIUS: All men are guilty of sin, are wicked, defiled, and impure in the sickness of their pride, and no one has ever lived sinless except Christ on whom all the sins of all men are heaped up, as on a lamb pure and spotless in every part for sacrifice. Therefore, why[357] is it not strange that God wished this victim who was most pleasing to Him to be sacrificed?

OCTAVIUS: If sacrifices of men or flocks atoned for another's sins, why does God repeatedly curse those who were confident that their sins were absolved by sacrifices and blood?[358]

FRIDERICUS: To instruct the Jews that sacrifices of blood had been a shadowy image of that eternal sacrifice which Christ, the greatest high priest of all, would offer for the salvation of all the world.[359] Moreover, when Philo the Hebrew was searching for the reason why the exiles were kept from returning to their paternal homes until the high priest had P. 293

[354] IV Kings (II Kings) 16:7–9.
[355] *iracundia percitum* M
[356] Lev. 22:20–30.
[357] *quid* M
[358] Hosea 6:6; Psalm 39 (40):7–9; Psalm 49 (50):7–15.
[359] Heb. 9, 10.

died,[360] he surely interprets that this high priest would not be a man but the Word of God, free from all sins; whose Father is God eternal, whose Mother is Wisdom. He seems to have hit the nail on the head with these words: namely, that Jesus would be that high priest who would, by His death, call back the human race into their ancestral homes of heaven.

SALOMON: How could Philo have reflected on Jesus' death as the high priest of souls since He had died before Philo had reached young manhood? Or why did he not mention in so many books the name of Jesus who had died recently? Lest anyone think that sins could be washed away with blood, the prophet Micah declared: "Shall I give my first born as an atonement for sin or the fruits of my belly as a sacrifice for the sin of my soul? I have shown you, O man, what is good and what God requires of you: namely, to make judgment, to love kindness, and to offer yourself humble to your God."[361] Thus since God was satisfied with Abraham's compliance and exceptional will, He refused the sacrifice of the son which He had ordered.[362] If God wished to be appeased by human blood, He would seem to have been most pleased in this most pure and innocent sacrifice.

OCTAVIUS: How much less would eternal God be pleased by the death of His Son Christ! Would not He rather curse this sacrifice as detestable? For when Solomon deprecates those who have plundered the goods of the week and needy and bring a part of them for sacrifices, he writes that they act in a manner corresponding to a father who sacrificed a son. He was making clear that nothing would be more detestable to God than if anyone sacrificed his own son who was most dear to him. Moreover, it is rather absurd that God, angered with mankind, exacts vengeance from Himself; equally foolish would it be if anyone, being severely wounded, demanded punishment not from the enemy but from himself and just as desperately ended his life by hanging.

CORONAEUS: The death of Christ not only was beneficial[363] in atoning for the sins of the wicked but also keeps us the more willingly from sin, when we realize that immortal God was so displeased by the sins of the wicked that He wanted His dearest Son to undergo the most loathsome death because of the sins of others. Moreover, can anyone not know that not only did the most precious blood of Christ bring forth eternal salvation for the human race but also the sign of the cross itself suddenly scatters evil demons and confounds aerial pests? Indeed, when Julian asked the

[360] See Num. 35:25; Josh. 20:6.
[361] Micah 6:6–8.
[362] Gen. 22:1–19.
[363] *profuit* M

demons why they fled, they did not hesitate to confess that they had been routed in terror[364] by the remarkable sign of the cross, as ecclesiastical writers have related. How deservedly is the Roman church accustomed to employ that song: "Hail, O cross, unique hope; increase justice for the pious and give pardon to the guilty."

CURTIUS: Coronaeus says this very excellently for his religion in which he was brought up. Still, I do not see how a piece of wood can grant pardon for sins to anyone; moreover, I believe evil demons have been accus- P. 294
tomed by these terrors to bind the unlearned and turn them away from the worship of God.

SALOMON: Having put aside the lifeless crosses, let us return to the crucified, not only in whom but also from whom salvation is believed to flow into all the human race. By the death of that One sins are expiated either for the dead or the living or those who were about to be born at that time; whose sins, please?

FRIDERICUS: All sins of all men have been cleansed by Christ's death: the sins of those who had believed He would come, and those who received Him when coming, and those who worshipped Him sincerely after His death.

OCTAVIUS: No high priest, I think, was so wicked as to think future sins were to be pardoned. For would not this be to propose the worst impunity for all crimes? For that reason Paul writes that past sins have been removed by Christ's death, but still not future sins.[365]

SALOMON: The removal of past sins by Christ's death is not consistent with divine law which would have been useless if pardon had been delayed up to the time of Christ; also useless would have been God's promises whereby He promised so often that He would be propitious to the penitent. Moreover, when God orders us to confess our sins and repent on the solemn fast day, He adds these words: "On this day all your sins will be forgiven, and you will be clean from all your defilements."[366] Certainly if He had wished to except[367] some disgraces, as the Roman pontiffs order sins of more serious impiety to be referred to them for indulgence, threatening punishment to lesser priests if they assume for themselves a more serious jurisdiction, and if He had deferred some sins until the advent of the future Christ, He would not omit this in bringing forth the

[364] *exterritos* M. The marginalia of M give the names of Cyril, Gregory of Nazianzus, and Nicephorus Callistius.

[365] Rom. 3:24–26. [366] Isaiah 33:24. [367] *excipi* M

law. However, He made no mention of this. And if anyone should think that the ancient prophets were less diligent in their interpretation of the law for our elders, understand, if you will, their teaching. They establish that sins against the commandments are expiated first by repentance—suppose, for example, that someone does not help one in need when he easily could; but if a man has sinned against a prohibitive law, for example, if he has injured another's reputation, this sin is sustained by repentance yet is abolished on the day of expiation. But if the punishment for a sin was to be death, as in the case of adultery, again by repentance and on the day of expiation the sin would be suspended. By punishments, however, which would be inflicted first by the judges, then by God, if the judges feigned punishment, their sin would be completely obliterated. This saying is relevant: "I shall visit their sins with lashes and blows and their disgrace with scourges."[368] But if anyone has desecrated the most sacred name of God with insult, his sin is suspended first by repentance, next by the day of expiation, and afterwards, also by punishments, and finally is abolished on the day of death. Nevertheless, punishments due for sin are generally lessened by outstanding actions, or surely weakened[369] by a
P. 295 superabundance of religious piety toward God, piety toward parents, and love toward the needy. It is clear from these examples that Jesus' death was useless in expiating the sins of men. Our elders have explained these things very fully, and they agree that no sin is so great that it is not washed away by continual repentance and noble and virtuous acts.

Coronaeus: On the contrary, our works are empty, our actions are empty, our supplications are empty without that most precious death of Christ. And since I could not attain with sufficient dignity in Latin verses the memory of so great a benefit and so great a salvation, I hoped that I could reach this in a holier way in Greek hymns:

"Christ, delicate flower of the sons of God, eternal Priest,
carried above the revolving heavens,
Master of the celestial plains where the strength of Your power is fixed;
from there You see all things and You hear all with Your excellent ears.
Your golden great eternal power rises above the world and the starry sky.
Exalted by this power and stimulating Yourself in Your splendor
You foster the infinite soul with perennial rivers.
You bring forth and shape incorruptible matter about which begetting wanders,

[368] Psalm 88 (89):33.

[369] *minui* M

since You have bound that matter with forms.
From this same mind the origin of holy kings who surround You have flowed, oh most powerful and most holy King of all.[370]
Born from You and having set out in their legations,
they are carried to You, begettor of their missions, and to Your power.
Moreover, You have created a certain third kind of kings who continually celebrate Your praises.
O best One, You have given mortals life by Your death."

OCTAVIUS: The Muse has allowed the Greeks to speak with polished tongue. We cannot possibly speak so elegantly. Indeed, I think it is impossible for these things to be rendered in Latin verses, not even if that man of yours[371] of Verona should come back to life, he who boasted that he had made sixty lines from one heroic verse.[372]

SALOMON: Indeed remarkable is that praise if it does not proceed from man to man. But if it is true that Christ's death gives life and removes sins, why do Christian priests require of sinners repentance, confession of sins, and even reparation? Or what more does the divine law require of man? Wherefore, nothing more destructive than the auricular confession of the Romans could be conceived: whether, for the fact that they think that man's sins are remitted by man, which is the greatest impiety toward God; or for the fact that by this conviction freedom to indulge in all sins is granted, and hope of pardon is set forth; or that all the lustiest sins are always kept in silence; or that conscience brings a desperation to those who are ashamed to confess their blackest sins which would be punished by death if they were known; or the fact that it is necessary to approach the pope to expiate the foulest sins; or that tyrants have open for themselves easy approaches for proscriptions and cruelties.

CORONAEUS: I, however, am convinced that there is no more efficacious amulet against all sins than auricular confession. For who would dare to commit a serious sin if he knows that there is no hope of pardon unless P. 296 he makes confession of the sin committed? Before the arrival of the Spanish, even the Indians and Peruvians, still uncivilized and sun worshippers, were accustomed to confess to their priests. The history of the Indians bears witness that it was a capital offense among them for the priest to divulge their sins.

[370] *Rex omniumque sanctissime* M [371] *vester* M

[372] The marginal note of M indicates that the man from Verona is Julius Caesar Scaliger.

CURTIUS: Since they served demons, can anyone doubt that they also learned this custom from demons and imitated it so that they sought and hoped for pardon from men, not from God? O wondrous amulet of wickedness, obviously unknown to God Himself for so many centuries, by which men may be restrained from sins. Moreover, their impiety advanced to the extent that they think that repentance is even unnecessary, and the word of the priest alone commonly removes the vilest sins. But how much repentance is necessary for obtaining pardon, Manasseh, king of the Jews, explains in an elegant and effectual statement to God. He said: "With infinite goodness You have decreed repentance, so that You can save from destruction those who would have perished under the fairest laws and judgments."[373]

FRIDERICUS: The death of Christ did not atone for those sins which hitherto had already been vindicated by repentance or just punishment. Neither did it atone for the sins of those who had no hope of a future Messiah, nor of those who scorned the remedy brought forth by Christ for recovering health [salvation]. However, it did atone for the sins of those who received the gratuitous beneficence of Christ. Those escape not only the guilt but also the most lenient punishments for all wickedness.

OCTAVIUS: To be sure, that decree seems very dangerous to me in that from faith, which each most wicked man can fortuitously accept about Christ's death, he merits forgiveness for sins. For what is this except to provide impunity for all and a wide path to all impieties for each most daring man?

FRIDERICUS: The death of Christ was especially necessary for mankind to purge the foulest Fall.

TORALBA: If there is no sin unless it is voluntary, as indeed all the theologians confess, original sin is not possible, because there is no will for sinning at birth. But if this is so, the troublesome question about the Trinity and much more difficult question about the incarnation of divinity, likewise about the ascension of God as man into heaven and other questions are solved as contrary to divine laws and the laws of nature.

CURTIUS: It is impossible that there is no original sin because nothing is more often discovered in the Old and New Testaments.

SALOMON: I do not doubt that Adam sinned, but not because he plucked
P. 297 the forbidden fruit, or tasted it when his wife offered it to him,[374] as people imagine in their childish error. Rather he sinned because he allowed

[373] Cf. II Paralip. (II Chron.) 33.

[374] *aut ab uxore oblata gustaret* M

his mind, led away from the contemplation of intelligible things, to be enticed and overcome by the allurements of sensual desires. Thus the most astute theologians of the Hebrews say that the name for woman indicates the bodily senses, but the name for man indicates the intellect; the word for serpent indicates pleasure, which, like a serpent, is accustomed to steal into the recesses of the body and to excite the avenues of sensation, yet it exerts its force especially in the teeth, and it creeps in the belly. But in whatever way Adam sinned, why did that sin spill over to his innocent posterity? Or, if faults are passed on to posterity, virtues must also be passed on, and much more so than faults, since it has been proven above that in universal nature goods have always been more powerful than evils. Moreover, all the philosophers as well as theologians have found from long experience as a guide that parents do not hand on to their descendants any virtues. Therefore, sins could not be transferred, since there is the same teaching of contraries.[375] Therefore, it follows that there is no original sin.

CORONAEUS: Indeed, that Pelagian heresy has for a long time been repudiated by the complete agreement of the theologians and driven out by the decrees of the councils. In our age the supreme authority of the Council of Trent crushed and rejected it. The decree is as follows: "Let there be anathema to him who denies that the sin of Adam was carried over to his posterity or who thinks that sin harmed only him [Adam] or that only corporeal weaknesses were transferred or could be abolished in any way except by the death of Christ." The words and teachings of Paul prove these words. As an example, Paul says: "Death held power for the damnation of all[376] because of the sin of one; thus by the death of one for all[377] grace is most fully propagated for salvation."[378] Why also did David complain with these words? "Behold, I have been conceived in sins, and my mother conceived me in sins."[379]

OCTAVIUS: Augustine said that the Manichaean heresy defended original sin.[380]

FRIDERICUS: Here Augustine meant the heresy of the Manichaeans who assumed two infinite principles of good and evil from eternity, a God of good and a God of evil with equal power. Augustine clung to this heresy

[375] *contrariorum* M

[376] *in omnium condemnationem* M

[377] *in omnes* M

[378] Rom. 5:17–18.

[379] Psalm 50 (51):7.

[380] *De civ. Dei* XIV. 5; *De haeres.* XLVI.

for a very long time. This is indeed a sin of origin.[381] But do not think that Augustine denies the Fall of human origin. His books and letters are full of original sin. Indeed he spoke thus against Pelagius: "All men are bound by original sin."[382]

TORALBA: If we attribute more to the authority of councils, which are yet rejected by the Swiss and Germans, than we do to reason, there will
P. 298 be no place for discussion and proof. Rather we must rashly agree on everything because Augustine, Jerome, Scotus, and Galatinus said it. But I beg our discussions to be drawn more clearly from reasons and arguments. For I saw no one who defended the opinion of Pelagius, the truest of all, in a worse way. Therefore, please discuss more carefully all the arguments of this question, since there will unfold from this the fruit of innumerable questions. Indeed, what is original sin except that the mother or father in conceiving sometimes indulged more in lust and pleasure than was fitting? Granted that this was so, why would there be sin for the son?

CURTIUS: Isn't it consistent with reason, when Toralba contends reasonably that a son as heir is bound by the obligation of his parents? Indeed, Plutarch, even though a pagan, wrote that this was consistent to natural equity.[383]

OCTAVIUS: I grant that hereditary debts must be paid. But who ever heard that revenge for sins or exaction of punishments was sought from heirs?

SALOMON: The divine laws very clearly forbid that a son be bound by a fault of his parents,[384] and we observe that this is rather often repeated.

CORONAEUS: We have witness that not only is original sin blotted out by the blood of Christ, but also the punishments for each private sin are revisited upon posterity.

SALOMON: Each man suffers punishment for his own sin, not for another's. When the Israelites complained that our elders had eaten sour grapes, and the children's teeth are set on edge,[385] God in a clear voice calls His people to witness that each man's integrity would benefit himself and each man's faults would harm himself, not others. The threat of vengeance to enemies of His name for the third and fourth generation has received this interpretation with theological accord: namely, if a worth-

[381] *originis* M

[382] *Sancti Augustini operum tomus* X (Paris, 1696). *Contra duas epistolas Pelagianorum* IV. 488c., Par. 29; *Contra Julianum Pelagianum* III. 558a., Par. 10.

[383] *De fraterno amore* XII. 484c.

[384] Ezech. 18:1–23.

[385] *ac filiorum dentes obstupuisse* M See Jer. 21:29; Ezech. 18:2.

less son follows a wicked parent, and a son follows him, unless he is better than his father and grandfather, then God, mindful of his parents, grandparents, and great-grandparents, would execute vengeance in such a way that henceforward there would be no recollection of their posterity, and their seed would be completely wiped out. But He pledged an oath that He would cherish the thousandth generation of those who worship and love Him to inform all peoples how much greater is God's mercy than His harshness. Nevertheless, He did not allow children to atone for the wickedness of parents; rather each one suffers his own punishment, not another's.

FRIDERICUS: Why then was it reported to the high priest Eli that no one of his descendants would be old or rich because he had left the impiety of his sons unavenged?[386]

SALOMON: This does not mean to punish the descendants who had not P. 299
yet been born and those who could have been prevented from being born, but to bless them less. An example is David's curse as he pleaded that there would be poverty, trouble, and sickness on the descendants of Joab who had wickedly killed Abner;[387] which is to say that the descendants of Joab were to be blessed less. Moreover, since nothing is dearer to anyone than his own children, nothing which can be loved more passionately; therefore God adds the most forceful threats, namely, that He would punish up to the third generation the injuries brought against Him. Nevertheless, it is right to remember the supreme kindnesses of God because it is better to be born, to grow, to live for a short time than never to have lived at all; and it is better to be lame than never to have existed.

FRIDERICUS: But the discussion is about the original sin of Adam being transferred to his descendants. The pagans themselves admit this as this passage of the lyrical poet[388] shows:

> For no one is born without faults; that man is
> best who is burdened with the
> least faults.

TORALBA: Let this be allowed to the poets. Surely those who blame the nature of any sin relate the sin not to themselves but to the parent of nature, and nothing is more deadly than this. Indeed, who sins in this which he could not avoid? Or can you imagine any sin which is sustained

[386] I Kings (I Sam.) 3:12–14.
[387] III Kings (I Kings) 2:5–6.
[388] Horace, *Sat.* I. 3. 68–69.

without the total will of the sinner? Now an infant is free from both. He cannot seek goods nor avoid evils, neither escape nor even understand the things which have been implanted in him by nature. Therefore, no sin can be charged to an infant. When there is no sin, no punishment ought to be sought. Since these things are so, there is no reason for a son to have been born from time eternal or no reason why that incredible and astonishing incarnation of God ought to be imagined. Finally, it is in vain to think that Christ suffered death to cleanse the stain of original sin.

FRIDERICUS: Indeed those beliefs are incredible, new, false and unheard of to philosophers. However, when Pelagius used reasons demanded by the philosophers to prove that there is no original sin, Jerome called him the patriarch of heretical philosophers. For if we give assent to the subtleties of the philosophers, we must reject faith and piety; and yet that argument is most insignificant, since that original sin did not proceed from an infant but from Adam who knowingly sinned, because of his own accord he departed from reason. Moreover, with whatever color the root is imbued, it imbues the trunk, branches, leaves, flowers, and fruits with the same flavor, odor, color, and poison. So it is that the nature of man, overturned from the foundation, seems to have no spark[389] of any good or virtue. The Teacher of Wisdom says: "Who can dare to say my heart is clean, I am free from sin?"[390] How much truer is this statement: "Every man is a liar,"[391] that is, a sinner! "For if I say that we are free from sin," that
P. 300 one said, "we deceive ourselves."[392] Moreover, salvation is proclaimed in one word: "Believe and you will be saved."[393]

OCTAVIUS: To what purpose is that except that wicked men, who believe they will get to heaven with the slightest faith, blame nature since they have wallowed in the foulest mire of pleasures, and having given up virtue, throw back upon God Himself, the Parent of nature, the efficient causes of all sins? All who have reached adulthood have strayed from the right path. This is not[394] understandable in the case of infants, but about those who have strayed from the laws of nature freely and with judgment. And indeed who can bear that Illyrian theologian when he writes that original sin pervades the intimate substance of souls and is produced and transformed by the devil himself and is removed by faith alone. Indeed that word seems dangerous to me.

[389] *scintillam* M
[390] Prov. 20:9.
[391] Rom. 3:4.
[392] I John 1:8.
[393] Acts 16:31; Mark 9:23.
[394] *non* M

FRIDERICUS:[395] What then did Paul mean when he said: "We were by nature the sons of anger"[396]—unless he was referring to original sin?

TORALBA: Let us pass over the authority of men and treat of necessary proofs! Who, indeed, can deserve praise and blame for those things which he drew from nature herself? Who can not seem worthy of compassion rather than of any punishment? We grieve for and pity those who are blind and deaf from birth; still these theologians do not feel pity for little infants. Now who can think that not only are we bound by sin before the birth of the first parent but also that in infants themselves there is a sin so ample and serious that it was necessary that God enter the womb of woman, suffer the conception of human flesh, and endure the tortures of a most loathsome death to free most innocent children from so great an enormity of sin?

CORONAEUS: Hear Cyprian, a theologian and the greatest martyr of his age.[397] He said: "Let him be completely afraid to die who is not reborn of water and the spirit and is delivered up to the fires of hell."[398] With these words he did not even make exception of infants. We truly believe that that taint of original sin is completely removed by baptism because baptism of Christ's blood is indicated by the pouring of water.

TORALBA: If original sin had been completely wiped away by the outpouring of Christ's blood, what need was there for Christ's baptism?[399] But if the stain is washed away by baptism, what need was there for Christ's suffering?[400] Nevertheless, I have rather often wondered at the rite of baptism. The priest asks the crying infant whether or not he wishes to be baptized. As if he could understand whether or not he can the more believe not only that but this![401] To what end are these questions?

CORONAEUS: The faith of relatives and parents accomplishes as much as if the child himself answered yes.

OCTAVIUS: It seems ridiculous to me that the faith of parents is useful to the crying baby for washing away original sin which, they affirm, came from those very parents.

[395] *Fridericus* M Continuation of Octavius' speech in N

[396] Eph. 5:8; Col. 3:8–9.

[397] St. Cyprian of Carthage suffered martyrdom in 258 at Carthage. He was the first bishop of Carthage to become a martyr.

[398] Cf. Cyprian, *De mortalitate* III.

[399] *baptismo* M

[400] *Sin baptismo macula diluitur, quid opus Christi supplicio?* M.

[401] *Quasi sensum ullum haberet; neque illud tantum, sed hoc amplius credat, necne?* M

p. 301 CURTIUS: This is the power of the blood poured out from the most precious wounds of Christ, God and man, by whose bath the parents have been washed.

SALOMON: But Paul writes that the death of Christ was effective for washing away only past sins.[402] Therefore, those who were born after Christ hold vain hope in His suffering. Indeed if your parents had been completely cleansed by a holier bath and the blood of Christ the Saviour, how is it possible that they again pass on to posterity that tainting sin?

CURTIUS: Baptism and the blood of Christ do not wash away sin in such a way that the root of sin does not remain implanted in the very secret darkness and thickets of desires.

TORALBA: But Christians advance this idea farther; they think that not only original sin but also all other sins are removed by Christ's death. In fact, either the most insignificant sins which have happened inadvertently through error or those sins contracted knowingly with no error or sins of more serious depravities are pardoned. Indeed, it has already been proved by divine law that the more trivial sins are removed by repentance alone; however, the more serious sins—I mean adultery, fornication, murder, poisoning, parricide, witchcraft, idolatry, blasphemy of God's name—have punishments instituted by divine and human laws. If a liar, a thief, an adulterer or a parricide should state before the praetors and judges of such matters that they had been baptized and were persuaded by constant faith that all their sins, past and future, were washed away by the most precious blood of Christ, the laws would be judged without effect after the death of Christ. Therefore, if just punishments for crimes are demanded from the living and the dead, useless is that benefit, and useless is the death of Christ for the impunity of sins.

CORONAEUS: Because of Christ's suffering, baptism has washed away all original sin. Although lust and desire and a hunger for sin remain, still they can harm no one who has been baptized, provided he wishes to resist them with reason as a guide, as the sanctions of the Council of Trent decree.

FRIDERICUS: Four councils I accept—namely, Nicaea, Constantinople, Ephesus, and Chalcedon,[403] which Pope Gregory considered in like manner as the Gospel. And I am willing to support the power of the princes

[402] Rom. 3:26.

[403] The Councils of Nicaea (325), Constantinople (381), Ephesus (431), and Chalcedon (451) are the first four ecumenical councils. See above, p. 358, note 232; p. 360, note 248; p. 374, note 315.

and popes who attended and who were leaders. But I cannot approve the other councils in which the popes were accustomed to alter ambitious decrees or to feign new ones. Indeed, Gregory Nazianzus openly wrote that he had never seen fortunate accomplishments of any synod.[404] And in truth, Nicolò, bishop of Palermo, the greatest supporter of the Roman church, weakening the authority of the councils,[405] said: "A simple layman who professes Sacred Scripture is more to be trusted than the whole Council." Therefore, it is safer to approve the opinion of Augustine in this matter; he wrote thus to Maximianus: "I am bound neither by the Synod of Rimini which approved the Arian doctrine nor by the Synod of Nicaea, P. 302
but I rely on the authority of Sacred Scriptures, that is, of the prophets, apostles and martyrs, who agree there is original sin."[406]

Toralba: I beg that we not allow the light of reason of our intelligence to be extinguished or blotted out by the authority of small councils or insignificant writers and unlearned men.

Curtius: But by what reasons, Toralba, do you believe that you can overturn divine matters and the most sacred and ancient decrees of the fathers, confirmed for so many centuries?

Toralba: If the active sin of Adam harmed not only the sinner, whatever punishment he took, but was transferred also to all his posterity, it must have been transferred either from body into bodies or from souls into souls or from both into both. Still a body itself cannot be proven guilty of any sin; otherwise animals themselves would also sin. But if every sin comes from the will and from the lapse of reason, as Christian theologians[407] agree, surely original sin cannot be in the souls of infants, since Christians, Ismaelites, and Hebrews agree that all the souls of all are created most clean and pure by God and immediately after creation flow into the human body. But if the soul [mind] comes pure from God, whence can sin creep into the soul of an infant? This reasoning gave the Master of the Sentences cause for wonder from whence that sin was de-

404 The marginal note in M indicates that this statement appears in *Epist. 42 ad Procop.*

405 Nicolò de Tudeschi (1386–1445) became bishop of Palermo in 1435. During the pontificate of Eugene IV, in which the question of whether the pope or the council should govern the church was hotly debated, Nicolò at first took the Pope's side but later allied himself with the anti-Pope Felix V. See *Cath. Encycl.*, XI, 69; also article, "Council of Basle," II, 334–38.

406 See *Sancti Augustini operum tomus* X (Paris, 1696). *Contra duas epistolas Pelagianorum* III. 466a–d., Par. 26.

407 The marginal note in M indicates Peter Lombard, Thomas Aquinas, Duns Scotus, Albertus, and Durandus.

rived. He said: "He who creates a soul does not sin; parents who beget a body do not sin, since this is consistent with universal nature." Therefore, through what cracks could sin penetrate among so many bulwarks of innocence? Aristotle did not even think that the soul of man was passed on through the seed, but that it was imparted extrinsically, as he states plainly enough in these words: "It remains that the mind alone comes from outside and alone is divine."[408] I interpret from the outside as from God, from heaven, from above.

SALOMON: When David Kimchi and Rabbi Saadias interpret those words—forming spirits in his presence—they say the soul is formed by God in the very perfection of the body. Not only does Rabbi Moses Aegyptius confirm this, but also the Stoics, along with the Christian and Ismaelite theologians, agree. They repudiate the opinion of the Platonists who say that souls indeed proceed from God, but think that at the beginning of the origin of the world all souls were made at one and the same time and in turn enter bodies.

P. 303 TORALBA: If it were true, as the Epicureans believed, that the souls of men as well as beasts are transferred with the seed itself (and we must admit this if we admit original sin), it would be necessary that sins increase to infinite force and number and are transmitted into all posterity. Experience and practice, the best teacher of all things, forces us to confess that this is absurd. We see that very few men were equal to Josiah in piety and justice and no one was superior to him, although his grandfather was Manasseh, the most cruel tyrant, who had surpassed the princes of his own nation with wickedness.[409] But if the soul is not transferred through the seed, but rather descends from heaven and is diffused into the body, no stain of original sin can be fashioned.

FRIDERICUS: We indeed admit that souls are not transmitted through the seed but are defiled by the contagion of the flesh because of the close union of body and soul. "You seek," Augustine said, "fault in boys; you will find that it is transferred from out of the flesh."[410] This is the same opinion as Peter Lombard's and of those who have come from his school.

TORALBA: This is boorish philosophy, since it is contrary to nature, that matter acts on form, that is, that body acts on soul. Matter is acted upon, but form is acting. And indeed Augustine himself concludes from this decree of nature that there is no action of bodies on minds.

[408] *De gener. animal.* II. 3. 736b. 28. [409] IV Kings (II Kings) 21–22.

[410] Cf. *Sancti Augustini operum tomus* X (Paris, 1696). *De gestis Pelagii* XXIII. 204d.

CURTIUS: Although Toralba uses Augustine's authority,[411] he is easily refuted by Augustine's authority. For thus Augustine wrote: "Believe this most forcefully and by no means doubt that those who die without baptism must be punished with eternal torments."[412] Augustine seems to have copied down these words from Cyprian's writings.

OCTAVIUS: Yet he denies the same thing in this same book; namely, that infants who died without baptism endure any punishments because they have enjoyed no sensual delight. From this it follows that there is no original sin if no punishment is ordained. Nor was there any reason why we should think that Christ ought to have endured such harsh punishments for the sin of Adam, transferred to posterity, because there is no [original sin]. In order to refute the old deeply rooted opinion of Christians concerning salvation obtained for the human race on account of Christ's death and in order, thereafter, to lead men from the hope of man to a trust[413] in immortal God, Mohammed wisely persuaded men that Christ had never been affected with torment.

FRIDERICUS: Still, do you think that no punishment is inflicted on the souls of infants from whom the hope of divine vision has been completely snatched away?

OCTAVIUS: Why then do Christians cherish the feasts of the infants slain by Herod's command as though the feasts of saints unless they [the infants] enjoy the vision of God?[414]

FRIDERICUS: Since they are thought to have been washed by Christ's blood like countless martyrs who were killed before they could have been baptized.

OCTAVIUS: If death excuses martyrs for the impossibility of baptism, P. 304
why will not sickness and premature death excuse infants, since often they will be more severely afflicted with sickness than those who die by the sword.

CURTIUS: Not the attack of diseases and swords, but the situation makes a martyr.

[411] *auctoritate* M

[412] *Sancti Augustini operum tomus* X (Paris, 1696). *De nuptiis et concupiscentia* I. 22. 291 ff.

[413] *fiduciam* M

[414] The children slain by Herod are mentioned in Matt. 2:16–18. The Latin Church instituted the feast of the Holy Innocents sometime between the fourth and fifth centuries. The churches of St. Paul's Outside the Walls and St. Mary Major are believed to possess the bodies of several of the holy innocents. See *Cath. Encycl.*, VII. 419. See above Book IV, note 88.

OCTAVIUS: I do not see what importance those washings of lustral water have in baptism except that the priests wash very lightly the dirt of the body, yet not all the dirt. And yet if baptism produces salvation, even tinkling bells and ships which you have very often seen baptized and christened with the sprinkling of lustral water and anointing would obtain salvation.

FRIDERICUS: The power of baptism washes away completely the filth of man's original sin and restores baptized men to the justice and integrity which Adam had at birth.

OCTAVIUS: If that lustral ablution of water, oil, salt, and spit cleansed to such a degree the stain of nature, what more could the death of Christ accomplish? Christian priests are exceedingly inconsistent in that they curse at one moment the sin of Adam which passed universally to his posterity, yet at another moment they say that it was necessary. Indeed, they use this solemn song on the day before Easter: "O necessary sin of Adam, which Christ's death removed!" Why is that sin which is so detestable said to be necessary? Or if it is necessary, why is it detestable?

CORONAEUS: It is said to be necessary because it had been anticipated many generations before by divine wisdom, which cannot be deceived.

TORALBA: Indeed, all who have any measure of understanding ought to feel that this is a deplorable argument: namely, that the innumerable souls are created by the offices of angels and by divine goodness and are derived from the very fountain of purity, and after their creation they penetrate bodies, and having penetrated they immediately produce the stain of dirt[415] by the contagion of the flesh; without any materiality of soul the compressed filth which otherwise is thought to be permanent is cleansed by the lightest sprinkling of water, and they become most just infants who are free from the senses. Nevertheless, we see that the materials of sins are the same for the clean and the dirty, for Christians as well as all others, and some are no more inclined than others to[416] pursue honor or shun baseness. Rather, to the extent that each pagan or Christian has been equipped with learning and trained from boyhood for true glory, so he excels with distinction in virtues, and the more so if there is a certain innate excellence of soul such as we hear in Aristides[417] the Just, Themis-

[415] *sordium* M [416] *ad* M

[417] From this list of excellent ancient Greeks and Romans only a few need identification. Aristides was the supreme commander of the Athenian army at Platea, and afterwards he worked with Themistocles in rebuilding the walls of Athens. His honesty became proverbial. Phocion held the constant respect of the

tocles, Socrates, Pericles, Phocion, Rutilius Torquatus, Papirius Cursor, the Fabii, the Scipios, and the Catos. What men they were! Among the philosophers also there were many men of great virtue and integrity, and no Christians ought to be compared with them. Erasmus spoke justly: "There is little to keep me from saying: 'Holy Socrates, pray for us!' "[418] And indeed Julian Augustus writes that Socrates was condemned to die when he struggled, on behalf of the eternal worship of God, since he had an angel as guide and teacher for his life.[419] Therefore, who is so void of understanding that he thinks that natural goods in men have been corrupted on account of the Fall of the first parent, but supernatural goods have been completely removed? Nevertheless, the Master of the Sentences himself writes thus from the opinion of Augustine. P. 305

CORONAEUS: Those who speak rather accurately about those matters say that justice is not restored to infants with the help of holy water but only the guilt is removed; that infants are not debtors of justice as Adam, who is said to have deserted the justice he received in the beginning of his lineage, not because of original sin, which he did not have, but because of actual sin. They say that in others the Fall is washed away, but the other sparks of sin remain. Indeed Augustine says: "In baptism sins are destroyed but not completely extirpated."[420]

TORALBA: To be sure this singular opinion is more probable than the

---

Athenians in the fourth century B.C., and was elected general forty-five times. Rutilius Rufus, a friend of Scipio Aemilianus, raised and trained the army which Marcus later commanded against the Cimbri. He combined Greek culture with the old Roman virtues. Manlius Torquatus was a striking embodiment of Roman virtue; according to popular tradition he killed a huge Celt in a duel and took his collar, hence the *cognomen* Torquatus. Papirius Cursor was the hero of the Second Samnite War (4th century B.C.); he was renowned for his bravery and his strictness and discipline.

[418] Erasmus' prayer to Socrates is more often cited than is its source documented. For example R. Nicol Cross, *Socrates, the Man and His Mission* (Freeport, N.Y., 1970, reprint of 1914 ed.), p. 2: "Erasmus, the great humanist and reformer, the flower of Christian scholarship in the sixteenth century, one not apt to fall into romantic admirations, gave him in his own heart a place among the saints of religion: 'Sancte Socrates, ora pro nobis.' " The documentation is *Opera omnia Desiderii Erasmi Roterodami, Colloquia* (Amsterdam, 1972), I, pt. 3, 254.

[419] There are many references in Julian's orations to Socrates as the ideal good man. See *The Heroic Deeds of Constantius,* 79, 96; *To the Uneducated Cynics,* 188, 190, 191; *To Sallust,* 249. Most explicit on his *daimonion* and devotion to universal religion: *To the Cynic Heradeios,* 239. Most explicit on the death of Socrates: *Letter to a Priest,* 295. See Book II, note 316; Book III, 7 and 8, and above, note 158.

[420] *Sancti Augustini operum tomus* V (Paris, 1683). *Sermo* CXXXI. 6. 643d.

opinion of those who think that the justice and integrity of origin is restored to infants by baptism; yet, those infants are said to be innocent because they have absorbed no part of justice or injustice. But this opinion has this disadvantage in that it has left the tinder of sin in the flesh, although it is in the senses and in the sensitive appetite. And there is great difference between the two, because the will commands the body with a master's mastery, but the appetite commands the body with civil and freeborn mastery. Indeed, with this reasoning no flesh can be transmitted although the kindling wood is defiled. And rightly does Anselm write that the soul is not defiled and dirtied by semen more than by blood. Still, in the pure causes of nature pleasure is characteristic of the sensitive appetite and in a pleasurable subject.

CURTIUS: Indeed let us grant this. But without the stain of origin that power of pleasure would not be excessive, as it is.

TORALBA: Then after baptism that power of pleasure would always be moderated, which is not true. For it is not in the power of the sensitive appetite not to be delighted, nor is there a measure of delight in it; but as much as it can, the appetite is delighted in that which is greatly delightful.[421] What, then, can passion add in addition to this which delights the senses in the highest grade of pleasure?

CORONAEUS: If the appetites were not ruled by reason, man would be no different from the judgment of the beasts.

TORALBA: What of this? Indeed we see that the beasts always follow the laws of nature.

SALOMON: All this discussion about the Fall of origin, which I think is no fall, has its beginning in the leaders of the Christian religion. In order
P. 306 to draw the souls of unlearned men to themselves, they convinced the unlearned that the punishment of their teacher and founder had been a salutary remedy for expiating sins; in addition, lest they seem to add a license for sin thereafter, they established that the sin of Adam which resided in himself was propagated into infinite posterity and for this sin eternal punishments, which bind all, are due. Hence[422] the seeds of errors began to creep far and wide through men's minds, because they decided that all mankind had been corrupted by that Fall of uncleanness so that no one could do or even think rightly nor obtain any part of justice. Why, they even thought that beasts, because of Adam's sin, had shaken off the yoke of natural obedience with which they had served man before. Nothing

[421] *delectabile* M

[422] *hinc* M

more removed from sacred history or from truth could be conceived. After the floods of all waters God ordered Noah to be of good and courageous spirit because He inflicted fear of man on all the beasts. Hence, the Psalmist extolls exceedingly that excellence and dignity of man among the other creatures and his mastery over the wild beasts, lest anyone be so foolish as to think that power after Adam's Fall had also been snatched from men and given to the beasts.[423]

CURTIUS: To what end then was that history of Adam, his Fall, his threatening, and his punishment so clearly recorded in the sacred scriptures?

SALOMON: Curtius, do you not see an elegant and divine allegory? Each man is Adam, and whatever things touched Adam, the same touch all who are delighted by the charms of the senses and by the sweet desire of excessive, indulgent pleasure and those who have established the highest good to be in that sweetness of the senses but the end of evils to be in griefs and calamities.[424] Adam is said to have returned to himself and to have recovered his senses; that is, he returned from the delight of the senses to the contemplation of intelligible things, which is to say, he enjoyed the tree of life, which Solomon interprets as true wisdom.[425] Next he fathered Seth,[426] clearly a divine man, for an image of himself. Thus it happens that even if we wander from the straight path and immerse ourselves in the filth and defilement of pleasures, finally we at some time rise up from the filth and return to the straight path of salvation. Although God had declared before to Adam that he would die when he had tasted of the fruit of the tree of the knowledge of good and evil, still He did not henceforth condemn him to eternal death. As God is merciful, so also does He always impose punishments lighter than the sins and laws. Indeed He even indicated to Adam a salutary remedy when He said: "Perhaps he will pluck the tree of life and live forever."[427]

FRIDERICUS: Salomon has caught himself in his own nets. Do you not see that by the tree of life the salutary wood of the cross of Christ[428] is clearly indicated in which we ought to establish the highest hope of salvation? P. 307

SALOMON: This interpretation corresponds with the word no more than a circle corresponds with a square. There is a Hebraic word *'ēts* which means fruit, not tree. And as Adam's repentance produced eternal salva-

[423] Psalm 8:6. [424] Philo, *Legum allegoriae* XLVI–XLVII.
[425] Prov. 3:13–18. [426] Gen. 4:25. [427] Gen. 2:9.
[428] *Christi* M Cf. Apocal. (Rev.) 2:7; 22:2.

tion, so it was possible and always will be possible for anyone with divine help which never fails to return from depraved desires to right reason, from the senses to intelligible things, and to obtain that salutary and everlasting life without any death and slaying of beasts or men.

OCTAVIUS: Indeed the divine mind in some way or other has inspired me, moved by the unworthiness of that opinion and the false propagation of sin, to put forth lamentable Phalaecean verse because of the lamentable complaint of Christians:

The heavenly Father heard the heavy[429] complaints of the human
 race
with difficulty excusing the origin of evils
because He flogs them for the first parent.
But if now He should rise from the tomb, renewed, thus
 He will wash away the sins[430] of His offspring:
At length stop violating My worthiness with an
 empty accusation.
As parent and founder of the human race, created from a
 better race
I have taught my sons the path of salvation.
I have instructed them in virtues, sciences,
and also a more liberal education which I first
 learned when God was my teacher.
We confess our frailty in that we have strayed from
 the teacher's path,
drawn away by the enticements of desires.
These sweeter fruits have been chosen
not from the tree of pleasure.
But they are made more learned by the senses,
and to foster the fruits of pleasure, Loves and
 Cupids to desert the mind's meditation
which would have languished and died unless it was
 recalled by its teacher
to the true glory of the supreme idea,
P. 308 so that I might take things celestial with knowledge as it were,
 as the true food for the mind.
The figure of trees displays this secret of hidden wisdom.

[429] *graves* M [430] *probra* M

This cultivation of divine love and fear has made me
joyful and has blessed me.
From thence it has established me free from the wearing away
of body[431] in the loftiest temples.
O incredible dumbness of those who falsely blame
themselves and their own
for their nearness to so many Iliads of evils
because we have delighted the tongue and the palate
with the taste of forbidden fruit.
The wrong doing of the father does not harm the son,
nor do the deeds of children keep their parents from
acquiring salvation
and enjoying divine resources.
We are entangled each one by his own fraud
each by his own madness,
and we are blessed by the good.

SALOMON: This is also my opinion. For how could it have happened that Abel was considered so pleasing to immortal God if he had brought from his mother's womb eternal stain and permanent blots of filthiness? Why were Noah, Enoch, Job, Moses, Samuel, and Elias so greatly praised by God himself for their piety, integrity, and justice if they had been so contaminated by their parents' sins that they could only be expiated by God becoming man and being condemned to the most shameful death? If that crime of birth which can be contracted without any fault of a poor little baby had kept man from an understanding of God, why did God speak to Moses, alive and breathing face to face, and as a friend to a friend?[432] Why also would God have filled Abraham, father of our race with so many and so great benefits that He opened the founts of divine goodness to all people because of him, if He had thought that Abraham was defiled by so great and so loathsome a sin? Rather, did not so great goods from God happen to Abraham because he surpassed all mortals in his singular love and faithfulness toward God and because he placed his hope not in a certain empty credulity and in human rewards, but in the goodness and power of one eternal God? Finally, why would God have offered Himself for consideration and enjoyment to so many prophets if they had been wicked from their very birth? The vision and enjoyment of the divine

[431] *cadaveris* M

[432] Ex. 33:9.

countenance happened to those clothed in flesh, which they think is most defiled. How much more[433] was it possible to enjoy the divine countenance without the garment of flesh? Yet Christians imagine that those most holy heroes had hidden among the shades and even in those very places of the
P. 309 earth most vast and squalid with densest dark for three or four thousand years and could not have tasted great happiness as Pindar[434] writes about Tantalus, before Jesus died, came down to those shades, snatched them from their vast and filthy prisons, and led them by the hand into heaven. Tertullian defines the shades as a ditch in the very vitals of the earth hidden by the vastness,[435] not, however, as this sublunar world, as Origen thought, although on the descent to the shades almost all are in disagreement. Still there is no[436] greater discrepancy than that the evangelists say that the soul of Lazarus, dead from hunger and fasting, was carried by the angels into Abraham's bosom,[437] although Jesus was not yet dead. But Abraham was deaf to the questions and sighs of the evil rich man when he was tormented among the shades, and he chided him with these words: "Between you and me there lies a great gulf and no approach from me to you nor from you to me is possible."[438] Still after a few months the soul of Lazarus fell from the sublime heavenly home into a smelly, half-decayed body so that Lazarus might die again after his soul transferred into its former prisons. How many errors have come from this conception of original sin!

FRIDERICUS: If I should wish to refute each point, I would have to wander farther afield than your patience would allow. And as mathematicians are prevented from speaking against those who overthrow and destroy the principles of the most certain sciences, so I should not speak against Salomon or Toralba, who surely cast doubt on the foundation of the Christian religion and destroy everything from the root, namely, the propagation of original sin in posterity. Yet if we are deceived by an erroneous opinon, why did Esdras cry out with such burning complaints: "O Adam, what have you done? A thing which did not rebound to your misfortune alone but also to each one[439] of us who have sprung from you!"[440] Indeed this one passage by Esdras, a leader of the Jewish race, can answer satisfactorily all the subtleties of all the heretics and Pelagians. Still, no Christian thinks

433 *magis* M
434 *Olym.* I. 60 ff.
435 *De anima.* I. 22.
436 *nulla* M
437 Luke 16:20–22.
438 Luke 16:25.
439 *quemque* M
440 IV Ezra (II *Esdras*) in *The Ezra-Apocalypse*, edited by G. H. Box and W. Sanday (London, 1912), Part I (Vision III), Chapter 7, Par. 4, p. 161.

that original sin is so great that it ought to separate man from the vision of divine light. It is wrong to be too inquisitive about the other things which are said about the prisons of the fathers before the death of Christ, since they have not been expressed in any decrees and placed in the secrets of divine knowledge. Only let us hold to this: that by Christ's death that original stain is cleansed and removed.

SALOMON: I think the fact does not escape anybody that the two later books which are attributed to Esdras are not considered to be among the sacred books and not even among those which Jerome calls apocrypha.[441] If indeed there were any confidence in such books, one would believe much more appropriately the book of Wisdom, which is counted among the Hagiographa in which the author introduces King Solomon speaking P. 310 thus: "I was a boy favored with a good character, having received a good nature; indeed since I myself was good, I obtained an uncontaminated body."[442] Solomon had been conceived by a mother who had formerly been an adulteress; yet he says that he had a pure soul and a pure body.

FRIDERICUS: The author Jesus Sirach shows well enough how reliable those writings are when he substitutes the name of King Solomon for his own. But how much truer are the words of Solomon's father: "Lo, I have been conceived in iniquities, and in sins my mother conceived me"[443] How much truer also are Job's words: "Who[444] will be clean, conceived from an impure seed?"[445]

SALOMON: Let us grant this, the mother sinned in conceiving, a thing which Christian theologians deny. What do we say in regard to birth?[446] The mother is impure, and the offspring is impure. On that account is he a sinner when only an infant? Not even the sun nor the angels are pure before God, yet they have not therefore the taint of original sin.

OCTAVIUS: The kernel of the discussion is that Adam recovered from sin, as indeed all admit, and his sin was not propagated to posterity. Although Cain's fratricide was more serious in all respects, still this [sin] remained in him and did not spread to his descendants. In truth, Adam did not die because he had fallen from the contemplation of intelligible things to sensible things. Even if he had remained in that innocence and integrity in which he had been created, he nevertheless was to die. For

441 See *Encycl. Judaic.* For a full discussion of IV Esdras or the Apocalypse of Esdras, see the introduction to *The Ezra-Apocalypse*, edited by Box and Sanday.

442 Wisdom 7. See *Encycl. Judaic.*

443 Psalm 50 (51):7.

444 *quis* M

445 Job 15:14–15.

446 *quid ad partum?* M

those are deceived who deny that Enoch and Elias died,[447] although they had derived their lineage from Adam. What fiercer punishment could have happened to those most divine men than to be confined to an eternal corpse? But while they were still alive, they had been snatched away by divine power lest they be worshipped as gods because of their integrity and virtue. God is said to have buried Moses in this way, yet in such a way that no mortal would know where he was.[448] Surely a thousand worlds would not enclose the posterity of Adam, if he were immortal. Therefore, as innocence would not have made his corpse immortal, so sin did not make him mortal.

CURTIUS: This opinion seems to be at war with that of Paul who said: "Through one man sin entered the world, from whence death followed, and through another justification for life."[449] Likewise: "From Adam down to Moses death reigned also in those who did not sin, on account of Adam's transgression."[450]

SALOMON: The fact that Paul extended the reign of death until the law which was promulgated by Moses makes clear that in that law was the
P. 311 most certain salvation for men. Likewise Paul calls the law of Moses holy and the commands holy, and he writes that officers of the law are justified by actions of the law.[451]

CURTIUS: The commands of Paul are clear and do not allow anyone to be in doubt of his opinion: namely, on account of the sin of one man death had crept into the world and overcome all down to the time of Moses. The death of the body is not meant, but the death of souls which are bound by eternal punishments. Then salvation was obtained from the law which states openly that those who followed the commands of the law would obtain salvation. However, since there had been no one nor was there hope that there would be one who could satisfy the law's demands, Paul shows in effectual proofs that no one could be justified by the actions of law. Hence those words flow: "The law causes anger. No one will be just from the works of the law. You who are justified according to the laws have been made void by Christ. The law leads no one to perfection. The law was given by Moses, but grace has been given through Jesus Christ."[452] A certain theologian interprets this passage to mean that there was neither truth nor any grace in the law of Moses.

[447] Gen. 5:24; Sirach 44:16; 49:14–16; 48:4–9.
[448] Deut. 34:4–6. [449] Rom. 5:16–17. [450] Rom. 5:14.
[451] Rom. 7:12; I Tim. 1:8.
[452] Rom. 4:15; Gal. 2:16, 5:4.

Salomon: Who was ever of such impiety and madness that he would thus trample upon the majesty of the divine law? How often does David exclaim: "All Your commandments are truth!"[453] Even Paul himself writes that those who follow the law itself are justified by the actions of the law.[454] Likewise he says Christ died in vain if we are justified according to the law. Because grace, life and salvation were offered for those who obeyed the law, we read a thousand times: "Do this and you will live; this is your life; this is your salvation." Or do we consider those promises of God to be lies? What of this? The very wise Solomon calls the divine law the tree of lives;[455] namely, of the present and future life, *ḥayyim*. And to be sure, when a certain divine and heavenly power once set me on fire to praise the divine law, in my youth I poured forth these songs:

You who suck with red mouth the swelling breasts
Whence the thundering father sent forth his songs,
Tell of the divine honors of the holy law.[456]
Then you who have learned to have loosened tongues
O gentle boys and tender girls,
Speak of the divine honors of the holy law!
Any of you who have just passed puberty,
Oh adolescents, it is always fitting to speak with polished phrase
  of the divine honors of the holy law.
And you, active youths, whose bodies are strong and
  whose souls have reached full power,
Speak of the divine honors of the holy law!
O men, famous and humble, and chaste mothers, P. 312
Whose lives have matured in praiseworthy manner,
Speak of the divine honors of the holy law.
And you whom old age with its fleeting years hastens
  toward[457] death, as you pray devotedly,
Speak of the divine honors of the holy law!
In like manner you who have been granted wisdom from
  heaven's bounty,
So that it is possible to watch the
secret aspects of holy scripture and the charming form,

[453] Cf. Psalm 118 (119).
[454] Rom. 7:8–12.
[455] Prov. 3:18.
[456] *Dicite divinos sacrosanctae legis honores* M
[457] *ad* M

Speak of the divine honors of holy law!
Happy souls, who have left in the ground bodies corrupted by decay,
and have flown swiftly back into the airs,
Speak of the divine honors of the holy law.[458]
Angelic choruses make haste, to whom
the holy page add light wings,
Separated in triple order,
To teach swift movements prepared for commands
Speak of the divine honors of the holy law!
And you living[459] stars of the flame-bearing heaven,
Who order the world by the nod of the great king
Speak of the divine honors of the holy law!

CORONAEUS: These divine songs befit divine law and those who follow the law. Moreover, who ever accomplished this except Christ alone? For this reason Paul calls the law the pedagogue for Christ, by which we are led as by hand to Him. Justin Martyr rightly asks what is the law. "The good news foretold! What is the good news? The law fulfilled."[460]

SALOMON: Why then did the lawgiver urge all classes to obey the law with the promise of great rewards? Finally in the assembly, when he was about to die, he made this speech: "Lo, I have offered to you life and good, death and evil."[461] Likewise, a little afterwards he said: "Today I call heaven and earth to witness that I have offered life and death to you, blessedness and destruction. Therefore, choose life, that you and your children may live; namely, love God and obey His voice and cling to Him, since He is your life."[462] Moreover, when he proclaimed in a clear voice the laws about everything and when he had given them whatever things pertain to the worship of God, to maintaining customs, to restraining passions, to safeguarding the society of men among men, finally all things—the most important, the moderately important, and the least important—which pertain to sacrifices, vows, rites and expiations, now would he have omitted that boon of which you boast, the origin of human salvation; namely, by the death of one man and God, the sins of the human race

[458] *Foelices animae, confecta cadavera putri*
Quae liquistis humo, ac celeres revolastis in auras.
Dicite divinos sacrosanctae legis honores. M

[459] *viventia* M

[460] Cf. *Dial. Tryph.* XLIII, XLV, XLVI.

[461] Deut. 30:15.

[462] Deut. 30:19.

and that taint of origin which mankind brought from the womb would be expiated after thousands of years? Can anyone think that he who had provided so carefully for the whole structure of the temple, for the curtains, the vestments, the buckles and bolts and for the selection of all food would have omitted a matter of such great importance for obtaining salvation? Therefore, divine salvation has been placed in the divine law. In vain does Christ or anyone else promise salvation by His death in order to lead men away from virtue, piety, integrity, observance of the law, and the true worship of eternal God to laziness, sin, and the wicked adoration of dead men, as if it were not in every man's power to execute the divine commands and as if the free will to follow the law had been snatched away from posterity by Adam's sin. P. 313

CURTIUS: Who can doubt that Adam by his sin lost the free will which was granted to him by God and also destroyed it for posterity?

CORONAEUS: Indeed, this is the decree of the Augsburg Confession, and many men who are filled with the new religion flock to this teaching. Contrary to this we observe the decree of the Roman church in all its teachings. And in truth, how does man differ from the judgment of the animals, if will is taken away from him?

FRIDERICUS: Indeed Adam did not lose the will of doing evil but of doing good. Paul said: "I do not[463] do this good which I wish, but I do this evil which I do not wish."[464]

TORALBA: I beg you, weigh what Paul wishes. If we give approval to that, no place for doing good or evil is left for man, nor will it be necessary to establish any rewards for good or any punishments for evils. Indeed who can blame one who sins from necessity? Or who can think a man worthy of the least punishment, since a wrong can be nothing unless it is voluntary, indeed, unless it is of one's free will? But if we admit that wicked men are rightly punished because they have free will of action with which to harness lewd desires and can be superior to the stars themselves, as that author says, what doctrine is it to deprive man altogether of the use of reason, that is, of free will? And yet, will cannot be spoken of as will, if it is forced, and therefore, men are loosed from laws when just fear or anger drives them to action.

CORONAEUS: Indeed I thus conclude that those who take away from men the free will of doing good seek hiding places for their own sins and open the doors to all crimes and call back the fatal necessity of the Stoics which

[463] *non* M

[464] Rom. 7:19.

has been discredited and silenced by the teachings of all theologians and wise men. Then comes that paradox: that many men are abandoned to eternal fires, since they cannot accomplish anything good even though they especially desire it, but certain men are chosen for salvation in such a way that they cannot become wicked even though they especially wish it.

TORALBA: This lazy reasoning of cowardly and lifeless men should be exploded, not with reasons, but with laughter, as did the Academician who mocked the Stoic who wondered whether he should marry for the
P. 314 sake of children. The Academician reasoned: "Why would you bring a wife home? For if it is children you want, you can have them even without a wife."

SALOMON: As innumerable errors follow from one error posited, so Christians think that free will of doing good is snatched away by original sin, which is nothing, and that by this men are bound to eternal punishments. But laws are commanded[465] in vain, and the promise of divine rewards would be empty if man has no power, nor even will, to follow divine laws.

CURTIUS: Indeed this is an excellent point. However, I do not see by what reason free will is granted to men after the fall of Adam, since he did not even have free will before the fall. For if divine foreknowledge cannot be deceived, it was necessary for Adam to sin. Moreover, God foreknows, even in the greatest distance of time, not only the words and deeds but also all the thoughts of all men, and He is never deceived. Therefore, it follows that we act good or bad not from will, but from necessity, nor has anyone ever had any power of free will.

SENAMUS: Although God sees, as if from a sublime tower, that a traveller will fall into the hands of robbers when he has turned from the right path, still it is not therefore necessary that it will happen, but rather because God saw that it will be. From this one knows that the things which God has foreseen do not happen from necessity.

CURTIUS: If God's providence followed human affairs, as indeed, Senamus, you believe, eternal God's foreknowledge would depend on the changeable and fallacious opinion of men, which is absurd. For as the knowledge of a present matter is in regard to present circumstances, so God's providence is in regard to future events. Truly, this which I know is now necessary that it be. Therefore, foreknowledge of the future is equally necessary in God who never opines; since this has been established,

[465] *juberentur* M

it is necessary that free will be removed. Otherwise, if God's providence is not necessary, His opinion is fallacious, which is wrong even to think. Therefore, in vain we turn away from base things or pursue honorable things.

TORALBA: I do not see how Aristotle satisfies the arguments of the Stoics. For although future contingencies could happen in one way or another, still divine foreknowledge cannot fail, because God sees an event not as future but as present, since all things are present to God; nothing can be past to Him, nothing future. Nevertheless, all things are free for men. Providence cannot seem to hang from your will, since it is changeable, but it foresees your future changes and therefore free will has not been removed from each man. Indeed, I assume this reasoning has satisfied all the deadly arguments of the Stoics.

SALOMON: I weigh neither the subtleties of the Stoics nor the reasons of the Peripatetics, but the prophecies of divine law. Moses in the assembly of the people called on heaven and earth to witness that he had offered life and death to the people. He said: "Choose life that you may live."[466] These P. 315
writings were promulgated two thousand years after Adam and the same number of years before Christ. Why would the people choose life if they had been destined for eternal punishment or if they had no power for choosing salvation? Or why would He wish man, whom He in fact had destined for eternal punishment, to be zealously attentive to divine laws? Useless would be labor, ridiculous the precepts of God, empty His promises; hope would be vain, vain would be desire; virtuous acts would be vain, vain, finally, all the piety of man, whom those think is condemned. Likewise, it would be false that God created man and left him to the mastery of his own will, after the laws had been disclosed to him. He said: "If you wish, you will keep the commandments, and they will preserve you. He has offered you fire and water. Stretch out your hand to whichever you wish. Life and death, likewise good and evil, have been placed before man. Whichever pleased him he follows."[467] In like manner Ezechiel said: "Give them My decrees. Who does them will live in them."[468] And indeed God repeated again to Moses, who was praying for the people to avert punishment and was begging that he rather be allowed to be removed from the book of life: "Whoever sinned against Me, I shall cast him from the book of life."[469] Thus, the Psalmist says everywhere: "All are

[466] Deut. 30:19. [467] Sirach 15:15–17. [468] Ezech. 20:11.
[469] Ex. 32:32.

inscribed in Your book."[470] Likewise: "Let them be destroyed from the book of the living."[471] Finally, to refute, in a word, the futile subtleties, listen to the voice of God crying out: "Your destruction is from you, Israel, but your salvation is from Me."[472]

OCTAVIUS: From this it follows that God wants all men to be saved and to be led to a recognition of Him.

CURTIUS: Octavius has explained this passage according to the evangelical writings. If he admits it, he borrowed. If he denies it, it is a theft.

FRIDERICUS: Indeed a sacrilege.

SALOMON: A sacred thing must be stolen from a sacred place without the guards' consent, although whatever is useful in the writings of the disciples and apostles, as much as there is, has been taken from the writings and books of our elders. Moreover, Paul's statement—"He wishes all to be safe"[473]—drove many into error, as if God with an imperious will had ordered this. Because nothing can withstand His command and will, it would be consistent that no one would suffer destruction. Since Christian theologians thought this was absurd, and not wanting anything that Paul wrote to seem foolish, they interpret those words thus: that God wants all to be saved who are saved, for the same reason by which He is said to illuminate men coming into this world, that is, whomever He illuminates. But it would be better to delete those words of Paul and John rather than to interpret them thus.

P. 316 SENAMUS: I cannot be persuaded that God designated anyone for eternal punishments before he was born, since Ezechiel wrote openly that He was never delighted by the destruction of the wicked.[474] How much less would He be pleased to designate most innocent babies to death, hell, and eternal torments.

SALOMON: Each proposition is most absurd: that some are so ordained for eternal life that they could not perish if they should especially wish it; that others are so rejected by God that they cannot be saved by any virtues or any uprightness. I beg you, understand the word, not of any man, but the word of eternal God to the prophet. He said: "Tell this to this people. When I shall say to a just man, you will live, and he relies on his integrity and justice and turned to crimes he will not be remembered for his prior integrity and virtues, but will die completely in his own sins. Again if I

470 Psalm 138 (139):16.
471 Psalm 68 (69):29.
472 Hosea 13:9.
473 I Tim. 2:4.
474 Ezech. 33:11.

shall say to a wicked man, most certainly you will perish, and yet he shall have turned from wickedness to piety, I shall forget his former impieties so that he may attain salvation."[475] And we have said this rather often: all are written in the book of life and in the roll of the blessed unless they suffer themselves to be removed by their own sinfulness. The fact that the Psalmist desires that the wicked be removed from the book of life could not have happened unless first the wicked had been inscribed in the roll of the blessed.[476] Also God very often removes punishments altogether which He had decreed in His own judgment, or He lessens them. When He had announced to David that the whole region was to be polluted by common diseases, although the angel of God stretched out his sword to threaten the city of Jerusalem, God began to grieve and be sorry for so much slaughter, so He ordered the angel to abstain from the destruction.[477]

CURTIUS: If God cast no one away from Himself, why do we see that He loved Jacob but hated his brother before they were born.[478]

SALOMON: Paul substituted these words, "before they were born," as he did many other words. Indeed the words do not appear in the prophet,[479] who, Paul says, is the author. For in his posterity Esau brought forth twelve leaders and peoples flourishing in arms and laws.[480] Likewise, in one chapter of the law he said: "You will not abominate Idumeus because he is your brother."[481] Although the Idumeans denied water to the Israelites who were offering to pay for it when they were in the most arid desert, God forbade that they be harmed or their fields invaded. However, when their children and their posterity tried to destroy the people of Israel and preferred to sacrifice to demons rather than to immortal God, then God justly hated them. Pertinent at the point are the words of Malachi, who wrote in the seventeenth century after the death of Esau. Moreover, if God prefers some to others, if He should wish to honor these with wealth, those with dignity, some with physical beauty, others with physical prowess, and some with excellent judgment, some with majesty of power or honor of the pontificate, and finally, if He should choose to adopt a very P. 317
few into His heavenly home, by what right can anyone think he should complain if He has granted more to these and less to those? "Would the clay say to the potter—'Why have you made me so'"[482] With this state-

[475] Ezech. 3:20.
[476] Psalm 68 (69):29.
[477] II Kings (II Sam.) 24.
[478] Rom. 9:13.
[479] Mal. 1:1–4.
[480] Gen. 36:15 ff.
[481] Deut. 23:8.
[482] Isaiah 45:9.

ment Isaiah shows that each one must be content with his own situation which was granted to him by God, since[483] the door of salvation lies open to every age, to every order, to every sex; since God embraces not only men, whom He placed in charge of the world, but also all creatures with supreme love. The statement—"I hold Esau in hate"—does not mean that God hates anyone from the womb, but we must understand that He loves these less, even blesses these less than those. For who could exist even for a moment if God pursue him with hatred?

CURTIUS: We must argue this question about predestination and repudiation and about free will with the Roman theologians. But let us return to Salomon.

CORONAEUS: Your argument is not only with the Roman church but also with the Hebrews and all the philosophers except the Stoics. Origen said: "Let them blush who deny that man has free will."

SALOMON: Moses Rambam, in a letter which he wrote against the astrologers, said: "All the theologians confirm that man has a will free for salvation." Then he adds these words. "For this reason we have great gratitude to immortal God."

CURTIUS: Let us not desert the proposed question whether anyone can obtain salvation from the actions of the law, even if free wills were granted to every one for following the good and avoiding the base. I still deny that anyone except Christ could satisfy divine laws. From Him the bulwarks of salvation must be sought and hoped for, so that He might absolve us from the antiquated law of Moses. Then when we are loosed from the old laws, He can teach us to put all faith in the death of His one Person and in the spilling of His blood. When the lawgiver Moses explained the curses on wicked men, in the last heading he interjects this statement: "Let him be cursed who does not exactly perform the letter of the law."[484] To these remarks all people will respond: "So be it!" From which Paul concludes that those who have placed their salvation in the actions of law are subject to this curse, as if no one has ever been innocent in regard to divine laws.[485]

OCTAVIUS: Why then does Paul boast that he had been without fault in the justice of the law? Indeed from this it follows that Christ's death
P. 318 availed him nothing, but for him Christ endured this curse when He hung

[483] N attributes this part of the speech to Fridericus, but I follow M and include it with Salomon's statement.

[484] Deut. 28:15.

[485] Gal. 3:10–11; Philip. 3:9.

on the cross. Paul said: "He became a curse and malediction so that He might snatch us from curse and malediction."[486]

SALOMON: Often Paul is caught cutting out words of the law and prophets or adding words or plainly changing the interpretation. The curse of divine law has been expressed by these words: *'arur 'asher lo' yaqim 'et divrê hattorah hazzot*, that is, be cursed who does not have the fixed words of this law that he might follow them. For the word *yaqim* means to confirm, to hold fixed, as both Jonathan and Onkelos the Chaldean interpret. Jeremiah explains this clearly: "Be cursed who has not heard the words of the contract which I have struck with your elders."[487] This interpretation differs completely from the words of Paul. He invokes a curse on those who have not fulfilled the law, which you never find written in divine law. Moreover, a man is considered worthy of being cursed who neither hears the divine law nor has a fixed covenant. Another error has sprung from this in that many think that he who has erred from one heading of the law stands accused by all the laws. So James writes in a letter[488] which Eusebius and Jerome, nevertheless, have rejected from the sacred letters. Eusebius said, "One must know that it is a corruption," when each made a decision about this letter. And indeed the one who will have been convicted for stealing another's cow is ordered by divine law to pay back five cows; if he steals a sheep, he is ordered to pay back four sheep. However, if he is not convicted but returns the stolen cow of his own free will and adds a fifth part of the price because he is sorry for his act, his sin is pardoned. But whoever commits adultery, kills or commits any other sin, if he is sorry and repentant for his past life, and requites the former sins by virtuous actions, he is in this circumstance that he seems to have transgressed in no way but to have fulfilled the law itself by repentance, as in truth Ezechiel's authority confirmed earlier. For if it were true what Paul writes, that no one would have satisfied the law except his teacher and no one could have secured perfection by the acts of the law, David would have been found guilty of a notorious lie when he witnessed to God thus: "I have guarded Your law; I have not strayed from Your law; I have not fallen away from Your commandments."[489] Moreover, he invokes God Himself as witness for his lie. Yet he had added adultery to homicide. However, because he repented and also gave compensation in part for his deed, he received pardon. This is what it means to obey the law, to follow the law,

[486] Gal. 3:13. [487] Jer. 11:3. [488] James 2:10.
[489] Psalm 118 (119):12–16.

to abide by the law, and finally, to fulfill the law. Moreover, it is false that a man who has sinned against one law is held liable by all the laws.

CURTIUS: Surely, if we are justified by the acts of the laws but not by the
P. 319 benefit of Christ "there is no grace altogether, and Christ, Redeemer of the human race, died in vain," as Paul said.[490] Likewise: "You are saved by the grace of God through faith, not from yourselves, lest anyone should boast."[491] In like manner: ". . . that we may be justified as heirs by the grace of Him."[492] Also: "Without Me you can do nothing."[493] Therefore, what do you deserve by yourself, if you can do nothing by yourself without Christ? It would be an endless task to gather together all the golden words of Augustine on this topic. He said: "All men lost their natural power in Adam and their free will by sinning."[494] Ambrose, Chrysostom, Jerome, Gregory, Bernard, and Augustine held this opinion.

OCTAVIUS: If one must contend with a multitude of witnesses and theologians or the excellence of doctrine, I shall add to those learned men Ismaelite theologians, who are far more famous than all the Christian theologians. I refer to Solyma, Zaid, Odmannus, Homarus, Balar, Abacherimus, Calbanus, Zepheninius, Elsarinus, Azebara, Achemula, Abaniphanus, Elfaridus,[495] and countless others who spread the law of Mohammed throughout almost all the world and called men back from the densest gloom to the brightest light and worship of one eternal God. They attribute much to virtues and[496] excellent acts, yet more to divine goodness and kindness, and they believe certain ones have been selected for salvation and others have been designated for destruction.

FRIDERICUS: I do not see why the brightest lights of Christian theologians ought to be compared by any reason[497] with that filth of the Mohammedans.

SENAMUS: If authority has precedence over reason, why can we not also summon the books of Verrius Flaccus[498] about the priestly law, and the things which the ancient priests and theologians of Jupiter and also the priests of Camarim Bahal and the priests of the Sabeans published in their ritual books.

490 Gal. 2:21. 491 Eph. 2:8–9. 492 Titus 3:7. 493 John 15:5.

494 *Enchir.* XXX.

495 See article, "Mohammedan Religion," in *Encycl. Brit.* (11th ed.), XVII, 417–24.

496 *ac* M 497 *ulla ratione* M

498 Flaccus, a freedman, was the most learned of the Augustan scholars and was the teacher of Augustus' grandsons. The books about the priestly law to which Bodin refers are the *Fasti praenestini.*

Toralba: If you continue to lead out with authorities, I shall summon all the families of philosophers who easily conquer those insignificant theologians by the excellence of their erudition and training. However, it is better to argue with the senses and clear reasons.

Salomon: Indeed this is true, except in obscure and ambiguous matters in which the human mind can find no way out. Surely it is needful that tragedians be punished. They call down God from the machine[499] and hear divine oracles from the mouths of the prophets and from the sacred books which the theologians, not only Hebrew, but also Christian and Ismaelite, have now for a long time approved, each in his own religion.

Fridericus: So far from accepting the innumerable errors of the Arabs and Jews who trust they can obtain justice by their own virtues and the acts of the laws, as if by the strongest protection, I do not even approve the opinion of Curtius, because he thinks the summit of salvation depends on faith, although I see this has pleased many. For if we are just because of our faith, grace in no way profits a man, since all of this which we believe, whatever it is, is completely ours. Action gathers nothing from that approbation, because unless it depends on the highest approbation of a free mind, faith ceases to be. Therefore, it is truer that we become just by the very justice of Christ, true God and man, all who have moved close to God. P. 320

Coronaeus: Augustine seems to strike the middle course between each opinion when he states that the excellent acts which precede faith accomplish nothing but rather those acts which follow faith.[500]

Toralba: I think it is utterly alien to all reason to confess with simple assent that Christ died for the salvation of the human race in order to secure not only pardon for immense disgraces but also supreme praise for justice[501] and integrity; but to avow that just men like Aristides, Solon, Lycurgus, Socrates, Chilo, Phocion, Plato, Camillus, Fabricius, the Scipios, Catos, Rutilii and Papirii,[502] who attained immortal honor in the judgment of all mortals because of their exceptional virtues, are tormented as if by the wicked and sinful eternal flames of hell and the most cruel punishments.

Fridericus: Either they were condemned to hell or snatched away and

499 Euripides quite often used the *deus ex machina* (god from the machine) in his tragedies to intensify the drama or provide a dramatic solution.

500 *Sancti Augustini operum tomus* II (Paris, 1679). *Epistola* CLXXXVI. 666c.

501 *iustitiae* M.

502 See above, pp. 402–3, note 417. Chilo was one of the Seven Sages.

saved from eternal punishments to which all men are bound because of the error of the first parent. But without a deliverer they cannot be saved or even become saved. Therefore, they are given up to eternal torments, or to act more mildly with those who have distinguished themselves by virtuous acts, they must be confined in the densest gloom and in the foulest hidden caverns of the earth.

OCTAVIUS: I think that surely Christians who have some judgment do not approve these statements. For if any virtue can make man most pleasing to God, faith and empty belief about Christ's death do not accomplish this, but rather constant trust in God eternal. Moreover, the man who is so graced with trust that he places hope for his own affairs neither in himself nor in human rewards burns with a unique love of God and necessarily plucks the sweetest fruits of true happiness. This is that faith, or rather a unique trust in God, which, having embraced all virtues, nourishes and safeguards them.

SENAMUS: I believe that each man is blessed by his excellent acts. The greater is his religion toward the gods, his piety for his native country, his regard for his parents,[503] his charity to his neighbors, his kindness toward those in need, his justice to all the more he is blessed, and the more
P. 321 he will be pleasing to immortal God, although he worships foreign gods in good faith and just error. What is fairer, what more consistent with nature, than for the greatest rewards to be granted to those who are especially deserving concerning the state, parents, neighbors, the poor, and finally concerning the whole human race, since concerning immortal God we can deserve nothing and not even make requital for His kindnesses toward us.

CORONAEUS: Indeed I always agree with the most holy and powerful decrees of the Roman church and the Council of Trent which place under anathemas those who think that faith without works and works without faith can justify. Indeed why did that prophet of divine prophecy cry out, "he is just; he lives by faith"?[504] He clearly says that faith will benefit the just, not the unjust; otherwise, demons and any most vile man may capture heaven with an empty belief about Christ's death.

CURTIUS: Since the apex of salvation is in justification, I think nothing should be discussed more accurately than this.

FRIDERICUS: When at the imperial Diet at Ratisbon the Emperor Charles V, in agreement with the German princes, had selected six most upright

[503] *cultu erga parentes* M

[504] Habakkuk 2:4.

theologians of each religion to settle the religious controversies of the Romans and Germans, as soon as they came together, they thought they should begin with the question of human justification.[505] When in this discussion three theologians of the Augsburg Confession had drawn the Catholics, Pflugius, Fabrus, and Groppeus, to their position and had likewise persuaded Cardinal Contarini, legate of the Roman See, of this point of view, namely, that man is blessed by faith alone and by no merit of his own, Eckius, one of the Catholics, became so angry against his colleagues that the Catholic bishops and princes, convinced by him, forced Charles V to dissolve the discussion twenty days after it had begun.[506] They were especially influenced by the speech of Azotus, a skilled Spanish theologian, since he said that in a short time the power of the Roman church would collapse and disappear because they admitted they had erred for so many centuries in a chief point of their religion. Moreover, a very shrewd man compared the Germans, whom he mocked as rude barbarians, to a wood cutter splitting wood; at first he makes a small fissure, but when he strikes the tree repeatedly with the ax, the wood is split into many parts. Since the Romans were influenced by this analogy, they forced the princes to dissolve this most dangerous discussion. Indeed, Cardinal Contarini, the most learned[507] Venetian patrician who was said to have agreed with the Lutherans,[508] died a little afterwards, and it was strongly suspected that he died from poisoning. Then, the bishops of the Roman church proposed that the ancient ceremonies and the old rites be increased and protected in every way lest they seem to have departed an inch from the primitive church, although many were ashamed of so many follies, P. 322 especially the relics; for example, the Virgin's milk, whose infinite supply has not yet diminished for so many centuries. It is shameful to refer to other things which you know better than I.

SALOMON: When the foundations are badly laid, whatever you build above falls at one and the same moment. When the founders of the Christian religion had turned from the true worship of God and had proposed that dead men be worshipped in place of immortal God, they declared

[505] The Diet of Ratisbon was held in 1541, and one of the main topics of discussion was the question of justification. Cardinal Gasparo Contarini was the special representative of Pope Paul III at the Diet. See Frederick C. Church, *The Italian Reformers, 1534–1564* (New York, 1932). See below, note 508.

[506] See Church, *Italian Reformers.*

[507] *doctissimus* M

[508] Cardinal Contarini had private meetings with the Lutherans, and it was said that he was very close to the Lutheran position on justification.

that the death of their God was salutary for the human race and necessary, lest it seem to have been ordained by right by the magistrates. That justice is obtained for any mortal by Christ's death or credulity towards Him is so far removed from the truth that this Christian belief is most distant from the true religion. Very close to this error is the fact that all Christian and Agarenian theologians think that justification is possible from acts of virtues or faith or both, not only among men but also with immortal God. For it often happens that a man most wicked in God's sight is considered most just in men's opinion. But in order for God to take away from men this arrogance and haughtiness, God clearly says: "No one of the living will be justified before Me."[509] The word for the living refers not only to men but also to the angels. This is clearly confirmed by these words: "Will a man be more just than his Maker?"[510] Lo, in His agents He does not find a stable work, and His angels are insane, the heavens impure, the stars unclean when compared with Him. And to lessen the ambiguity, this is often repeated. Then he adds "How much more removed from consummate perfection are those who build mud houses,"[511] meaning men who are made from clay. Likewise: "Who, born from woman, would be pure?"[512] Since not even the brightest stars before God are pure, how much less pure are frivolous and vain men who can be reckoned as putrid worms. At this point I am impelled to ponder the wondrous majesty and holiness of God:

O who will be pure and sinless? Who
will be free of blame before God
Whose brightness makes the sun obscure and dull.

His cleanness is so great and so great
the honor of His majesty that the
brightest countenance of angels
seems marked with disease.

O three times holy Parent! O non-
violable Godhead of eternal mind
whose power is so august.

Toralba: Salomon's opinion is unfolded in the teachings of the more holy philosophers; namely, whatever has any concreteness of matter is impure. Justly did Porphyry say that nothing is material which has not

[509] Psalm 52 (53):4.
[510] Job 4:17.
[511] Job 4:19.
[512] Job 25:4.

been rendered unclean to immortal God.[513] This is not to say that there is any evil or fault in matter itself, as many philosophers think, which they call something doing ill, for earlier this has been proved to be false. Rather, matter is farthest removed from that highest and pure excellence[514] of divine nature because it is changeable, transient, and fleeting. P. 323

CURTIUS: We do not demand that man's justice be equal to the justice of God, and we do not even hope it would be, for it would be necessary for men to be gods. But we hope that there is as much justice as is possible in human life and nature. Although men are defiled not only by their materiality but also by that stain of origin, which we have often mentioned, and by their own sins, still by the grace of God through Christ, God as well as man, they are completely cleansed so that in a certain way they seem just.

SALOMON: The angels enjoy a much greater grace of God and happiness, and they are nearer to eternal God. Still in respect to God they bear no trace of purity and justice. And so when God granted Noah the highest praise of justice and integrity, He added the phrase "in his own kind,"[515] that is, a squinting man among the half blind. Since these things are so, who can agree rightly with John writing so confidently? He said: "We know if God has appeared, we shall be like Him, and whoever hopes in this purifies himself, just as God is pure."[516] If Adam had remained in his God-given integrity and innocence as great as is possible in man, he would not even for that reason be considered just before God. That another said: "God alone is just, and except for Him no other one is."[517] If no one is upright, if nothing is pure, nothing clean, if the sun itself and the angels who are closest to the divinity of immortal God are not bright, that whole discussion about the justification of man, whether it stems from faith or from honorable actions or from both, or also from the grace of God alone, is completely empty, since justification cannot belong to man. It is much more trivial that they think that highest integrity must be weighed by man's measures, not God's. But those who think they will obtain justice by their own actions, let them hear the harsh reproach which Elihu uses[518] to a man most laudable according to the most serious testimony of all. "If you are just, what then? Or what are your deeds to God, whether they are base or noble?"[519] You may profit or harm yourself and others, yet this adds or subtracts nothing from God.

[513] Cf. Augustine, *De civ. Dei* X. 24; XXII. 26.
[514] *praestantia* M
[515] Cf. Gen. 6:9.
[516] I John 3:2.
[517] Sirach 18:1–2.
[518] *utitur* M
[519] Job 35:7–8.

TORALBA: If you merit nothing good for doing good, you also ought to bear no punishment for doing bad. However, it was stated earlier that the actions of each man must be examined by the most just measures.

OCTAVIUS: I think Ismaelites are far superior to Christians, especially in acts of virtue, that is, in piety, justice, love, courage, and temperance, be-
P. 324 cause they have been instructed in such a way that they believe the summit of salvation has been placed in virtuous acts. Nevertheless, most loathsome of all are those who think that all wickedness is erased by the power of masses, which are acquired with money; or those who have established that salvation is in faith alone, which opinion leads far and wide to a destruction of states.

CORONAEUS: I have always held back from this opinion. Surely all divine and human laws would perish if there were no rewards for deeds performed well and no punishments for sins. Why would God say to Abraham: "I have sworn on Myself, because you have done this, I shall bless you, and because of you, all peoples."[520] He did not say: I shall bless you uniquely and freely because of Me; but rather because of this which you have done. Likewise God said: "Whoever has heaped up on Me praises, on him I shall heap up honors."[521] Likewise: "He will return to man according to his justice."[522] And again: "There is much recompense in observing Your commands."[523] Likewise, Noah, Job, and Daniel freed their souls by their own justice.[524] Likewise: "Redeem your sins by alms."[525] Also: "God saw the works of those who were repentant, and He pitied them."[526] Likewise: "Do I not benefit him who walks uprightly?"[527] I would go on forever if I recounted all the passages where it is openly declared that each man will reap rewards or punishments according to his very works.

FRIDERICUS: No reward is owed for a duty. If there is anyone who lives justly (but no one does), he does nothing except according to duty. Therefore, he who lives justly is worthy of no reward; indeed, a reward is contrary to duty. But he who does wicked things acts contrary to duty; he who acts contrary to duty deserves punishment. Therefore, the wicked are rightly punished; still the just, if there are any, do not deserve any re-

[520] Gen. 22:16. [521] Psalm 49 (50):23. [522] Job 34:11.
[523] Prov. 13:13. [524] Dan. 9:5 ff.
[525] Psalm 50 (51):3; Sirach 7:10. On almsgiving, cf. Augustine, *De civ. Dei* XXI. 27.
[526] Sirach 18:13; cf. Psalm 102 (103):13.
[527] Psalm 83 (84):12.

wards. For this reason, when Christ, true God and man, urges men to salvation, He said: "When you have done all things which must be done, then say: 'We are useless servants, whether we owe this from duty or because no usefulness to God is derived from these actions.' "[528] Therefore, no justice can be provided for any one from outstanding actions.

Salomon: I grant that no one is made just by actions, however worthy they may be, much less by an empty belief in a dead Jesus. Rather each man is blessed by eternal God according to honorable actions, and the more justly and honorably each man has lived, the more blessed and the more pleasing he will be to immortal God. Indeed all creatures and also demons are blessed more or less in accordance with the goodness of the giver or the capacity of the receiver or the unworthiness of him who rejects the abundant light brought to them. Indeed, it is one thing to be blessed, another to be justified. Christian theologians have confused these issues or understood them too little, and in this discussion they have pro- P. 325
duced serious obscurities and errors. For if no one except the just is blessed, no one would ever be blessed. Yet all creatures are blessed, although no one is justified, and no one is free from stain and impurity. So as to understand better the difference of these matters which has been confused, let us pretend, for example, that a most powerful king gave swift horses to his servants as a gift, some better than others, in accordance with his benevolence toward each servant, as he loved each man either more or less. Nevertheless, he stipulated that all run in the stadium; but those who were reluctant or who refused the course from fear or laziness would have their horses taken away. The death penalty was declared for any man who violated the horse of another or toppled a fellow rider from his horse so that it could not run, or stole the horse of the master.[529] The king offered the racers rewards of different kinds, bronze, silver, gold, garments, and precious stones. The quicker each one reached the goal, the better was his reward. When the race was completed, the king gave in good faith the rewards which he had promised and according to the rules which he had made. Those who had refused the race lost their horses because of their laziness. Those who had not only been unwilling to run but also had hindered others or had driven away the horses were pursued, caught, and killed. Will we not say that each man deserved his rewards?

Curtius: I suppose so.

[528] See Acts 16:17; Rom. 6:16, 22; I Pet. 2:16.
[529] *furto domini equum* M

SALOMON: Why so? Since the king owed his servants nothing, for they were his own, he could by right, without any rewards, have forced them to the race, sold them, or killed them.

FRIDERICUS: Granted. But since he promised, he would think it contrary to honor and dignity to go back on his word.

SALOMON: Therefore, there is an obligation, not because God is the debtor of man, and man, the creditor, as it were, may demand rewards by his right. Rather, the dignity of the one promising resides in the promise of those things which he promised, although he did not owe them by right. But if those horsemen who exerted their energies in the race because they had been properly trained not only will not claim for themselves any glory but also will graciously thank their king for his largess, they will credit their victory to him, because he trained the servants and not only prepared them for the race, but also he provided the most spirited and fleet horses for running the course. How much more ought we to credit all things received to immortal God because He created us from nothing. He gave us body and mind; He prescribed laws for running well, and He taught us; He helped us to run in the stadium of virtues; He sustained us when we were falling; He often helped us after we had fallen; He led us to the goal when we had been up. Indeed the Master of Wisdom spoke in elegant words thus: "Be unwilling to boast before the king!"[530] In another place he said more clearly: "Be unwilling to justify yourself before God for our salvation depends on Him."[531] When Job, the most upright man of all in God's judgment, vehemently complained that, although he
P. 326 had always lived most justly and most saintly, still he was overwhelmed by a multitude of all misfortunes, Elihu refuted the errors of Job's associates and friends who said that he suffered as he deserved and through the consciences of his sins, and he forcefully explained that God brings injury to no one.[532] Although Job had always lived with the highest integrity, still God could rightly recall and reclaim the things which were His own and which He had lent to Job to enjoy for a time, namely, wealth, children, servants, houses, good health, even mind and life itself; and this without injury to anyone. When finally God had tested his constancy and bravery, He paid back abundantly and above measure the things which he had taken from Job. Which is to say, He doubled his wealth, his flocks and cattle; He also blessed his wife in fruitfulness, and finally He preserved Job's life with sound mind and body for one hundred and fifty

[530] Sirach 10:23, 25. [531] Sirach 10:5. [532] Job 34:1–15.

years.[533] Moreover, He gave that which is the summit of happiness—Himself to be enjoyed and perceived. Herein lies the peak of human happiness, not of justification or justice which man cannot reach. Finally we must be advised that no glory of justice is brighter than the glory of those who love God with the whole force of their mind and follow His commands with no hope of reward, although they know for certain that a reward will never be lacking to good men.

CURTIUS: Indeed those are noteworthy remarks except that Salomon has missed the mark since he denies that Christ is God, who heaps up rewards for all, not from a debt but from grace, and who alone cleanses the stains of origin and all sins by His blood. On the other hand, Salomon in a certain way acknowledges the Fall in that he admits that all men are unjust, impure, and unclean even from the womb.

OCTAVIUS: If sin is in man because he is as far as possible from the purity and holiness of his Creator, we shall say that even the angels and stars, which are impure before God, are bound by original sin. If these things are absurd, the things which follow from them must also seem absurd. They are the more absurd, the less that imperfection can be perfected, unless a creature becomes God. From this it is deduced that Christ, if He had died, which the Ismaelites constantly deny, would not, and indeed could not, if He had especially desired, have cured that uncleanness or Fall of origin, as it is pleasing to call it. He could not, not even if He had been God, as Christians believe that He was, since that which is born cannot become clean and pure; much less that which is born of woman, as Christ was, unless He becomes a creator, as it were, a creature, a thing which not even God can do.

CORONAEUS: We must beware lest anything escape us, which is alien to divine majesty. Indeed I cannot approve those statements of the Scholastics which seem to have the flavor of impiety; namely, that God cannot make God, that He cannot produce contradictories that are true at one P. 327
and the same time. It is fitting to say more truly and more soberly that a creature cannot become God. Certainly the power of the creator is not lessened because of the weakness of the creature and subject. Therefore, no impotency is attributed to God because men and angels are not just nor ever were nor ever will be. Rather an angelic and human creature is not capable of perfect and consummate justice, much less of that divine excellence and purity which we do not even reach in our understanding. It is

[533] Job 42:10–17.

not even able to effect and give that good which each excellent man desires; Paul complained of this impossibility in himself.[534]

SALOMON: The divine law commands nothing which you cannot easily do if you wish. I am amazed that Paul, whom you value so highly, wrote this, when at another time he boasts that he was blameless in the justice of the law.[535] But what lawgiver was ever so cruel that he commanded his people to do something which was impossible? If anyone so cruel existed anywhere, and I know of no one, still to think this about the best and most kind lawgiver of all is a crime; to think of it is wrong; to speak it is a capital crime. That another said: "Taste and see how sweet God is."[536] Likewise: "How sweet and good is the Lord."[537] It is so far removed from God's nature for Him to command anything which cannot be done as for Him to blame a man for breaking all the law when he had erred from one commandment, that even a man who has violated all the commands of the law and returned to honor after repentance, attains pardon for all his sins. David said: "I shall not delay before I confess the sin which you have already forgiven."[538] On the other hand, what does Paul say? "Reconsider, I beg you. If we have sinned willingly after the accepted recognition of truth, no more sacrifice remains for our sins, but a dreadful expectation of judgment and vehement fire which will devour us."[539] You see that man does not even leave room for confession or repentance. Yet there are those who think the divine law is harsher than the Christian law! Indeed[540] I think they have turned very far aside from the truth.

SENAMUS: Here is one passage where Paul caused many to despair of salvation. Some believe that this letter to the Hebrews is not Paul's, and they reject it completely.

FRIDERICUS: I do not think this letter ought to be rejected, since the councils endorsed it; however, I feel that this passage was written in hyperbole to frighten the wicked, since everywhere in Scripture pardon is offered for the repentant. It is not true that God orders anything which cannot be done. Cyprian spoke thus: "Whoever says that God commands the impos-
P. 328 sible, let him be accursed."[541] But the weakness of human frailty and the fury of our passions is so great that we always need Christ, true God and man, as advocate and mediator. Moreover, since the sacrifices of animals

[534] Rom. 7:19. [535] Philip. 3:6. [536] Psalm 33 (34):9.
[537] *Item. O quam suavis ac bonus Dominus* M. Cf. Psalm 118 (119):103.
[538] Psalm 31 (32):5. [539] Heb. 10:26. [540] *nam* M
[541] Marginalia in M on this passage indicate *In sermone de baptizmo Petri Lombardi*, dist. XXXIX. lib. 3.

and the old rites of the Jews were abrogated by His death, when the thorns were removed as it were, He imparted a much easier and clearer path by the promulgation of the new laws by which all sins are washed away. And so calling sinners to Himself and inviting them to His table, as it were, He said: "Come to Me all who are heavy laden; I shall give you rest. My yoke is sweet and My burden light."[542]

OCTAVIUS: I do not see that Christ commanded any law[543] or had the power of commanding, and much less did he repeal the laws which were given by God. Moreover, he openly declared: "I have not come to destroy the laws but to fulfill them."[544] The heart of the old law is in the two tablets of the decalogue which Christ no more wanted to repeal, or could repeal, than the laws of nature, since nothing is contained in the two tablets except what is most fair by the law of nature, as was shown above. I cannot but wonder why Martin Luther said the decalogue did not pertain to Christians, unless he judged that the Christian law could not stand along side the decalogue.

FRIDERICUS: I believe that Luther, who was abundantly praised, led Christians by his great piety and learning from their errors into the straightest and safest path, as his writings and actions openly declare. Nobody should think that he wished to abrogate the decalogue. Rather, he wanted all to understand that we cannot obtain enough help for attaining eternal salvation in the decalogue unless first we rejoice in the death of Christ, true God and best and greatest Savior, since no one could ever follow the laws of Moses.

SALOMON: Clearly the teachings of the evangelical writings are not only harsher and more difficult than the divine law, but also they are such that no mortal can fulfill them, as Trypho the Hebrew said to Justin.[545] Here are a few examples from many. They forbid any divorce unless a wife is convicted of adultery, and those who hand down judgments know well enough how difficult this is. And if the wife is not adulterous, what is more unjust than to conquer the unconquered with a domestic enemy or to plot against the innocent so that he is put to death, or to call into open danger the reputation of the wife or of another family; or to cause one or the other to die from poison or hidden plots, since Christ forbids divorce. It is also contrary to nature that we forbid marriages to those who are divorced because of adultery. For with this reasoning either adultery

[542] Matt. 11:28–30. [543] *legem ullam* M [544] Matt. 5:17.
[545] See Justin, *Dial. Tryph.*

or public whoring or pollution or something worse than all these things is inevitable. Moreover, the divine law concerning divorce, common to all people except Christians, and comprehended by the most just laws of the ancient Romans, has influenced not only women to be more temperate but
P. 329 also men to be more compliant because of fear of divorce. This had also removed violent deaths and domestic and secret poisonings. Moreover, what is more alien to nature, to the purity of sacred things, to divine holiness than that we see the rights of marriage forbidden to priests by the Christians? What is more fatal than for countless girls to be bound by eternal vows of chastity, since this is unnatural? As a result, lusts for both sexes are indulged in, also violent abortions, murders, adulteries, harloting and whoring even in the temples themselves, and the unredeemable defilement of all sacred things, the likes of which not even the pagans did allow. Even the Romans had once forbidden a flamen of Jupiter to renounce his wife, and when the wife died, they ordered him to resign from the priesthood.

Coronaeus: I see that you disapprove of celibacy in the priesthood of Christians of both sexes because of impending dangers which forced Augustine to write openly that prostitutes ought not to be driven from the state. He said: "Take prostitutes away from human affairs, and you will have thrown everything into confusion because of lust."[546] However, if divine law forbids a priest to touch his wife for three days before he enters the sanctuary, how much more just is it for Christian priests who daily touch that most sacred body of Christ, God and man, and daily enter the holy of holies in regard to Him to live in perpetual celibacy.

Salomon: Divine law forbade a priest who expiated the people to touch his wife for three days before. However, the day of expiation occurred only once a year. But they forbid marriage for the length of the priesthood, yet they do not forbid prostitutes. Similar is the fact that divine law forbade priests to use wine when they enter the sanctuary. Why, then, do Christian priests not abstain from wine forever, as they do from a wife and wedlock? Nevertheless, they do not abstain from prostitutes, as they do not abstain from wine. Rather, they have been accustomed by their constant pandering and pimping to exchange prostitutes of one sex for the other with the greatest shame for the whole Christian church, lest they be bound by the marriage laws by which they bind others. As a result, when they leave their

[546] *Sancti Augustini operum tomus* I (Paris, 1679). *De ordine* II. 335b.

churches they sprinkle themselves with holy water. The orator Lycurgus spoke thus to the flatterers of Alexander the Great who they were proclaiming was God: "O such a God, that those who leave his temples must be sprinkled with holy water!"[547] Still, of all Christian proclamations none is more impossible than that which commands a man to turn his left cheek to the one who strikes his right cheek[548] and also to allow his cloak to be taken by him who has seized his stole and for him who has called someone a fool to be bound by eternal fires of hell.

TORALBA: Surely it is contrary to nature for him who has received a blow on the cheek to ask that he be struck or robbed again.

SALOMON: How much easier are the commands of divine law, which Paul himself boasts that he has observed so scrupulously that he was guiltless in the justice of the law. Likewise Luke witnesses that Zacharias and Elizabeth lived blameless before God in all His precepts and commands.[549] Justin Martyr openly uses these arguments to show that the divine law P. 330 forbids or commands nothing which cannot be done by man, provided he wants to.[550] Moreover, what is the total justice of the law? It is for man to love God more than himself, but his neighbor as himself; a thing which each one can do. Then he proposes why it is customarily said that no one is justified according to the law. It is not said because they cannot, but because they will not. Indeed, we are accustomed to use the will for things which can be done. Therefore, the Christian law is much more difficult in many areas than the divine law. "I pass over the empty rites (there happens to be a multitude of them)," Augustine said, "so that the condition of Christians seems much[551] worse than that of the Jews."[552] What if Augustine could see the daily ceremonies of the Roman church today? Indeed, those very ones who throw up to us the sacrifices of cattle which have been outmoded for a long time continually eat, break, and tear up Jesus in a sacrifice, for so they call it.

CURTIUS: We who have followed the Helvetian church embrace those bloodless sacrifices and praises, to use the words of Cyril and Eusebius, or we sacrifice to eternal God the bulls of our lips, as the prophet Amos says.

547 Plutarch, *Regum et imperatorum apophthegmata.*

548 Matt. 5:39–42. 549 Luke 1:6. 550 *Dial. Tryph.* XLIV.

551 *conditio multo deterior* M

552 *Sancti Augustini operum tomus* V (Paris, 1681). In *Psalmum XXX.* Enarratio III. 157a–f. Augustine says that evil Christians live worse than Jews or pagans, but he does not specifically mention "empty rites."

But so as not to stray from the question at hand, I wonder why Salomon is so much in favor of divorce, since Valerius Maximus[553] praises the Romans especially for the fact that they had seen no divorces for more than five hundred years, and Spurius Camillus[554] was blamed because he had formerly divorced his wife. Moreover, what is more wicked than for a public corruptor to trick any girls he desires under the appearance of marriage, and after he has corrupted them, to be able to send them away.

Salomon: Although many troubles have been pointed out, the more serious must always be avoided. It is more serious and more perilous to poison and commit adultery than to divorce. However, who would wish to give his daughter in marriage to a man who without cause divorces an honest and chaste wife?

Curtius: Having moved from the discussion of divorce, we must investigate the excellence of the lawgiver more than the ease of following the law of Christ. For if any sin will be committed, always at hand is a pleader, a speaker, a patron, and the same lawgiver Christ, whom the Jews and poor Ismaelites do not have. Indeed, whence can a man hope for salvation if he has not received Christ, true God and man who comes to him, and has cast aside His offer? Paul said: "He is our sanctification."[555] Likewise: "He died for our crimes and rose for our justification."[556] What of Jerome who said: "A prayer which does not go through Christ is a sin."[557] Therefore, since no man ought to hope for salvation without Christ-God, why do we hold any longer to the Mosaic laws which have already passed away because of their age? "Through Christ alone," Cyril said, "the door lies open to the kingdoms of heaven."[558]

P. 331 Octavius: If you have Christ alone as speaker and pleader, why does Christ console his disciples by saying: "I shall ask[559] My Father, and He will give you another advocate."[560] Why do you Christians invoke infinite

[553] Valerius Maximus, a Roman historian of Tiberius' reign, wrote a handbook of illustrative examples for rhetoricians. The book, *Factorum ac dictorum memorabilium libri* IX, was dedicated to Tiberius. The subject matter of the book contains headings about Omens, Moderation, Gratitude, Chastity, and Cruelty. This compilation was frequently used in the Middle Ages. See *Ox. Class. Dict.*, p. 935.

[554] Spurius Camillus was the son of the famous M. Furius Camillus. See Smith, *Dictionary* (1844 ed.), I, 591–92.

[555] I Cor. 1:30.

[556] Rom. 4:24.

[557] The marginal note in M indicates this is from Jerome's commentary on Psalm 109 (110).

[558] The marginal note in M indicates that Cyril's statement is found in his commentary on the third chapter of John.

[559] *rogabo* M

[560] John 14:16.

thousands, that is, just as many dead men, in addition to those orators and patrons, although religious entreaty is due to God alone? "Call on me, and I shall rescue you. Call on Me and you will live."[561] We read this rather often. Nevertheless, you honor the orders of all the angels and saints with prayers and solemn feasts just as you do God eternal, and many honor them more zealously and eagerly than God Himself, for whom no day free of sacred rites remains in the calendar. How much better are the Ismaelites who not only have established for themselves the worship of one eternal God but also consider it a capital crime to have a picture for the public's enjoyment.

FRIDERICUS: This is our quarrel with the Roman church which teaches men to honor the assemblies of angels and the blessed with vows, although only one advocate ought to be proposed, Christ-God, in whose name we fashion our vows and through whom we pray for favors and deprecate adversities.

CORONAEUS: Indeed I have been so shaped by teaching and so influenced by my elders that I consider it wrong to depart even a half-inch from the decrees of the Roman church which alone is the church of God. To be sure, we recognize only one mediator, the high Priest of the human race, Christ. But what prevents us from having patrons inferior to Christ? I am speaking of pleaders, the angels, the Virgin Mary and groups of apostles and martyrs; not that they grant us salvation, since there is only one Savior of mankind, Christ, but that they offer petitions for us. And yet, your Luther, Fridericus, admits that the souls of the blessed must be reverenced, and Bucer follows his authority. When the Jews had been oppressed with the help of Christians and driven out from their homes in Jerusalem, O immortal God, what an influx of men there was to the holy places, what holiness of the city, the tomb, the manger, the cross, all the monuments! Why, moreover, would Jerome have written so accurately against Vigilantius, not only in behalf of honors for the saints but also for their relics, that he even confirmed that demons were routed with the help of relics?[562] Why did Ambrose, Gregory of Tours, Augustine, and the rest cherish the saints with so many honors and praises, if they thought it was a sin?

CURTIUS: It is noble both to feel and to write honorably about illustrious

[561] Jer. 29:12; Joel 2:12–13.

[562] Jerome quarrelled with Vigilantius on questions of ecclesiastical usages rather than doctrine. Vigilantius was principally opposed to the veneration of saints and relics and the monastic life. See *Cath. Encycl.*, VIII, 343.

men, nor would I wish to lessen their dignity with words nor disparage them in any manner of speech. Still, I would not wish to pray to them, to worship them, or to invoke them, for these are special evidences of adoration. The law said: "You will adore God eternal, and you will serve
P. 332 Him alone!"[563] Although the Virgin Mary conceived Christ, true God and man, in her womb and gave Him birth, nevertheless, we abstain from the adoration of her. When Epiphanius in his age saw Christian people, and especially the heretical Collyridians,[564] incline to worship of her, he railed against them harshly, saying: "If we are forbidden to worship angels, we are forbidden all the more from worshipping Mary, the daughter of Ann." Moreover, Julian Augustus' most serious objection to Christians was the fact that they worshipped martyrs in place of gods and eagerly sought martyrdom in the hope of divinity so that they might be inscribed in the register of gods.[565] When he had realized that the elders had nothing more than this secret for strengthening religion, he repressed the deaths and punishments of Christians. Cyril, in answer to these charges, said: "We say that holy martyrs are not gods nor are we accustomed to worship them."[566] Likewise Chrysostom: "See the prudence of the Canaanite woman; she does not ask Jacob; she does not beseech John; she does not hasten to Peter nor does she direct herself to the group of Apostles. She seeks no mediator for herself, but in place of all these she has received repentance as a companion with which she has filled the place of the absent advocate." A little later he says the same thing: "Wherever you shall call upon God, He hears you. There is no need for a doorkeeper, a mediator, nor attendants; nor is there need of the help of a patron." Likewise: "They are accustomed to use the poor excuse that they can come to God through those, just as they may gain access to the king through his courtiers, and they worship fellow slaves while abandoning God." In regard to God there is no need of a supporter. He very carefully describes all these things and especially that which He calls worship, when we use the saints as advocates and mediators.

[563] Deut. 6:4–5.

[564] The Collyridians or Philomarianites offered little cakes to the Mother of God, but this practice was condemned not only by Epiphanius (Migne, *Patrologia Graeca* XCIV. 728) but also by John Damascene and Leontius Byzantius. See article, "Intercession," *Cath. Encycl.*, VIII, 70–72.

[565] Julian's satire is biting. Whereas Jesus despised unclean sepulchres, his followers "grovel among tombs." *Against the Galileans*, 343. See above, note 419.

[566] The marginal note in M indicates the reference is from *Adversus Julianum* VI. For Chrysostom, in the next lines, Homily XII, *De fructu evangelii.*

CORONAEUS: The Lutherans have used these passages to which we can easily answer: we follow God in the adoration of service (*latreia*) for the right of His majesty, and this worship the creature owes to the Creator alone. Hence the interpreters add to this: "Worship the footstool of His feet," the phrase, "in the adoration of service," because it is fitting for God alone. However, they call the footstool the flesh of Christ, which Damascenus and Scotus deny must be adored, since it is creature, contrary to the opinion of Peter Lombard. But there is a certain veneration of the service (*douleia*) but another for the sake of the service (*hyper douleia*). One of these is the veneration granted to the blessed Virgin Mary, the other to saints and angels. Otherwise, if we follow the latter words, who can doubt that the word for adoration is granted to man by man in the Scripture. Abraham adored the people of the land; Jacob adored his brother, Joseph his brothers, and Moses himself adored his father-in-law.

FRIDERICUS: If *latreia* (service) is accepted everywhere for worship and honor, and *douleia* for servitude, we would grant less to eternal God than to angels and saints because we venerate God, but we are in servitude to P. 333
angels and saints. Yet servile obedience is much more vile and demeaning than worship itself. The Hebrew word *hishtaḥāweh* "to bend down" has the same meaning as *tisgur* in Chaldean, *prosḳunein* in Greek and *adorare* in Latin, that is, to bend down the body. Pliny writes of a mutual salutation because the Gauls, as they worship, turn the body around.[567] But whatever words we use or whatever gesture we use, no one doubts that religious veneration or worship and adoration is owed only to immortal God, since every kind of *douleia* (servitude) and *latreia* (service) is understood from this chapter of the law—"You will adore your God and serve Him alone."[568] Moreover, the word for honor and servitude in divine affairs is owed to God alone. God bears clear witness to this: "I shall not give my glory to another."[569] Augustine spoke thus: "We honor the saints in love not servitude."[570] Indeed, because divine law prohibits us from building steps to the altars of God, in a more secret meaning, we are forbidden to direct to creatures petitions through which we go to the Maker. That prohibition is soon added to the decalogue, where no permission is made for sacrifice or altars, so that all may know that we must come to God directly, even if we were certain that angels and the minds of the eternal blessed would hear our vows.

[567] Cf. Curtius X. 8. 23. [568] Deut. 6:4–5. [569] Isaiah 42:8.

[570] *Sancti Augustini operum tomus* I (Paris, 1679). *Liber de vera religione* 786b, Par. 108.

Curtius: I think that God has granted to each angel to bear[571] petitions for those whom the angel joins as guardian. Thus the word for pleader is used in the Scriptures when an angel as leader and guardian in divine matters is meant; still, for that reason we must not entreat or adore the angel to bear our petitions. When John tried to do this, the angel said: "Beware of doing this; indeed I am your fellow-servant. Worship God."[572] We read this twice repeated. When David was honoring God with all praises, he turned to the angels and said: "Adore Him, all His angels."[573] He is so far removed from wanting to beseech and worship angels that He urges them in their function, that is, to fear and reverence God. For this reason, we often read that angels in the Scriptures conceal[574] their names so that they do not seem to have presented any opportunity for adoration.

Coronaeus: Does it seem to you a crime if I ask you—a thing which I do most willingly—to pray to immortal God for me? So also does Pharaoh address Moses and Aaron and the people address Samuel. He said: "Pray to your God for us." And they granted his request. Why, then, is it not allowed to beseech angels and saints to conceive prayers for us?

Fridericus: Since this has been forbidden, the other not likewise. And yet, who would dare to affirm whether or not the saints hear us? Or if they hear, who would say whether or not they wish to pray for us? That they do not pray for us God attests in Jeremiah: "If Moses and Samuel
P. 334 should stand before me, my mind would not incline to that people."[575] In that time especially, when the city was being surrounded on all sides by the enemy, it was fitting for Moses and Samuel to address God in heaven with entreaties and prayers, since they had done this so eagerly on earth so many times, though not asked. But when they died, God testifies that there was no one who could offer a request for the happiness of the people when the Chaldeans were devastating the region. He said: "I sought a man to set up a fence and stand opposite Me for the land lest I destroy[576] it, and I did not find him."[577]

Coronaeus: Since the assembly of the saints knew (for what would lie hidden to them?) the decree of God whereby He had determined to overthrow the city. For when Samuel was alive and was still grieving over the death of Saul, God turned to him and said: "How long will you grieve for Saul? I have cast him aside from ruling."[578]

Curtius: It is foolish to think that the minds of the saints see the inti-

[571] *ferre* M
[572] Apocal. (Rev.) 19:10.
[573] Psalm 148:2.
[574] *celare* M
[575] Jer. 15:1.
[576] *dissiparem* M
[577] Ezech. 22:30.
[578] I Kings (I Sam.) 16:1.

mate feelings of men, as Solomon so aptly explains in his speech of dedication for the temple. He said: "You alone, eternal God, see all the thoughts of all men."[579] If all the saints heard and saw all things, still not on this account should we entreat them.

CORONAEUS: When Moses prays for the disgrace of the people, why does he say: "Be mindful, Lord, of Abraham, Isaac, and Jacob?"[580]

CURTIUS: He does not pray to Abraham that he beseech God, but he asks God to be mindful of the covenant which God had struck with them and to pardon the people. And yet, it is dangerous to affirm who ought to be counted among the saints. Thus, not without cause did a certain theologian exclaim that Christians worshipped many bodies whose souls were tormented in hell. The Romans worship Cyprian as a martyr brought into the register of saints, and yet they call him a heretic and Anabaptist.[581] Therefore, Augustine spoke rightly: "We honor the saints for imitation; we do not adore them for religion."[582]

CORONAEUS: I shall never be ashamed to use David's word: "Praise God in His saints."[583]

CURTIUS: The Hebrew word *biqodsho* means "on account of His holiness," as Pagninus and Campensis correctly state.[584] However, the Chaldean interpreter says "in the abode of His sanctuary." From this it is observed that many things are distorted by Christian theologians. The seventy-two interpreters change it to *tois hagiois* (the holy things), since the Greeks call *ta hagia* (holy things) the sanctuary, but the Latins understood *tous hagious* (the saints).

579 II Paralip. (II Chron.) 6:30. 580 Ex. 32:13.

581 For a discussion of the life of St. Cyprian, bishop of Carthage and martyr, and especially of his conflict with Novatian, see *Cath. Encyl.*, IV, 583–89. The allusion to Cyprian as an Anabaptist probably refers to his contention that Rome should not interfere in internal affairs of a bishopric and that uniformity was not desirable.

582 *Sancti Augustini operum tomus* I (Paris, 1679). *Liber de vera religione* 786b, Par. 108. Also see *tomus* IV (1681). *Enarratio in Psalmum XCVI.* 1048d, Par. 12.

583 See especially Psalms 145–150.

584 Santes Pagninus (1470–1541), an Italian Dominican, was one of the leading philologists and Biblicists of his day. His interlinear translation of the Old and New Testaments adhered to the original languages and won the favor of contemporary rabbis as well as the Christians. It found favor also with the Reformers. The expense of its publication was assumed by Pope Leo X. A revision of Pagninus' translation, resulting in an even more literal text, was made by Arias Montano. See B. Rekers, *Benito Arias Montano (1529–1598)* (Leiden, 1972). Montano's work appeared in the Antwerp Polyglot (1572).

FRIDERICUS: The worship of saints and[585] angels has stemmed from the ancient pagans, especially in the age of Epiphanius, as is clear from the things which he wrote against the heretical Collyridians[586] who first be-
P. 335 gan to worship the Virgin Mary. Afterwards, Augustinus rather often curses those Marian worshippers.[587] And he did not even allow any prayers to be offered to the angels themselves who are higher in dignity than all the saints; nor did he think there was any approach to the Father except through the Son. Chrysostom, Ambrose, and Theophylactus[588] went along with this same opinion.

CORONAEUS: It has often been said, and it must be said more often, that no worship is offered, but only that which is also asked of friends still alive, namely that they formulate prayers for us and take these requests to God. No salvation of body or soul is sought or hoped for from those, but from the very source of salvation.

FRIDERICUS: Why, then, do they come on bended knees to the saints when the head of the priest is uncovered? Indeed, at the feast of the Immaculate Conception, they say to Mary: "You are the consolation for the oppressed; you are the medicine for the sick; you are all things to all men." What is left to immortal God?

OCTAVIUS: Nothing completely. When I was living among Christians in Greece, I happened on the day on which the Romans celebrate the visitation of Mary and the Greeks celebrate the cloak of the Virgin Mary. On December 31 a feast is held in honor of the Robe of the Virgin at the Blachernae,[589] which was a temple consecrated to Mary at Constantinople.[590] I cannot remember anything that the pagans did which was more foolish than this.

585 *ac* M

586 See above, note 564.

587 Antonius Augustinus (1517–1586), Spanish historian of canon law, displayed a positive and critical treatment of the ancient materials of canonical jurisprudence. Augustinus is one of the foremost figures in the Counter-Reformation. His most important work was *Emendationum et opinionum libri IV*, the first critical study on Gratian's *Decretum*. See *Cath. Encycl.*, II, 105–106.

588 Theophylactus, archbishop of Bulgaria in the 11th century, was one of the most famous Greek Catenists. The medieval writers in their commentaries used passages from the Fathers which they connected as in a chain (catena). See *Cath. Encycl.*, IV, 159–160.

589 in *Blachernis* Mazarine fonds latin 3529

590 The major feasts in honor of the Virgin in the Byzantine rite are Memory of the Mother of God on Dec. 26, birthday of Our Lady on Sept. 8, Presentation in the Temple on Nov. 21, Conception on Dec. 9, Falling-asleep on Aug. 15, and Keeping of Her Robe at the Blachernae on July 2. Bodin is in error on the date of the keeping of Her Robe; perhaps he had it confused with the feast of the Memory of the Mother of God which is in December. See *Cath. Encycl.*, IV, 315.

Basel 1544

TORALBA: There was that ancient superstition of the Academicians who thought that the only way to approach the Parent of all gods was to direct prayers little by little to heroes so that one might go from the souls of heroes to demons, from demons to the lesser gods, and from these to the major gods so that they might draw the Parent of all gods and men to themselves because of the approval which was secured for them by entreaty. So thought Iamblichus, the greatest of the magicians of his age, whom Porphyry said he saw carried in the air, when he was sacrificing to Isis. He also was in familiar conversation with demons.[591] Yet when he had used alectryomancy to find out who would be Emperor Valens' successor, and when this was discovered, he took his life by drinking poison, since death was the punishment for companions of impiety and witchcraft.

FRIDERICUS: You have heard, I suppose, that Magdalena de la Cruz, abbess of a convent at Cordova and noblest of all the witches of her day, had often been lifted up by a demon in the church itself during Mass on solemn feast days.[592] Finally, when Pope Paul III had heard of her crimes, he granted her pardon after a written confession of her crimes.

TORALBA: Still, is it not much easier and more excellent to approach that most ancient principle of all things and the efficient cause of the lower gods? For the orders of intelligences and angels and indeed all creatures P. 336
are in attendance, after this principle has been persuaded (moreover, what is easier to persuade?). It is an infinite task to reconcile the lower divinities which are innumerable. Moreover, who can say whether good demons, heroes, lesser gods, or higher gods, whether angels and helpers next to God, hear our vows and prayers? Or if they do hear, who can say whether they grant our prayers, or want to grant them, or can grant them? Sacrifices are offered not only to those gods and major and minor divinities, but also to ashes, bones, and statues, and these sacrifices are performed on bended knees, with outstretched hands and burning eyes, and even with torches and candles accompanied by gift offerings. Eternal God, however, is hardly ever worshipped, unless perhaps for the sake of appearance. There is surely

591 See Iamblichus, *On the Mysteries*, translated by Thomas Taylor, pp. 321–26.

592 Magdalena de la Cruz (1487–1560), a Franciscan nun, was believed to have the stigmata and to take no other food than the Eucharist. The Host was said to fly to her tongue from the priest's hand at Communion, and at such moments she was raised from the ground. She was so universally venerated that noble ladies had her bless garments prepared for their expected children. St. Ignatius, however, had always regarded her with suspicion. When she became seriously ill in 1543, Magdalena confessed to a career of hypocrisy, saying that demons which possessed her were responsible for her miracles. See *Cath. Encycl.*, VII, 700–701.

less sin, if people worship the creators of images and statues rather than their creatures. For who would not consider Phidias,[593] the sculptor of Pallas, more important than the Pallas itself, although the statue was made from ivory or gold.

CORONAEUS: Those are the old arguments of the iconoclasts who can be answered in a word. Statues are due to virtue in order that the unlearned may look at them and imitate their virtue. Pope Gregory the Great is praised because he called statues the books of the illiterate. However, you who mock at the garment of Mary and the Feast of the Girdle, have you not heard that the cloak of Elias, the bones of Elisaeus, the fringe of Christ's garment, the handkerchiefs of Paul,[594] indeed even the shadow of Peter, were responsible for so many miracles and portents that the sacred Scriptures bear witness to them?[595] What is the reason, then, why honors ought not to be given to the relics of the saints?

CURTIUS: If the learned do not need images and the ignorant use these images for evil adoration, what could be more appropriate than for images to be cast aside completely, since the holy Scriptures everywhere strongly prohibit images. Lactantius says: "There is no religion where an image exists."[596] Moreover, the Teacher of Wisdom harshly curses not only statues but also that baneful art. Indeed I have often thought it strange that the Baltic cities of Lower Germany which have rejected the Roman rites could admire the statues still in all their churches.

SENAMUS: Rude and ignorant men have a weaker mind and are concerned with only that which is at hand, just like animals who know nothing except that which their senses receive. Therefore, if you take away from these men the statues and images which are appendages of the mind, as it were, they will not believe that they have any religious obligation. And yet, Eusebius explains there is remarkable power in the statues of saints. He says that there was a statue of Christ at Caesarea near the statue

[593] *Phidiam* M. Phidias was the most famous sculptor of Athens in the 5th century B.C. His Athena Promachos, a bronze statue thirty feet high, stood on the Acropolis near the Propylaea. His chryselephantine Athena Parthenos, famed in antiquity, survives in several copies. Equally famous was his chryselephantine Zeus of Olympia. Phidias was also responsible for the design and composition of the sculptures of the Parthenon.

[594] *sudaria Pauli* M

[595] See article, "Relics," *Cath. Encycl.*, XII, 734–38.

[596] Lactantius (4th century A.D.) was called the "Christian Cicero" by the humanists. His most important work is "The Divine Institutions," a systematic apology intended to show the futility of pagan beliefs and to establish the truth and reasonableness of Christianity.

of that woman who had been cured of hemorrhage, placed[597] on a column where a plant had grown, which had remarkable curative power for all sickness after it had gotten so large that it touched the thread of the gar- P. 337 ment of Christ's statue; only from this touching of the garment did the plant receive curative power.

Octavius: Those who want the untutored masses to waste away in coarsest errors are accustomed to use fables of this sort. Therefore, there is need of examples and[598] sound teaching.

Coronaeus: I am amazed, Octavius, that you hate images so much. God Himself ordered not only the screens of the sanctuary to be adorned with angels, that is, with figures of winged youths,[599] but also golden statues of Cherubim overhanging the propitiatory[600] on both sides. He also ordered a bronze serpent to be erected so that those who had been bitten by serpents might be snatched from the risk of sickness because of the sight of the snake.[601]

Salomon: This conversation concerns me as much as Octavius. God wanted to signify that the worship of angels should be completely avoided when He added angels as attendants. But He wanted the Israelites to see the bronze serpent, but not to worship it, because of a remarkable secret in the serpent. He wanted to indicate that we should extinguish in us the mad desire for delicacies (which is indicated by the word for serpent) and would thus attain eternal life. For the chief power of the serpent is in its teeth. Since the people eagerly desired the elegant foods and foulness of the Egyptians in their desert loneliness, God had sent a serpent, from whose bite many perished, so that they might eat the purest manna which had fallen from heaven and forget their old delicacies. However, when King Ezechias had realized that the ignorant were worshipping that bronze serpent as a divinity, he ordered it to be burned publicly.[602]

Curtius: Why, then, do Christian princes not imitate the illustrious deed of Ezechias?

Octavius: So far distant are they from the piety and holiness of that king that they even allow the idolatry to be increased more and more. For what is more remarkable, what is more incredible, what is more alien to the senses and finally to all reason than that through five words ("For this is my body," or as an emaciated priest in a multitude of crusts would say, in order to speak fitly, "For these are my bodies,") six hundred thousand gods

[597] *superposita* M
[598] *ac* M
[599] *puellorum.*
[600] Ex. 25:18–20.
[601] Num. 21:8–9.
[602] II Paralip. (II Chron.) 31:1.

can be procured in a moment from the same number of crusts. Christian theologians have persuaded so many people of this that it can be doubted whether posterity will believe that, as Basil says, a people of gods can be persuaded by a little man who sacrifices to come into being in one moment. Much less will future offspring believe that these words could have been committed to public books and literature, which words Christian priests say when sacrificing: "He who created me is created through me."

CORONAEUS: We ought to wonder at that most sacred sacrament of all and receive it according to the precepts of Christ Himself, true God, rather than to seek subtly what sort it is, and we ought to temper our speech and thought about matters so deep and so removed from human understand-
P. 338 ing. Indeed Thomas Aquinas, that most celebrated theologian, mocking at the roots of subtleties and the fibers of impiety, said: "He diminishes omnipotence who says that anything can be understood in creatures which cannot be done by God."[603]

TORALBA: Those sacrificing priests think that they are creating the Creator. The question for our consideration does not concern divine power but the power of the priest; namely, can he effect God from this material which was not God before?

SALOMON: I am accustomed to be amazed at the secrets of divine things which I understand less, and we ought not to be too inquisitive concerning them. But, as the divine law orders us to hurl to the flames the remains and bones of the paschal lamb which no one can eat, and the ancient Latins customarily imitated this when they were committing wantonness in their sacrifices, so I also am accustomed to consume the secrets of difficult matters which I cannot understand with the fire of divine love. Yet in this secret of the sacrament I wonder whether or not God's presence depends on the will and power of the priest, as they say. For if the most insignificant priest wished it, the crust will be God; if he did not wish it, the crust will not be God. If he pronounced that holy song and turned his mind elsewhere, he will accomplish nothing. If he does not wish God to be created, that is, if he does not wish a thing created to be consecrated, the bread remains. If he wishes, that which was not God before will be God in a moment.

CURTIUS: They participate in the sacrifice when that salutary host is elevated both for viewing and adoration. What will the people at the rear

[603] Cf. *Summa theologica*, Prima pars, Quaest. LXXIX, art. 3, pp. 603–604.

do if they doubt whether or not the priest wished the host to be God? For the mind can be distracted very often of its own accord, and also rather often by another occurrence.

SENAMUS: Astesanus[604] the theologian had this doubt and thought that he should pray with this condition: "If You are God, I worship You; but if you are less than God, I do not worship you."

CURTIUS: We do not even allow the legitimate act to take place although a condition has been added. To be sure, I remember a priest of Lyons who, in order to avenge the parishioners against whom he had brought a lawsuit, pretended that he was offering that sacred God-making song in the liturgy. At length, after he had lost the lawsuit, he proclaimed in a loud voice that all parishioners were idolators because they had worshipped pure bread instead of God. When the matter was brought into the open, he was condemned to death and burned in the avenging flames.[605]

CORONAEUS: I beg you, by immortal God, that you do not discuss the most sacred matters except with the most reverent attitude. Can you think that He who through His Word made the shining stars, the sun, and the elements, who executed remarkable things by His Word or command, had been weakened in His power?

CURTIUS: No one surely is doubtful that He can make what He wishes except Himself. But what does this mean in regard to the priest? They confess in those mystical words—"This is My body"—that there is no causative power of God because if the sacrificer does any thing else while he is pronouncing those words, he effects nothing.

CORONAEUS: If you are not doubtful concerning God's power, how much less can you doubt His will, since it is obvious from Paul's perceptive interpretation that Christ, true God and man, had offered Himself under the P. 339
appearance of bread and wine to His disciples to eat, and that He ordered this to be an eternal memorial of Him. Moreover, it is most likely that He can do much more than He wishes.

CURTIUS: This opinion has been refuted by the most clear-sighted theologians and does not need my eloquence. The records, the books, the volumes of the libraries are full of this. Still no one is more effectual and

604 *Astesanus* M. Astesanus was an Italian theologian born at Asti in 1330. He is the author of *Summa de casibus conscientiae*, which was widely read. See *La grande encyclopédie* (Paris, n.d.), IV, 357–58.

605 The marginal note in M indicates that this took place in 1548, when Henry II was king of France.

concise than Augustine. He said: "Indeed it is miserable servitude to receive signs for things."[606] If an outrage is commanded, the speech is figurative. When Christ orders His flesh to be eaten and His blood to be drunk, the speech is figurative. When Christians transferred this figurative speech to the thing itself, not to the symbol, they gave the Ismaelites and Jews an unlimited opportunity for mocking them. Tertullian said: "Christ made the bread received into His body, when He said: 'This is My body,' that is, the form of My body."[607] These are the words of the most ancient and holy theologian.

SALOMON: If it were right to worship Jesus, already dead for a long time, under the form of bread, as the Romans do, or with bread, as the Germans do, or without bread, as the Zwinglians think must be done, how much more is it permissible for Israel to worship God in the molten calves? When the calf was cast, Aaron, the priest, ordered the trumpet to proclaim that the next day would be a feast day, sacred to eternal God.[608] He used the name, Tetragrammaton, which was communicable to no creatures, to indicate that it was He who had snatched the people from cruel servitude. Therefore, they were worshipping God under the form of the golden calf, which had been most sacredly forbidden them. Moreover, if God avenged that capital crime with such anger that He immediately ordered three thousand men who committed that disgrace to be killed by the hands of kinsmen and consecrated the hands, which were bloody with brothers' blood, in an eternal covenant to God, how great vengeance do you think there would be for those who say they can sacrifice, not the Creator under the appearance of a calf, but a man overcome with punishment under the form of bread and wine at each moment and everywhere and honor Him with the greatest adoration in place of eternal God?

CORONAEUS: Christ is not sacrificed in the most holy sacrifice of the Mass, but the priest as suppliant offers Christ on the altars to the eternal Father, and begs from Him that because of the beneficence of the Son He grant eternal life to the suppliants. In like manner did Themistocles,

[606] *Sancti Augustini operum tomus* III (Paris, 1680). *De doctrina Christiana* III. 13. 49a.

[607] Did this famous statement from Tertullian imply the real presence? This has been much debated. If the form (figura) referred to the body present, then Curtius cannot use this term to refer to the body absent. Tertullian does not make this explicit. Although he has been interpreted in the Calvinist tradition of symbolism, there are grounds for using *Contra Marcionem* as a defense of physical presentation. *Cath. Encycl.*, XIV, 524.

[608] Ex. 32:4–5.

when an exile, having embraced his son near the altars, beg from Admetus, king of the Molossians, that he spare him because of his love toward his son.[609]

Octavius: Nevertheless, He is worshipped whether as Christ or a host or form or that which is truer, as wheat bread. Not only is He worshipped with the greatest veneration and burning tapers but also as God living and breathing. He is torn by hands and teeth; He is eaten and consumed so that He is changed into the flesh and fiber of man. For they think that Christ, whom they call God and man, thus becomes one and the same with the one receiving the bread. Others who cannot endure these monsters of words think that Christ was hurrying back into heaven from the P. 340
mouth of the one receiving the bread; however, that He is not received by the wicked, although there is serious controversy about this among them. Averroës used to say that it seemed very strange to him that Christians were greedily swallowing so many thousands of gods whom they boasted they created in a moment under the appearance of piety. Moses set before its worshippers the molten calf, broken into dust and poured into water, and gave it to them to drink in disgrace.[610] Moreover, there is no greater proof of severity and hatred than to eat the flesh of an enemy.

Coronaeus: May the name of the atheist Averroës be abolished by eternal oblivion. Finally, it is necessary to admit that in the most holy feast the true flesh of Christ, God and man, and His most precious blood is offered to us in the form of the bread and wine, or we are tormented by the eternal tortures of fire.

Toralba: As a creature is incapable of deity, so also is he incapable of eternal torment.

Fridericus: There is no one, I believe, who thinks that a creature can become God. Nevertheless, because it occurs so often in sacred Scripture that the wickedly willful are punished by eternal torments, I think it is wrong to cast doubt upon it.

Coronaeus: Not only will those who violated certain divine and human laws because of their complete stubbornness and have never repented be punished with the eternal torments of hell, but also those who committed one mortal sin and died before they had repented.

Senamus: Therefore, we must first define of what kind is that sin which they call mortal or capital, since it is still under dispute. A certain most

[609] Plutarch, *Themistocles.* See Plutarch, *The Lives of the Noble Grecians and Romans,* The Modern Library (New York, n.d.) p. 149.

[610] Ex. 32:19–20.

astute theologian writes that he strongly doubts whether any sin is mortal, when all things which the interpreters say are taken into consideration. Jerome defines mortal sin as transgressing the command of God. Some say it is to sin against the Holy Spirit, while others say it is not to confess a sin and not to want to repent. Others say otherwise.

CURTIUS: Christ Himself seems to define that which is neither remitted in this life nor the next as when one sins against the Holy Spirit.

SALOMON: It has been said previously that, according to that definition, the Holy Spirit becomes greater than[611] the Father and the Son, from whom it is said to be derived, because a sin is the greater and more serious, the greater and more serious is the one against whom the sin is committed.

OCTAVIUS: This definition of mortal sin has a greater disadvantage in that a sin of this type could not be abolished by any persistence, by any merits, and almost all the theologians have decided against this. And although Augustine felt somewhat different, still of his own accord he withdrew from that opinion.

TORALBA: If nothing is eternal in its own nature except God, as we have proven earlier, no eternal punishment can be ordained.

P. 341 SALOMON: The theologians all agree that God always bestows greater rewards to the good and lighter[612] punishments for the wicked than are deserved. God said: "I am God eternal who renders judgment, justice, and pity. And I take special delight in these words."[613] Punishment is decided by judgment, but reward is decided by justice. However, pity pertains to the fact that greater rewards are granted to the just man than is his merit, and lighter punishments to the sinner than is his sin. God likewise renewed this promise to Moses who was praying for the people. "I am God eternal, merciful, kind, gentle, of infinite goodness and truth; I am accustomed to safeguard inviolably the pledge and covenant even to the thousandth generation and to abolish crimes and sins; and still I do not allow disgraces to go unpunished, but I require payment to the third and fourth generation."[614] Apropos is David's statement that pity stands at the right hand of God to teach that mercy is more powerful than harshness.[615] Indeed Solomon writes thus that wisdom has at the right hand the long duration of life, but on the left riches and glory, which are weaker than

[611] *spiritum sanctum Patre . . . maiorem fieri* M.
[612] *leviores* M
[613] Jer. 9:24.
[614] Ex. 34:6–7.
[615] *acerbitate potentiorem* M. Psalm 15 (16):10–11.

the blessed life.[616] But if divine compassion is more powerful than harshness, surely no punishment can be eternal.

SENAMUS: For this reason, I think, the Athenians dedicated temples to compassion, none to harshness, as Pausanias writes.[617] The ancient Greeks imagined three avenging deities, *Poinē, Dikē*, and *Erīnys*; the first punishes the sins by loss of goods, the second snatches away good health or breathing life from their bodies; the third brings innumerable sicknesses to their minds; nevertheless they decreed no eternal punishments.

CURTIUS: The travails of living men cannot last longer than their bodily life. In order to lessen them through a soft statement, Epicurus said that pains would be lighter if they were of long duration; however, the harsher pains would cease in a short death. But since the life of the soul is eternal, I do not doubt that punishments will also be eternal.

TORALBA: I think no one except the Epicureans doubts that souls survive bodies. However, it has been proven earlier that they are eternal not by their own nature; still they can become eternal by the goodness[618] and power of God.

CURTIUS: Indeed this is most certain according to the authority of Christ, since He says that He must be feared who can destroy not only the body but also the soul.

SALOMON: Although the Hebrews say that punishments are demanded from the wicked, first when living, then when dead, still they have defined no certain punishments for those who are dead lest they affirm anything rashly in matters so difficult. However, they have decreed various punishments for bodies in accordance with the variety of crime. For sins are committed either by the unwilling or the errant or the willing or the stubborn. He who sinned unwillingly is bound by no punishment because P. 342
that sin cannot even be said to be his own. He who sinned through error is not punished but he is excused with a warning.[619] If a man does not wish to be taught, his punishment is Maltut or Mardut,[620] which is more serious than pecuniary punishment. If a man sins from a certain stubbornness of heart and scorn of the divine law, he is punished with death, even if he offends in the most insignificant part of the law. In truth he who was more abusive toward God not only is punished by the most dreadful death but also his money, clothing, and whatever he has of value is burned

[616] Prov. 8:1–11.
[617] *Attica* VIII. 2.
[618] *bonitate* M
[619] *admonitione* N var.
[620] *Mardut* M

lest he leave any of his profit[621] or his desire to his heirs. Even his estates are ordered to be abandoned, as if accursed, barren land.

CORONAEUS: Christ clearly announced that eternal punishment had been decreed for the depravity of willful men.[622]

SENAMUS: Indeed these punishments are useful also for the terror of the wicked.

CURTIUS: I think nothing better or more useful can happen than to propose eternal torments for the disgraces of evil men, either because it will thus come to pass, as indeed I believe, or to instill terror in the wicked or for both reasons. Those who think differently truly seem to indulge their desire for sinning with great harm to public institutions and religions.

TORALBA: Those who have once passed beyond the limits of wickedness think they must be violently and imprudently wicked, and they believe those terrors have been proposed for the ignorant and the womanish. Others who believe in the truth of the punishments of hell, broken with desperation, despair of attaining pardon, and they grow old in perpetual wickedness. This has been recorded concerning Cain, for example, who complained that he had sinned too seriously to obtain pardon.[623]

FRIDERICUS: I believe the words of Christ pertain not only to fear but also to the truth of the matter, since he who has committed an infinite sin must be punished by a certain infinite punishment. Moreover, he who sins against God surely commits an infinite sin.

TORALBA: With this reasoning, not only are all sins infinite, because one always sins against God, but also all sins are equal, since all infinite things are equal among themselves. Indeed that which is infinite in no way recognizes an increase or extension, more or less. Likewise, it would follow that an infinite evil is contrary to an infinite good, and there would be two infinites in the act, contrary to the clear proofs of nature which we have touched on earlier. Wherefore, I cannot approve the opinion of those who say that nothing is contrary to God formally, to use their words, but only virtually.[624] Indeed, it is necessary that the power of evil and the infinite power be equal to the supreme and infinite good, which would confound the glory and majesty and remarkable harmony of nature in constant wars.
P. 343 When contraries are under the same species, it would be necessary for God also to be added to this species. Since these things are absurd, it follows that no sin is infinite. It would be truer to state that the souls of the

621 *lucrum* M

622 Matt. 18:32–35; Mark 3:28–29.

623 Gen. 4:13.

624 The marginal note indicates *Scotus II. dist. 2. quaest 2.*

wicked perish completely after punishments have been exacted, as the words of Job declare. He said: "As warmth melts the snows, so hell consumes the wicked."[625]

FRIDERICUS: In Christ's opinion the man who has called anyone a fool is said to be worthy of the fire of gehenna. Therefore, all sins are equal and death-bearing, since God is the judge. Nevertheless, these sins are punished less severely than proposed.

SENAMUS: Draco[626] held this same opinion. He who was a parricide and he who stole an apple were equal in regard to the death penalty. However, when the Athenians were complaining about the harshness of the law, he said that he would apply a punishment worse than death for parricides, if he had such a punishment. And so Demosthenes fitly stated that Draco's laws had been written in blood.

SALOMON: For a long time the Stoics' opinion about equal sins has been refuted. Indeed, the divine law, a unique example of all the best laws, appointed the severity of punishments in relation to the size of the crime. The one who has borne false testimony is bound with the same punishment which he tried to divert onto another, whether the testimony pertained to the smallest fine of money or to the death penalty. Moreover, there are seven grades of penalties in the Pandects[627] of the Hebrews. They are stoning, burning, decapitation, suffocation, destruction, unexpected death, and beating inflicted with leather thongs, the blows being limited by divine law to forty lest anyone become completely helpless from the wounds derived from the blows. They call death *mawet*, that is, when anyone dies from divine vengeance before his appointed end of life. Pertinent to this point is the statement which often occurs in the sacred Scriptures:

[625] Job 24:19. The Douay considers verses 18–24 spurious and does not print verse 19. St. Jerome, however, translates verse 19: "Let him pass from the snow waters to excessive heat, and his sin even to Hell."

[626] Draco was an Athenian lawgiver of the 7th century B.C., who drew up a code of laws with fixed penalties. Homicide could no longer be dealt with by families as blood-feuds; rather the state provided courts to try all cases of homicide. Solon revised all of Draco's laws, except those dealing with homicide, because they were too severe. See *Ox. Class. Dict.*, p. 298.

[627] "Pandects" properly refers to the digest of Roman law prepared under Justinian. But not only this collection of passages from the Roman jurists but also any collection, arranged and subdivided under titles according to subject matter, can be embraced by the term "pandects." Jewish law allows mitigating circumstances to reduce the penalty prescribed for transgressions. Among the dozen grounds for establishing innocence are: ignorance of the law, mental incapacity, unconsciousness, illness, torture, threat, failure to complete an action, acting as another's agent, or involvement with another. See "Penal Law," *Encycl. Judaic.*, 13, 222–27.

"Those who will do this will be cut off from their people." The Christian theologians falsely interpret this to mean eternal damnation. Since divine punishment is always lighter than the sin, if the punishment were infinite, the punishment would be more severe than the transgression and harshness more lasting[628] than compassion, and this is opposite to all we are taught from Scripture. Therefore, if punishment is less severe than the sin whether in extension of time or in intensity of pain, it is sure that it cannot be said to be infinite.

CORONAEUS: It is one thing to deserve punishment, another thing to be punished. For if a man who has called someone a fool deserved eternal punishment in the judgment of Christ, true God, it does not follow that he will therefore suffer eternal punishment.

TORALBA: And if there is an equality of punishments, surely there is also an equality of crimes. Likewise, eternal punishment is infinite if not in the intensity of pain, still, it is infinite in the extension of time. If all the sins of all men were heaped up into the same act, still, in no way could they make up an infinite; likewise, infinite action and suffering cannot happen in any way in a finite creature. Therefore, since a creature, which is always finite, cannot endure infinite punishment in the intensity of grief
P. 344 or extension of time, and since all creatures are fettered by birth and death, it follows that there will be no eternal punishments. For this reason, perhaps, Origen said that demons would finally obtain salvation at some time.

FRIDERICUS: This heresy has been rejected for a long time and cast aside by the opinions of the theologians and all their calculations.

SENAMUS: Since the equality of sins is absurd, and also the infinite gravity of sins, since some wrongs are more serious than others even in divine and human laws, still those sins are not many altogether inasmuch as they may be abolished by good deeds or punishments or by some satisfaction; and all the deeds of all must be brought into judgment, as the "Preacher"[629] concludes his sermon, it necessarily follows that there are various punishments and also various kinds of rewards; and all the wicked do not deserve the same punishments of hell nor do the good deserve the same celestial rewards. Paul approves of this when he writes that some stars are brighter than others, and that the same applies to the situation of the blessed.[630]

CURTIUS: There are two exits for souls: some go to a blessed life, others to eternal punishments. There is no third. This can be confirmed in many

[628] *durior* M [629] Eccles. 12:14. [630] I Cor. 15:41.

places of sacred scripture in which these ideas are often expressed: to some the path lies open to life; to others the path lies open to eternal destruction. "Whoever will have believed will be saved, but whoever will not have believed will be condemned."[631] But if there had been a safe path[632] from hell to heaven, why would Christ represent Abraham speaking thus from heaven to the complaints of the evil rich man: "There is a great distance between you and me, so that neither can pass over to the other."[633] Why would Augustine speak likewise: "There are two habitations: one in eternal fire, the other in the eternal kingdom."[634] Likewise: The Catholic faith believes there is a kingdom of heaven, next, a hell;[635] we are completely ignorant of a third.

Octavius: To be sure, the Ismaelites established only two abodes for immortal souls according to *Azora* 45 of the Koran: one for pleasures and delights; the other for torments and griefs. They think there is none in between.

Senamus: The Indians of the West used to say there was a certain cleansing place in addition to hell and heaven which was not harmful because of fire and flames but because of iciest cold. This belief completely upsets the investigations of those who deny the fires of purgatory subsist without matter or that matter is found which cannot be dissolved[636] or consumed by any fires (as an asbestus or pure stone, commonly called an alum pillow), because there is no power of cold for consuming.

Toralba: I would say they philosophize foolishly and unsuitably who deny that matter is eternal in the fires of purgatory. Indeed we see the fires of Aetna and the fire of Ireland, Iceland, and the regions of Peru and torrid zones. These regions have taken their name "fiery earth" from the P. 345
perpetual flames, which do not lack matter.

Coronaeus: What supplies so much and so everlasting food for these flames?

Toralba: Indeed I formerly thought that food was supplied by the underground waters which continually water the rocks, just as in furnaces black asphalt hardened with a dense material burns hotter when sprinkled with water. However, when the marl of the stone is completely consumed, water accomplishes nothing more. For fire is not fed by water but by the dense marshy earth; otherwise, the mass of waters already would have

631 Mark 16:16. 632 *via munita* M 633 Luke 16:26.
634 *Sancti Augustini operum tomus* II (Paris, 1679). *De fine saeculi.* Epist. CXCIX. 754b–g.
635 *gehennam* M 636 *liquari* M

been consumed by fire. And so we see that the porous rocks from Aetna, which they call pumice-stones, are thrown up after the dense matter has been burned, and nonetheless the fires endure.

Octavius: But in order to return from physics to metaphysics, it is logical that there are various kinds of punishment consistent with the variety of crimes, whether the immortal soul is more or less punished by the duration of time, by the harshness of grief, by flames or the terror of cold, by murky gloom or the foulest stench, by contrary persons, or by most loathsome and vile treatments. However, there is a certain divine power which is spread abroad in the earth which avenges the impiety of the wicked. Crimes are never able to be unavenged, lest hiding places from disgrace are sought, because of the faith of the man nailed to the cross. It is clear that wicked men who have spent all their lives in every kind of pleasure very often die without any sense of pain,[637] although good men often die in prisons and torments with the greatest grief of the good. It is proper that these good men are marked for a better life and those wicked ones for punishments, as Solomon indicated when he said that certain men hasten to a kingdom from chains and prisons, but a king hastens to poverty.[638] Therefore, it is necessary that certain punishments exist after this life by which the wicked are chastened. Indeed, God would not seem to be a just judge if He left so many disgraces unavenged and on the other hand punished all the failings of noble and good men as long as they live. But if eternal punishments for all sins have not been established after this life, it is necessary that they are limited by time and place. When punishments have been exacted, souls must die, or they must live more blessed and happier, because a third alternative cannot be imagined.

Toralba: There is an ancient belief which has been handed down from antiquity that the souls of those who have given themselves to bodily pleasures and violated human and divine rights by their impulse slip out of their bodies and fly around the earth in torment; nor will they return to that heavenly home and abode of the blessed, that is, as Plato says, to the spotless dwelling, unless they have been tormented for many centuries.[639] Hence the ancients thought that in this way they were excellently dealt with. They also thought that those who had suffered severe
P. 346 punishments as long as they lived on the earth were snatched away from great evils. So Plato writes the same thing: "To suffer punishment is

[637] Job 21:7–17. [638] Eccles. 4:14. [639] *Phaedo* 81b–e, 108b–c.

release from the greatest evil, namely wickedness."[640] These opinions have indicated that crimes are not unavenged nor will punishments be eternal.

CURTIUS: If we determine purgatory fires or iciest regions for punishments and for expiating sins so that from there an entrance to the homes of the blessed may be provided, we must take care lest we admit infinite kinds of punishments in hell; for universal nature abhors infinity. Therefore, it is better to establish only two places: one for rewards, the other for punishments.

CORONAEUS: If immortal God has any concern for right and justice (and we believe His concern is supreme), we must admit that at the final breath of life the sins of the penitent are not completely destroyed by absolution[640a] but in a certain way they are diminished. Let us take for example two men. One had lived his whole life in excellent virtue and piety; he never committed injustice; he worshipped eternal God with no hope of rewards but only out of divine love in which resides the consummate perfection of justice. Nevertheless, at the end of his life he committed adultery and was killed without repentance. Now the other man had lived his whole life in debauchery, adulteries, murders, parricides, strife, and the greatest impiety toward God. Nevertheless, with his final breath he repented of the way he had spent his life and died after having made an humble confession of his sins. This man, Curtius and Fridericus believe, is carried by angels to the loftiest homes of the blessed. But the other man, they think, is tormented by the eternal punishments of hell. Weigh now, if anything can be more unjustly decided?

CURTIUS: This is the ancient complaint of the Israelites who did not hesitate to accuse God of injustice for this reason. He spoke through the prophet, saying: "The soul which has sinned will die; neither will the son sustain the sins of the parent nor a parent the sins of the sons. But if a wicked man turns away from his sins and embraces all My decrees, judgment, and justice, that man will live, and his past sins will not be remembered. So also if a just man turns himself away from uprightness to impiety, there will be no future remembrance of his former virtues, but he will die in his sins. Still you have said: " 'The judgments of God are not fair.' Hear, house of Israel, whether or not My judgments are fair. Perhaps you are not fair."[641] From these statements, it follows that there are only two ends for souls.

[640] *Gorgias* 478d. [640a] *absolutione* N var. [641] Ezech. 18:20–25.

SALOMON: Ezechiel did not say that that wicked man who was detestable because of all his disgraces and sins would obtain salvation, if, with his last breath, he was ashamed of the way he had lived. However, if he turned from impiety and lived justly, God would forget his former impi-
P. 347 eties. Likewise, the most upright man who committed a sin at the last moment of life must not be tormented by eternal punishments; however, he will indeed perish at death if he turned himself altogether to impieties and sins.

CORONAEUS: I believe that man who has repented of his sins will be expiated by the fires of purgatory: not only do the sacred scriptures support this idea but also the authority of Martin Luther himself.

SALOMON: I think that repentance at the last breath of life is of no profit for the wicked.

CORONAEUS: Nevertheless, we think he is free from blame who has secured pardon by the divinely granted power of the priest.

SALOMON: Nothing seems more detestable to me than for the priests of the Roman church to claim the power of pardon for sins or to forgive those who confess their sins, since this is fitting for immortal God alone in behalf of the right of His majesty.

CORONAEUS: But Christ most openly bestowed this power upon His disciples so that whatever things they might bind or loose on earth the same would be loosed and bound in heaven.[642]

CURTIUS: I do not know why the Roman priests have twisted the words for binding and loosing to mean the abolition of sins, unless they thought they would be more important if they took possession of things which were communicable to no creature according to the right of divine majesty and procured a limitless amount of gold from indulgence of all faults. Indeed we see those priests pardon not only sins that have been committed but also sins that are about to be committed. Although they do not loose the unlearned from divine and human laws without great reward (to themselves), they very often grant pardon for strong impieties when money flows. Hence the pontifical selling[643] of venial indulgences, an invention of Pope Gregory grew to such proportions that pardon for a thousand years was sometimes bestowed.[644]

CORONAEUS: To be sure, sin is pardoned so that those who have repented are not bound by eternal torments, but when expiated by the fire of pur-

[642] Matt. 18:18.

[643] *pontificiae nundinationes* M

[644] See article, "Indulgences," in *Cath. Encycl.*, VII, 783–88.

gatory, as Paul himself says, they obtain eternal life at some time or other.[645]

CURTIUS: I believe that a heavenly life awaits those who repent and confess their sins to God without the fires of expiation, which are nothing. But when our garments are washed in the most precious blood of Christ-God and in the bath by which He washes us clean of all iniquities, we are summoned to the heavenly nuptials. Otherwise, it would be inconsistent to torment most cruelly with blows, beatings, torments, and burnings the one whom you wish to receive at the banquet of solemn nuptials.

TORALBA: The hypothesis suggested by Coronaeus earlier pertains to this: that deserved punishments are first required from each one before we grant that those dirtied with the stains of sins are thrust into the holiest abodes of the angels.

SALOMON: Thus I believe that no sin is unpunished; but vengeance, as long as a man lives, will be more excellent, as the Master of Wisdom shows in these words: "Behold, the just are indeed punished on the earth; how much more are the sinners?"[646] This is to say that punishments for sins are demanded from the just, as long as they live, but they are demanded from the wicked after death. Nevertheless, both are punished less than they deserve. For if all crimes were examined according to merit and punishments decreed likewise, who could endure these? However, with repentance many sins will be removed or punished very lightly, the more so if unusual actions of virtues are added to repentance, such as duties toward orphans, widows, and strangers, and actions of greatest kindness[647] toward inferiors.[648] And so Daniel urged King Nebuchadnezzar to diminish through kindness the punishment decreed by divine judgment, since by nothing else are sins more quickly abolished.[649] Although God forgives those who pray for pardon and repent, still in these words He says they will not be unpunished: "He will purge us by purging."[650] David Kimchi interprets the passage to mean that the things which[651] God forgave still He may punish in a certain way. Rabbi Abraham and the Chaldean interpreter think that God pardons completely, which must be interpreted about sin. Although He had said that He had pardoned the people[652] because of Moses' prayer, still He declares that He will avenge

P. 348

[645] Rom. 6:22.
[646] Prov. 11:31.
[647] *summae . . . benignitatis* M
[648] Ezech. 18:5–9.
[649] Dan. 4:24.
[650] Cf. Psalm 78 (79):9; Isaiah 1:25; Ezech. 20:38.
[651] *quae* M
[652] *populo* M

the sin and diffidence of the people, as He did.[653] All those who had gone out from Egypt, with two exceptions, perished in the desert. In like manner He pardons David when he repents; still He inflicted punishment, first by the death of his adulterous son, next by incests and parricides[654] of his children.[655]

Octavius: Indeed the wicked are nourished on the destruction of the good, and they often spend their whole life in the luxury of all wealth and pleasures which are the rewards of the things they have done rightly. Thus, there is no good deed for which God does not grant a just reward and one that is greater than the merit, because no one is so altogether wicked that he has done nothing good. About the just and unjust who are already dead, the Teacher of Wisdom writes thus: "The wicked will proceed, terrified[656] by the memory of their sins. Then the just will stand face to face with their oppressors, at whose sight the wicked, struck with fear and afflicted with unexpected dumbness and grief, will cry out. 'That is the one whom we formerly held in mockery; foolish were we who thought his life was mad and his death disgraceful. And so he has been enrolled in the register of the sons of gods and has secured his lot among the holy. But what have our riches and pride profited us?' "[657]

Senamus: Truly this is the class of those who like beasts have had no concern at all for divine or human affairs; they are said to suffer death of the body and soul at the same time. To be sure, God can kill both body and soul.

P. 349 Curtius: It is difficult to make a judgment about these things. Nevertheless, we believe that the souls of those who have spent their lives not in the innocent manner of beasts but have contaminated their existence with crimes and disgraces will not die before they have suffered the most just punishments for their detestable sins. The last words of Isaiah speak to this point: "They will see the bodies of those who have failed Me since their worm will not die and their fire will not be extinguished, but they will be a disgust to all."[658] These words attest that their punishments will be eternal.

Salomon: Rabbi Elieser spoke somewhat plainer: "Surely you know all the words and deeds of men are measured by their just weights, nor should an evil spirit drive you into deceit, as if the tomb were, as it were, a future

[653] Num. 15:30–31.
[654] *parricidiis* M
[655] II Kings (II Sam.) 12:13–31.
[656] *perterriti* M
[657] *Quid nobis opes ac superbia profuere?* M Wisdom 5:1–6.
[658] Isaiah 66:24.

refuge for security and impunity, for you will stand face to face with God eternal, the Judge of the whole world."

CURTIUS: The Roman church owes great thanks to you because by the power of your arguments and the ardor[659] of your eloquence you have stirred up the fires of purgatory which had almost died out. Indeed in those fires the power of bequests and donations is enormous and seems to exist not only in a persuasive cause, as the lawyers say, but also in a final cause, so that annual sacrifices of masses are made for the salvation of the soul of the donor.

FRIDERICUS: Even if it were clear from evident proof that the sins of the wicked are expiated after this life by avenging flames, still for this reason it would not follow that sacrifices would benefit the dead.

CORONAEUS: Why not?

FRIDERICUS: Since the divine laws forbid it. Ambrose said: "He who does not receive forgiveness for sins here will not receive them there. Moreover, this forgiveness will not be possible because he did not want to come to eternal life."[660] Likewise Cyprian said: "When a man departs this world, no other place remains for repentance or sanctification. Here life is lost or retained."[661] Augustine declared: "After this life each man will have that which he acquired in this life. Now is the time for mercy; afterwards is the time for judgment."[662] Also Jerome said: "When you will have come before the throne of Christ, neither Job nor Daniel will be able to pray for you."[663] Likewise Chrysostom: "As soon as[664] we shall have departed from here, we are not permitted to repent or remove our sins. Also he who does not wash away his sins in his present life will have no consolation afterwards."[665] Solomon's statement about the fallen tree is

[659] *eloquentiae ardoribus* M

[660] Most of Ambrose's writings are homilies, spoken commentaries on the Scriptures that were taken down by his hearers. Few of his discourses have reached us exactly as spoken by the great bishop. The marginal note in M indicates this statement is from *De bono mortis.*

[661] Marginal note in M reads *contra Demetrianum.*

[662] *Sancti Augustini operum tomus* IV (Paris, 1681). *In Psalmum XXXII.* Enarratio II. 10. 194d–e. Fridericus has used Augustine's statement out of context. The statement is: "He [God] loves mercy and justice. Do these things because He does them. Direct your thoughts to mercy and justice. Now is the time for mercy and afterwards there will be time for justice."

[663] Marginal note in M states *Homil. 10 in John 13. quaest. 2.*

[664] *simul ac* M

[665] *Concione 2 de Lazaro; Homil. 4 ad Hebr. c. 2.* in the marginal note of M.

also apropos. He says that wherever a tree has fallen, whether to the north or to the south, it will remain in that spot forever.[666]

CORONAEUS: Lest I set theologians against you theologians, it is sufficient to note the unusual passage in sacred Scripture from Maccabees. It says:
P. 350 "Unless they hoped that those who are dead would live again, in vain would prayers for the dead be conceived."[667] Hence Judas, a Jewish prince, ordered the dead for the safety of his country to be expiated by solemn sacred rites so that they might be loosed from the stain of sins.

CURTIUS: Not only the Hebrews but also all the old Christian theologians judge the books of the Maccabees to be among the apocrypha, and the most holy decrees of the Council of Laodicea[668] repudiated them.

CORONAEUS: But in the later councils and according to the decrees of the Council of Trent, they are approved in a remarkable manner, as if holier.

TORALBA: Indeed, not only because of the authority of theologians and academicians but also because of most certain proofs do I not doubt that there will be purgations of souls and expiations for crimes after this life. However, I cannot be satisfied that they are cleansed by any prayers or entreaties. Indeed Plato writes that the human race could be persuaded of nothing more dangerous or deadly.[669] For, the more wicked a man is and the more riches he has amassed from thefts and rapings of orphans and widows, the more confidently he will think the cruelty of his own disgraces will be blotted out by another's prayers and sacrifices.

SALOMON: We are often warned by divine laws that sins are not expiated by any sacrifices except those sins which are admitted to be from probable error. In truth, the stolen goods, especially of the poor, of widows and orphans, consume, as if a flaming fire, all the wealth of the rapers. Since these things are so, who can think that any prayers or sacrifices benefit the dead?

CORONAEUS: If the prayers of the living do not help the dead in any way, why do the Jews, as they carry their dead to the tombs, sing their own "laying in" song, in which they use these words: "May the Spirit of the Lord make N. rest in the garden of Eden in peace, him and all the dead Israelites."? The people answer Amen to the voice of this one praying. Why does Augustine pray thus for his mother, Monica: "Release her, oh Lord, release her, I pray, lest You enter into judgment with this one."?[670]

666 Eccl. 11:3. 667 II Macc. 12:44. 668 A.D. 320.
669 Cf. *De leg.* V. 735d–4, IX. 871b–d, 873c–d. Also see III. 688c.
670 *Conf.* IX. 13.

Why also would the Mohammedans themselves, who believe that the punishments of hell will be eternal, pray so ardently that their dead friends be snatched from the questioning of both black angels?

Octavius: Indeed that prayer is made by Mohammedans before they go to judgment, not because they think that those once damned are ever rescued from judgment.

Salomon: I do not mock at the authority of the Maccabees or Augustine. But we do not use solemn anniversaries, sacrifices, or prayers for the souls of the dead because we know that nothing will avail; moreover, that "laying in" song is nothing other than the word for those desiring that their friends, relatives, and parents be blessed.

Coronaeus: If there was any doubt whether the prayers of the living help the dead, as indeed I think they do, would it not be better to do this which in no way harms the dead rather than to desert them in doubtful P. 351 hope when they are about to be tortured? As wise men forbid this which you doubt is just, so they order us to do this which you doubt will be beneficial or not. For this reason Cato the Censor reaps praise. When he was speaking about the immortality of souls, whose power and sensation certain untrustworthy Epicureans thought was blotted out with death, Cato said: "If I am mistaken in this, the fact that I believe souls are immortal, I am unwilling, for as long as I live, to be freed from this error in which I delight; or if souls are mortal, as certain insignificant philosophers believe, I am not afraid that they will mock me when dead."[671] How much more carefully and willingly ought we to supplicate for our dead friends, if it is certain, as I hope, that the Roman church cannot stray from true piety.

Senamus: I have learned from the Roman pontiffs that no one is a heretic who defends one or the other opinion as is pleasing from among two or more opinions of learned men which are at variance about religion.

Coronaeus: Indeed I agree, if the discussion is about indifferent things, but I do not agree if the discussion is about a keypoint of religion or about principles of faith.

Senamus: In this very matter there is a grave controversy as to what are the principles of faith. For the theologians at the Sorbonne have substituted for the twelve principles of the Christian faith one hundred and twenty,

[671] Cicero, *De senectute* XXI.

and have abandoned to capital punishments those who thought otherwise. Among these principles it was decreed that Peter must be called Saint Peter, not Peter; and Paul, Saint Paul, not Paul.

TORALBA: I see that Jews differ from both Christians and Saracens in the key point of religion. Also the Saracens have serious controversies among themselves about faith, and at least one hundred and twenty heresies among Christians are mentioned by Tertullian and Epiphanius. Not only are heretics of the major groups disagreeing with each other but also those who seem to know more than the others. I mean Damascenus disagrees with Chrysostom, Cyprian with Tertullian, Epiphanius with Eusebius, Jerome with Augustine, Gregory with Jerome, Origen with the others, Abelard with Bernard, Thomas with Scotus, Henry with Durand, Albert with Henry; and finally each beats the writings of their predecessors[672] black and blue. Why even the Master of the Sentences was accused by the young theologians of the Sorbonne of twenty-five heresies. Greek Christians are refuted by Latin Christians, Romans by Germans, Swiss and French by both, Luther by Zwingli, Calvin by Stancari,[673] Beza by Castellio.[674] In short, almost everyone is at odds with everyone; all are angry at all with curses and ill words for all. Although the Jews seem to protect the purity of their religion with greater steadfastness, still the eastern Jews differ from the western Jews in rites. Since these things are so, is it not better to embrace that most simple and most ancient and
P. 352 at the same time the most true religion of nature, instilled by immortal God in the minds of each man from which there was no division (I am speaking of that religion in which Abel, Enoch, Lot, Seth, Noah, Job, Abraham, Isaac, and Jacob, heroes dearest to God, lived) than for each one to wander around uncertain in the midst of so many various opinions and have no sure abode of the soul in which to find peace?

SALOMON: If we were like those heroes, we would need no rites nor ceremonies. However, it is hardly possible and even impossible for the common people and the untutored masses to be restrained by a simple assent of true religion without rites and ceremonies.

CURTIUS: I do not like a multitude of ceremonies which overturn the

672 *quemque superiorum scripta sugillare* M.

673 Francesco Stancari was a notorious Italian "Judaizer" who arrived at the University of Cracow in 1546 to teach Hebrew.

674 Castellio spoke out against Calvin's burning of Servetus in 1554 in a pamphlet entitled, "Ought heretics to be persecuted?" It is considered the earliest plea for toleration in modern times, and in this it is akin to the *Colloquium heptaplomeres*. See above, Book IV, p. 177, note 161.

worship of true God, for example, those ceremonies of the pagans and those who are not far from the pagans, the Catholics.

Octavius: I think that the Ismaelites worship eternal God more purely[675] with fewer[676] ceremonies than every other kind of religion.

Salomon: But now they have strayed from the path, and they wear themselves out with continuous pilgrimages to the tombs of Naphissa Mohammed and some one or other of those prophets. The Jews perform only the ceremonies of divine law, not those devised by the will of men, with the worship of the true eternal God so that they easily hold the souls of the common people as well as of the educated in duty without any sacrifices.

Coronaeus: I believe that the Roman pontiffs have handed down the true Religion to posterity in a continuous line from Christ, true God, and the most holy apostles and the disciples, and that they protect with constant faith the splendor and honor of their worthiness among the shattered remains of heretics, Jews, and Turks, Pagans, and Epicureans. And although I cannot persuade you of this which I do not despair will come to pass, I shall not cease praying to Christ, true God and man, and His hallowed parent, the honor of virgins, all the hosts of angels, martyrs, and confessors, and the orders of all saints that they render eternal God propitious to you and bear entreaties for your salvation.

Salomon: We owe unusually great thanks to Coronaeus for so many kindnesses and especially for his exceptional piety and love toward us, which we in turn must imitate and pray, each one for the other, to eternal God that He lead us in the right path of salvation, purged from all the brambles and thorns of errors. *

Fridericus: Whoever doubts whether his own religion is true or not, or whoever confesses a false religion for the true religion does not seem able to pray effectively for others. But he who is certain of his religion in which he must find rest, if he has the true religion, will pray effectively for others, not so for himself, in order that[677] he may advance[678] on the right path which he holds securely,[679] with God as his guide.

Salomon: No mortal was ever more certain about divine will than Moses, who, although he had brought God's laws to the people, still invoked God in prayers, saying: "Show me Your ways that I may know You."[680] Also David, the most skilled interpreter of divine laws, said:

[675] *purius* M
[676] *paucioribus* M
[677] *ut* M
[678] *ingrediatur* M
[679] *securus* M
[680] Ex. 33:13.

* Faltenbacher S. 96f. Sieht hier bereits ein Ende des Gesprächs!

P. 353 "Show me Your ways."[681] He had said at another time: "You have made the ways of life known to me in order that God might enlighten those to understand the secrets of the law."[682] Indeed in the fortieth year after the law had been given, Moses, in an assembly of the people, added this: "God thus far has not given you a heart to understand nor eyes to see nor ears to hear."[683] From which it is known that without help from the divine light the laws of God and His commands cannot be understood or perceived. Hence the Psalmist exclaims: "Unveil my eyes that I may see the wondrous secrets of Your law."[684] Therefore, how much more zealously than those men ought we to pour out mutual prayers to immortal God, since we live in so great a variety of contradictory opinions about the true religion.

SENAMUS: Then what is there to keep all of us at the same time from earnestly asking immortal God, on behalf of us all, that we advance in the right path, if only we have attained the true path. But if we have turned from the true path or life, may we be set on the straight path with divine goodness as our guide. As missiles of war sent forth one by one[685] do not shake fortresses with as great force as when many are hurled together in the same attack, so prayers of the multitude strike heaven itself with such strength that they seem to exert force on God Himself.

SALOMON: Still the prayer of one most upright man has more weight with God than the prayers of all the people, as indeed Moses, Samuel, and Elias often declared, since in a multitude the impiety of one man blocks the others; yet the prayers of good men are always heard.

OCTAVIUS: The prayer of the multitude is efficacious if it has beseeched eternal God with a sincere mind. But if one worships a false God for a true God or joins a creature to the creator in the communion of worship, the same charge can be hurled at that one which Elias hurled at his people: "How long will you waver now in this part, now in that? If Bahal is king, worship him, etc."[686] He said to the priests who were calling to Bahal in a most eager voice: "You must cry out more loudly, because Bahal is involved either in sleep or domestic computations."[687] Worse also if they doubt whether or not there is a God whom they may solicit, since doubt in divine worship always brings the taint of impiety. Who can receive the amulet of the theologian Astesanus,[688] who is about to venerate the

[681] Psalm 118 (119):27.
[682] Psalm 118 (119):33; 152 (153):8.
[683] Deut. 29:4.
[684] Psalm 118 (119):18.
[685] *singillatim* M
[686] III Kings (I Kings) 18:21.
[687] III Kings (I Kings) 18:27.
[688] See above, note 604.

wheaten host, if they doubt whether or not it was consecrated, since it is in the power and will of the priest, namely, of him who commands or denies the mystical words whether or not God is present because it touches the hands.[689] He said: "If You are God, I venerate You; but if not, I do not venerate you."

SENAMUS: All men recognize that God is the Parent of all gods, as far as I know. Although many join creatures with the Creator by sharing honors, still they confess that He is the head. Porphyry and Plato call Him Father of the gods and almighty One. Octavius, Salomon, and Toralba P. 354
declare that He alone must be worshipped and all others cast aside. Fridericus and Curtius agree in all other points, yet they differ in this, that they say that that God, the Parent of nature, or what is the same, that His Son, coessential and coeternal, had assumed human flesh in the womb of a virgin and had endured death for the salvation of the human race; they are nearly in agreement on the other matters except for the banquet, confession, and statues. Coronaeus, as he is the most religious of all, does not think that there should even be the slightest departure from the ceremonies of the Roman church. But I, lest I ever offend, prefer to approve all the religions of all rather than to exclude the one which is perhaps the true religion.

SALOMON: I would prefer that you were hot or cold rather than lukewarm in religion, Senamus. And yet, how is it possible to defend the religions of all at the same time, that is, to confess or believe that Christ is God and to deny that He is God, that He has been overcome by death and snatched from torment, that bread becomes God, and does not become God, which things cannot happen at the same time through nature.

SENAMUS: I wish neither to agree lightly nor deny rashly the things which the theologians turn upside down in doubtful discussion. However, I consider Paul's opinion more excellent to follow. He said: "I have become a Jew to the Jews, a Gentile to the Gentiles, and to those who are without laws, as if I were devoid of law. I have become all things to all men so that I might make all men a profit."[690] Hence that harmony of the citizens of Jerusalem seemed most pleasing to me. There are eight Christian sects there, Latins, Greeks, Jacobites, Armenians, Gregorians, Copts,

689 *Quis enim ferat Astesani Theologi Amuletum qui adoraturus hostiam siligineam quam dubitent consecrata sit, necne; quoniam in arbitrio ac potestate sacerdotis est scilicet verba mystica jubentis aut vetantis Deus sit necne quod manibus contrectat.* M

690 I Cor. 9:20–21.

Abyssinians, Nestorians, then the Jews and Mohammedans, and each sect has its own temples in which their religious services are held separately with separate rites and ceremonies. Nevertheless, those sects cherish the public tranquility with supreme harmony. I enter the temples of Christians and Ismaelites and Jews wherever possible and also those of the Lutherans and Zwinglians lest I be offensive to anyone, as if I were an atheist, or seem to disturb the peaceful state of the republic. Still I attribute all things to that best and greatest Prince of the gods. Therefore, what hinders us from appeasing with common prayers the common Author and Parent of all nature, so that He may lead us all into a knowledge of the true religion.

SALOMON: Indeed, we must do that in order that each individual[691] conceive prayers for every single person; however, all cannot remain in safe piety for each one at the same time in so great a variety of religions. Moses could not even allow the people to offer sacrifices in Egypt, since Pharaoh permitted it. He said: "It is not proper that we sacrifice the abomination of the Egyptians to our God. If this were done forthwith, we would be covered over with stones."[692] And for that reason, even from the farthest recollection our elders forcefully obtained from princes, and at great cost, the right for us to practice our religion separately in chapels and sanctuaries. For this reason, we were accustomed to bestow a gold crown on the
P. 355 Roman popes and the empresses and the Rights of the Girdles on the German emperors. When a colony of our elders were prohibited by the inhabitants on the island of Delos from practicing their religion because the island was considered sacred to Apollo and Diana, Caesar[693] the dictator, giving a rescript,[694] said: "I am not pleased with the decree by which you prohibit our Jewish friends from practicing their ancestral religion or bringing money into the sacred rites since these things are not even prohibited at Rome."[695] A letter of Dolabella, proconsul to the Ephesians, makes the same statement that the Jews[696] are not to be prevented from practicing their religion in the towns and cities of Asia. Nevertheless, we have often been disturbed in our religion and have been injured by the violence of the raging mob.

CURTIUS: To protect publicly[697] the authority of different religions in the same city has always seemed to me to be the most difficult matter of all.

[691] *pro singulis vota singuli* M

[692] Ex. 8:22.

[693] *Caesar* M

[694] *rescribens* M.

[695] Philo, *De legatione ad Caium* XL. 311–18. See also above, Book III, note 134.

[696] *Judaei* M

[697] *publice* M

However, in this matter, the common people have been accustomed to claim power for themselves, and it is not even safe for princes to resist them. When Phocas, emperor of the Greeks, had ordered the statues to be hurled down, he was killed in the basilica of Sophia by the very dregs of the mob.[698] Moreover, it is more dangerous to perform private sacrifices than public ones because of the secret conspiracies of citizens, which finally at some time erupt into destruction of the state. For this reason Trajan commanded Pliny, the proconsul of Asia, to forbid nighttime gatherings of Christians. When the magistrate of the city of Münster had allowed the Anabaptist sects to hold nocturnal meetings, they gradually increased to the point that they took over the rule of the city. In private religious services and especially in gatherings at night where men and women come together, there is the greatest suspicion of pandering. When these disgraces had been found at Rome in the sacred rites of the Bacchanalia, lewdness and sexual debaucheries and murders, they were forbidden by perpetual decree in all of Italy.[699] Christians who attended the nightly religious gatherings out of fear for the magistrates could never escape this infamy of suspicion, although they especially wanted to, as is clear from the apologetics.

SENAMUS: If all people could be persuaded as the Ismaelites, Octavius, and I are that all the prayers of all people which come from a pure heart are pleasing to God, or surely are not displeasing, it would be possible to live everywhere in the world in the same harmony as those who live under the emperor of the Turks or Persians.

CORONAEUS: The princes of this city allow the foreign rites of the Jews and Greeks to be performed publicly, yet the same privileges are not granted to others. However, it is possible for each man to enjoy liberty provided he does not disturb the tranquility of the state, and no one is forced to attend religious services or prevented from attending.

OCTAVIUS: Indeed, that is a wise judgment as are all the institutions of this city, by which it has flourished for a very long time in an aristocratic form of government and will continue to flourish. In this kind of state no more dangerous pest can arise than civil discord.

CORONAEUS: Still, piety ought to be placed before public utility, and P. 356

[698] Phocas was emperor of Constantinople from A.D. 602 to 610. He was bloodthirsty and intolerant. Because of his order that all Jews in the empire must be baptized, terrible riots broke out in Alexandria. See Smith, *Dictionary* (1856 ed.) III, 338–39.

[699] Tertullian, *Apol.* I. 6. Also see Livy XXXIX.

piety concerning religion ought to be sought and even those who are unwilling ought to be forced to go to public religious services, as the most holy decrees of the Roman church warn. This statement is pertinent: "Compel those to enter."

OCTAVIUS: I believe that statement has to do with those called to nuptials. If they are unwilling to be present, it would seem very rude and unfitting to wish to force them with blows or capital punishment, if indeed we understand *to biazesthai* (to do violence) from the word *anagkazein* (to force).

CURTIUS: In regard to this consideration Tertullian wrote thus: "It is not for religion to compel, which ought to be undertaken of one's own accord, not by force."[700] Indeed, it was decreed by the Councils of Nicea, Constantinople, Ephesus, and Chalcedon that heretics must be defeated not by arms but by doctrine, nor are the tares to be separated before the harvest. I see that this opinion pleased Augustine, Jerome, and Bernard. Hilary said: "God does not need necessary compliance. He does not require forced confession; He does not receive it unless the confession is made willingly. God must be sought with simplicity, He must be known by confession; He must be loved with charity; He must be worshipped with fear; He must be kept by an upright will. But priests are forced in chains to fear God, are commanded by punishments, are held in prison; virgins are stripped for punishment, and their bodies which have been made sacred to God are put on public display for the enjoyment of a spectacle and interrogation." And so for this reason the Priscilliani[701] were condemned of heresy because they thought heretics must be tortured by punishments.

SALOMON: The divine law orders that all males present themselves to God every year on solemn feast days with gift offerings.[702] Still, the law desired that no one be forced. Indeed, what more serious insult against God can be conceived than to wish to force anyone to obey Him, since no one can approach Him in love with a soul sufficiently eager. It is wrong that God is worshipped by the reluctant and unwilling. If anyone of our nation seeks a foreign god and foreign sacred rites, after he has deserted the worship of God, he is ordered to be stoned, and the city to be destroyed.

[700] *Ad Scapulam* II.

[701] Priscillianism originated in Spain in the 4th century and was derived from the Gnostic-Manichaean doctrines.

[702] Deut. 16:16.

The same punishment follows those who have not acquiesced to the high priest's dictum. Pertinent to this matter is that contract which King Asa made with the tribes of Judah and Benjamin,[703] by which the life of the man who had deserted eternal God is damned;[704] yet in this contract nothing is stipulated about foreigners. And although the people of Israel were ordered to destroy the people, and to overturn the temples, places, and altars, when they had come into their promised land, nevertheless, they did not force the neighboring people to change their religion. When David had subjoined the Ammonites, Moabites, and Idumeans to his kingdom and had imposed taxes, he still allowed them to practice their own religion and sacred rites. And I believe this is the intention of the emperor[705] Julian in the book which he wrote against the Galileans, since he believed that the Mosaic law forbade that temples and shrines of other nations be destroyed. P. 357

CURTIUS: This question whether anyone must be forced to forswear his own religion has been the center of great strife in the senate of the Portuguese under King Emanuel. When Ferdinand of Aragon[706] and king of Castile had expelled all the Jews from the boundaries of his empire, a part fled into Narbonne. After a while they were driven out of there by King Francis, except a few who had changed their religion out of fear of proscription or pretended to change their religion. The greatest number went to Portugal. King Emanuel summoned a council and ordered it to determine whether the Jews must be forced to profess the Christian religion. At length, it was decided that no one must be forced; nevertheless, the Jews were not to be permitted to practice their own religion. Moreover, they were advised by decree to depart from the land in a short time, unless they preferred either to forswear their religion or submit to the yoke of harsh servitude. Those who did not have the opportunity to leave either because of the difficulty of sea voyages or because of poverty chose to be baptized because of the fear of impending slavery. When a meeting was being held in the capital of Lisbon, the wound of the crucified Christ which was painted red appeared to be flowing with blood when the light of the sun struck it. When a preacher saw this, crying out loudly he said: "Look at the wounds of Christ the Savior, as they flow with blood." The people in their amazement gave assent to these words. At this point a certain Jewish neophyte who pretended to be a Christian, in a loud voice

703 II Paralip. (II Chron.) 15:8–13.
704 *damnatum* N var.
705 *Imperator* M
706 *Aragoniae* M

rebuked the astonished crowd, saying: "Why does that wood image of a dead man move you?" After the Jew spoke, the preacher bitterly cursed the man and his whole race as wicked and filthy because he lied with despicable deception that he was a Christian. The mob was incited by these words, and like mad men they dragged the Jew from the sanctuary and stoned him. Not content with this, the mob sought out the Jews everywhere in the city and killed about three thousand. When the king learned of this affair, he was gravely disturbed because he had forced the Jews to desert their own religion. And so he crucified the leaders of the uprising along with the preacher.

SALOMON: There is nothing which I bear more grievously than for piety implanted with the deepest roots, to be mocked; from this source civil disturbances and uprisings spring which are too numerous to recount. However, I shall say a few things from many. When the Jews were performing their sacred rites in a solemn feast day in the city of Jerusalem, a certain garrison soldier took off his clothes in the temple itself and defiled the most holy rites with the foulest insult of words. He was seized by the people for punishment; still about twenty thousand people were killed because of this disturbance. Moreover, many rulers wickedly present an appearance of piety for the purpose of seizing the wealth of the innocent. For example, Louis of Hungary, Dagobert and Philip Augustus of France, and Ferdinand, king of Aragon, proscribed Jews who were summoned on false charges. When they lacked evidence for prosecution, they openly applied force. As a result, all the Jews of Cracow in the memory of our grandfathers were killed except for the young, who were instructed
P. 358 early in the Christian religion. They also burned the homes of those slain, and all Cracow burned in this conflagration.

OCTAVIUS: After Ferdinand, king of Aragon, from a certain wicked piety or rather from an insatiable greed for money, had driven out the Jews and despoiled those Jews who had pretended to be Christian and had been baptized out of fear of losing their wealth, he forced the Moors of Granada, who were of the Arabic religion, to forswear Mohammed. Still, this did not take place before he forced Alphaguinus, a priest of the Moors who had been subjected to prison and torture for a long time, to be baptized. He also ordered 5,000 books which the Ismaelites held sacred to be burned. Then, after their religion had been changed, public informers were given the opportunity to proscribe those who were said to be pretending to be Christians. All these things happened at the instigation of Cardinal Ximenez, when as bishop of Toledo he should have remembered[707] a decree of the Council of Toledo forbade that any one be forced against his will to profess the Christian religion.[708]

FRIDERICUS: The opinion of Theodoric, emperor of the Romans and Goths, is worthy to be inscribed in golden letters on the door posts of princes. When the Roman Senate advised him that he should bring the Arians to the Catholic faith by punishments, he replied that we are unable to command religion because no one can be forced to believe against his will.

CURTIUS: Indeed, he spoke excellently. Even better is the statement of Emperor Jovianus.[709] After he proposed an edict of union, which he called Henoticon, to gather together the Pagans, Christians, Arians, Manichaeans, Jews, and almost two hundred sects in harmony, he constantly urged speakers to use restraint, lest they confound the people and the order of the state by seditious gatherings, but he urged them to challenge the people to piety, uprightness, and mutual love.

Since everyone approved of these things, Coronaeus bade me to summon the boys to whom he offered the song: "Lo, how good and pleasing it is for brothers to live in unity, arranged not in common diatonics or chromatics, but in enharmonics with a certain, more divine modulation." All were most sweetly delighted with this song, and they withdrew, having embraced each other in mutual love. Henceforth, they nourished their piety in remarkable harmony and their integrity of life in common pursuits and intimacy. However, afterwards they held no other conversation about religions, although each one defended his own religion with the supreme sanctity of his life.

[707] *meminisse* M

[708] "In 1500 [Ximenez] had the Moors of Granada baptized and gave orders to burn thousands of Korans, but to save the Arabic books on medicine, philosophy, and history. His burning of the Korans, which was approved by almost all contemporaries, has been condemned by many modern critics who do not understand the circumstances of the time." See the article, "Ximeney de Cisneros, Francisco," *New Catholic Encyclopedia* (New York, 1967), XIV, 1063. Henry Charles Lea, *A History of the Inquisition in Spain*, 4 volumes (New York, 1907), gives a hostile account in great detail, especially in Vol. 3, Book VIII, Chapter II, "Moriscos."

[709] Jovianus was the Roman emperor (363–364) who followed Julian the Apostate. He restored to the Christian church the privileges abrogated by Julian. In a general edict of toleration Jovianus established freedom of worship for all religions, even paganism, but forbade magical sacrifices. He reintroduced the religious toleration proclaimed in Constantine's Edict of Milan of 313. The Henoticon, however, was not proposed by Jovianus, but by the Emperor Zeno in order to conciliate Catholics and Monophysites. The Henoticon (union) was published in 482 and was meant to satisfy all. See *Cath. Encycl.*, VII, 218–19; VIII, 529–30.

Index

INDEX

INDEX

Library of Congress Cataloging in Publication Data

Bodin, Jean, 1530-1596.
Colloquium of the seven about secrets of the sublime.

Translation of Colloquium heptaplomeres de rerum sublimium arcanis abditis.
Bibliography: p.
Includes index.
1. Religions. 2. Catholic Church—Relations. 3. Religion—Philosophy. I. Title.
B781.B33C6413 1975 291 73-2453
ISBN 0-691-07193-4